THE GREEN GUIDE London

Colourful Pageantry of the foot guards photo: Ph. Gajic/MICHELIN

THEGREENGUIDE **LONDON**

Editorial Director	Cynthia Clayton Ochterbeck
Editorial Manager	Gwen Cannon
Contributing Writer	Siân Lezard
Production Manager	Natasha G. George
Cartography	Peter Wrenn
Photo Editor	Nicole D. Jordan
Photo Researcher	Siân Lezard
Interior Design	Chris Bell, cbdesign
Layout	Siân Lezard, Nicole D. Jordan, Natasha G. George
Cover Design	Chris Bell, cbdesign, Christelle Le Déan
Cover Layout	Natasha G. George
Contact Us	Michelin Travel and Lifestyle North America One Parkway South Greenville, SC 29615 USA travel.lifestyle@us.michelin.com www.michelintravel.com Michelin Travel Partner Hannay House 39 Clarendon Road Watford, Herts WD17 1JA UK ☏01923 205240 travelpubsales@uk.michelin.com www.ViaMichelin.com
Special Sales	For information regarding bulk sales, customized editions and premium sales, please contact us at: travel.lifestyle@us.michelin.com www.michelintravel.com

HOW TO USE THIS GUIDE

PLANNING YOUR TRIP

The blue-tabbed PLANNING YOUR TRIP section at the front of the guide gives you **ideas for your trip** and **practical information** to help you organise it. You'll find tours, practical information, a host of outdoor activities, a calendar of events, information on shopping, sightseeing, kids' activities and more.

INTRODUCTION

The orange-tabbed INTRODUCTION section explores London's **History**, spanning Roman Londinium to Henry VIII and to the modern day. The **Art and Culture** section covers architecture, art, literature and music, while **London Today** delves into modern London.

DISCOVERING

The green-tabbed DISCOVERING section features Principal Sights by region, featuring the most interesting local **Sights** and **Walking Tours**. Admission prices shown are normally for a single adult.

ADDRESSES

We've selected the best hotels, restaurants, cafés, shops, nightlife and entertainment to fit all budgets. See the Legend on the cover flap for an explanation of the price categories. See Your Stay in London for a comprehensive list of hotels and restaurants.

Sidebars

Throughout the guide you will find blue, peach and green-coloured text boxes with lively anecdotes, detailed history and background information.

A Bit of Advice

Green advice boxes found in this guide contain practical tips and handy information relevant to your visit or to a sight in the Discovering section.

STAR RATINGS★★★

Michelin has given star ratings for more than 100 years. If you're pressed for time, we recommend you visit the ★★★, or ★★ sights first:

★★★ **Highly recommended**
★★ **Recommended**
★ **Interesting**

MAPS

- Principal Sights map
- Suburbs map
- Local town maps
- Local area maps

All maps in this guide are oriented north, unless otherwise indicated by a directional arrow. The term "Local Map" refers to a map within the chapter or Tourism Region. A complete list of the maps found in the guide appears at the back of this book.

PLANNING YOUR TRIP

INTRODUCTION TO LONDON

DISCOVERING LONDON

CONTENTS

YOUR STAY IN LONDON

Welcome to London

As Samuel Johnson so famously said, "when a man is tired of London, he is tired of life" and indeed, there are enough attractions, sights and sounds in Europe's most exciting city to keep even the most jaded traveller happy for many weeks. The UK's capital is known not only for its British traditions but also for its thoroughly modern multicultural outlook, and you'll find facets of almost every global culture have made their mark.

Juggler in the Piazza, Covent Garden

WEST END *(pp90–118)*

The beating heart of London, this vibrant district of theatres, restaurants, pubs and bars, centres around the cobbled piazza of Covent Garden with its famous street performers and the tight-knit grid of streets which make up the edgier entertainment district of Soho. This is an area to spend some quality time, whether relaxing at a pavement café, taking in a musical or dancing the night away at a buzzing nightclub.

MAYFAIR, MARYLEBONE, REGENT'S PARK *(pp119–132)*

Two of the city's most upmarket areas, Mayfair and Marylebone, are located on the western edge and feature wide, quiet streets, leafy squares and luxurious shops and restaurants. Major shopping thoroughfare Oxford Street divides them, while to the North, Regent's Park attracts Londoners and visitors alike to stroll in the grounds and picnic or play games on the grass, and visit the world-famous zoo.

POLITICAL CENTRE *(pp133–158)*

Westminster is both London's political centre and the home of the Monarchy, with HM The Queen's official residence, Buckingham Palace, located to the west, and both the Houses of Parliament (Britain's seat of government) and Westminster Abbey (site of coronations and royal weddings for centuries) near the banks of the Thames in the east. Whitehall, lined with the offices of almost every government department, links this area with the West End.

KENSINGTON AND CHELSEA *(pp159–186)*

Long the preserve of the wealthy and influential, the twin royal boroughs of Kensington and Chelsea are located to the West of Westminster, on the north bank of the Thames. South Kensington, the home of several major national museums, is the area many visitors gravitate towards, while Hyde Park is a serene place for a stroll. The chic boutiques of Knightsbridge and the King's Road provide ample opportunity for window shopping.

BLOOMSBURY AND HOLBORN *(pp187–203)*

Known for its literary history, Bloomsbury, just north of Covent Garden, is today home to several universities and the incomparable British Museum. Chancery Lane, in Holborn, is London's legal centre.

CAMDEN AND ISLINGTON *(pp204–215)*

With some of London's most desirable residential addresses, Camden and Islington are also pulsing centres of nightlife, home to more restaurants, bars and clubs than even the most energetic party animal could visit in a lifetime. Camden is well known for its fabulous markets, while Islington has a pleasant village vibe.

THE CITY *(pp216–255)*

One of the world's leading financial centres, the City of London may be important but it's certainly not all work and no play in London's oldest area. Cultural venues such as the Barbican Centre and Museum of London are located here, in addition to sights such as St Paul's Cathedral and the Bank of England, as well as a thriving traditional pub scene.

SOUTHWARK, LAMBETH AND WANDSWORTH *(pp256–275)*

Though generally referred to as the "other side" of the river, the southern boroughs of Southwark, Lambeth and Wandsworth are destinations in their own right, featuring the Tate Modern, the Southbank Centre, the London Eye and numerous theatres and galleries.

EAST LONDON *(pp276–290)*

Perhaps London's most exciting area, and site of the successful 2012 Olympic Games, East London is home to a wide range of different cultures and communities. An eclectic mix of bohemian art galleries, lively curry houses (especially around Brick Lane) and new developments give the place a unique character. The Queen Elizabeth Olympic Park will continue the transformation.

MAJOR CENTRAL LONDON MUSEUMS *(pp291–337)*

London is home to some of the world's finest museums. The British Museum showcases its collection of artefacts from around the globe; the Science Museum focuses on stories of human endeavour; the Imperial War Museum explores every element of conflict; and the National Gallery exhibits a wide range of breathtaking artworks.

NORTHWEST LONDON *(pp340–349)*

London's suburbs are not all urban sprawl; there are many pleasant places in the outlying areas. Hampstead Heath is one of the best, offering an easy escape from the bustle of the city. Wembley Stadium, one of Europe's largest sporting and music venues, is located in this part of the city.

SOUTHEAST LONDON *(pp350–361)*

Across the river from Docklands are some of London's best and most convenient day-trips: the UNESCO World Heritage Site of Maritime Greenwich, home of the beautifully restored Cutty Sark; Eltham Palace's unique combination of Medieval and Art Deco architecture; and kids' favourite, the Horniman Museum.

SOUTHWEST LONDON *(pp362–395)*

Some of the city's most attractive areas are found here, including villagey Richmond, with its vast royal park where deer roam, riverside Chiswick, and the Royal Botanic Gardens at Kew. There are several stately homes too, such as Ham House, Osterley Park and the splendid Hampton Court Palace.

St Pancras International Station

Key to maps

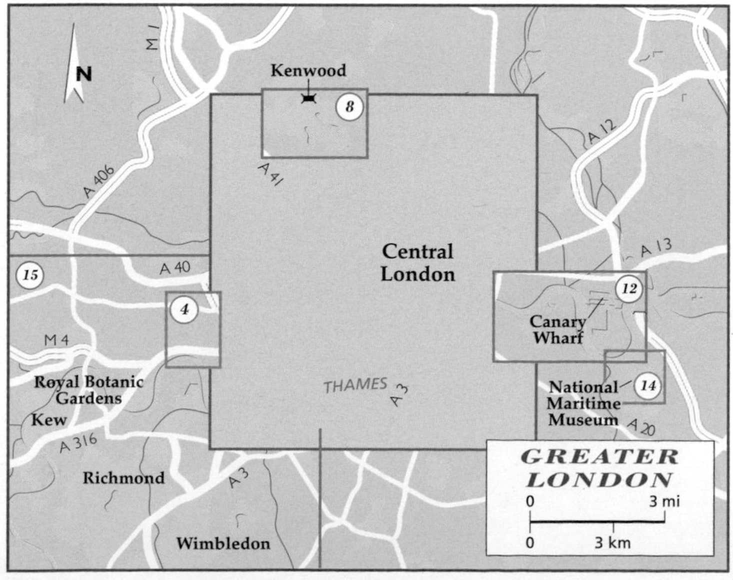

N
M 1
Kenwood
8
A 406
A 41
A 12
Central
London
A 13
15
A 40
4
12
Canary
Wharf
M 4
Royal Botanic
Gardens
THAMES
A 3
National
Maritime
Museum
14
Kew
A 20
A 316
GREATER
LONDON
0
3 mi
0
3 km
Richmond
A 3
Wimbledon

Key to maps

Soho, Covent Garden, Trafalgar Square, The Strand

Whitehall, Westminster, Buckingham, St James's, Pimlico

Knightsbridge, Kensington, Chelsea, Earl's Court

Hyde Park

Hammersmith & Chiswick

Notting Hill, Bayswater & Paddington

Marylebone, Mayfair, Regent's Park

Camden Town [illegible]

Hampstead, Highgate

Bloomsbury, Holborn

The City

Clerkenwell, Islington

Hoxton, Shoreditch, Spitalfields, Whitechapel

Docklands

Lambeth, Southwark [illegible]

Greenwich

[illegible]

PLANNING YOUR TRIP

When and Where to Go

WHEN TO GO

SEASONS

The **busiest period** is the summer (roughly from Easter to September) and particularly during the UK school holidays in July and August. The **summer** season is marked by traditional events: the Chelsea Flower Show, Trooping The Colour (*see Calendar of Events*), the pomp and circumstance of The Proms and outdoor concerts and theatre at many stately homes. Alongside these, more eclectic celebrations such as the Notting Hill Carnival provide colour. In winter most sights remain open, although some operate reduced hours. **Autumn** and **winter** are the best times for visiting museums or for shopping, as places are less crowded, except throughout December when the city gears up for Christmas. During the **Christmas** holidays, baubles flash in the windows of stores such as Liberty of London, Hamley's and Harvey Nichols; Oxford, Regent and Bond Streets light up with Christmas lights and decorations. **Spring** and **autumn** are ideal for visiting parks and gardens when the flowers are in bloom or the leaves are turning colour. The Oxford and Cambridge Boat Race along the Thames in late March/early April, or the Lord Mayor's Show in the City on the second Saturday in November, are good opportunities to get outside.

School Holidays

UK schools have roughly six weeks off in **late July** and **throughout August** and about two weeks off for each of the **Easter** and **Christmas** holidays. There are also week-long half-term breaks in **February**, **May** and **October**. At these times expect higher visitor numbers.

IDEAS FOR YOUR VISIT

A LONDON UNDERGROUND MAP is located on the inside back cover of this guide to help you plan your visit.

WALKING TOURS

WALKWAYS

Discover dramatic sights by following these signed walks with viewpoints throughout the city:

Silver Jubilee Walkway

10mi/16km in the heart of London

Marked by special pavement markers and including two spurs to the Barbican and Bloomsbury and 10 **viewpoints** with indicators identifying the neighbouring buildings: **Leicester Square** – **Parliament Square** – **Lambeth Palace** –**Jubilee Gardens** – **National Theatre** – **Tate Modern** – **Southwark Cathedral** – **Hays Galleria** – **Tower Hill** – **Mansion House** and the **Royal Exchange**. Maps can be bought from the London Tourist Board Information Centres.

Millennium Mile

A pleasant riverside walk along part of the Silver Jubilee Walkway starting from Westminster Bridge and continuing past the London Eye, Tate Modern and The Globe, Shakespeare's theatre, to London Bridge; the second part of the walk along the green path from Butler's Wharf takes in London Bridge, the City area and goes inland to Waterloo.

London Wall Walk

Less than 2mi/1.2km long

Marked by 21 panels, it follows the line of the City wall between the Tower of London and the Museum of London.

Thames Path

180mi/228km

A National Trail marked by acorn signs, running from the Thames Barrier to its source in the Cotswolds; for more information, contact www.nationaltrail.co.uk/thamespath, or call 01865 810 224.

GUIDED WALKS

London features a vast range of **guided walking tours** and **guides** include trained actors, historians, professional Blue Badge holders, botanists, and authors. Common **themes** include: the City of London, Fleet Street, Legal London, Pubs, London Theatres, the West End, Westminster, the East End, Jewish London, Docklands, the Thames, Royal London, Literary London, (Shakespeare's London, Dickens' London, Sherlock Holmes' London etc.), Beatles' London, the Swinging 60s, London Ghost Tours, London Film Locations, and many more.

If you'd rather go it alone, London for free, *www.londonforfree.net*, offers information on eleven **self-guided walks** around different areas of the city, while *www.tfl.gov.uk/gettingaround/walking* lists seven top walking routes in and around London.

A number of **museums** and **exhibitions**, including the City of London Museum, the Museum of Docklands, the London Canal Museum, the Theatre Museum and Shakespeare's Globe, also offer themed walks in their specialist subjects; for details see the main listings for each attraction in the *Discovering London* section *(see Index also).*

Big Bus Tours

A choice of three guided walking tours, which come free with the cost of your bus ticket *(020 7233 9533; www.bigbustours.com).*

Discovery Walks

One of the city's most experienced and compelling guides offers a wide variety of walks with all the usual sights joined by village walks in areas such as Hampstead, Highgate, Chelsea and many others, including ghost tours, Charles Dickens, Shakespeare and a Harry Potter themed walk. 020 8530 8443. www.discovery-walks.com.

Original London Walks

Long-established company offering a huge range of walks, including night walks. 020 7624 3978; 020 7624 WALK *(9255) (recorded information).* www.walks.com.

Mystery Walks

Evening tours, including Jack the Ripper and Ghosts and Executions. 020 8526 7755 or 07957 388 280. www.tourguides.org.uk.

THEMED TOURS

Most museums and art galleries organise guided tours and lectures. For information, see the individual museum or gallery entry.

Official Blue Badge guides permitted to operate in London may be contacted through the tourist information offices; they may be hired for the day or for a series of visits. For more information, visit www.blue-badge-guides.com.

ART

London is packed with art venues. Besides the renowned National Gallery, National Portrait Gallery, Tate Modern and Tate Britain, which present European Art, there are several smaller galleries, which hold many treasures, such as the Courtauld Institute Galleries *(one of several excellent collections in Somerset House)*, the Wallace Collection, the Royal Academy, the Dulwich Picture Gallery and the controversial, cutting-edge Saatchi Gallery in the Duke of York's HQ, Chelsea. Maritime art is on view at the National Maritime Museum in Greenwich.

Splendid works of art belonging to the Royal Collections are on display in royal palaces: Buckingham Palace, the Queen's Gallery, Kensington Palace, Hampton Court and Windsor.

Noble mansions such as Apsley House, Kenwood House, Ham House, Syon Park and Osterley Park also boast superb holdings of fine art.

Well-presented temporary exhibitions devoted to major artists and schools are held at the Royal Academy in Piccadilly and the Hayward Gallery on the South Bank. The ICA in the Mall, the Whitechapel Art Gallery in the East End, the White Cube Gallery in Hoxton, and many other small specialist galleries present contemporary art. Check the press for fine-art exhibitions put on by art dealers in Mayfair, St James's and Knightsbridge. The public is also welcome at auction houses such as Sotheby's.

SCIENCE

Besides the **Science Museum**, do not miss the **Royal Observatory** in Greenwich and the **Planetarium**. The **Kew Bridge Steam Museum** charts industrial advances.

BIRD'S-EYE VIEWS

The biggest overview of the capital is from the **London Eye**. However, the viewing areas on the top floors of **Tate Modern** also afford wonderful perspectives of the City of London, with the dome of St Paul's Cathedral in the foreground; there is a fine view up and down the Thames spanned by the elegant **Millennium Bridge**. The outlook from the dome of **St Paul's Cathedral** is spectacular. The view from the elevated walkway of **Tower Bridge** embraces the graceful **Tower of London** and **Canary Wharf** on the horizon. In the **City**, the **Monument** offers sweeping views in all directions. **Wellington Arch** at **Hyde Park Corner** is a good viewpoint over **Hyde Park**, **Buckingham Palace** and **Knightsbridge**. To enjoy an unusual view of the rooftops of neighbouring buildings, of **Nelson's Column** and of the vista down **Whitehall**, go to the top floor café of the **National Portrait Gallery**. Visitors to **Kenwood House**, in Hampstead, should not miss the viewpoint in the grounds, which pinpoints the capital's distant landmarks. **Primrose Hill**, just north of Regent's Park, and **Greenwich Park**, to the south of the Thames, are great places to enjoy city views while picnicking or walking.

FOOD AND DRINK

London is a world leader when it comes to eating out. You'll find restaurants and cafés on virtually every corner in Central London, with particular concentration around Covent Garden and Soho.

The city's multicultural population makes for an eclectic and exciting range of fare, with every cuisine from **Polish** to **Peruvian** represented. London is particularly known for its **Indian** and **Bangladeshi** cuisine, with every local high street in the suburbs home to at least one curry house – **Brick Lane** is the epicentre of this trend. **Chinese** (especially **Cantonese**) food is also extremely popular and easy to come by – especially, of course, in **Chinatown**. For cheap eats, there is a wide range of farmers markets across the city (don't miss **Borough Market**, near **London Bridge**), as well as numerous cafés and budget restaurants serving up hearty, affordable fare. The top end of the market is also well served, and the city has attracted many top-flight chefs, including British favourites Gordon Ramsay, Jamie Oliver and Heston Blumenthal.

Places to drink run the gamut from cosy local pubs to high-class bars and clubs. Londoners tend to spend a large amount of time in the city's various watering holes and wherever you choose to go, you're likely to find a lively crowd. Most pubs serve traditional real ales, with **Fuller's London Pride** *(brewed in Chiswick)* being the most prolific. All pubs and bars serve a range of wines and many places now also mix a wide variety of cocktails.

Overall, whether you're eating or drinking, prices tend to be high but quality usually follows suit. *For more information and suggestions of places to eat, see the red-cover Michelin Guide.*

GARDENS

Gardens are a national passion and there's no better way to enjoy the great outdoors than to visit **Kew**

Gardens, which makes for a glorious show in all seasons *(lilac, bluebells, azaleas, magnolias, cherry blossom in spring; rhododendrons and roses in summer; heathers in autumn-winter)*.
In spring the rhododendrons of **The Isabella Plantation** in **Richmond Park** gladden the eye, but summer is the best time to visit the city, if gardens are what you're coming to see. The heady fragrance of **Queen Mary's Rose Garden** in **Regent's Park** and of the rose garden in **Syon Park** are among the delights of summer in London, while the fine gardens of **Buckingham Palace**, which were previously enjoyed only by privileged guests at royal garden parties, are now accessible as part of a visit when the palace is open to the public from July to September.
The Edwardian sunken garden and the Flower Walk are the glories of **Kensington Gardens**, while the intricate Knot Garden, the Privy Garden and the Great Vine are special features of **Hampton Court**.
Deliciously aromatic herb gardens are to be found at the delightful **Garden Museum** in Lambeth and at the **Chelsea Physic Garden**.
In addition to the more formal gardens, do not miss out on the city's green lungs – **Hyde Park**, **Holland Park**, **St James's Park**, **Green Park** and **Regent's Park** all offer expansive greenery and plenty of places to sit and smell the flowers.
Further afield are the **Valley Gardens**, with shrubs and trees, and the landscaped **Savill Gardens**, both in Windsor Great Park *(Egham, Windsor, 25mi/40km west of London)*.

ROYAL LONDON

From the earliest times the sovereigns have built their palaces in and around London. **The Tower of London**, built after the Norman Conquest, is one of the earliest royal residences and the glittering **Crown Jewels** are one of its most popular attractions.
All that now remains of the 11C **Westminster Palace** is the majestic **Westminster Hall**, a magnificent large building, which has played a central role in British history for over 900 years.
There are Tudor remnants of **Whitehall Palace** near Whitehall, where Henry VIII held court. Also on the site is the harmonious **Banqueting House** with its wonderful interior décor. This, along with the elegant **Queen's House** in Greenwich, encapsulates the sophistication of the Stuarts.
St James's Palace is a splendid example of Tudor architecture but due to its role as the London residence of several members of the royal family, it is not open to the public. **Clarence House** nearby, formerly the home of Queen Elizabeth, was also the home of the late Queen Mother *(1900–2002)* after the death of George VI in 1952. It is now the official residence of the Prince of Wales and the Duchess of Cornwall.
The red-brick **Kensington Palace**, built in Jacobean style, has undergone major refurbishment; this is where Diana, Princess of Wales, lived, and is where the Duke and Duchess of Cambridge live when in London.
The royal standard flies when the sovereign is in residence at **Buckingham Palace**. The palace is open to the public in season and the fascination of wandering through the State Rooms is irresistible. Do not miss the **Changing of the Guard**, or the elaborate pageantry of state, such as **Trooping The Colour** or the **Opening of Parliament**.
In addition to the central palaces, it is well worth making an excursion out to **Hampton Court** in its riverside setting, or to the majestic **Windsor Castle** and the town of Windsor *(25mi/40km west of London)*.

STATELY HOMES

Several mansions in the vicinity of London retain the rural prospect enjoyed by their original owners. As they were built when the Thames was the main highway, many have a riverside setting.

To the west of London, **Chiswick House**, which was intended for entertaining friends of the Earl of Burlington, epitomises 18C refinement. **Syon Park**, near Kew, an imposing mansion with royal associations, reflects the tastes of discerning patrons of the arts. **Osterley Park** is an elegant stately home with splendid furnishings in the Adam style *(18C)*. Richmond's handsome 17C **Ham House** in the Jacobean style and the charming 18C Palladian **Marble Hill House** in Twickenham also boast many treasures.
To the North of the city, **Kenwood House**, which was built as a country retreat in the 18C, stands amid splendid grounds on Highgate Hill; it has been the setting for several award-winning films.

MILITARY LONDON

London boasts several outstanding collections of arms and armour, which are sure to satisfy even the most demanding of amateur historians.
The **Royal Armouries Collection** in the **Tower of London** is an assemblage of arms, armour and artillery dating from antiquity to the present day.
At the **Imperial War Museum**, you can find out about all aspects of warfare and visit galleries devoted to the World War I and II, while the tale of the British Army over five centuries is traced at the **National Army Museum** in Chelsea.
Excellent displays are presented at the **Wallace Collection**, **Hampton Court** and the **Victoria and Albert Museum**. The **Guards Museum** near Buckingham Palace shows the history of the great Household regiments.
One of the world's oldest military museums, **Firepower, The Royal Artillery Museum** at the **Royal Arsenal** in **Woolwich**, tells the history of artillery from catapult to rocket and features the ground-shaking "Field of Fire" audiovisual show.

LITERARY LONDON

A plethora of writers and dramatists have plied their trade in London and are household names in the history of the English language.
The most illustrious of all is William Shakespeare, whose fame is associated with **The Globe** and other theatres on **Bankside**, an area also haunted by his contemporaries, Ben Jonson and Christopher Marlowe.
Geoffrey Chaucer is linked with **Westminster Abbey**; his pilgrims started from the inns of **Southwark** and made their way to Canterbury.
The poet John Milton is recorded as living in the City in the 17C and the great diarist Samuel Pepys chronicled life in London in the late 17C, from the Plague to the Great Fire.
The renowned 18C scholar Dr Johnson compiled his Dictionary and drafted his essays while living off **Fleet Street**.
Several novels by Charles Dickens are set in Victorian London, where he spent a difficult childhood, living in **Bloomsbury** with his family. The Bloomsbury Group, whose famous members included Virginia Woolf, EM Forster, Dora Carrington, Lytton Strachey and many others, also flourished here, around the leafy squares. Other celebrated figures include the poet Rupert Brooke, novelist DH Lawrence and the philosopher Bertrand Russell.
Thomas Carlyle, Hilaire Belloc, Oscar Wilde and AA Milne all resided in **Chelsea**, as did Mark Twain, Henry James and TS Eliot. Elizabeth Barrett and Robert Browning are associated with **Marylebone**, which also lays claim to Sir Arthur Conan Doyle.
Lord Byron won fame while living in **St James's**, while Thomas Hardy and George Bernard Shaw were famous residents of the **Adelphi**, on the **Strand**. The nearby **Savoy Theatre** was where Gilbert and Sullivan founded the D'Oyly Carte Company.
Further north, Karl Marx haunted the reading room of the **British Library**, near King's Cross, while researching and writing *Das Kapital,* and is buried

in **Highgate Cemetery**, while the leafy groves of **Hampstead** nurtured the poet John Keats, crime writer Agatha Christie and James Bond creator Ian Fleming.

CRUISES

One of the best ways to see the city is to join an organised cruise and float past the main sights.
The **London Eye** runs boat tours, while the **Tate to Tate** boat connects the **Tate Britain** and **Modern** galleries. For information about **Thames Cruises**, contact www.visitlondon.com.

City Cruises

Year-round between Westminster, Waterloo *(London Eye)*, Tower and Greenwich piers: daily 10am–6pm, with later sailings in summer; £11 one way, £14 round trip *(child £5.40/£7)* Westminster–Greenwich; other legs cheaper. **River Red Rover** one-day hop-on-hop-off ticket, £15.30 *(child £7.65)*. A **Family Red Rover** is available online for 2 adults and up to 3 children *(£39.50)*. There are also lunch, tea, dinner, disco and cabaret cruises, plus Christmas and New Year buffet and dance cruises.

- **Cherry Garden Pier,** London SE16 4TU. ☎020 7740 0400. www.citycruises.com.

Circular Cruises

Round trip of London's famous landmarks, which starts at Westminster Pier and calls at Festival, Bankside, and London Bridge City piers before turning at St Katharine's pier for the return journey. One way £8.40, return £11 *(child £4.20/£5.50)*.

- **The Old Pump House,** Blackfriars Pier. ☎020 7936 2033. www.crownrivercruise.co.uk.

London Duck Tours

A 75min adventure on an amphibious vehicle; road tour of Westminster followed by a river trip. Departs from Chicheley Street *(behind the London Eye)* daily 10am–sunset. Adult £21, child £14. ☎020 7928 3132. www.londonducktours.co.uk.

Westminster Passenger Service Association (WPSA)

Scheduled service from Westminster to Kew, Richmond and Hampton Court. Daily from April–October. Westminster-Hampton Court £15.00 single, £22.50 return *(child £7.50/£11.25)*; other legs cheaper. Journey time 3hr.

- **Westminster Pier**, Victoria Embankment, London SW1A 2JH ☎020 7930 2062/4721. www.wpsa.co.uk.

Lunch and Evening Cruises

- **Bateaux London**
  Lunch and dinner cruises. ☎020 7695 1800. www.bateauxlondon.com.
- **Woods' Silver Fleet**
  Upmarket private dining. ☎020 7759 1900. www.silverfleet.co.uk.

CANAL BOATS

Services operate on Regent's Canal between Little Venice and Camden Lock, via London Zoo; dinner cruises, too.

London Waterbus Company

From Little Venice to Camden Lock. Daily summer 10am–4/5pm. £7.20 single *(50min), £10.30 round trip (110min)*; child £6/£8.40. More for London Zoo. Reduced service in winter. ☎020 7482 2550. www.londonwaterbus.com.

Jason's Trip

1.5hr round trip from Little Venice to Camden Lock on former working boats with live commentary. April–November only, 10.30am–3.15pm *(additional later service June–August)*; £8 single, £9 return *(child £7/£8)*.

- Departs from opposite 42 Blomfield Road, London W9 2PE. ☎020 7286 3428. www.jasons.co.uk.

What to See and Do

OUTDOOR FUN

CYCLING

Cycle routes run throughout the capital, across the Royal Parks and along many bus routes.

Barclays Cycle Hire

All around the city you will see 'Boris bikes', as they are known after the mayor (Boris Johnson) who introduced them. They can be booked online, or you can pay at one of the many docking stations (*see p33*). They are a fun and inexpensive way to explore London's parks, but caution is advised if you plan to cycle on the streets. Cycling in London is not for the faint-hearted. 020 8216 6666. www.tfl.gov.uk/roadusers/cycling.

The London Bicycle Tour Company

As well as hiring bicycles, this company offers three **guided cycle tours of London** (*see p33*). Gabriel's Wharf, 56 Upper Ground SE1 9PP. 020 3318 3088. www.londonbicycle.com.

BOATING

For details on boating, cycling and angling on and along the canals contact:

- **London Waterways**
  Canal & River Trust, Docklands Office , 420 Manchester Road, London E14 9ST. www.canalrivertrust.org.uk.

Self-Drive Boat Hire

- **Lee Valley Boat Centre**
  Old Nazeing Rd. Broxbourne, Herts EN10 6LX. 01992 462085. www.leevalleyboats.co.uk.

HORSE RIDING

Hyde Park Stables *(020 7723 2813; www.hydeparkstables.com)* offer horse riding along Hyde Park's 5mi/8km of bridleways, plus lessons in an outdoor arena for all abilities.

ACTIVITIES FOR KIDS

Children's playgrounds are to be found in most parks and there are plenty of activities for kids of all ages in London. Museums and galleries have special programmes, from treasure hunts to storytelling, and even sleepovers to engage young imaginations. The wonderful exhibits at the **Natural History Museum** bring ecological and environmental issues to the fore, while next door at the **Science Museum**, children can take part in experiments relating to scientific and technological advances. The mummies at the **British Museum** have a gruesome appeal, while thrilling sea shanties are told at the **National Maritime Museum**. Possibly the best of the museums for kids is the **Horniman Museum** in south London, which has a wonderful array of activities for youngsters, many based around its superb collection of musical instruments.

Children will also enjoy experiencing the spartan conditions on board the **Golden Hinde** and exploring the World War II light cruiser **HMS Belfast**, which bristles with 12 x 6in (15cm) guns. At **London Zoo**, families can observe the antics of the inmates (monkeys are a particular favourite) and even adopt an animal, while **city farms** in **Hackney**, **Shoreditch**, **Mudchute** and elsewhere are particularly popular with younger kids. The **Planetarium** and the **Royal Observatory** at **Greenwich** have exciting presentations of the heavens. The grisly exhibits of the **London Dungeon** and the **Chamber of Horrors** at **Madame Tussaud's** will bring a thrill to some and scare others senseless, while **Pollock's Toy Museum and Shop** and the **V&A Museum of Childhood** strike a nostalgic note. The delightful shows at the **Polka Theatre for Children** in Wimbledon and the **Little Angel Theatre** in Islington will enchant the young ones; older children can take up **brass rubbing** at Westminster Abbey, in the crypt of St Martin-in-the-Fields and at All Hallows by the Tower. As well as all the other theatres and cinemas, there are **IMAX** screens in Waterloo and at the Science Museum. *Visit London runs a special section for families: www.visitlondon.com; and Time Out, a listings magazine (www.timeout.com) carries special children's supplements during the school holidays.*

SIGHTSEEING

BUS TOURS

Some tours are non-stop; others allow passengers to hop on and off and continue on a later bus with the original ticket. Ticket prices vary *(from £18)* and some include entry and guided tours of sights. Sightseeing tours on open-top double-decker buses (weather permitting) are an excellent introduction to London.

The Original London Tour

Hop-on-hop-off service, which operates on three different routes and has a recorded commentary in 8 different languages. *Every 15–20min from 9am–6/7pm (seasonal variations). Adult ticket £26 (£23 online), child £13 (£11 online), family (2 adults and 3 children) £91 (£78 online). Starting points at Piccadilly Circus, Trafalgar Square, Woburn Place (near Russell Square), Grosvenor Gardens (near Victoria) and Hyde Park Corner. 020 8877 1722. www.theoriginaltour.com.*

The Big Bus Experience

Hop-on hop-off service, choice of live commentary (Red Tour) or recorded in a choice of 8 languages (Blue Tour). Every 10–20min from 8.30am–6pm *(4.30pm Oct–Mar).* Adult £29, child £12, (online £25/£10), family *(2 adults and 2 children*) £70 (£60 online). Ticket includes three guided walking tours *(Royal London Walk, Ghosts by Gaslight and Harry Potter film locations),* a river cruise and a voucher booklet. Tickets available online or when boarding. Main departure points are Baker Street, Green Park, Marble Arch and Victoria. 020 7233 9533. www.bigbustours.com.

Evan Evans Tours

Guided bus tours of London including tours of major sites and excursions to Windsor, Oxford, Stratford-upon-Avon, Stonehenge, Bath, Leeds Castle and Canterbury. *020 7950 1777. www.evanevanstours.co.uk.*

Visitors Sightseeing Tours

Half-day and full-day tours of London, themed events and tours outside London. *020 7636 7175. www.visitorsightseeing.co.uk.*

TAXI TOURS

Black cab drivers in London must pass "The Knowledge" – a two- to four-year training course with countless exams – in order to drive in London. Besides themed tours of central London, there are also visits to "London's Villages": Hampstead, Richmond, etc.

Door-to-door pickup and a 2hr *"Sights of London"* tour costs £130 *(£135 Sat, Sun and Bank Holidays)* per taxi *(8am–6pm);* "London by Night" costs £140 *(£145 Sat, Sun and Bank Holidays)* per taxi (6pm–midnight). Half-day tours to Hampton Court or Windsor are £295.

Black Taxi Tours of London

7 Durweston Mews, London W1U 6DF. 020 7935 9363. www.blacktaxitours.co.uk.

DISCOUNTS

Spending time in London is expensive. Visitors wishing to keep costs down will find information on **budget accommodation** *( )* in the section *Your Stay in the City (see pp398–409).* If you are travelling by train to the capital, contact 2for1 London (www.daysoutguide.co.uk), which offers discounts for entry to hundreds of London attractions.

Calendar of Events

Listed below are some of the most popular annual events. For specific dates and full details, visit any tourist information centre or log on to www.visitlondon.com.

JANUARY

New Year's Day Parade
Boat Show at Earls Court Exhibition Centre *(starts first Thursday)*
Chinese New Year in Soho *(Jan/Feb)*

FEBRUARY

Start of RBS 6 Nations Championship (Rugby Union) at Twickenham
Clowns' Church Service at Holy Trinity, Dalston *(First Sunday)*
Destinations Travel Show at Earls Court Exhibition Centre
Great Spitalfields Pancake Race *(Shrove Tuesday)*

MARCH

Chelsea Antiques Fair, Old Town Hall, Chelsea

The Boat Race

The annual Oxford and Cambridge Boat Race, brainchild of Charles Merivale, a Cambridge student, and Oxford student Charles Wordsworth (William Wordsworth's nephew), was first held at Henley-on-Thames in 1829. The clash transferred to the tideway between Putney and Mortlake in 1845, and on race day each March draws some 250 000 spectators to line the banks and pubs along the course. Competition is fierce: crews train for seven months for this one epic race of 4mi 374yd/6.8km. In 2012 the race was stopped when a protester swam between the boats. Famous Boat Race oarsmen include actor Hugh Laurie and Olympic gold medalist, Matthew Pinsent.

Head of the River Race from Mortlake to Putney *(420 crews leaving at 10 second intervals)*
Oxford and Cambridge Boat Race from Putney to Mortlake
Ideal Home Exhibition at Earls Court Exhibition Centre
St Patrick's Day Parade and party, Hyde Park to Trafalgar Square

EASTER

Service and distribution of hot cross buns at St Bartholomew-the-Great *(Good Friday)*
Carnival Parade in Battersea Park *(Easter Sunday)*

APRIL

RHS London Orchid Show and Botanical Art Show at Westminster
London Marathon from Docklands to Westminster

MAY

Royal Windsor Horse Show held in Home Park, Windsor
Chelsea Flower Show at the Royal Hospital, Chelsea
F A Cup Final, Wembley Stadium
Chelsea Pensioners' Oak Apple Day Parade at the Royal Hospital, Chelsea
Covent Garden May Fayre and Puppet Festival – Punch & Judy, that stalwart of the English seaside
Open-air theatre seasons start at Shakespeare's Globe and Regent's Park Open-Air Theatre *(to September)*

JUNE

Beating Retreat at Horse Guards Parade, Whitehall
Trooping The Colour at Horse Guards Parade *(Queen's Birthday)*
Hampton Court Music Festival at Hampton Court Palace
Spitalfields Annual Music Festival
Taste of London food festival in Regent's Park
AEGON Grass Court Championships at Queen's Club

Royal Ascot Racing Week
British Polo Open Championships at Cowdray Park
Royal Academy Summer Exhibition at Burlington House, Piccadilly
Wimbledon Championships at the All England Club, Wimbledon *(2 weeks)*
Cricket Test Matches at Lord's and The Oval

JULY
Hampton Court Palace **Flower Show**
The Proms – Sir Henry Wood's Promenade Concerts at the Royal Albert Hall *(8 weeks)*
The City Festival is celebrated in the City Churches and Halls
Swan Upping on the River Thames, when the swan population is counted along stretches of the river
Doggett's Coat and Badge Race rowed by 6 new freemen of the Watermen and Lightermen's Company from London Bridge to Chelsea Bridge
Opera and ballet at the Holland Park Outdoor Theatre

AUGUST
Great British Beer Festival – Olympia Exhibition Hall
RHS Summer Flower Show in Westminster
London Mela – Asian arts and culture festival
Notting Hill Carnival in Ladbroke Grove *(Bank Holiday Weekend)*

SEPTEMBER
Friends Provident Trophy Final at Lord's Cricket Ground
Costermongers' Harvest Festival and Church Parade, with Pearly kings and queens, from Guildhall to Cheapside
Great River Race, the Thames – 150 crafts, from dragon boats to Hawaiian war canoes
Mayor's Thames Festival – free festival with carnival and fireworks on the South Bank of the Thames
Open House Weekend – fascinating buildings usually closed open their doors for one weekend a year

OCTOBER
Goldsmith's Fair, Goldsmiths Hall *(First week)*
London Film Festival organised by the BFI *(three weeks)*
Chelsea Crafts Fair at Chelsea Town Hall
Opening of the Michaelmas Law Term: Procession of Judges in full robes to Westminster Abbey

NOVEMBER
London to Brighton Veteran Car Run departing from Hyde Park Corner *(First Sunday)*
Lord Mayor's Show held in the City *(Saturday nearest to 9 November)*
Remembrance Sunday Cenotaph, Whitehall *(11am service; Sunday nearest to 11 November)*
State Opening of Parliament by HM the Queen at Westminster
Regent Street Christmas lights are switched on
Open-air ice-rinks at Hampton Court, Somerset House, Greenwich and elsewhere *(to January)*

DECEMBER
Lighting of the **Norwegian Christmas Tree** in Trafalgar Square
Carol Services throughout the capital's churches

Ice-skating rink at Somerset House

Know Before You Go

USEFUL WEBSITES

London offers a dizzying array of entertainments and attractions. Use these websites to gather information and plan an itinerary before you leave home.

www.visitlondon.com
The **tourist office** runs a comprehensive website with full details of events and sightseeing.

www.thisislondon.co.uk
London's newspaper, the *Evening Standard*, has the latest news on the capital and good entertainment listings. This is its online version.

www.timeout.com/london
The weekly magazine, *Time Out*, has comprehensive entertainment listings.

www.londontown.com
Comprehensive information on sightseeing, entertainment, services, shopping and many other topics is available on this website.

www.freelondonlistings.co.uk
Site listing attractions and events with **free** or nearly free access.

www.officiallondontheatre.co.uk
Search theatre listings and buy tickets for West End shows.

TOURIST OFFICES

INTERNATIONAL

The **Visit Britain tourist authority** provides assistance in planning a trip to London and has an excellent range of brochures and maps. For all overseas offices, refer to www.visitbritain.org/aboutus/contactus/officefinder.

- **Australia**
  Level 16, The Gateway,
  1 Macquarie Place , Sydney,
  NSW 2000 , Australia
  ✆+61 (0)2 8247 2272
- **Canada**
  160 Bloor Street East , Ontario
  Toronto, M4W 1B9
  Canada
  ✆+1 416 646 6674
- **France**
  BP70-154
  75363 Paris Cedex 08
  Paris, 75008
  France
  ✆+33 (0) 1 44 51 34 95
- **United States**
  Los Angeles
  11766 Wilshire Blvd
  Suite 1200
  Los Angeles 90025
  California
  USA
  ✆+1 310 481 2989

  New York
  845 Third Avenue, 10th Floor
  New York, NY 10022
  USA
  ✆+ 212 850 0336

LOCAL

The main information centres operated by **Visit London** (www.visitlondon.com) are located as follows:

- **City of London Information Centre**
  St. Pauls Churchyard,
  London EC4M 8BX
  ✆020 7332 1456
- **Kings Cross St Pancras Travel Information Centre**
  LUL Western Ticket Hall (through brick arches at St Pancras to LUL),
  Euston Road
  London N1 9AL
- **Piccadilly Circus Travel Information Centre**
  Piccadilly Circus
  Underground Station
  London W1D 7DH
- **Victoria Station Travel Information Centre**
  Opposite Platform 8,
  Victoria Railway Station
  London SW1V 1JU

INTERNATIONAL VISITORS

EMBASSIES AND CONSULATES

Australian High Commission:
Australia House, Strand, WC2B 4LA
020 7379 4334
www.australia.org.uk

Canadian High Commission:
1 Grosvenor Sq, W1K 4AB.
020 7258 6600
www.canada.org.uk

Republic of Ireland:
Embassy of Ireland, 17 Grosvenor Place, SW1X 7HR
020 7235 2171
www.gov.ie

New Zealand High Commission:
80 Haymarket SW1Y 4TQ
020 7930 8422
www.nzembassy.com

South African High Commission:
South Africa House, Trafalgar Square, WC2N 5DP
020 7451 7299
www.southafricahouseuk.com

United States Embassy:
24 Grosvenor Square, W1A 2LQ
020 7499 9000
www.usembassy.org.uk

ENTRY REQUIREMENTS

Passports

EU nationals will need their **passport** or **national ID card** to enter the UK. Non-EU nationals may also require a **visa** in addition to their passport. Loss or theft should be reported to the appropriate embassy or consulate and to the local police. It is sensible to photocopy the relevant pages of your passport and keep the photocopy separate from the passport itself.

Visas

A **visa** to visit the United Kingdom is not required by nationals of member states of the European Economic Area (EEA), the Commonwealth (including Australia, Canada, New Zealand and South Africa) and the USA. Nationals of other countries should check with the British Embassy and apply for a visa, if necessary, in good time.
Entry visas are required by Australian, New Zealand, Canadian and US nationals for a stay exceeding three months. All visitors from areas outside the EEA must apply for a visa before travelling if they plan to stay for more than six months.
For up-to-date official information on visas, visit www.ukvisas.gov.uk.
US citizens should view *Tips for Traveling Abroad* online *(travel.state.gov)* for general information on visa requirements, customs regulations, medical care, etc.
American nationals can download a passport application from the website of the **National Passport Information Center**: http://travel.state.gov/passport or call 1 877 487 2778.

CUSTOMS REGULATIONS

Tax-free allowances for various commodities are governed by EU legislation except in the Channel Islands and the Isle of Man, which have different regulations. Details of these allowances and restrictions are available at most ports of entry to Great Britain.
The UK Customs Office produces a leaflet on customs regulations and the full range of "duty free" allowances; in the United Kingdom a sales tax of 20 percent is added to most retail goods. Non-EU nationals may reclaim this tax when leaving the country; paperwork should be completed by the retailer at the time of purchase.

Prohibited Items

It is against the law to bring into the United Kingdom any drugs, firearms and ammunition, obscene material featuring children, counterfeit merchandise, unlicensed livestock *(birds or animals)*, anything related to endangered species *(furs, ivory, horn, leather)* and certain plants *(potatoes, bulbs, seeds, trees)*. It is also an offence to import duty-paid goods *(to a maximum value of £145)* from the EU other than for personal use.

HM Revenue & Customs (HMRC)

The website customs.hmrc.gov.uk has information on import to and export from the UK. For US visitors, the website http://travel.state.gov/travel has a comprehensive section on travelling abroad.

Domestic Animals

Domestic animals *(dogs, cats)* with vaccination documents are allowed into the country. However, animal import legislation is complex and animals may require a period of quarantine. It is strongly suggested that you take advice several months in advance of travelling if you wish to bring your animals with you.
Contact **DEFRA Animal Health***:* ✆08459 335 577; from outside the UK ✆+44 20 738 6951; ww.defra.gov.uk.

HEALTH

Medical care in the UK is free to all British residents, excepting charges for prescriptions, dentistry, hearing and sight tests.
Visitors to Britain are entitled to treatment at the Accident and Emergency Departments (A&E) of National Health Service hospitals. For an overnight or longer stay in hospital, payment may well be required.
Visitors from EU countries should apply to their own National Social Security Offices for the **European Health Insurance Card (EHIC)**, which entitles them to free medical treatment.
If you are not entitled to free reciprocal medical care, it is crucial to take out comprehensive travel insurance, including medical cover, prior to departure as treatment in the UK may be extremely expensive.
For minor complaints, pharmacists may be able to assist – there are numerous pharmacies in all parts of London. Alternatively, for a free 24hr phone or online consultation with a nurse or doctor, contact **NHS Direct** *(✆0845 4647; www.nhsdirect.nhs.uk)*.
To contact a doctor for **first aid** or **emergency medical advice**, visit or call the walk-in medical centre Medicentre *(✆020 7510 0300, www.medicentre.co.uk)*. There is a charge for this service.
If you are treated by a doctor in the UK, remember to ask for a photocopy of any prescriptions so you are able to receive any follow-up treatment back home.
American Express offers a service, "**Global Assist**", for any medical, legal or personal emergency, *call collect from anywhere:* ✆715 343 7977.

Emergencies

In case of an emergency, dial the free nationwide number *(999) and ask for Fire, Police or Ambulance.*

ACCESSIBILITY

The sights described in this guide that are easily accessible to those with reduced mobility are indicated in the admission times and charges by the ♿ symbol.
The range of possible facilities is great but readers are advised to telephone the attraction in advance to check on availability.
The red-cover **Michelin Guide Great Britain and Ireland** indicates hotels with facilities suitable for those with disabilities. Booklets for the disabled are published by organisations such as VisitBritain, the National Trust and the Department of Transport. Many ticket offices, banks and other venues are fitted with hearing loops.
The **Royal Association for Disability and Rehabilitation** *(RADAR)* publishes a guide to hotels and holiday centres, transport, accommodation for children and activity holidays.

RADAR

12 City Forum, 250 City Road, London ECIV 8AF. ✆020 7250 3222, www.radar.org.uk.

Artsline

Artsline provides up-to-date information on cinema, theatre and gallery access for disabled people. The website allows you to search through over 1000 arts venues across London.

- C/o 21 Pine Court
  Wood Lodge Gardens
  Bromley BR1 2WA.
  www.artsline.org.uk.

Transport

Transport for London *(☏020 7222 1234; www.tfl.gov.uk)* publishes information on wheelchair-accessible bus routes and underground stations. There are no passes or discounts on London public transport for visitors with physical disabilities.

Getting There and Getting Around

BY PLANE

Hundreds of airlines operate services to the five airports serving London – **Heathrow**, **Gatwick**, **Luton**, **Stansted** and **City**. Information, brochures and timetables are available from the airlines and from travel agents.

Details of how to get to the airport may be found on the **London Tourist Board** website *(www.visitlondon.com)*; for **Heathrow** and **Stansted**, visit the **British Airports Authority:** *www.baa.com.*

HEATHROW AIRPORT

Heathrow handles most major airlines' scheduled flights. It is situated 20mi/32km west of London, off the A4/M4.

- **Airport Information**
  ☏0844 335 1801
  www.heathrowairport.com

To and From the Airport

By Rail – **Tube/Underground** services to and from Central London are provided by the **Piccadilly line** with connections to other lines *(see LONDON UNDERGROUND MAP on the inside back cover)*. It takes about 50 minutes to reach central London. Alternatively, take the **Bakerloo**, **Circle**, **District** or **Hammersmith & City** lines to London Paddington and board the **Heathrow Connect** *(www.heathrowconnect.com)* service, which takes about 25 minutes to reach the airport or the faster **Heathrow Express** *(see box)* from London Paddington National Rail Station.

At night the N9 bus shuttles between Heathrow *(Terminals 1,2,3 and 5)* and Trafalgar Square/Aldwych roughly every 20min. For further information, contact **Transport for London** *(TfL)* on ☏0843 222 1234 or visit www.tfl.gov.uk.

By Coach/Bus – National Express operates a coach service from Heathrow Airport Central Bus Station to London Victoria Coach Station, which takes 35–75min and operates every 10–50min *(to Heathrow: 5.35am–11.59pm; from Heathrow: 5.35am–9.40pm)*. Tickets cost £6 *(single)*; £11 *(return)*. ☏08717 818 178. www.nationalexpress.com.

By Taxi – Subject to road traffic conditions, a taxi will take around 40min on a good day to reach Marble

Heathrow Express

With a journey time of 15–20min, the **Heathrow Express** train provides a frequent, fast rail link between London Paddington Station and Heathrow Central *(Terminals 1, 2 and 3)*, and on to Terminal 5. To reach **Terminal 4**, take the regular free shuttle train service. *www.heathrowexpress.com.*

Arch (but it is best to allow at least an hour) – approximate cost £90-£110. There are taxi desks and taxi ranks at all terminals. Services may be booked in advance on ✆020 7908 0207 if paying by cash, ✆020 7432 1432 if paying by credit card *(Computer Cabs)*.

GATWICK AIRPORT

Gatwick airport is located 30mi/48km to the south down the M25/M23. Two terminals *(**North** and **South**)* handle flights to destinations worldwide, including scheduled, charter and low-cost flights.

- **Airport Information** ✆0844 892 0322. www.gatwickairport.com.

To and From the Airport

By Rail – The rail link **Gatwick Express** shuttles to and from Victoria Station *(30min; 35min at night and on Sun. Departures every 15min from 5am until midnight plus some earlier services)*. Tickets cost £19.90 (child £9.95; online £17.75/£8.85) for a single journey (£15.95/£7.95 online) and £34.90 (child £17.45) for a return (£31.05/£15.55 online). ✆0845 850 1530. www.gatwickexpress.com. Slower (but cheaper) services are also offered by other companies such as **First Capital Connect** *(✆0845 026 4700; www.firstcapitalconnect.co.uk)* and **Southern** *(✆08451 272920; www.southernrailway.com)*. **Gatwick Railway Station** has more than 900 services daily to all parts of the UK; contact **National Rail Enquiries** *(✆08457 48 49 50)* for more details.

By Coach/Bus – National Express *(www.nationalexpress.com)* runs a coach service from **London Victoria Coach Station** to **Gatwick Airport** *(every 30min to an hour from 7am–11.30pm; journey time is 1hr5min–1hr35min)*.
National Express also runs a coach service between **Gatwick** and **Heathrow Airports**.
easyBus runs a direct service from **both terminals** to **Earl's Court** *(every 15–20min; 24 hours a day)*. Journey time is approximately 65min and tickets cost from £2 one way and £4 return if you buy online at www.easybus.co.uk.

By Taxi – Taxi services from both terminals are provided by the airport's official concessionaire, **Airport Cars Gatwick**. There is a quoted fare system and the cost of the journey is made known to customers in advance. Taxis can be pre-booked and all fares may be paid in advance by cash or credit card or at the end of the journey by cash only:
Airport Cars Gatwick ✆01293 550 000, www.taxis.gatwickairport.com. *(Allow 65–90min to reach central London and expect to pay around £100 one way)*.

STANSTED AIRPORT

Located near Bishop's Stortford, Essex, about 34mi/54km northeast of London *(✆0844 335 1803 www.stanstedairport.com)*.
This is home to mostly low-cost carriers (it is Ryanair's base), but it is also heavily used by charter services during the summer.

To and From the Airport

By Rail – Stansted Express runs from **Liverpool Street Station** to **Stansted Airport** every 15–30min. Journey time is 50min and tickets cost £23.40 single, £32.80 return *(child £11.70/£16.40)*. There's a £1 discount (child 50p) each way for booking online *(✆0845 600 7245; www.stanstedexpress.com)*.

By Coach/Bus – National Express coaches run every 20min between Stansted and Victoria daily *(✆08717 818 178; www.nationalexpress.co.uk)*.
easyBus operates a 24hr service to Baker Street. Departures are every 20min and journey time is approx. 65min. Tickets cost from £2 one way and £4 return if you buy online at www.easybus.co.uk.

By Taxi – Taxi services are provided by **24x7**: ✆01279 661 111. www.24x7stansted.com.

CITY AIRPORT

City Airport lies 6mi/9.6km east of central London. The airport generally services European business centre destinations.

- **Airport Information** ✆020 7646 0088. www.londoncityairport.com.

To and From the Airport

By Rail – Docklands Light Railway (DLR) connects the airport to East London. Departures to London every 15min (7min to Canning Town or Woolwich Arsenal; 22min to Bank).

By Coach/Bus – Bus no. 473 runs between the airport, Stratford, Silvertown, North Woolwich (for the free Woolwich ferry and foot tunnel) and Prince Regent DLR station; **bus 474** runs between the airport, Canning Town, North Woolwich Station and East Beckton via West Silvertown rail station.

LONDON LUTON AIRPORT

Located in Luton, Bedfordshire, 32mi/51km north of London.

- **Airport Information** www.london-luton.co.uk.

To and From the Airport

By Rail – First Capital Connect trains and **East Midlands trains** run from St Pancras *(35min)* to Luton Airport Parkway, where there is a free airport shuttle bus *(5–10min)*.

By Coach/Bus – National Express runs coaches to London Victoria every 10–30min; 24 hours a day. *Tickets cost £15 one way (child £12) and £16 return (child £13).*
There are also services to Gatwick and Heathrow airports. *✆08717 818 178; www.nationalexpress.co.uk.*
easyBus runs an express service every 15min between Luton and Baker Street. Journey times are approx. 80min and tickets cost from £2 one way and £4 return *(buy online at www.easybus.co.uk; tickets bought from the driver cost considerably more).*

Parking

There are short- and long-term car parks at all the London airports and free shuttle buses to the terminals at regular intervals. For the best prices, book online in advance.

BY SHIP

There are numerous cross-Channel passenger and car ferries and other ferry or shipping services from the Continent, the Channel Islands and Ireland. For details, apply to travel agencies or to the ferry companies.

- **Brittany Ferries** ✆0871 244 0744 www.brittanyferries.com
- **Norfolkline** ✆0871 574 7235 www.norfolkline.com
- **Irish Ferries** Dublin ✆00 353 818 300 400 www.irishferries.com
- **P & O Ferries** *✆08716 642121 www.poferries.com*

BY TRAIN

London has 13 mainline terminals connected by the Underground and in some cases by inter-station buses. *(Tickets and information are available from the terminals. Tickets can be expensive, but long-distance tickets are considerably cheaper if you travel off-peak and book in advance.)*. Train services are operated by about 20 different companies. It is important to check whether any ticket you purchase restricts you to one operator, in order to avoid travelling with another company and incurring a penalty fine. Many outlying areas of Greater London and much of south London are served by overground commuter trains. Travel from stations within the six zones is included on the daily and weekly travelcards and Oyster cards (*see p31*). Try to avoid

The London Pass

The **London Pass** offers options with or without transport as well as entry to 60 London attractions and fast-track entry. Purchase from London Transport Information Centres, tourist information centres and major train and bus stations. It may be more economical to buy the version without transport, starting at £47 for one day and going up to £91.80 for six days per adult *(www.londonpass.com).*

all mainline stations during rush hours *(8am–10am, 4.30pm–6.30pm).*

Note for Travellers with Disabilities: It is important for disabled travellers to check in advance on procedures and facilities and to arrange assistance at stations before undertaking your journey; smaller British stations are not particularly wheelchair-friendly. *0845 605 0525; www.disabledpersons-railcard.co.uk.*

Rail Information and Bookings

Information on fares and timetables, on special deals for unlimited travel or group travel in Europe, on rail services and on other concessionary tickets, including combined train and bus tickets, is available from **National Rail Enquiries** 08457 48 49 50; www.nationalrail.co.uk.

Websites such as www.qjump.co.uk, www.thetrainline.co.uk and www.raileasy.co.uk offer reduced priced tickets for all operators.

For European services, including Eurostar and railcards, contact **Rail Europe**: 0844 848 4078. www.raileurope.co.uk.

Transport for London

Windsor House, 42–50 Victoria Street, London SW1H 0TL. 020 7222 1234 *(24hr)*; deaf callers 020 7918 3015. www.tfl.gov.uk. **Oyster Cards** *(see p31).*

MAIN LONDON STATIONS

Charing Cross – Services to south-east England.

London Bridge – Services to south, central and south-east England, and the suburbs of Greenwich, Eltham and Dulwich.

Cannon Street – Services to south-east England.

Blackfriars – Services to south-central and south-east England.

Fenchurch Street – Local commuter services to south Essex (including Basildon and Southend).

Euston – Local commuter services to the north of London (including Watford, Hemel Hempstead and Northampton). Intercity services to the West Midlands; North Wales; Northwest England; Scotland via the West Coast; Northern Ireland; Republic of Ireland.

King's Cross – Local commuter services to the North of London including St Albans, Hitchin, Bedford, Stevenage and Cambridge. Intercity services to East and Northeast England; Scotland via the East Coast.

Liverpool Street – Local and intercity services to Essex and East Anglia and the **Stansted Express**.

Marylebone – Services to Birmingham, including Stratford-upon-Avon.

Paddington – Intercity services to the West of England and South Wales. Local commuter services to the West of London (including Maidenhead, Reading and the Thames Valley). Also home to the **Heathrow Express** *(15–20min service every 15min to Heathrow Airport, see p25).*

St Pancras – Eurostar services continental Europe; East Midlands services the Midlands and northern England (including Nottingham, Derby, Sheffield and Leeds); regular First Capital Connect services run from Bedford and Luton through London to Brighton).

Victoria – Local commuter services around south London. Services to Gatwick Airport and southern England, including the **Gatwick Express**.

The **Orient Express** also operates out of Victoria: ✆0845 077 2222 www.orient-express.com.
Waterloo – Services to southwestern England and Windsor. Local commuter services around south London (including Richmond, Wimbledon and Hampton Court).

EUROSTAR

Eurostar runs regular services from London (**St Pancras International Station**) to Calais, Brussels, Lille and Paris Gare du Nord, from which there are excellent onward connections across France, and direct trains to Disneyland Resort Paris. Prices are comparable with the airlines and the service is far quicker, with a 45min check-in *(1hr for Avignon and ski services)*, and travelling time of 2 hrs 20min to Paris. ✆*08432 186 186 (bookings); www.eurostar.com*.

BY COACH/BUS

Coach services are operated by **National Express** in association with other bus operators. Special season ticket rates, such as the Familysaver passes, are available.
Details of ultra-cheap international coach services to Great Britain from all parts of Europe, plus coach-based travel passes are available from **Eurolines**.
Most coaches depart from Victoria Coach Station *(Gate 10)* in Buckingham Palace Road *(5min walk from Victoria Railway Station)* or from Marble Arch.

- **National Express**
  ✆08717 818 178
  www.nationalexpress.com
- **Eurolines**
  ✆08717 818 178
  www.eurolines.co.uk
- **Greenline Coaches**
  ✆0844 801 7261
  www.greenline.co.uk
- **Megabus**
  ✆0871 266 3333
  http://uk.megabus.com

BY CAR

See also DRIVING IN THE UK, p35.
The Michelin companion maps and plans for this guide are listed at the back of the guide.
Most visitors travelling to London by car enter the country through the Channel ports *(Dover, Folkestone, Newhaven, Portsmouth, Bournemouth, Weymouth and Plymouth)*, through the Welsh ports *(Swansea, Pembroke Dock, Fishguard, Holyhead)* or by the East Coast ports *(Harwich, Hull, Newcastle upon Tyne)*.

EUROTUNNEL

Eurotunnel runs shuttle services for vehicles through the Channel Tunnel from Folkestone, Kent, to Calais, France. ✆08443 353 535/08444 630 000 *(24hr information service)*; www.eurotunnel.com.

GETTING AROUND

London is a sprawling city, but it has a comprehensive transport network, which makes it easy to get about. However, the system is overloaded and can be overcrowded at times. Serious efforts are underway to improve public transport with many new buses and long-term plans for additional underground lines and Crossrail, a fast East to West rail line through the centre of London, which should be operational by 2018.
The Docklands Light Railway is a quick and comfortable way to travel to the East of the city and City Airport, connecting with the underground at Bank and Canary Wharf stations.

Rush Hours

Unless you have no option, avoid travelling during the morning and evening rush hours *(Mon–Fri 7am–10am; 4.30pm–7pm)* when Londoners travel to and from work.

BY BUS

With 8,500 scheduled buses running daily on more than 700 different routes, the famed red London buses provide an economical and efficient way of exploring the capital.

Bus maps are available from underground ticket offices, tourist information points and online at www.tfl.gov.uk. Bus apps are available to tell you when the next bus is coming. Routes are displayed in bus shelters as well as inside the buses themselves; note that most bus stop signs will bear the name of the stop, but if in doubt ask a passenger or the driver. Where there are a number of routes at key points, the different bus stops have a letter (A, B, C, etc.) – check that you are at the correct stop and travelling in the right direction on the map at the bus stop sign.

On some routes reduced services operate through the night – most of them converging on Trafalgar Square. If you're on board a bus and wish to alight, you need to press the bell to alert the driver. Night buses *(prefixed with "N" or on a blue tile located on the bus stop)* stop only if requested.

Central London Bus Routes

For timetable information and bus routes in central London, visit www.tfl.gov.uk.

In 2005, the last of the classic and much-loved Routemaster buses were taken out of service, but they continue to run on two heritage routes *(numbers 9 & 15)*. A new, eco-friendly and fully-accessible bus inspired by the Routemaster began running in 2012 between Victoria and Hackney *(no. 38)*. The bus has a conductor, three entrances and the ever-popular hop-on, hop-off rear platform.

Bus tickets

Buses are cheaper than trains or the Underground, but they are also slower. *Tickets cost £2.40 cash for a single journey of any length (you must pay again if you change buses during your journey); £19.60 all zones for a 7-day pass. It is much cheaper with a pre-pay* **Oyster Card** *(see box opposite), with a single fare costing £1.30.*

Children *under the age of 16 years travel free but above the age of 11 must have a child Oyster photocard, which has to be obtained in advance (£10 admin. fee).* In central London, you must buy a ticket before you board. There are ticket machines at every bus stop within the pre-pay area.

BY TRAIN

Docklands Light Railway (DLR)

The Docklands Light Railway consists of four lines in East London: Tower Gateway to Beckton; Bank to Woolwich; Bank to Lewisham; Stratford International (for the Olympic Park) to Lewisham. *Services are reduced at weekends. DLR trains are fully wheelchair-accessible.*

The London Overground

Trains run from Richmond, Clapham and Croydon in the South, looping round through West and East London to Watford in the North, Barking and Stratford in the East and Euston in central London.

THE LONDON UNDERGROUND (THE TUBE)

The London Underground network is divided into six main zones with Zone 1 covering central London (and almost all the tourist sites). There are 11 different lines running mostly north of the Thames and covering anywhere you're likely to want to go. Each has a different name and colour; trains, stations and tube maps feature these colours to help with navigation.

Trains run from Central London Mon–Fri 5.30am–12.30am, Sun 7.30am–11.30pm; trains coming in from the suburbs start and finish earlier. To calculate an estimated journey time, count three minutes between stations.

Services are disrupted at weekends due to engineering works; check www.tfl.gov.uk for closures.

The LONDON UNDERGROUND MAP is located on the inside back cover.

TICKETS/PASSES

Single or return tickets can be purchased only at underground stations. They must be retained after passing through the electronic barrier at the start of your journey and after any barriers during it as they are required to exit the final station. Inspectors may also do spot checks so do not destroy or deface your ticket. Passengers must have a valid ticket for their complete journey or they may be liable to pay on-the-spot penalties of up to £50 on bus, Tube, London Overground, Tramlink and DLR services. All children under the age of 11 years travel free on the Underground when travelling with an accompanying fare-paying adult. Those aged 11–15 travel at a discount if they have a photocard.

For the most efficient and least expensive travel, purchase an Oyster Card (*see opposite*).

Travelcards

Whether or not you buy an Oyster Card, do use the multi-journey zoned passes, which are capped to allow you to hop on and hop off transport throughout the day without worrying about the cost.

There are two versions; those that allow you to travel day and night *(up to 4.30am the following day)* and cheaper off-peak versions *(after 9.30am Mon–Fri, all day Sat, Sun and public holidays)*. Price is relative to the number of zones you wish to travel in.

Penalty charges apply for travelling outside your ticket's zone.

- A **One Day** card is £8.80 peak *(child £4.40)* and £7.30 off-peak *(child £3.40)* for Zones 1 and 2.
- A **Seven Day** Card is £30.40 *(child £15.20)* for Zones 1 and 2. There is no off-peak version.

A **photocard** is required by children using a Seven Day Travelcard. It is also required by 11- to 15-year-olds as a qualifier for child fares. Applications for photocards must be made several weeks in advance. *Visit www.tfl.gov.uk or call 0845 330 9876.*

Oyster Cards

The cheapest way to travel in London is with an Oyster Card, available from designated newsagents, online and at ticket desks. This is a blue plastic smart card *(£5)*: load it up with as much money as you choose and reload as and when you need to *(check the amount remaining as you swipe it at the turnstiles)*. Simply hold it against a reader terminal on the bus or as you enter the Tube or pass through a National Rail ticket barrier. It acts as a single-journey ticket until it reaches the cost of a day's bus pass or travelcard (depending on which form of transport you use) when it automatically converts itself to a day pass for the rest of the day *(until 4.29am the following day if you first touch in after 9.30am)*. Cards are valid on the underground, buses, trams, DLR, London Overground and National Rail services. Fares are considerably cheaper with an Oyster (particularly for single journeys) than standard tickets.

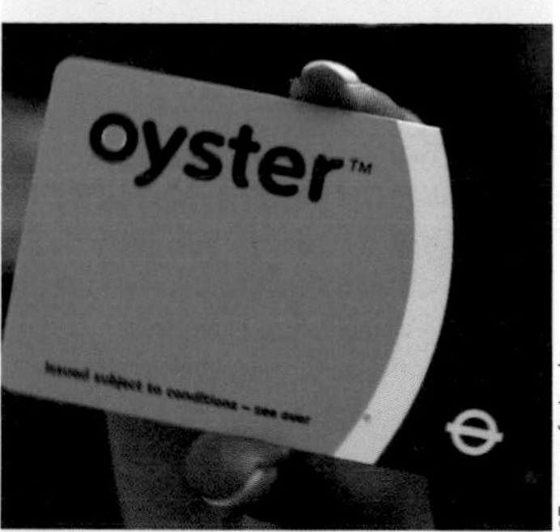

©Transport for London

BY TAXI

The traditional London black cab is available at railway terminals, airports, taxi ranks and cruising the streets. An orange roof-light is displayed when the taxi is free to be hailed. There are plenty around although you may find it difficult to hail one during rush hour,

Travel Discounts

Rail travel in the UK is not cheap, but there are various passes to help make it a little lighter on your pocket.

If you have either a UK passport or driving licence you can buy a railcard. Those aged between 16 and 25 can buy a 16-25 Railcard *(www.16-25railcard.co.uk)* and over 60s a Senior Railcard (www.senior-railcard.co.uk); both cost £28. Each lasts a year and awards you a third off most fares.

Everyone else can buy a Network Railcard for £28. It offers a third off selected fares around the Southeast.

For all visitors to Europe, including the UK, **www.railrocket.com** gives information and highlights the discounts available, such as BritRail, Eurail and Point-to-Point tickets.

between about 10.30pm–11.30pm or if it is raining. ✆0871 871 8710.

Minicabs

Outside the centre, there are also many local licensed minicab companies that must be booked by phone *(look on www.tfl.gov.uk)*. They do not have meters, so be sure to check the price when booking.

Never use the unlicensed, illegal minicabs that cruise the city centre at night and have no meter. At best, you are uninsured and at worst in danger, especially lone females.

To receive the telephone numbers of the two nearest minicabs and one black cab number, text CAB to 60835 from your smartphone *(charge)*.

Fares

All black cabs are metered. The minimum fare is £2.40. Fares rise between 8pm–10pm on Mon–Fri and at weekends, and again from 10pm–6am and on public holidays. All fares are set, so any negotiating in central London is pointless. Journeys beyond the limits of Greater London are subject to negotiation. Taxis are not obliged to go outside Greater London nor more than 6mi/9.6km or one hour from the pick-up point *(20mi at Heathrow)*.

Few cabs accept credit cards. Those who do will have a CC sign; let them know when you get in that you will be using a card and expect a handling fee of at least £1 or 12.5 percent of the metered fare. Tips are discretionary but up to 10 percent is usual.

BY BICYCLE

Cycling in London is more and more popular, especially with the success of the Barclays Cycle Hire scheme. However, it is not recommended unless you are a confident experienced cyclist, or you are intending to stick to the parks and cycle lanes.

Bikes can be hired from Barclays Cycle Hire docking stations which are scattered all over the city. *Bikes are available 24 hours a day and do not need to be booked in advance – simply pay as you go using a credit or debit card. For 24-hour access there is a charge of £2; the first 30min is then free, an hour is £1 and two hours £6; make sure the green light comes on when you return the bike or you will continue to be charged.* The bikes are intended for short journeys only and prices can rise as high as £50 for the maximum 24-hour period. You must be over 18 years old to purchase access and over

Barclays Cycle Hire

14 to ride. www.tfl.gov.uk/roadusers. A folding bicycle may be taken on all forms of transport without restriction (at the driver's discretion on buses; and only in a container on the DLR). *London Cycle Guides* are available free from:

- **Transport for London** (www.tfl.gov.uk) and **London Cycling Campaign** (2 Newhams Row, London SE1 3UZ; ✆020 7234 9310; www.lcc.org.uk).

- **London Bicycle Tour Company** Rental £20 first day, £10 subsequent days, £50 first week and £25 second week. 2.5hr central London bike tour daily; 10.30am *(£18.95)*. 56 Upper Ground SE1 9PP. ✆020 3318 3088 www.londonbicycle.com.

BY BOAT

A novel way of getting about London is by river, with many of the boats offering excellent guided sightseeing tours, either upstream to Kew and Hampton Court or down the river to Greenwich.

To encourage Londoners to make more use of the river, piers have been built and regular commuter services introduced, with hop-on-hop-off fares and valid all-day tickets; travelcard holders (including Oyster Card holders with a loaded travelcard) are entitled to a 33 percent discount off some river service fares.

Transport for London offers downloads of timetables and fares *(www.tfl.gov.uk)*.

Some companies operate only on weekdays and in summer, others do so all week and year round.

City Cruises
✆020 77 400 400;
www.citycruises.com
Victoria Embankment, London.
Mon–Fri only (except bank holidays); £6.90–£11.50 adult; £3.45–£6.75 child.

Thames Clippers
✆020 7001 2222;
www.thamesclippers.com
Waterloo–Embankment–Blackfriars–Bankside–London Bridge–Tower–Canary Wharf–Greenland–Masthouse Terrace–Greenwich. *Daily; £6 single (child £3); £13.60 River Roamer (child £6.80).*

Crown River Cruises
✆020 7936 2033;
www.crownrivercruise.co.uk
Westminster–St Katharine's pier
Hop-on-hop-off service daily; £8.40 single, £12.30 return (child 50 percent discount).

BY CABLE CAR

London's first and only cable car, Emirates Air Line, runs above the Thames between North Greenwich and the Royal Docks. It's a great way to enjoy a bird's eye view of the city, especially the river and the Olympic sites. You can use your Oyster Card or buy a ticket (more expensive); www.tfl.gov.uk.

BY CAR

If you are arriving by car, it is advisable to find a place to stay on the outskirts and travel to the city centre by public transport, as London traffic is dense and parking very expensive – up to £30 a day in the centre. Traffic in and around towns is heavy during the rush hours, as well as on major roads at the weekend, particularly in summer and more so on bank holiday weekends. Never leave anything of value in an unattended vehicle.

CONGESTION CHARGE

A £10 daily charge is levied on any vehicle *(except motorcycles and "greener" vehicles registered with TFL)* entering the central zone Mon–Fri 7am–6pm, except public holidays. Payment must be made in advance or before midnight on the day of travel – £2 surcharge for next-day payment – by post, by text *(SMS)*, online, by telephone and in shops displaying the logo. There is a £120 penalty for non-payment, which must be paid within 28 days (reduced to £60 for payment within 14 days). ✆0845 900 1234; www.tfl.gov.uk/roadusers.

ROAD REGULATIONS

The **minimum driving age** is 17 years. Traffic drives **on the left** and overtakes on the right. Go clockwise round roundabouts. Headlights must be used at night and in poor visibility. Important **traffic signs** generally correspond to international norms.

Seat Belts

In Britain the compulsory wearing of **seat belts** includes rear seat passengers (when rear belts are fitted) and all children under 14 years of age. Infants and small children are required to be seated in specifically designed car seats.

Bus Lanes

Blue road signs indicate the hours between which certain lanes are reserved for buses and taxis. Most bear a sign permitting use by motorcylists and cyclists too.

Pedestrian Crossings

Give way to pedestrians on black-and-white crossings (known as zebra crossings) and when traffic lights flash amber or are red.

MAXIMUM SPEED LIMITS	
70mph/112kph	Motorways or dual carriageways
60mph/96kph	Single carriageways
30mph/48kph	In towns and cities

PARKING

Off-street parking is indicated by blue signs with white lettering *(Parking or P)*; payment is made on leaving or in advance for a certain period. In some boroughs, such as Westminster, a Pay by Phone option is available *(call to set up an account: ✆020 7005 0055; or visit www.westminster.gov.uk/services to download an app).*

PARKING RESTRICTIONS	
Double red line	No stopping at any time
Double yellow line	No parking at any time
Dotted yellow line	No parking for set periods, as indicated on panel
White zigzag lines at a zebra crossing	No stopping or parking at any time

To find a convenient car park, visit www.ncp.co.uk or www.247parking.com.
There are also parking meters, disc systems and paying parking zones; in the last case tickets must be obtained from ticket machines *(small change necessary)* and displayed inside the windscreen. Parking meters are usually time-restricted and also heavily policed.
Residential parking: Parking within London is very limited and quite a few places are restricted to local residents, who pay handsomely for the privilege. Watch for the signs. Different boroughs operate varying restrictions and since enforcement has been granted to independent operators, ticketing, clamping and removal is common.

PENALTIES

Drinking and Driving: There are severe penalties for driving after drinking more than the legal limit of alcohol. The legal limit is 80mg of alcohol per 100ml of blood – how much you can drink depends on your body weight, metabolism and other factors, but assume that two small glasses of wine or one pint of beer will put you close to or over the limit. The police can breathalyse you on the spot. Penalties may vary from points on your licence to losing it altogether, fines of up to £5, 000 and even custodial sentences for causing injury or death while driving under

the influence of alcohol or drugs. *For more information, see ww.drinkdrivinglaw.co.uk.*
Speeding: Roadside cameras (indicated) record vehicles exceeding the speed limit; fines and points on your licence follow.
Parking: Illegal parking is liable to fines and also in certain cases to the vehicle being clamped or towed away. To release your car costs £45 plus a fine of £50–100 *(50 percent discount if you pay within 14 days)*. To get your car back if it has been towed will cost up to £200 plus fine. If your car has been clamped, you will be given a notice of the payment centre to contact. *If your car has been towed away, contact the nearest police station or call the* **Trace service** *hotline on* ✆020 7747 4747.

PETROL/GASOLINE

Unleaded petrol and **diesel** are available at all service stations. Most service stations are self-service. Payment is usually taken inside the attached shop; credit card payments at the pump are increasingly common.

MOTORING ORGANISATIONS

The major UK motoring organisations are the **Automobile Association** *(AA; ✆0906 888 4322 (travel information); 0800 88 77 66 (breakdown helpline); www.theaa.com)* and the **Royal Automobile Club** *(RAC; ✆0800 197 7815 (breakdown helpline); www.rac.co.uk)*.

RENTAL CARS

There are car rental agencies at airport terminals, railway stations and in all large towns throughout Great Britain. Hire cars usually have manual transmissions, but automatic cars are available on demand; the driver sits on the right. An internationally recognised driving licence is required for non-EU nationals. Most companies will not rent to those aged under 25 (21 in some cases).

Rental Car Agencies

- **Avis** www.avis.com
- **Budget** www.budget.co.uk
- **easyCar** www.easycar.com
- **Europcar** www.europcar.co.uk
- **Hertz** www.hertz.com
- **National Car Rental** www.nationalcar.co.uk

Alternatively, sign up for a car sharing scheme such as Zipcar *(www.zipcar.co.uk)*, which has short-term rental cars across London. Annual membership is £59.50 and gives you access to any of the company's cars from £5/hour, £49/day, £275 for the week, slightly more at weekends. Register for free online and once you receive your membership card, you can book a vehicle up to six months in advance. Bookings can be made online and by phone *(✆0333 240 9000)*.

DRIVING IN THE UK

EU nationals require a **valid national driving licence**; non-EU nationals require an **international driving permit** *(IDP)*. A permit is available from local branches of the **American Automobile Association** or from the **National Automobile Club** *(✆+1-650 294 7000; +1 800 622 2136; www.thenac.com)*. You also require the vehicle's **registration papers** *(log-book)* and a **nationality plate**. Insurance cover is compulsory; the **International Insurance Certificate** *(Green Card)*, though no longer a legal requirement, is the most effective proof of insurance cover and internationally recognised by the authorities. Certain UK motoring organisations run accident insurance and breakdown service schemes for members, including **Europ Assistance**, the **AA** and the **RAC** *(check before travelling; see under Motoring Organisations, left)*.

Basic Information

ADMISSION TIMES
CHURCHES

Some small churches are locked when not in use for services. The cathedrals charge an entrance fee for sightseers; other churches are free but would appreciate a donation.

SHOPS

Most larger shops are open Mondays to Saturdays from 9am until about 9pm in central London and 6pm elsewhere. On Sundays, shops may only trade for 6 hours and often open from 11am–5pm. Some supermarkets are open 24 hours, and many local corner shops stay open until 10pm (or later in residential areas).

TICKET OFFICES

These usually close 30min before the attraction itself; only exceptions are mentioned.

ADMISSION CHARGES

The charge given is for an individual adult. Major state-owned museums in London are all free. Most places offer reductions for families, children, students, senior citizens *(old-age pensioners, OAPs)* and the unemployed; it may be necessary to provide proof of identity and status. Large parties should apply in advance, as many places offer special rates for group bookings.

DATES

Dates given in this guide are inclusive. The term "weekend" means Saturday and Sunday; "holidays" means bank and public holidays, when shops, museums and other monuments may close or vary their times of admission. The terms "school holidays" and "half-term" refer to the breaks between terms at Christmas, Easter and during the summer months and to the short mid-term breaks, which are usually in February, May and October.

ELECTRICITY

The electric current is 230 volts AC *(tolerances +10 percent and -6 percent) (50 HZ)*; 3-pin flat wall sockets are standard. An adaptor or multiple point plug is required for non-British appliances.

EMERGENCIES

Call **999** for all emergency services *(no charge nationwide)*; ask for Fire, Police or Ambulance.

LOST PROPERTY

Do not despair, precious possessions are sometimes handed in.
For property lost in the street, enquire at the local police station.
For property left on an underground train, London Bus or licensed taxi cab, enquire in person at the **Transport for London Lost Property Office**, 200 Baker Street, NW1 5RZ *(Mon–Fri 8.30am–4pm; closed weekends and bank holidays)*; enquiry forms also available from any TFL bus garage or station. ✆0845 330 9882 *(recorded)*. Lost property forms also available on www.tfl.gov.uk/lostproperty.
For property left on mainline trains, enquire at the station itself.

MAIL/POST
OPENING HOURS

Post offices are generally open Mon–Fri 9.30am–5.30pm and Sat mornings 9.30am–12.30pm. Late and Sun collections are made from William IV Street, at the principal sorting offices at Paddington, Nine Elms, Mount Pleasant and St Paul's.
Stamps are available from many newsagents and tobacconists. *Poste Restante* items are held for 14 days; proof of identity is required. Airmail delivery usually takes 3 to 4 days in Europe and 4 to 7 globally.

MONEY

Currency is the British pound sterling (100 pence = £1), used throughout Great Britain; Scotland has different notes, including £1 and £100 notes, which are valid in the UK.

The common currency – in descending order of value – is £50, £20, £10 and £5 *(notes)*; £2, £1, 50p, 20p, 10p, 5p *(silver coins)* and 2p and 1p *(copper coins)*. Some high street shops and department stores in central London will also accept euros (€).

BANKS

Opening Hours

Banks are generally open from Mon–Fri 9/9.30am–4.30/5pm; many are open 9.30am–12.30/3.30pm on Sat; all banks are closed on Sundays and bank holidays (*see Public Holidays*). Most banks have 24hr cash dispensers *(ATMs)* that accept international credit cards and some debit cards, such as Maestro. Check with your card issuer. Exchange facilities outside banking hours are available at airports, bureaux de change, travel agencies and the bigger hotels.

Traveller's Cheques

Some form of identification is necessary when cashing traveller's cheques in banks. Commission charges vary; hotels usually charge more than banks.

CREDIT CARDS

The main credit cards *(EuroCard, MasterCard, Visa, Barclaycard)* are widely accepted. Cash machines *(ATMS)*, which accept international credit cards, are commonplace, particularly near banks but also in some small shops *(transaction fee applies)*. Report any **loss or theft** to the police, who will issue a crime number for use by the insurance or credit card company.

NEWSPAPERS

Britain has an excellent selection of daily newspapers from the more serious "broadsheets" – *The Times*, the *Daily Telegraph*, the *Independent*, the *Guardian* and the *Financial Times* – to mid-market papers such as the *Daily Mail* and the *Express*, and tabloids such as the *Sun*. Most also have Sunday equivalents and all have websites.

Event Listings

Time Out – this weekly magazine *(free from tube stations and bigger museums and galleries)* contains up-to-date listings on venues, events and shopping, plus reviews of theatre, cinemas, exhibitions, concerts, nightlife, restaurants, guided walks, etc.

Useful websites include:
freelondonlistings.co.uk;
www.standard.co.uk;
www.officiallondontheatre.co.uk;
www.visitlondon.com/events

PUBLIC HOLIDAYS

The following days are statutory or discretionary holidays, when banks, museums and shops may be closed, or may vary their times of admission: It is advisable to check boat, bus and railway timetables for changes. Most tourist sights are open on these days.

1 January	New Year's Day
Good Friday	Friday before Easter Day
Easter Monday	Monday after Easter Day
First Monday in May	May Day
Last Monday in May	Spring Bank Holiday
Last Monday in August	Bank Holiday
25 December	Christmas Day
26 December	Boxing Day

SMOKING

Smoking inside public places is banned throughout England. Customers wishing to smoke must step outside, though be aware that it is also illegal to smoke in some outside spaces, such as on train platforms.

TAX

VAT

Many stores in London participate in the Retail Export Scheme *(look for the sign "Tax Free Shopping")*.

This means that customers may be entitled to receive a refund of VAT paid on goods (currently 20 percent) exported to destinations outside the European Union. There is no statutory minimum sale value although retailers may set a minimum transaction value (for example, £50), below which they will not operate the scheme. Ask the sales assistant for the form for reclaiming the tax and present this at the point of exit from the UK for the refund to be passed onto you.

GIFT AID AND DONATIONS

Gift Aid is a government scheme of tax relief on money donated to UK charities, which may be applied at visitor attractions with charitable status.

The scheme is only for UK residents and you will be asked for your postcode and name, which will be verified instantly by a machine. You will then be given the choice of buying a ticket with or without Gift Aid – the former is 10 percent higher. Be aware that in some cases you may be asked for the Gift Aid inclusive price straightaway.

If you choose to pay the higher price, you may be given an incentive in the form of a voucher redeemable towards purchases in the shop or refreshments. If you spend the full amount of this voucher (which in most cases will only amount to the price of a coffee or less) then you will pay less overall but the charity/visitor attraction will still gain extra revenue.

Within this guidebook we have given admission prices without Gift Aid/charitable donation.

TELEPHONES

The **UK mobile/cell phone** networks use the European-standard GSM networks. US and Canadian visitors will need a tri-band phone.

PHONECARDS

It is possible to buy very cheap **pay-as-you-go SIM cards**. If you wish to make and receive a lot of overseas calls, call ℘020 7107 9700 or visit www.sim4travel.com to find international SIM cards with cheap rates. Newsagents often list prices of calls to various countries.

Prepaid **British Telecom phonecards** of varying value are available from post offices and many newsagents; they can be used in booths with phonecard facilities for national and international calls. Most public telephones accept credit cards. Call 100 for the operator and 118 500 for directory enquiries *(charge)*.

INTERNATIONAL CALLS

To make an international call, dial 00 followed by the country code, the area code *(without the initial 0)* and finally the number you wish to reach.

Many newsagents sell **pre-pay phone cards** that offer cheap international call rates; ask shop assistants and study the various adverts to find the best for your destination.

SOME INTERNATIONAL DIALLING CODES (00 + CODE)	
Australia	℘61
Canada	℘1
Republic of Ireland	℘353
New Zealand	℘64
United Kingdom	℘44
United States	℘1
International Operator	℘155
International Directory	℘118

TIME ZONE

In winter, **standard time** throughout the British Isles is Greenwich Mean Time *(GMT)*. In summer *(last Sun in March to last Sun of Oct)*, clocks are advanced by an hour to give **British Summer Time** *(BST)*.

CONVERSION TABLES

Weights and Measures

1 kilogram (kg)	**2.2 pounds (lb)**	**2.2 pounds**	*To convert kilograms to pounds, multiply by 2.2*
6.35 kilograms	14 pounds	1 stone (st)	
0.45 kilograms	16 ounces (oz)	16 ounces	
1 metric ton (tn)	**1.1 tons**	**1.1 tons**	
1 litre (l)	**2.11 pints (pt)**	**1.76 pints**	*To convert litres to gallons, multiply by 0.26 (US) or 0.22 (UK)*
3.79 litres	1 gallon (gal)	0.83 gallon	
4.55 litres	1.20 gallon	1 gallon	
1 hectare (ha)	**2.47 acres**	**2.47 acres**	*To convert hectares to acres, multiply by 2.4*
1 sq kilometre (km^2)	**0.38 sq. miles (sq mi)**	**0.38 sq. miles**	
1 centimetre (cm)	**0.39 inches (in)**	**0.39 inches**	*To convert metres to feet, multiply by 3.28; for kilometres to miles, multiply by 0.6*
1 metre (m)	3.28 feet (ft) or 39.37 inches or 1.09 yards (yd)		
1 kilometre (km)	**0.62 miles (mi)**	**0.62 miles**	

Clothing

Women			
	35	4	2½
	36	5	3½
	37	6	4½
Shoes	38	7	5½
	39	8	6½
	40	9	7½
	41	10	8½
	36	6	8
	38	8	10
Dresses & suits	40	10	12
	42	12	14
	44	14	16
	46	16	18
	36	6	30
	38	8	32
Blouses & sweaters	40	10	34
	42	12	36
	44	14	38
	46	16	40

Men			
	40	7½	7
	41	8½	8
	42	9½	9
Shoes	43	10½	10
	44	11½	11
	45	12½	12
	46	13½	13
	46	36	36
	48	38	38
Suits	50	40	40
	52	42	42
	54	44	44
	56	46	48
	37	14½	14½
	38	15	15
Shirts	39	15½	15½
	40	15¾	15¾
	41	16	16
	42	16½	16½

Sizes often vary depending on the designer. These equivalents are given for guidance only.

Speed

KPH	10	30	50	70	80	90	100	110	120	130
MPH	6	19	31	43	50	56	62	68	75	81

Temperature

Celsius (°C)	0°	5°	10°	15°	20°	25°	30°	40°	60°	80°	100°
Fahrenheit (°F)	32°	41°	50°	59°	68°	77°	86°	104°	140°	176°	212°

To convert Celsius into Fahrenheit, multiply °C by 9, divide by 5, and add 32.
To convert Fahrenheit into Celsius, subtract 32 from °F, multiply by 5, and divide by 9.

NB: Conversion factors on this page are approximate.

INTRODUCTION TO LONDON

Tower Bridge

London Today

Enduring, domineering and utterly idiosyncratic, London is a city which has truly stood the test of time. From historical powerhouse to modern-day metropolis, London thrives as Britain's capital and Europe's most visited city. From iconic sights and world-renowned attractions to cutting-edge culture and superlative dining, the London of today has it all – and then some.

THE RIVER THAMES

London's river is once again its focal point. Join a boat tour to soak up the atmosphere of one of Europe's most important waterways, before visiting the countless venues along its banks. Explore celebrated museums and historic attractions, flex the credit card in designer shops and gourmet restaurants, or simply indulge in that most British of traditions – a pint in a local pub. As darkness descends, take in a show at one of the world-class theatres or concert halls, stroll the light-strung banks or gaze at illuminated landmarks from a nighttime cruise.

From the King's Reach bend *(at Waterloo Bridge)* the view embraces two traditional monuments: to the East is the imposing dome of St Paul's Cathedral and to the West the multi-turreted Houses of Parliament. Across the water, adding a note of fantasy to the South Bank, rises the London Eye, a giant observation wheel, which affords a unique panorama of London extending to the far horizon.

EVENTS AND CELEBRATIONS

Events on the Thames feature prominently in the social calendar. Tradition is kept alive with **Doggett's Coat and Badge Race**, a long-established rowing contest from London Bridge to Chelsea, and the **Swan Upping** ceremony at Teddington Lock (run since the 12C), when the beaks of the swans are marked by the guilds which own them (those owned by the Crown are left unmarked); both events are held in July.

Sporting challenges such as the long-running **Oxford and Cambridge Boat Race** *(March/April)* attract large crowds, while regular regattas are held up and down the river during the summer; the highlight of the season is the five-day **Henley Royal Regatta** *(July)*, which has been running since 1839.

The annual **Greenwich and Docklands Festival** *(June/July)* features events on or by the Thames; while the exotic **Dragon Boat Festival** *(June)* is inspired by Chinese culture. For special celebrations, including New Year's Eve,

Millennium Bridge over the Thames with St. Paul's Cathedral

spectacular fireworks displays on the river light up the night sky.

A CHANGING SCENE

The Thames, England's longest river *(215mi/346km long)*, meanders gently through typically English countryside of low hills, woods, meadows, country houses, pretty villages and small towns. Marinas provide moorings for private craft and locks add to the fun of a leisurely outing on the river with majestic swans and other waterfowl gliding by.

By the time the river reaches London it is a broad tidal waterway bustling with activity; barges used to ply their trade along here, and today various craft offer daytime excursions downstream to the Tower, Greenwich and the Thames Barrier or upstream to Kew and Hampton Court, as well as evening cruises with entertainment. At low tide the muddy banks are also frequented by archaeologists and treasure-seekers in search of precious artefacts, lost or discarded objects, old ship timbers and other salvage items.

Near Woolwich, the **Thames Barrier**, an impressive engineering feat, was built to protect London from tidal surges and is one of the largest movable flood barriers in the world. Further downstream, the marshlands of the estuary are a haven for wintering birds, waterfowl and endangered species.

Old and new now coexist as modern developments rise side by side with the old docks and warehouses. The cowls of the Thames Barrier dominate the scene at Woolwich and imaginative conversions of wharves *(Butler's, Chelsea)* and power stations *(Bankside, Battersea)* have turned these relics of the industrial era into the latest landmarks.

MAIN THOROUGHFARE OF LONDON

Throughout the centuries the kings and nobles of England built palaces along the river from Greenwich to Hampton. Many of these grand buildings have been destroyed, but Ham House, Hampton Court and Syon Park still survive.

Until the late 17C the Thames was the capital's main highway and old engravings show craft of every size thronging the waterway. The royal household, the City Corporation and the city livery companies had their own barges; ordinary citizens hired the services of the watermen plying for business at the many landing stages, called Stairs; cargo ships and men o'war added to the congestion.

The first regular steamer services began around 1816 and by mid-century were carrying several million people. On weekdays the boats were crowded with workers going into the docks and boatyards, the Arsenal and South Bank factories; fares were a penny from one pier to the next. At other times they carried families and friends for an evening trip or for an excursion, often to the estuary or the seaside towns of Herne Bay, Margate and Ramsgate.

POOL OF LONDON

London's historical importance is intertwined with its status as a port. From the 16C to the mid-20C, the commercial prosperity of the city derived from the wharves and docks in the Pool of London stretching from London Bridge to Tower Bridge and the shipbuilding yards downstream. The yards at Deptford, founded by Henry VIII in 1513, grew rapidly and are associated with many historical events *(see GREENWICH)*.

Merchantmen unable to sail under London Bridge or to approach the wharves across the mudflats, moored in midstream and depended on a vast fleet of lighters *(3,500)* for loading and unloading. This system provided many opportunities for pilfering by river pirates, night plunderers, scuffle hunters and mudlarks.

Today, such river activity is a thing of the past: wharves and warehouses have gradually been rebuilt and transformed into business and shopping centres *(see BANKSIDE – SOUTHWARK, Hay's Galleria)* and World War II light cruiser HMS *Belfast*, moored along the South

Bank of the river, is an annexe of the Imperial War Museum (*see BANKSIDE – SOUTHWARK, HMS Belfast*).

COMMERCIAL DOCKS

The first enclosed commercial dock, designed to cut down the opportunities for theft, was built early in the 19C. By the end of the century, there were four systems of enclosed docks extending beyond Tower Bridge over 3,000 acres/1,214ha with 36mi/58km of quays and 665 acres/270ha of dock basins: London Docks *(1864)*, Surrey Commercial Docks *(1864)*, East and West India Docks *(1838)*, and Royal Docks *(1855–80)*.

During World War II the docks suffered severe damage from bombing and by the 1960s closure was threatened as a result of the transfer of cargo handling to specialised riverside wharves and the dock at Tilbury.

Today, some of the surviving docks provide facilities for watersports, such as the Royal Albert Dock, now home to the London Regatta Centre. City Airport, Excel Exhibition Centre and the Millennium Dome *(now the 02 Arena)* are also built on former docks.

WATER SUPPLY

In the Middle Ages water supplies came from the Thames, its tributaries and from wells *(Clerkenwell, Sadler's Wells, Muswell Hill)*. After 1285, conduits of leather or hollow tree trunks were provided by the City fathers to bring water from the Tyburn, Westbourne and Lee waterways to lead cisterns in the City, where it was collected by householders and by water carriers, who later formed a guild. During the next 300 years these provisions were augmented by private enterprise. The first pump driven by horses was set up in Upper Thames Street in 1594.

The Industrial Revolution brought steam pumping, gradually introduced from 1750, with cast-iron pipes: wooden mains could not sustain the higher pumping pressures. The widespread introduction of the water closet after 1820 resulted in sewage being discharged into the streams and rivers, polluting the water supply and bringing epidemics of typhoid and cholera *(1832 and 1848)*. Filtration *(1829)*, the requirement to draw water from the non-tidal river above Teddington *(1856)* and chlorination *(1916)* made London's water safe to drink.

Today, supply is maintained by reservoirs situated on the periphery of London at Datchet, Staines, Chingford and Walthamstow. In 1974 the Thames Water Authority was constituted to take over from the Metropolitan Water Board *(1903)*. It levied its own rate and was responsible for the management of the Thames throughout its length and for London's water supply, sewage disposal and pollution control. The National Rivers Authority (Thames Region) was responsible for flood defence and pollution control from 1989/90 to 1996, when it was replaced by the Environment Agency. Throughout the 1980s and 1990s initiatives to clean up the pollution of the tideway were successful and meant that fish began to descend the stream and re-enter the estuary. Since 2006, some 125 species, including sole, cod, bass and even the odd seahorse, have been documented in the Thames. Licences for eel fishing are in demand and salmon, in particular, have returned in quantity after an absence of more than 150 years.

RIVER CROSSINGS

London grew around a fishing village at Southwark, where the only crossing was by a wooden bridge built by the Romans (*see THE CITY, London Bridge*). After the Norman Conquest *(1066)*, Richmond Bridge was the first to span the river *(1139)* upstream; this was followed by Putney Bridge *(1729)* and Westminster Bridge *(1750)*. Tower Bridge *(1894)* with its high-level walkway and hydraulic lifts is a major landmark.

Albert Bridge, festooned by lights at night, was at the cutting edge of 19C progress with its cantilever suspension structure. The tallest liners can pass under Dartford's Queen Elizabeth II Bridge *(1991)*, the UK's second largest suspension bridge.

Thames Tributaries

Most now flow in underground pipes, some have been dammed to form lakes and there is little except street names to recall the course of these lost waterways. Among the northern tributaries are *(East–West)*: the Lee *(or Lea)*; the Walbrook in the City; the Fleet *(two branches)* from Hampstead and Highgate; Tyburn via Marylebone to Westminster *(traced by Marylebone Lane)*; Westbourne via Paddington and Kensington to enter at Pimlico; Stamford Brook, which enters at Hammersmith; River Brent, which enters at Kew. Among the southern tributaries are *(East–West)*: the Ravensbourne, which enters at Deptford Creek; Effra River, which enters in Brixton; Falcon Brook, which enters in Battersea; River Wandle, which enters at Wandsworth.

The building of the Rotherhithe Tunnel *(Rotherhithe–Wapping)*, the first underwater tunnel by Marc Brunel *(1824–43)*, and the foot tunnel *(1902, Greenwich–Isle of Dogs)* by his son, Isambard Kingdom Brunel, with its two distinctive cupolas, introduced innovative engineering techniques that were later refined for the construction of the Channel Tunnel. The original Hungerford Bridge was built by Brunel; two modernistic structures for pedestrians are elegant new features. The advanced design of the pedestrian Millennium Bridge *(2000)*, a steel suspension bridge, evolved from the collaboration of the architect Sir Norman Foster, the engineers Ove Arup and the sculptor Anthony Caro. Initially nicknamed "the wobbly bridge" after swaying with high volumes of pedestrians crossing was reported, the futuristic structure underwent modification and is now an architectural landmark, linking Tate Modern on the South Bank with St Paul's Cathedral on the North.

A RECURRING THEME

The Thames has inspired many artists. Canaletto's celebrated views are of great historical interest, while Monet and Turner were both enthralled by the play of light on the water. The great bend of the Thames framed by idyllic scenery at Richmond was captured with great artistry by Reynolds and Turner, and Whistler's paintings of Battersea Bridge (entitled *Nocturne*) are evocative works.

The following literary works and their writers found inspiration in the Thames; the plays of Shakespeare and Ben Jonson, the musings of John Evelyn, Samuel Pepys, Samuel Johnson and James Boswell, the poetry of Edmund Spenser, William Blake and TS Eliot, and the novels of Charles Dickens, Jerome K Jerome, Joseph Conrad and Virginia Woolf.

GOVERNMENT

THE REALM

Great Britain comprises England, Wales, Scotland, the Channel Islands and the Isle of Man.

The **United Kingdom**, which is ruled from London's Palace of Westminster, comprises England, Wales, Scotland and Northern Ireland, but does not include the Channel Islands or Isle of Man, which have their own parliaments and are attached directly to the Crown. Major recent constitutional reforms include devolution of some powers to a Scottish Parliament and a Welsh Assembly.

MONARCHY

The United Kingdom is a constitutional Monarchy, a form of government in which supreme power is vested in the **Sovereign** (King or Queen). In law the Sovereign is the head of the **executive** *(government elected by a majority, headed by a prime minister and implemented by civil servants)*, an integral part of the **legislature** *(the Houses of Commons and Lords responsible for deciding on matters of law)*, head of the **judiciary** *(Criminal and Crown*

Courts of law), commander-in-chief of the Armed Forces, temporal head of the Church of England and symbolic Head of the Commonwealth. In practice the role is strictly a formal one. During the reign of Queen Victoria *(1837–1901)*, the Monarch's right in relation to ministers was defined as "the right to be consulted, to encourage and to warn." The Monarchy also acts as a last line of defence against coup as the Monarch has the right to force the removal of a prime minister and call a new election in extreme circumstances.

PARLIAMENT

The United Kingdom has no written constitution as such, but several important statutes underpin the institution and conventions of government.

The **Magna Carta** *(1215)* sealed the King's promise to refrain from imposing feudal tax, save by the consent of the Common Council of the Realm, and instituted a fundamental human right: "To no man will we deny or delay right or justice". The **Petition of Right Act** *(1628)* confirmed that no tax should be levied by the King without the consent of Parliament and that no person be detained without lawful cause. The **Bill of Rights** *(1689)* ensured ultimate supremacy of Parliament. The **Act of Settlement** *(1701)* established the independence of the Law Courts and regulated the succession to the Crown of England. The **Race Relations Act** *(1968)* aimed to prohibit prejudice on account of race, colour or ethnic origin; the **Representation of the People Act** *(1969)* gave the vote to all persons over the age of 18 listed on the Electoral Register save acting members of the House of Lords and those incapacitated through insanity or imprisonment.

The supreme legislature is Parliament, consisting of two bodies: the **House of Commons** and the **House of Lords** within the Palace of Westminster (see *CITY OF WESTMINSTER)*. Regular Parliament meetings were assured after the Bloodless or Glorious Revolution *(1688)*, when Parliament repealed James II's rule by "divine right" and appointed William III and Mary II; both houses were dominated by "landed gentry" until the 19C *(MPs were paid a salary from 1911)*.

Horses and carriages carrying HM The Queen leave Buckingham Palace for the State Opening of Parliament

©Gary Lee/UPPA/Photoshot

HOUSE OF COMMONS

Three major political parties dominate the House of Commons: the Conservatives *(or Tories)*, the Labour party and the Liberal Democrats. Since the 17C power has been held by one (or more) of these three parties.

The United Kingdom is divided into around 650 constituencies, each calculated to hold approximately 65,000 voters. A Member of Parliament *(MP)* is elected by a majority vote secured at a General Election to appoint a new government or at a by-election if the seat falls vacant in the interim. Government term is for a maximum of five years. The House is presided over by the Speaker, appointed at the beginning of each session. MPs sit on parallel benches: members of the Government Cabinet sit in the first row opposite the members of the Shadow Cabinet *(frontbenchers)* while members of their respective parties sit behind *(backbenchers)*.

Their combined function is to decide upon legislation: each act is subjected to two Readings, a Committee and a Report Stage and a Third Reading before going to "the Other House" and obtaining Royal Assent.

HOUSE OF LORDS

A major reform of the House of Lords is under way. The House of Lords Act 1999 removed the rights of most hereditary peers to sit and vote in the House. An amendment enabled 92 hereditary peers, **Lords Temporal**, to remain in the House until a Royal Commission reports on the role, functions and composition of the second chamber.

Life Peers include the Lords of Appeal *(Law Lords)* and distinguished persons honoured for service to the Land *(since 1958)*; the **Lords Spiritual** are the archbishops and bishops of the Church of England.

This body of the legislature debates issues officially without the bias of party politics. It also acts as the highest court of appeal in the land, although only the Law Lords are involved in such proceedings. The main body of the legal establishment, the Royal Courts of Justice and Chambers, reside between Westminster and the City, where the Strand gives way to Fleet Street.

LOCAL GOVERNMENT

Since the early Middle Ages the City has been administered by the Corporation of the City of London. After the Dissolution of the monasteries *(1539)*, Westminster and Southwark, the other urban districts, were given into the care of newly appointed **parish vestries**, which differed in character and probity. Their powers overlapped and were insufficient to control, even where they thought it necessary, the speculators who erected tall houses with inadequate sanitation, which thus polluted the water supplies and let off each room to one, or often several, families. Conditions were not, of course, uniformly bad – the "good life" was led with considerable elegance in St James's and Whitehall, in Mayfair, Marylebone, Knightsbridge, Kensington and westwards beyond.

In the 19C reform began, spurred on by traffic congestion and the dangers of poor sanitation. In 1855, the Government established a central body, the **Metropolitan Board of Works**, with special responsibility for main sewerage.

Slum clearance began as new roads were built to ease traffic congestion. Through its chief engineer, **Joseph Bazalgette**, the board reconstructed the drainage system for central London and built the embankments.

In 1888 the County of London was created with the **London County Council** *(LCC)* as the county authority with responsibility for an area equivalent to the present 12 inner London boroughs *(Outer London has 19 boroughs)*.

In 1965, in the newly defined area of Greater London, the LCC was superseded by a regional authority, the **Greater London Council** *(GLC)*. Greater London comprised the former County of London and former local authority areas surrounding London, in all a total of 610sq mi/1 579km, with a population of about 6.7 million.

Following the 1983 general election, the structure of local government was reformed by Margaret Thatcher and the GLC and other metropolitan councils were abolished *(1986)*. The GLC's functions were devolved largely to the borough councils.

For more than a decade London was without a voice. A referendum in 1998 proved in favour of an elected Mayor for London and elections were held in 2000. Since then, London has had an elected Mayor *(Ken Livingstone from 2000–2008 and Boris Johnson since 2008)*, whose chief functions are transport, policing, fire and emergency planning, economic development, planning, culture, environment and health. The Mayor's work is assisted and carefully monitored by a 25-strong elected Greater London Assembly. In the last mayoral election, in May 2012, Boris Johnson was elected for a second term.

Greater London is made up of 32 boroughs, which currently have responsibility for education *(excluding the universities)*, personal welfare services, housing, public health, environmental planning and traffic management.

Discussions are ongoing about whether the Mayor will also take increasing responsibility for policing, housing and education in the city, moving much of the city's power away from the boroughs into a more centralised control.

LOCAL TAXATION

In 1601 a statute was passed requiring householders to pay rates to provide a dole for vagrants and the destitute, since the traditional almoners, the monastic foundations, had been suppressed by Henry VIII in 1539. For centuries the major part of the levy was employed for the relief of the poor; in 1813 out of £8.5 million raised nationally, £7 million went in relief and only £1.5 million on all other local necessities. Today, the Council Tax that supports local government is levied per property, whether owned or rented, and is based on price bands. The Greater London Authority is financed by government grant and council tax.

URBAN IMPROVEMENTS

The so-called Improvement Acts of 1762 began the transformation of every street in the capital. Paving became the responsibility of the parish vestries, who replaced the deep central drains *(kennels)* with shallow underground sewers and lateral gutters. They provided scavengers and sweepers to clear the streets of night soil and garbage, which were still thrown out of doors.

By the 17C streets were wider and in all but the worst areas, cleaner; the squares were cleared of accumulated refuse and enclosed and planted.

The same 1762 Acts also instituted house numbering and street lighting. Change had begun in 1738, with the installation by the vestries of 15,000 oil-fed lamps with cotton wicks that burned from sunset to sunrise in such main thoroughfares as Oxford Street. In 1807, 13 gas lamp-posts were set up in Pall Mall. Seventy years later *(1878)*, electricity was available and the first major street lighting project was inaugurated with the illumination of the Embankment.

One of the greatest and least visible improvements to the city came after three bouts of cholera killed more than 30,000 people and the "Great Stink" of 1858, when Joseph Bazalgette proposed, designed and built the London sewer system, a design later copied across the world.

The corollary to the 1762 Improvement Acts came with the passage of the Clean Air Acts *(1956, 1962)* controlling the burning of coal in furnaces and open grates, so banishing the notorious London pea-soup fogs. Air quality in the capital has had a further boost with the introduction of the London Low Emission Zone in 2008, to deter lorries, coaches, large vans and other high-emission vehicles from driving in key areas. A congestion charge *(or penalty charge for non-payers)* is levied Monday to Friday for those vehicles wishing to drive in the zone that do not meet the LEZ emissions standard.

EDUCATION

A century ago in the capital there were only the schools of ancient foundation such as Westminster *(1371)* and St Paul's *(1510)*, charity schools, Sunday schools and a few groups run by the Ragged Schools' Union, founded in 1844, attended by an estimated 12.5 percent of the child population.

The Education Acts of 1870 and 1876 provided schools and laid upon parents the duty of seeing that their children "received elementary education in reading, writing and arithmetic" *(the Three Rs)*. Responsibility later devolved on the LCC *(1903)* and subsequently *(1965)* on the Inner London Education Authority *(ILEA)*. When the ILEA was disbanded in 1986, education in inner London became the responsibility of the individual boroughs as it is in outer London. Under later legislation some schools opted out of local authority control. In 2005, discussions began on the possibility of transferring control of education in Greater London to the Mayor's office and Greater London Assembly. Today, London faces challenges in its state school system: the

problems of struggling schools in less affluent inner-city areas are exacerbated by high property prices, which means teachers cannot afford to live near to their work. Recruitment drives to attract and train more teachers and the Key Worker Living Scheme, which provides affordable housing for teachers *(and other so-called key workers)*, are currently aiming to offset these problems.

LIVING IN LONDON
GREEN LONDON

London is a very green city, endowed with millions of trees, mostly cypress, sycamore, ash, plane and cherry. The Royal Parks include St James's Park, Green Park, Hyde Park and Kensington Gardens at the very heart of Inner London, while Regent's Park, Holland Park, Greenwich Park, Richmond Park and Bushy Park extend beyond.

Many residential areas in the inner city are built around garden squares, most either lined by houses, completely hidden from the road, or locked behind high railings and only accessible to local householders with a key. Some, in areas taken over by business, are now open to all and are popular summer picnic sites among local workers. In addition, many residential streets are tree-lined and the average English house remains a lowrise block with a small back garden. Some residential areas in the outer suburbs still have allotments – areas set aside to rent out for growing vegetables.

There are some 3,500 acres/1,416ha of "common land". These are preserved today in local "commons", such as Streatham Common and Tooting Bec in south London.

Most parks are tended by the borough councils and some have sports facilities: football and cricket pitches, bowling greens, golf courses, tennis courts, bandstands, children's summer zoos and playgrounds.

In 1976 the first ecological park *(the temporary and now-defunct William Curtis near Tower Bridge)* was created out of inner city wasteland, turning it into a renewed natural refuge, where urban wildlife could thrive and bringing nature to the city-dweller for serious study or simple enjoyment. Several parks, as well as numerous city farms, continue this purpose today.

In the 1930s a Green Belt (covering 840sq mi/ 2,179sq km) was designated to run through the home counties encircling London at a radius of 20–30mi/32–48km. Although in some sections the belt has completely disappeared, it has had some success in defining the limits of London and halting the metropolitan sprawl. However, with an agreed government target of 32,700 new homes to be built annually in southeast England between now and 2026, the Green Belt is under greater threat from developers than at any time since it was first created.

Environmental focus in London has increased dramatically in recent years. The Recycle for London initiative was launched in 2003 by the Mayor to encourage recycling and many London Boroughs now run their own programmes, with recycling banks, green box collections and other schemes. The Low Emissions Zone (*see Urban Improvements*) aims to improve air quality by taxing high-emission vehicles, while the introduction of an easy-to-use bike hire system by the Mayor of London has seen an increase in two-wheeled traffic on the city's streets.

The City

There is little room within the square mile for parks but since 1878 superb tracts of land "for the recreation and enjoyment of the public" have been acquired by the Corporation: Epping Forest *(6,000 acres/2,400ha)*, Highgate Wood *(70 acres/28ha)*, Queen's Park in Kilburn *(30 acres/12ha)* and West Ham Park *(77 acres/31ha)* among others. The Corporation has also converted Bunhill Fields into a garden; it maintains a bowling green at Finsbury Circus and has created gardens and courts in churchyards *(for example, Postman's Park by St Botolph's)* and in the shells of blitzed or deconsecrated churches: 142 patches of green with over 2,000 trees.

SOCIAL LIFE

The green open spaces scattered across the city greatly contribute to London's social life: each of the many villages that were joined together and progressively formed the city has its own park, green or common, which becomes the centre of social life as soon as the sun shines. Sport, music, summer fairs, picnics and local festivals bring residents from all walks of life together in collective celebration.

There have been times during the long history of the city when being a Londoner has taken on a deeper meaning, and people of various origins and walks of life have found a common ground in the face of adversity and responded with courage and determination. Such was the case during the Blitz of 1940–41, when 30,000 civilians were killed, during the wave of IRA bombings in the 1970s–80s and again during the terrorist bombings of July 2005.

One aspect of London which greatly enriches its social life is its cosmopolitan character: it has always attracted people from countries around the globe, and today it has the largest number of immigrants of any city in the world. This accounts for the great diversity of the capital's social and cultural events. Some of these events, such as the **Brick Lane Festival** *(Bengali)* or the **Notting Hill Carnival** *(Jamaican)*, reach far beyond the communities who initiated them and have become part of the traditional and very British London Season.

The **Season** goes back to the 16C and 17C, when London began to influence taste and fashion in the rest of the country. Originally, it coincided with the sitting of Parliament, starting soon after Christmas and finishing around midsummer. It concerned the upper social classes and included social and charity events, opera and theatre performances, as well as ballroom dances during which aristocratic families hoped to find suitable and advantageous matches for their sons and daughters.

Today, the Season has considerably changed: it extends from April to August, is accessible to a wide public and main events are now mostly sponsored by major companies. One of the first large events of the Season is the **Chelsea Flower Show** in May, while June sees a celebration of HM The Queen's Birthday in **Trooping The Colour**. The summer cultural scene boasts **Glyndebourne** *(a high-quality opera festival in Sussex)*, the **Proms** *(a series of classical concerts given at the Albert Hall)* and the **Royal Academy Summer Exhibition**. Sporting events include the Oxford and Cambridge Boat Race between Putney and Mortlake, international cricket test matches at **Lord's**, the **Wimbledon Tennis Championship** and the **Henley Royal Regatta**.

In addition to the Season, the social life of London rolls continuously; the **Theatreland** of the **West End** dazzles with the latest shows and musicals, the ENO and Royal Opera House host world-class ballet and opera performances, and music and performance of all varieties fills The South Bank, Royal Albert Hall, 02 Arena and Wembley Stadium. Smaller venues, such as the 02 Shepherd's Bush Empire, the 02 Academy Brixton and the HMV Forum in Kentish Town provide alternative live music and gigs, stand-up comedy shows and sporting events, such as Snooker.

Dining out is also a major part of the London social scene, from Michelin-starred restaurants to the buzz of small eateries and lively bars in places such as Soho. With the introduction of the indoor smoking ban in 2006, the streets are even more lively on warm evenings and weekends now, with many establishments putting tables outside to sit at – both for smokers and for those who embrace café culture, despite the sometimes chilly temperatures.

LONDON TOMORROW

Even in uncertain global economic times, London continues to move forward with determination. As a world capital, the pace of life quickens relentlessly, entrepreneurial spirit prevails and people are working harder than ever: Britain has the longest working hours in Europe.

Yet this is offset by the capital's natural dynamism, which stimulates regeneration programmes and projects, from new retail developments such as the vast Westfield shopping centres in Shepherd's Bush and Stratford to Heathrow Airport's new Terminal 5, and revamped entertainment venues such as the **02 Arena, Wembley Stadium** and the **Royal Festival Hall**.

Aside from the Olympics (*see p290*), London's largest project in recent years has been Crossrail, a new 73.3mi/118km railway line, which will run East–West across the city, calling at 37 stations between Maidenhead and Heathrow airport in the West and Shenfield and Abbey Wood in the East. The completed line should be operational in 2018 and promises to lighten the load currently placed on the city's overstretched transport system.

COSMOPOLITAN LONDON

London has attracted people from the four corners of the earth, who have integrated into the London social fabric. The city has more than 35 ethnic groups, with a population of over 100,000, leading to one of the most vibrant and cosmopolitan communities in the world.

African and Caribbean

The Afro-Caribbean communities who originally settled in Brixton and Notting Hill have since spread out all over the city, especially in northwest and south London. The Notting Hill Carnival is now an international event and the lively markets in Brixton, Shepherd's Bush and Tooting, and at the North end of Portobello Road, are packed with exotic produce. The Africa Centre in King Street, Covent Garden, provides a concert venue for music and entertainment, and a craft shop. The arts of Africa are on display at the **British Museum** and at Forest Hill's **Horniman Museum**.

Jewish

London's Jewish community was well established at the time of the Norman conquest *(1066)* and, after many difficulties throughout the ages, has become an economic force through hard work and perseverance. The principal Jewish communities now reside in northwest London: Golders

Green, Hendon, Stanmore, Barnet, Redbridge and around.

The **Jewish Museum** *(see ST PANCRAS)* gives an introduction to the history and culture of London's Jewish community. The museum has recently undergone extensive renovation, but walking tours, temporary exhibitions, events and activities are still being held in partnership with different organisations *(see www.jewishmuseum.org.uk).*

Indian, Pakistani and Bangladeshi

Principal communities are located in the East End *(Shoreditch and Whitechapel)*, Tooting, Shepherd's Bush, Southall and Ealing. Foodstuffs, fashion and crafts are available around the city and the area around **Brick Lane** in the East End and **Southall** are notable for their restaurants. The **Neasden Temple** *(Sri Swaminarayan Mandir, off the North Circular)*, the first traditional Mandir temple in Europe, opened in 1995.

There are displays of the most exquisite jewellery and artefacts at the **Victoria and Albert Museum** and an exhibition on Hinduism – daily life, sacred places and devotional practices in Southern India at the **Horniman Museum**.

Far Eastern

Chinese, Thai, Malaysian, Vietnamese and Filipino communities thrive in London. At the heart of the capital is **Chinatown★**, an Asian enclave that offers all kinds of services *(legal advice, traditional medicine, supermarkets)* and hosts the annual celebration of Chinese New Year. Limehouse in the East End is the area where the Chinese first settled. Japanese expatriates, who live mostly in the affluent suburbs to the West and Northwest, run their own schools and shops *(Oriental City, 399 Edgware Road, NW9)*. Japanese designer stores *(including Muji)* are famous for their simple forms, practical raw materials and plain colours.

Chinese New Year in Chinatown

The **Percival David Foundation** *(see BLOOMSBURY)* is dedicated to the appreciation and study of Chinese culture and important collections of Far Eastern art are on view at the **British Museum** and the **Victoria and Albert Museum** *(see MAJOR CENTRAL LONDON MUSEUMS)*. The **Peace Pagoda** in Battersea Park and Wimbledon's Thai temple are distinctive landmarks.

Mediterranean

Soho and parts of north London have been the preserve of Italian, Greek and Cypriot immigrants for decades. Spaniards and Portuguese congregates around the top end of Portobello Road, while Greek shopkeepers have been attracted to the vicinity of **Aghia Sophia** on Moscow Road, W2.

Middle Eastern

The Edgware Road and the Bayswater area, Shepherd's Market, Kensington High Street and Westbourne Grove are frequented by the Turkish, Lebanese, Syrian and Iranian communities. The golden dome of the **Islamic Cultural Centre and London Central Mosque** *(146 Park Road, NW8)* dominates the skyline in Regent's Park and there are mosques in Whitechapel and other areas of the city.

The Ismaili Centre in South Kensington promotes Islamic culture. Rich collections of Islamic art are exhibited at the **British Museum** and the **Victoria and Albert Museum** *(see MAJOR CENTRAL LONDON MUSEUMS)*.

History

The strategic importance of the site of London as a bridgehead and trading port was recognised by the Romans almost two millennia ago.

TIME LINE

CELTS AND VIKINGS

When the Romans invaded Britain, a Celtic fishing village had already existed since the 5C BC on the north bank of the Thames. The Romans built on the twin hills above the river crossing and Londinium grew into a major town defended by walls, with a permanent stone bridge over the Thames. The decline of the Roman Empire left the city open to Saxon and Viking invasions.

AD

43 Roman Londinium founded.
60 Revolt against the Romans by Queen Boudicca.
2C Roman wall constructed.
5C Londinium evacuated by the Romans.
8C–10C Viking raids and Barbarian invasions.

SAXONS AND NORMANS

Trade continued throughout the Dark Ages, despite the siege and fire of Germanic and Danish invasions. In the 8C London was recognised as the "mart of many nations by land and sea".
Under Alfred for a brief period the kingdom was united and London was constituted a major city, but an attempt to establish the metropolitan see in London was unsuccessful. Slowly the **City** developed into an ordered and rich community. In the 11C, when King Canute exacted tribute, the citizens contributed £10,500, an eighth of the total paid by the whole of England. The last Saxon king, **Edward the Confessor**, on being elected King by the people of the City of London, went upstream to **Westminster**; here he rebuilt the abbey and constructed a royal palace; since then the Monarch and Parliament have been separate from the business community in the City.

Remains of an original Roman wall in the City of London
©Chris Harvey/Bigstockphoto.com

Two months after the Battle of Hastings *(1066)*, the citizens of London submitted to **William the Conqueror**, Duke of Normandy, who was crowned William I and soon built the Tower of London, Baynard's Castle and Mountfichet Castle on the river, East and West of the City, less to defend it against future invaders than to deter the citizens from reconsidering their submission.

1016 Edmund Ironside elected King by the assembly *(gemut)* of London; died the same year; succeeded by **Canute**.
1042–66 Reign of **Edward the Confessor**.
1065 Westminster Abbey founded.
1066 Norman invasion. Coronation of William I. First royal charter granted to the City, whereby government, laws and dues devolved directly upon the citizens themselves.
1066–87 Reign of William I *(**William the Conqueror**)*.
1067–97 Construction of the Tower of London.
1087–1100 Reign of William II (Rufus).
1087 Construction of Westminster Hall.
1100–35 Reign of Henry I; Royal Charter granted to the City.
1135–54 Reign of Stephen.
1136 St Paul's Cathedral and many wooden houses destroyed by fire.

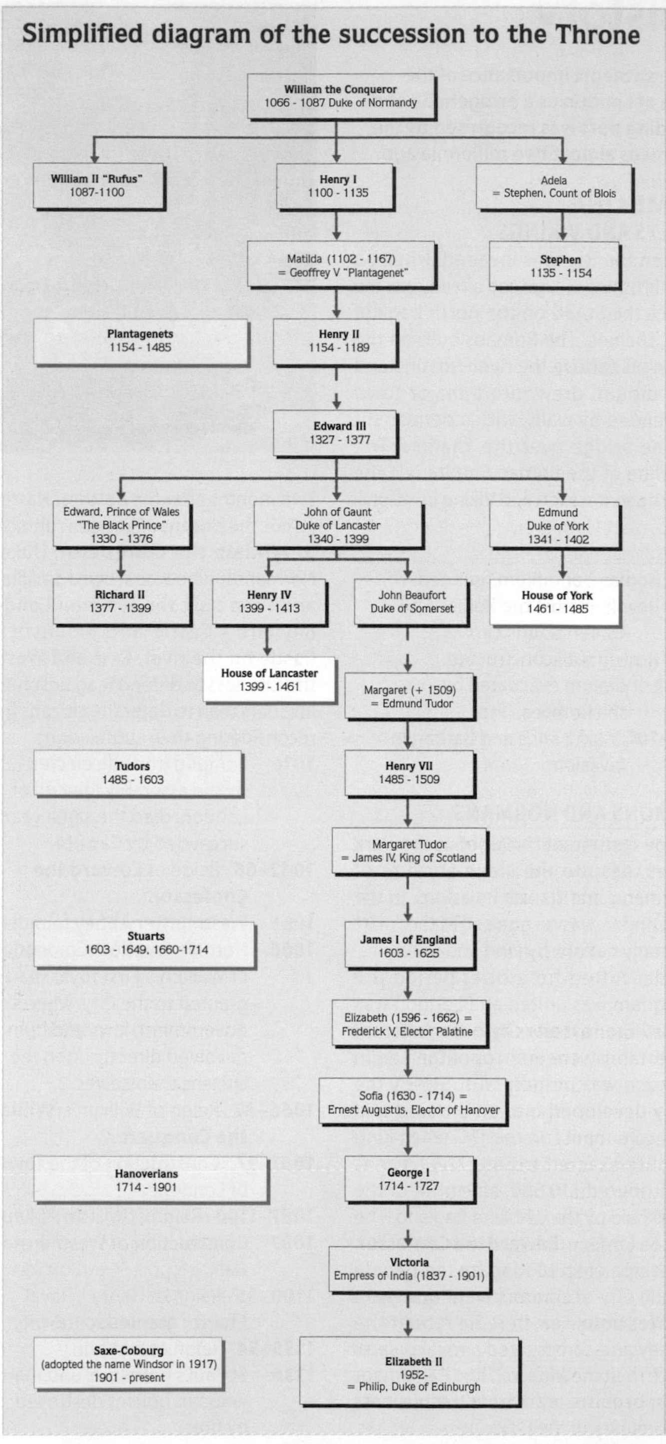
Simplified diagram of the succession to the Throne
William the Conqueror
1066 - 1087 Duke of Normandy
William II "Rufus"
1087-1100
Henry I
1100 - 1135
Adela
= Stephen, Count of Blois
Matilda (1102 - 1167)
= Geoffrey V "Plantagenet"
Stephen
1135 - 1154
Plantagenets
1154 - 1485
Henry II
1154 - 1189
Edward III
1327 - 1377
Edward, Prince of Wales
"The Black Prince"
1330 - 1376
John of Gaunt
Duke of Lancaster
1340 - 1399
Edmund
Duke of York
1341 - 1402
Richard II
1377 - 1399
Henry IV
1399 - 1413
John Beaufort
Duke of Somerset
House of York
1461 - 1485
House of Lancaster
1399 - 1461
Margaret (+ 1509)
= Edmund Tudor
Tudors
1485 - 1603
Henry VII
1485 - 1509
Margaret Tudor
= James IV, King of Scotland
Stuarts
1603 - 1649, 1660-1714
James I of England
1603 - 1625
Elizabeth (1596 - 1662) =
Frederick V, Elector Palatine
Sofia (1630 - 1714) =
Ernest Augustus, Elector of Hanover
Hanoverians
1714 - 1901
George I
1714 - 1727
Victoria
Empress of India (1837 - 1901)
Saxe-Cobourg
(adopted the name Windsor in 1917)
1901 - present
Elizabeth II
1952-
= Philip, Duke of Edinburgh

MEDIEVAL LONDON

The Roman wall, which had fallen into decay, was rebuilt in the Middle Ages largely on the original foundations with an extension to the West; ruined sections are visible at London Wall and by the Tower.

In 1215, under King John, Londoners were empowered to elect annually their own mayor *(elsewhere, a royal appointee)* who had only to submit himself formally at Westminster for royal approval; this was the origin of the Lord Mayor's Show *(see The CITY – Mansion House)*.

By the 13C the **City of London** had become a rich port and the capital of the kingdom. The wealthy City merchants loaned or gave money to Edward III and Henry V for wars on the Continent and apart from the risings of Wat Tyler and Jack Cade, kept clear of strife, even during the Wars of the Roses. Indeed, the City never encroached on Westminster; with a few notable exceptions, citizens held no office under the Crown or Parliament.

Many of the merchants, insurance brokers and bankers were related to landed families; younger sons, such as Richard Whittington *(d. 1423)*, and the Hanseatics, who had arrived by 1157, were sent to seek their fortune in the City: they traded in everything and anything, particularly wool and cloth, building great timber-framed and gabled mansions and buying country estates in the West End and the outskirts of London.

Many **monasteries and magnificent churches** were erected in the City of London by the religious orders. The Dominicans, who arrived in England in 1221, constructed Blackfriars in 1276; the Franciscans *(1224)* began Greyfriars Church in Newgate in 1306; the Carmelites *(1241)* had a house off Fleet Street; the Austin friars *(1253)* settled near Moorgate; St John's Priory, the London Charterhouse and Rahere's priory with St Bartholomew's medical school were established on the north side of the City. At the **Dissolution of the Monasteries** *(1539)*, Henry VIII seized their riches, destroyed the buildings and nominated himself refounder of the hospitals – St Bartholomew's and Bedlam; this did not spoil his relations with the City, which became the home of the royal wardrobe. Under Edward VI, St Paul's Cathedral, one of the great Gothic cathedrals of Europe, was stripped of its holy statues and remaining riches.

1154–89 Reign of Henry II.

115 Arrival of Hanseatic merchants in the City of London.

1189–99 Reign of Richard I *(Richard the Lionheart)*.

1192 Election of Henry Fitzailwin as first Mayor of the City.

1199–1216 Reign of John *(Lackland)*.

1209 Construction of the first stone bridge *(London Bridge)* replacing the Roman bridge.

1215 *Magna Carta* signed by King John at Runnymede under pressure from his rebellious barons.

1216–72 Reign of Henry III.

1224 Law courts established at Westminster.

1290 Jews banished from the City of London.

1272–1377 Reigns of Edward I *(1272–1307)*, Edward II *(1307–27)* and Edward III *(1327–77)*.

1349 Black Death: population of London reduced by half to 30,000.

1337–1453 The Hundred Years' War between England and France began during the reign of Edward III and ended during the reign of Henry VI.

1377–99 Reign of Richard II.

1381 The Peasants' Revolt led by Wat Tyler.

1399–1461 Reigns of Henry IV *(1399–1413)* and Henry V *(1413–22)*.

1450 Rebellion of the men of Kent headed by Jack Cade; they occupied London for three days.

1453 Wars of the Roses between Lancaster and York; Henry VI imprisoned in the Tower of London.

1461–83 Reign of Edward IV.

1476 First English printing press set up at Westminster by William Caxton.

1483 Edward IV's sons assassinated *(The Little Princes in the Tower)*.

1483–85 Reigns of Edward V *(1483)* and Richard III *(1483–85)*.

1485 The battle of Bosworth marked the end of the Wars of the Roses and the beginning of the reign of Henry VII, the first Tudor King.

ELIZABETHAN LONDON

The reign of Elizabeth I dominated the second half of the 16C and marked the capital's golden age: demographic, urban and economic expansion, as well as cultural revival, particularly in literature.

Queen Elizabeth I, during whose reign the population doubled, passed the first of many Acts prohibiting the erection of any new houses within 3mi/5km of the City Gates. The reason for the royal alarm was twofold; it was feared that the newcomers (poor country people) might easily be led into rebellion and that water supplies, sewerage and burial grounds were inadequate. These and later decrees were, however, largely ignored or circumvented.

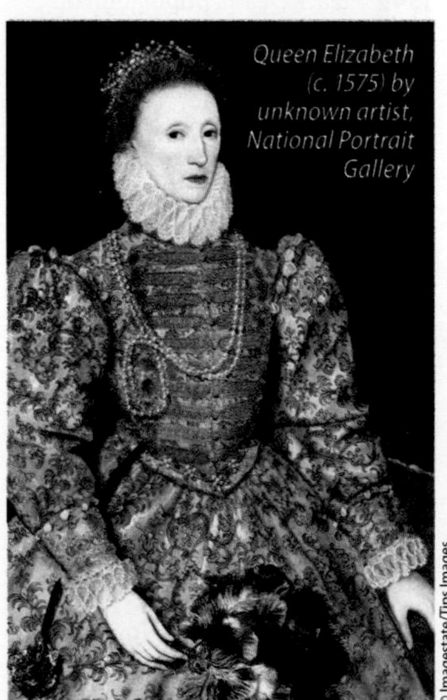

Queen Elizabeth (c. 1575) by unknown artist, National Portrait Gallery

© Imagestate/Tips Images

The Queen tried vainly to curb the growth of suburbs outside the walls. James I, however, subsidised the New River scheme, which brought fresh drinking water to the City.

In the age of exploration the City raised loans and fitted out and financed merchant venturers. The Elizabethan navigators were knighted by the Queen but funds for the voyages of Drake, Frobisher, Hawkins and Raleigh were raised by the City. The aim of the adventurers was to make their fortune of the City to establish trading posts. The result was a worldwide empire.

In 1600, under a charter of incorporation, Queen Elizabeth I granted a monopoly of trade between England and India to a new undertaking, the **East India Company**.

1509–1547 Reign of Henry VIII.

1530 Construction of St James's Palace.

1536 Beheading of Anne Boleyn, second wife of Henry VIII.

1536–39 **Reformation**: Papal authority rejected by the English Church; suppression of the monasteries.

1547–58 Reigns of Edward VI *(1547–53)* and Mary I *(1553–58)*.

1555 Restoration of Catholicism during the reign of Mary I *(Bloody Mary)*. Execution at Smithfield of 300 Protestants. Founding of the Muscovy Company.

1558 Population reaches 100,000.

1558–1603 Reign of Elizabeth I *(Good Queen Bess, the Virgin Queen)*.

1567 First Exchange established in the City.

1581 Founding of the Turkey *(later Levant)* Company.

1599 Inauguration of the original Globe Theatre in Southwark.

1600 Charter of incorporation granted to the **East India Company**.

Great Fire of London – Ludgate is in the foreground and old St Paul's is in the distance

THE CIVIL WAR AND THE RESTORATION

Conflict between the King and Parliament led to civil war. The City merchants sided with Oliver Cromwell and his supporters against Charles I, who was always forcing loans, applying restrictions to trade and requiring gifts, ship money and tonnage.

The Jews, who had been banished in the late 13C, returned in strength during the **Commonwealth** *(1649–60)*, a republic established by Cromwell after the execution of the King.

During the second half of the 17C, London was devastated first by the **Great Plague**, which killed almost one-fifth of the population, and a year later, by the worst fire in the history of the capital.

The **Great Fire** *(1666)*, which burned for four days, destroyed four-fifths of the buildings within the City walls. The Act for Rebuilding the City of London of 1667 stipulated all future structures, houses included, should be of brick, thus reducing the risk of fire.

Christopher Wren was the main architect in charge of rebuilding the City. His great achievement was undoubtedly **St Paul's Cathedral**, but he also rebuilt many of the City's churches with money granted under acts of parliament, which increased the dues on coal entering the Port of London.

1605 The **Gunpowder Plot** *(see CITY OF WESTMINSTER)*.

1616 Queen's House at Greenwich, the first Classical building in England, was designed by Inigo Jones.

1635 Completion of the Covent Garden district.

1642 The beginning of the **Civil War:** Charles I opposed by Parliament; Royalists confront Roundheads at Turnham Green.

1649 **Execution of Charles I** on Tuesday, 30 January 1649 outside the Banqueting Hall in Whitehall.

1649–60 **Commonwealth.**

1653 Cromwell named Lord Protector of the Commonwealth.

1660 **Restoration.**

1660–85 Reign of Charles II *(the Merry Monarch, the Black Boy)*.

1660 Royal warrants permitting theatre performances in Covent Garden.

1661 Design of Bloomsbury Square, the first London square.

1665 **Great Plague:** records give the total mortality as 75,000 out of a population of 460,000, rapidly spreading through London from St Giles-in-the-Fields and causing the most

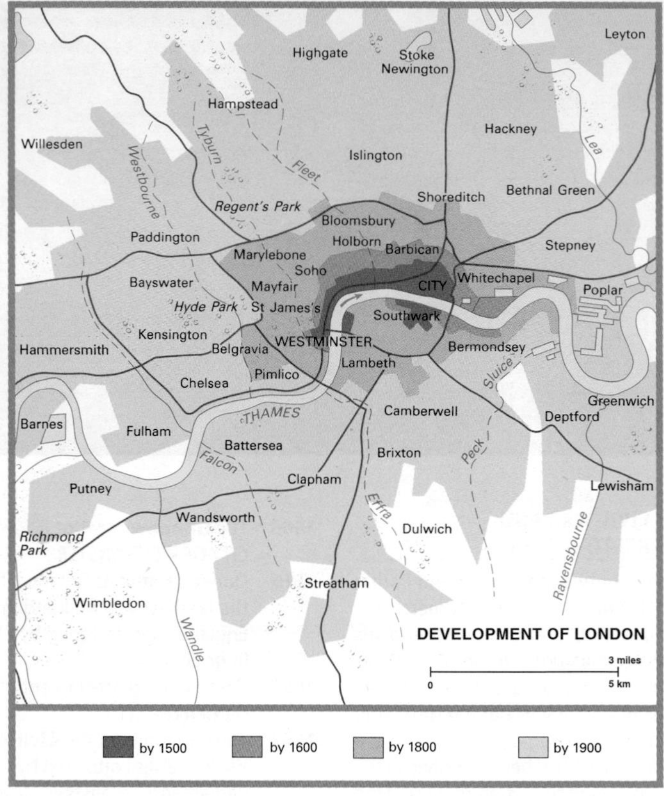

deaths in the poorest, most over-crowded districts on the outskirts of the City *(Stepney, Shoreditch, Clerkenwell, Cripplegate and Westminster)*. In June 1665 the King and the Court left London, only to return the following February; Parliament met briefly in Oxford. A vivid account of these events is given by Daniel Defoe in his *Journal of the Plague Year (1722)*.

1666 Publication of the first London newspaper.

1666 **The Great Fire of London** *(2–5 September)* destroyed four-fifths of the City: St Paul's Cathedral, 87 parish churches, most of the civic buildings and over 13,000 houses.

1666–1723 Reconstruction of St Paul's Cathedral and the City churches by Sir Christopher Wren.

1670 The founding of the **Hudson Bay Company**, with a monopoly that lasted until 1859 in the fur trade with the North American Indians, led to British rule in Canada.

1682 The Royal Hospital in Chelsea is founded for veteran soldiers.

1685 Arrival of Huguenot refugees from France following the Revocation of the Edict of Nantes.

1688 **Glorious Revolution:** flight into exile of James II; crown offered to William of Orange.

1689–1702 Reigns of William III and Mary II until her death in 1694 and then of William alone.

1694 Founding of the Bank of England.

1700 Population 670,000.

1702 Publication of the *Daily Courant* newspaper.

GEORGIAN LONDON

As the London merchants established trading posts abroad, great changes were simultaneously evolving at home as a result of the Industrial Revolution. By the mid-18C people hitherto employed in agriculture were moving into London to work in the new factories and settling east of the City in the docklands, which came to be known as the **East End**. By contrast, fashionable society migrated westwards resulting in the development of the **West End**, with its life of elegance and leisure.

Improved methods of transport were developed. All roads and railways, both literally and metaphorically, converged on London. Easier travel led to the development of the **London Season**, as men coming to London on business brought their wives and particularly their grown-up daughters in search of husbands.

In the 18C, during the **Age of Enlightenment**, the city began to develop from a community of merchants, bankers and craftsmen into a forum for men of letters and the arts.

1714–1830 Reigns of George I *(1714–27)*, George II *(1727–60)*, George III *(1760–1820)* and George IV *(1820–30)*.

1750 Construction of Westminster Bridge.

1753 British Museum established.

1756–63 Seven Years' War.

1775–83 American War of Independence.

1780 Gordon Riots against Roman Catholics.

1801 First census: population 1,100,000.

1811–20 Reign of the future George IV as Prince Regent.

1812 Regent Street created by **John Nash**.

1824 Opening of the National Gallery.

1828 Founding of University College.

1831 Founding of King's College.

1836 **University of London** incorporated by charter as an examining body.

VICTORIAN LONDON

In the 19C as more bridges were built and traffic increased, new wide streets were created to relieve congestion: King William Street as a direct route from the Bank of England to the new London Bridge; Queen Victoria Street, the first street to be lit by electricity.

One of the problems brought on by overpopulation was the Great Stink, which caused engineer Joseph Bazalgette to design London's sewer system, with over 1,000 miles of tunnels and drains.

Public transport was developed through the introduction of omnibuses and the first underground railway.

Several prestigious museums were built and London hosted the first World Fair.

1837–1901 Reign of Queen Victoria.

1835–60 Reconstruction of the Palace of Westminster *(Houses of Parliament)*.

1851 First World Fair in Hyde Park. Population 2.7 million.

1852 Founding of the Victoria and Albert Museum.

1856–1909 Building of the South Kensington museums.

1860 Horse-drawn trams introduced.

Statue of Queen Victoria

1863 First underground railway excavated.
1888 Jack the Ripper stalks the East End, murdering five prostitutes.
1894 Opening of Tower Bridge.
1897 First omnibuses *(buses)* introduced.

20C TO TODAY

The first half of the 20C was marked by a spectacular increase in the population of London, which reached almost nine million on the eve of World War II. At the same time a large proportion of Londoners settled in the **suburbs**. The 1930s saw economic depression and social unrest with an unprecedented rate of unemployment.

In 1940–41, at the beginning of World War II, German air raids concentrated on London left the City and the East End in ruins for over a decade. In the 1950s the importance of the **Port of London** faded: her smog-inducing industries were relocated and the demands for warehousing and docking dwindled. Instead efforts were concentrated on the service industries: company administration, banking, commerce and insurance.

Post-war London offered a contrast of moods: the late fifties, marred by race riots, were followed by the carefree **Swinging Sixties**, which in turn gave way to the aggressive **punk rock culture** of the seventies against a background of IRA bombings.

In the past decades, the **City** has changed beyond all recognition as a result of the "Big Bang" reforms of the 1980s *(computerised share dealing, monitoring of transactions and investment business by government-appointed regulators, removal of restrictions on foreign ownership)*; the rise and fall of Lloyd's of London; Black Monday *(the collapse of the London Stock Exchange in 1987)* and other financial crises; the collapse of venerable banking institutions; foreign takeovers; Bank of England independence and the growth of the European Union. In view of these developments there is a determination

City of London coat of arms

to reassert the City's pre-eminence by forging new alliances in Europe and London remains one of the greatest financial and business centres in the world.

The City is governed by the **Corporation of London**, which acts through the Court of Common Council. The latter, numbering 25 Aldermen and 159 Councilmen, who represent the different wards, is presided over by the Lord Mayor and meets in Guildhall. It has its own police force. Territorial boundaries are marked by the winged dragon of St George and street signs bear the City coat of arms.

Over the first decade of the 21C **London** has continued to evolve. The double centre remains the **City of London** for business and **Westminster** for politics and although to the outward eye the villages may have coalesced into a great urban sprawl, they are claimed with local pride by their residents.

During World War II, the City and the East End suffered greatly from bombing, but as in previous periods, new amenities in tune with the age have risen from the ruins. The docks, which stimulated the growth of the city, have mostly been replaced by modern industries driven by the latest technology and by the financial sector expanding east from the City, as well as massive areas of dormitory accommodation in converted riverfront warehouses. The East End in particular continues to benefit most from the **2012 Olympic Games**, with large infrastrucutre,

City Livery Companies and Ancient City Guild Halls

There are in existence 100 guilds, of which 12 make up the so-called Greater Companies: Mercers, Grocers, Drapers, Fishmongers, Goldsmiths, Skinners, Merchant Taylors, Haberdashers, Salters, Ironmongers, Vintners and Clothworkers. Most are successors of medieval religious fraternities, craft or social guilds, some of which adopted uniforms and were thus styled livery companies. The number of their halls has been reduced to 25 by the Great Fire, local fires, changes of fortune and incendiary bombs – the Master Mariners have adopted a floating hall, the frigate HMS *Wellington*, which is moored in the Thames off the Victoria Embankment below the Strand.

New guilds are created by the modern professions. The Worshipful Company of Information Technologists, whose ranks number 100, held its first meeting in 1992 in Guildhall. The requirements for a new livery company are a minimum of 100 freemen, £100,000 in charitable funds and a record of charitable and educational good works.

Although in 1523 Henry VIII "commanded to have all money and plate belonging to any Hall or Crypt", many halls have collections or pieces dating back to the 15C, which they either managed to hide from the King or repurchased. Notable collections reside at the Mansion House; Clothworkers' Hall *(Mincing Lane)*; Founders' Hall; Fishmongers' Hall; Tallow Chandlers' Hall *(Dowgate Hill)*; Skinners' Hall *(Dowgate Hill)*; Innholders' Hall *(College Street)* – salts and spoons; Vintners' Hall *(Upper Thames Street)*; Mercers' Hall *(Ironmonger Lane)*; Haberdashers' Hall *(Staining Lane)*; Ironmongers' Hall *(Aldersgate Street)*; Barber-Surgeons' Hall *(Monkwell Square)*.

development and legacy projects. It is, of course, the inhabitants of London who make "London town": Londoners born and bred, adopted Londoners from the provinces, refugees from political persecution abroad *(14C–17C Flemish and French Huguenots, political theorists such as Marx and Engels, post-war ex-monarchs, 20C Chileans and Ugandan Asians, to name just a few)* or economic immigrants attracted by a higher standard of living, men and women who achieve international recognition as artists and actors, writers and statesmen, high-flying business men and women, and the nameless millions who ply their daily trade with wit and humour.

1901–10 Reign of Edward VII.

1901 Population 6.6 million.

1909 Establishment of the **Port of London Authority** to manage the docks.

1910–36 Reign of George V.

1914–18 Zeppelin raids on London.

1918 After years of campaigning by the Suffragette movement, led by the Pankhurst family, women over-30 get the vote for the first time.

1919 American-born Nancy Astor becomes Britain's first female MP.

1933 Establishment of London Transport to coordinate public transport: underground, bus and railway.

1936 Accession and abdication of Edward VIII.

1936–52 Reign of George VI.

1938 Establishment of the **Green Belt** to protect land from development.

1939 Population 8.61 million.

1940–41 **London Blitz** *(aerial bombardment of London)* began in 1940 after the British retreat from Dunkerque *(Dunkirk)* and the Battle of Britain. The first heavy raids on London by the German Air Force *(Luftwaffe)* began on 7 September; for 57 consecutive nights hundreds of bombers flew over London dropping heavy explosive or incendiary bombs. Only adverse weather conditions brought respite.

1951 **The Festival of Britain**, an echo of the Great Exhibition of 1851, was promoted as a "tonic to the nation" to bring colour, light and fun to the postwar scene.

1952 Elizabeth II is crowned Queen.

1958 First female peers introduced to the House of Lords. Gatwick Airport opened.

1966 Founding of the City University.

1971 15 February: introduction of decimal coinage.

1975 Population 7 million.

1976 National Theatre opens.

1979 Margaret Thatcher elected the first female Prime Minister.

1981 **London Docklands Development Corporation** *(LDDC)* set up to regenerate the redundant London Docks. First London Marathon run. Violent confrontations in London betweeen Punks and the National Front. Marriage of Prince Charles to Lady Diana Spencer at St Paul's Cathedral.

1982 Barbican Centre opened in the City of London; Thames Barrier raised.

1986 Deregulation of trading on the Stock Exchange. Abolition of the Greater London Council.

1988 Jets begin landing at City Airport.

1995 Opening of the Channel Tunnel, linking Britain with continental Europe for the first time.

1995 National Lottery launched.

1996 After 700 years the Stone of Scone returns to Scotland.

1997 Inauguration of the British Library, St Pancras. Opening of the Globe Theatre.
31 August: Diana, Princess of Wales killed in a Paris car crash. London mourns.

1999–2000 London gains new landmarks to mark the third Millennium: the Dome *(now the O2 Arena, Greenwich)*, the Jubilee Line extension, Millennium Bridge and Tate Modern *(Bankside)* and the London Eye *(South Bank)*.

2000 Ken Livingstone becomes the first elected Mayor of London, with an elected Greater London Assembly.

2005 London wins the bid for the 2012 Olympic Games leading to massive redevelopment of east London.
7 July: terrorists explode four bombs on London's transport network, killing 52.
Prince Charles marries Camilla, Duchess of Cornwall.
Population 7,600,000.

2006 HM The Queen celebrates her 80th birthday.

2007 Tony Blair stands down as Prime Minister. Gordon Brown is appointed in his place through an internal Labour party election.
International Eurostar rail services move to St Pancras.

2007 New Wembley Stadium opens.

2008 Conservative Boris Johnson defeats Labour's Ken Livingstone in the Mayoral election.

2009 Iconic music venue, The Astoria, closes after 33 years and is demolised to make way for Crossrail.

2009 G-20 London Summit held at the Excel centre.

2010 David Cameron, Conservative, becomes Prime Minister in coalition with Nick Clegg, Liberal Democrat.

2011 Half a million people take to the streets to protest against government cutbacks.

2012 The London 2012 Olympics. The Queen celebrates her Diamond Jubilee. Boris Johnson wins second term as Mayor of London.

2013 Imperial War Museum undergoes major refurbishment.

Art and Culture

As London reinvents itself to suit the demands of the time, the architecture of the capital reflects its dynamic character. Tradition is an inherent part of the modern environment and a walk around London reveals an abundance of cultural landmarks. The extension of the City to the East and commissions for major buildings have provided architects with an opportunity to show a renewed sense of flair and innovation as old buildings are put to new uses and new architectural concepts brought into play.

St Bartholomew-the-Great, City of London

© Pictures Colour Library

ARCHITECTURE

ROMAN INFLUENCE

None of the City gates has survived but their existence is recalled in the names of the modern streets or neighbouring churches: Ludgate, Newgate, Aldersgate, Cripplegate, Moorgate, Bishopsgate, Aldgate. The wall built by the Romans c. AD 200 was partially rebuilt between the 12C and the 17C.

Demolition began in the 18C and by the 19C most of it had disappeared. The line of the old wall can be traced by excavated outcrops, usually consisting of an upper area of medieval construction resting on a Roman base *(Barbican, St Alphage Church, All Hallows Church, Sir John Cass College and the Tower of London)*. The street known as London Wall more or less follows the line of the Roman Wall between Aldersgate and Bishopsgate; Houndsditch marks the course of the old ditch outside the wall.

The **London Wall Walk** *(just under 2mi/3km; about 2hr)* between the Museum of London and the Tower of London is well mapped out, with 21 descriptive panels.

MATERIALS

Timber was, for a long time, the cheapest material. Stone, quarried in Kent or imported from Normandy, was brought upriver to the Tower of London; **Portland stone** was first brought to London for St Paul's Cathedral *(17C)*; **Yorkshire stone** for the Houses of Parliament *(1835–60)*. **Bricks** were made locally in Kensington and Islington. In the City, roofs were for the most part thatched until the 15C or 16C and were not uniformly tiled or slated until after the Great Fire *(1666)*.

THE NORMAN CONQUEST

Edward the Confessor grew up in exile in Normandy before assuming the throne of England *(1042–66)*, it was therefore natural for him to model his designs for Westminster Abbey on the Abbey at Jumièges as a symbol of the Church Militant.

The best examples of Norman architecture can be found at St Bartholomew-the-Great, St John's Chapel in the Tower of London and the extant parts of Westminster Abbey rebuilt by Edward the Confessor before the arrival of William the Conqueror.

The boldness of design and sheer scale of the Norman style are reflected in the White Tower and in Westminster Hall – the largest to be built north of the Alps *(240ft/73m long)*.

THE TUDOR AND JACOBEAN ERAS

The greatest examples in the public domain are St James's Palace and Hampton Court, which have the typical multi-storey gateway. At Hampton Court are preserved decorative chimney-

© Stephen Finn/Bigstockphoto.com

stacks, internal courtyards and the great hall with its hammerbeam roof. The first such roof and the most impressive *(spanning 70ft/21m)* is that in the hall of the Palace of Westminster, while other examples survive in the Middle Temple Hall, Charterhouse and Eltham Palace *(c. 1479)*; decorative pendants used at Hampton Court also survive at Crosby Hall in Chelsea. Tudor brickwork with diaper patterning is visible at Charterhouse and Fulham Palace.

THE GOTHIC STYLE

Gothic arrived in England from the continent in the 12C with the expansion of the Benedictine and, in the North, the Cistercian Orders. It remained the predominant style for 400 years, evolving in three main phases.

Early English emerged as a distinctive style at Salisbury and was confirmed at Westminster *(1220)*, where the fabric of the building was essentially conceived as a framework for traceried windows. In the 13C, Henry III assumed the role of pre-eminent patron of architecture in the country – an example continued until the reign of Henry VIII. When the King decided to remodel Westminster church to his taste, he selected the best craftsmen from home and abroad. The result is an English interpretation of French Gothic: Westminster was consolidated with flying buttresses *(cloister side of the nave)*. The elevation consisted of a high arcade, narrow triforium and tall clerestory with rose windows. However, what is distinctly English is the window tracery, so delicate and fluid as no longer to be considered stone masonry as such; the use of polished stone column shafts; the overall richness of applied decoration and the use of iron tie-rods as an alternative to flying buttresses.

Decorated Gothic emerged in the late 13C and is distinguished by the richness and wealth of design in geometrical and later curvilinear tracery; from the 1290s, lierne vaulting became widespread. In essence, a spirit of experimentation and variety of approach pervaded this transitional phase.

Perpendicular, which overlapped with the previous style for 50 years, inspired architects on occasion to abandon the quadrangular in favour of the polygonal, thereby giving greater visual play to the windows and the illusion of a more coherent space. In some cases this led to the use of timber rather than stone for roofing.

During the 15C and 16C, after the Hundred Years' War and the Wars of the Roses, the Crown returned to being the leading patron leaving southeast England three Royal chapels, including Henry VII's Chapel in Westminster Abbey *(1503–19)*. Otherwise, this Perpendicular phase was the great age for secular building and parish churches. Many of the London churches were damaged by the Reformation and/or destroyed in the City by the Great Fire *(1666)*.

The rebuilding that followed, to designs by **Sir Christopher Wren** *(1632–1723)*, marked the end of the evolution of Gothic architecture and the dawn of a different Continental influence.

EARLY CLASSICISM OR PALLADIANISM

The turning point in the evolution of English architecture comes in the mid-16C when the Duke of Northumberland sent a certain John Shute to Italy "to confer with the doings of the skilful masters in architecture". His findings, however, only superficially influenced decorative designs applied to Elizabethan country houses.

At the turn of the century, **Inigo Jones** *(1573–1652)* emerged as the first British architect with a definable personality moulded by the Renaissance Humanist ideal, by his affinity with Palladio's work on Italian architecture (*I Quattro Libri dell'Architettura*) published in Venice in 1570, and by his visits to Venice *(1601 and 1605)*, Padua and Rome *(1613)*.

Important projects to survive undertaken for the Crown by Jones include the Banqueting House completed in 1622 (*see WHITEHALL*) and the Queen's House(*see GREENWICH*).

Banqueting House

Historic Royal Palaces/newsteam.co.uk

CLASSICAL BAROQUE AND THE CLASSICAL REVIVAL (17C18C)

In the wake of Jones comes **Sir Christopher Wren**, who is perhaps a contender for the Top 10 of greatest Englishmen. Wren left England only once for Paris in 1665, where he met Bernini, the famous Baroque sculptor, architect and designer from Rome. On his return to London, he drew up a series of designs for the rebuilding of the Old St Paul's inspired by Lemercier's dome at the Church of the Sorbonne. In the run-up to the millennium a redesign of the area around St Paul's was based in part on Wren's plans, opening up a view of the cathedral from the river.

The City Churches

Although only a few of the parish churches were drawn in detail by Wren, most were planned by the Royal Surveyor, and later supplied with steeples. The most complete surviving Wren churches include St Bride's, St Mary le Bow, St Stephen Walbrook, St Vedast, St Clement Danes and St James's.

St Paul's Cathedral

What is remarkable is that Christopher Wren lived long enough to see the completion of his masterpiece *(1675–1710)*, which has provided later generations of architects with inspiration and solutions to design problems.

Wren also worked on Hampton Court Palace *(south and east wings)*, the Chelsea Hospital and the Greenwich Hospital, where he was certainly assisted by Hawksmoor and Sir John Vanbrugh *(1664–1726)* – both use Classical elements with boldness and imagination to dramatic effect.

The Clerk of Works who followed Wren, **Nicholas Hawksmoor** *(1661–1736)*, developed his own form of English Mannerism *(St Mary Woolnoth in the City; St Alfege in Greenwich; St Anne's, Limehouse; St George-in-the-East, Stepney; St George, Bloomsbury; west towers of Westminster Abbey)*.

NEOCLASSICISM

The rise of a new aristocracy, together with the Duke of Marlborough's great military victories, provided new opportunities for patronage and travel to the Continent. During the first decades of the 18C, **Colen Campbell** *(d. 1729)* published *Vitruvius Britannicus*, a compilation of British buildings in the Antique manner – a veritable manifesto for Palladianism; the other two mainstays of the movement were **Lord Burlington** *(1694–1753)* and **William Kent** *(1685–1748)*, who together went on to forge a powerful partnership that provided architectural designs, interior decoration and layouts for extensive gardens-cum-parks in the manner of Palladio's Brenta villas *(Chiswick Villa)*.

The man who bridges the gap between Wren and the new surge of Palladianism is **James Gibbs** *(1682–1754)*, the architect of St Martin-in-the-Fields. Gibbs was a great follower of Wren – his St Mary-le-Strand is a stylistic and physical neighbour of Wren's St Clement Danes along the Strand.

GEORGIAN ELEGANCE

The next generation of eclectic designers is dominated by two rivals: **Sir William Chambers RA** *(1723–96)*, an upholder of tradition, and the more innovative **Robert Adam** *(1728–92)*.
Chambers, who had travelled to the Far East, was asked to remodel Kew Gardens and embellish them with exotic temples and a pagoda. He gained particular favour with George III, which allowed him to exercise his taste and judgement in such important commissions as Somerset House *(see STRAND)*.
Adam also travelled extensively, to France, Italy and Dalmatia, to explore the Classical style and draw inspiration direct from the example of Antique domestic architecture. In interior decoration he borrowed extensively from descriptions of Pompeii and Herculaneum and from artefacts excavated from Palmyra and Greece, most especially from Greek vase painting – he developed a light touch and delicacy that, having found favour at Osterley Park and Syon House, was quickly assimilated into 18C aesthetic movements. Few Adam town houses survive intact: Home House at 20 Portman Square, the South and East sides of Fitzroy Square, single houses in St James's Square *(no 20)*, Chandos Street and behind the Adelphi.
English Neoclassicism evolved into an informal reinterpretation of the Antique and affected all the decorative and applied arts. Multi-disciplined designers like Adam and Chambers were content to accommodate other revivalist styles in the form of follies, bowers and bandstands. **Gothic** was limited to private houses *(Strawberry Hill)*; **chinoiserie** to garden pagodas *(Kew)*; **Rococo** to follies or pleasure gardens *(Vauxhall)*; the **Picturesque** contrived to imitate untamed Nature, as depicted in painting – dead trees were planted and "ruins" artificially assembled in gardens.

THE REGENCY PERIOD (1811–30)

The main thread of the Regency style came from pre-Revolution France, copied from picture books and interpreted by Continental craftsmen. The key figure of this phase is probably **Henry Holland** *(1745–1806)*, who designed Brooks's Club in St James's.
The period up to the death of George IV is also dominated by three men: **Sir John Soane** *(1753–1837)*, whose principal legacy was the Bank of England, now largely destroyed; **John Nash**, favourite architect of George IV, who was responsible for laying out Regent Street, the terraces of elegant residences for Members of Parliament surrounding Regent's Park *(1810–11)*, for designing the grand Carlton House Terrace, Buckingham Palace (although much changed), the Brighton Pavilion and various country houses.
Thomas Cubitt, quality builder and property developer, worked from George Basevi's designs to create Belgrave Square and other large sections of Belgravia *(1825)*, Pelham Crescent *(1820–30)*; other squares, crescents and streets stretch from Putney and Clapham to Islington, Kensington to the Isle of Dogs.

THE VICTORIAN AGE (19C)

A population explosion provoked a huge demand for urban housing that in turn necessitated a change in building practices. Materials began to be industrially manufactured *(by the 1840s whole buildings were pre-fabricated and concrete was being tested in the 1860s)* and transported cheaply by rail.
The main phases may be identified as **Early Victorian**, characterised by earnest historicism and the use of plainish materials, **High Victorian** *(1850s–1870s)*, which reacted against archaeological correctness with bright colour, contrasting materials and strong

Architectural Terms used in this guide

Ambulatory: continuation of the aisles around the east end sanctuary.

Apsidal or radiating chapel: apsed chapel radiating from the ambulatory or sanctuary.

Barrel vaulting: most basic form of tunnel vaulting, continuous rounded or pointed profile.

Blind arcading: decorative frieze of small, interlacing, arches and intervening pilaster strips; typical of Romanesque architecture in Lombardy and West Country Transitional.

Buttress: a structural member placed along the exterior wall to reinforce and counter side thrust of a vault

Capital: head or crowning feature of a column. In Classical architecture there are four orders: Doric, Ionic *(with volutes)*, Corinthian *(leaf decoration)* and Composite *(Ionic and Corinthian)*. Other forms include a Cushion capital *(Romanesque cut from a cube)* and a Crocket capital *(decorated with stylised Gothic leaves terminating in volutes)*.

Caryatid: female figure used as a column *(atlantes are male caryatids)*.

Clerestory: upper section of the elevation containing large windows.

Flamboyant: latest phase *(15C)* of French Gothic architecture; name taken from the undulating *(flame-like)* lines of the window tracery.

Flying buttress: buttress of masonry decorated with pinnacles.

Fresco: mural paintings executed on wet plaster.

Gable: triangular part of an end wall carrying a sloping roof or steeply pitched ornamental pediment of Gothic architecture.

Gargoyle: waterspout projecting from the parapet, often ornamented with a grotesque figure, animal or human.

Groined vault: produced by the intersection of two perpendicular tunnel vaults of identical shape.

Lady Chapel: chapel radiating or extending from the sanctuary dedicated to the Virgin Mary.

Lierne: a tertiary rib that neither springs from the main springers nor passes through the central boss.

Lintel, transom: horizontal beam or stone bridging an opening of a door or window.

Pediment: low-pitched gable over a portico, usually triangular, in Classical architecture.

Pier: solid masonry structural support as distinct from a column.

Pilaster: engaged *(attached)* rectangular column.

Pinnacle: small turret-like decorative feature crowning spires, buttresses.

Quadripartite vaulting: one bay subdivided into four quarters or cells.

Rib vault: framework of diagonal arched ribs carrying the cells.

Rood screen: carved screen separating the chancel from the nave, sometimes surmounted by a gallery.

Semicircular arch: round-headed arch.

Tracery: intersecting stone ribwork in the upper part of a window.

Transept: transverse section of a cross-shaped church bisecting the nave.

Triforium: arcaded wall passage running the length of the nave above the arcade and below the clerestory.

Triptych: three panels hinged together, chiefly used as an altarpiece.

Capitals of Carlton House Terrace

St Pancras Station

© Douglas Freer/iStockphoto.com

sculptural effects, and **Late Victorian**, which reverted to smooth contours and soft textures, intricate decoration and delicate colour.

A key figure who straddles all three phases was **Sir George Gilbert Scott** *(1811–78)*. He applied his confident Gothic style as easily to religious buildings *(St Mary Abbotts, Kensington)* as to secular developments: St Pancras Station and Hotel, Albert Memorial, Broad Sanctuary, West of Westminster Abbey. His grandson **Sir Giles Gilbert Scott** *(1880–1960)* proved himself to be a far more sensitive and inspired product of the Late Victorian age, bequeathing such individual landmarks of the post-industrial age as Battersea Power Station *(1932–34)*, Waterloo Bridge *(1939–45)* and Bankside Power Station.

London's singlemost famous building, the Houses of Parliament, with its signature clocktower housing Big Ben, was added to the medieval Westminster Hall by **Sir Charles Barry** between 1840 and 1888.

At the same time, functional cast-iron building became an art in itself *(Lewis Cubitt's King's Cross Station 1852, Brunel's Paddington Station 1850)*.

Red-brick developments were instituted by the London County Council, who drew inspiration from **Philip Webb** for Bethnal Green and Millbank. Another successful exponent of this practical, unfussy style was **Richard Norman Shaw** *(1831–1912)*, who designed Lowther Lodge in Kensington *(1873, now the Geographical Society)*, Swan House in Chelsea *(1876)* and four houses in Cadogan Square *(60a, 62, 68 and 72)*. The interior decoration and furnishings were left to the firm of the socialist **William Morris** *(1834–96)* and as such soon became identified with the **Arts and Crafts Movement**.

Against the tide of mass production came a revival of craftsmanship in architectural sculpture, stained glass, practical hand-made furniture, block-printed fabrics and wallpapers. While **Alfred Waterhouse** *(1830–1905)* designed the Natural History Museum, combining naturalistic observation with fantastic imaginary beasts applied to some great Germanic Romanesque fabric, De Morgan tiles and Morris screens spurned the development of art nouveau.

A surge in **church building** was provoked by demand to serve the new suburbs. Perpendicular spires spiked the sky as a new interest in Gothic architecture culminated in the latest designs for the Palace of Westminster.

As in the 18C, fads and fashions proliferated ,prompting a revivalist taste for neo-Norman, neo-Early Christian and, in the mid century, for neo-Italian Romanesque.

20C AND EARLY 21C

Not until the 1920s was the neo-Gothic tradition broken when **Edward Maufe** provoked a change of direction by building truly modern **churches**: St Columba's in Pont Street, St John's in Peckham.

The International Style formulated by the Belgian **Henry van der Velde** *(1863–1957)* and the German **Peter Behrens** *(1868–1940)* – both painters turned designer and architect – were followed by **Walter Gropius** *(1883–1969)*. They advocated quality in building and practical functionality – factories and power stations should not be dressed to look like schools or cathedrals. Meanwhile, steel-frame construction

(Ritz Hotel, 1904) and the use of concrete led to ever-shorter building time-frames. Distinctive **modern housing** is rare: 64–66 Old Church Street in Chelsea *(c. 1934)* by the International Modernist **Mendelsohn** and Chernayeff, the Sun House in Hampstead *(1935)* by **Maxwell Fry**, Highpoint One and Two in Highgate *(1936–38)* by the reclusive **Berthold Lubetkin** and Tecton, **Goldfinger's** custom-built 2 Willow Road and Cheltenham Estate *(Kensal Rise)*. Lillington Gardens, Pimlico *(1960s)* and Aberdeen Park in Islington *(1980s)* by Darbourne and Darke show that council housing need not be unattractive.

Today, important contemporary developments abound on the South Bank, in the City, Docklands and around Heathrow, Gatwick and Stansted airports, while imaginative conversions proliferate along the Thames and within London's mainline railway stations and disused markets *(Billingsgate, Spitalfields)* and power stations *(Bankside)*. Notable landmarks on London's skyline include Centre Point, the South Bank Complex, Barbican, the BT Tower, **Richard Rogers'** Lloyd's Building, Tower 42, Chelsea Harbour, Vauxhall Cross, and 1 Canada Square – known simply as Canary Wharf. The Millennium Dome in Greenwich and the new offices of the Mayor of London in Bermondsey *(City Hall)* add a futuristic note to the riverside. The distinctive Swiss Re building designed by **Sir Norman Foster** *(2002)* and known to locals simply as "the Gherkin" continues the trend for eco-friendly buildings. Other architects have applied their skills to the 2012 Olympic Games project and to the redevelopment of the **Lower Lee Valley** around Stratford, where several innovative buildings have sprung up in recent years – not all of them destined to become sports venues.

MUSIC AND THE PERFORMING ARTS

It is acknowledged that the best way to capture the spirit of a place is to take part in its cultural activities. London has a proud reputation as an eclectic capital for the performing arts and Londoners have open minds and show a refreshing willingness to share new experiences. The profusion of venues and the range and quality of the offerings attest to the vibrancy of the musical and theatrical scene. The diversity of this multicultural city is a further asset to which artists from all over the world also make a contribution.

A MUSICAL MOSAIC

London is one of the concert, opera and pop capitals of the world. Tradition and modernity are often juxtaposed

City Hall and Tower Bridge

to reflect diverse cultural influences at play; nowadays pop musicians and classical orchestras collaborate with great success. This significant development is a consequence of the fusion of genres, as audiences show a willingness to experiment with new musical forms. It is not unusual to mark events of national interest in a musical idiom fusing the popular and traditional styles. Opera performances are held in more accessible venues, such as the arena at the Royal Albert Hall and the piazza in Covent Garden. Happy crowds enjoy the "Last Night of The Proms" in **Hyde Park** and the open-air concerts at **Holland Park**, **Hampton Court** and **Kenwood**.

Popstars are equally at home at the Royal Albert Hall, The 02 Arena, Wembley Arena and the London Arena in Docklands; the Royal Festival Hall and the Barbican host jazz, folk and world music, along with a superb array of classical concerts.

THE SWINGING CAPITAL

London's dizzying musical atmosphere is characterised by four prestigious orchestras, two celebrated opera companies, a multitude of pop groups and a wide range of musical entertainment, from buskers to lunchtime church concerts and from polished orchestral performances to professionally staged rock shows and techno raves. The creative energy of the music scene, which fosters inventive new styles, shows no sign of abating.

A FORMIDABLE TRADITION

The light airs of Tudor England *(e.g. Greensleeves, attributed to Henry VIII)* developed into rounds, canons and finally a golden age *(1588–1630)* of madrigals. Much instrumental dance music was written with variations to display the performer's virtuosity; **John Dowland** excelled at solo songs accompanied by lute and viol. At the same time **Thomas Tallis** and **William Byrd** were composing religious music for the organ and voice in masses and anthems, set to the Latin and English liturgy; only in Elizabeth's reign did a distinctive Anglican style emerge.

In the latter half of the 17C composers extended their range with *Te Deums* and songs, and incidental music for the theatre. **Henry Purcell** *(1659–96)*, who dominated his own and subsequent generations, produced the first full-length opera *(Dido and Aeneas)* in 1689. Italian opera then became popular and was firmly established with *Rinaldo (1711)* by **Handel**, who had arrived in England that year. Handel resided at 25 Brook Street, Mayfair until his death in 1759 and he produced operas based on mythological subjects, which were satirised by John Gay in *The Beggar's Opera (1728)*, occasional pieces such as the *Fireworks* and *Water Music*, and a great succession of oratorios about religious heroes: *Esther, Messiah*.

Mozart composed his first symphony in 1764 while residing at 180 Ebury Street; his name is perpetuated in Mozart Terrace in Pimlico. **Haydn** stayed in London in the 1790s when he was the greatest musical figure in Europe. **Mendelssohn** came to London early in the 19C and began work on the *Scottish Symphony* and incidental music to *A Midsummer Night's Dream*, which he completed some 20 years later.

THE MODERN AGE

At the end of the 19C, English music became widely popular. The Savoy operas – *Libretto* by **WS Gilbert** and music by **Sir Arthur Sullivan** *(1875–99)* appealed to a wide audience. As radio became widespread in the 1930s, the BBC began to broadcast the **Promenade Concerts**, which had been inaugurated in 1895 by the conductor Henry Wood in the Queen's Hall and later held in the Albert Hall. The programmes, organised by the BBC, include orchestral works and opera by classical and modern composers, performed by national and visiting musicians and conductors. The promenaders make a spirited contribution to the Last Night, when traditional pieces are played (including Elgar's *Pomp and Circumstance*).

The opening of the 20C also saw the appearance of a host of new British composers: **Edward Elgar** (*Enigma Variations, 1899, Dream of Gerontius,* 1900), Delius, **Vaughan Williams** *(nine symphonies)* and **Gustav Holst** (*The Planets, 1914–16*). They were joined in the 1920s by Bax, Bliss and William Walton (*Belshazzar's Feast, 1931*).
After the war they were reinforced by **Michael Tippett** (*A Child of Our Time, 1941, The Midsummer Marriage, 1955*) and **Benjamin Britten**, who produced a magnificent series of works – *Peter Grimes*, 1945, *Albert Herring, Let's Make an Opera, Billy Budd, Midsummer Night's Dream, The War Requiem* and the operetta, *Paul Bunyan.*
The second half of the 20C saw the establishment of permanent centres of opera at Covent Garden and the London Coliseum, the construction of concert halls on the South Bank and at the Barbican, the restoration of the Wigmore Hall and the birth of numerous provincial *(summer)* festivals.

THE BRITISH MUSICAL

From the late 1960s musicals achieved huge popularity, dominated by the talented and prolific **Andrew Lloyd-Webber**, who initially collaborated with Tim Rice *(Jesus Christ Superstar* and *Evita*) and the producer Cameron Mackintosh *(Cats)*. The shows, where the story is partly told in song, set the trend for spectacular staging, strong but simple melody and large casts. Other thrilling shows, such as *Oklahoma!, My Fair Lady, Les Misérables* and *Phantom of the Opera*, have enjoyed long runs in the West End. Recent revivals have included *Mary Poppins, Saturday Night Fever* and *Guys and Dolls*.
The successful shows are staged in cities worldwide and have won a huge following. *The Lion King*, with music by **Elton John**, combines animation, music and song in a novel way, and there is a new trend towards reusing great pop music as the background for a plot, with smash hits such as *Mamma Mia!* (Abba) and *We Will Rock You* (Queen).

CODA

The rich legacy of the music-hall tradition and the fantastic success of contemporary musicals are evidence of the happy fusion of two genres. Jazz music, which took over from the big dance bands, has a solid following and jazz clubs are flourishing with a high calibre of performers such as the saxophonist Courtney Pine.
Since the Swinging Sixties, the **Britpop** music scene has never been so dynamic, with a proliferation of new styles, the thundering rhythmic output of famous rock and dance venues and nightclubs, the chart-topping popstars and bands and independent groups performing in pubs and clubs.
Prestigious orchestras and celebrated artists make regular appearances at famous concert halls, opera houses, cathedrals and churches throughout London. Besides the classical repertoire, there is a drive to introduce music by modern composers to a wide public.

THE LONDON STAGE

The success of the London stage has been built on a unique tradition spanning more than five centuries. Talented playwrights and actors have helped to establish the reputation of British theatre worldwide but the capital is also receptive to foreign influences and new talent is applauded by enthusiastic and knowledgeable audiences.
Today, high standards and international reputations are maintained by the Royal Shakespeare Company and the Royal National Theatre. Experimental theatre starts in the provinces and on London's fringe circuit before moving to the West End. During the summer, open-air venues in Holland Park, Regent's Park and the Globe Theatre are an unusually historical and informal way to enjoy performances, while several stately homes and parks, including Hampton Court and Kew, are now hosting short seasons of open-air Shakespeare. Behind all of this, the suburbs support many smaller theatres, shared by touring productions and enthusiastic local amateur groups.

A RICH THEATRICAL HISTORY

During the Middle Ages plays were performed outside the city boundaries as the City of London authorities remained steadfast in refusing to allow theatrical performances within their jurisdiction. The courts of Henry VIII and Elizabeth I at Nonsuch Palace and Hampton Court attracted contemporary dramatists and entertainers for their private functions.

The first regular "public" performances were held in Clerkenwell and Shoreditch, where **James Burbage** founded the first English playhouse and then moved south of the river to Southwark.

The legal fraternity also provided facilities for the performance of plays, masques and revels; in the late 16C *The Comedy of Errors* was staged in Gray's Inn and *Twelfth Night* was played beneath the hammerbeam roof of the Middle Temple Hall.

The true theatrical tradition, however, is descended from the popular genre, whose most famous exponents include **William Shakespeare** *(1564–1616)*, **Christopher Marlowe** *(1564–93)*, Ben Jonson *(1572/3–1637)*, Wycherley, Congreve, Sheridan, **Oscar Wilde**, Tom Stoppard and **Harold Pinter**.

FROM RESTORATION COMEDY TO MUSIC HALL

The social climate of the Restoration is reflected in the witty comedy of manners of **William Congreve** (*The Way of the World* and *Love for Love*). The Theatres Royal of Drury Lane, Haymarket and Covent Garden opened under royal patronage in that period. The most famous performer was Nell Gwynne, a royal favourite. The 18C was an era of great acting talent, such as David Garrick, the Kembles, Sarah Siddons and Dorothea Jordan. *The School for Scandal* by **Sheridan** was a triumph. In the 19C the stage was dominated by Henry Irving, Ellen Terry and the great Shakespearean actor Edmund Kean.

In the Victorian era, the growth of the urban population brought about new forms of entertainment: melodrama reflecting the popular taste for sentimentality and music hall combining song and ribald comedy.

Wilton's Music Hall

The popularity of the latter genre – the star was the glamorous singer Marie Lloyd – led to grander theatres, known as Palaces of Variety, such as the London Palladium. The Hackney Empire, Collins Music Hall in Islington and Wilton's Music Hall in Wapping are rare survivals. Variety gave way to French-style revue, combining songs and sketches. Its undisputed masters were **Ivor Novello** and **Noël Coward**, who epitomised the glamour and sophistication of the period.

A WAVE OF INNOVATION

Farce and "kitchen sink drama" were new vogues introduced by the English Stage Company at the Royal Court Theatre, which opened in 1870. Coined as the "bad boy of West End theatre," this famous institution was the launch pad for **GB Shaw** (1904–09), **John Osborne** *(Look Back in Anger, 1956)* and Arnold Wesker, among others who dealt with current social and political issues. The innovative style of **Harold Pinter**, his sparse use of language and challenging political themes were in tune with the mood of the time. In 2005, Pinter won the Nobel Prize for Literature.

The National Theatre Company was established to stage original works which might not be produced in the West End owing to commercial pressures. The Old Vic under Lilian

Baylis had set the scene. Famous performers include many of the greatest: Sir Laurence Olivier, Sir John Gielgud, Sir Ralph Richardson, Sir Paul Scofield, Dame Peggy Ashcroft, Dame Maggie Smith and Dame Judi Dench have all won acclaim internationally. The playwrights David Hare, Alan Ayckbourn, David Storey, Edward Bond, Michael Frayn and Tom Stoppard have achieved pre-eminence on TV and in film, as well as on the stage.

THE FRINGE

Alternative theatre dealing with experimental or controversial themes is performed in pubs, converted churches and small venues such as the Royal Court *(Sloane Square)*, the King's Head *(Islington)*, the Bush *(Shepherd's Bush)*, the Gate *(Notting Hill)* and the Battersea Arts Centre. The Donmar and the Almeida are reputed for staging intelligent and provocative plays and for attracting famous names. The fringe is the proving ground of many leading writers, directors and actors.
Stand-up comedy comes into its own at The Comedy Store, Jongleurs and a host of other venues. There is an atmosphere of fun and the shows are usually of a good quality with young hopefuls trying their luck and established comics running through new routines.

DANCE

The London dance scene is arguably the world's most dynamic, with sophisticated shows, both home-grown and international, gracing the stage of the city's major venues year-round. Sadlers Wells presents a rolling programme of eclectic, cutting-edge shows, while the Royal Opera House is home to the internationally renowned Royal Ballet. A range of smaller spaces around the city, such as the Laban Centre in Lewisham and The Place in Euston, play host to contemporary and innovative performances, while centres such as Danceworks and Pineapple Dance Studio run daily dance classes in all styles, from flamenco and tap to jazz and salsa.

LITERATURE

A CAPTIVATING CITY

Not all have felt with William Dunbar "London, thou art the flower of cities all" nor even with Dr Johnson that "there is in London all that life can afford," but at some point in their careers many writers lived in London and English literature from detective stories to diaries, and from novels to biographies, is permeated with scenes of the City. Despite their numbers there has been no regular forum for writers down the years: groups have shifted from the pubs near Blackfriars Theatre to those on Bankside and along the Borough High Street, close to the Globe; to Highgate, to Chelsea and, for a charmed circle, centred on **Virginia Woolf**, to Bloomsbury; at the turn of the 20C a group around **Oscar Wilde**, which included Aubrey Beardsley and Max Beerbohm, and artists of the day met at the Café Royal.
Since many writers begun or earned a living as journalists, the first regular haunts were the coffee houses around Fleet Street; Addison and Steel frequented the George and Vulture and subsequently Button's at both of which they wrote copy for the *Tatler* and *Spectator*; **Dr Johnson** called at many coffee houses and taverns, but nearest his own house was The Cheshire Cheese where, tradition has it, many of the great conversations took place.

VERSE

Geoffrey Chaucer *(1340–1400)* was a courtier and diplomat; he drew on the rich tradition of contemporary French, Latin and Italian literature to recount his *Canterbury Tales* about pilgrims journeying between Southwark and Canterbury. The Elizabethan Age is encapsulated in **Sir Edmund Spenser**'s *Faerie Queene*, a long poem populated with personifications of Justice, Temperance, Holiness, Chastity, etc. The two great masters of theatre **Christopher Marlowe** *(1564–93)* and **William Shakespeare** *(1564–1616)* used free verse enriched with powerful imagery and varied syntax.

Oscar Wilde

It was not until **John Milton** *(1608–74)* emerged that the poetic genre heralded the Age of the Enlightenment. Intellectually provocative, Milton carefully expressed his Puritan anti-Royalist politics in prose and his views on the Fall of Man in verse *(Paradise Lost, Comus, Lycidas)*. The first Poet Laureate, **John Dryden** *(1631–1700)*, recorded contemporary events in his poetry, criticism, drama and translations: his clear, precise verse heralds the rational climate of the period of **Alexander Pope**, **Jonathan Swift** *(Gulliver's Travels)* and **Samuel Johnson** *(compiler of the first Dictionary, 1755)*.

Such **Romantic poets** as Blake, Burns, Wordsworth and Coleridge are great and distinctive figures but, like the Brontës, Hardy and Eliot, wrote largely outside the London scene, turning instead to spirituality, Scottish patriotism and Nature for inspiration. The quintessence of the movement exists in the tragically short life and inspired output of **John Keats** *(1795–1821)*, who came to London to study medicine. **William Wordsworth** mused on Westminster Bridge but lived in the Lake District; **Lord Byron** enjoyed high society.

For the Victorians, Imagination must reign over Reason – the Poet Laureate *(1850–92)* **Tennyson** *(Morte d'Arthur)* specialised in mellifluous poetry, **Browning** in more exclamatory verse and **Arnold** in descriptions of the moral dilemmas of life deprived of religious faith. Pre-Raphaelite poets such as **DG Rossetti**, his sister **Christina**, **William Morris** and **Swinburne** drew their subject matter from the timeless myths and legends, and from ancient ballads. The **Aesthetes** of the 1890s, including **Oscar Wilde** *(1854–1900)*, **Beerbohm** and **Beardsley**, were greatly impressed by the philosophical writings of Henri Bergson *(1859–1941)* and affected by Huysmans' Symbolist novel *A Rebours (Against the Grain* alluded to in Wilde's *Picture of Dorian Gray*). The counter-reaction this provoked was a move towards realism led by **WB Yeats** *(1865–1939)* and **Rudyard Kipling**, whose verse was full of colloquial language, natural rhythm and vitality. The Georgian poets, including **TS Eliot** *(The Waste Land, Old Possum's Book of Practical Cats, Murder in the Cathedral)*, **DH Lawrence** and Walter de la Mare, defined the transition to Modernism; their work is haunted by the devastating effect of war – poignantly captured by the War Poets (**Sassoon**, **Owen** and **Brooke**).

The 1930s era of depression is recorded by **WH Auden**, **Cecil Day Lewis**, **Louis MacNeice** and **Stephen Spender**: contemporaries at Oxford, their verse is direct in appeal, colloquial in language and anti-establishment in politics. **Dylan Thomas** *(1914–53)*, on the other hand, explores childhood and innocence, while **Ted Hughes** *(1930–98)* describes the inherent violence of Nature. **Carol Ann Duffy** is the current – and first female – Poet Laureate (Britain's "official" poet).

THE LIGHTER TOUCH

Truly English in quality is the gently humorous and entertaining light verse. Many of the major writers dabbled in it, but it is the likes of **Edward Lear** *(1812–88 – Book of Nonsense)* and **Lewis Carroll** *(1832–98 – Alice in Wonderland)*, who have been the most enduring masters of nonsense and limerick. **Hilaire Belloc** *(1870–1953 – Cautionary Tales)* and **AA Milne** *(1882–1956 – Winnie the Pooh)* contributed their verse to *Punch* magazine – a venue that in the pictorial arts had already long perfected the parallel genre of caricature and cartoon. Perhaps the most typically English of the comic writers were **Sir John Betjeman** *(1906–1984)* and **PG Wodehouse** *(1881–1975)*.

THE NOVEL

"The object of a novel should be to instruct in morals while it amuses," observed **Anthony Trollope**. The first of a line of great novelists is **Daniel Defoe** *(c. 1661–1731)*, who managed, in *Robinson Crusoe* and *Moll Flanders*, to describe ordinary middle-class characters in credible plots. Following Defoe comes **Samuel Richardson** *(1689–1761)*, originator of the epistolary novel with *Pamela* and *Clarissa*, which explore human thought and emotion, and the popular playwright before he became a novelist, **Henry Fielding** *(1701–54)*, whose *Tom Jones* is the story (moralistic in tone) of a man of unknown birth, who goes to London to seek his fortune. At the turn of the century Oliver Goldsmith, Fanny Burney and Sir Horace Walpole found fame with single works prompting an interest in the Picturesque as well as mystery and terror – a tradition which was to inspire Mary Shelley's *Frankenstein (1818)*.

The Romantic movement is dominated by the prolific **Sir Walter Scott** *(1771–1832)*, a specialist of the historical novel, where characters seem powerless pawns before external political predicaments *(Waverley, Rob Roy, Ivanhoe)*. In contrast, **Jane Austen** *(1775–1817)* drew her six novels from personal experience – notably in matters of love and marriage; she writes with a wry humour and sensitivity, which give her novels an enduring popularity.

The Victorian chapter is dominated by **Charles Dickens** *(1812–70)*, who animates his great catalogue of novels, set in and around London, with colourful characterisation, inventive plots, humour and pathos (*Pickwick Papers, Oliver Twist, Nicholas Nickleby, A Christmas Carol, David Copperfield, Bleak House, Little Dorrit* and *Great Expectations*). Published as serials, his stories quickly found a large audience and stirred contemporary Humanists to reform social conditions for children, the poor and the deprived. **William Thackeray** *(1811–63)* sets his *Vanity Fair* in Regency England, reproaching hypocrisy and double standards.

Writing at the turn of the century, **HG Wells** *(1866–1946)* drew on his studies at London University to create scientific romances that lead the way for the science fiction of John Wyndham *(1903–69)*. Travel and free thought are the principal themes of a new phase in literature: **EM Forster** *(1879–1970)* explored the frailty of human nature; **Virginia Woolf** *(1882–1941)* saw herself as an artist retaliating against the narrow-mindedness of Victorian London; she is certainly one of the most discerning and psychological novelists. **Evelyn Waugh** *(1903–66)* depicts social circumstances with wit, black comedy and farce that develop to realism in the face of the threat of war – a realism that pervades the work of **George Orwell** *(1903–50)* and his haunting images in *1984* of a spiritless, futuristic age.

The 20C was marked by various versatile personalities living and working in London but taking a global view, informed by travel abroad: **Graham Greene, Kingsley Amis, Muriel Spark, Doris Lessing, Iris Murdoch** and **Anthony Burgess**.

The end of the 20C saw the emergence of novelists belonging to various ethnic minorities, in particular Indian-born **Salman Rushdie**, whose controversial *Satanic Verses* divided Islamic opinion and led to a *fatwa* death sentence being pronounced on him. The 21C has seen the continuation of this trend with novels such as *White Teeth* by half-Jamaican **Zadie Smith** and *Brick Lane* by Bangladesh-born Monica Ali – which both focus on the experiences of those who have immigrated to London – enjoying huge literary and commercial success.

London remains a rich and inspiring subject to the present day, with recent novels such as **Zoë Heller**'s *Notes on a Scandal*, **Ian McEwan**'s *Saturday* and *Her Fearful Symmetry* by **Audrey Niffenegger** drawing on the city's character to inform their narrative and provide the setting.

PAINTING

THE TUDOR ERA

The Renaissance master **Hans Holbein the Younger** *(1497/8–1543)* first came to London in 1526 with an introduction from the Humanist scholar **Erasmus**. His great draughtsmanship, penetrating eye and delicate colour suggest the artist's concern for capturing an accurate resemblance of physique and personality – formal portraits show the master keen to emphasise the exquisite detail of a jewel, brooch, brocade, silken velvet, fur or other such mark denoting status *(The Ambassadors* 1533, National Gallery*)*. Holbein joined the court of Henry VIII and was subsequently sent abroad to paint the King's prospective brides *(Duchess of Milan*, National Gallery*)*.

Hans Eworth, who came from Antwerp in 1549, fused his own style *(Sir John Luttrell*, Courtauld Institute Galleries*)* with that of Holbein in order to be promoted to court painter by Mary I and influence the likes of British-born **Nicholas Hilliard** *(c. 1547–1619)*, who rose to become the most eminent Elizabethan portraitist in about 1570. Having been apprenticed to a goldsmith, Hilliard's jewel-like precise style was eminently suited to miniature painting *(works in the* **Wallace Collection, V&A** *and* **Tate Britain***)*. His greatest disciple and later rival was **Isaac Oliver** *(d. 1617)*.

THE STUARTS

Thomas Howard, Earl of Arundel, Charles I and George Villiers, Duke of Buckingham emerge as three great patrons of the age. Religious troubles continued to provoke restlessness on the Continent and artists were obliged to seek patrons where they could. **Van Somer** settled in London in 1616 and quickly found favour at the court *(Queen Anne of Denmark,* 1617, Royal Collection*)*. **Daniel Mytens** came to England c. 1618 from The Hague bringing a new sense of confidence in both his bold style of painting and the stances given to his subjects; he was appointed Painter to Charles I in 1625. He, together with London-born **Cornelius Johnson** *(1593–1661)*, a master of technique, was superseded in popularity by **Sir Anthony van Dyck** *(1599–1641)*, whose full-length official portraits project an air of gracious ease and elegance. Van Dyck's Baroque compositions are a symphony of colour and texture – shimmering silk set against a matt complexion, heavily draped curtains contrasting with solid objects that represent a distinctive attribute pertinent to the sitter. His portraits of the English royal family set a benchmark for future generations perpetuated through Dobson, Lely, Reynolds, Gainsborough, Romney and Lawrence *(Charles I in Three Positions,* Royal Collection, *Charles I on Horseback,* National Gallery*)*.

"The most excellent painter England hath yet bred," **William Dobson** *(1610–46)*, was born in London and grew up to become a staunch Cavalier (Royalist). His natural style, influenced by Italian art, is less refined than Van Dyck's whom he succeeded as court painter *(Endymion Porter,* Tate Britain*)*.

Sir Peter Lely *(1618–80)* was born in Germany of Dutch parentage. His early works *(1640s)* in England are narrative religious pieces. At the Restoration he became Principal Painter to Charles II (1661) and produced stylised portraits celebrating the image of languorous Beauty *(Windsor Beauties* at Hampton Court*)* or the masculine Admiralty *(Flagmen* at Greenwich*)*: one honouring virtue, the other victory in the Second Dutch War. His "history" pictures meanwhile satisfied a less prudish market, depicting the same modish voluptuous ladies (*Sleeping Nymphs* at Dulwich) in more sensual poses.

The reign of James II saw the appointment of a new Principal Painter, **Sir Godfrey Kneller** *(1646/9–1723)*. Official portraits in the style of Lely are dignified, if not beautiful in the Classical sense; well executed, they conform to a taste for formality and noble bearing *(42 portraits known as the Kit-Cat series showing the head and one hand,* *see MAJOR CENTRAL LONDON MUSEUMS – National Portrait Gallery*).

Decorative Schemes

Peter Paul Rubens *(1577–1640)* evolved his highly energetic Baroque style from studying works by Titian, Raphael, Velázquez and epitomised the best of contemporary Continental art. In 1635, he completed the ceiling of the Banqueting House in Whitehall, a complex allegorical painting commissioned by Charles I. The impact on the English court of this bold political celebration of Charles's kingship should not be underestimated, nor should his influence on subsequent court painters be dismissed.

Lesser decorative schemes for stairways and ceilings were undertaken by foreign artists, paid by the square foot: **Antonio Verrio**, a Neapolitan, is registered in the service of the Crown from 1676 until 1688 at Windsor, St James's Palace and Whitehall. **Louis Laguerre** was trained in the Classical French tradition before coming to England at the behest of the Duke of Montagu, who was building Montagu House in Bloomsbury. **Pellegrini**, a follower of Ricci, was invited to England by the Earl of Manchester; he later became a founding member of the Royal Academy. The Venetian **Sebastiano Ricci** was responsible for the dome painting at Chelsea Hospital and a pair of large mythological paintings that hang in Burlington House. The great skill of these craftsmen, their ability to suggest luminosity and movement on a grand scale have secured their reputation as well as that of **Sir James Thornhill** *(1675/6–1734)*, the British Baroque master of decorative painting who followed their example when engaged on such important commissions as the Painted Hall at Greenwich, the Prince's Apartments at Hampton Court and the dome of St Paul's Cathedral. Taste veered away from this French art in the manner of Lebrun only when the Neoclassical designer **William Kent** clinched the commission to decorate Kensington Palace.

Landscape

William van de Velde was an official war artist employed by the Dutch navy to document battles against the British fleet. Works at the National Maritime Museum Collection, Greenwich confirm his ability to record precise detail – a quality that endeared him to the British authorities, who persuaded him to work for them. It is, however, his son William who left the more lasting impression on the evolution of British marine painting; he painted tranquil riverside views as well as warships at sea. Other Dutch painters recorded such social events as hunting scenes and the construction of major buildings; this generated a taste for sporting pictures, still-life paintings with game and flowers, topographical landscapes: genres that were to flourish throughout the 18C.

18C

The Age of Enlightenment promoted connoisseurship in the Italian art of the Renaissance and Classical art from Antiquity, either from travel to the continent to study the styles at first hand or from drawings, engravings and folios. Another, less intellectual but no less accomplished influence came from Versailles in the form of a highly decorative French Baroque. Taste was a matter for stimulating debate much as the politics of the day; preference for a particular style, therefore, varied from patron to patron.

In 1757 Edmund Burke published his treatise *A Philosophical Enquiry into the Origin of Our Ideas of the Sublime and Beautiful*. The Sublime was defined as an artistic effect that could provoke the greatest emotional feeling. The influence and impact of this work was considerable, both in Burke's own life time and on subsequent generations.

William Hogarth *(1697–1764)* was apprenticed as an engraver, and became popular through his "conversation" pieces like *The Beggar's Opera*. In his

Antonio Canaletto (1697–1768)

During the 1740s, the War of the Austrian Succession prevented British noblemen from undertaking the Grand Tour and so Italian artists who had hitherto relied on their patronage decided to come to England (1746–56). Canaletto transposed the sparkle and lucidity of the Venetian landscape to reaches of the Thames *(pictures are in the Sir John Soane Museum, and the collections of the Bank of England, Courtauld Institute Galleries and the National Gallery)*.

treatise *The Analysis of Beauty (1753)* he upholds the importance of a national style at a time when foreign artists were achieving greater success; he propounded theories on naturalism, observing that figures conform to standard expressions, gestures and stances appropriate to age; he advocated the use of the serpentine line as a basis of artistic harmony and beauty in composition *(inscribed on his palette in his self-portrait in Tate Britain)*. Perhaps Hogarth's greatest follower was **Thomas Rowlandson** *(1756–1827)*: a fine caricaturist and supreme draughtsman, he produced pictures drawn from low-life and populist subjects. His talent is Rococo in its freshness, although the humour and wit are undoubtedly English.

Woman in Blue – Portrait of the Duchess of Beaufort (c. 1778) by Thomas Gainsborough

George Lambert *(1700–65)* is widely regarded as "the father of British oil landscape", although his pictures were often executed in collaboration with a figure painter *(Hogarth)* or a marine painter *(Scott)*.

Richard Wilson *(c. 1713–82)* was given a classical education by his father. When he arrived in London in the 1740s he came as a portrait painter, although early landscapes survive from 1746. In 1750 he is recorded working in and around Rome, forging a new style in the tradition of Claude and Vernet: idyllic landscapes composed of clumped trees, buildings, paths and rivers, and populated with figures (usually drawn from Classical literature or mythology). On his return to England, the Roman Campania gently gave way to views of his own green and pleasant land.

Sir Joshua Reynolds *(1723–92)*, a key figure in the development of British painting, was the son of an educated Devon family, a respected figure associated with the circles of Dr Johnson, David Garrick, Goldsmith and Burke. He drew inspiration from Van Dyck and the Old Master paintings known in England by engravings *(Rembrandt self-portrait)* or from posing his sitters according to Classical statues from Antiquity (Apollo Belvedere). He spent the years 1752–54 in Rome and studied High Renaissance Art. Returning to London via Venice, he resolved to merge the taste for the Italian "Grand Style" with the demand for "face-painting" at home. In 1768 he was rewarded with the Presidentship of the new Royal Academy and during his tenure outlined the way a British School of History might be forged. His history portraits endorsed his theories (*Three Ladies Adorning a Term of Hymen – The Montgomery Sisters* in Tate Britain) and provoked a shift in fashion towards simple Neoclassical "nightdresses" rather than billowing gowns of damask. Upon his death the position of Painter to the King was taken by **Sir Thomas**

Lawrence *(1769–1830)*. Lawrence was commissioned by the Prince Regent, later George IV, to paint portraits of all the leading men who had opposed Napoleon; a large collection of sovereigns and statesmen are now hung in Windsor Castle.

Thomas Gainsborough *(1727–88)* developed his own natural style while painting landscapes and "fancy pictures" for his personal pleasure. After residing several years in Suffolk, in Ipswich and in Bath *(1759)*, he settled in London *(1774)* in the wake of Fashionable Society. In Bath, his portraits became more assured, full-length, life-size and set in arcadian gardens. His landscapes, meanwhile, echo the Dutch style of Hobbema and Ruisdael. The rich palette used for his wooded country scenes is evidently drawn from Rubens: these small pictures seem to exude naturalism although the composition is carefully contrived. Gainsborough's textured rendering of foliage heralds Constable, while his skilled technique in capturing haze and flickering light foreshadows Turner.

George Stubbs *(1724–1806)* began as a portrait painter while studying anatomy in York. He visited Rome in 1754 in order to prove that the study of art was secondary to the observation of Nature; there he witnessed a horse being devoured by a lion, a scene that was to provide inspiration for later works. On his return to England, he applied himself to the study of the skeleton and musculature of the horse by minute observation, dissection and from Renaissance drawings with a view to publishing his *Anatomy of a Horse* in 1766. Stubbs painted in oils, but preferred to use enamels because of their assured durability, even if the medium demanded an exacting and meticulous technique.

19C

Landscape

John Constable *(1776–1834)* developed his personal style and technique from observation and experimentation; his landscapes suggest topographical accuracy *(Salisbury Cathedral, Hampstead Heath)* when in fact realism has been compromised for the sake of art: trees, perspective or other such elements are contrived to better the overall composition, which in turn is unified by *chiaroscuro* (patches of light and shade). Constable refused to depend upon formal patronage and therefore was able to explore a new relationship between man and the landscape, contradicting the 18C view of Nature as a force to appease and tame rather than accept and admire for its own sake. He considered how to convey the atmosphere of a pastoral landscape *(The Haywain*, National Gallery*)* by comparison with the fear and dread of a storm at sea; it is interesting to note how, from 1828, after the death of his wife Maria, Constable seemed to betray a fascination for sombre skies and disturbed seas. He conveyed in landscape as much drama as any grand gesture or emotion in "high art".

Constable arrived at his theories by sketching from nature – in oil, a medium which took time to dry and therefore intensified his awareness of fleeting effects of light, ephemeral phenomena like rainbows and transient cloud patterns and formations. As his work met with little success, he resolved to compete in terms of size and embarked upon a series of "six-footers" *(Flatford Mill* in Tate Britain*)*, for which he was forced to make scale sketches. In 1816 he settled permanently in London, spending the summer months in Hampstead and capturing scenes of kite flying high on the Heath. In 1824 he was awarded gold medals for two pictures exhibited at the Paris Salon *(The Haywain*, National Gallery*; View on the Stour)*, which provoked great interest from the members of the Barbizon School of outdoor painters and artists associated with the Romantic Movement, notably **Delacroix**.

Watercolour is a medium that found particular favour with English artists looking to capture changing qualities of light or the distance through rolling green fields to a far horizon and blue sky; for travellers on the Grand Tour it

provided an efficient way of recording atmospheric details to complement topographical pencil drawings or thumb-nail sketches (hence **John Ruskin**'s near-obsessional realism).
Unlike Continental predecessors, the English artists used opaque white paper which, if left blank, provided bright highlights. The leading watercolourists include Paul Sandby *(1725–1809)*, JR Cozens *(1752–97)*, JMW Turner (*see below*) and **Thomas Girtin** *(1775–1802)*.

Drawings and Illustration

Henry Fuseli *(1741–1825)* explored the realms of the imagination, dreams and nightmares, full of drama and extravagant movement, stylised form in vivid, if horrifying detail *(Lady Macbeth Seizing the Daggers)*; in 1787 he met the visionary poet **William Blake** *(1757–1827)*, whose spirit contradicts the Age of Reason and heralds the advent of Romanticism. A large collection of Blake's works on paper is to be found at **Tate Britain**.
Joseph Mallord William Turner *(1775–1851)* showed precocious talent at painting topographical watercolours: by 1790, his work was hanging at the RA; six years later his *Fishermen at Sea* demonstrated his ability to handle oils and to show man in a natural world full of light, moving water and changing sky. Subsequent paintings confirmed his preoccupation with the same themes: *Snowstorm, Shipwreck* 1805; *Snowstorm, Hannibal and his Army crossing the Alps*. Meanwhile he continued to produce atmospheric studies of landscape *(London from Greenwich*, 1809*)*.
He went to France and Switzerland and made several trips to Italy *(1819–40)* cataloguing his impressions as he went. In his sketchbooks Turner managed to suggest reflected sunlight, its blinding brilliance, its translucence and somehow its transience (*Norham Castle, Sunrise*). In 1842 his Romantic predisposition to experience "atmosphere" at first hand was pushed to extremes: the drama captured in *Steamboat off a Harbour's Mouth* resulted from the artist insisting on being strapped to the mast of a ship pitching at sea in squally weather. Turner also studied the work of Claude, the first artist really to attempt to paint the sun at dusk setting over rippling water (*see MAJOR CENTRAL LONDON MUSEUMS* – **National Gallery**).

Pre-Raphaelite Brotherhood

The initials PRB began to suffix Rossetti's signature in 1849 following discussions between the coterie of RA School artists **WH Hunt** *(1827–1910)*, **DG Rossetti** *(1828–82)* and his brother William, **JE Millais** *(1829–96)*, Collinson, the sculptor Woolner and Stephens. The Pre-Raphaelites considered the 15C Renaissance paintings by Raphael to be too sophisticated and therefore sought to develop a style that might have predated Raphael: elaborate symbolism charged with poetic allusion, strong colour heightened by natural light and meticulous detail. Their success came with Ruskin's defence of their art before harsh criticism from Charles Dickens (especially directed at Millais' *The Carpenter's Shop*, **Tate Britain**). During the early 1850s, the group was dissolved.
Associated in style but independent of the Brotherhood is Sir **Edward Burne-Jones** *(1833–98)*, a fine technician with an excellent sense of style and visual appeal honed by travels in Italy with Ruskin, for whom he executed a number of studies of Tintoretto *(1862)*; the influences of Mantegna and Botticelli are also apparent in his flat and linear designs for tapestries and stained-glass windows. In a similar vein is the **Aesthetic Movement** (*see MAJOR CENTRAL LONDON MUSEUMS* – **Tate Britain**) immortalised by **Oscar Wilde** in his *Portrait of Dorian Gray*, and represented by Frederic, Lord Leighton *(1830–96)*, Albert Moore *(1841–93)* and Whistler.

Foreign Artists

The American **JA McNeill Whistler** *(1834–1903)* trained as a Navy cartographer, hence his etching skills, before going to Paris to study painting. In 1859 he moved to London and earned notoriety for falling out with a patron over the so-called Peacock Room décor *(now in the Freer Gallery of Art, Washington, DC: www.asia.si.edu)*, and later with Ruskin, who accused the painter of "flinging a pot of paint in the public's face" when he exhibited *Nocturne in Black and Gold (now in Detroit)*. Having been influenced by Courbet, Fantin-Latour, Degas and Manet during his life in Paris, Whistler introduced new perspectives to Victorian England, notably in the form of Japanese art.

Born of American expatriate parents in Italy, **JS Sargent** *(1856–1925)* settled in London to paint his vivid portraits and capture the elegance of Edwardian High Society with all its brilliance.

French Impressionism came to England in the form of a large exhibition put on in London in 1883: the Impressionists used pure pigments to capture the effects of bright sunlight on coloured forms; vibrancy was achieved by contrasting complementary shades; texture and movement suggested by bold brushstrokes. Simple family scenes, informal portraiture and landscape provided them with engaging subject matter. The portrayal of circus performers and cabaret entertainers for what they are was explored by Degas, Seurat and Toulouse-Lautrec; in turn they provided subjects for Walter Sickert and Aubrey Beardsley. As for Monet, he immortalised on canvas some of London's most famous landmarks.

In 1886 the New English Art Club was founded to provide a platform for artists ostracised by the Royal Academy: **Philip Wilson Steer** *(1860–1942)* and **Walter Sickert** *(1860–1942)* went on to set up an alternative exhibition entitled "London Impressionists", at the **Goupil Gallery**.

20C

In 1910, the critic and painter **Roger Fry** organised a major show of modern French art: "Manet and the Post-Impressionists" comprised 21 works by **Cézanne**, 37 by **Gauguin**, 20 by Van Gogh and others by **Manet**, **Matisse** and **Picasso**. In 1912 he organised the "Second Post-Impressionist Exhibition", dedicated to Cubist art and large compositions by Matisse.

Augustus John's reputation as a leader in modern British art hinged on *The Smiling Woman*, a portrait of his mistress exhibited in 1909; a famous series of contemporary luminaries followed.

Sickert conformed with the philosophy of Impressionism, which he assimilated while living in Paris. In 1910 he produced a series of works depicting the Old Bedford Music Hall, its performers, stage and audience with sympathy *(Ennui, La Hollandaise)*; in 1911 he founded the **Camden Town Group**, which attracted Robert Bevan, Spencer Gore, Harold Gilman and Charles Ginner. Bold colour, strong outlines and broad brushstrokes were dedicated to depicting the urban landscape.

The **Bloomsbury Group** brought together writers and artists: the biographer Lytton Strachey, economist Maynard Keynes, the novelist Virginia Woolf, her publisher husband Leonard Woolf, Clive Bell, Henry Tonks, Marc Gertler and members of the **Omega Workshop**. Vanessa Bell, Roger Fry and Duncan Grant all used bright colour to delineate bold form in the manner of Matisse; by 1914 they were experimenting with abstraction.

The **Vorticists**, led by Wyndham Lewis, responded to Cubism and the dynamics of Futurism in painting and sculpture. Jessica Desmorr, Epstein and Gaudier-Brzeska were later joined in spirit by David Bomberg. Strong axes, parallel lines, harsh angles, stepped geometric forms and lurid colours proliferate, mesmerising the eye.

Pure Abstraction, which inspired **Nicholson**, Moore, Hepworth and Nash, explored form in relation to landscape. In 1936 the "International Surrealist Exhibition" was held in London, which was a high point in the city's avant-garde artistic circles.

Among **post-war artists** are Graham Sutherland, painter of religious themes, landscapes and portraits as well as scenes of urban devastation; Sir Stanley Spencer, whose visionary Biblical scenes are set in familiar surroundings and who explored eroticism as a means of exorcising the violence of war. Peter Blake, David Hockney and Bridget Riley were the exuberant exponents of **Pop Art**, while the disturbing portraits and figures of **Francis Bacon** and **Lucian Freud** evoke a darker outlook.

Tate Modern, Whitchapel Gallery and the Saatchi Gallery all put on shows by artists such as **Gilbert and George**, Paula Rego, Beryl Cooke, Julian Opie, Damien Hirst, Tracy Emin and Rachel Whiteread among others, exploring new idioms – collages, installations and conceptual and performance art, which challenge preconceptions and at times provoke strong reactions.

The success of the **Young British Artists** group is measured by the popularity of the White Cube Gallery, Jerwood Space, LUX art exhibits, the Wapping Project and the South London Gallery, as well as alternative and artist-run spaces exhibiting contemporary art, their exhibitions and the controversial annual **Turner Prize** attracting much media interest, which in turn is successful in drawing a young public.

Stuckism was founded in 1999 by Charles Thomson and Billy Childish in reaction to contemporary Postmodernism and in favour of a return to some form of figurative painting. Since then it has developed into an international art movement.

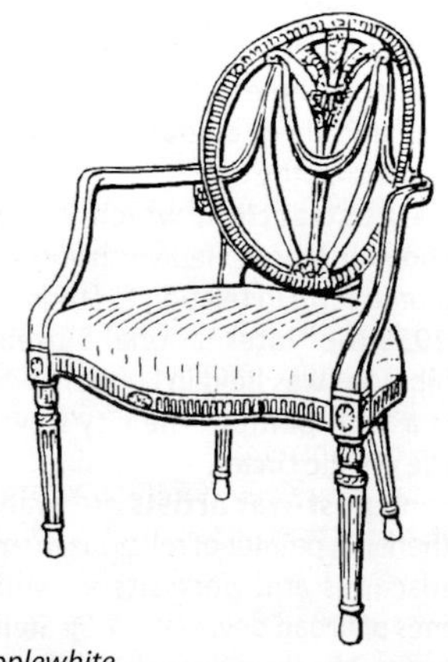

Hepplewhite

Chippendale

DECORATIVE ARTS

FURNITURE

Antique English furniture has long enjoyed favour. Distinctive types have evolved to suit changes in lifestyle and tastes in dress. Influences have been exerted by waves of craftsmen seeking refuge from Holland or France, and by the arrival of foreign pieces from Japan, China, India and other far corners of the Empire. The most complete display is to be found in the **Victoria and Albert Museum**, while the majority of the large houses provide period contexts in which original fixtures, fittings and furnishings may be appreciated *(Ham, Osterley, Kenwood, Fenton)*.

The height of English furniture-making came in the **18C**, when oak was replaced by imported mahogany and later by tropical satinwood, before a return was made to native walnut. These new woods were embellished with carving and enrichments of brass in the form of inlays and gilded mounts, hardwood veneers and marquetry.

A handful of names dominate English furniture of the period. Thomas Chippendale *(1718–79)* imported incomplete furniture from France, which his workshops then finished off *(1769)*. His reputation as the pre-eminent cabinetmaker of his day was secured by his publication of *The Gentleman and Cabinet Maker's Director* (1754). Perhaps the most original Chippendale designs were made for the great Neoclassical houses designed or remodelled by

Robert Adam and his contemporaries, by the second Thomas Chippendale *(1749–1822)*, who went on to produce an anglicised version of Louis XVI and archetypal Regency furniture. John Linnell *(1729–96)* began as a carver but soon expanded his workshops in Berkeley Square to include cabinet-making and upholstery. His reputation was secured by his association with William Kent, Robert Adam and Henry Holland *(mirrors and chairs)*. The partnership of William Vile *(1700–67)* and John Cobb *(1751–1778)* produced the most outstanding pieces; better crafted than Chippendale, if less original.

George Hepplewhite *(d. 1786)* achieved widespread recognition two years after his death when *The Cabinet Maker and Upholsterer's Guide* was published. This codified 300 designs for Neoclassical interiors, epitomising Adam's principles of uniting elegance with utility. It became the standard handbook for country gentlemen commissioning furniture from artisans. Hepplewhite pieces are considered as country furniture, simple, rational, extremely elegant and stylish.

Post-Hepplewhite but pre-Regency comes **Thomas Sheraton** *(1751–1806)* whose rectilinear designs dominate the 1790s, a perfect foil to Adam's intricate yet restrained interior stuccowork. His designs are recorded in *The Cabinet-Maker and Upholsterer's Drawing-Book (1791–94)*. He particularly exploits the grain and textures of wood with contrasting inlays, relief panels and highly polished surfaces. Inspiration is drawn from Louis XVI furniture.

The Goliath of Victorian taste is undoubtedly **William Morris** *(1834–96)* whose firm of Art Decorators at Merton Abbey supplied the full gamut of furnishings: furniture – mostly designed by Philip Webb, textiles, wallpapers, carpets, curtains, tapestries *(often in collaboration with Burne-Jones)*, tiles, candlesticks and brassware. Many designs were collated by Morris himself, who drew inspiration from historic patterns found in churches, paintings or books and natural forms. Some Arts and Crafts work, which was based on craftsmanship and pre-industrial techniques, is on show at the **William Morris Gallery**.

In the following generation, Sir Ambrose Heal *(1872–1959)* designed simple solid oak furniture, sometimes inlaid with pewter and ebony, in collaboration with Charles Voysey. He supplied middle-class homes with inexpensive alternatives to flimsy reproduction or expensive Arts and Crafts furniture – a market now supplied by retail outlets such as Conran's and Habitat.

CERAMICS

Tin-glazed Earthenware

The **Lambeth Potteries** *(founded c. 1601)*, are famous for their dark blue earthenware with a raised white ornamentation known as **Lambeth delft**.

The leading factory in the early 17C was the **Southwark Potteries**, founded by Dutchman Christian Wilhelm in 1618. In 1628, he secured a 14-year monopoly for producing blue and white pieces in imitation of Chinese Ming.

Porcelain

The **Bow Factory** *(identified by a variety of marks – incised, impressed or painted in underglazed blue and/or red)*, together with that at Chelsea, were the first porcelain factories in England. It was founded by an Irish painter, Thomas Frye, with a glass merchant, Edward Heylyn, in the East End *(Stratford Langthorne)*. In 1744 it registered a patent for wares crafted from a white clay *(unaker)* imported from America. In 1748, Frye also patented the use of bone ash to make **bone-china**, softer than hard-paste and cheaper to manufacture. Early pieces include plain white figures; later on, items were decorated with sprigs of flowers and foliage, or painted in underglazed blue or enamelled with colour or transfers.

The earliest pieces identified with the **Chelsea Factory** *(incised with a triangle)* are dated 1745, most modelled on shapes, then current for silver plate. The name "soft-paste" derives from the texture and translucence of the material, similar to white glass. After the first manager Charles Gouyon departed, the concern was headed by Nicholas Sprimont, a silversmith of Flemish Huguenot origin *(raised anchor period 1749–52, followed by the red anchor period, 1752–58 and the gold anchor period, 1758–69)*. From 1750–70, the factory enjoyed great commercial prosperity, owing to the high technical quality of the product and the adoption of new colours, including a red tint known as claret: influence shifts from Meissen prototypes – attractive, animated figures, Sir Hans Sloane's botanical specimen plants – to a taste for French Sèvres. Despite the flavour of Continental Rococo, the highly varied Chelsea wares *(vegetable tureens, vases, chandeliers, figurines, busts, etc.)* are somehow very English, their style of painted decoration highly naturalistic.

METALWORK

Gold and Silver

English gold and silversmiths were already known for their work in the Middle Ages and by 1180 had formed a guild in London. In the Elizabethan period the pieces produced showed a bold and elegant line, which gave way to greater austerity in the reign of James I. The 17C was an extravagant period for London silver, which was particularly influenced by Dutch Baroque. Under Charles II the French style predominated

© MICHELIN

Dolphin lamp-post

© MICHELIN

Bench, Victoria Embankment

as highly skilled Huguenots *(Protestant Calvinists)* were expelled from France following the Revocation of the Edict of Nantes *(1685)*.

Under Queen Anne, in the early 18C, Dutch silver design ceded to more sophisticatedly ornate designs – cut card work, strap design, cast ornaments with scrolls, escutcheons, boss beading, repoussé and chasing. The rocaille style of Paul de Lamerie *(1688–1741)* was followed by more sober designs produced by William Kent *(1684–1748)* and others working within the delicate Adam style.

Important collections of silver plate *(tableware, church vessels, commemorative pieces, etc.)* are on view at the Tower of London, the Victoria and Albert Museum, Apsley House, the Courtauld Institute Galleries, Bank of England, the National Maritime Museum in Greenwich and the various military museums. Significant private collections, to which public access is restricted, survive at the Mansion House and in the halls of the City guild and livery companies.

Iron

London offers many fine examples of decorative gates, railings, balconies and balustrades ranging from the work of masters such as **Jean Tijou** *(active 1689–1712)* at Hampton Court to the modern design of the Queen Elizabeth Gates in **Hyde Park**.

Many City churches contain elaborate wrought-iron **sword rests** that date from the Elizabethan period *(16C)*, when it was customary to provide a pew for the Lord Mayor of London in his own parish church furnished with a sword rest, where he could deposit the Sword of State during the service.

In the 19C, design and iron casting complemented each other in the production of **street furniture**: the Egyptian-inspired bench ends along the Victoria Embankment by Cleopatra's Needle; the cannon ball and barrel bollards marking the Clink in Southwark; the beautiful dolphin lamp standards of 1870, which line the Albert Embankment; and the pair of George III lamp-posts in Marlborough Road, St James's.

Many of the city's iron railings were melted down for munitions during WW II; the discussion still continues about whether or not to replace them.

The first **pillar boxes** in London, 15 years after the introduction of the penny post in 1840, were erected in Fleet St., the Strand, Pall Mall, Piccadilly, Grosvenor Place and Rutland Gate. They were rectangular with a solid round ball atop the pyramidal roof. Subsequent hexagonal, circular, fluted, conical designs followed: flat-roofed, crowned or plain, and most bearing with the royal cipher. A few hexagonal boxes *(1866–79)* survive, as do some from the 1880s "anonymous" series which the Post Office forgot to mark with its name. Pillarboxes were promoted by the writer Anthony Trollope, a Post Office official, and were first painted red in 1874.

Brass

From the Middle Ages until the 17C **brass tomb plates** were very popular and a variety still to be found in several London churches. The design was engraved with a triangular-headed engraving tool and the groove sometimes filled with enamel, or black or coloured wax. A study of these brasses shows how fashions in dress changed over the centuries: warriors clothed from head to toe in chain mail were followed by knights in armour wearing a helmet. The appearance of wives of such nobles ranges from the veiled simplicity of the 14C, via the rich dress and complicated headdress of the 15C, the plainer style of the Tudor period to the ribbons and embroidery of Elizabeth's reign. In the 16C the brasses of the great churchmen were removed. In their place were rich merchants, with short hair, clean-shaven in the 15C and bearded in the Elizabethan period. **Brass-rubbing** is organised at All Hallows-by-the-Tower, St Martin-in-the-Fields and Westminster Abbey.

The long-standing tradition and patronage of fine craftsmanship and design in London is maintained today by the **Chelsea Craft Fair** and the **Goldsmith's show** at the Guildhall, where international buyers come to explore ideas that will launch new trends worldwide.

Sculpture

The quick pace of change in popular culture has a powerful impact on all forms of art. Sculpture is no longer restricted to traditional materials and a young generation of artists has the freedom to experiment with new forms, which elicit a mixed public response. As more public spaces are created, monumental sculpture becomes an interesting feature of the cityscape.

In sculpture the evolution from Gothic tomb effigies to modern abstract form begins with **William Torel**, citizen and goldsmith of London, who modelled Henry III and Eleanor of Castile *(1291–92)*, and the visiting *(1511–20)* early Renaissance Florentine **Torrigiano**, who cast the gilt bronze figures of Henry VII *(in the Victoria & Albert)*, his queen, Elizabeth, and mother, Margaret, Duchess of Richmond. After the Reformation, contact with Italy was suspended; dominant influences were imported from France and Flanders.

Actual portraiture appears in the 17C in the works of, among others, Nicholas Stone *(John Donne)*, the French Huguenot **Le Sueur** *(bronzes of Charles I and James I)* and **Grinling Gibbons** *(statues of Charles II and James II)*. Gibbons

Henry Moore Sculptures in London

West Wind 1928/9 *(St James's Park Underground)* was Moore's first open-air sculpture and first public commission. It reflects his empathy for Mexican sculpture. In *Three Standing Figures* 1947/8 *(west end of the lake in Battersea Park)*, Moore explores spatial unity of the 3D group. *Time-Life Screen* 1952/3 *(New Bond St, inset on the second floor of the former Time-Life Building)*. The 11ft/3.3m bronze *Upright Motives* 1, 2 and 7 1955/6 *(Battersea Park)* show Moore working on a grand scale specifically for the outdoors. *Two Piece Reclining Figure No 1* 1959 (Chelsea School of Art). *Knife Edge Two Piece* 1962/5 *(Abingdon Gardens)*. *Locking Piece* 1963/4 *(Millbank)* was inspired by two pebbles. *Two Piece Reclining Figure No 5* 1963/4 *(Kenwood House)*. *Circular Altar* 1972 *(St Stephen Walbrook, City)*. *Large Spindle Piece* 1974 *(Spring Gardens)*. *The Arch* 1979/80 *(Kensington Gardens)*. *Mother and Child: Hood* 1983 *(St Paul's Cathedral)*.

is better known and celebrated as a woodcarver of genius and great delicacy, who often signed his work with a peapod.

In the 18C, as a Classical style began to appeal to graduates of the Grand Tour, the Flemings, Michael Rysbrack and Peter Scheemakers, the Frenchman **François Roubiliac,** Englishmen **John Bacon**, **John Flaxman** and **Nollekens** executed hundreds of figures until the genre became stylised and empty in the 19C. Many examples of their work are to be found in the nave and north transept of Westminster Abbey.

Vigour began to return in the 20C in portraiture and religious sculptures with works by **Jacob Epstein**, in human, near abstract and abstract themes by **Henry Moore**, and pure abstract by **Barbara Hepworth**. In the 1930s after Dada and Surrealism had swept through Paris to touch all forms of artistic consciousness, a number of painters, sculptors and architects emigrated, while others settled in Hampstead, which hosted a new move towards pure abstraction: Roland Penrose, Lee Miller, Henry Moore, Barbara Hepworth, Ben Nicholson.

In addition to a large collection of mainly military dignitaries, whose statues guard the streets of London, some fine contemporary sculpture adorns the open spaces created by modern town planning: the *Horses of Helios*, the Sun God, with the three Graces above, by Rudi Weller *(corner of the Haymarket and Piccadilly Circus)*; *Boy with a Dolphin* in bronze by David Wynne *(north end of Albert Bridge in Chelsea and outside the Tower Hotel in Wapping)*; *Fulcrum* by Richard Serra *(Broadgate)*; a *Dancer (Bow Street, opposite the Royal Opera House)*; *Horse* by Shirley Pace *(The Circle, Bermondsey)* and *The Navigators* by David Kemp *(Hays Galleria, Southwark)*. Modern works temporarily displayed next to traditional statues in Trafalgar Square have aroused much public interest in recent years, with a public vote to decide what will be displayed on the square's so-called "Fourth Plinth".

Cinema

1926 **The Lodger: A Story of the London Fog** tells the story of the unsolved Whitechapel Murders of 1888; directed by Alfred Hitchcock.

1929 **Blackmail**, directed by Alfred Hitchcock, this is considered to be the first British talkie.

1941 **Dr Jekyll and Mr Hyde** is an evocative story of identity; directed by Victor Fleming.

1942 **Mrs Miniver**, with Walter Pidgeon and Greer Garson, filmed in America, portrays London during the War.

1946 **Great Expectations,** filmed in London after the War under the directorship of David Lean, retells Dickens' classic story.

1948 **Oliver Twist**, Dickens' most well-known tale, with stage sets recreated by David Lean from Gustave Doré's *Portrait of London* (1870).

1949 **Passport to Pimlico** is a British comedy filmed, in fact, in Lambeth; directed by H Cornelius.

1953 **Genevieve** is a comedy about a car taking part in the London to Brighton veteran car run.

1955 **The Lady Killers**, set in Barnsbury, captures the Copenhagen Tunnels, outside King's Cross, on celluloid.

1964 **My Fair Lady**, based on Bernard Shaw's *Pygmalion*, re-creates an evocative, if sentimental interpretation of London's class divisions. Stars Audrey Hepburn and Rex Harrison.

1966 **Blow-Up**, a photographer on a fashion shoot accidentally witnesses a murder. David Hemmings stars.

1966 **Alfie** tracks Jack-the-lad, south-London-born Michael Caine and the easy life.

1971 **A Clockwork Orange**, Stanley Kubrick's banned cult film, is about the terrors of anarchy.

1979 **The Long Good Friday** charts the decline of the Docklands.

1980 **The Elephant Man** is a provocative story set in Victorian England; directed by David Lynch, and starring John Hurt, Anthony Hopkins, Anne Bancroft and John Gielgud.

1985 **My Beautiful Launderette** explores racial tensions in south London; directed by Stephen Frears.

1988 **A Fish called Wanda**, a comedy starring John Cleese, Kevin Kline and Jamie Lee Curtis, in and around London and the Docklands.

1992 **Chaplin** re-creates the life of Charlie Chaplin in south London in the 1880s; directed by Richard Attenborough.

1994 **The Madness of King George**, Nigel Hawthorne in Alan Bennett's play about the mad monarch. Supported by Helen Mirren; directed by Nicholas Hytner.

1995 **Richard III**, Shakespeare's classic, with a cast led by Ian McKellen, exploits several London landmarks (Battersea and Bankside Power Stations, St Pancras).

1999 **Notting Hill**, romantic comedy set in Portobello Rd.

2003 **Love, Actually**, an ensemble cast portrays the mixed-up love lives of a disparate group of Londoners at Christmas.

2005 **The Libertine**, Johnny Depp's portrait of the debauched 2nd Earl of Rochester in Restoration London.

2005 **Mrs Henderson Presents**, Judi Dench and Bob Hoskins star in this portrait of the Windmill Theatre in WWII.

2007 **Cassandra's Dream**, Woody Allen's story of two working-class brothers (Colin Farrell and Ewan McGregor), who commit murder to preserve their selfish lifestyles.

2008 **RocknRolla**, director Guy Ritchie's stylistic slice of London's criminal underworld.

2009 **London River**, moving story set in the wake of the 2005 London terrorist attacks.

2009 **Sherlock Holmes**, action mystery based on Conan Doyle's famous character.

2010 **The King's Speech** tells the story of King George VI.

2012 **Skyfall,** the 23rd outing for James Bond, becomes the most successful film in British box office history.

Portobello Market, Notting Hill
©Peter Phipp/World Pictures/Photoshot

To many people London *is* the West End – a vibrant area of cultural attractions, shops, restaurants, bars and nightclubs. Visitors flock here in their thousands to take in a show at one of the numerous theatres around Shaftesbury Avenue and Covent Garden, to shop in the stores along Oxford Street or to indulge in the hedonistic nightlife of Soho. The area itself is the big draw here and the streetlife is an attraction all on its own.

Highlights

1. Soak up the streetlife in buzzing **Trafalgar Square** (p94)
2. Discover a world of art at the **Courtauld Gallery** (p100)
3. Take in a show at one of **Covent Garden**'s grand theatres (p104)
4. Find out how the city took shape at its **Transport Museum** (p106)
5. Indulge in afternoon tea at the opulent **Ritz Hotel** (p116)

A Bit of Geography

The West End pivots around the key areas of Soho and Covent Garden, where you'll find the largest concentration of shops, restaurants and bars. Covent Garden piazza is a good place to start your exploration of the area, strolling south to the Strand and River Thames, north into the Seven Dials, or west to Leicester Square and Piccadilly Circus. North of here the grid-pattern streets of Soho, lined with more restaurants and bars than you could visit in a year, stretch north to the shopping throughfare of Oxford Street. The best way to explore the West End is on foot, particularly during the evening rush hour, when thousands of Londoners flow into the area to unwind or blow off steam. Most attractions and venues are close together and it's while walking between them that you are most likely to uncover the real West End anyway.

A Bit of History

The West End has been the beating heart of London for several centuries, squashed between the City of London to the East and Westminster to the West. As the city began to burst at the seams during the 17C *(and people were forced to relocate after the Great Fire of 1666)*, the area became a fashionable place to live, favoured by the elite for its location upwind of the smoke drifting from the crowded city to the east.

Covent Garden was originally part of the Convent of St Peter at Westminster, but after the dissolution of the monasteries in the 16C, the land was granted to the First Earl of Bedford, John Russell. It was the Fourth Earl, Francis Russell, who finally did something concrete with the area, engaging architect Inigo Jones to build houses here, "fitt for the habitacions of Gentlemen." Influenced by Italian Palladian architecture, Jones constructed London's first square. In the late 16C a fruit and vegetable market opened here and numerous coffee houses sprang up to cater for the fashionable gents who frequented the area.

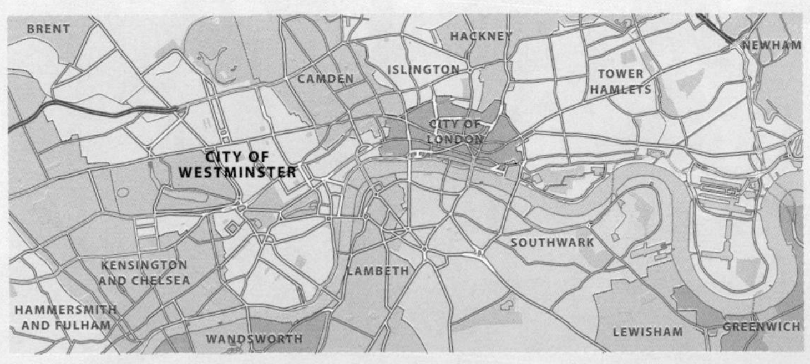

Soho, Covent Garden, Trafalgar Square, The Strand (see map)

WHERE TO STAY

- Chancery Court 1
- Piccadilly Backpackers 2
- YHA Oxford Street 3
- Savoy 4
- St Martins Lane 5
- Strand Palace Hotel 6
- W London 7

WHERE TO EAT

- Andrew Edmunds 1
- Bali Bali 2
- Busaba Eathai 3
- Café des Amis 4
- Café in the Crypt 5
- Carluccio's 6
- Clachan (The) 7
- Endurance 8
- 5th View 9
- Food for Thought 10
- Fortnum & Mason 11
- Golden Dragon 12
- Imperial China 13
- J. Sheekey 14
- Kulu Kulu Sushi 15
- Les Deux Salons 16
- Masala Zone 17
- Meza (Carom) 18
- Nando's 19
- Neal's Yard Salad Bar 20
- Patara 21
- Pearl 22
- Ritz (The) 24
- Rules 25
- Sarastro 26
- Simpson's-in-the-Strand 27
- Souk Medina 28
- Stockpot 29
- Ten Ten Tei 30
- Vita Organic 31
- Wagamama 32
- Wasabi 33
- Whole Foods Market 34
- World Food Café 35
- Yauatcha 36
- Zizzi 37

CAFÉS

- Flat White 1
- Maison Berthaux 2
- Milkbar 3
- Monmouth Coffee Company........ 4
- Pâtisserie Valérie 5
- Primrose Bakery 6

BARS, PUBS & NIGHTLIFE

- Argyll Arms 7
- Bar Rumba 8
- Borderline (The) 9
- Chinawhite 10
- Cross Keys (The) 11
- Dirty Martini 12
- English National Opera 13
- Floridita 14
- Globe (The) 15
- Gordon's 16
- Jazz After Dark 17
- Lamb & Flag 18
- Madame Jo Jo's 19
- Marquis of Anglesey 20
- Nell of Old Drury 21
- Opera Tavern (The) 23
- Pizza Express Jazz Club 23
- Punch & Judy 24
- Salsa 25
- Sherlock Holmes (The) 26
- St Martin-in-the-Fields 27
- TKTS 28
- Two Floors 29

LEISURE

- Odeon Cinemas 30

SHOPPING

- Agent Provocateur 31
- Algerian Coffee Stores 32
- Berwick St 33
- Birkenstock 34
- Cecil Court 35
- Foyle's 36
- Gerry's 37
- Hamleys 38
- Hatchards Booksellers 39
- Jubilee Hall Market 40
- Liberty 41
- Lush 42
- Milroy's of Soho 43
- Neal's Yard Dairy 44
- Neal's Yard Remedies 45
- Paul Smith 46
- Penhaligon's 47
- Tea House (The) 48
- Ted Baker 49
- Topshop 50
- Twining 51
- Vinmag.com 52
- Waterstone's Booksellers 53

After the Restoration *(1660)* two theatre companies were licensed to perform and the Theatre Royal *(later, the Theatre Royal, Drury Lane)* opened its doors, followed by the Haymarket Theatre and the Theatre Royal, Covent Garden. The area has since been the home of London theatre.

Soho began its journey to cultural prominence as a rural idyll chosen by Henry VIII as a royal park *(its name is believed to derive from a hunting call)*. In the 17C, like Covent Garden, it became a residential area, though populated mostly by immigrant communities, first Greek Christians and French Protestants *(Huguenots)*. The

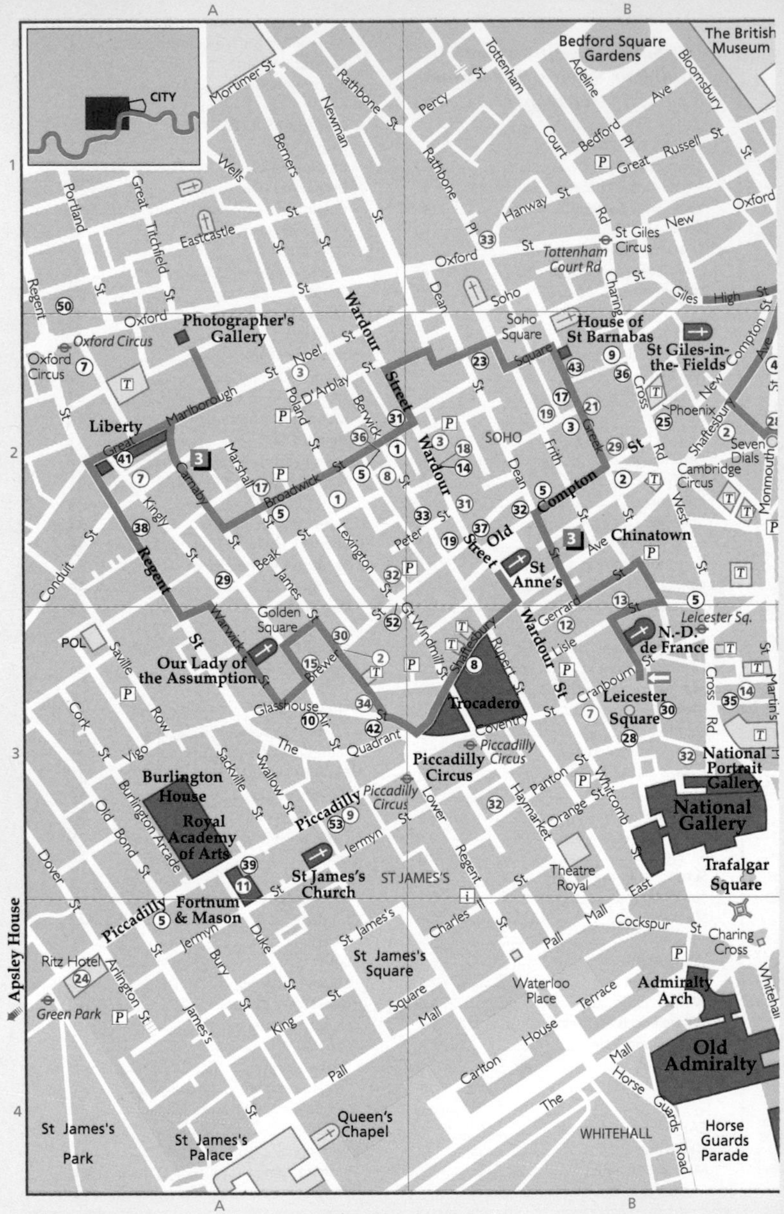

area became one of Britain's worst slums in the 19C *(Regent Street was designed to keep it separate from well-to-do Mayfair)* before showgirls and prostitutes started moving in during the 20C. Artists and musicians followed, playing gigs and boozing here, *(including Francis Bacon and Pink Floyd)*. Since the 1980s crack-down on the sex industry the area has cleaned up its act and is known for its gay culture and happening nightlife.

The West End Today

The density of attractions and eating and drinking venues in the West End draws a constant flow of tourists and

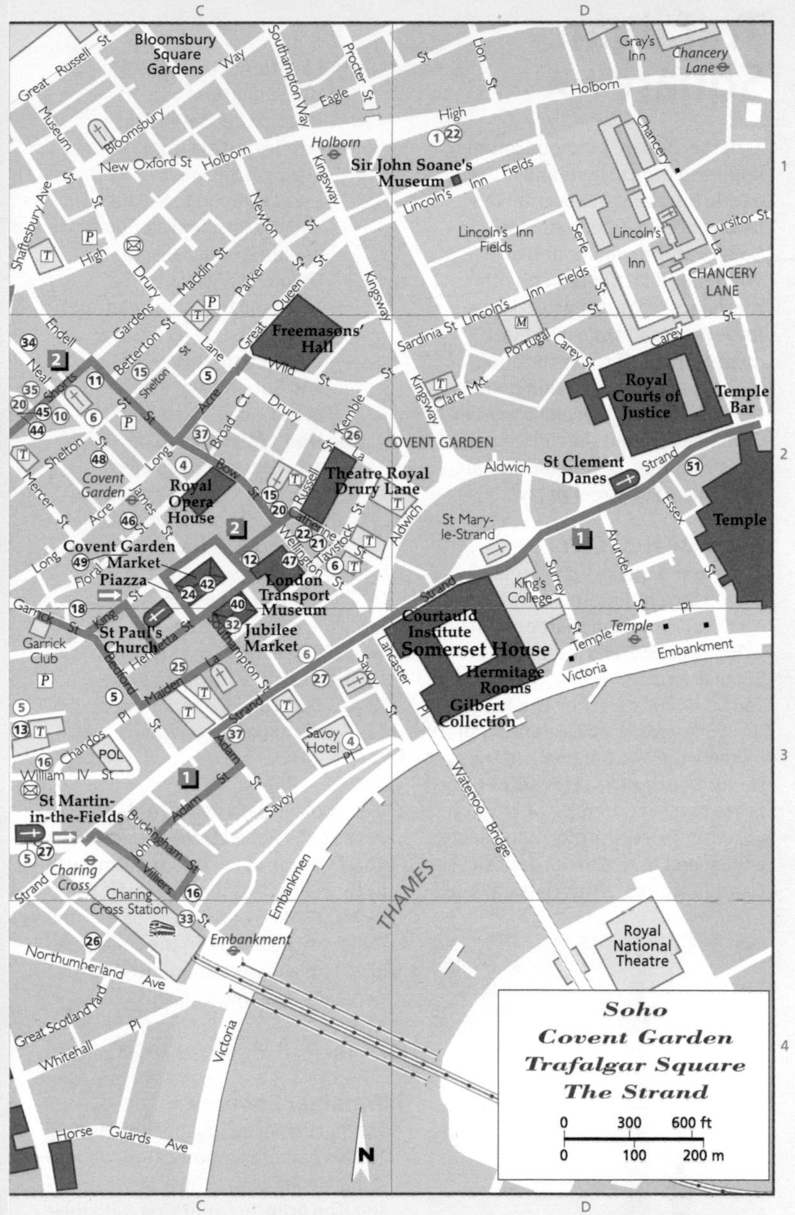

Londoners "into town" to work or play. Nowhere in the capital (and arguably nowhere in Europe) can compete with the area's vibrant, unique and at times downright bizarre streetlife, and one of the joys of a visit here is in watching it pass you by. The area pulses with all walks of life, from drag queens and street performers to dolled-up clubbers and laidback theatregoers: the area challenges New York's Broadway for the title of "best place on earth to catch a show", new restaurants and hip bars are constantly opening up and the streets and squares are popular places for people to congregate, both day and night.

Trafalgar Square★★

Trafalgar Square's famous column, imposing bronze lions and gentle fountains are overlooked by the monumental National Gallery at the culmination of Whitehall, which connects with the Palace of Westminster. Since its pedestrianisation it has lost most of the traffic, but continues to serve as a congregation point in times of strife or joy: political rallies, Christmas around the Norwegian Christmas tree, or the traditional New Year's Eve street party.

- **Location:** Map pp92–93. *Charing Cross; Westminster.* Several main arteries radiate from Trafalgar Square, with buses running to St Paul's and the City, to Waterloo and the South Bank, to Oxford St and Marble Arch, and to Victoria and Chelsea. Leicester Square, Covent Garden, the Mall and Buckingham Palace are all easily accessible.
- **Don't Miss:** Changing artworks exhibited atop the "fourth plinth" in the NW corner of the square.
- **Timing:** Start from Trafalgar Square in the morning, have lunch and then take time to visit at least one sight.
- **Kids:** The Horse Guards, particularly a mounting or dismounting ceremony.

A BIT OF HISTORY

Trafalgar Square – The square celebrates Britain's naval prowess following Nelson's victory at the Battle of Trafalgar *(20 October 1805)* and the full glory of her Colonial Empire.

To the North stretches the length of the world-renowned **National Gallery** (*see NATIONAL GALLERY*); to the East stands **South Africa House**, designed by Herbert Baker in 1933, where pickets rallied for the release of Nelson Mandela and an end to apartheid; opposite sits **Canada House**, a Neoclassical building of golden Bath stone *(1824–27)*, conceived by Sir Robert Smirke in fact for the Royal College of Physicians. **Admiralty Arch**, built across the Mall by Sir Aston Webb in 1906–11, takes its name from the Admiralty buildings on the south side. In 2013 plans were announced to turn Admiralty Arch into a hotel.

Nelson's Column, Trafalgar Square

WALKING TOUR

Trafalgar Square★★

The Square was laid out by **John Nash** in 1820 as part of a proposed North–South route linking Bloomsbury to Westminster. The **granite fountains**, with their mermaids and dolphins, were added in 1845 and remodelled in 1939 by Lutyens. The Square was completed at the turn of the 20C by **Sir Charles Barry**, who also constructed the north terrace in front of the National Gallery.

Major improvement plans have created a majestic piazza with steps sweeping down from the National Gallery.

Nelson's Column rises from a pedestal, decorated with bronze reliefs commemorating the Battles of St Vincent, Aboukir, Copenhagen and Trafalgar cast from French cannon, via a fluted granite column, to a bronze Corinthian capital supporting the admiral – a full 185ft/56m overall. **Landseer**'s four magnificent bronze lions *(20ft/6m long, 11ft/3m high)* were mounted in 1867.
Against the north terrace wall are **Imperial Standards of Length** *(1 inch, 1 foot, etc.)* and busts of 20C Admirals; the northeast pedestal is occupied by a bronze equestrian figure of **George IV**, originally commissioned by the King for Marble Arch; on the south corner plinths are mounted two 19C generals. The fourth plinth was originally intended for an equestrian statue, but lay empty for years. It is now topped by temporary, specially commissioned sculpture.
On the outside of the Square, before and behind the National Gallery, are figures of **James II** by Grinling Gibbons, **George Washington** after Houdon and Henry Irving. On the island *(NE)* is Nurse **Edith Cavell**.

St Martin-in-the-Fields★

Opens daily 8.30am (Sat 9.30am, Sun 3.30pm), closes daily 6pm (Wed & Sun 5pm). Audio tours (6 languages, £3.50; booking in advance is advised). Lunchtime recitals: Mon–Tue and Fri 1pm; evening concerts: various dates 7.30pm; jazz nights Wed 8pm. Tickets available from the Crypt box office (Mon–Sat 10am–5pm) or by telephone. 020 7766 1100. www.stmartin-in-the-fields.org

The church is famous not only for its architecture – particularly its elegant spire – but, since the 1930s, as a shelter for the homeless, and also gives its name to the world-famous chamber orchestra, the **Academy of St Martin-in-the-Fields**, which maintains the church's long-standing tradition for classical music with recitals and concerts. The present edifice was designed by Gibbs in 1722–26. The steeple rises in five stages to a pillared octagonal lantern and concave obelisk spire. The triangular pediment crowning the Corinthian portico bears the royal arms; this is justified by the fact that Buckingham Palace stands within the parish boundary. The spacious galleried interior is barrel vaulted; the stucco work is by the two Italians Artari and Bagutti; the pulpit is by Grinling Gibbons.
In the vaulted crypt is the **London Brass Rubbing Centre**, which has replicas of brasses from churches in all parts of the country and from abroad, including some Celtic engravings (*open Mon–Wed 10am–6pm, Thur–Sat 10am–8pm, Sun 11.30am–5pm; closed 25 Dec; brass rubbings including all materials according to size from £4.50; 020 7766 1122).*
In the alley behind the church, Maggi Hambling's *(1998)* bronze commemorates **Oscar Wilde**.

Walk up to St Martin's Lane.

Beyond the Post Office stands the striking Edwardian **Coliseum**, home to the English National Opera (*see Your Stay in the City: Entertainment).*

Retrace your steps to the Square and cross to reach the western side of

A National Hero

Horatio Nelson, 1st Viscount *(1758–1805)*, was the son of a Norfolk clergyman. He went to sea aged 12 and rose through the ranks to become captain in 1793. During various French revolutionary actions, he lost his right eye *(1794)* and his right arm *(1797)*, before defeating the French at Aboukir Bay *(1798)*, and destroying their fleet at Trafalgar. It was during this final campaign that he died from a musket wound to the shoulder *(the ball is conserved at the National Maritime Museum in Greenwich, as are many letters, personal possessions and memorabilia)*.
Nelson's ship, HMS *Victory*, on which he died, is at the Historic Dockyards in Portsmouth.

Hidden History of the Square

A Noble Emblem – In the southeast corner of Trafalgar Square was the early 17C Northumberland House *(demolished in the 19C to make way for Northumberland Avenue)*, identified by the Northumberland lion, now at Syon Park *(see pp374–375)*, which stood above the gate.

Eleanor Cross – In 1290 Edward I erected 12 crosses to mark the route taken by the funeral cortège of his queen on its journey to Westminster. It was here, in Trafalgar Square, that the last of the solid-looking octagonal structures of marble and Caen stone was placed; it was destroyed by the Puritans but a 19C reproduction now stands in the forecourt of Charing Cross Station. A mural in the Underground station *(Northern Line)* shows the Medieval cross being built.

Whitehall , noting Charles I's statue on the island beneath Nelson's Column.

Hubert Le Sueur's equestrian statue of **Charles I** was cast in Covent Garden in 1633; in 1655 it was discovered in the crypt of St Paul's by Cromwell's men, who sold it to a brazier, so making a fortune from its supposed "relics". Eventually it was purchased by Charles II and set up in 1675 overlooking the execution site. From this point mileages from London are measured *(plaque in pavement behind statue)*.

ADDRESSES

LIGHT BITE

Café in the Crypt, *St Martin-in-the-Fields, WC2N 4JJ. Charing Cross. 020 7766 1158. www.stmartin-in-the-fields.org. Mon–Tue 8am–8pm, Wed 8am–10.30pm, Thur–Sat 8am–9pm, Sun 11am–6pm.* The self-service café in the lovely 18C vaulted crypt is one of the best places in the area for a quick, inexpensive snack; all proceeds go to the famous church.

PUBS AND BARS

Gordon's, *47 Villiers St. Embankment or Charing Cross. 020 7930 1408. www.gordonswinebar.com. Daily 11am–11pm.* Set in a vaulted cellar which has been serving wine since 1364, this bar is one of London's most atmospheric. The wine list is particularly attractive and the atmosphere is friendly. You can sit outside in the summer by the square.

The Sherlock Holmes, *10–11 Northumberland St. Charing Cross. 020 7930 2644. Mon–Fri 11am–11pm, Sat 11am–midnight, Sun noon–10pm.* This quaint pub, named after the famous detective, offers an interesting selection of English beers and ciders. Upstairs is a dining room serving typical British dishes.

ENTERTAINMENT

English National Opera, *The Coliseum, St Martin's Lane, WC2N 4ES. Leicester Square or Charing Cross. 020 7845 9300. www.eno.org. Box office: Mon–Sat 10am–8pm. £10–85.* This beautiful Edwardian theatre has been occupied by the ENO since 1968. It was built in 1904 by Oswald Stoll and deserves a visit in itself. A wide-ranging programme of opera and ballet is performed in English.

St Martin-in-the-Fields, *WC2N 4JJ. Charing Cross. Evening concerts: Tue, Thu–Sat at 7.30pm; tickets available from the Crypt box office (Mon–Sat 10am–5pm) or by telephone: 020 7766 1100. www.stmartin-in-the-fields.org.* Candle-lit evening concerts held in this historic church make for a highly romantic experience.

Strand★★

Bordering Covent Garden and on the edge of the city, the Strand holds many attractions despite the relentless traffic. Lined with ornate buildings recalling its aristocratic past, it boasts elegant hotels, lively theatres and fabulous art galleries at Somerset House. Fleet Street and Temple are intrinsic parts of entirely different traditions: the former is the national press, the latter is British law.

- **Location:** Map pp92–93. ⊖*Temple; Charing Cross.* Strand is adjacent to Covent Garden, Trafalgar Square and the City. Waterloo Bridge and Hungerford Bridge provide direct access to the South Bank.
- **Don't Miss:** The Impressionism, Post-Impressionism and Fauvism collections of the Courtauld Institute; Temple Church; the spire and crypt of St Bride's Church.
- **Timing:** Allow 2hr to see the Courtauld Institute Galleries, the rest of the day to stroll through the area.
- **Kids:** The ice rink at Somerset House in winter.

A BIT OF HISTORY

The Strand was an ancient track, midway between the Thames, London's main thoroughfare, and the highway leading west out of the City.

Only the churches have survived from the Medieval period. Up to Hanoverian times the street was lined with law students' hostels (inns) and provincial bishops' town houses.

After the Dissolution of the monasteries, the palaces and mansions were purchased by the nobility as local street names testify: Essex Street recalls the House owned by a famous Elizabethan favourite and Arundel Street the great house of the Howards.

In 1624 **James I** presented York House, one-time palace of the Archbishop, to George Villiers, Duke of Buckingham, an event recalled by York Place and Villiers Street. Between the big houses and down the side lanes were hundreds of small houses, ale houses, brothels, coffee houses and shops. The **New Exchange** *(1609–1737)* was an arcade of shops, mostly milliners and mercers, patronised by royalty and later by **Samuel Pepys**. The Grecian, later the Devereux public house and a favourite with Addison, is now the Edgar Wallace with an Edwardian decoration and interesting mementoes.

In the late Victorian and Edwardian era, the Strand was known for its restaurants and hotels – the Cecil (now Shell-Mex House) had 1,000 bedrooms, the Metropole, the Victoria and the Grand, and for its theatres: a popular 19C music-hall song was *Let's All Go Down the Strand.*

WALKING TOUR 1

Start from Charing Cross Station.

STRAND★

Today the Strand links Trafalgar Square to Fleet Street and the City. The elegant open-glazed building of **Coutts Bank** *(no. 440)* was designed by **Sir Frederick Gibberd** to be sympathetic to its 19C neighbours in the style of John Nash. The bank was transferred to this address in 1904 by Thomas Coutts.

Across the Strand, down Craven St, on the west side of Charing Cross Station, is the **Benjamin Franklin House**, in which the statesman, scientist and inventor *(1706–90)* lived between 1757 and 1775. An actress in period costume conducts guided tours that recall Franklin's busy social life in 18C London and his role as mediator between Britain and America in the years that preceded the Declaration of Independence *(36 Craven St; Architectural tour Mon noon, 1pm, 2pm, 3.15pm and 4.15pm; £7; The Historic Experience Show same times; £7; under 16 free; 020 7925 1405 or 0207 839 2006; www.benjaminfranklinhouse.org).*

Charing Cross Station
The street frontage is scaled to pleasing proportions alongside EM Barry's neo-Gothic **Charing Cross Station Hotel** *(1863–64)*. The modern station buildings, conceived by Terry Farrell *(1990)* as part of a larger project spanning both banks of the Thames, feature a great white arch over and beyond the station viaduct. This giant glazed railway "hangar" is lodged between four granite-faced corner service towers.
In the forecourt of Charing Cross Station stands a reproduction, designed by EM Barry, of the original **Eleanor Cross**, which stood in Trafalgar Square.

▶ Leave the Strand to walk down Villiers St. towards the river.

Hungerford Bridge
As one of London's Millennium projects, the old rail bridge, a plain lattice girder structure *(1862)*, has been sandwiched between two pedestrian suspension bridges designed by Lifshutz Davidson, their soaring cobweb of struts and cables beautifully lit at night to provide easy access to the South Bank.

▶ Enter Embankment Gardens and exit at the rear onto Buckingham St.

Buckingham Street
17C and 18C brick houses still line both sides *(nos. 12, 17, 18, 20 date from the 1670s)* down to Victoria Embankment Gardens. Pepys lived at no. 12 in 1679–88. At the south end stands **York Water Gate**, a triple arch of rusticated stone, decorated with the Villiers arms and a scallop shell, built in 1626 at the water's edge by Nicholas Stone, mastermason to George Villiers, 1st Duke of Buckingham.

▶ Continue up to John Adam St. and turn right.

The Adelphi
The riverfront retains the name, although the Royal Adelphi Terrace, erected by Robert Adam in 1768–72, was demolished in 1937. The Adam brothers – *adelphi* is the Greek word for brothers – transformed the area by the construction along the foreshore of a towering embankment arcade, the Adelphi Arches, supporting a terrace of 11 houses. The end houses were pedimented and decorated to form advanced wings to the terrace. It was the first and possibly finest of Thames-side concepts; now only a few houses remain to give an idea of how the quarter must have looked in the 18C. George Bernard Shaw *(1896–1927)* lived at no. 10a.
John Adam Street: no. 8 was built by Adam for the **Royal Society of Arts** in 1772–74, with a projecting porch surmounted by a giant order of fluted columns. The RSA was founded in 1754 "to embolden enterprise, to enlarge science, to refine art, to improve our manufacture and extend our commerce".
Adam Street: the east side has a run of houses beginning with no. 10, Adam House; neat and compact with a rounded corner and curved ironwork; 9 and 8 are the street's standard, with attractive pilastered doors; no. 7, in the axis of John Adam Street, is a typical example of the Adam decorative style, including his favourite acanthus leaf motif applied to pilasters, cornice and ironwork.

▶ Return to the Strand and turn right.

The Savoy
The Savoy is now a precinct that comprises a chapel, a **theatre** *(the first public building in the world to be lit throughout by electricity)* and a **grand hotel**, built by D'Oyly Carte in 1889.
The name dates from 1246, when Henry III granted the manor beside the Thames to his queen's uncle, Peter of Savoy. The estate then passed to the Dukes of Lancaster and as "the fairest manor in England" became, until his death, the "lodging" of King John of France, captured by the Black Prince at Poitiers *(1356)*. The **Savoy Hotel** is one of the most famous in London, while the theatre was the original home of the D'Oyly Carte Opera Company, who first staged all Gilbert and Sullivan's much

loved operettas. The little access road at the front of the hotel is in fact the only road in Britain on which you drive on the right.

Walk down Savoy Hill to Savoy Pl. and Victoria Embankment Gardens.

The Queen's Chapel of the Savoy (Chapel of the Royal Victorian Order)

Savoy Hill. Open (services permitting) Oct–Jul Mon–Thur 9am–4pm (Sun 10am). 020 7836 7221.

The chapel was largely rebuilt after the war and dates back to the construction of a hospital for 100 "pouer, needie people" in 1510–16. The hospital was dissolved in 1702, but the chapel and burial yard survived to be made into the Chapel of the Royal Victorian Order in 1937. **Savoy Hill** is famous as the site of the BBC's first studios and offices from 1923 to 1932 *(plaque on the Embankment façade of no. 2 Savoy Place).*

The **Victoria Embankment Gardens★**, complete with their bandstand for summer concerts, were created in 1864. Opposite the gardens on the river front, flanked by great bronze lions stands **Cleopatra's Needle**, erected after a long saga in 1878. One of two great Egyptian obelisks covered in hieroglyphs uncovered at Heliopolis *(c.1450 BC)*, it was first offered to George IV by Mehemet Ali of Egypt. Similar obelisks stand in Paris (Place de la Concorde) and New York. Note the dolphin lamp standards and decorated bench ends.

Walk back to the Strand, turn right and cross Lancaster Pl.

Simpson's in the Strand landmark restaurant replaces a coffee house – The Grand Cigar Divan, founded by Samuel Reiss in 1828.

Somerset House★★

The present building was erected in Portland stone in 1776–86 to the designs of **Sir William Chambers**; it was built on the site of the palace begun by Protector Somerset in 1547 and still incomplete when he was executed in 1552. The narrow Strand façade of Somerset House, inspired by Inigo Jones' Palladian riverside gallery, has a triple gateway and giant columns beneath a balustrade decorated with statues and a massive statuary group by Bacon.

Through the arch is a vast courtyard surrounded by ranges of buildings treated like rows of terrace houses round a square. A continuous balustrade punctuated by vases unites the fronts. The riverside front stands on a continuous line of massive arches, which in the 18C, were at the water's edge.

The Strand block of Somerset House is the most elaborate and has two advanced wings. It contains the so-called **Fine Rooms**, which are notable for their pleasing proportions and hand-

Somerset House

some plasterwork. These were originally designed for three learned societies. Somerset House now houses major art collections, including The Courtauld Collection *(see below)* and a variety of temporary exhibitions, workshops and events.

Fountains adorn the grand piazza, which is used for public entertainment throughout the year, including musical performances and a full-scale open-air cinema with a giant screen and surround-sound in the summer *(advance booking necessary)*. An open-air ice rink takes up residence each winter *(advance booking necessary)*, offering timed skates, Christmas music and a café with mulled wine and hot chocolate.

At any time of the year, fine **views**★★ of the Thames may be enjoyed from the riverside façade *(020 7845 4600 ; www.somersethouse.org.uk)*.

COURTAULD GALLERY★★

Somerset House. Open daily 10am–6pm (last admission 5.30pm); 24 Dec 10am–4pm. Closed 25–26 Dec. £6; £3 Mon (including bank holidays). 020 7848 2526. www.courtauld.ac.uk/gallery.

This fine collection includes recognised masterpieces from a wide range of periods, stretching from the Gothic to Modernism. The collection totals around 530 paintings, 6,000 drawings, 20,000 prints as well as sculpture and decorative arts; the highlights are displayed.

COLLECTIONS

The colour schemes throughout the galleries conform, where possible, to William Chambers' original specifications. Works are grouped by benefactor.

Gallery 1: *Ground Floor.*

Between 1830 and 1870 **Thomas Gambier-Parry** *(1816–88)* collected 14C Italian Primitives whose simplicity he greatly admired. Displays in Gallery 1 include a Crucifixion polyptych by **Bernardo Daddi**, a limestone statue of the *Virgin and Child* attributed to **André Beauneuveu** and three **Fra Angelico** *predella* panels.

Galleries 2–4: *First Floor.*

Samuel Courtauld began collecting Impressionist and Post-Impressionist paintings in 1923. His perceptive eye and discerning taste selected some of the most famous expressions of the modern masters.

Light is the main preoccupation of the 19C French landscape painters at Barbizon and their followers, the Impressionists. Boudin *(Deauville)*, Cézanne *(The Lac d'Annecy)*, Sisley *(Boats on the Seine)*, Seurat *(The Bridge at Courbevoie)* and Monet *(Autumn Effect at Argenteuil)* all explored watery landscapes.

Of particular interest in **Gallery 2** are *La Loge* by **Renoir**, which was exhibited in

Detail of A Bar at the Folies-Bergères *(1882) by Edouard Manet*

the first Impressionist exhibition in 1874; and *Antibes* by **Claude Monet**, who was influenced by Japanese prints.

In **Gallery 3**, **Manet**'s sketch for *Le Déjeuner sur l'Herbe* was intentionally controversial: while being "modern", Manet desperately hoped to earn respect from the Salon establishment. *A Bar at the Folies-Bergère*, his last major work, is presented as a bold portrait of a young working woman; the wealthy members of the audience seem oblivious to the trapeze artist suspended in the corner.

Cézanne on the other hand, who is considered to be the "father of modern art", builds a suggestion of space and depth into still-life *(Still-life with Plaster Cupid)* and landscape *(Montagne Sainte Victoire)* by means of colour (blues and greens give depth; reds and oranges relief) and form arranged in the foreground, middle ground and background. His figures *(The Card-players)*, meanwhile, are strong and direct studies of personality. *Nevermore* and *Te Rerioa*, painted at the height of **Gauguin**'s Tahitian period, in which naturally posed figures are shown in harmony with a primitive way of life, contrast with *Haymaking*, his bucolic Breton landscape.

Gallery 4 is devoted to Post-Impressionism. Two examples of **Van Gogh** are on display: *Peach blossom in the Crau* works in the mainstream Impressionist manner where fractured light is boldly captured by strong brushstrokes of thick paint. In his world-famous *Self-portrait with Bandaged Ear*, the artist is dressed in a greeny-blue coat, which gives his eyes a haunting look. **Georges-Pierre Seurat** mechanically painted in dots of colour, a technique known as pointillism, which if seen from a distance merge into tonal values. This accentuates the dusty interior scene of *Young Woman Powdering Herself*. **Amedeo Modigliani**'s *Female Nude* uses influences from Egypt, with her elongated face and early Italian art in the flat surface of the painting.

Gallery 5: Viscount Lee of Fareham, having given his first collection and Elizabethan manor house "Chequers" to the Nation in 1917 for use as a country retreat for Prime Ministers in office, began building his second collection after retiring from politics in 1922. Italian Renaissance paintings include **Botticelli**'s *Holy Trinity*; **Giovanni Bellini**'s *Assassination of St Peter Martyr*; **Paolo Veronese**'s *Baptism of Christ*; **Parmigianino**'s *The Virgin and Child* (the elegance and poise of the Virgin reflects the artist's refined idea of beauty).

Galleries 6–7: Count Antoine Seilern *(The Princes' Gate Collection)* was Austrian by extraction but British by birth. As he had undertaken research into the Venetian sources of Rubens' ceiling pictures while in Vienna, 32 paintings and over 20 drawings by the master make up the bulk of his important donation. In **Gallery 6**, several works by **Rubens** demonstrate his ability to treat historical and religious subjects, portraits and landscape with equal adeptness. Strong contrasts of light and texture, gesture and emotion characterise the colourful, restless compositions.

The early tradition of Netherlandish painting is represented by **Pieter Bruegel the Elder**: religious subjects set in vast landscapes, balanced composition, bands of colour to emphasise spatial recession *(Landscape with the Flight into Egypt)*, austere composition and monumental figures *(Christ and the Woman Taken in Adultery)*. *Adam and Eve (1526)* provides **Lucas Cranach the Elder**, friend and ally of Luther, with an opportunity to represent nude figures.

Gallery 7 is devoted to 18C portraits and to Tiepolo. Portraiture became an important genre in the 17C, with **William Dobson** and **Sir Peter Lely** emerging as masters of a style pioneered by Van Dyck and providing modern viewers with a strong idea of dress and attitude. In the 18C portraiture became an uncontroversial subject matter in which English artists achieved new heights: **Gainsborough**, **Reynolds**, **Raeburn**, and **Romney** sought to preserve natural likenesses of the leading thinkers, intellectuals, leaders and the gentry of the Age of Enlightenment.

Sketches for altarpieces and ceiling frescoes in luminous colours reveal

Giovanni Battista Tiepolo's *(1696–1770)* technical mastery and deep, religious feeling.

The gallery also contains the **collection of silver** *(1710–80)* made by three generations of the Courtauld family, who fled religious persecution in France due to their Protestant beliefs. The service is arranged according to their use and includes tea and coffee sets, dining and display silver.

Gallery 8: *Second Floor*

This gallery displays small bronzes by **Degas**, along with his *Two Dancers on Stage*. Note also *Woman at a Window* and his pastel *After the Bath*. **Toulouse-Lautrec** uses paint as if it were pastel, faces are lit and even distorted by artificial light *(Tête-à-tête Supper)* and volumes are flattened.

Galleries 9–14: *Second Floor*

20C collections. Informality seems to pervade the layout of the early-20C collections. **Gallery 9** is devoted to **Matisse** *(Woman in a Kimono)* and Fauvism. Matisse and others such as **André Derain** and **Maurice de Vlaminck** used vivid colours in their landscapes. **Gallery 10** displays French Painting from the early 20C, such as **Pierre Bonnard**'s unconventional *The Seine in Paris: The Pont du Carrousel*.

Galleries 11a and **11b** house the Roger Fry Collection. **Roger Fry** *(1866–1934)* was an emminent art historian, critic and painter who collected contemporary works by **Duncan Grant** (*Lily Pond* four-fold screen) and **Vanessa Bell**, who were associated with the **Bloomsbury Group** and the **Omega Workshop** during the 1930s (*see Introduction to LONDON – Painting*). His personal taste was for Bonnard, Derain, Friesz, O'Connor, Rouault and Sickert. This collection of works by British artists should be considered a selection made by individuals for their own personal pleasure rather than for a major public museum and as such, modern art is presented as highly approachable. Following on in **11b** is a display of sketches by Seurat in his pointillist style.

Gallery 12 is devoted to a series of drawings and prints, while **Galleries 13** and **14** deal with **Expressionist Art** and **Modernism**, with works by German artists such as **Max Pechstein**, **Alexej von Jawlensky** and above all, Russian-born **Wassily Kandinsky**, who moved to Munich at the age of 30. **Gallery 15** houses temporary exhibitions.

Return to the Strand and cross to the island in its centre.

St Mary-le-Strand

Open Tues–Thur 11am–4pm, Sun 10am–1pm. 020 7836 3126 (church warden). www.stmarylestrand.org.

This compact, Baroque miniature *(1714–24)* was the first commission to be undertaken by **James Gibbs**. It is sober and ordered: a simple apsed space that is light and harmoniously proportioned. The tower rises in four tiers over the rounded porch and first-floor pediment to a gilded weather vane. Fine carvings decorate the exterior, but it is perhaps the Italianate plasterwork ceiling which is particularly worthy of note: executed by English craftsmen, the stylised flower heads are especially delicate. It is known as the "Cabbies' church".

Cross back to the main pavement.

King's College

Founded in 1829, King's College was housed from its earliest days in the East extension of Somerset House; the Strand front *(1970s)* is in an unrelated, modern style. The courtyard, long and narrow, is terminated by the colonnaded pavilion which completes the Somerset House river front.

Continue along the Strand and cross to reach Aldwych.

Aldwych

The sweeping semicircle was laid out in 1905. The huge half-moon island on the Strand is occupied by massive buildings: Australia House, India House *(reliefs)* and, in the centre, the 1925–35 **Bush House**, base of the BBC External Services. Above the lintel the motto "To the friendship of English speaking

peoples" is inscribed. Today the BBC World Service, at 81 years of operation and broadcasting all round the world in 28 languages (including English), is seen as a lifeline to many living under repressive regimes.

Continue along the Strand.

St Clement Danes★

Strand, WC2R 1DH. Open daily 9am–4pm. Closed bank holidays. Oranges and Lemons carillon operates daily at 9am, noon (except Sun), 3pm (except Sun), 6pm. Leaflets (6 languages). 020 7242 2380.

St Clement's was designed by **Christopher Wren** in 1682 on the site of a 9C church built by Danish merchants married to Englishwomen. The building, featuring an open spire in three diminishing pillared stages – the steeple was added by **James Gibbs** *(1719)* – was burnt down on 10 May 1941 and rebuilt as the RAF church in 1955–58. The dark oak panelling, first-floor galleries beneath a richly decorated vault and plasterwork Stuart coat of arms conforms to Wren's original design, now embellished with Air Force mementoes that include badges carved in Welsh slate and inlaid in the pavement, memorials of the Commonwealth air forces and the Polish squadrons, a USAAF and other shrines. The grand pulpit is the original one by Grinling Gibbons.

"Oranges and lemons say the bells of St Clement's" refers to the boats that came up the Thames to land fruit for sale in Clare Market *(on the site of Kingsway)* and paid a tithe in kind to the church; the carillon rings out the **nursery rhyme** four times a day.

At the east end stands a statue of **Dr Samuel Johnson**, a worshipper at the church, who lived nearby.

Continue along the south side of the Strand.

Lloyd's Law Courts Branch

No. 222. The **Palsgrave Tavern**, as frequented by the dramatist Ben Jonson, was named after Frederick Palsgrave, later King of Bohemia, who married Elizabeth, daughter of James I. All three figures are commemorated in the singular glazed earthenware decoration supplied by Royal Doulton. Inside the building, a branch of Lloyds bank since 1895, is panelled with American walnut and sequoia, inset with tiles.

Further along the Strand at *No. 216* is **Twinings** *(see Addresses)*. Several generations have witnessed changes in tea trading over the last centuries. Today Twinings manufacture over 150 blends of tea and infusions. At *Nos. 229/230* is the building of the famous **Wig and Pen Club**, which survived the Great Fire of 1666 and now comprises two narrow 18C town houses with dark wood panelling. The club has now closed.

Cross the Strand.

Royal Courts of Justice

The Law Courts date from 1874–82. The centrepiece inside is the Great Hall, a vaulted arcade decorated with foliated doorways, blind arcades, diapering and a seated statue of the architect. The early courtrooms *(there are still more than 20)* lead off the hall, which is marked outside by a needle spire, offsetting the long arched façade, the heavy tower and polygonal west end. There is a small exhibition of legal costumes. Here the Strand gives way to Fleet Street, enclosed within the confines of the City of London: the boundary is marked by the Temple Bar.

ADDRESSES

SHOPPING

Twining & C°, *216 The Strand, WC2R 1AP. Temple. 020 7353 3511. www.twinings.co.uk. Mon–Fri 8.30am–7.30pm, Sat 10am–5pm, Sun 10am–4pm.* This famous teahouse has had a shop on the Strand since 1717. In addition to finding your favourite teas and infusions, you can visit the museum tracing the history of the Twining family and their company, which celebrated its 300th anniversary in 2006.

Covent Garden★★

Lively crowds enjoy the animation of the central piazza until a late hour, with street entertainers and quality craft and antique markets. The refurbishment of the opera house and its facilities have given a new cachet to Covent Garden, which recalls its heyday in the 19C. Old warehouses have been carefully adapted to accommodate enticing small shops and boutiques selling off-the-peg designer clothing, while long-established businesses continue to thrive. Street cafés cater to the browsers by day and smart restaurants feed the throngs of theatregoers by night.

- **Location:** Map pp92–93. ⊖*Covent Garden; Leicester Sq; Charing Cross.* Covent Garden is the area delineated by Strand, Kingsway, Charing Cross Rd and New Oxford St.
- **Don't Miss:** The Floral Hall, now the sleek foyer of the Royal Opera House.
- **Timing:** Spend the afternoon at the London Transport Museum or window-shopping around Neal Street, then enjoy the lively atmosphere of the Piazza in the evening.
- **Kids:** The London Transport Museum.

A BIT OF HISTORY

In the Middle Ages, Covent Garden was a 40 acre/16ha walled property belonging to the Benedictines of Westminster. Following the dissolution of the monasteries and the confiscation of the garden, Henry VIII granted the land to the Earl of Bedford. In the 17C the 4th Earl commissioned Inigo Jones to create the country's first public square here. Drawing on his enthusiam for the classical, especially the Palladian style of architecture, Jones created the piazza and the church of St Paul.

In approximately 1654 the first fruit and vegetable market begain operating in the square and when the theatres, hitherto principally in Southwark, reopened after the Restoration *(1660)*, **Charles II** granted two royal warrants for theatres here: the first was the **Theatre Royal, Drury Lane** *(1663)*; the second, the **Theatre Royal, Covent Garden** *(1732)*. Covent Garden has since been the home of London theatre. When the monopoly of the royal theatres was broken by the Theatre Regulation Act in 1843, some 40 new theatres mushroomed within as many years; and in 1987 the Theatre Museum opened in the old Covent Garden Flower Market *(since relocated to the Victoria and Albert Museum)*.

WALKING TOUR 2

Start from the Piazza.

The Piazza★★

The 1631 licence gave **Inigo Jones** the opportunity to design London's first square, which he modelled after those he had seen in Italy, lining the grand space on two sides with terraces of three-storey brick houses rising tall above a stone colonnade; behind the covered walkway nestled shops and coffee houses. The garden wall of the Earl's new town house ran on the south side. Bedford House was demolished in 1700 and the area was developed. Today the piazza is a meeting place for Londoners and visitors alike for both relaxation and entertainment.

Covent Garden Market

The long-established market was regularised by Letters Patent in 1670 and in 1830 royal permission was granted for special buildings to be erected. The **Central Market Buildings** were designed by **Charles Fowler** *(1832)* and linked by glass canopies in 1872.

By the turn of the 19C/20C, the market spilled into the neighbouring streets and in November 1974, it moved to

Nine Elms (see SUBURBS – BATTERSEA), leaving Eliza Doolittle's flower market to franchised shops, canopied cafés, vaulted pubs and wine bars. Today you'll find stalls in the covered Jubilee Hall Market (see Addresses) instead. Located at the far end of the Piazza, this small market has around 120 stalls, and sells arts and crafts, antiques and general goods depending on the day of the week *(open Mon 5am–4pm (antiques), Tue–Fri 9.30am–6.30pm (general), Sat–Sun 9.30am–5.30pm (crafts); 020 7836 2139; www.jubileemarket.co.uk).*

St Paul's Church★

Entrance from Bedford Street.

The Earl was unwilling to afford anything "much better than a barn" so Jones, declaring he should have "the handsomest barn in England," designed a classical church with a pitched roof. Since its completion, the church has been closely associated with the world of entertainment: actors, artists, musicians and craftsmen. Overlooking the square is the famous Tuscan portico, from which on 9 May 1662, **Pepys** watched the first ever **Punch and Judy** show in England; much later, **George Bernard Shaw** set the opening scene of *Pygmalion* there. Today it provides a dramatic backdrop to a variety of buskers.

Leave the square on King St. and turn right onto Garrick St.

Pubs and Clubs

The district's oldest tavern is **The Lamb & Flag** (see Addresses) *on an alley off King St.* A traditional old-school club is also still flourishing near here: the **Garrick** *(15 Garrick St.)*, founded in 1831 and named after the actor David Garrick.

Walk down to Bedford St. and turn left onto Maiden Lane.

Maiden Lane is home to several good places to eat. At no. 35 is **Rules**, London's oldest restaurant, established in 1798. See Your Stay in the City.

At the end of Maiden Lane, turn left up Southampton St. to return to the Piazza.

Coffee Houses Past and Present

The fashion for coffee houses was introduced to London during the Commonwealth *(1652)*. Originally they served as meeting places in the City for the exchange of business intelligence but by 1715 there were over 500, not only in the City but also in Covent Garden and the Strand, St James's, Mayfair and Westminster. Customers with similar interests would gather regularly, even daily, in the same houses or call at several to pick up messages or to read the news sheets, which at first circulated here. Later, newspapers *(Daily Courant, 1702)* were available to customers for the price of a single cup of hot chocolate or coffee. Of the 17C and 18C coffee houses for which Covent Garden was famous, none remain, though many have become pubs. However, coffee culture remains alive and well in London and many Londoners socialise and do business in modern versions of the traditional coffee house such as Monmouth *(Monmouth St.)* and Canela *(Earlham St.)* in Covent Garden, and Flat White *(Berwick St. Market)* and Milk Bar *(Bateman St.)* in Soho.

Monmouth Coffee Company

Type B Bus, London Transport Museum

London Transport Museum★

Covent Garden Piazza., WC2E 7BB. Covent Garden. Open Sat–Thu 10am–6pm (5.15pm last admission), Fri 11am–6pm (5.15pm last admission). £15; under 16s free (all tickets allow free return entry for a year). For details of special events, check the website. 020 7379 6344. www.ltmuseum.co.uk.

The London Transport Museum, housed in the Flower Market building in Covent Garden, brings alive the development of one of the world's earliest and largest transport networks, from trams and trolleybuses to London's beloved Routemaster bus.

Let your imagination run wild as you are transported back in time by the Museum's historical and interactive galleries, which are packed full of real vehicles. You can take the wheel of an old double-decker bus, try your hand as a Tube conductor or bump around with the other passengers in the back of a train. Enjoy the Museum's mixture of modernity and nostalgia, and discover the cultural and design elements of the Underground. The stamps you collect as you go round the museum appeal to children of all ages.

You can stop in at the shop, which showcases London's leading designers and sells a variety of souvenirs, or grab a coffee at the Upper Deck café.

Return to the Piazza and leave the square via Russell St.

Theatre Royal, Drury Lane

The present Georgian theatre is one of London's largest *(2,283 seats)* with symmetrical staircases rising beneath the domed entrance to a circular balcony. The first theatre, opened in 1663, was frequently patronised by Charles II, who met Nell Gwynne there in 1665. The second theatre, designed by **Wren**, knew a golden age under **Garrick** *(from 1747 to 1776)*; it was replaced in 1794 by a third building, opening with **Sheridan**'s new play *The School for Scandal.* The present house, to designs by **Wyatt**, was erected in 1812. Kean, **Irving** and Ellen Terry all played there; **Ivor Novello**'s dancing operettas were also staged there.

Bow Street

In the mid-18C, when **Henry Fielding**, novelist, dramatist and magistrate and his half-brother John, the **Blind Beak**, moved into a house opposite the Opera House, they began their crusade for penal and police reform, which included the organisation in 1753 of the **Bow Street Runners**, mainly intended to fight prostitution.

The present building on the site of their house dates from 1881; in 1992 the police moved to new premises at Charing Cross.

Royal Opera House★

Charles II's patent was secured by **John Rich**, who opened his Theatre Royal, Covent Garden in 1732. In 1847, the theatre was remodelled and renamed **Royal Italian Opera**. The present house, inaugurated in 1858, became the Royal Opera House in 1892. A hundred years later, major renovation work was needed and the house was largely reconstructed between 1996 and 2000. Extensions to the West *(in the 1858 style)* house new dressing rooms and rehearsal facilities. The opera house now boasts an exquisitely restored auditorium with air conditioning and modern facilities for staging big productions. The iron-and-glass **Floral Hall** is used to great theatrical effect as the main foyer, with escalators rising to the mezzanine galleries, which accommodate bars and restaurant, with panoramic **views** of the piazza from the loggias. **The Royal Ballet** performs here regularly and it is also the city's premier venue for opera and visiting dance companies.

▶ At the top of Bow St. turn right onto Great Queen St.

Great Queen Street

The Masons occupy the greater part of Great Queen Street, which includes 18C houses *(nos. 27–29)* and the Art Deco **Freemasons Hall** *(1927–33)*.

▶ Walk up Endell St. and turn left onto Shorts Gardens.

Neal's Yard

The picturesque **Neal's Yard★**, complete with period hoists, dovecote, trees in tubs and window-boxes, has attracted fashionable and eco-friendly shops.

Seven Dials

A 40ft/12m Doric column, adorned with a sundial on each face, was erected at the centre of seven radiating streets in the early 1690s. It was pulled down by a mob in 1773 on a rumour that treasure was buried underneath it. A replica of the pillar has been erected on the original site.

▶ Walk up Mercer St., turn right and take Shaftesbury Ave to Princes Circus. Turn left into St Giles High St.

St Giles-in-the-Fields, which is of ancient foundation, was rebuilt in 1734 by Flitcroft after the styles of **Wren** and **James Gibbs**; the steeple rising directly from the façade echoes St Martin-in-the-Fields *(open daily 9am–6pm and for services; 020 7240 2532; www.stgilesonline.org)*.

ADDRESSES

LIGHT BITE

Food for Thought, *31 Neal St., WC2H 9PR. Covent Garden. 020 7836 9072. foodforthought-london.ukay.com. Mon–Sat noon–8.30pm, Sun noon–5.30pm.* You cannot miss this discreet address nestled among the shops of Neal St., thanks to the queue it attracts at lunchtime. The vegetarian food is fresh and tasty, and portions are very generous. Take away or eat in a small room in the basement.

Neal's Yard Salad Bar, *Neal's Yard, WC2H 9DP. Covent Garden. 020 7836 3233. Daily 9am–9pm.* Good vegetarian and vegan cuisine (salads, quiches, soups, hot dishes) for consumption on or off the premises. Pleasant terrace.

Pâtisserie Valérie, *44 Old Compton St., W1D 4TY. Leicester Square. 020 7437 3466 www.patisserie-valerie.co.uk. Mon–Tues 7.30am–9pm, Wed–Fri 7.30am–11pm, Sat 8am–11pm, Sun 9am–9pm.* This French patisserie is well established across London and offers a wide selection of cakes and pastries. Breakfasts and light lunches also available. *(Also at 15 Bedford St., WC2E 9HE. Covent Garden. 020 7379 6428. Mon–Fri 7.30am–9pm, Sat 8.30am–9pm, Sun 9am–8pm.)*

Primrose Bakery, *44 Tavistock St., WC2E 7PB. Covent Garden. 020 7836 3638. www.primrose-bakery.co.uk. Also at 15 Bedford St., WC2E 9HE. Mon–Sat 10am–7.30pm, Sun noon–5pm.* This diminutive cupcake store and café is slightly off the beaten track, so can be a calming place to take a break. A delicious range of cupcakes are for sale, both to takeaway and to eat in, along with a pot of tea or cup of coffee.

World Food Café, *14 Neal's Yard, WC2H 9DP. ⊖Covent Garden. ✆020 7379 0298. www.worldfoodcafénealsyard.co.uk. Mon–Sat noon–5pm.* Overlooking the quaint and eco-friendly Neal's Yard, this first-floor vegetarian restaurant is known for its hearty recipes from exotic lands around the globe, particularly Asia and Africa. Shared pine tables around a central kitchen counter. If you are pressed for time, pick up a healthy snack at one of the ground-floor outlets.

PUBS AND BARS

Argyll Arms, *18 Argyll St., W1F 7TP. ⊖Oxford Circus. ✆020 7734 6117. Mon–Sat 10am–11pm, Sun 10am–10.30pm.* This historic pub *(1716)* has retained its superb 18C interior: enormous mirrors, carved woodwork and mahogany bar. This alone makes it worth a visit and its location in bustling Oxford Circus means it is crowded at all hours. Small outside area.

The Cross Keys, *31 Endell St., WC2H 9EB. ⊖Covent Garden. ✆020 7836 5185.Mon–Sat 11am–11pm, Sun noon–10.30pm.* Located in a quiet street in Covent Garden, this 19C pub has a pretty floral façade and eclectic décor, with walls covered in photos and prints from various periods and bric-a-brac antiques hanging from the ceiling. Relaxed atmosphere.

Dirty Martini, *11/12 Russell St., Covent Garden, WC2B 5HZ. ⊖Covent Garden. ✆0844 371 2550. www.dirtymartini.uk.com. Mon–Wed 5pm–1am, Thur–Sat 5pm–3am, Sun 5pm–11pm. Fri/Sat over-21s only.* Basement bar serving a delicious range of decadent cocktails plus beers, wines and spirits to a young, stylish crowd. Free entry all night, every night and a generous happy hour.

The Globe, *37 Bow St., WC2E 7AU. ⊖Covent Garden. ✆020 7379 0154. www.theglobebowstreet.co.uk. Mon–Sat 11am–midnight, Sun 11am–11pm.* Opened in 1682, The Globe is one of eight historic pubs on Bow Street. There's no shortage of character inside the ancient wooden interior and the atmosphere is pleasant, especially in the evenings when the place is filled with an eclectic clientele.

The Lamb & Flag, *33 Rose St., WC2E 9EB. ⊖Covent Garden. ✆020 7497 9504. Mon–Sat 11am–11pm, Sun noon–10.30pm.* This pub, nestling in a tiny alley, is the oldest and perhaps the most pleasant in the area. It opened in 1623 as the Cooper's Arms and became known unofficially as the Bucket of Blood from 1679, after an incident involving John Dryden, who was attacked outside while on his way home to Long Acre. Good selection of beers. Best enjoyed during off-peak hours, though make an exception for popular free jazz nights on Sundays.

Marquis of Anglesey, *39 Bow St., WC2E 7AU. ⊖Covent Garden. ✆020 7240 3216. www.themarquess.co.uk. Mon–Thur 11am–11.30pm, Fri–Sat 11am–midnight, Sun noon–10pm.* Located on a busy corner of Bow Street, this fairly spacious pub gets packed in the evenings but at other times has a pleasant laidback atmosphere (and comfy chairs!). The décor is more modern than traditional and upmarket pub grub is served all day.

Nell of Old Drury, *29 Catherine St., WC2B 5JS. ⊖Covent Garden. ✆020 7836 5328. www.nellofolddrury.com. Mon–Fri noon–3pm, 5pm–11.30pm, Sat noon–midnight.* This friendly pub is popular with theatregoers heading to the nearby Theatre Royal. The décor echoes the area's theatrical tradition with photos and posters of past productions. Good selection of beers and ciders.

The Opera Tavern, *23 Catherine St., WC2B 5JS. ⊖Covent Garden. ✆020 7836 3680. www.operatavern.co.uk. Mon–Sat 11.30am–11pm, Sun 10am–10.30pm.* Another unpretentious historic pub *(1879)*, also located opposite the Theatre Royal. Gets crowded before and after each performance.

Punch & Judy, *40 The Market, WC2E 8RF. ⊖Covent Garden. ✆020 7379 0923. Mon–Sat 10am–11pm, Sun noon–10.30pm.* This touristy pub has a terrace overlooking the Piazza, which makes it Ideal for watching the street performances that animate Covent Garden. Gets very crowded in the evenings, though.

SHOPPING

Birkenstock, *70 Neal St., WC2H 9PA. ⊖Covent Garden. ✆020 7240 2783. www.birkenstock.co.uk. Mon–Wed, Fri–Sat 10.30am–7pm, Thur 10.30am–8pm, Sun noon–6pm.* Small, popular shop selling over 100 different styles, colours and textures of comfortable, good-quality footwear developed by Birkenstock, the German family who designed the first flexible arch support that mirrors the shape of the foot.

Cecil Court *between Charing Cross Rd and St Martin's Lane, WC2H 9PR. ⊖Leicester Square. www.cecilcourt.co.uk.* Pedestrianised street, which is home to numerous antiquarian booksellers.

Jubilee Hall Market, *1 Tavistock Court, The Piazza, WC2E 8BD. ⊖Covent Garden.* Stallholders sell a wide range of antiques *(Mon)*, general goods *(Tue–Fri)* and handmade crafts *(Sat–Sun)*.

Lush, *The Piazza (unit 11), Covent Garden (⊖Covent Garden) ; ✆020 7240 4570; Quadrant Arcade, 80–82 Regent St. (⊖Piccadilly Circus) ; www.lush.co.uk. Open daily.* Range of fresh, handmade cosmetics made from fruit, vegetables and natural oils (no animal products): soaps, shampoos, skin creams, body butters, massage bars, etc.

Monmouth Coffee House, *27 Monmouth St., WC2H 9EU. ⊖Covent Garden. ✆020 7379 3516. www.monmouthcoffee.co.uk. Mon–Sat 8am–6.30pm (closed bank holidays).* A small shop operated by true coffee connoisseurs, who will give you excellent advice on your perfect cup of java. The range of coffee changes regularly and you can sample it on the spot. Also at Borough Market, *⊖London Bridge or Borough.*

Neal's Yard Dairy, *17 Shorts Gardens, WC2H 9AT. ⊖Covent Garden. ✆020 7240 5700. www.nealsyarddairy.co.uk. Mon–Sat 10am–7pm.* This popular cheese merchant sells fabulous dairy products from the British Isles only. The house classics include Montgomery's Cheddar, Colston Bassett Stilton and Cashel Blue (a creamy Irish cheese).

Neal's Yard Remedies, *15 Neal's Yard, WC2H 9DP. ⊖Covent Garden. ✆020 7379 7222. www.nealsyardremedies.com. Mon–Wed, Fri, Sat 10am–7pm, Thur 10am–7.30pm, Sun 11am–6pm.* Established in 1981 by Romy Fraser and identifiable by its dark blue packaging, this popular brand of beautycare products and cosmetics prides itself on using only natural ingredients. Here you will find aniseed toothpaste and rosemary shampoo. There's a herbalist and homeopath; nine therapy rooms.

Paul Smith, *40–44 Floral St., WC2E 9DG. ⊖Covent Garden. ✆020 7379 7133. www.paulsmith.co.uk. Mon–Wed & Fri 10.30am–6.30pm, Thur 10.30am–7pm, Sat 10am–7pm, Sun 12.30–5.30pm.* Fashion for men, women and children, designed by the man who revolutionised the British fashion world. Fans should also drop into Smith's Notting Hill boutique (122 Kensington Park Rd.) in a former house and designed as an exhibition hall, or the Grade II listed building at 13 Park St., Borough Market, *⊖London Bridge or Borough.*

Penhaligon's, *41 Wellington St., WC2E 7BN. ⊖Covent Garden. ✆020 7836 2150. www.penhaligons.com.* Perfume supplier to the aristocracy since 1870, Penhaligon counts the Royal Family among its clients. Favourite scents are "Hammam Bouquet", still made according to the original 1872 composition, or "Blenheim Bouquet", one of Churchill's favourite scents.

The Tea House, *15 Neal St., WC2H 9PU. ⊖Covent Garden. ✆020 7240 7539. Mon–Wed 10am–7pm, Thur–Sat 10am–8pm, Sun noon–7pm.* True lovers of England's national beverage will find a wide selection of black, green, smoked, fruit and herbal tea leaves and bags in this lovely tea emporium.

Ted Baker, *9-10 Floral St., WC2E 9DS. ⊖Covent Garden. ✆020 7836 7808. Mon–Wed, Fri 10.30am–7.30pm, Thur 10.30am–8pm, Sat 10am–7pm, Sun noon–6pm.* Oh-so-British funky fashions for men and women from this quirky label.

ENTERTAINMENT

Opera and Ballet Nights in the Piazza

In summer, live opera and ballet productions are broadcast from the Royal Opera House and Royal Ballet onto giant screens to enthusiastic crowds. It is a great opportunity to enjoy world-class singers and dancers in major productions in a congenial al fresco atmosphere. Enquire at the box office and check online for dates. Tickets are free but cannot be booked in advance, so be sure to get there early.

Soho★

Soho is the beating heart of the West End, one of the greatest theatre centres in the world ("Theatreland"). By day it is the hub of London's creative advertising and film industry: by night the place takes on new life as lights flicker in the windows of the various clubs, bars, restaurants (French, Italian, Greek and Chinese), jazz venues, nightclubs, cinemas and theatres, thronged with night owls. Soho has its louche side, with risqué shows and shops, but it has a solid core of loyal residents among its otherwise transient population; its Bohemian appeal has always attracted artists, writers and foreign immigrants. Soho was the centre of book reatailing adjacent to Bloomsbury's publishing houses, immortalised in Helene Hanff's novel *84 Charing Cross Road*. Centred on Gerrard Street, just north of Leicester Square, is London's Chinatown.

- **Location:** Map pp92–93. *⊖Leicester Square; Piccadilly Circus; Tottenham Court Road*. Extending north from Piccadilly Circus and Leicester Square, the area is bounded by Oxford Street, Charing Cross Road, Regent St. and is to the West of Covent Garden. It is London's theatre and cinema heartland.
- **Timing:** You can spend anything from 1hr to a day here. Window-shop along stylish Regent St. then make your way to Soho in the early evening, where you can: have a meal in Chinatown, see a film or a play, or just join the crowd in one of the many bars and clubs.

A BIT OF HISTORY

In the Middle Ages Soho was a chase, named after the cry of the Medieval hunt, which was often found in the vicinity of St Giles-in-the-Fields (*see COVENT GARDEN*).

Street names *(Brewer St., Glasshouse St.)* reflect the area's early activities. By the mid-19C (after a fashionable spell in the 17C–18C), Soho included the worst slums in the capital. The building of Regent Street divided the West End from its disreputable neighbour and two new streets were built to penetrate the fetid tangle: Charing Cross Road *(1880)* and Shaftesbury Avenue *(1886)*.

People of All Nations – Refugees began to arrive in the 17C: Greeks fleeing the Ottoman Turks; persecuted Huguenots after the revocation of the Edict of Nantes *(1685)*; Frenchmen hounded by the Revolution and later by political changes – these established French restaurants and cafés (**Wheeler's** *at 19 Old Compton Street, founded by Napoleon III's chef; the* **York Minster** *pub at 49 Dean Street)*. Waves of Swiss, Italian and Spanish immigrants followed. Then came the Chinese from Hong Kong, Singapore and the docks to transform Gerrard Street into a **Chinatown★**.

Commerce – The southern end of Shaftesbury Avenue is known for its theatres; the area around Golden Square is dominated by the film industry, television production companies,

A Roll-Call of Luminaries

William Blake was born in Soho *(1757)*, Hazlitt died there *(1830)*; Edmund Burke, Sarah Siddons, Dryden, Sheraton lived there; Marx, Engels, Canaletto, Haydn lodged there; Mendelssohn and Chopin gave recitals at the 18C house in Meard Street of Vincent Novello, father of Ivor and founder of the music publishers. John Logie Baird *(1888–1946)* first demonstrated television in Frith Street in 1926.

cinema advertisers, photographers; sleazy parts boast peep-shows and sex shops below lurid neon signs; this is also the home of London's mainstream jazz scene – instruments, specialist music shops and clubs pepper Shaftesbury Avenue, Charing Cross Road and Denmark Street.

WALKING TOUR 3

Leicester Square★

The Square, now a pedestrian precinct surrounded by cinemas and places to eat, is one of the busiest meeting places in London, with some 22 million visitors each year. At the centre stands the Shakespeare Memorial Fountain *(1874)* facing a statue of **Charlie Chaplin** *(north side)* by John Doubleday *(1980)*, while around the railings sit busts of famous local residents – Reynolds, Newton, Hunter, Hogarth; panels tell the history of the Square from Leicester Fields to the building of the **Empire**. Around the edge of the central gardens the **handprints** of many famous actors and movie stars are set into the pavement. The Square is also a traditional site for royal and red-carpet premieres, where film stars meet, greet and pose for assembled crowds of onlookers.
On the south side of the central garden is the popular **TKTS Ticket Booth** (*see YOUR STAY IN THE CITY – Entertainment, Theatre*).

Leave Leicester Sq. on Leicester Pl.

Inside the circular Roman Catholic church of **Notre Dame de France**, an Aubusson tapestry hangs above the altar; mosaic ornaments and paintings by Jean Cocteau on the walls *(open daily 9.30am–8pm; brochure in 2 languages; 020 7437 9363; www.rcdow.org.uk)*.

Turn right into Lisle St., then left into Newport Pl. to Gerrard St.

Chinatown★

Gerrard Street is the centre of this colourful area marked by oriental gates, which abounds in restaurants, supermarkets selling exotic foodstuffs, oriental medicine centres, etc. It is the scene of great festivities at Chinese New Year *(a movable feast in Jan or Feb)* celebrated in traditional and colourful fashion.

Walk up Gerrard Pl. and turn left onto Shaftesbury Ave then right onto Dean St.

St Anne's Church *(1686)*, at *No. 55*, was bombed in the war. The tower, now occupied by the Soho Society, was restored in 1979.

Continue up Dean St. and turn right onto Old Compton St.

Old Compton Street, at the heart of Soho, is lined with pubs, eating places, wine merchants, pastry shops, Italian food stores and frequented by a spirited gay crowd.

Continue along Old Compton St. then turn left onto Greek St.

House of St Barnabas

1 Greek St. Check times before visiting. Closed Easter and Christmas. Donation appreciated. 020 7437 1894. www.hosb.org.uk.
The House of Charity was built c.1750. The exterior is plain except for two obelisks at the entrance; the interior, one of the finest in Soho, has beautiful plasterwork ceilings and walls, and an unusual crinoline staircase. The proportions of the small chapel, built in 1863 in 13C French Gothic style, are unique.

Soho Square

The pleasant Square, laid out in 1680 between Greek Street and Frith Street, is adorned by a fountain topped by a statue of Charles II. Two churches stand to the East and Northwest.

Leave by Carlisle St., cross Dean St to Great Chapel St., turn left into Sheraton St. and left onto Wardour St.

Wardour Street and its immediate vicinity *(Beak Street, Dean Street and Soho Square)* conjures up the **film**

industry from the creators of blockbuster movies and catchy commercials.

Continue on Wardour St. then turn right into Broadwick St., cutting across Berwick St.

Many of the houses along Berwick Street are 18C. The **Berwick Street Market**, which dates from 1778, is one of the finest fresh produce markets in central London; the surrounding shops include Aladdin's caves of extravagant fabrics used by couturier designers and the frills and fantasy of theatrical costumiers.

Continue to Carnaby St.

The largely pedestrianised area in and around **Carnaby St.**, which was a high spot of the Swinging Sixties, has now reinvented itself as a centre of stylish shops, trendy bars, eateries and clubs.

Walk up to Great Marlborough St. and turn left onto Ramillies St.

Photographer's Gallery

16–18 Ramillies St. Open daily 11am–6pm. 020 7087 9300. www.photonet.org.uk.

The largest public gallery dedicated to photography in London hosts exhibitions by well-known artists and emerging talent, and has been in instrumental in establishing photography as a serious art form. The newly developed three-storey building is light and airy and features a street-level café-bar and large bookshop and print store. A wide variety of projects, talks and events take place here; check the website to find out what's on.

Retrace your steps back to Great Marlborough St., turn right and continue to the end, at Regent St.

Regent Street★★

Liberty, Jaeger, Hamleys Toy Shop, Aquascutum, the Café Royal and Austin Reed all line this elegant street sweeping southwards to Piccadilly Circus and the heart of the West End.

Liberty★★ *(see p435)* was founded by Arthur Liberty in 1875. It soon acquired the dignified title of "Emporium", stocking broad ranges of exotic silks imported from the East, Japanese porcelain, wallpapers and fans, and became associated with the Aesthetic Movement. Furniture, made in workshops in Soho, supplemented the imported ranges. Own brand fabrics were made to different weights after traditional Indian prints and from designs by artists sympathetic to the Aesthetic and Arts and Crafts movements.

The Liberty jewellery came from the Continent, where Art Nouveau was flourishing and from where furniture was imported. The success of the Art Nouveau style lasted until the outbreak of war in 1914, after which furniture manufacture reverted to Queen Anne and Tudor styles. Liberty fabrics and jewellery, however, continue much in the same traditional vein.

Note the splendid **pediment** on the Regent Street façade. The **Tudor Building** *(1922–24)* in Great Marlborough Street was built from timbers taken from the Royal Navy's last two sailing ships.

Proceed down Regent St., turn left into Beak St. and right into Warwick St.

Tucked away off Regent Street stands **Our Lady of the Assumption**, a Catholic church *(1788)* with only a pediment as decoration *(open Mon–Fri 7am–6pm, Sat–Sun 10am–6pm; 020 7437 1525)*.

Turn left into Brewer St. and left again into Lower John St.

The attractive **Golden Square**, with gardens enclosed by railings, is the preserve of the media and fashion industries.

ADDRESSES

LIGHT BITE

The Clachan, *34 Kingly St. ⊖Oxford Circus. ✆020 7494 0834. Mon–Thur 10am–11pm, Fri–Sat 10am–11.30pm, Sun 10am–10.30pm.* Located just behind Liberty's, away from the bustle of Regent Street and Carnaby Street, this spacious pub offers a menu of classic dishes in plentiful portions. The original woodwork *(1898)* lends it a traditional atmosphere.

Whole Foods Market, *20 Glasshouse St. ⊖Piccadilly Circus. ✆020 7406 3100. Mon–Fri 7.30am–9.30pm, Sat 9am–9.30pm, Sun 10am–6pm.* The coffee shop in this deli-grocer serves a great selection of salads, sandwiches and divine pastries.

Kulu Kulu Sushi, *76 Brewer St. ⊖Piccadilly Circus. ✆020 7734 7316. Also at 39 Thurloe Place ⊖Covent Garden. ✆020 7240 5687. Mon–Sat noon–3.30pm, 5pm–9.30pm.* This small sushi bar is a pleasant surprise. Prepared before your eyes, a wide variety of delicious Japanese dishes are placed in small dishes on the conveyor belt in front of you. Diners are requested to spend a maximum of 45 minutes at the counter.

Masala Zone, *9 Marshall St. ⊖Oxford Circus. ✆020 7287 9966, www.masala zone.com. Mon–Sat noon–11pm, Sun 12.30pm–10.30pm.* Part of the same chain as famous restaurants Amaya, Chutney Mary and Veeraswamy, Masala Zone modernises the concept of the British Indian restaurant: simple décor, warm lighting and functional food. The thalis (platters) are especially good value.

Stockpot, *18 Old Compton St. ⊖Leicester Square. ✆020 7287 1066. Mon–Sun 9am–11.30.* A reliable neighbourhood restaurant serving simple, hearty dishes to fill even the hungriest stomachs. About the cheapest place to eat in Soho.

Vita Organic, *74 Wardour St. ⊖Piccadilly Circus. ✆020 7734 8986. www.vitao.co.uk. Mon–Sat noon–11pm, Sun noon–9pm.* This strictly "Ayurvedic" vegetarian restaurant serves a rich and varied menu in a tiny dining room. You pay depending on the size of the dish (from £2.50–7.50). Choice of teas.

Wasabi, *58 Oxford St. ⊖Tottenham Court Road. ✆020 7580 0062. Mon–Sat 10.30am–11pm, Sun 10.30am–8pm. Other branches of Wasabis in London include: 34 Villiers St. ⊖Charing Cross. ✆020 7807 9992. Mon–Fri 10.30am–10pm, Sat–Sun 11am–8pm. www.wasabi.uk.com.* Japanese specialties to go, with a choice of hot dishes and a wide variety of sushi.

CAFÉS

Flat White, *17 Berwick St., W1F 0PT. ⊖Tottenham Court Road or Oxford Circus. ✆020 7734 0370. Mon–Fri 8am–7pm, Sat–Sun 9am–6pm.* Antipodean-style café serving a wide range of coffees, all-day brunch dishes and sweet treats. Sister café **Milkbar** *(3–5 Bateman St., W1D 4AG; ⊖Tottenham Court Road; ✆020 7287 4796)* offers a similar choice of food and drink, with changing art on the walls.

Maison Bertaux, *28 Greek St. ⊖Leicester Square. ✆020 7437 6007. www.maisonbertaux.com Daily 8.30am–11pm.* This small patisserie claims to be London's oldest and is known for its cream cakes. Everything is baked on the premises and can be eaten in or out.

Yauatcha, *15 Broadwick St. ⊖Piccadilly Circus. ✆020 7494 8888. www.yauatcha. com. Mon–Sat noon–11.30pm, Sun noon–10.30pm.* This contemporary, open-plan dim-sum teahouse offers an all-day grazing menu of light bites, served with a range of specialty Chinese and Indian teas. One to savour.

ENTERTAINMENT AND NIGHTLIFE

The Borderline, *Orange Yard, access from 16 Manette St. ⊖Tottenham Court Road. ✆ 020 7734 5547 (reservations); www. meanfiddler.com. Box office: Mon–Sat 5pm–10pm. £10–20.* This small room, in a basement near Tottenham Court Road, hosts a varied programme of gigs covering all musical styles throughout the week. Indie-focused club nights take over at weekends *(11pm–3am, £5–7)*.

Floridita, *100 Wardour St. ⊖Tottenham Court Road. ✆020 7314 4000. www. floriditalondon.com. Tue–Sat 7.30pm–2am. £10 entrance fee.* The London version of the famous Havana bar invites you to party Cuban-style. There's an impressive selection of cigars and cocktails, including the traditional daiquiri and mojito, and live music of a South American flavour to get everyone dancing.

Jazz After Dark, *9 Greek St. ⊖Tottenham Court Road. ✆020 7734 0545. www.jazzafterdark.co.uk. Mon–Thur 5pm–2am, Fri–Sat 5pm–3am. £5–15.* Cocktail bar with live blues, jazz and Latin music. Dinner and tapas served.

Salsa, *96 Charing Cross ⊖Tottenham Court Road. ✆020 7379 3277. www.bar-salsa.com. Mon–Thur 5pm–2am, Fri–Sat 5pm–3am, Sun 5pm–1am.* Salsa classes every night to teach you the moves, followed by lively club nights so you can put them into practice. Classes are cheaper earlier in the week. The restaurant serves Latin-infused dishes and the bar serves great cocktails. A hen party favourite.

Two Floors, *3 Kingly St. ⊖Oxford Circus. ✆020 7439 1007. www.twofloors.com. Mon–Thur noon–11.30pm, Fri–Sat noon–midnight.* This friendly, unassuming bar is the place to go for a quiet drink with friends. Sink into the deep leather sofas and relax as you sip beer, wine or cocktails.

SHOPPING

Agent Provocateur, *6 Broadwick St. ⊖Oxford Circus. ✆020 7439 0229. www.agentprovocateur.com. Mon–Sat 11am–7pm (Thur 8pm), Sun noon–5pm.* Founded in 1994 by Joseph Corre, the son of Vivienne Westwood and Malcolm McLaren, this luxurious lingerie brand is chic and sexy without being vulgar.

Algerian Coffee Stores, *52 Old Compton St. ⊖Leicester Square. ✆020 7437 2480. www.algcoffee.co.uk. Mon–Wed 9am–7pm, Thur–Fri 9am–9pm, Sat 9am–8pm.* Connoisseurs of caffeine will be familiar with this long-running tea and coffee supplier, located here since 1887. There are over 140 varieties of coffee, 200 types of tea, and more coffee and teapots than you could shake a teabag at.

Berwick Street, W1 *⊖Piccadilly Circus*, is known for its various music stores, including Vinyl Junkies (no. 94), which specialises in house, disco, funk, techno, jazz and soul, and Music and Video Exchange (no. 95), where everything from rock and pop to drum'n'bass is for sale on all formats.

Foyle's, *113–119 Charing Cross Rd. ⊖Tottenham Court Road. ✆020 7434 1574. www.foyles.co.uk. Mon–Sat 9.30am–9pm, Sun noon–6pm, bank holidays 11am–8pm.* For more than one hundred years, this literary institution has been selling books to the British public. Browse the shelves for that title you've always been looking for or simply indulge in the latest must-read blockbuster.

Gerry's, *74 Old Compton St. ⊖Leicester Square. ✆020 7734 2053. www.gerrys.uk.com. Mon–Thur 9am–6.30pm, Fri 9am–7.30pm, Sat 9am–6.30pm, Sun noon–6pm.* Whatever tipple you're looking for, you're almost sure to find it in this quaint shop. Impressive selection of wines, aperitifs, spirits and liqueurs from around the world.

Hamleys, *188–196 Regent St. ⊖Oxford Circus. ✆0871 704 1977. www.hamleys.com. Mon–Wed 10am–8pm, Thur–Fri 10am–9pm, Sat 9.30am–8pm, Sun noon–6pm.* Every kid's paradise, this five-floor temple to childhood fun sells everything from classic toys like Paddington Bear to the latest video games and consoles. Activities and demonstrations happen most days to entertain the ever-present hoards. Once you're in, expect to lose several hours!

Milroy's of Soho, *3 Greek St. ⊖Tottenham Court Road. ✆020 7437 2385. www.milroys.co.uk. Mon–Sat 10am–7pm.* This specialist whiskey supplier offers no less than 700 varieties of whisky (and whiskey!) from around the world. Tastings can also be arranged.

Vinmag.com, *39–43 Brewer St. ⊖Piccadilly Circus. ✆020 7439 8525. www.vinmag.com. Mon–Wed 10am–7pm, Thur 10am–8pm, Fri–Sat 10am–10pm, Sun noon–8pm.* A treasure trove for lovers of vintage, this friendly store has over 250,000 original magazines ***(Vogue, Elle, Life, Picture Post, Playboy)*** and vintage posters, arranged by decade, from 1930 onwards. A great place to buy gifts.

Piccadilly★

This busy thoroughfare, lined with stately buildings, elegant shops and hotels, is the dividing line between fashionable Mayfair and dignified St James's. To the East, Piccadilly Circus, famous for the statue of Eros and its illuminated hoardings, is a major hub and meeting place. At the west end is the quiet elegance of Apsley House set against the luxuriant greenery of Hyde Park.

Location: Map pp92–93. *Piccadilly Circus; Green Park; Hyde Park Corner.* Several thoroughfares converge on Piccadilly Circus, which is a short distance west of Leicester Square and within easy access of Soho. On the other side of Green Park are Buckingham Palace and the Mall.

Timing: Allow 2hr for a stroll along Piccadilly, lined with exclusive shops. Add another 1.5hr to visit one of the sights.

Kids: The attractions inside the Trocadero.

A BIT OF HISTORY

The name "Piccadilly" is derived from Pickadill Hall, an imposing family mansion built by a Somerset tailor, who had made a fortune manufacturing frilled lace borders known as "pickadills", beloved by fashionable Elizabethans.

WALKING TOUR

Piccadilly Circus★

The circus still draws the crowds, chiefly as the heart of nighttime London between the West End theatres and the clubs and restaurants of Soho. It was created by **John Nash** as part of his new Regent Street plan. The statue of **Eros**, officially the Angel of Christian Charity, crowns a memorial fountain erected in 1892 to the philanthropist, **Lord Shaftesbury**.

The south side of the circus is occupied by the **Criterion**, a Victorian building containing a hotel and restaurant. The 19C mosaic ceiling is still visible in the Criterion Brasserie; the **Criterion Theatre** was one of the first theatres to be lit by electricity. On the southeast corner *(at the top end of Haymarket)* stands a four horse fountain by Rudy Weller: high above, three divers reach for the sky.

The north side is taken up by the **London Pavilion**, redeveloped in the 1980s to contain shops and restaurants.

Trocadero

Open Sun–Thu 10am–midnight, Fri–Sat 10am–1am. Closed 25 Dec. Charges for individual attractions. www.londontrocadero.com

A place of gentle entertainment throughout the Victorian and Edwardian eras when waltzing to Strauss was all the rage has been redeveloped to accommodate a range of lively attractions aimed firmly at families and teens. **Funland** *(daily 10am–1am; closed Christmas Day and after 10pm New Year's Eve)* features a ten-pin bowling centre with 10 full-size lanes, UV lighting and pulsing music, an American Pool lounge, dodgems and a range of video games. **Ripley's Believe It or Not** *(daily 10am–midnight, last entry 10.30pm, £26.95)* is home to more than 800 mind-bending exhibits, including a chewing-gum sculpture of the Beatles, fossilised dinosaur eggs and a four-metre-long model of Tower Bridge made entirely from matchsticks.

Cross to the south side of Piccadilly (*St James's Church is described in ST JAMES'S*).

Piccadilly★
The shops here display their merchandise with flair: silk, leather, cashmere, tweed; wines and spirits, even rifles and guns. Of the most traditional establishments, it is worth noting **no. 203** *(formerly Simpson's, now Waterstone's)* for its fine, elegantly proportioned building *(1935)*; **Hatchard's** (**no. 187**) established in 1797 and still trading from its original 18C building; the foodie wonderland that is **Fortnum and Mason's**, founded 1707; when the clock *(1964)* above the Piccadilly entrance chimes the hour, Mr Fortnum and Mr Mason emerge and bow to one another *(see Addresses)*.

Cross over to the north side.

The Albany
The harmonious building, designed by **Sir William Chambers,** is named after the Duke of Albany, George III's second son. The prince sold the 18C house to a builder who converted it into "sets" or "chambers" for bachelors and widowers' which remain to this day. The building, as altered by Henry Holland in 1804, is in the shape of an "H"; the front, with a forecourt on Piccadilly, is of brick, with a central pediment and porch. Its residents have included Gladstone, Byron, J B Priestley and Graham Greene. To preserve the peace, trustees rule that occupants are not allowed to whistle or keep cats, dogs or children under the age of 13!

Burlington House★
The Earl of Burlington's 17C town house was remodelled and refaced in the Palladian style *(1715–16)* and altered again in the 19C (twice) to its present neo-Italian Renaissance appearance.
The **Royal Academy of Arts** *(see Sights)* now occupies the main building on the northern side of the courtyard. Note the upper portico of giant columns and the magisterial statues decorating the façade. The adjacent wings of the complex accommodate five learned societies, including the Geological Society, the Royal Astronomical Society and the Society of Antiquaries.

The **Burlington Arcade**, built in 1819 along the west side of Burlington House, is a delectable retail experience, with traditional purveyors of luxury goods: table linen, fine antique jewellery, cashmere knitwear, leather and shoes. The arcade is patrolled by beadles; the gates are closed at night and on Sundays.

Near Old Bond St. (*see MAYFAIR*) –cross to the south side.

William Curtis-Green *(1875–1960)* designed **no. 160** as a car showroom *(1922)* for Wolseley Motors and later transformed the interior into a banking hall. The building *(now a restaurant)* is in the "Big Bow-Wow style of Corinth USA" on the outside and inside, decked in the most sumptuous red, black and gold exotic decoration.

Ritz Hotel
The 135-bedroom hotel was opened on 24 May 1906 by César Ritz, a Swiss waiter turned entrepreneur, at the height of the Edwardian era. It was an immediate success, bordering on the decorous and the decadent! Externally, the early frame structure was fashioned to the French Classical style, while inside all was gilded Louis XVI decoration and marble. Regular patrons have included royalty (the Duke of Windsor and Wallis Simpson), the rich (Aristotle Onassis), the glamorous and showbiz (Rita Hayworth) and just the plain famous (Charlie Chaplin, Winston Churchill).
Tea at the Ritz showcases the height of English style and sophistication: cucumber sandwiches, cream scones and Earl Grey, with a harpist in the corner. Book up to six weeks ahead.

Walk on past Green Park towards Hyde Park Corner.

The west end of Piccadilly is lined by late Georgian houses occupied by a growing number of hotels following the demise of the gentleman's clubs.
No. 94, an 18C town house, with a Venetian window beneath the central pediment, was formerly the residence

of George IV's son, the Duke of Cambridge *(1829–50)*, and from 1854–65 of Lord Palmerston. **No. 128** harbours the **Royal Air Force Club**. On the south side of Piccadilly, by the Hyde Park Corner underpass stands a **porters' rest**, a solid plank of wood at shoulder height, on which porters could rest their backpacks without unloading them.

SIGHTS

Apsley House★

Open Nov–Mar Sat and Sun 10am–4pm; Apr–Oct Wed–Sun, bank holiday Mon 11am–5pm. Closed Good Fri, May Day, 24–26 Dec, 1 Jan. £6.50, no charge 18 June (Waterloo Day). Audioguide (4 languages). 020 7499 5676. www.english-heritage.org.

Apsley House stands on the site of the old lodge of Hyde Park. As the first house beyond the turnpike, it became known in the 19C as no. 1, London.

The present house was purchased by Wellington in 1817, having been designed nearly 40 years before by **Robert Adam** for Baron Apsley. It was subsequently altered by the Duke and his architect Benjamin S Wyatt: the exterior was given a pedimented portico and refaced entirely in golden Bath stone; the interior, meanwhile, was rearranged *(save the Portico and Piccadilly Drawing Room)* and in 1812, extended. The transformation was such as to befit the town residence of the victorious general and national hero (later Prime Minister). On the ground floor it provided for the Muniment or Plate and China Room to house a priceless collection of treasures and on the floor above, the splendid Waterloo Gallery. In 1947 the 7th Duke presented the house to the nation.

Waterloo Gallery, Apsley House

©English Heritage Photo Library

Wellington Museum★ – Most of the objects displayed have significant associations with Wellington himself: orders and decorations include the silver Waterloo Medal, the first-ever campaign medal, and 85 tricolours paraded on 1 June 1815 in Paris.

The museum includes his highly personal collection of objects selected as supreme examples of quality and artistry: porcelain and silver, beautiful jewellery, orders of chivalry, field marshal's batons and snuffboxes. Of the paintings by English, Spanish, Dutch and Flemish masters, more than 100 were appropriated from the Spanish royal collection by Joseph Bonaparte and acquired from him in 1813 after the Battle of Vitoria.

Plate and China – The opulent splendour of the Egyptian, Prussian, Saxon and Austrian porcelain services compares well with the glorious gold and silver plate (Wellington Shield, solid silver candelabra), silver and gilt services that would be used for lavish celebratory banquets. Meanwhile, the rich gold, enamelled and jewelled snuffboxes reflect a more personal appreciation for quality.

In the basement are displayed the **Duke's death mask**, his uniforms and garter robes, his and Napoleon's swords from Waterloo, a panorama and a programme, printed on silk, of his remarkable funeral and a commentary on his political career by newspaper cartoonists of the day *(1852)*.

Standing in the staircase vestibule is a Carrara marble *(11ft 4in/3.5m)* likeness of Napoleon, posed like the god Apollo, sculpted by **Canova**. Other portraits of *Napoleon* by Lefèvre and Dabos, of the *Empress Josephine* and *Pauline Bonaparte* by Lefèvre hang upstairs.

Art Collection – On the first floor, the most striking room is the **Waterloo Gallery**. The early Waterloo Day *(18 June)* reunion dinners, with only the Generals present, used to be held in the dining room; but by 1829, with

Wellington now premier, the guest list had grown to such an extent that he added the gallery *(90ft/27m long)*. This he had decorated in 18C French style, setting a fashion favoured until the end of the Edwardian era. The windows that would once have had a rural view are fitted with sliding mirrors to enhance still further the glittering gold decoration, chandelier, silver centrepiece and blue-and-red uniforms with their gold buttons and braid.

The **paintings** are dominated by portraits of Charles I and the Goya portrait of the Duke himself in the standard Spanish heroic pose on horseback – recent X-rays have revealed that it was painted prematurely and the head of Joseph Bonaparte overpainted with that of the victor. Other major masterpieces hung here include works by **Murillo, Rubens, Ribera**, **Velázquez** and the Duke's favourite, *The Agony in the Garden* by **Correggio**. Many of these were seized in 1813 from Joseph Bonaparte, who had in turn stolen them from the King of Spain.

The Yellow Drawing Room is hung with yellow damask resembling that originally in the Waterloo Gallery, while the striped drawing room is devoted to *The Battle of Waterloo* by Sir William Allan.

In the Dining Room, the amazing portrait of George IV in Highland dress by Wilkie overlooks the banqueting table set with the silver centrepiece *(26ft/8m)* from the Portuguese service.

Royal Academy of Arts

Burlington House. Open daily 10am–6pm (10pm Fri). Closed 24–25 Dec. £9–£17 exhibitions. Restaurant. Café. Shop. Live jazz Friday evenings in the restaurant. 020 7300 8000 (switchboard); 020 7300 5608 (restaurant). www.royalacademy.org.uk.
The Royal Academy of Arts, founded in 1768, is the oldest fine arts institution in Britain. It is universally renowned for hosting some of the capital's finest temporary and touring exhibitions, including the annual Summer Exhibition.The light and versatile Sackler Galleries, designed by **Sir Norman Foster**, were opened in 1991 by HM The Queen. The Academy's treasures, on permanent display in the lavishly restored John Madeski Fine Rooms, include paintings by members (Reynolds, Gainsborough, Constable, Turner), 18C furniture, Queen Victoria's paintbox, **Michelangelo**'s unfinished marble tondo of the *Madonna and Child*, and the famous copy of **Leonardo da Vinci**'s *Last Supper*.

ADDRESSES

LIGHT BITES AND AFTERNOON TEA

5th View, *203 Piccadilly (in Waterstone's), W1V 9LE. Piccadilly Circus. 020 7851 2433.* This stylish bar-restaurant, on the 5th floor of Waterstone's, affords far-reaching views over the rooftops of Westminster, and serves an eclectic menu and cocktails.

Fortnum & Mason, *181 Piccadilly, W1A 1ER. Piccadilly Circus. 0845 300 1707. www.fortnumandmason.co.uk.* This internationally famous purveyor of fine products, established in 1707, operates several restaurants in which to savour afternoon tea.

The Ritz, *150 Piccadilly, W1J 9BR. Green Park. 020 7493 8181; 020 7300 2345 (tea reservations). www.theritzlondon.com. Tea served daily at 11.30am, 1.30pm, 3.30pm, 5.30pm and 7.30pm (booking essential).* To join the illustrious in the English ritual of afternoon tea – Chaplin, De Gaulle, King Edward VII – in the magical Louis XVI lounge, you'll need to reserve six weeks in advance.

SHOPPING

Hatchards Booksellers, *187 Piccadilly, W1J 9LE. Piccadilly Circus. 020 7439 9921. www.hatchards.co.uk.* This large, traditional bookshop is the official book supplier to Her Majesty the Queen. The five floors cover all subjects.

Waterstone's Booksellers, *203–206 Piccadilly, W1J 9HD. Piccadilly Circus. 0843 290 8549. www.waterstones.co.uk.* Occupying 6 floors of an attractive listed 1930s building, this is reputedly the largest bookshop in London. It has a good national and international press section.

One of London's most affluent areas, this is also one of the city's least touristy. Despite being home to attractions such as Madame Tussaud's, this upscale area with fantastic shopping is mostly focused on the needs of its residents, including the numerous businesses and embassies located along its streets and around its squares. That said, it is also one of London's most attractive neighbourhoods, and a walk around its beautiful architecture is extremely rewarding.

A Bit of Geography

Regent's Park is located to the North of the city centre and just west of King's Cross and Euston. The park has the shape of a slightly squashed circle and is bordered by Marylebone to its south and west. Immediately south of the park is Marylebone Road, off which run Baker Street and Portland Place, both heading south towards Oxford Street; Portland Place is also the eastern boundary of the area; beyond here is Bloomsbury. Edgware Road runs along the area's western edge, providing a border with Paddington. On the southern side of Oxford Street is Mayfair, running down to Piccadilly in the South. Regent Street divides the wider streets of this well-to-do area from the narrower, more down-at-heel streets of Soho, while to the West, Park Lane marks the end of Mayfair and the beginning of Hyde Park. Attractions here are relatively spread out but the area's numerous squares provide plenty of places to rest.

Highlights

1. Window shop in **Mayfair** (p122)
2. Get snapped with the celebrities at **Madame Tussaud's** (p127)
3. Stroll in **Regent's Park** (p129)
4. Meet the animals at **London Zoo** (p131)
5. Hear the sound of leather on willow at **Lord's Cricket Ground** (p132)

A Bit of History

Marylebone was the site of Tyburn manor, which appears in the Domesday Book *(1086)* and got its name from a small stream which flowed from here into the Thames, along the path of what is now Marylebone Lane. In the 16C the northern part of the estate was enclosed by Henry VIII as a deer park; it later became Regent's Park. The southern half passed through the hands of various noblemen. Many of the street names reflect past landowners and most of the area is retained by these families today. The name "Marylebone" is a contraction of the 15C parish church St Mary by the Bourne, which was located at the top of what is now Marylebone High Street; St Marylebone Parish Church stands on the site.

Regent's Park

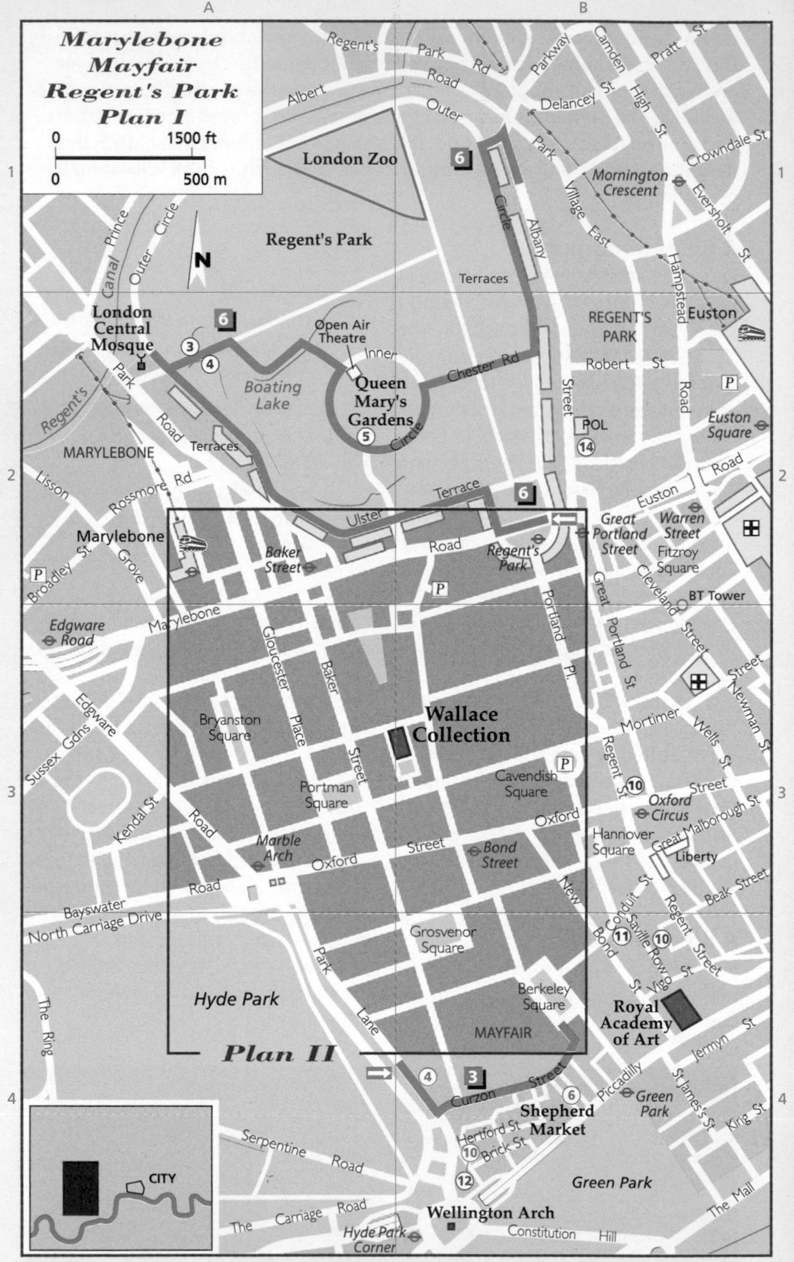

Mayfair was once rolling green fields, but was bought by the Grosvenor and Berkeley families in the mid-17C. They built a fashionable residential neighbourhood on the land throughout the 18C, developing the series of squares surrounded by elegant townhouses, which remain today. Mayfair's name comes from the annual fortnight-long fair, which was held here each May from 1686 until 1764, when it moved to Bow.

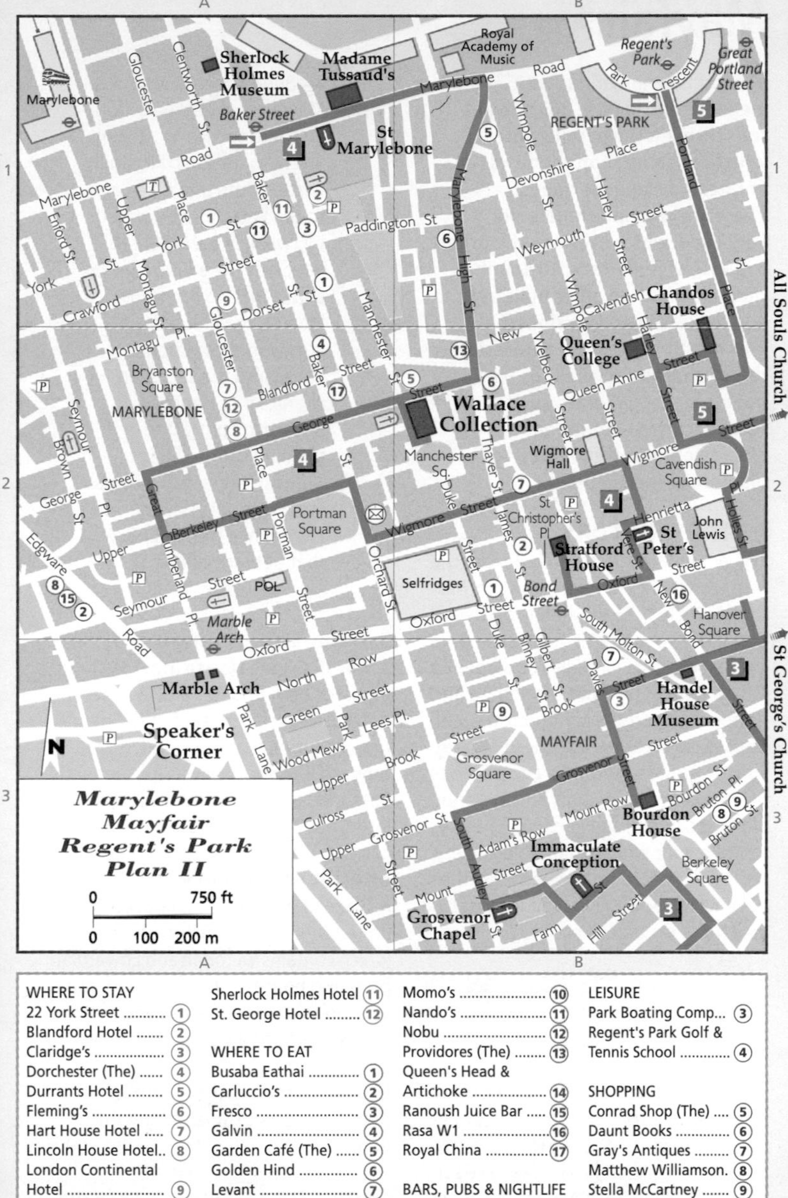

The Area Today

These are two of London's most genteel districts, with a quiet air of sophisticated grandeur palpable in both. Marylebone, now rebranded as Marylebone Village, is a fashionable area full of boutiques and upmarket restaurants, while Mayfair is home to some of London's most attractive squares (especially Grosvenor and Berkeley) and the city's most upmarket shopping street, Bond Street.

Mayfair★

Mayfair is synonymous with elegance and luxury; Bond Street runs through the middle, agleam with handsome shop windows full of rare and exquisite goods. There are luxurious hotels along Park Lane, which overlook the green expanse of Hyde Park. Although there are modern office buildings and the Georgian mansions are now mostly offices and embassies, the area retains its prestige with numerous art galleries, auction houses, casinos, boutiques and restaurants frequented by glamorous society people.

Location: Map pp120–121. ⊖*Bond Street; Green Park.* Mayfair is edged by Oxford Street to the North, Regent Street to the East, Piccadilly to the South and Park Lane to the West; and bordered by two vast parks: Green Park and Hyde Park.

Don't Miss: Shepherd Market, the affluent atmosphere of Bond Street and the secluded character of Hanover Square in contrast to bustling Oxford Street.

Timing: Allow half a day to stroll through Mayfair, and experience the sheer luxury that pervades the area.

A BIT OF HISTORY

The name Mayfair is derived from the fair, which was held annually in May until 1706. In 1735 the architect Edward Shepherd took a 999-year lease on a site just north of Piccadilly and opened a food market. Around the square and dependent streets he erected small houses, so creating Shepherd Market. Large squares were the centrepiece of vast estates; elegant streets lined with Georgian mansions and houses found favour with fashionable society. Artisans' mews houses and stables have now been converted into desirable homes.

WALKING TOUR 3

Start in Park Lane.

Once a winding road on the edge of **Hyde Park**, **Park Lane** is now an eight-lane highway. At the north end a few houses with graceful balconies have survived; elsewhere the town residences of local estate owners have been replaced by hotels: the **Grosvenor House** *(1930)*, the **Dorchester** *(1930)*, the **London Hilton** *(1960s)*, the **InterContinental**.

Walk down Curzon St.

Curzon Street, part residential and part commercial, is lined with 18C houses at the Park Lane end. **Disraeli** died in 1881 at **no. 19 Crewe House** (**no. 15**), standing back behind gates and lawns is the only surviving example of an 18C gentleman's London mansion. Built in 1730 by **Edward Shepherd**, it was subsequently extended to its present seven bays, with large, bow-fronted wings at either end.

Shepherd Market★

A maze of alleyways and paved courts linked by archways forms the market, which contains Victorian and Edwardian pubs and houses with small shop fronts serving as pavement cafés and antique shops. It retains a village atmosphere.

Return to Curzon St., turn left onto Chesterfield St. and right on Charles St.

Charles Street contains several gracious 18C houses, some remodelled in the 19C, such as **no. 37**; there is a small 19C–20C pub in a cobbled yard at the end.

Berkeley Square

The square, lined with 200-year-old plane trees, was laid out in 1737. On its west side a few 18C houses with ironwork balconies, lamp holders at the steps and torch snuffers survive: the façade of **no. 52** is in Charles Street; stone-faced and pedimented **nos. 46** and **45** have balustraded balconies on their first floors.

Leave the square on Hill St. and turn right into Farm St.

The **Church of the Immaculate Conception**, the 1844–49 church of the Jesuit community, has a fine high altar by **Pugin** *(open daily 7am–6.30pm; 020 7493 7811)*.

Continue onto South St. then turn right onto South Audley St.

South Audley Street

The **Grosvenor Chapel** *(1739)* has a distinctive Tuscan portico, square quoined tower and octagonal turret. The garden became the burial ground of St George's Hanover Square *(see below; open Mon, Tues, Thur, Fri 9am–1pm; 020 7499 1684; www.grosvenorchapel.org.uk)*. Purdeys, the gun and riflemakers at **no. 57**, established in 1881, bears the royal coat of arms above the door.

A leisurely air pervades **Mount Street**, lined by tall, gabled terra-cotta brick houses of 1888 and 1893. At street level, window after window displays antique furniture, Lalique glass, porcelain, pictures and Oriental screens.

Grosvenor Square

The square *(1725)*, one of London's largest, was redesigned in the 20C. The original circular garden is now square with a memorial to **Franklin Roosevelt** and a monument to the RAF American squadrons.

The first American resident (at **no. 9**) was **John Adams**, the first Minister to Britain and later President. For several decades the neo-Georgian buildings to the North, East and South were almost all US State Department offices, while the 1960 listed building designed by Eero Saarinen, which dominates the entire western side, is home to the US Embassy. Today, the embassy is making plans to move to a more secure site in Wandsworth; the building has been purchased by a Qatari company.

Leave the square via Grosvenor St. and turn left onto Davies St.

Davies Street runs north from Berkeley Square to Oxford Street. At **no. 2** stands **Bourdon House**, built in 1723–25 as a manor-house amid fields and orchards.

Turn right into Brook St. past Gray's Antique Market and across New Bond St.

Hanover Square

A bronze statue of **William Pitt** graces the spacious square, which was laid out c.1715 as part of a large estate, which included a parish church.

Leave the square via St George St. and turn right onto Maddox St.

St George's Church

Open Mon–Fri 8am–4pm, Wed till 6pm, Sun 8am–noon. Handel Festival (Apr–May). 020 7629 0874. www.stgeorgeshanoversquare.org.

The church *(1721–24)* is a distinctive landmark, with its portico projecting across the pavement flanked by two cast-iron game dogs. The interior is white and the reredos is from the workshop of Grinling Gibbons, framing a painting of *The Last Supper* by William Kent *(1724)*. Since it was first built, the church has been renowned for its society weddings, including Shelley's, Benjamin Disraeli's and Teddy Roosevelt's.

Bond Street★

Bisecting Mayfair from north to south is Bond Street. The area around **Old Bond Street** was developed first. **New Bond Street** was constructed in 1720 and soon boasted such residents as (Lord) Nelson, Byron, Boswell and Beau Brummell. Bond Street soon became renowned for retailing elegance, the unique and the luxurious. It is lined with specialist shops offering handmade leather goods *(Hermès, Louis Vuitton, Loewe, Gucci)*,

New Bond Street

© C. Eymenier/Michelin

stationery *(Smythsons)*, perfume and toiletries *(Fenwick)*, antique furniture and fine art *(Bond Street Antique Centre, Wildenstein, Partridge, Fine Art Society, Mallett)*, not forgetting haute couture *(Betty Barclay, Cerruti, Louis Féraud, Guy Laroche, Lanvin, Ballantyne, Max Mara, Valentino, Céline, Yves St Laurent)*.

At **no. 35** is **Sotheby's**, which began in 1744 as a book auctioneer and is now the biggest art auctioneer globally – the first big sale on 9 February 1798 was of Marie Antoinette's pictures. Nearby are art and antique dealers.

Beyond the bronze group of Churchill and Roosevelt extends **Old Bond Street★**, lined with well-established institutions specialising in fine porcelain, jewellery and watches *(Cartier, Tiffany, Boucheron, Asprey & Garrard)*, Antiques and fine art *(Agnew, Marlborough Fine Art, Colnaghi)*.

▶ Take Royal Arcade to Albemarle St.

Several gracious 18C houses still survive in **Albemarle Street,** for instance **no. 21**, which is now occupied by the **Royal Institution** (f. 1799) and the **Faraday Museum** *(Mon–Fri 9am–6pm; ☎ 020 7409 2992; www.rigb.org)*, where you can explore over 200 years of science and discover Michael Faraday's original laboratories (from 1799).

ADDRESSES

SHOPPING

Oxford Street, London's main shopping street, is home to the flagship stores of dozens of high street brands.

Bond Street: the boutiques of international fashion designers such as Chanel, Gucci, Louis Vuitton, Ralph Lauren and Prada are concentrated here.

South Molton Street: an attractive precinct lined with fashion boutiques.

Savile Row: the home of tailoring since the 19C, Savile Row is lined with small bespoke tailors who can make you the perfect suit or made-to-measure shirt.

Matthew Williamson, *28 Bruton St. ⊖Green Park. ☎020 7629 6200, www.matthewwilliamson.com. Mon–Sat 10am–6pm (Thur 7pm).* Matthew Williamson is known for colourful prints and glamorous, yet feminine tailoring.

Stella McCartney, *30 Bruton St. ⊖Green Park. ☎020 7518 3100, www.stellamccartney.com. Mon–Sat 10am–6pm (Thur 7pm).* The creations of talented Stella are not within reach of every budget, but the store is worth a look, even if only to windowshop.

Vivienne Westwood, *44 Conduit St., W1S 2LY. ⊖Piccadilly Circus. ☎020 7439 1109. www.viviennewestwood.co.uk.* The designer who brought respectability to punk still displays tremendous talent and extravagance plus an exquisite eye for tailoring. Menswear store at 18 Conduit St.

Marylebone★

The appeal of Marylebone is in the contrast between the intense activity along Oxford Street and the calm atmosphere of the dignified squares lined with attractive buildings. Famous department stores, elegant outlets along Wigmore Street and tiny shops in quaint alleyways make for a shopper's paradise. Marylebone High Street itself is lined with high-end shops. There's more to the area than shopping: there are splendid 18C mansions built for high society; one now houses a museum *(The Wallace Collection)* **and another is used as an exclusive club** *(Stratford House)*. **Harley Street is famous as a centre of medical expertise, and cultural interest is provided by Broadcasting House, the home of the BBC, and Wigmore Hall.**

- **Location:** Map pp120–121. ⊖ *Baker St; Regent's Park; Bond Street.* The main thoroughfares are Oxford Street, Wigmore Street, Portland Place and Regent Street, Baker Street and Marylebone Road.
- **Don't Miss:** The Wallace Collection (*see MAJOR CENTRAL LONDON MUSEUMS*), the department stores on Oxford St.
- **Timing:** mid-morning and mid-afternoon are the best times to shop on Oxford Street, when it is less crowded.

A BIT OF HISTORY

The only remaining traces of St Marylebone village are Marylebone High St and Marylebone Lane, which followed the winding course of the Tyburn River. The land was confiscated by **Henry VIII**, who built a hunting lodge.

On old maps **Oxford Street★** appears variously as Tyburn Road, Uxbridge Road and Oxford Road. A turnpike just before the junction with Park Lane marked the western limit of what soon became London's prime shopping street.

Cavendish Square was developed early in the 18C. By the end of the century St Marylebone village and the surrounding wasteland was covered by the most complete grid layout of streets in any area of London. In 1756 Marylebone Road was created to link the City directly to Paddington and west London.

WALKING TOUR

4 NORTH OF OXFORD ST★

Start from Baker St. Station (the Sherlock Holmes Museum, *see Additional Sights*, is just north of the station) and walk along Marylebone Rd. past Madame Tussaud's (*see Additional Sights*).

Marylebone Road is a six-lane highway, bordered by several buildings of interest. On the north side is the **Royal Academy of Music** accommodated in an attractive building *(1911)* in red brick and stone, with a large, elaborately decorated pediment.

Across the road is the early 19C **St Marylebone Church** by Thomas Hardwick, a large balustraded building with a three-stage tower ending in gilded caryatids upholding the cupola. The pedimented Corinthian portico was added by **Nash. Elizabeth Barrett** and **Robert Browning** were secretly married in the church in 1846. A sculptured panel commemorates **Charles Dickens**, who lived in a house on the site *(♿ leaflet in 6 languages; ☎020 7935 7315; www.stmarylebone.org).*

Turn right onto Marylebone High St., then right into George St. and left into Spanish Pl.

Manchester Square

This elegant square, surrounded with late Georgian houses, developed to the South of Manchester House from 1776. The house served as residence

to the Spanish ambassador and then to his French counterparts *(Talleyrand and Guizot, among others)*. In 1872 the house was bought by **Richard Wallace, Marquess of Hertford**, who renamed it **Hertford House** and remodelled it entirely to display the **Wallace Collection★★★** *(see MAJOR CENTRAL LONDON MUSEUMS)*.

Return to George St., turn left and cross Baker St. and Gloucester Pl.

On your right are two early-19C squares, **Montagu Square**, notable for its houses with shallow, ground-floor bow windows – at **no. 39** lived the novelist Anthony **Trollope** *(1873–80)* – and **Bryanston Square**, graced with long stucco terraces.

Turn left onto Great Cumberland Pl. and left again into Upper Berkeley St.

At the northwest corner of **Portman Square★** are two fine houses (**nos. 20–21**). **No. 20** *(1772–77)* is by **Robert Adam**.

Leave the square via Wigmore St.

Wigmore Hall

36 Wigmore St. 020 7935 2141. www.wigmore-hall.org.uk.

The concert hall, famed for its intimate atmosphere conducive to chamber music and solo recitals, borrows its name from the street.

Turn right on Wimpole St. and right again into Henrietta Pl.

St Peter's

Vere St. Open Mon–Fri 9am–5pm. Guidebook. 020 7399 9555. www.licc.org.uk

This attractive small, dark brick building *(1721–24)*, designed by the architect **James Gibbs**, may have been an experimental model for St Martin-in-the-Fields *(see TRAFALGAR SQUARE)*. The unexpectedly spacious interior includes galleries supported on giant Corinthian columns with massive entablatures. The quite lovely stained-glass windows were designed by **Edward Coley Burne-Jones** and made by **William Morris & Co** at their Queen's Square premises.

Continue on Henrietta Pl., turn left onto Marylebone Lane and right onto Oxford St.

Stratford Place is a quiet cul-de-sac closed at its north end by **Stratford House** (now the **Oriental Club**), an imposing mansion designed in 1773 in the Palladian style.

Further on is **St Christopher's Place**, a narrow pedestrian passage restored to its Victorian appearance and well known for its outdoor cafés and small specialist shops. This is a great place for lunch, if shopping on Oxford Street.

5 SOUTH OF PORTLAND PLACE

Start from Regent's Park Station, walking south along Portland Place.

Portland Place

In the 18C the street was a fashionable promenade; the north end was closed by gates; both sides were lined by houses designed by **Robert and James Adam**; its width was dictated by the façade of Foley House at the south end *(replaced in 1864 by the Langham Hotel)*.

Only one **(no. 46)** of the Adam houses has survived. The tall stone corner building (**no. 66**)was erected in 1934 to celebrate the centenary of the **Royal Institute of British Architects** (**RIBA**). Note the distinctive curved front of **Broadcasting House**, home to BBC Radio *(1931)*.

All Souls Church

Open Mon–Fri 9.30am–5.30pm; Sun 9am–2pm, 5.30pm–8.30pm. 020 7580 3522. www.allsouls.org.

The church was designed by **John Nash** as a pivot between Portland Place and Regent Street. Its unique feature, a circular portico of tall Ionic pillars, surmounted by a ring of columns supporting a fluted spire, was designed to look the same from whatever angle it was approached.

Take Portland Pl. opposite and turn right into Chandos St.

At the north end of **Chandos St.**, facing south, stands the perfectly proportioned **Chandos House** *(1771)*, designed by **Robert Adam**. It is built of Portland stone and the only embellishments are a narrow frieze above the second floor, the square porch and the 18C iron railings.

Turn left into Queen Anne St. and left again into Harley St. south.

Harley Street is an architectural mixture, dating from the original Georgian to the present. The Tuscan pillared stucco portico (**nos. 43–49**) is the entrance to **Queen's College**, the oldest English school for girls.
Before it was monopolised by the medical profession, Harley Street was home to many eminent figures, notably **Wellington** *(11)*, **Florence Nightingale** *(47)* and **Turner** *(64)*.

Cavendish Square

On the north side of the square *(1717)* stands a pair of stone-faced Palladian houses of the 1770s *(opposite John Lewis)*; these are now linked by a bridge designed by Louis Osman *(1914–96)* against which stands a moving composition of the *Madonna and Child* by **Jacob Epstein** *(1950)*. There are late-18C and 19C houses, much altered, along the east side; **no. 5** was the home of Nelson in 1787. Where John Lewis, the department store, now stands used to be the house where Lord Byron was born *(1788)*.

Leave the square to the South via Holles St. to return to Oxford St.
A piece by British sculptor Barbara Hepworth, Winged Figure, is on the side wall of John Lewis.

Oxford Street★

Oxford Street, stretching west to **Marble Arch** and **Hyde Park★★★** beyond, is the main shopping centre of London, with major shops including **Selfridges** *(opened in 1908)*, **John Lewis**, **House of Fraser**, **Debenhams** and **Marks and Spencer**; just round the corner in Regent Street is **Hamleys**, the world's finest toy shop. Eastwards, this major thoroughfare becomes **New Oxford Street** and stretches to Bloomsbury.

ADDITIONAL SIGHTS

Madame Tussaud's★

⊖Baker Street. Advance booking recommended, especially in high season. ♿ Open Mon–Fri 9.30am–5.30pm, Sat–Sun and during peak times 9am–6pm. Closed 25 Dec. £30 (online £22.50). Brochure (5 languages). 0871 894 3000. www.madametussauds.com.

Marie Grosholtz *(1761–1850)* acquired her modelling skills from Philippe Curtius, a doctor and talented modeller who mixed with the French aristocracy. For nine years she was employed at Versailles as an art tutor and later narrowly escaped the guillotine. She survived the French Revolution by taking death masks of its victims, many of whom she had known personally. In 1802, she emigrated with her two children to England and toured the country before settling in at the Baker Street Bazaar. The waxworks moved to their present site in 1884.
Figures are arranged by theme in separate exhibitions and are regularly updated to reflect changing times. **A-List Party** and **Premiere Night** allow visitors to mingle and be photographed with contemporary rich and famous personalities drawn from the "showbiz" worlds of entertainment and sport. The politicians, from Gandhi to Barack Obama, are gathered in the **World Leaders** section.
The **Culture Zone** presents some of the world's best known scientists, artists and writers. Downstairs, the **Chamber of Horrors**, which should be by-passed by the very young and faint-hearted, lines up famous murderers and serial killers in your path.
The **Spirit of London** is a dark ride *(5min)* in a simulated black London taxi cab on a whirlwind tour of the history of

© L. Maisant/hemis.fr

Statue of Sherlock Holmes in front of Baker Street Station

London, but at a gentle enough pace to make it suitable for children.

Interactive exhibition **Music Megastars** offers you the chance to become a singing star for the day, or star in a Beatles' album cover. Finish on a light note and watch the auditorium's new experience, **The Marvel Superheroes 4D Experience** in the Stardome next door, with high impact special effects.

Sherlock Holmes Museum

Open daily 9.30am–6pm. Closed 25 Dec. £6. Brochure (7 languages). 020 7224 3688. www.sherlock-holmes.co.uk. The interior of 221b Baker Street, a fine-looking narrow townhouse built in 1815, has been arranged as described in the novels by **Sir Arthur Conan Doyle**: note in particular the familiar pipes and deerstalker hat, the magnifying glass, telescope and field-glasses, the chemical apparatus and copies of *The Times*, as well as photos and paintings of the period.

ADDRESSES

LIGHT BITE

Fresco, *31 Paddington St. Baker Street. 020 7221 2355. www.frescojuices.co.uk. Mon–Sat 8am–10.30pm, Sun 9am–10.30pm.* Worth visiting for its excellent fresh juices, this juice bar also does great sandwiches, falafel and mezze. Take away or eat in the small bright dining room.

Golden Hind, *73 Marylebone Lane. Bond Street. 020 7486 3644. Mon–Sat noon–3pm, 6pm–10pm.* This veteran of the fish and chips scene has been dishing up crispy battered fish since 1914. Supplies arrive fresh from Grimsby daily; try the haddock, rock or plaice with a large portion of chips and mushy peas. BYO alcohol.

Ranoush Juice Bar, *43 Edgware Rd., Marble Arch. 020 7723 5929. Daily 9am–3am.* Fast food-style Lebanese cuisine and fresh juices.

PUB

The Barley Mow, *8 Dorset St. Baker Street. 07967 484 596. Mon–Sat 11am–11pm, Sun noon–10.30pm.* This quaint pub situated on a quiet street is one of the oldest in the area *(1791)* and exudes a certain village charm.

NIGHTLIFE

Salt Whisky Bar, *82 Seymour St. Marble Arch. 020 7402 1155. www.saltbar.com. Mon–Sat noon–1am, Sun noon–12.30am.* Whisky connoisseurs will love this chic bar-lounge, which offers no fewer than 200 varieties of the stuff, drunk straight or in cocktails. Good wine (and champagne) list too. DJ every night.

SHOPPING

The Conran Shop, *55 Marylebone High St. Baker Street. 020 7723 2223. www.conranshop.co.uk. Mon–Fri 10am–6pm (Thur 7pm), Sat 10am–6.30pm, Sun 11am–5pm.* Furniture and interior design from reputed British designer Terence Conran.

Daunt Books, *83 Marylebone High St. Baker Street, 020 7224 2295. www.dauntbooks.co.uk. Mon–Sat 9am–7.30pm, Sun 11am–6pm.* This Edwardian-style bookshop, with its long, panelled gallery topped by a canopy, is one of the most beautiful in the capital. Its wide selection of guides and travel books makes it a must for globetrotters.

Regent's Park★★★

The harmonious composition of the park – orignally known as Marylebone Park – is a unique achievement, combining nature and artistic flair. Bounded by Regent's Canal to the North, the park is surrounded by dazzling terraces and villas.
Visitors young and old enjoy the attractions of the Zoo. The fragrant rose garden, the spirited performances at the open-air theatre and band music in the park are highlights of the summer season. The superb amenities include a boating lake and tennis courts.

Location: Map pp120–121. ⊖*Regent's Park; Great Portland Street; Baker St.* Regent's Park can also be reached by boat or bus from Camden Town *(⊖Camden Town)*, famous for its markets, and by boat from Little Venice *(Bloomfield Rd., ⊖Warwick Avenue)*. To the North and West are the desirable residential areas of Primrose Hill and St John's Wood.

Timing: At least half a day, including 3–4hr at the Zoo.

Kids: The London Zoo, with its Sumatran tigers, Squirrel Monkeys, megabugs and meerkats.

A BIT OF HISTORY

The Proposal – In 1811, **Nash** was commissioned to draw up a plan to make use of former royal hunting grounds in the Marylebone area and build a direct route from north London to Westminster. He devised a tree-landscaped park with a serpentine lake bounded by a road along which, on all except the north side, was to be left open for the view of Primrose Hill and the heights of Hampstead and Highgate. There would be a series of terrace-palaces for the noble and fashionable. Within the park would be a circus, ringed by houses; elsewhere would be a summer pavilion for the Prince of Wales, approached along a wide avenue *(the Broad Walk)* on an axis with Portland Place. Numerous other villas were planned to nestle, half-hidden, among the trees, while the central feature would be the proposed Regent's Canal.

The Constraints – Portland Place, a successful speculation begun by the Adam brothers in 1774, consisted of a private road lined by substantial mansions and closed at the south end by Foley House, whose owner insisted on an uninterrupted view, thereby dictating the street's 125ft/38m width. Between the place and park ran New Road *(Marylebone Road)*, a psychological barrier that bisected the area. Portland Place, which Nash greatly admired, would be extended south across Oxford Street and Piccadilly to arrive at Carlton House. The section south of Oxford Circus would be lined with a continuous arcade of shops sheltered by colonnades, with balconied houses above.

The Realisation – In essence, the plan survived, though the pleasure garden never materialised, nor did seven of the planned villas. However, an Inner Circle was laid out as a botanic garden, which has been transformed into the **Queen Mary's Gardens**.

The approach from Portland Place was modified to form the open-armed Park Crescent and Park Square. The extension south from Portland Place was given a pivoted turn by the construction of the circular porch of All Souls and the angle at the south beautifully swept round by means of the Quadrant. The project took eight years to complete *(1817–25)*.

New Street, as it was at first called, was a fashionable success; the houses along the park were snapped up. Nash himself probably designed only a few of the **terraces★★**, houses and shops, but he set the style sufficiently explicitly for different architects to draw up plans. Giant columns, generally Ionic or Corinthian, are used throughout to articulate the centre and ends of the long façades which, in addition, were usually advanced and sometimes pedimented. Columns of a different order formed arcades; balustrades and continuous first-floor balconies of iron or stucco ran the length of the long fronts, uniting them into single compositions. In 1828 **London Zoo★★** opened on the north side of the Park beside the canal.

WALKING TOUR

6 TERRACES★★

Start from ⊖Regent's Park Station.

Park Crescent *(1821)*, which surrounds the station, is characterised by paired Ionic columns in a continuous porch, a balustrade and a balcony which emphasise the classical curve of the Crescent. The **East and West** *(1823–24)* buildings which flank **Park Square** are embellished by single Ionic columns.

The **terraces** are named after the titles of some of George III's 15 children. Beyond Ulster Terrace lies **York Terrace** *(1821; west end now named* **Nottingham Terrace***)*, which is 360yd/329m long (nearly half the width of the park) and comprises two symmetrical blocks, York Gate in the axis of St Marylebone Church (*see MARYLEBONE*) and some detached houses.

The attractive **Cornwall Terrace** *(1822)* has a 187yd/170m front that is marked at either end and in the centre by Corinthian columns and divided into a number of receding planes. Note the lodge with rounded windows and pitched slate roof. **Clarence Terrace** *(1823)* boasts a heavily accented Corinthian centre and angles above an Ionic arcade. Notable features of **Sussex Place** (1822; **London Graduate School of Business Studies**) include the most surprising, finialled, slim, octagonal cupolas in pairs, crowning the ends and framing the pedimented centre of the terrace.

Hanover Terrace *(1822–23)* is marked by pediments coloured bright blue as a background to plasterwork and serving as pedestals for statuary silhouetted against the sky. Hanover Gate has a small, octagonal lodge with heavy, inverted corbel decoration and niches with statues beneath a pitched slate roof and central octagonal chimney.

The **Mosque** *(1977)*, marked by its minaret *(140ft/43m high)*, white with a small gold coloured dome and finial crescent, stands on the site of one of Nash's villas *(Albany Cottage)* and was designed by **Sir Frederick Gibberd**. Other new buildings accommodate a school and the Islamic Cultural Centre.

Hanover Lodge, one of the 18C villas, has a large modern brick addition; note the row of three modern villas alongside and across the Outer Circle, a neo-Georgian house *(1936)*: **Winfield House**, now residence of the US Ambassador.

The **boating lake**, which curves picturesquely around the Inner Circle, is a popular spot for sport and recreation. There are boats and deckchairs for hire and live bands in the summer.

Inner Circle

The **Open Air Theatre** *(℘0844 826 4242; www.openairtheatre.com)* presents a summer season of open-air performances of plays by Shakespeare and other playwrights; also popular musicals.

The Holme is one of the 18C villas.

Regent's College is on the site of South Villa and St John's Lodge, rebuilt and enlarged last century in red brick.

Queen Mary's Gardens were created out of the original Botanic Garden and are a delightful haven. **The Rose Garden**, filled with heady perfumes in summer, is very romantic.

Leave the Inner Circle via Chester Rd and walk along Broad Walk to the Outer Circle.

Outer Circle

The southern section of the park is flanked by the **Avenue Gardens**, which were relaid according to the designs prepared by William Andrews Nesfield in

1862. A tesserae-faced building by Denys Lasdun extending squarely forward is the home of the **Royal College of Physicians** *(1964)*.

Cambridge Gate *(1875)* is a Victorian, stone-faced block with pavilion roofs; the adjacent **Cambridge Terrace**, dating from 1825, has been restored.

The longest unbroken façade *(313yds/286m)* of **Chester Terrace** *(1825)* has Corinthian columns rising from ground level to emphasise the ends, centre and mid-points between; at either end triumphal named arches lead to the access road to the rear.

The Ionic pillars of the façade *(267yd/242m long)* of **Cumberland Terrace** *(1826)* recur in the intervening arches. Britannia, science and the arts are represented in the central pedim ent behind squat vases. Angle pediments with plasterwork against red-painted tympana and surmounting statues mark the main terrace of **Gloucester Gate** *(1827)*.

Pass through the gate and make a short detour to Albany St.

Park Village West, *Albany Street.* This attractive street is lined with small houses and modest terraces in Nash's country cottage style, although they were not designed by him.

LONDON ZOO★★

Open daily from 10am, closing time varies; roughly Mar–mid-Jul and Sept–Oct 5.30pm; Jul & Aug 6pm; Oct–Feb 4pm. Last admission 1hr before closing. Closed 25 Dec. winter £20 adult, £15.50 child; peak season £24 adult, £17 child. Restaurant, refreshments. 0844 225 1826. www.zsl.org.

The Zoological Society of London (ZSL), founded in 1826 by Sir Stamford Raffles (of Singapore fame) and Sir Humphry Davy, opened two years later on a site *(5 acres/2ha)* in Regent's Park with a small collection of animals looked after by a keeper in a top hat and striped waistcoat. The first big cats came from the menagerie at the Tower of London *(closed by William IV)*; the first giraffes, unloaded in the Docklands, were led through the City to Regent's Park *(May 1836)*. During World War II, the most dangerous animals were destroyed in case the zoo was bombed. Today, the zoo's objective is to promote international conservation efforts to save rare species around the world. ZSL (which runs London Zoo and Whipsnade Zoo) cooperates in European and global breeding programmes for rare animals. The zoo's architecture reflects its long History.

The **Aquarium** was built in 1853 and was the first of its kind in the world; the **Reptile House** was built in 1902.

The iconic **Berthold Lubetkin Penguin Pool** (1934), although no longer home to the penguins, is a Grade I listed building, while the **Casson Pavilion** (built in 1961) is a classic of its kind; the roof was designed to mimic the watering hole of the elephants it used to house. The rhinos and elephants have now been moved to greener pastures at Whipsnade. In March 2013 a flagship exhibit called **Tiger Territory** opened, home to Jae Jae and Melati, a pair of Sumatran tigers. The exhibit features high feeding poles to encourage the tigers' natural predatory behaviour and tall trees for them to scale. You can see them hanging out in their custom-built pool, or relaxing on heated rocks in their indoor dens. Tiger Territory means that ZSL can breed the critically endangered tigers and try to reverse the bleak fate of these animals. Other popular zoo exhibits include **Gorilla Kingdom, Butterfly Paradise, Rainforest Life** and Komodo dragons. **Penguin Beach** is England's biggest penguin exhibit, housing more than 50 of the birds.

Domestic animals are presented at close quarters in the revamped children's zoo, **Animal Adventure,** which also has underground and water zones. Children love the high jinks in the Meet the Monkeys area and the Meerkats. Rainforest Life re-creates a South American rain forest through which visitors can wander at canopy and floor levels.

The **B.U.G.S** exhibit is devoted to biodiversity and conservation of invertebrates. Other recent additions include two walk-through exhibits: the **Butter-**

fly Paradise, with clouds of free-flying butterfly species, and the tropical birds in the restored Victorian bird house, the **Blackburn Pavilion**.

Danish Church

Open Tue–Fri 9am–1pm, Sat noon–3pm, Sun 10am–5pm. Keys available at 5 St Katherine's Precinct, Regent's Park. 020 7935 7584. www.danskekirke.org.

The neo-Gothic church *(1829)* in stock brick, built for the **St Katharine Royal Hospital Community** *(see East London: DOCKLANDS)*, was taken over in 1950 by the Danish community, whose own building in Limehouse had been bombed. Inside are a coffered ceiling and beside the modern fittings, John the Baptist and Moses, two of the four figures carved in wood by the 17C Danish sculptor **Caius Cibber** for Limehouse.

EXCURSIONS
ST JOHN'S WOOD

St John's Wood, west of the park, developed rapidly in the first half of the 19C as a residential district following the expansion of Marylebone and Nash's development of Regent's Park. Its rural character was swept aside as villas, broad-eaved and often in pairs, were erected.

St John's Wood Church

Lord's Roundabout. Open daily 9am–5pm. Concerts. 020 7586 3864. www.stjohnswoodchurch.org.uk.

The church is of the same date, 1813, and by the same architect, **Thomas Hardwick**, as **St Marylebone** Parish Church *(see MARYLEBONE)* and, similarly, has a distinctive, cupola-topped turret.

Lord's Cricket Ground

St John's Wood Road. Guided tour (inc museum) Mon–Sun noon & 2pm, weekends & Apr–Sep also 10am, 11am. Closed on match days, cup finals, preparation days and certain public holidays. £15. 020 7432 1000 (info), 020 7616 8595 (tours). www.lords.org.

Marylebone Cricket Club, which owns Lord's, began life in 1787. The first match MCC played at the original Lord's ground *(Dorset Fields)* was against Essex on 1 June 1787. The present ground was inaugurated with a match against Herts on 22 June 1814.

The first test matches at Lord's were played in 1884. The main gates were erected in memory of **Dr WG Grace** *(d. 1915)* in 1923; Father Time, removing the bails, was placed on the grandstand in 1926. The much-acclaimed **Mound Stand** combines various building techniques used between 1898 and 1987, while the futuristic Media Centre *(1999)* breaks new ground.

The best introduction to the ground is by guided tour through the famous **Long Room** in the Pavilion, the "real" tennis court, the Mound Stand and the **MCC Museum**, which was founded in memory of all the cricketers who lost their lives in World War I and displays the famous **Ashes**, along with other memorabilia, from batting lists to snuff boxes. The **Library** is perhaps the world's most important cricket archive.

Just around the corner from Lord's, up Grove End Road beyond the junction with **Abbey Road**, is the zebra crossing immortalised by the eponymous Beatles album recorded nearby.

ADDRESSES

LIGHT BITE

The Garden Café, *Inner Circle, Regent's Park. 020 7935 5729. Daily 9am–8pm (winter 4pm).* In the heart of the park, the café offers light meals all day.

ACTIVITIES

Regent's Park *0300 061 2300. www.royalparks.org.uk.* Sports in the park include football, rugby and cricket.

The Regent's Park Golf & Tennis School, *Outer Circle. 020 7724 0643. Daily 8am–9pm.* Tennis courts and a floodlit driving range.

Park Boating Company, *Boating Lake. April–Sep daily 10am–6pm.* Canoes and pedalos to rent. *£5.50/30min or £7.50/hr.*

Canal cruises – Short cruises on Regent's Canal between Little Venice and Camden Lock (*see PLANNING YOUR TRIP*).

London's political centre is a thriving part of the city. Filled with buildings of great significance to both the political and the royal apparatus of modern Britain, Westminster and the surrounding areas are the powerhouse of one of the world's oldest parliamentary democracies. Decisions affecting the city and the country which it serves are made here, so a walk around Westminster's streets is infused with a sense of significance few other urban areas can bestow. The area buzzes during the day as people from around the world visit parks, palaces and soak up the atmosphere, but as night falls the streets become significantly quieter as visitors and workers alike leave the area for the livelier neighbourhoods that border it. However, stick around and you'll find that the streets into which the corridors of power lead are home to a host of traditional English pubs in which to debate the day's events.

A Bit of Geography

Westminster stretches west away from Trafalgar Square on the north bank of the River Thames and is separated from the City of London by the leisure-oriented West End. Whitehall, lined with government offices along its length, runs parallel to the Thames and ends in Parliament Square, dominated by Big Ben and the Houses of Parliament. West of here the green lungs of St James's Park and Green Park lead to royal residence Buckingham Palace, while towards the South are the major railway terminus of Victoria and the leafy streets of upmarket Pimlico.

Highlights

1 Wonder at one of London's most beautiful and significant buildings, the **Houses of Parliament** (p137)

2 Overhear political debate in a traditional Whitehall **pub** (p143)

3 Follow in Prince William's footsteps down the aisle of **Westminster Abbey** (p144)

4 Tour **Buckingham Palace** (p151)

5 Relax in **St James's Park** (p153)

A Bit of History

There has been an abbey on the site of Westminster Abbey for over one thousand years, since Benedictine monks first established a site for daily worship here in the middle of the 10C. It is the abbey that gives the surrounding area its name. Derived from the moniker "the West Minster", the name was intended to differentiate the Abbey from St Paul's in the City of London.

The core of Westminster is built on the former Thorney Island and was initially developed as a distinct area from the

Ceremonial mounting of the Queen's Life Guard, Horse Guards

© London on View

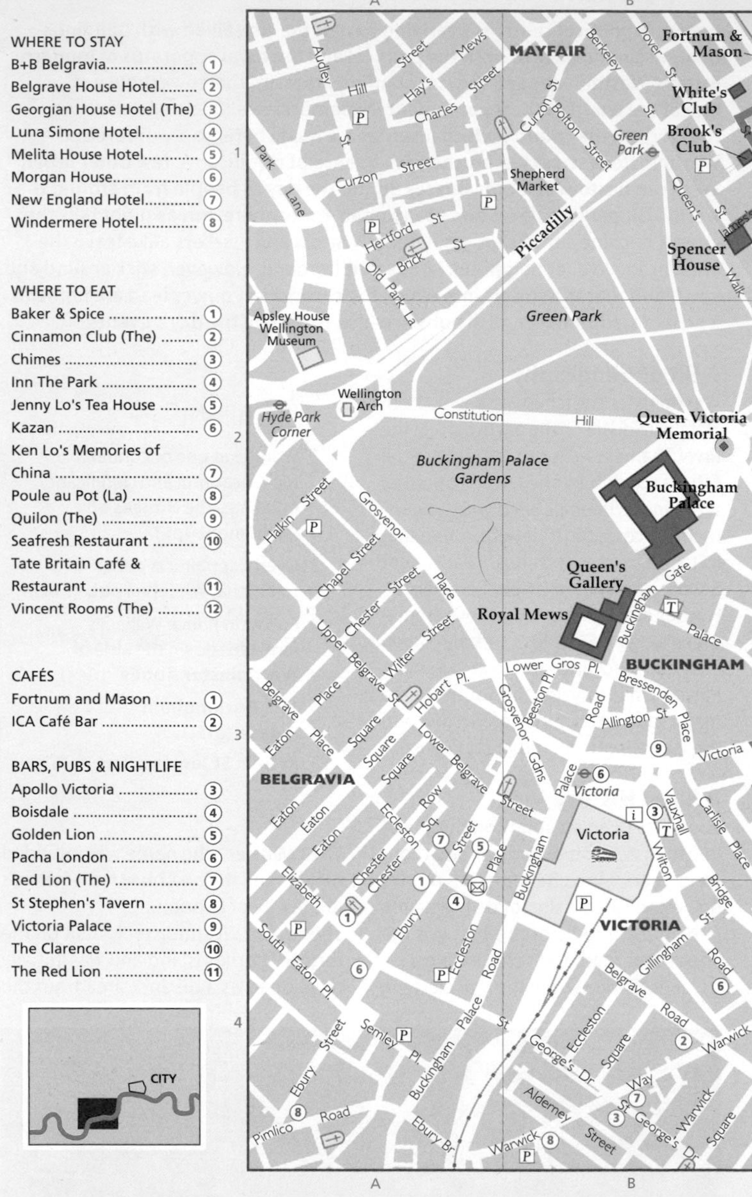

WHERE TO STAY

- B+B Belgravia .... ①
- Belgrave House Hotel .... ②
- Georgian House Hotel (The) ③
- Luna Simone Hotel .... ④
- Melita House Hotel .... ⑤
- Morgan House .... ⑥
- New England Hotel .... ⑦
- Windermere Hotel .... ⑧

WHERE TO EAT

- Baker & Spice .... ①
- Cinnamon Club (The) .... ②
- Chimes .... ③
- Inn The Park .... ④
- Jenny Lo's Tea House .... ⑤
- Kazan .... ⑥
- Ken Lo's Memories of China .... ⑦
- Poule au Pot (La) .... ⑧
- Quilon (The) .... ⑨
- Seafresh Restaurant .... ⑩
- Tate Britain Café & Restaurant .... ⑪
- Vincent Rooms (The) .... ⑫

CAFÉS

- Fortnum and Mason .... ①
- ICA Café Bar .... ②

BARS, PUBS & NIGHTLIFE

- Apollo Victoria .... ③
- Boisdale .... ④
- Golden Lion .... ⑤
- Pacha London .... ⑥
- Red Lion (The) .... ⑦
- St Stephen's Tavern .... ⑧
- Victoria Palace .... ⑨
- The Clarence .... ⑩
- The Red Lion .... ⑪

City of London, allowing the political and economic parts of the city to remain independent of each other.

Westminster Palace was built on the banks of the Thames here during the Middle Ages and was the monarch's principal residence for many years, as well as the seat of Parliament, which is its function today.

In 1837, with the accession of Queen Victoria, the official royal residence was moved to Buckingham Palace, former home of the Duke of Buckingham, and remains so to this day. This area has always been inextricably linked with royalty.

After William the Conqueror invaded in 1066 he was crowned monarch in

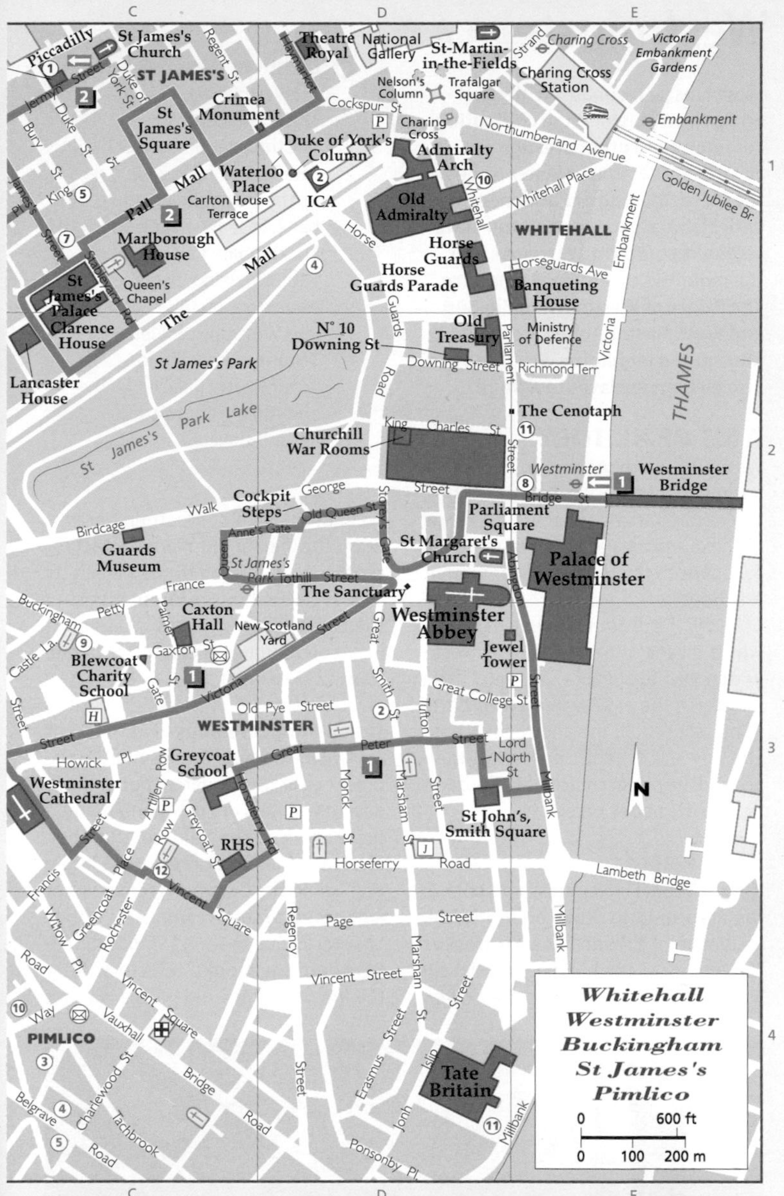

Westminster Abbey and since then all monarchs have been crowned here. The building is also the traditional venue for royal weddings – most recently on 29 April 2011 when heir to the throne Prince William married Catherine Middleton here.

Westminster Today

Westminster is little changed from its original function and remains the seat of both government and monarchy. Whitehall is home to most major government offices, including that of the Prime Minister, and many members of the royal family have their principal residences in this area.

Westminster★★★

Westminster resonates with royal and political history: the coronation ceremony and other prestigious royal events at Westminster Abbey, the State Opening of Parliament with elaborate pageantry, and state visits with glittering carriages and the mounted cavalry in attendance. The Palace of Westminster, Big Ben and Westminster Abbey are the undisputed highlights, but there are also elegant enclaves to admire.

Location: Map pp 134–135. ⊖*Westminster; Victoria.* The South Bank is over Westminster Bridge; for Tate Britain, follow the river upstream on the north bank. St James's Park and Buckingham Palace are within walking distance. For excursions on the Thames, visit Westminster Pier.

Timing: Allow 2hr for Westminster Palace and Abbey; 1hr to stroll around the area.

A BIT OF HISTORY

Westminster embodies two important institutions of state: Westminster Abbey, where coronations and royal weddings are held, and the Palace of Westminster, seat of both the Houses of Parliament *(the House of Commons and the House of Lords)*. The district acquired its name, which means "the minster in the west", as opposed to St Paul's Cathedral, "the minster in the east", when Edward the Confessor rebuilt the abbey church on Thorney Island; he also built a royal palace and the parish church of St Margaret next to the abbey precincts.

Royal Palace

King William I built much at his palace, for, according to Stow, he found the residence of **Edward the Confessor** "far inferior to the building of princely palaces in France." Unlike the Tower, William's palace at Westminster was never fortified but remained intact for centuries. Hemming in the palace on all sides were houses for members of the court who, as representatives of local communities or commons, began from 1332 to meet apart as the House of Commons.

The **opening ceremony of Parliament** took place then, as it does now, in the presence of the Monarch, but in those days, it was held in a richly ornamented hall known as the Painted Chamber. The Lords then adjourned to the White Hall, while the Commons remained or adjourned to the Westminster Abbey Chapter House (*see WESTMINSTERABBEY*) or to the monks' refectory. After the fire of 1512 the old palace was not

Houses of Parliament

The Gunpowder Plot

Robert Catesby, Thomas Winter, Thomas Percy and John Wright intended to blow up the House of Lords, the King and Queen and heir to the throne. They rented a cellar extending under Parliament and enlisted **Guy Fawkes**, a little-known mercenary from York, just returned from war abroad, to plant the explosive in the cellar: at least 20 barrels of gunpowder camouflaged with coal and faggots. Seeking to recruit additional support, Catesby approached Francis Tresham, who warned Lord Monteagle, his brother-in-law, not to attend Parliament on the fateful day. However, Monteagle alerted the Government and Guy Fawkes was discovered in the cellar late on 4 November. Under torture on the rack he revealed the names of his fellow conspirators. Catesby and Percy were killed while resisting arrest. The others were tried, hanged, drawn and quartered on 31 January 1606. Guy Fawkes Day is celebrated every 5 November with fireworks.

rebuilt, and **Henry VIII** had no royal residence in Westminster until he confiscated York House from Wolsey in 1529. In 1547 St Stephen's Chapel was granted by **Edward VI** to the Commons as their chamber, where they continued to sit until the 19C. The Lords, so nearly blown up in the **Gunpowder Plot** *(1605)*, continued to meet in the White Hall until the night of 16 October 1834, when a devastating fire swept through Westminster Palace; the only buildings to survive were Westminster Hall, St Stephen's Crypt, St Stephen's cloister and the Jewel Tower. The new Parliament buildings designed by **Charles Barry** and **Augustus Pugin** were completed in 1860; there were more than 1,000 rooms, 100 staircases and 2mi/3km of corridors spread over 8 acres/3hectares.

HOUSES OF PARLIAMENT (PALACE OF WESTMINSTER)★★★

Guided tours (75min) available. Call or see website for details. 0870 906 3773, 020 7219 4272 (House of Commons information office). www.parliament.uk/visiting.

Barry's ground plan is outstandingly simple: two chambers are disposed on a single, processional north-south axis so that the throne, the Woolsack, the bars of the two chambers and the Speaker's chair are all in line. At the centre is a large common lobby. Libraries, committee rooms and dining rooms, parallel to the main axis, overlook the river. Above the central lobby rises a lantern and slender spire (originally part of the ventilation system). The ends of the complex are marked by dissimilar towers: the Victoria Tower over the royal entrance, the other housing a clock.

The long waterfront is articulated from end to end with Gothic pinnacles and windows, and decorated with medieval tracery, carving, niches and figures, individually designed by Pugin in Perpendicular Gothic.

Royal Entrance and Staircase

On ceremonial occasions, such as the State Opening of Parliament, the Sovereign is met by high officers of state at the entrance to the Victoria Tower; members of the Household Cavalry line the flight of stairs leading up to the **Norman Porch**, which is square in shape and Perpendicular in style with gilded vaulting.

Robing Room★

Here the Sovereign assumes the Imperial State Crown and crimson parliamentary robe. The room, like the Lords' Chamber, presents Pugin's most remarkable concentration of decorative invention: note in particular the elaborately ornamented panelled ceiling.

Royal Gallery

The gallery *(110ft/33.5m)*, the Sovereign's processional way, is decorated with frescoes by Daniel Maclise, gilt bronze statues of monarchs from Alfred to Queen Anne and portraits of all the sovereigns and their consorts since George I. In the following **Prince's Chamber** are representations of the Tudor monarchs and their consorts, including all six wives of Henry VIII.

House of Lords★★

The "magnificent and gravely gorgeous" chamber is the summit of Pugin's achievement; a symphony of design and workmanship in scarlet, gilding and encrusted gold. At one end of the chamber on a stepped dais stands the throne beneath a Gothic canopy. The Woolsack, symbol of England's Medieval wealth, is said to be "most uncomfortable". The benches are covered in red buttoned leather; the one with arms is for the bishops. The cross benches are between the clerk's table and the bar of the house, behind which the members of the House of Commons stand when summoned by Black Rod to hear the speech from the throne at the State Opening of Parliament in November. Between the windows are statues of 18 barons who witnessed King John's assent to **Magna Carta**.

Central Lobby★

The octagonal lobby *(75ft/23m high)* is the hub of the building, where constituents waiting to see their MP may spot many well-known political figures. Every element of the design is by Pugin: Perpendicular arches framing the windows and entrances, decorated with English sovereigns, life-size 19C statesmen, mosaics over the doors, gilded and patterned roof ribs and the chandelier. When the **Commons Lobby**, destroyed in an air raid in 1941, was reconstructed, stones from the original fabric were incorporated in the **Churchill Arch**; it is flanked by his statue in bronze by Oscar Nemon and a statue of Lloyd George.

House of Lords

House of Commons★

The chamber, also destroyed in the 1941 raid, was rebuilt without decoration. Parallel benches in the traditional green hide provide seating for 437 of the 651 elected members.

At the end is the canopied Speaker's chair; before it are the seats of the Clerks and the table of the house bearing the mace and the bronze-mounted despatch boxes. Red stripes on either side of the green carpet mark the limit to which a member may advance when addressing the House.

The Government sits to the Speaker's right, the Prime Minister opposite the despatch box. When a division is called, members leave for the tellers' lobbies past the Speaker's right for Aye and through the far end for No.

The **libraries**, overlooking the river, are oases of silence. The **Lords' library**, decoration by Pugin, contains the warrant for the execution of Charles I signed by Cromwell and the Council.

The **terrace** is reserved for Members of Parliament and their guests; a very special place to take tea.

St Stephen's Hall

The long narrow hall, the public entrance to the Central Lobby, was constructed by Barry to look like the 14C St Stephen's Chapel. At the end are two superimposed arches, the upper filled with a mosaic of St Stephen between King Stephen and Edward the Confessor. Brasses on the floor mark the limit of the old Commons chamber *(60 x 30ft/18 x 9m)*.

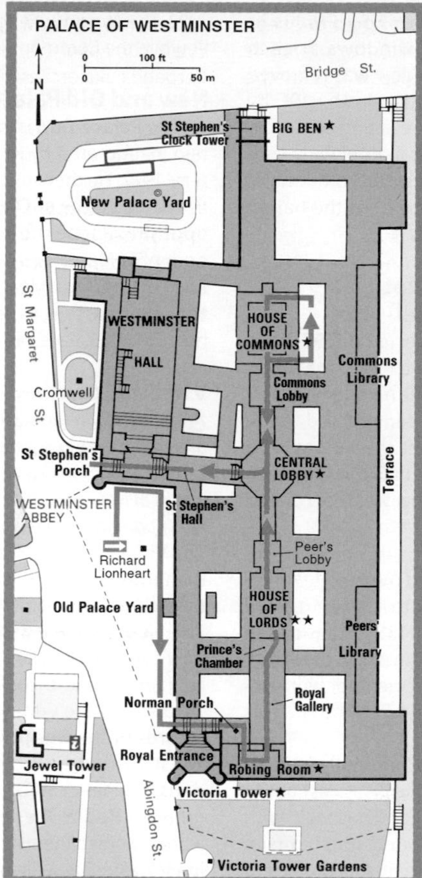

Westminster Hall★

The Hall was added to William I's palace by his son, **William Rufus**, in 1097. Throughout the Middle Ages it was used for royal Christmas feasts, jousts, ceremonial events and as a place of assembly. **Sir Thomas More** *(1535)*, **Somerset** *(1551)*, **Northumberland** *(1553)*, Essex *(1601)*, **Guy Fawkes** *(1606)* and **Charles I** all stood trial here.

Westminster Hall was later appointed the permanent Seat of Justice until the Royal Courts of Justice (*see STRAND*) moved to the Strand in the 1870s. During this century monarchs and Churchill have all lain in state there. The superb **hammerbeam roof ★★★**, probably the finest timber roof of all time, was constructed by Henry Yevele, master mason, and Hugh Herland, carpenter, at the command of **Richard II** in 1394. The roof rises to 90ft/27m at the crest and depends on projecting hammerbeams. Now reinforced with steel, the beams are carved with great flying angels.

An Innovator

On the opposite side of nearby Great Smith Street stood the almonry, where the well-to-do cloth merchant **William Caxton** set up his press in 1476, using as his imprint William Caxton in the Abbey of Westminster *(publishing* **Chaucer's** *Canterbury Tales, Malory's Le Morte d'Arthur and Aesop's Fables).*

The hall *(238 x 70ft/69.5 x 21m)* is lit by Perpendicular windows at each end. The south window was removed to its present position in the 19C by Barry; beneath the resulting arch, now flanked by six 14C statues of early English kings, Barry inserted a dramatic flight of steps rising from the hall to **St Stephen's Porch**.

St Stephen's Crypt (St Mary's Chapel)

The domestic chapel *(built 1292–97 by Edward I)* was on two levels, the upper being reserved for the royal family. After St Stephen's had been granted to the Commons, the lower chapel was used for secular purposes until the 19C, when the Medieval chamber was redecorated as a chapel.

Big Ben's Clock Tower★

St Stephen's clock tower *(316ft/97m)* was completed by 1858–59. Inside is a luxurious prison cell in which the leader of the militant movement for women's suffrage, Emmeline Pankhurst, was detained in 1902.

The name **Big Ben** originally applied only to the bell, which was cast at the Whitechapel Foundry. The clock, with its electrically wound mechanism, proved reliable until it succumbed to metal fatigue in 1976 and subsequently required major repairs. Big Ben's chimes were first broadcast on New Year's Eve in 1923. The Ayrton light above the clock is lit while the Commons is sitting.

Facts and Figures

Measuring 9ft/3m in diameter and 7ft/2m in height, **Big Ben** weighs in at 13tons 10cwts 3qtrs 15lbs. It also has a 4ft/1m crack, which developed soon after it was installed. The **clock mechanism** weighs about 5 tons. The dials of cast-iron tracery *(diameter 23ft/7m)* are glazed with pot opal glass; the figures are 2ft/60cm long and the minute spaces are 1ft/30cm square. The 14ft/4m long minute hands are made of copper, weigh 2 cwts and travel 120mi/193km per year.

New and Old Palace Yards

In **New Palace Yard** is the Jubilee Fountain inaugurated by HM The Queen in May 1977. Farther south a plinth supports the statue of **Oliver Cromwell**; opposite, above the small northeast door of St Margaret's Church is a small head of **Charles I**. Meanwhile, **Richard the Lionheart** sits patiently astride his horse in Old Palace Yard.

Victoria Tower★

Open Mon–Fri 9.30am–5pm, preferably by appointment. Closed certain public holidays and the last two weeks of Nov. 020 7219 4272. www.parliament.uk/visiting.

The Victoria Tower *(336ft/102m)*, taller than the clock tower, was designed as the archive for parliamentary documents The **House of Lords Record Office** now contains 3 million papers, including journals of the House of Lords from 1510 and of the Commons from 1547, records of the **Gunpowder Plot**, etc. The statuary in the **Victoria Tower Gardens** includes a cast of the great bronze group by **Rodin**, *The Burghers of Calais*, who ransomed themselves to Edward III in 1347, as well as a slim statue of the suffragette leader **Emmeline Pankhurst**.

Jewel Tower

Open April–Oct daily 10am–5pm, Nov–Mar Sat–Sun 10am–4pm. Closed 24–26 Dec, 1 Jan. £3.90. 020 7222 2219. www.english-heritage.org.uk.

The L-shaped tower, with a corner staircase turret, dates from 1365 when it was built as the King's personal jewel house and treasury, and surrounded by a moat. There is a brick-vaulted strongroom on the first floor with a later iron door *(1612)*. When Westminster ceased to be a royal palace, the tower became the archive for parliamentary papers and subsequently the weights and measures office.

Adjoining the Jewel Tower in Abingdon Garden stands the sculpture *Knife Edge to Edge* by Henry Moore *(1964)*.

WALKING TOUR 1

Start from Westminster Bridge, then cross to Parliament Square.

Westminster Bridge★

The stone bridge *(1750)*, where Wordsworth composed his famous sonnet *(1807)*, was the second to be built, after London Bridge. It was replaced in 1862 with a flat stone structure by Thomas Page, comprising seven low arches. From the bridge there is a fine view of the terrace and riverfront of the Houses of Parliament. At the bridge foot is a sculpture of **Boadicea** heroically riding in her chariot during her campaign against the Romans.

Parliament Square

The Square and Parliament Street, which were laid out in 1750 at the time of the building of the first Westminster Bridge, were redesigned in 1951. There are bronze statues of Victorian statesmen such as **Lord Palmerston**, **Benjamin Disraeli** and **Robert Peel**, but one's attention is inevitably drawn to the powerful statue of **Churchill** by Ivor Roberts Jones.

Cross the square to the South and walk past St Margaret's Church (*see Additional Sights*) and Westminster Abbey (*see WESTMINSTER ABBEY*).

The Sanctuary

In the monastery's day, the right of sanctuary extended over a considerable area. The quarter became so overbuilt with squalid houses and the right so abused by vagabonds, thieves and murderers that it was first restricted and finally abolished in all but name under James I. The Gatehouse in which **Sir Walter Raleigh** spent his last night before execution and **Richard Lovelace** penned the line "stone walls do not a prison make nor iron bars a cage" was demolished in 1776; on the site stands a red granite column erected in memory of former pupils of Westminster School, who died in the Indian Mutiny and the Crimean War.

The Sanctuary buildings, designed by Sir Gilbert Scott with an archway through to the Dean's Yard (*see WESTMINSTER ABBEY*), are in marked contrast to the 1970s **Queen Elizabeth II Conference Centre** and **Central Hall** opposite, designed as a Wesleyan church with the third-largest dome in London by Rickards and Lanchester in 1912 and now used as an examination hall or hired out for public events.

Turn right up Storey's Gate and left into Old Queen St., which is lined with several 18C houses (note ***No. 28***).

Cockpit Steps now lead to Birdcage Walk and St James's Park (*see BUCKINGHAM PALACE*) but in the days of Whitehall Palace they led down to a cockfighting pit. Flanked by the Home Office buildings on the left, is **Queen Anne's Gate**, an L-shaped street of substantial three-storey terraced houses dating from the reign of Queen Anne *(1704)*. Several pilastered doorways are protected by flat wooden hoods, decorated with rich carving and hanging pendants. The street's hallmark is the white satyr's mask set in place of a tablet stone above the ground and first-floor windows of every house.

Take Broadway and Tothill St. back to the top of Victoria St.

Victoria Street

The street was cut through the Georgian slums to link Parliament to Victoria Station in 1862. It is now lined with 20C buildings – tower blocks in steel and brown glass, faced in marble, stone and concrete, providing offices for government ministries and international companies. Buildings of interest include: **New Scotland Yard** *(1967)*; **London Transport's headquarters** *(1927–29)* by Charles Holden, with decorative statuary groups by **Jacob Epstein** and reliefs by **Eric Gill**, **Henry Moore** and others; **Caxton Hall** *(1878)*, once famous for register office weddings; the old **Blewcoat Charity School** *(Buckingham Street)*, a delightful square red-brick building

erected in 1709 to house the school, which was founded in 1688 and is now the property of the National Trust *(the National Trust shop and information centre are no longer open).*

At the west end of the street stands **Little Ben**, a model *(30ft/9m high)* of Big Ben. **Victoria Railway Station** was built in the 1870s, but the present buildings are from the 1900s.

Walk back to Westminster Cathedral piazza, turn right into Ambrosden Ave, left onto Francis St. then right onto Emery Hill St. to Vincent Square.

Vincent Square

The large square was laid out in 1810 to provide playing fields for Westminster School *(see WESTMINSTER ABBEY)*.

On the northeast side is the **Royal Horticultural Society** *(f.1804)*, a square brick building with the New Horticultural Hall *(1923–28)* at the back, where monthly flower shows are held *(open to non-members).*

Leave the square via Elverton St. and turn left along Horseferry Rd. to Greycoat Place.

Greycoat School

Greycoat Place.

The grey uniform of this Westminster Charity school, founded in 1698, can be seen on the small wooden niche figures, contrasting puritanically with the bright royal coat of arms set between them on the pedimented stucco. It is now a girls' school.

Turn right along Great Peter St. and then right into Lord North St.

Smith Square

The Square, the four streets midway along each side and the streets to the North include many original Georgian houses: **Nos. 6–9** Smith Square, all Lord North Street except at the northern end, and at the south end of Cowley Street *(occasional date stones 1722, 1726).*

Today, the Square is associated with politics; in the southwest corner is **Conservative Central Office**, while many properties all around accommodate MPs' offices or lodgings.

At the centre stands **St John's**, **Smith Square**, a tall Baroque church *(1714–28)*, designed by Thomas Archer, now serving as a concert hall. Its four ornate corner towers having been compared by the Queen to an upturned footstool gave rise to its nickname "Queen Anne's Footstool". It was badly bombed during World War II but the interior has been restored with giant Corinthian columns and an 18C chandelier.

Turn left down Dean Stanley St. then left along Millbank to return to Parliament Sq.

Westminster Cathedral★

Open daily 8am–7pm (5.30pm bank holidays). 020 7798 9055. www.westminstercathedral.org.uk.

Set back from Victoria Street and graced by a modern piazza towers the remarkable neo-Byzantine Roman-Catholic cathedral. Cardinal Manning and his successor Cardinal Vaughan determined on early Christian inspiration for the architecture of the new cathedral. The architect **JF Bentley** travelled widely in Italy before producing *(1894)* plans for an **Italianate-Byzantine** building; construction started promptly in 1895 and was completed so far as the fabric was concerned by 1903. The brick building *(360ft/109m long x 156ft/47m wide)* is distinguished by a **domed campanile** *(273ft/83m high).*

Interior

The initial impression is of vastness and fine proportions. The widest nave in England is roofed by three domes. Decoration is incomplete; above the marble and granite lower surfaces and piers rise unpointed brick walls, awaiting mosaics. The altar, beneath its baldachin supported on yellow marble columns, is dominated by a suspended crucifix. On the main piers are the 14 Stations of the Cross.

The body of the English martyr **John Southworth**, hanged, drawn and quartered at Tyburn in 1654, lies in the second chapel in the north aisle. The south transept contains an early-15C alabaster statue of the Virgin and Child, carved by the Nottingham school, which originally stood in Westminster Abbey but was removed to France in the 15C and returned in 1955; there is also a bronze of **St Teresa of Lisieux** by Giacomo Manzù and a Chi-Rho, executed in flat-headed nails, by David Partridge.

St Margaret's Church★

Open Mon–Fri 9.30am–3.30pm, Sat 9.30am–1.30pm, Sun 2pm–4.30pm. www.westminster-abbey.org/st-margarets.

The Parish and Parliamentary Church built by Edward the Confessor to serve local parishioners was rebuilt in the mid-14C. A third reconstruction *(1488–1523)*, scarcely completed at the time of the Reformation, would have been demolished had not the parishioners "with bows and arrows, staves and clubs and other such offensive weapons so terrified the workmen that they ran away in great amazement". Much of the church's present late-Perpendicular appearance derives from the radical restoration by Sir George Gilbert Scott in the mid-19C. St Margaret's is the church of the House of Commons, not only because the Palace of Westminster lies within the parish, but by a tradition inaugurated on Palm Sunday 1614, when the Commons met for the first time for corporate communion and being mostly Puritans, preferred the church to the Abbey.Each year in November a **Garden of Remembrance**, composed of commemorative Flanders poppies, blossoms in the churchyard.

Interior

The interior presents Tudor monuments: **Blanche Parry**, chief gentlewoman of Queen Elizabeth's privy chamber *(to the right side of the porch on entering)*, a Yeoman of the Guard *(d. 1577 at 94)*, **Richard Montpesson**, kneeling by his wife's tomb. There are two plaques *(by the east door)* and fragments of a window *(north aisle)* as memorials to **Caxton**, buried in the old churchyard; **Walter Raleigh** executed in Old Palace Yard on 29 October 1618 and buried beneath the high altar is commemorated in a tablet near the east door and in the west window, presented in the late 19C by citizens of the USA. The carved lime-wood reredos *(1753)* is based on Titian's *Supper at Emmaus*. The east window is special, having been made in Flanders in 1501 at the behest of Ferdinand and Isabella of Spain to celebrate the marriage of their daughter Catherine to Prince Arthur; by the time it arrived Arthur was dead and the Princess affianced to the future Henry VIII. The window was duly despatched outside London and retrieved only in 1758, when the House of Commons purchased it for 400 guineas and presented it to the Church.

ADDRESSES

PUBS

St Stephen's Tavern, *10 Bridge St. ⊖Westminster. ✆020 7925 2286. Mon–Sat 10am–11.30pm, Sun 10.30am–10.30pm.* Facing Big Ben, this popular Victorian pub has a beautiful interior and a cosy atmosphere. Try the real ales.

The Clarence, *53 Whitehall. ⊖Westminster or Charing Cross. ✆ 020 7930 4808. Mon–Sat 11am–11pm, Sun noon–10.30pm.* Now owned by upmarket pub chain Geronimo Inns, this inviting bar has plenty of seating, a wide range of wines and decent pub grub. Real ales too. Attracts a fairly well-heeled crowd but gets busy in the evenings as office workers congregate for post-work drinks.

The Red Lion, *48 Parliament St. ⊖Westminster or Charing Cross. ✆020 7930 5826. Mon–Sat 10am–11pm, Sun 10am–9pm.* Traditional British pub located between the Houses of Parliament and Downing Street, and the closest pub to the PM's residence. It's unlikely that you'll see him in here but several MPs are frequent guests and rumour has it there's a division bell, which rings to alert them to any votes taking place in nearby parliament. Good real ales and a friendly atmosphere.

Westminster Abbey★★★

The Collegiate Church of St Peter at Westminster – better known as Westminster Abbey – is as rich in architectural splendour as it is in history and culture. Moreover, its potent historical associations make it a most glorious monument. For centuries it has hosted the funerals and weddings of statesmen and royalty, witnessed the coronation of many kings and queens, and today hosts cultural events, concerts and festivals. The Abbey has a strong musical tradition and its carol concerts are an enjoyable feature of the Christmas period.

Location: Map pp 134–135. ⊖*Westminster.* The Abbey, at the heart of Westminster, is close to many important tourist sites. The area is on several bus routes from Victoria Station and Trafalgar Square.

Don't Miss: There are 12 bells that ring, generally between noon and 1pm, on great occasions and on some 25 days of festival and commemoration, including 25, 26 and 28 December, 1 January, Easter and Whit Sundays and HM The Queen's official Birthday.

Timing: The Abbey can easily be visited in under an hour as part of a tour of the whole area of Westminster.

A BIT OF HISTORY

Westminster Abbey, for centuries a royal mausoleum, became a national shrine owing to its situation next to the Palace of Westminster, once the Sovereign's residence and now the seat of Parliament.

Since the coronation of William I on Christmas Day in 1066, all but two of the kings and queens of England have been crowned here. In more recent times, it hosted the marriage of the future George VI to Elizabeth Bowes-Lyon *(1923)*, Prince Andrew to Sarah Ferguson *(1986)* and the funeral of Diana, Princess of Wales *(1997)*.

A Saxon monastery stood on the site in the 6C. **Edward the Confessor** built a new Norman-style abbey church, which was consecrated on 28 December 1065. In 1220, inspired by the Gothic style of Amiens and Rheims, the Plantagenet king **Henry III** began to rebuild the church.

By the late 13C, the east end, transept, choir, the first bay of the nave and the chapter house were complete; work then came to a halt and another two centuries passed before the nave was finished.

Henry VII's Chapel *(1503–19)*, built in Perpendicular Gothic style, is the jewel of its age, more delicate, with finer niches and pinnacles than any other part of the Abbey.

Later additions, notably the upper parts of the west towers *(1722–45)* by **Wren** and **Hawksmoor**, and repairs by Sir George Gilbert Scott and others have echoed the Gothic theme. Recent additions *(1998)* on the west front are limestone statues of modern Christian martyrs (Grand Duchess Elizabeth of Russia, Maximilian Kolbe, **Martin Luther King** and Oscar Romero, among others) placed in niches above figures depicting truth, justice, mercy and peace.

Royal Peculiar – When **Henry VIII** ordered the Dissolution of the monasteries in 1540, the Abbey's treasures were confiscated but the buildings were not destroyed. The 600-year-old Benedictine community was disbanded and the Abbot dismissed.

In 1560, **Elizabeth I** established the Collegiate Church of St Peter, with a royally appointed dean and chapter of 12 prebendaries *(canons)* and also the College of St Peter, known as **Westminster School**, which replaced the monastic school.

VISIT

Abbey usually open Mon–Fri 9.30am–4.30pm (Wed till 7pm), Sat 9.30am–2.30pm. Sun and religious holidays services only. Last admission 1hr before closing. Chapter House Mon–Sat 10am–4.30pm. Cloisters open daily 8am–6pm, Wed 4pm; museum and Pyx Chamber Mon–Sat 10.30am–3.30pm. £18, children £8, museum free with main ticket. Leaflet (8 languages). Audio-guide. Verger guided tours (90min) £3 (English only). 020 7222 5152. www.westminster-abbey.org. Confirm opening times in advance by phone.

Enter by the north door.

The **monuments** to national figures, which crowd the Abbey, date from the early Middle Ages.

The older monuments, the figures on the ancient tombs, are mostly in the chapels east of the high altar. In the 18C and 19C there was a surfeit of monuments sculpted by the great artists of the day: **Roubiliac**, the Bacons, Flaxman, Le Sueur, Westmacott, Chantrey. Permission to be buried in the Abbey or for a memorial to be erected is granted by the Dean.

Nave – The soaring vaulting retains its original beauty; the carving is delicate, often beautiful, sometimes humorous. At the west end of the nave is the memorial to the **Unknown Warrior (1)**, set in the pavement and surrounded by red Flanders poppies.

Against the first south pier is the **painting of Richard II (2)**, the earliest known painting of an English sovereign. In the north aisle, low down, is the small stone that covered the upright figure of the playwright "O rare Ben Johnson" **(3)** (misspelt).

On the north side, along Musicians' Aisle, you can see the graves and memorials of famous musicians including **Henry Purcell**, a former organist of the Abbey. The **North Transept**, known as Statesmen's Aisle, contains the graves and memorials of famous national figures.

Choir – The choir screen, which faces the west door, is a 13C structure of stone, with lierne vaulting under the arch.

Sanctuary – This is where the Monarch is crowned and receives the peers' homage in the **coronation ceremony**. The floor is laid with a 13C Italian pavement of porphyry and mosaic. Behind the altar is the 19C high altar screen. To the right is a large 15C altarpiece of rare beauty. Beyond is an ancient 13C sedilia painted with full-length royal figures *(Henry II, Edward I)*. On the left are three tombs, each a recumbent figure: Aveline of Lancaster *(**4**; d. 1274)*, renowned for her beauty; Aymer de Valence, Earl of Pembroke *(**5**; d. 1324)*, cousin to Edward I; Edmund Crouchback *(**6**; d. 1296)*, youngest son of Henry III, Aveline's husband.

North Ambulatory – On the left is the chapel of Abbot Islip, known for its rebus – an eye and a slip or branch of a tree clasped by a hand.

The **Chapel of Our Lady of the Pew**, in the thickness of the wall, contains a modern alabaster Madonna and Child, modelled on the original, which is now in Westminster Cathedral.

Queen Elizabeth Chapel – In the north aisle of Henry VII's Chapel is the tomb of **Queen Elizabeth I (7)** in white marble; beneath is the coffin of Mary Tudor without any monument. At the east end are memorials to two young daughters

Westminster Abbey

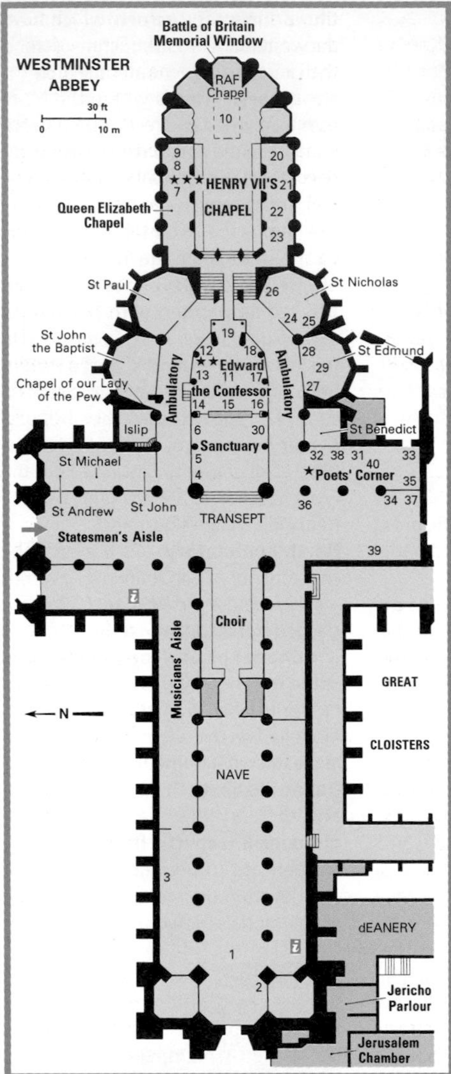

of James I **(8)** and, in a small sarcophagus, the bones found in the Tower of London presumed to be those of the Little Princes **(9)**.

Henry VII's Chapel★★★ – Note the superb fan-vaulted roof and the banners of the Knights Grand Cross of the Order of the Bath, hanging still and brilliant above the stalls, which are crowned with pinnacles, helmets and coifs; the witty and inventive misericords date from the 16C to 18C. The chapel was first used for the knights' installations in 1725, when **George I** reconstructed the order.

At the east end is the tomb of Henry VII and Elizabeth of York **(10)**. Beyond, in the **RAF Chapel**, is the **Battle of Britain Memorial Window** *(1947)*, a many-faceted, brightly coloured screen containing the badges of the 68 Fighter Squadrons who took part.

The great double gates at the entrance are decorated with the royal emblems of Henry Tudor and his antecedents: the roses of Lancaster and York, the leopards of England, the fleur-de-lys of France, the falcon of Edward IV, father of Elizabeth, Henry's queen.

Chapel of Edward the Confessor★★ – The chapel contains the tombs of five kings and three queens around the **Confessor's Shrine (11)**. Against the north wall are **Queen Eleanor of Castile** *(**12**; d. 1290)*, in whose memory the Eleanor crosses were erected (*see WHITEHALL*) by the master goldsmith William Torel; Henry III *(**13**; d. 1272)*, builder of the chapel; **Edward I**, Longshanks *(**14**; d. 1307)*, the first king to be crowned in the present abbey *(1272)* and the Hammer of the Scots, who brought south the Scottish regalia and the stone of Scone in 1297.

The carved **stone screen**, which closes the west end of the chapel, was completed in 1441. At the centre stands the **Coronation Chair (15)**; for coronations the chair is moved into the sanctuary.

Against the south wall are Richard II **(16)**; the gilt bronze figure of Edward III *(**17**; d. 1377)*, surrounded by the bronze representations of his children, and his queen, Philippa of Hainault *(**18**; d. 1369)*, who interceded for the Burghers of Calais. At the east end is the oak figure of the young Henry V *(**19**; d. 422)*.

South Aisle of Henry VII's Chapel – Here are buried, in a royal vault **(20)**, Charles II, William III and Mary, Queen Anne and her consort, George of Denmark. Three grand tombs occupy the centre: Lady Margaret Beaufort *(**21**; d. 1509)*, a masterpiece by **Torrigiano** in gilt bronze; **Mary Queen of Scots (22)** in white marble; Margaret Douglas, Countess of Lennox *(**23**; d. 1578)*, niece of Henry VIII, mother of Darnley and grandmother of James I, a beautiful woman carved in alabaster.

South Ambulatory – St Nicholas' Chapel contains the tomb of Philippa, Duchess of York *(**24**; d. 1431)*; the vault of the Percys **(25)**; the tomb of Anne, Duchess of Somerset *(**26**; d. 1587)*, widow of the Protector. In St Edmund's Chapel are the tomb of William de Valence *(**27**; d. 1296)*, half brother of Henry III, and the marble effigy of John of Eltham *(**28**; d. 1337)*, second son of Edward II. In the centre, on a low altar tomb, is the Abbey's finest **brass** of Eleanor, Duchess of Gloucester *(**29**; d. 1399)* beneath a triple canopy. On the north side of the ambulatory are Sebert's tomb **(30)** and the sedilia painting of the Confessor.

Poets' Corner★ – This famous corner in the south transept contains the tomb of Chaucer **(31)**; statues of the court poets Dryden **(32)** and Ben Jonson **(33)**, William Shakespeare **(34)**, John Milton **(35)**, William Blake **(36)** *(bust by Epstein, 1957)*, Robert Burns **(37)**, Longfellow **(38)**, Joseph Addison **(39)**. Plaques and stones are now more the order of the day: Thomas Hardy, Dylan Thomas, Lewis Carroll **(40)**. Oscar Wilde, who died in Paris, is honoured with a window.

Great Cloisters

Preserved in the Abbey's precincts are a number of historical buildings.

Chapter House – The octagonal chamber *(1248–53)* features a fine vault supported by a central pier braced with shafts of Purbeck marble. Under Edward I, the Chapter House became the **Parliment House of the Commons** and continued after the Dissolution. By the 19C it had become an archive for the state papers. When the damage caused during World War II was repaired, the windows were reglazed with clear glass, decorated with the coats of arms of sovereigns and abbots, and the devices of the two Medieval master masons who designed and built the Abbey.

Chapel of the Pyx – The 11C chamber became the monastery treasury in the 13C–14C. At the Dissolution it passed to the Crown and was used as the strongroom, in which gold and silver coins were tried against standard specimens kept there in a box or pyx. Today it is used to display church plate from the Abbey and from St Margaret's Church *(see WESTMINSTER)*.

Westminster Abbey Museum – The museum is housed in the low 11C vaulted Norman undercroft. It contains historical documents, gold plate and a number of unique wax and wood funeral effigies. Edward III and Katherine de Valois, both full-length, are of wood. The wax figure of **Charles II** in his Garter robes is unforgettable. **Nelson** was purchased by the Abbey in 1806 in an attempt to attract the crowds away from his tomb in St Paul's Cathedral.

Among the museum's collection of treasures are the saddle, sword, helm and shield of Henry V carried at his funeral in 1422, Mary II's coronation chair, replicas of the coronation regalia that were used for coronation rehearsals and the armour of General Monck, which was carried at his funeral in 1670.

Dean's Yard – The yard, the old heart of the Abbey precinct, is now a tree-shaded lawn. A low arch through the eastern range is the entrance to **Westminster School** *(private)*. The south side of Dean's Yard is filled by **Church House** *(1940)*, containing the circular Convocation Hall, where the General Synod of the Church of England meets, and the Hoare Memorial Hall, where the Commons sat during the war.

Whitehall★

Running between two of London's most famous squares, Whitehall links the vibrant streets of the West End with the more sedate corridors of power of Britain's political centre. Some of the country's most important buildings are located here and all the major government departments are represented, including that of the Prime Minister himself – the area is so known for its political clout that its name is synonymous with government itself.

Location: Map pp 134–135. ⊖*Westminster; Charing Cross*. Whitehall links Trafalgar Square to the North with Parliament Square to the south and runs parallel to the Thames.

Don't Miss: Peering through the gates at Downing Street, ceremonial mounting of the Queen's Life Guard.

Timing: Allow at least 1hr to soak up the atmosphere of Britain's political centre.

Palace of Whitehall – In 1529, Henry VIII confiscated Cardinal Wolsey's London palace dating back to the mid-13C. Wolsey made it his personal property, rebuilding, enlarging and enriching it. Henry VIII continued building and increased the royal precinct until it extended from Charing Cross to Westminster Hall, from the river to St James's Park. In 1996 archaeologists confirmed the discovery, below the Ministry of Defence of a sophisticated type of Turkish bath, fitted with a 12ft/3.5m stove and lined with British-made tiles.

The early owners of Whitehall had shown respect for a parcel of land known as Scotland, which until the 16C had been the site of a Scottish royal palace. When it was eventually built over, the streets were named Little, Great **Scotland Yard** etc. The newly formed Metropolitan Police, given an office there in 1829, became known by their address and retained it when they moved along the Embankment in the 1890s and later, in 1967, to Victoria Street.

William and Mary disliked Whitehall Palace and after a disastrous fire in 1698, did nothing to restore it. All that remains are the Tudor walls and windows behind the **Old Treasury** *(visible from Downing Street)*, the end of Queen Mary's Terrace, a riverside quay and steps that were built in 1661 by Wren *(NE corner of the Ministry of Defence)* and the highly decorative Banqueting House *(see Additional Sights)*.

Old Admiralty★

The Old Admiralty of 1722–26 was, in Horace Walpole's phrase, "deservedly veiled by **Mr Adam's** handsome screen", a Classical portico erected in 1759–61.

Horse Guards★★★

Ceremonial mounting of the Queen's Life Guard★★★ *daily by the Household Cavalry at 11am (10am Sun) on Horse Guards Parade; dismount ceremony daily 4pm in the Front Yard of Horse Guards. The Cavalry rides along the Mall between Horse Guards and their barracks in* **Hyde Park★★★**. *020 7414 2353. www.royal.gov.uk.*

The low 18C stonefaced edifice, designed symmetrically by **William Kent** around three sides of a shallow forecourt, is pierced by a central arch and marked above by a clock tower. The plain building acts as the official entrance to Buckingham Palace and as such is where all dignitaries of State on an official visit are greeted. To this end it is guarded by mounted sentries. When HM The Queen is in London this comprises an officer, a corporal major to bear the standard, two non-commissioned officers, a trumpeter and 10 troopers *(Long Guard)*; otherwise there are two non-commissioned officers and 10 troopers only *(Short Guard)*. Sentry duty alternates between the Life Guards in scarlet tunics and white plumed helmets, and the Blues and Royals in blue with red plumes. The west front *(through the arch)* overlooks the parade ground, where the Colour is Trooped in June. Among the statues and memorials is a huge French mortar from Cadiz *(1812)* and the **Guards' Memorial** *(1926) (on the far side)* backed by St James's Park *(see BUCKINGHAM PALACE)*.

Cross for Banqueting House.

The 18C **Dover** and **Gwydyr Houses**, both named after 19C owners and facing each other across Whitehall, are home to the **Scottish and Welsh Offices**.

Ministry of Defence

In front of the monolithic building stands the small but jaunty bronze of **Sir Walter Raleigh**, who was beheaded nearby. Next to him stands "**Monty**", a 10ft/3m solid bronze statue of Field Marshal Viscount Montgomery of Alamein by Oscar Nemon, unveiled in 1980.
The façade of **Richmond Terrace**, dating from 1822, has been restored to its original design.

Cross the street again.

Treasuries have stood on the site since the 16C. The present one of 1845 by Barry used the columns from the previous building by Soane.

Downing Street

No. 10 has been the residence of the Prime Minister since 1731, when Sir Robert Walpole accepted it *ex-officio* from George II. The row of four or five very large houses, erected in the 1680s by Sir George Downing, was rebuilt in the 1720s. No. 10 contains the **Cabinet Room** and a staircase, on which hang portraits of each successive resident. The Chancellor of the Exchequer lives at **No. 11**.

The Cenotaph

The slim white monument by **Lutyens** *(1919)* is the country's official war memorial. A service is held on Remembrance Sunday *(the Sunday nearest to 11 November)* in the presence of HM The Queen.

The two Victorian-Italian palazzo style buildings on either side of King Charles St. are best known for the Treasury door on Great George Street, from which the Chancellor goes to the House on Budget Day, and the former Home Office balcony, from where members of the Royal Family watch the Remembrance Day service.

At the far end of King Charles St. are the Churchill War Rooms (*see Additional Sights; for description of Parliament Square, see WESTMINSTER*).

ADDITIONAL SIGHTS

Banqueting House★★

Open daily 10am–1pm; call to check for afternoons. Closed bank holidays, 24–26 Dec and 1 Jan. £5 (including multi-language audio guide). 020 3166 6154/5. www.hrp.org.uk.
The palladian-style hall, all that remains of Whitehall Palace, has been called a memorial to the Stuarts. It was built by Inigo Jones for James I *(1619–22)*; Charles I then had the sumptuous ceiling paintings done by Rubens in 1629 and stepped on to the scaffold in Whitehall through one of its windows on 30 January 1649; 11 years later, Charles II received the Lords and Commons in the hall on the eve of his restoration.
Although the exterior has been refaced in Portland stone *(1829 by Soane)* and a new north entrance and staircase added by Wyatt in 1809, and despite the interior having been used as a chapel and museum from the 18C to the 20C, it now looks as splendid as it might have done in the 17C and still serves superbly beneath the chandeliers for occasional official functions.
Inside it is a single empty space, conceived as a double cube 110ft/33.5m x 55ft/17m x 55ft/17m with a balcony supported on gilded corbels on three sides. Above, richly decorated beams quarter the ceiling decorated with Rubens' flamboyant **paintings** in praise of James I.

Sir Winston Leonard Spencer Churchill (1874–1965)

Churchill was perhaps Britain's most charismatic leader: his speeches – broadcast worldwide by the BBC – rallied military troops into action, civilians at home and in occupied Europe, prisoners, spies, friends and foes. He is still remembered for his bursts of anger and impatience by those who knew him, but respected for his brilliance, staunch patriotism and remarkable use of the English language. His school report (aged nine) describes him as "very bad, a constant trouble to everybody and is always in some scrape or other" – a far cry from the man who was to rise through Harrow, soldiering, to the war premiership and become an elder statesman through the Cold War crisis. On the whole he was a creature of habit. He would wake at 8.30am, hold court from his bed throughout the morning until it was time for his bath (mid/late morning); he would then lunch, take a nap and maybe another soak before going out to dinner and dealing with business late into the night. Meals were preferably accompanied by champagne and punctuated by a dozen or so cigars smoked throughout the day. His presence lives on in the Cabinet War Rooms while his distinctive silhouette watches over the House of Commons from Parliament Square.

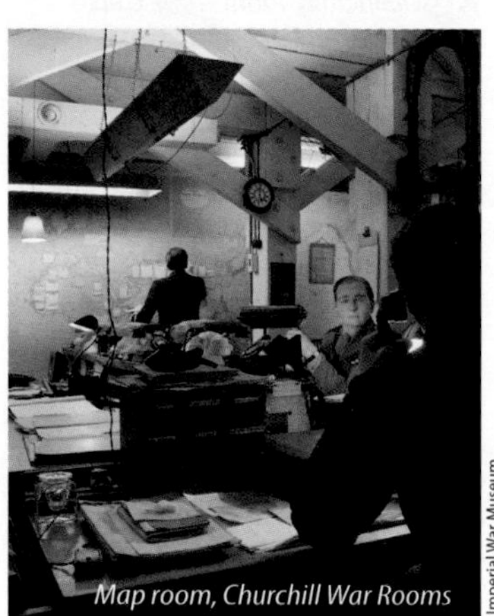
Map room, Churchill War Rooms

© Imperial War Museum

Churchill War Rooms★★

Clive Steps, King Charles Street. Open daily 9.30am–6pm (last admission 5pm). Closed 24–26 Dec. Audio guide (8 languages). £17 (includes voluntary donation of £1.55). Cafeteria. 020 7930 6961. www.iwm.org.uk.

The underground emergency accommodation provided to protect **Winston Churchill**, his War Cabinet and the Chiefs of Staff of the Armed Forces from air attacks, was the nerve centre of the war effort from 1939 to 1945. The 19 rooms on view include the Cabinet Room, the Transatlantic Telephone Room *(for direct communication with the White House)*, the Map Room bedecked with original maps marked with pins and coloured strings, the Prime Minister's Room and the room from which Churchill made direct broadcasts to the nation. Also in situ are the wedged wooden supports that were installed by the Naval team assigned to reinforce the premises against collapse during shelling.

Within his private quarters is now a **museum**. It tells a surprisingly intimate tale of the man in five sections: Young Churchill (1874–1900); Politician to Statesman (1900–1929); Wilderness Years (1929–1939); War Leader (1939–1945); and Cold War Statesman (1945–1965 and legacy). A 50ft (15m)-long, interactive **Lifeline**, using documents, photos, film and sound archives, is matched by some 150 original objects including Churchill's baby rattle, a red velvet siren suit and painting materials.

ADDRESSES

LIGHT BITE

ICA Café Bar – *The Mall, SW1Y 5AH. Charing Cross. 020 7930 8619. Tue–Sun 11am–11pm. www.ica.org.uk.* Bright and airy space between galleries at the Institute of Contemporary Arts serving light dishes. with live music and events in the evening. *Also see Café in the Crypt, St Martin-in-the-Fields, page 96.*

Buckingham Palace★★

The ceremonial heart of London is a focal point for Londoners and visitors alike. State occasions are marked with the pomp and circumstance associated with the Sovereign. The Palace is a congregation point when national events arouse strong emotions.

- **Location:** Map pp 134–135. *⊖Green Park; St James's Park; Victoria.* East of the Palace is Westminster, with Trafalgar Sq. to the northeast and St James's and Piccadilly to the North. Constitution Hill leads to Hyde Park Corner.
- **Don't Miss:** The Royal Mews, the Palace Gardens, St James's Park.
- **Timing:** Visit the Palace and the Mews and/or the Guards' Museum in the morning, then stroll through St James's Park at lunchtime when the park throngs with Londoners working nearby.
- **Kids:** The Changing of the Guard; the Guards' Museum.

A BIT OF HISTORY

Mulberry Garden to Royal Palace – In 1703 a piece of land, partly planted by **James I** as a mulberry garden, was granted by Queen Anne to the Duke of Buckingham, who built a town residence of brick on it. In 1762, **George III** purchased the property for his bride, Charlotte, and named it Queen's House. In 1825 **John Nash** was commissioned by **George IV** to turn the house into a palace. He extended it, added a cladding of Bath stone, a grand entrance portico and a range of rooms overlooking the garden.

The work was completed by Edward Blore in 1837. Three weeks after her accession **Victoria** took up residence and at last the royal standard flew on the **Marble Arch**, which Nash had designed. Ten years later a new east range enclosed the courtyard; it contains the famous **balcony**, where members of the Royal Family greet the crowds in the Mall on state occasions. In 1851, Marble Arch was moved to northeast Hyde Park.

Henry VIII acquired **St James's Park** in 1532 for hunting purposes. **James I** established a menagerie of animals and exotic birds here. **Charles II** aligned aviaries along what came to be called Birdcage Walk and opened the park to the public. In the 19C Nash replaced the wall by iron railings and landscaped the park itself.

Buckingham Palace viewed from St James's Park

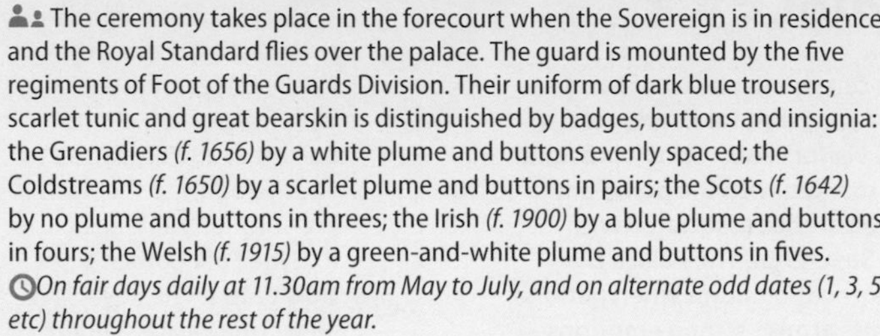

Changing of the Guard★★★

The ceremony takes place in the forecourt when the Sovereign is in residence and the Royal Standard flies over the palace. The guard is mounted by the five regiments of Foot of the Guards Division. Their uniform of dark blue trousers, scarlet tunic and great bearskin is distinguished by badges, buttons and insignia: the Grenadiers *(f. 1656)* by a white plume and buttons evenly spaced; the Coldstreams *(f. 1650)* by a scarlet plume and buttons in pairs; the Scots *(f. 1642)* by no plume and buttons in threes; the Irish *(f. 1900)* by a blue plume and buttons in fours; the Welsh *(f. 1915)* by a green-and-white plume and buttons in fives. *On fair days daily at 11.30am from May to July, and on alternate odd dates (1, 3, 5 etc) throughout the rest of the year.*

BUCKINGHAM PALACE★★

Open late Jul–Aug daily 9.30am–7pm (4.45pm last admission), Sept 9.30am–6.30pm (3.45 last admission). Timed ticket including audio tour £19; combined ticket with Queen's Gallery and Royal Mews £33.25. Guided tours (2–2.5hr). Brochure (6 languages). 020 7766 7300. www.royalcollection.org.uk.

The interior presents the suite of Edwardian-style state rooms, decorated with treasures from the Royal Collection: Sèvres porcelain, 18C French clocks and furniture, royal portraits and chandeliers. From the Ambassadors' Entrance pass into the courtyard, dominated by the entrance portico; the pediment bears carvings of Britannia in her chariot. The Entrance Hall leads to the **Grand Staircase**, lit by a domed skylight. 18C Gobelins tapestries and magnificent chandeliers adorn the **Guard Room** leading to the **Green Drawing Room**, which has an extravagant coved white-and-gold plaster ceiling. Red and gold predominate in the **Throne Room**; note the frieze depicting the Wars of the Roses. The two chairs were used at the Coronation *(1953)* by HM The Queen and the Duke of Edinburgh.

In the **Picture Gallery** hang masterpieces from the Royal Collection: by Van Dyck *(Charles I)*, Rembrandt, Vermeer *(A Lady at the Virginals)*, Rubens and other artists.

On the west front are the state rooms: the **Dining Room** is adorned with royal portraits (*George IV* with his hand resting on the Commanders' Table, commissioned by Napoleon in 1806 and presented to George IV by Louis XVIII in 1817). In the **Blue Drawing Room** stands the **Commanders' Table**, decorated with the head of Alexander the Great surrounded by 12 commanders of Antiquity in Sèvres porcelain with gilt-bronze mounts. The gilded ceiling of the **Music Room** features the rose of England, the thistle of Scotland and the shamrock of Ireland with a border of fleur-de-lys.

The ornate **White Drawing Room** has Corinthian pilasters, a piano in a gilt case painted with figures and a roll-top desk by Riesener. Don't miss two graceful sculptures by Canova, *Mars and Venus* and *A Fountain Nymph (by the Ministers' Stairs and Marble Hall)*.

From the garden , there is a superb view of the west front of the Palace.

Royal Mews★★

Open Apr–Oct daily 10am–5pm; Nov and Feb–late Mar Mon–Sat 10am–4pm. Last admission 45min earlier. Closed during state visits and selected days in May and June. £8.50. Combined ticket with Buckingham Palace, state rooms, Royal Mews and Queen's Gallery £33.25. 020 7766 7300. www.royalcollection.org.uk.

The mews were built by **Nash** in the 1820s. The blocks around the tree-shaded courtyard house stables, harness rooms and coach houses displaying, among other royal carriages, the gold State Coach *(1762)*, which has been used at every coronation since 1820.

Queen's Gallery★★

Open daily 10am–5.30pm. Timed ticket £9.25, combined ticket with Buckingham Palace, state rooms and the Royal Mews £33.25. 020 7766 7300. www.royalcollection.org.uk.
The gallery holds constant temporary exhibitions of treasures drawn from the Royal collections (Holbein watercolours, Canaletto paintings, furniture, sculpture, ceramics, silver and gold).

Wellington Barracks

On the south side of the parade ground stand the Wellington Barracks, built in 1833. Inside, the **Guards' Museum** *(Birdcage Walk, SW1; daily 10am–4pm, last admission 3.30pm; £5; 020 7414 3428; www.theguardsmuseum.com)* is devoted to the Guards Regiments and charts its history from Civil War origins to today.
Guards' Chapel – *Open as a museum (except some ceremonial days).* The chapel, destroyed by a flying bomb in June 1944 *(apart from the apse lined with mosaics)*, was rebuilt in 1963.

ADDITIONAL SIGHTS

St James's Park★★

London's oldest park is known for its flower borders and pelicans and wildfowl on the lake. Stroll by the lake or relax on the grass and enjoy band music. From the bridge there is a fine view of Buckingham Palace. St James's Park pelicans have a long-standing history: the first one, from Astrakhan, was a gift to Charles II given by a Russian ambassador in 1664 – it promptly flew off and was shot over Norfolk.

The Mall★★

In 1910 the 17C Mall was transformed into a processional way by **Sir Aston Webb**, who designed the **Queen Victoria Memorial**.
At the far end the thoroughfare stretches through Admiralty Arch to Trafalgar Square, while the processional route leads right to **Horse Guards**.
The north side is flanked by **Green Park** and **Carlton Terrace**. A memorial statue to HM The Queen Mother, who died in 2002, aged 101, was unveiled here in February 2009.

The ICA

Open Tue–Sun 11am–11pm. 020 7930 3647. www.ica.org.uk.
The Institute of Contemporary Arts is a multi-disciplinary arts centre established by a collection of artists in 1947. The two galleries, two cinemas and a theatre host a range of exhibitions and events covering all art forms. There's a small bookshop selling arthouse DVDs, a wide selection of art and design magazines and souvenirs, as well as a licensed café-bar serving food.

ADDRESSES

LIGHT BITE

Jenny Lo's Tea House – *14 Eccleston St., SW1W 9LT. Victoria. 020 7259 0399. Mon–Fri noon–2.55pm & 6pm–9pm.* This popular, authentic Chinese restaurant has an imaginative menu. Come early to avoid queues.

CAFÉ

Baker & Spice, *54–56 Elizabeth St. Victoria. 020 7730 5524. www.bakerandspice.uk.com. Mon–Sat 7am–7pm, Sun 8am–6pm.* Great selection of breads, pastries and dishes made daily and based on organic produce (soups, salads, pies). Take away or eat in.

NIGHTLIFE

Boisdale, *15 Eccleston St. Victoria. 020 7730 6922. www.boisdale.co.uk/belgravia. Mon–Fri noon–1am, Sat 6pm–1am.* This cosy bar hosts live jazz every night (closed Sundays) and has a pleasant outdoor courtyard.

Pacha London, *Victoria St. 0845 371 4489. www.pachalondon.com. Fri 10am–5am, Sat 10pm–6pm; ticket price around £18–£22 depending on show.* Like its Ibizan counterpart, this up-for-it club belts out progressive electro beats to an energetic but sophisticated crowd.

St James's★★

St James's is one of London's most exclusive addresses. This elegant area is home to a royal palace and garden, dignified mansions used as royal residences, gentlemen's clubs, specialist shops and theatres. Wander through the warren of alleyways to discover traditional pubs, or pause with office workers lounging on the grass or in deck chairs (available for hire).

- **Location:** Map pp 134–135. ⊖*Piccadilly Circus; Green Park*. The area is hemmed in by Piccadilly, Haymarket and the Mall; Trafalgar Square and Leicester Square are to the East, Mayfair and Belgravia to the West.
- **Don't Miss:** The passages linking King Street and Pall Mall.
- **Timing**: Allow half a day to stroll through the streets lined with historic mansions and window-shop along St James's St and Jermyn St.

A BIT OF HISTORY

Henry VIII built a palace on the grounds of a former lepers' hospital dedicated to St James the Less of Jerusalem.

The domain was given by Charles II at the Restoration to his loyal courtier, Henry Jermyn, who speedily developed the empty fields into an elegant suburb for members of the re-established court. The founder of the West End, as he has since been described, laid out his estate around a square: to the East was a large market bordered by the Haymarket, to the North lay Jermyn Street, the local shopping street, and in the axis of Duke of York Street stood the church.

At the end of the Stuart monarchy, vacated private houses were taken over by the clubs. The latter had originated in taverns and coffee and chocolate houses, which they finally took over, employing the owner or publican as manager and enhancing the amenities, particularly the food for which many became famous. Numbers grew until by the turn of the 20C there were nearly 200 in the West End; now there are fewer than 30, including eight in St James's St and five in Pall Mall.

Their character has also changed from 18C flamboyance to 19C silence and reserve, and now to a modified social function or gaming.

St James's has remained a masculine world of bespoke boot and shoemakers, shirtmakers and hatters, sword, gun and rod makers, antique and 18C picture dealers, wine merchants, cheese vendors, jewellers traditional and modern and fine art auctioneers.

WALKING TOUR 2

St James's Church★

Open daily. Morning prayer: Mon, Tue, Wed, Fri at 8.30am. Thu–Sat at 7.30pm. Markets are held in the courtyard of the church: Mon 11am–5pm (food), Tue 10am–6pm (crafts and antiques), Wed–Sat, 10am–6pm (crafts) . Lectures, seminars. ℘020 7734 4511. www.st-james-piccadilly.org.

The new parish church by **Christopher Wren** in 1676 was a plain basilica of brick with Portland stone dressings and balustrade and a square tower. Plain glass windows line the north and south walls and a Venetian window fills the east end. In the 19C new entrances were made on both sides of the tower.

The galleried interior is roofed with a barrel vault with stucco ornamentation. The organ was donated by Queen Mary, daughter of James II; its case is original, as is the altarpiece of gilded wood carved by **Grinling Gibbons** and the marble font. Several artists are buried here *(plaque in vestibule)* in what is the parish church of the Royal Academy.

Jermyn Street★

The narrow street has shirtmakers, pipe makers, antique dealers, antiquarian booksellers, a chemist with real sponges,

Paxton and Whitfield (**No. 93**) selling fabulous cheese, a perfumer (**No. 89**), modern jewellery (**No. 80**), restaurants, bars, chambers and the Cavendish, a luxury hotel on the site of the famous Edwardian rendezvous.

Piccadilly Arcade★, bright with bow-fronted shops, links Piccadilly to Jermyn Street.

St James's Street★

This street was lined with town houses by the end of the 17C, including those of merchants who fled the City after the **Plague** and **Great Fire** *(1665–66)*. It retains an atmosphere of quiet elegance with shops, restaurants and clubs.

Famous buildings (north to south) include: **White's Club** (**No. 37**), established 1693, is the oldest London club and Tory in character; its bow window was added in 1811. **Boodle's Club** (**No. 28**) dates from 1762 and the building from 1765. **The Economist** (**No. 25**) complex consists of three canted glass towers around a courtyard *(1966–68)*. **Brooks's Club** (**No. 60**) was founded as the rival Whig club to White's in 1764. The house was designed by **Henry Holland,** Robert Adam's rival, in 1778.

The narrow **Park Place** is filled with the buildings of the **Royal Overseas League** *(founded 1910; 50 000 members)*. **No. 14** was once Pratt's Club.

Next on the right is **Blue Ball Yard**. The far end of the gaslit yard is lined by stables of 1742, now garages, but still with round niches in the walls, where iron hay baskets once hung.

St James's Place

This L-shaped street is lined by 18C houses, some with decorative fanlights and continuous iron balconies.

The Royal Ocean Racing Club (**No. 20**) is a neat Georgian town house. At the far end is Spencer House (**No. 27**, *see Additional Sight*).

Continue down St James's St.

The **Carlton Club** (**No. 69** St James's St.), founded in 1832 by the Duke of Wellington, is housed in an early 19C Palladian stone building. **No. 74**, formerly the Conservative Club, was designed by **George Basevi** and **Sydney Smirke** in the mid-19C in modified Palladian style. Note **No. 86**, a magnificent Victorian golden ochre stone building *(1862)*.

On the opposite side of the street stands **Byron House** (**Nos. 7–9**), built in the 1960s on the site of the house in which Byron awoke to find himself famous after the publication of his *Childe Harold (1811)*. Long-established businesses in the vicinity include **Lobb's** the bespoke bootmaker (**No. 9**); **Lock's** hatters (**No. 6** since 1700) and **Berry Bros & Rudd** (**No. 3**), the wine merchants "established in the XVII century". The half-timbered passage beside the shop leads to **Pickering Place**, a gaslit court of 18C houses reputed to be the site of the last duel to be fought in London.

St James's Palace★★

In 1532 the "goodly manor" built by **Henry VIII** was converted into a crenellated and turreted palace entered through the **Gate House** at the bottom of St James's Street. The original palace buildings, partly destroyed by the fire of 1809, are of the traditional 16C Tudor red brick, with a diaper pattern and stone trim along the line of the crenellations. They surround four courts: Colour, Friary, Ambassadors' and Engine.

Many kings and queens have been born or died in the Palace. **Charles I** spent his last night in the guardroom before walking across the park to his execution at the Banqueting House on 30 January 1649. After Whitehall Palace burned down in 1698, St James's became the chief royal residence and ambassadors are still accredited to the Court of St James. Today the Palace serves as the official residence of the Duke and Duchess of Kent and Princess Alexandra.

Chapel Royal – *Ambassadors Court.* *Open for services only early Oct to Good Fri, Sun at 8.30am (Holy Communion) and 11.15am (Choral Eucharist/Mattins); 12.30pm Prayer Book Saints' days.* *020 7839 1377.* The huge Tudor Gothic window, visible from the exterior to the

A Traditional Establishment

Pickering's, later known as **Berry Brothers & Rudd Ltd**, has occupied this site, identified as Henry VIII's tennis court, since 1731. The sign of the coffee-mill hanging outside **No. 3** was put there by the Widow Bourne to mark her grocer's shop *(1690s)*. As the shop was handed down through the generations, business, which had included "arms painting and heraldic furnishings", moved into spices, smoking tobacco, snuff, fine teas and coffee, to become one of the most comprehensive grocer's of the day, judiciously placed for the 18C Beau Monde by St James's Palace. The variously fashionable commodities were carefully weighed from the great brass weighing beams. Indeed, a Register of Weights has been kept since 1765. The last remaining stocks of groceries were sold in 1896.

right of the palace gateway, lights the Chapel Royal and its so-called Holbein ceiling. The choir is famous for its long tradition since the Medieval period and choristers wear scarlet and gold state coats at services. Several royal marriages have taken place here, including that of Queen Victoria to Prince Albert *(1840)*.

Clarence House – *Guided tours (45 mins) early Aug–early Sep Mon–Fri 10am–4pm, Sat–Sun 10am–5.30pm, last admission 1hr earlier. Timed ticket and advance booking only. £9. 020 7766 7300. www.royalcollection.org.uk.*
The distinctive white stucco mansion – the former home of HM Queen Elizabeth, the Queen Mother, and now the residence of the Prince of Wales and Duchess of Cornwall – was built in 1825 by **John Nash** for the Duke of Clarence, the future William IV. It is best seen from the Mall. The tour takes in five rooms used for official functions, in which the Queen Mother's collection of 20C British art is displayed, with works by John Piper, Graham Sutherland, WS Sickert and Augustus John.
Across Stable Yard stands **Lancaster House★**, the golden Bath stone mansion designed by Benjamin Wyatt in 1825 for the Duke of York. For many years in the 19C it was the setting for grand balls and soirées; today it is the Government's hospitality centre.
The acres now known as **Green Park** were added to St James's Park in 1667 by Charles II, who in the early morning would regularly walk up a path to what is now Hyde Park Corner – hence **Constitution Hill**. From the east side of the park there is a fine view of Spencer House.

Continue towards the Mall for a good view of Buckingham Palace and then turn left into Marlborough Road.

On the corner overlooking the Mall note the life-like relief of Queen Mary, consort of George V, by Reid-Dick and the gaslight lanterns crested with gilded crowns.

Queen's Chapel★

Past a large Art Nouveau bronze group in memory of Queen Alexandra *(1926)* is the entrance to the Queen's Chapel *(open for services only from Easter Day to last Sunday of July; 020 7930 4832)*. intended for the Infanta Maria of Spain but completed in 1625 for Charles I's eventual queen, **Henrietta Maria**, by **Inigo Jones**. It was the first church in England designed completely outside the Perpendicular Gothic tradition.

Marlborough House

While John Churchill, **Duke of Marlborough**, was winning the final victories in the seemingly endless War of the Spanish Succession *(Blenheim 1704, Ramillies 1706, Oudenaarde 1708)* and the Duchess, one of the Ladies of the Bedchamber to Queen Anne, was supervising the construction of Blenheim Palace *(1705–24)*, **Christopher Wren** designed and completed Marlborough House in two years *(1709–11)*. It was altered in 1771 by **William Chambers** and enlarged in the 19C.

Turn right into Pall Mall.

Pall Mall

The ancient way from the City to St James's Palace gets its name from the game brought over from France early in the 17C and much favoured by the Stuarts.

Crown Passage *(opposite Marlborough House, under 59–60)* is a narrow alley leading past the 19C **Red Lion** pub *(see Addresses)* into King Street, where the two world-famous establishments have their headquarters: **Christie's (No. 8)**, fine art auctioneers, founded in 1766 at the height of the fashion for doing the Grand Tour, and **Spinks (No. 5)**, specialists in coins, medals and orders, as well as antiques of all kinds.

Angel Court leads back past the **Golden Lion** *(see Addresses)*, gleaming with mirror glass and mahogany, to Pall Mall.

Lord Palmerston founded the exclusive **Oxford and Cambridge Club (No. 71)** here in 1830.

The dark red brick exterior of **Schomberg House (Nos. 80–82)** dates from 1698; Nell Gwynne lived next door (**No. 79**).

The **Army and Navy Club (No. 36**, founded 1839) was rebuilt in 1963 – not to be confused with the Naval and Military Club in St James's Square.

The **RAC** (Royal Automobile Club) is a vast building *(1911)* constructed by the builders of the Ritz.

Walk up the west side of St James's Square and then round clockwise.

St James's Square★

The Square, with a Classical equestrian statue of William III *(1807)* beneath very tall plane trees, is encircled by modern offices and 19C residences except on the north and west sides, where there are still Georgian town houses. The most notable are **No. 4** of 1676, remodelled in 1725, where Nancy Astor once lived and now the home of the **Naval and Military Club**; **No. 5** of 1748–51, with 18C and 19C additions; **No. 13** of 1740 with faked mortar uprights to give an all-header effect to the blackened brick wall; **No. 15, Lichfield House**, of 1764–65, **James "Athenian" Stuart**'s Classical stone façade with a continuous iron balcony; and **No. 20** built by Adam in 1775, with **No. 21** its 20C mirror image. **No. 31**, Norfolk House, where George III was born, served as **General Eisenhower's headquarters** in 1942 and 1944.

No. 14 *(of 1896)* is the **London Library** and **Nos. 9–10**, Chatham House, the Royal Institute of International Affairs *(f. 1920)*. The houses date from 1736 and **No. 10**, in its time, has been residence of three Prime Ministers: William Pitt 1757–61, Edward Stanley 1837–54 and William Ewart Gladstone, 1890.

Return to Pall Mall and turn left to continue east.

The **Reform Club (Nos. 104–105)**, which was established in opposition to the Carlton by Whig supporters at the time of the Reform Bill in 1832, is housed in a 19C Italian palazzo building.

The **Travellers' Club (No. 106)**, also an Italian palazzo building (19C), was founded in 1819 with a rule that members must have travelled a minimum of 500 miles *(now 1,000)* outside the British Isles in a straight line from London.

Waterloo Place★

Pall Mall is intersected by Waterloo Place, designed by John Nash as a broad approach to Carlton House and demolished in 1829. In the northern half stands the **Crimea Monument**. The beginning of the southern half is marked by two clubs, both planned by Nash, which face each other across the place. The **Athenaeum (No. 107)**, designed by Decimus Burton, is a stucco block *(1829–30)*, with Classical touches: torches, Roman Doric pillars supporting the porch, the gilded figure of Pallas Athene and the important Classical frieze in deference to the membership of the club, founded as a meeting place for artists and Men of Letters.

Carlton Gardens is a small grass plot shaded by plane trees and surrounded by four grand houses. **No. 4** *(demolished and rebuilt in 1933)* served as the headquarters of the Free French Forces *(1940–45)*. A tablet is inscribed with

General de Gaulle's famous call to arms, broadcast on 18 June 1940.

Carlton House Terrace★

Carlton House *(1709)*, which stood on the south side of Pall Mall, was taken over in 1772 by the Prince Regent. **Henry Holland** transformed it into the most gorgeous mansion in the land. In 1825, however, five years after his accession to the throne, **George IV** grew tired of the house and transferred his attention to Buckingham Palace.

Carlton House was demolished in 1829 and the Government commissioned **John Nash**, who had just re-developed Regent's Park, to design similar terraces here; only two were built. Between the two terraces at the top of the steps leading down to the Mall is the pink granite **Duke of York's Column**, tall enough according to contemporaries to place the Duke out of his creditors' reach.

▶ Go back up Waterloo Pl. to Pall Mall.

At **No. 116** stands a building of similar size and style to the Athenaeum opposite, designed by Nash but remodelled by Burton in 1842. The delightful row of bow-fronted shops, known as the **Royal Opera Arcade★**, was designed by **Nash** and **Repton** in 1817 as one of three arcades surrounding the then Royal Opera House.

▶ Walk up Haymarket.

Her Majesty's (The King's)

On the corner of Charles II Street is a Victorian, French pavilioned building with an ornate interior plan, constructed by Beerbohm Tree in 1895–97. The theatre now stages major musicals.

Theatre Royal, Haymarket★

John Nash designed the theatre in 1821 to stand, unlike its predecessor of 1720, in the axis of Charles II Street and so enjoy a double aspect. The interior *(remodelled)* is decorated in blue, gold and white.

ADDITIONAL SIGHT

Spencer House★★

Guided tour (1hr) Sun (except Jan and Aug), 10.30am–5.45pm (last admission 4.45pm). £12. Children must be accompanied by an adult, no child under 10yrs. No photography. 020 7514 1958. www.spencerhouse.co.uk.

The house was built in 1756–66 for John, 1st Earl Spencer, who initially employed the Palladian architect **John Vardy**. In 1758 Vardy was replaced by James "Athenian" Stuart, who was responsible for the Greek detail of the interior decoration; the house is one of the pioneer examples of the Neoclassical style. In 1942 the house was stripped of original fixtures, with chimney-pieces, panelling, mouldings and architraves being removed to Althorp.

Spencer House has been restored to the splendour of its late-18C appearance. The eight State Rooms are complemented by a collection of paintings and furniture: *(ground floor)* Morning Room or Ante Room; Library; Dining Room; the Palm Room, designed by Vardy with carved and gilded palm trees framing the alcove; and *(first floor)* the Music Room, Lady Spencer's Room, the Great Room and the Painted Room decorated in Stuart's Greek style.

ADDRESSES

CAFÉS

Inn The Park, *St James's Park. Charlng Cross. 020 7451 9999. www.inntheprark.com. Open Mon–Fri 8am–5pm, Sat–Sun 9am–5pm.* In the heart of the park, serving local produce.

PUBS AND BARS

Golden Lion, *25 King St. Green Park. 020 7925 0007. Mon–Fri 11am–11pm, Sat noon–8pm.* Traditional British pub, which dates from 1762.

The Red Lion, *23 Crown Passage Green Park. 020 7930 4141. Mon–Fri 11am–11pm, Sat 11.30am–11pm.* Small pub in an off-the-beaten-track location, which attracts a distinguished crowd of local workers.

KENSINGTON AND CHELSEA

Genteel and monied, Kensington and Chelsea is one of London's most elegant areas, knitted around a patchwork of squares, dazzling white town houses converted into flats for central urbanites and mews houses down leafy backstreets – all with millionaire pricetags. The area cradles key London attractions, from South Kensington's range of world-class museums to the shopping hubs of Kensington High Street and the King's Road. Trendy Notting Hill is just to the North, with its bohemian village vibe, café culture, the Portobello Road antiques market and tranquil Little Venice.

Highlights

1. London's grandest park: **Hyde Park** (p162)
2. Explore the elegance of royal residence, **Kensington Palace** (p166)
3. High-end shopping and coffee on the **King's Road** (p175)
4. Cutting-edge contemporary art at the **Saatchi Gallery** (p178)
5. Find a must-buy at Notting Hill's lively **Portobello Market** (p181)

Geography – The borough of Kensington and Chelsea lies to the West of Westminster, on the other side of Hyde Park from Mayfair. Fashionable Knightsbridge is ranged along the park's southern edge, with the museum district of South Kensington immediately south and the shopping area of Kensington High Street immediately west. Notting Hill is located to the North of here, while Chelsea is situated below South Kensington and runs down to the north bank of the River Thames to the West of Pimlico and East of Fulham.

History – Traditionally an area populated by the city's richer residents, Kensington and Chelsea also has numerous royal connections. Two of Henry VIII's wives lived in Chelsea, as did Queen Elizabeth I, and the King's Road itself was named for Charles II – he used to use it as a private route from London to his palace at Kew. The manor of Kensington was mentioned in the Domesday Book under the tenancy of Aubrey de Vere, later Earl of Oxford. Queen Victoria was born in Kensington Palace and conferred Royal status on the borough. Later palace residents included Diana, Princess of Wales.

In the 19C and early 20C the area became a creative and radical crucible: painters Rosetti, Whistler and Singer Sargent all lived and worked here, as did writer Oscar Wilde. It rose to prominence again as a "Swinging Sixties" centre, with seminal shops and groovy residents such as Biba and the Beatles setting up homes and businesses on the King's Road (which was also the birthplace of Punk in the 1970s, thanks to designer Vivienne Westwood and musician and music manager Malcolm McLaren). Kensington and Chelsea were amalgamated into the Royal Borough of Kensington and Chelsea in 1965.

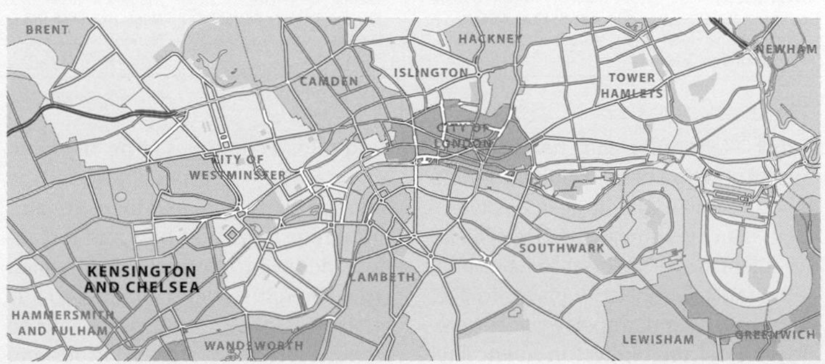

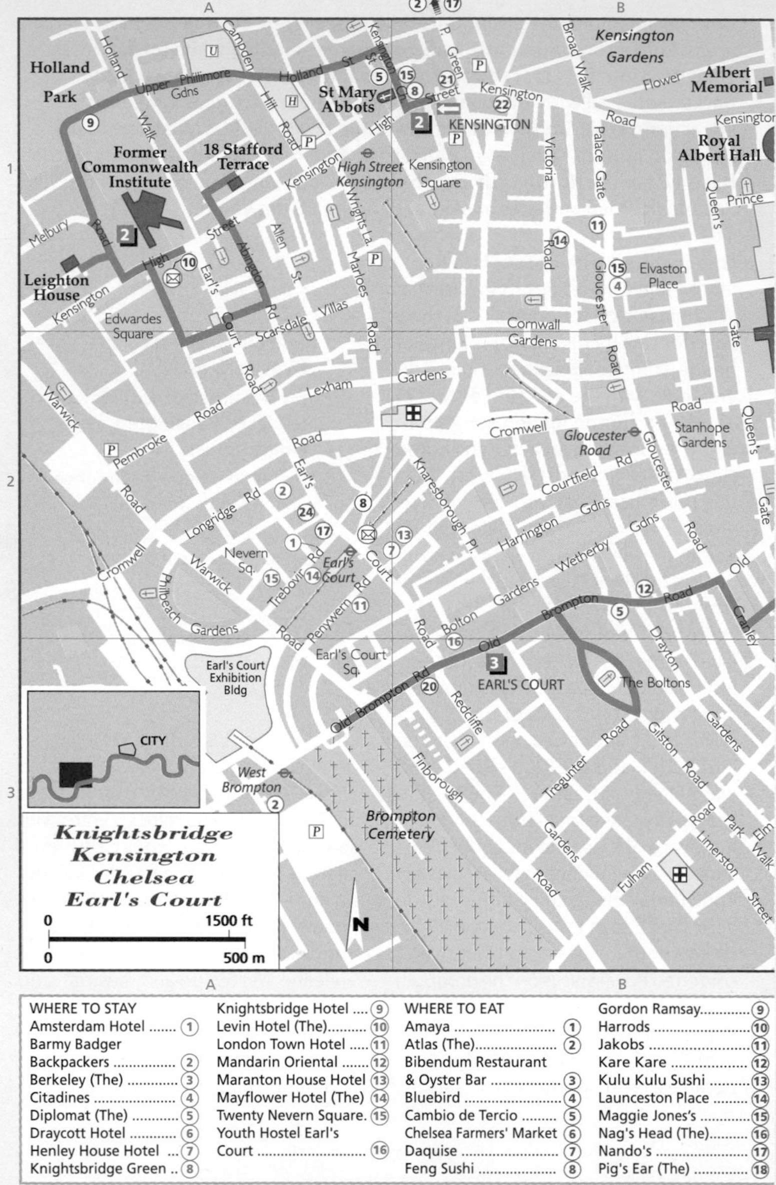

Today – Kensington and Chelsea is now better known for being a nightlife haunt of young royals and upper-class wannabes than a progressive hotbed of creative talent. Nevertheless it remains one of the most sought-after places to live in the capital and property prices here are some of the highest in town. The King's Road continues to be an enjoyable place to shop, especially around the Sloane Square end, and there are also numerous upmarket bars and restaurants here which attract a well-heeled crowd. Knightsbridge continues to pull in the designer shoppers, thanks to iconic department stores Harrods and

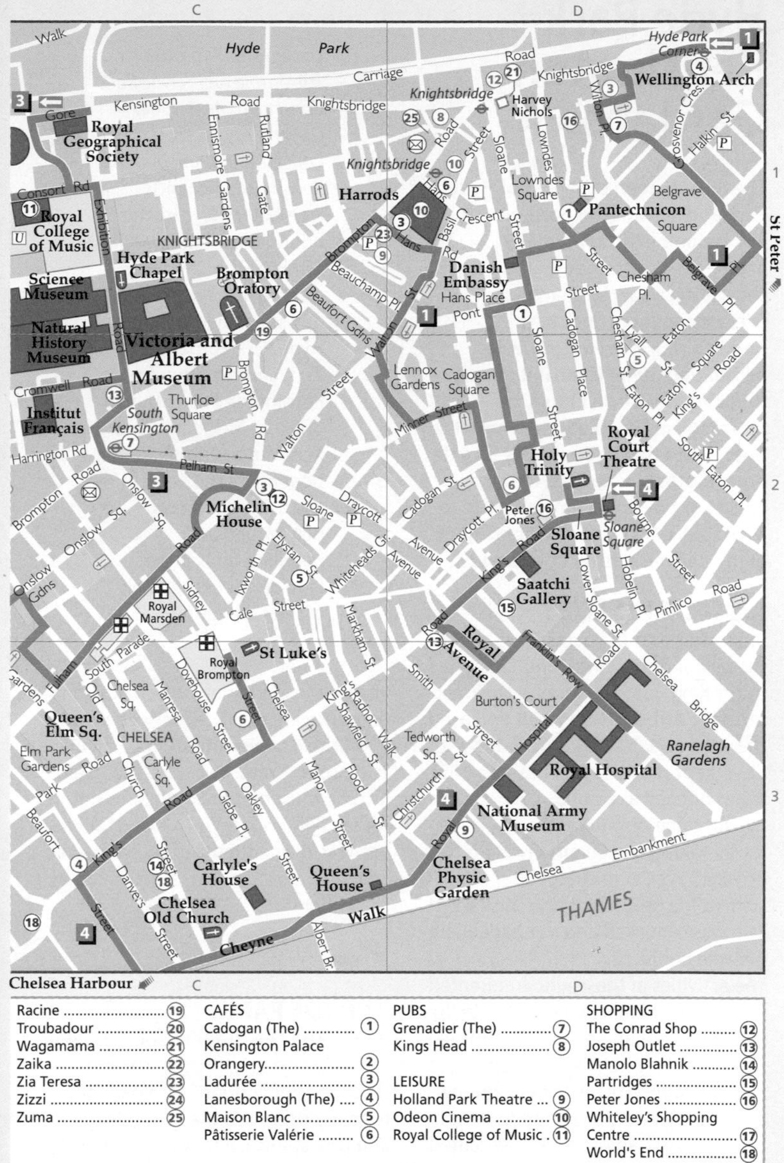

Harvey Nichols, although Kensington High Street is feeling the effects of the nearby Westfield Shopping Centre, which opened in Shepherd's Bush in 2008, and has seen something of a downturn.

The Saatchi Gallery near Sloane Square brought the creative impulse back to the area when it moved here in 2008 from the South Bank, while South Kensington sees a steady stream of visitors heading for the cultural meccas of the Victoria and Albert Museum, the Science Museum and the Natural History Museum (see *CENTRAL LONDON MUSEUMS*).

Hyde Park – Kensington Gardens★★

The linked green expanses of Hyde Park and Kensington Gardens at London's heart offer many attractions in all seasons and give the capital a special charm. Every day people flock to the parks to walk the dog, jog, ride, go boating, swim (even if it means breaking the ice on Christmas morning), in-line skate, sail model boats, feed the pigeons, play bicycle polo, football, rounders, tennis, cricket or bowls – even archery is available. Concerts and celebrations in the park also attract the crowds.

- **Location:** Map p163. *⊖Marble Arch; Hyde Park Corner; Knightsbridge; Queensway; Lancaster Gate; Park Lane; Knightsbridge.* Kensington Rd. and Bayswater Rd. mark the boundaries of the two parks.
- **Timing:** This chapter is divided into two walks: one starting from either Hyde Park Corner or Marble Arch and the other from Kensington Palace. Allow one day, including a tour of Kensington Palace and/or boating on the Serpentine.
- **Kids:** The children's playground and paddling pool at the Lido on the south bank of the Serpentine.

A BIT OF HISTORY

In Saxon times the acres were part of the Manor of Eia which, until "resumed by the King" in 1536, belonged to **Westminster Abbey**. **Henry VIII** enclosed the area and, having stocked it with deer, kept it as a royal chase. In 1637 it was opened as a public park and the crowds came, only to be debarred when it was sold by the Commonwealth to a private buyer, who charged for admission. At the Restoration the contract of sale was cancelled and the park again became public.

The activities of those who frequented the park were even more diverse in the 18C and 19C than now: the last formal royal hunt was held in 1768; pits were dug to supply clay for bricks; gunpowder magazines and arms depots sited in isolated parts; soldiers were executed against the wall in the northeast corner; at the same time it was a fashionable carriage and riding promenade, first round the road known as **the Tour** and then **the Ring** (originally a small inner circle) or along the Row **(Rotten Row)**.

The **Great Exhibition of 1851**, conceived and planned by Prince Albert, was housed in the **Crystal Palace**, a vast iron and glass structure. Queen Victoria, Wellington and some 6,030,195 others visited the exhibition, which aimed to demonstrate man's inventiveness and 19C British achievement in particular. The profit it made was used to establish the museums in South Kensington (*see KENSINGTON*). The Crystal Palace was dismantled and re-erected at Sydenham, where it was destroyed by fire in 1936.

WALKING TOUR

1 HYDE PARK

It was **Pitt the Elder** in the 17C who aptly called the former deer park, "the lungs of London". The park is put to many uses: as a place of relaxation and free speech, a rallying ground for parades and royal salutes, and since 1800 a burial ground for pet dogs *(at the Victoria Gate)*.

Marble Arch

At the northeast corner stands a fine triumphal arch of Italian white marble with three bronze gates. Modelled on the Arch of Constantine in Rome by **John Nash** *(1827)*, it was intended to stand before Buckingham Palace, a monument

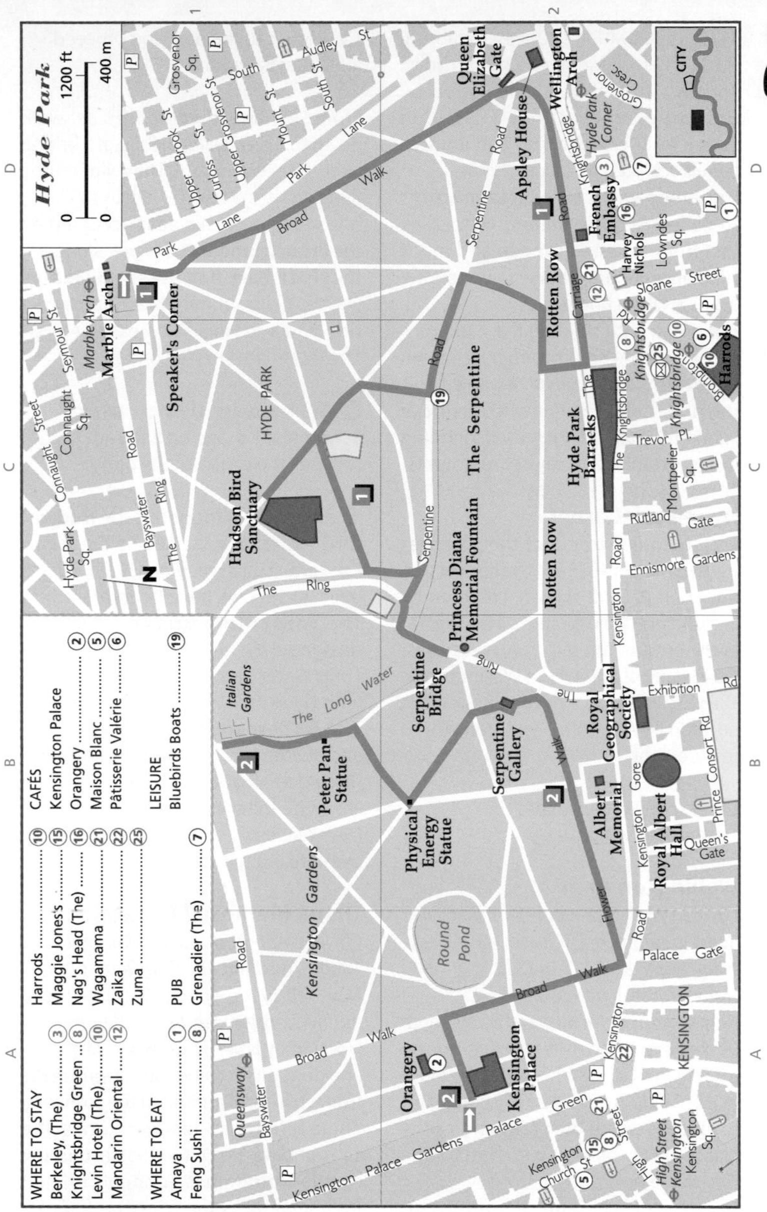

to celebrate the end of the Napoleonic wars, but the central archway was not wide enough to accommodate the Gold Stage Coach. The arch was dismantled *(1837)*, and in 1851 was rebuilt where the **Tyburn gallows** had stood until 1783. **Speakers' Corner** is a relatively modern feature of the park. Anyone may mount their soap box and address the crowds so long as they do not blaspheme or incite a Breach of the Peace.

Walk down Broad Walk.

At the bottom end of Park Lane stands the **Queen Elizabeth Gate**, erected in

1993 in celebration of Queen Elizabeth, the late Queen Mother's 93rd birthday. The two sets of gates, designed by **Giuseppe Lund**, provide a cast-iron screen for the central lion and unicorn panels sculpted by David Wynne.

Inside the park is **Richard Westmacott**'s so-called **Achilles** statue *(18ft/5.5m)*, cast from captured cannon and modelled on an Antique horse tamer on the Quirinal Hill in Rome.

The riding path through the park, running parallel to Knightsbridge, is known as **Rotten Row** *(originally Route du Roi)*, the first road in Britain with artificial lighting *(1690)*. Today it is used for riding by local stables and cavalry regiments.

Hyde Park Corner

The southeast corner of the park was transformed in 1825–28 by the erection of a triple arched **screen**, crowned by a sculptured frieze and a **triumphal arch** surmounted by a colossal equestrian statue of the Duke of Wellington. In 1883 the arch was moved to its present position but the statue was transferred to Aldershot.

Take the underpass to the central reservation.

Wellington Arch

Open Wed–Sun 10am–5pm (longer hours in summer). Closed 24–26 Dec, 1 Jan. £4. 020 7930 2726. www.english-heritage.org.uk.

Hemmed in by the busy traffic, this arch has been restored to its former glory. An exhibition relates the history of the landmark. Go up to the viewing platforms to enjoy views of the parks and of the Palace of Westminster, with the London Eye on the horizon.

The present **Wellington Monument**, placed before the entrance to Apsley House (*see PICCADILLY*), is by Boehm *(1834–90)*; cast from captured guns, it shows the Duke mounted on his horse Copenhagen, guarded by a Grenadier, a Royal Highlander, a Welsh Fusilier and an Inniskilling Dragoon.

Return to the park and proceed along Carriage Rd.

From Carriage Road *(south side)* walk down to Albert Gate, the site of a bridge over the Westbourne. The twin houses flanking the gate were built in 1852; the house on the east side is occupied by the **French Embassy**. Further along are the **Hyde Park Barracks and stables** *(1970–71)*. From here the Guardsmen ride down to Horse Guards' when HM The Queen returns to London.

Walk through the park, along Serpentine Rd. and up any path towards the centre of the park.

At the centre of the park is the **Hudson Bird Sanctuary**, marked by the **Jacob Epstein** sculpture *Rima* (1925), where over 90 species have been recorded. The **Serpentine Bridge** (1826–28), designed by John Rennie, spans the Long Water and the Serpentine. It also links Hyde Park to Kensington Gardens. **The Serpentine** is used for boating and swimming, with a children's paddling pool. If you like to watch people shiver, it's the site of London's traditional New Year open-air swim. There is a café overlooking the water.

Diana Memorial Fountain

Open Apr–Aug 10am–8pm; Sept 10am–7pm; Mar and Oct 10am–6pm; Nov–Feb 10am–4pm. May be closed during extreme weather conditions.

Opened by HM The Queen in July 2004 and dogged for some time by problems from children slipping on the stones to engineering hiccups that turned the surrounding area into a marsh, this low circular fountain is London's official memorial to Diana, Princess of Wales, who died in 1997.

2 KENSINGTON GARDENS

See Kensington Palace, p166.

The Gardens were at their prime under the Royal gardeners, **Henry Wise** and his successor in 1728, **Charles Bridgman**. An octagonal basin, the **Round**

Pond, was constructed facing the palace with avenues radiating from it. Other features of the period that persist are the **Broad Walk** and the **Orangery★**, a lovely place for tea or a light lunch. Later additions are the Edwardian **sunken garden**, the statue of **Peter Pan** *(1912)* to the West and **The Arch**, sculpted by **Henry Moore** in 1979, and the **Flower Walk**, north of the Albert Memorial. The **Diana Memorial Playground**, in the northwest corner, is a fabulous spot for children, with a life-size pirate ship at its centre.

Take the Broad Walk and continue along the Flower Walk.

Albert Memorial★

The epitome of mid-Victorian taste and sentiment, this memorial was commissioned by a heartbroken Queen Victoria to commemorate her beloved husband Prince Albert, who died of typhoid in 1861. It was designed by **Sir George Gilbert Scott** *(1872)* as a neo-Gothic spire *(175ft/53m)*, ornamented with mosaics, pinnacles and a cross. At the centre is a brilliantly gilded figure *(14ft/4m)* of the Prince Consort.

For details of Royal Albert Hall and surrounding buildings across Kensington Road, see KENSINGTON.

Follow the path to the Gallery.

Serpentine Gallery

Kensington Gardens, W2. Open daily 10am–6pm. No charge. 020 7402 6075. www.serpentinegallery.org. This is one of London's best loved galleries, housing a small collection of modern and contemporary art in a delightful building shaded by trees. A striking pavilion is built in the grounds every summer.

Serpentine Sackler Gallery

A new gallery opened in July 2013 a stone's throw away from the Serpentine Gallery. Prize-winning architect Zaha Hadid has redeveloped The Magazine, a Grade II listed building near the Serpentine Lake, into a dynamic new space, the Serpentine Sackler Gallery *(www.serpentinegallery.org)*. The dramatic modern extension, used as a café/restaurant and social space, presents the best in emerging talent across all art forms.

Take a diagonal path towards the Statue of Physical Energy.

The **Statue of Physical Energy** is a bronze equestrian statue by GF Watts, which depicts a powerful horse and its muscular rider, and is said to borrow heavily from Ancient Greek tradition, despite dating from the 19C. From here, branch right towards the Serpentine to view the statue of **Peter Pan**, sculpted in 1912 by Sir George Frampton to a plan by J.M. Barrie himself.

Continue north around the edge of the Serpentine to the Italian Fountains.

Italian Fountains

At the northern end of the Serpentine are the Italian Gardens, where you'll find five fountains flanked by numerous works of classical statuary and sculpture. Separating the gardens from the Bayswater Road are the railings where artists exhibit their works for sale in an open-air market most Sundays.

KENSINGTON PALACE★★

Open Mon–Sat 10am–5pm (last admission 4pm). Closed 24–26 Dec. Guided tour. £14.50, guided tours free. Audio-guide. No photography. 0844 482 7777. www.hrp.org.uk.

The State Apartments have undergone major redevelopment, with improved accessibility.

In 2012 Kensington Palace reopened its doors after a two-year programme of refurbishment. The palace has been transformed, with many new rooms open to the public. The new Jubilee Garden reconnects the Palace to Kensington Gardens, and has at its centre a restored statue of Queen Victoria.

Kensington Palace

Since its purchase in 1689 by **William III**, Kensington Palace has passed through three phases: the Monarch's private residence with **Wren** as principal architect; a royal palace with **William Kent** in charge of alterations and, since 1760, a residence for members of the royal family, notably the late Diana, Princess of Wales, and now HRH the Duke and Duchess of Cambridge.

Victoria Revealed

A major new exhibition about the life of Queen Victoria, who was born at Kensington Palace and lived here until she became queen at 18, is among the highlights of the palace.

Previously unexhibited items include a gold locket given to Queen Victoria on her first birthday in 1820, containing a lock of hair from her parents, the Duke and Duchess of Kent, and Prince Albert's dressing kit, featuring razors, brushes and a tongue scraper, one of his rarest surviving personal items.

The King's and Queen's State Apartments, once the epicentre of royal and political life, have been brought to life with new multi-media installations, interactive theatre, and costumes from the Royal Ceremonial Dress Collection.

The Queen's Apartments

The **gallery** *(84ft/25.6m long)* is rich in carving, with cornice and door heads by **William Emmett** and sumptuous surrounds to the gilt Vauxhall mirrors above the fireplace in the gallery by Grinling Gibbons *(1691)*. Portraits in the rooms are personal: *Peter the Great* in armour by Kneller in commemoration of his visit in 1698, *William III* as King and Prince of Orange, *Queen Mary* by Wissing, *Queen Anne* and *William, Duke of Gloucester* by Kneller. In the **Drawing Room** Kneller painted *Queen Anne* in profile and the first Royal Gardener, *Henry Wise*.

The King's Apartments

The **King's Grand Staircase** *(Wren, 1689)* links the circuit of rooms which make up The King's Gallery. It was altered in 1692–93, when the **Tijou** iron balustrade was incorporated and again in 1696 by Kent, who covered walls and ceiling with grand *trompe-l'œil* paintings.

The lofty 18C rooms bear William Kent's strong decorative imprint. The **Privy Chamber** has an allegorical ceiling of George I as Mars; the **Presence Chamber**, a red and blue-on-white ceiling with arabesque decoration by Kent *(1724)*.

The King's Gallery was limited to simpler ornamentation as it was intended to display the greatest pictures in the royal collection.

Although the 19C **Victorian Rooms** were redecorated by Queen Mary, all else belonged to and epitomises **Queen Victoria** and her family: furniture, ornaments, portraits and toys. The **Council Chamber** at the far end of the east front contains mementoes of the 1851 Exhibition and a massive carved Indian ivory throne and footstool. Only the ceiling of arabesques, figures and medallions remains of Kent's Baroque decoration in the **King's Drawing Room**.

ADDRESSES

SHOPPING

Whiteleys Shopping Centre *Queensway, W2 4YN. ⊖Queensway or Bayswater. ✆020 7229 8844. www.whiteleys.com.* Formerly a department store – the UK's first and supposedly saved from World War II, as Hitler wanted it for his UK HQ – this is now a modern shopping mall with smart boutiques, food outlets and a cinema multiplex.

Knightsbridge – Belgravia★★

Knightsbridge and Belgravia are the most exclusive residential districts in the capital and the fashionable emporia and designer shops along Brompton Road, Sloane Street and Beauchamp Place are temples of delight. It is a pleasurable pastime to mingle with the leisured classes and to admire the stylish displays. The area also boasts some of the finest hotels and restaurants.

- **Location**: Map pp 160–161. *⊖Knightsbridge; Hyde Park Corner; South Kensington.* This area is bounded by Hyde Park to the North, the museum district of South Kensington to the West, and Buckingham Palace Gardens to the East.
- **Don't Miss:** Belgrave Square, Harrods, the neo-Baroque Brompton Oratory.
- **Timing:** Allow half a day to stroll through the area, more if you decide to browse through Harrods or visit the Victoria and Albert Museum (*see MAJOR CENTRAL LONDON MUSEUMS*).

A BIT OF HISTORY

Until the end of the 18C **Knightsbridge** was an unkempt village outside London and on a major highway, with its fair share of cattle markets, slaughterhouses, taverns and pleasure gardens.
In 1831 **Benjamin Harvey** opened a linen draper's *(Harvey Nichols)*; in 1849 **Henry Harrod** took over a small grocer's shop. These stores, which over the years have become household names for luxury shopping, attract an elegant and wealthy clientele.
It was probably **George IV**'s decision to transform Buckingham House into Buckingham Palace that provided the impetus for the development of **Belgravia**, part of the Grosvenor Estate. By 1827 **Wilton Crescent**, **Belgrave Square**, **Eaton Place** and **Eaton Square** had all been erected.
Basevi (the architect) and Cubitt (the builder) were probably responsible for the adjoining square and streets: **Chester Square**, **Belgrave Place** and **Upper Belgrave Street**.

WALKING TOUR 1

Start from Hyde Park Corner. *For Apsley House See PICCADILLY.*

The Lanesborough Hotel

This handsome building *(1827–29)* on Hyde Park Corner, originally designed by **William Wilkins** to house St George's Hospital, has a central porch with square columns flanked by two wings.

Walk along Knightsbridge and turn left into Wilton Pl.

The 17C brick terraces of **Wilton Place** predate St Paul's Church by a century, erected in 1843 on the site of a Guards' barracks, still recalled in local street and pub names. **Wilton Crescent** is lined by stuccoed terraces.

Make a short detour to Wilton Row to visit the Grenadier pub (*see Addresses*), then return to Belgrave Sq.

Belgrave Square★★

The square *(10 acres/4ha)* is bordered by twinned, but not identical ranges consisting of three-storeyed, white-stuccoed houses. The centres and ends are in the Corinthian style, with urns and balustrades, pillared porches and an attic screen decorated with statues; there are detached houses in three of the corners. The ironwork matches the fence enclosing the central garden; a bronze statue of Simon Bolivar stands at the southeast corner. Seaford House was the residence of the statesman, Lord John Russell. Today the Square is home to several embassies.

Leave the Square via Upper Belgrave St. to reach Eaton Sq.

St Peter's Church, at the northeastern end of Eaton Square, was erected in 1827 in the Classical style as part of the original development project. The interior was refurbished after a fire in 1988.

Proceed along Eaton Sq,, turn right onto Belgrave Pl., left into Chesham Pl. and right onto Belgrave Mews to reach Halkin Pl. and West Halkin St.

Pantechnicon

The august Doric-columned warehouse dates from 1830. On either side and in **West Halkin Street** and **Halkin Arcade** are a number of small shops dealing in luxury goods. Just north along **Lowndes Street** is **Lowndes Square**, developed separately in the mid-19C and largely rebuilt in the 20C.

Retrace your steps and turn right into Cadogan Pl. towards Sloane St.

Sloane Street

The street, first developed in 1773 to link Knightsbridge to Chelsea and the river, has been rebuilt piecemeal. The **Danish Embassy** *(1976–77)* was designed by Ove Arup. The area west of Sloane Street, known as **Hans Town,** dates from the late 18C. The tall red brick buildings date mainly to the Cadogan Estate.

Turn right into Pont St.

On the right is **Hans Pl.**, a pleasant residential area. On the left is **St Columba's**, the London Church of Scotland *(1950–55)*, designed by **Edward Maufe** with a square stone tower capped by a green cupola *(open Mon–Fri 9.30am–1pm, 2pm–5pm; 020 7584 2321; www.stcolumbas.org.uk)*.
In the late 19C the area around **Cadogan Square** and **Cadogan Gardens** was rebuilt in unfading red brick, nicknamed "Pont Street Dutch".

Turn right onto Walton St. to Walton Pl., then left onto Hans Rd.

Harrods

Since 1905 this shop, which claims to sell everything, has been housed in the familiar terra-cotta building with towers and cupolas; the lofty **food halls** are decorated with art nouveau wall tiles (*see YOUR STAY IN THE CITY – Shop-*

Brightly lit Harrods on Brompton Road

ping). It is still regularly voted the world's finest department store. Owned by Mohammed al Fayed, there is a memorial to Princess Diana and Dodi al Fayed on the ground floor.

Harvey Nichols

This is the other great landmark department store in Knightsbridge, which featured in the British comedy *Absolutely Fabulous*. Opened in 1831, Harvey Nichols is famous for its high-end fashion and original store windows showcasing British design and creative flare.

Cross Brompton Rd. and follow the map to explore the charming streets and squares, past the following:

Brompton Road

The triangle between Kensington Road and Brompton Road developed as a residential district in Georgian fashion around a series of squares: **Trevor Square** *(1818)*, **Brompton Square** *(1826)*, **Montpelier Square★***(1837)*; the houses have stucco ground floors and basements with brick upper storeys and balconies. Narrow streets link the squares, with mews and closes lined by colour-washed cottages with handkerchief-sized front gardens.

Oratory of St Philip Neri (Brompton Oratory)

Open daily 7am–6pm. 020 7808 0900. www.bromptonoratory.com.

The main body of the church was designed *(1881)* by **Herbert Gribble** in the Italian Baroque style in Portland stone; the dome and lantern, meanwhile, was planned by **George Sherrin** *(1895–96)* so as to span the exceptionally wide and lofty nave.

The 18C Italian Baroque statues of the Twelve Apostles by Giuseppe Mazzuoli *(1644–1725)* used to stand in Siena Cathedral. The Baroque pulpit and much of the mosaic decoration are by **Commendatore Formilli**. The inlaid wooden floor and carved choir stalls inlaid with ivory date from the previous church. The altar is early-18C Flemish Baroque.

ADDRESSES

CAFÉS

Kensington Palace Orangery, *Kensington Gardens. Queensway. 020 3166 6113. Generally 9am–6pm (5pm Oct–Feb); check website as may close for functions. www.hrp.org.uk.* Light lunches and afternoon tea served in a delightful setting in Queen Anne's 18C Orangery next to the palace. This is one of the nicest places to have tea in London.

Ladurée, *inside Harrods, 87–135 Brompton Rd. Knightsbridge. 020 3155 0111. Mon–Sat 9am–9pm, Sun 11.30am–6.30pm.* The famous French pâtisserie, known for its delicious macaroons, has a concession on the ground floor of Harrods. A lovely place for a snack.

Pâtisserie Valérie, *215 Brompton Rd. and 32–44 Hans Crescent. Knightsbridge Mon–Sat 8am–6pm, Sun 9am–6pm.* Handmade cakes and patisserie served in elegant surroundings.

The Cadogan, *75 Sloane St. Knightsbridge or Sloane Square. 020 7235 7141. www.cadogan.com. Afternoon tea daily 3–6pm.* This luxurious hotel serves afternoon tea in a cosy living room with a warm, inviting atmosphere. The scones, baked on demand, are to die for! Choice of teas and pastries from £4.50 or set tea for £17.

PUB

The Grenadier, *18 Wilton Row, Belgravia. Hyde Park Corner. 020 7235 3074. Daily noon–11pm (Sun 10.30pm).* This lovely historic pub was once frequented by the Duke of Wellington and his grenadiers. indoors, dark wood walls are covered with military memorabilia and it is said that the place is haunted by a murdered officer, who was convicted of cheating. Good selection of beers.

The Nag's Head, *53 Kennerton St, Belgravia. Knightsbridge. 020 7235 1135. Mon–Sat 11am–11pm, Sun noon–10.30pm.* Like a pub from an old movie, this traditional boozer has a picturesque bar and dozens of nick-knacks to make you feel at home. Dine on solid pub fare to the sound of Anglo-Irish folk music, and all without the nuisance of ringing mobile phones, which are banned!

Kensington★★

The Royal Borough of Kensington takes great pride in its aristocratic connections. Elegant residential streets are spacious and white-stuccoed houses boast all the trappings of affluence. It is also famous for its world-class museums and fashionable amenities.

Location: Map pp 160–161. *⊖High Street Kensington; South Kensington; Notting Hill Gate; Holland Park.* Kensington and South Kensington are to the South and West of Kensington Gardens.

Don't Miss: The Science Museum and the Natural History Museum *See MAJOR CENTRAL LONDON MUSEUMS.*

Timing: Allow an hour or two to explore the leafy avenues and elegant squares lying south of Kensington High Street.

Kids: The adventure playground in Holland Park.

A BIT OF HISTORY

The village of Kensington was for centuries manorial, with a few large houses at the centre of fields. It slowly increased from small houses lining the main road to squares and tributary streets as estates. Before long, separate parcels of land were sold. Among the famous mansions were Nottingham House (later Kensington Palace), Campden House, Holland House and, on the site of the Albert Hall, Gore House, the home of **William Wilberforce** until 1823 and for 12 years from 1836 the residence of "the gorgeous" Lady Blessington, whose circle included Wellington, Brougham, Landseer, Tom Moore, Bulwer-Lytton, Thackeray, Dickens, Louis Napoleon and other such poets, novelists, artists, journalists and French exiles.

A Visionary Enterprise – When the **Great Exhibition**, held in 1851 in Hyde Park was over, **Prince Albert**, its initiator, proposed that the financial profit, a vast £200,000, be spent in establishing a great educational centre in South Kensington. The money was used to buy the land on which the world-famous museums and colleges, including the Natural History and Science museums, are to be found today *(see MAJOR CENTRAL LONDON MUSEUMS).*

WALKING TOUR 2

KENSINGTON VILLAGE

Kensington High Street

In 1846 when **Thackeray** and his daughters moved into a house in Young Street, the eldest described Kensington High Street as "a noble highway, skirted by beautiful old houses with scrolled iron gates." Within a few years the population was to multiply from 70 to 120,000; shops spread along both sides of the High Street.

Down Young Street is **Kensington Square**, with houses dating from the 17–19C, as varied in design as the people who have lived in it: Sir Hubert Parry (**No. 17**), John Stuart Mill (**No. 18**) and Mrs Patrick Campbell (**No. 33**). The two oldest houses are Nos. 11 and 12 in the southeast corner; a cartouche over the door mentions previous owners including the Duchess Mazarin (Henrietta Mancini, niece of the Cardinal), 1692–98.

The **Roof Garden** at **No. 99** Kensington High Street *(entrance in Derry Street)* was laid out in the 1930s and has mature trees, grass and flamingos high up above the bustle of High Street Kensington. *Open (private functions permitting) daily 11am–5pm by appointment. 020 7937 7994. www.roofgardens.virgin.com.*

On the corner of **Kensington Church Street** and the High Street an unusual vaulted cloister leads to the neo-Gothic parish church of **St Mary Abbots**, which boasts an unusually tall spire *(278ft/85m high).*

Walk west along Kensington High St.

Holland Park

Open daily 7.30am until 30min before dusk (check signs); open-air opera, Jun–Aug; café; sports facilities (golf range, tennis courts, cricket pitch and nets, football pitch); 020 7631 3003 (enquiries); 0300 999 1000 (opera; open late Apr–Aug); 020 7602 2226 (sports bookings).

It is nearly 400 years since Holland House was built by the City merchant and courtier Sir Walter Cope in the scattered village of Kensington. The mansion soon became a place of entertainment for King and Court. Advanced wings on either side of the central range were added by Cope's daughter, whose husband was made Earl Holland in 1624.

In the mid-18C Holland House was acquired by the politician Henry Fox, who was also created Baron Holland. He was rich, knew everyone and entertained lavishly; his grandson, 3rd Baron Holland, politician, writer and literary patron, was the last great host of Holland House. Among those who dined and visited frequently were the Prince Regent, Sheridan, Byron, Talleyrand, Louis Napoleon, William IV and, almost the last visitor, Prince Albert.

Today, the restored **East Wing** and **George VI Hostel** serve as a youth hostel. In summer the forecourt is canopied to accommodate open-air performances of opera and dance. A restaurant occupies part of the 17C stable block; the **Ice House** and **Orangery**, meanwhile, are used for functions and exhibitions. The woodland has been re-established and the gardens replanted after long neglect; peacocks flaunt their plumages in the gardens and water tinkles through the **Japanese Garden**.

Former Commonwealth Institute Building

Kensington High Street.

The unique tent-shaped building, with its four peaked, green copper roofs supported on glass curtain walls, was opened by HM The Queen in 1962 to replace the former Imperial Institute, opened in 1893 by Queen Victoria, of which only the imposing **Queen's Tower** survives. Currently closed for refurbishment, the building will house the Design Museum from 2014.

Turn right along Melbury Rd. then left into Holland Park Rd.

Leighton House★

12 Holland Park Road. Call or see website for times. 020 7602 3316. www.leightonhouse.co.uk.

The Victorian painter **Lord Leighton** *(1830–96)*, President of the Royal Academy, remains most originally reflected in the house that he built for himself in 1866. The **Arab Hall** is covered with panels of glazed tiles imported from the Middle East. A mosaic floor spreads around a bubbling, cool fountain.

To the North of Kensington, the fashionable residential area of **Notting Hill** has many excellent restaurants and bars. *See p181.*

Return to Kensington High St. and cross the road to Edwardes Sq.

Edwardes Square

Tucked away behind the Odeon Cinema and the uniform brick range of large houses known as **Earl's Terrace** *(1800–10)* is this elegant square. The East and West ranges are composed of more modest three-storey houses *(1811–20)* complete with balcony, garden and square ironwork. In the southeast corner stands the **Scarsdale Arms**, a Victorian pub bedecked with flowers, established in 1837 *(see Addresses)*. To the South is **Pembroke Square**, lined on three sides with Georgian ranges, matching iron balconies and in the southeast corner, its pub.

Return to Kensington High St., then turn left onto Phillimore Gardens and right onto Stafford Terrace.

18 Stafford Terrace★

18 Stafford Terrace. Open mid-Sept–mid-June. Guided tours Sat–Sun 11.15am and Wed 11.15am and 2.15pm (conventional guide), Sat–Sun 1pm, 2.15pm and 3.30pm (costumed guide). £8. To book 020 7602 3316 (Mon–

Fri 9am–5pm), ✆020 7938 1295 (Mon–Sat 10.15am–5pm). www.rbkc.gov.uk
Edward Linley Sambourne, a leading *Punch* cartoonist and book illustrator, moved into this Victorian town house in 1874. The original wall decoration by **William Morris** and the furniture have survived largely unaltered. Cartoons by Sambourne and his contemporaries line the stairs.

WALKING TOUR 3

SOUTH KENSINGTON

The **Royal College of Art**, with eight floors of studios and workshops, dates from 1961. The college evolved from a fusion of the Government School of Design and the National Art Training School *(1896)* and has nurtured many eminent artists, architects, sculptors and industrial and fashion designers.
In contrast, the elaborately decorated building next door is the former home of **The Royal College of Organists** *(1875)*; note the frieze of Putti carrying musical instruments and garlands incorporating the "VR" monogram around the door.

Royal Albert Hall★

Kensington Gore, SW7. Guided tours Thu–Tue 10.30am–3.30pm. £9.50. ✆020 7838 3105 (tours); 020 7589 8212 (box office). www.royalalberthall.com.
The round hall, almost ¼ mile/0.4km in circumference, built of red brick with a shallow glass-and-iron dome, is the foil in shape and ornament to the Albert Memorial *(see HYDE PARK – Kensington Gardens)* opposite, since its only decoration is an upper frieze of figures illustrating the Arts and Sciences.
Reunions, pop and jazz sessions, exhibitions, boxing, political meetings, conferences and concerts, particularly the eight-week summer series of **Promenade Concerts** *(known as "The Proms")*, fill the hall with up to 7,000 people at a time.
Behind the Albert Hall stands a monument to Prince Albert, a driving force behind the 1851 Great Exhibition. *See Kensington Gardens.*

Return to Kensington Rd. and turn right.

Imperial and Royal Colleges and Society

Virtually next door, the **Royal Geographical Society** founded in 1830, has been a cornerstone of Britain's exploration of the world ever since. Statues of explorers **Shackleton** and **Livingstone** adorn the outer wall. The collections contain many objects linked to the great explorers, from HM Stanley's boots to Livingstone's compass. The **Map Room** contains 30,000 old and historic maps. ***Map Room and Library:*** *open Mon–Fri 10am–5pm.* ***Picture Library:*** *open Mon–Fri 10am–5pm by appointment. ✆020 7591 3000. www.rgs.org.*
To the south, in Prince Consort Road, stands the dark-red brick **Royal College of Music**, built in 1893 in neo-Gothic style. Inside is the highly prized **Museum of Instruments**, which has over 600 items, including a spinet played by Handel and Haydn's clavichord. *Open Tue–Fri 11.30am–4.30pm; free. ✆020 7591 4842. www.rcm.ac.uk.*
Imperial College of Science and Technology extends from either side of the Royal College of Music in Prince Consort Road south to the Science Museum, apart from the small enclaves occupied by Holy Trinity Church *(1909)*, the Edwardian Post Office Building and the Underground exit. With the exception of the neo-Georgian 1909–13 **Royal School of Mines**, the vast, clean-lined buildings date from the mid-50s. In their midst, guarded at its foot by a pair of lions, rises the old **Queen's Tower** *(280ft/85m high)*, last relic of the Imperial Institute *(1887–93)*, erected following the Colonial Exhibition of 1886.
Opposite, the Sir Alexander Fleming building, with a stepped double-glazed roof designed by **Sir Norman Foster**, combines architectural flair and high technology.
Exhibition Road has been redesigned as a shared space in a dynamic new urban redevelopment; there are no pavements, and cars do not take priority over pedestrians.

Continue south on Exhibition Rd.

Hyde Park Chapel

Exhibition Road.
The stylish Mormon chapel, dating from 1960, is surmounted by a needle spire of gilded bricks.

Continue to Cromwell Rd. and cross.

The distinctive modern **Ismaili Centre**, faced in grey-blue marble and adorned with slim windows, serves as a religious and cultural centre for Ismailis.

Walk West along Cromwell Rd.

The buildings of the **Institut Français**, founded in 1910, although in Art Nouveau style, date from only 1938. Many of the students enrolled here and at the nearby Lycée are English.

Retrace your steps and turn right into Cromwell Pl. to Thurloe St. and past the station on Pelham St. to the left.

Michelin House

This striking 1910 building is the former UK headquarters of Michelin Tyre PLC. Its original *art nouveau* **decoration★** has been restored and tiled tyre-fitting bays preserved. It houses the restaurant Bibendum and the iconic Conran Shop.

Turn right along Fulham Rd.

Elizabeth I is said to have sheltered under an elm tree during a storm here, giving the Tudor **Queen's Elm Square** its name.
There are 19C artisan cottages in **Elm Place** *(across Fulham Rd., right)* and its immediate vicinity. Turn right past a pleasant pub, then left to **Onslow Gardens**, a mid-19C development of stuccoed houses with pillared porches.

Cranley Gdns leads to Old Brompton Rd; turn left.

Bolton Place, on the left, leads to **The Boltons**, where fine white-stuccoed houses are laid out in a mandorla crescent. Further on along Brompton Road is the entrance to **Brompton Cemetery** *(see infobox p179)*.

ADDRESSES

LIGHT BITE

Jakobs, *20 Gloucester Rd. Gloucester Road. 020 7581 9292. Daily 8am–11pm.* Simple cuisine, with Mediterranean influences, served in generous portions.

Kulu Kulu Sushi, *39 Thurloe Pl. South Kensington. 020 7589 2225. 12.15pm–2.45pm (Sat 3.45pm), 5.30pm–10.30pm.* Conveyor-belt style sushi place serving a wide range of tasty small dishes.

CAFÉS

The Lanesborough, *Hyde Park Corner. Hyde Park Corner. 020 7259 5599. www.lanesborough.com. 4pm–6pm.* With its beautiful glass roof, the Conservatory is an elegant venue for afternoon tea. Prices start at £38 per person.

ENTERTAINMENT

Holland Park Theatre, *Holland Park, 020 7631 3570 or 030 0999 1000 (Mon–Fri 10am–6pm, open late Apr–Aug). Holland Park. www.operahollandpark.co.uk. Ticket office (Old Stable Block, Park Office): Mon–Fri 1pm–6pm (8pm on show days).* Between June and August each year the outdoor theatre in Holland Park hosts performances of opera, theatre and dance.

Royal College of Music, *Prince Consort Rd. 020 7591 4314 or 4331. Knightsbridge or Gloucester Rd. www.rcm.ac.uk. Box office: Mon–Fri 10am–4pm.* Classical music concerts, most of them free.

SHOPPING

The Conran Shop, **Michelin House**, *81 Fulham Rd., South Kensington, SW3 6RD. South Kensington. 020 7589 7401. www.conran.com.* Conran's flagship store, opened in 1987 in this beautiful building, sells furniture and stylish accessories for the home and garden.

Partridges, *17–21 Gloucester Rd., 020 7581 0535. Gloucester Road. Daily 8am–11pm.* High-end grocery store stocked with typically British delights: chutneys, pickles, jams, teas and biscuits.

Chelsea★★

Chelsea is synonymous with a fashionable lifestyle, but its artistic associations still hold fascination. The lively atmosphere, still redolent of 60s Bohemia, draws those seeking the limelight and the trendy social scene. People-watching is an entertaining pastime and there are plenty of elegant boutiques, antique shops, cafés and restaurants to indulge one's fancy. Explore the King's Road and the residential squares, and walk along Chelsea Embankment for views of the Thames to appreciate the charm of the area.

- **Location:** Map pp 160–161. ⊖*Sloane Square.* Chelsea extends on the north bank of the Thames from Chelsea Bridge west along Chelsea embankment and Cheyne Walk, and from Sloane Square to Brompton Cemetery.
- **Don't miss:** Chelsea Physic Garden for its historic associations, Cheyne Walk for its Georgian terraces and the Kings Road for its boutiques.
- **Timing:** Allow one day to explore the area along the route suggested in the Walking Tour *(see below)*, soaking in the atmosphere of the King's Road at the end and taking a well-earned break in one of the local cafés.

A BIT OF HISTORY

The completion of the Embankment in 1874 removed forever the atmosphere of a riverside community: boats drawn up on the mud flats, trees shading the foreshore, people walking along a country road, as painted by **Rowlandson** in 1789 *(Chelsea Reach)*, watched in his old age at sunset by Turner and captured by **Whistler** *(Old Battersea Bridge)*.

Chelsea had royal connections, but the only royal building to survive is the **Royal Hospital**. Architectural interest lies in the churches, squares, terraces and attractive houses of all periods.

Henry VIII's Palace – The river still served as the main access when the King's riverside palace, a two-storey brick mansion, was built in 1537, near Albert Bridge. Owned by the Cheynes in the 17C, it later belonged to **Sir Hans Sloane** and was demolished when he died in 1753.

Sir Thomas More, Henry VIII's Chancellor, built a house at the water's edge. One regular guest in the 12 years he lived in Chelsea, before sailing downriver to his execution in 1535, was **Erasmus**.

A Fashionable Set – Chelsea has been the setting for many a new or revived fashion: the exclusivity of the Pre-Raphaelites and the individuality of Oscar Wilde's green carnation. The opening of Bazaar in 1955 and the launch of **Mary Quant's** mini skirt; in the 1960s Chelsea was the "navel of Swinging London" and the King's Road a Mecca of the avant-garde. In 1971 **Vivienne Westwood** opened her clothes shop at 430 King's Road; it became the centre of punk fashion. Today the King's Road has weathered into a well-heeled shopping area.

WALKING TOUR

4 SLOANE SQUARE

The Square boasts two very different institutions: **Peter Jones**, the upper-middle-class department store with a stunning exterior *(1936)*; and the **Royal Court Theatre** *(020 7565 5000; www.royalcourttheatre.com)*, which has assumed a pioneering role since 1956, when the English Stage Co under George Devine presented John Osborne's *Look Back in Anger*.

Holy Trinity

A short way up Sloane Street. Open Mon–Fri 9am–6pm, Sat 9.30am–6pm. Concerts. 020 7730 7270. www.holytrinitysloanesquare.co.uk.

The church was rebuilt in 1888 by a leading exponent of the **Arts and Crafts movement**, John Dando Sedding *(1838–91)*. **Burne-Jones** *(see INTRODUCTION – Art and Culture, Decorative Arts)* designed the 48-panel east window with Apostles, Patriarchs, Kings, Prophets and Saints – St Bartholomew by **William Morris**. All decoration is of the period and harmonises with the High Altar marble crucifix and candlesticks. Note also the bronze panels in the choir stalls, the gilded organ case, golden lectern and unusual railings outside on Sloane Street.

Walk round Sloane Sq. to the King's Rd.

The King's Road

This used to be the private route taken by **Charles II** when calling on **Nell Gwynne** at her house in Fulham; in fact, the King's Road was only opened to the public in 1830. At the height of the Swinging Sixties, it was the home of Mary Quant and other high fashion designers. It is now famous for its shops selling fashion accessories and antiques, restaurants and pubs, while the small streets around are lined by traditional cottages once built for artisans and now selling for a king's ransom.

Turn left into Royal Avenue.

Between the King's Road and the Royal Hospital lies the playing field **Burton's Court**, flanked by **St Leonard's Terrace** – a mid-18C Georgian row (**Nos. 14–31**). At the centre of the terrace is **Royal Avenue**, planned in the late 17C to extend as far as Kensington Palace but never completed.

The Royal Hospital★★

Open Nov–Mar Mon–Sat 10am–noon, 2pm–4pm; Apr–Oct daily 10am–noon, 2pm–4pm. ***Grounds*** *open Mon–Sat 10am–noon, 2pm–4pm, with late closures during summer. Leaflet (8 languages). 020 7881 5516. www.chelsea-pensioners.org.uk.*

Chelsea Pensioners have been colourful members of the local community for over 300 years. Inspired by Les Invalides, built by Louis XIV in Paris in 1670, **Charles II,** who had re-established a standing army in 1661, commissioned **Sir Christopher Wren** to build a veterans' hostel. The architect designed a quadrangular plan with a main court open on the south to the grounds and the river. The main entrance is beneath the lantern-crowned **Octagon Porch**

Statue of Charles II in Figure Court, Royal Hospital

Chelsea Luminaries

A varied group of notable people has lived in Chelsea: the famous actresses Nell Gwynne, Dame Ellen Terry, Dame Sybil Thorndyke (who inspired GB Shaw to write *St Joan* for her); Sir Joseph Banks (botanist, explorer and President of the Royal Society); Sir John Fielding (a respected magistrate, who was blind from birth), the engineers **Sir Marc Isambard Brunel** and his son Isambard Kingdom; Charles Kingsley (author of *The Water Babies)*; Mrs Elizabeth Gaskell (novelist); the **Pre-Raphaelite** poets and painters **Dante Gabriel Rossetti**, his sister Christina, Burne-Jones, William and Jane Morris, Holman Hunt, Swinburne and Millais.

Other artists include **William de Morgan**, Wilson Steer, Sargent, Augustus John, Orpen and Sickert. Mark Twain, **Henry James** and TS Eliot are among Chelsea Americans. Smollett lived in Lawrence Street; **Oscar Wilde** at 34 Tite Street; AA Milne at 13 Mallord Street. Hilaire Belloc, the Sitwells and Arnold Bennett were also in residence.

in the north range of the original **Figure Court**, so-called after the Classical statue of Charles II by **Grinling Gibbons** at the centre.

From the **Octagon Porch** steps rise on either side to the **Chapel and Great Hall**, both panelled beneath tall rounded windows. The Chapel has a barrel vault and at the end, a domed and painted apse by Ricci. The end wall of the Hall is decorated with an 18C mural of Charles II on horseback before the hospital. The **Council Chamber** *(West Wing)* was decorated by both Wren and Robert Adam; Van Dyck painted the portrait of Charles I and his family. The **Museum**, located on the east side, displays Wellington mementoes and illustrates the history of the Hospital.

Since 1913 the **Chelsea Flower Show** *(see Addresses)* has been held in the grounds by the **Royal Horticultural Society**. In 1805 the Hospital purchased the celebrated **Ranelagh Gardens** *(1742–1805)*, which offered patrons *alfresco* meals, concerts and spectacles in the Rotunda.

Walk west along Royal Hospital Rd past the National Army Museum *(see Additional Sights).*

Chelsea Physic Garden

66 Royal Hospital Rd., SW3 (entrance on Swan Walk). Open Apr–Oct Tue–Fri, Sun and bank holidays 11am–6pm, noon–6pm, Jul–Aug Wed till 10pm; last admission 30min before closing. £9 Guidebook. No dogs allowed. Plants for sale. Refreshments. 020 7352 5646. www.chelseaphysicgarden.co.uk.

The botanical garden, frequented by such leading lights as **Linnaeus**, was founded in 1673 by the Worshipful Society of Apothecaries of London on land leased from Sir Hans Sloane. His statue by Rysbrack stands in the centre. The record of the garden is remarkable: Georgia's cotton seeds came from the South Seas via the Physic Garden, India's tea from China, her quinine *(cinchona)* from South America and Malaya's rubber from South America.

Cheyne Walk★

The terraces of brick houses standing back from the river front are rich with memories of artists, writers and royalty. Corinthian pilasters mark the entrance to **No. 4**, where **George Eliot** spent her last weeks. Beautiful railings and fine urns distinguish **No. 5**; **No. 6** is remarkable for the Chinese-Chippendale gate and railings. The **Queen's House** (**No. 16**) was the home of the poet and painter **DG Rossetti**, where the Pre-Raphaelites used to meet. In the gardens opposite stands a fountain bearing a portrait bust of Rossetti by Seddon. **No. 18** was the popular Don Saltero's coffeehouse and museum. **Nos. 19–26** occupy the site of Henry VIII's riverside palace.

For Albert Bridge *See* *BATTERSEA.* *For Carlyle's House, 24 Cheyne Row, see Additional Sights.*

In **Lawrence Street** flourished the **Chelsea China Works** *(1745–84)* before being transferred to Derby (*see INTRODUCTION – Decorative Arts).* The **King's Head and Eight Bells** *(now a restaurant)* dates back to the 17C.

Chelsea Old Church

Open Tue–Thu 2pm–4pm. *020 7795 1019.* *www.chelseaoldchurch.org.uk.*

The pre-Norman church, with a 14C chapel remodelled by **Sir Thomas More** in 1528, was reconstructed after suffering bomb damage. Many monuments were rescued from the rubble: note in particular the 17C altar, rails and small marble font; the **chained books** presented by Sir Hans Sloane; the reclining figure of Lady Jane Cheyne *(1699)*, the massive Stanley monument of 1632 and More's self-composed inscription against the south wall of the sanctuary. The novelist **Henry James** is also buried here, while in the churchyard a **statue** of a sombre, seated black-robed figure with gilded face and hands commemorates **Sir Thomas More**.

Roper's Garden, once part of More's orchard, is named after his son-in-law. The stone relief of *A Woman Walking against the Wind* is by **Jacob Epstein**, who lived in Chelsea *(1909–14)*.

Crosby Hall, the Medieval great hall transferred from the City to Chelsea in 1910, was part of the residence of a 15C wool merchant.

From Cheyne Walk there is a fine view of Battersea Bridge (*see SUBURBS–BATTERSEA).* **Nos. 91–92** were built in 1771 and have several Venetian windows. **Nos. 93** and **94** date from 1777. Whistler resided at **No. 96**.

The large **Lindsey House** with mansard roof-storey, built in 1674 on the site of Sir Thomas More's farm and divided later, was home to the Brunels, commemorated in the modern **Brunel House** on the corner at **No. 105**.

Continue along the Embankment.

104–120 Cheyne Walk

Several writers and artists lived along this stretch: the essayist and historian **Hilaire Belloc** *(1873–1953)*, the landscape painter **PW Steer** *(1860–1942)* and above all, **Turner** *(1775–1851)*, who spent his last years at **No. 119**.

Chelsea Harbour, where barges once unloaded coal, is now a modern riverside development organised around a 75-berth marina and comprising a series of elegant and exclusive apartments, offices, a hotel, shops and restaurants: those that face onto the river enjoy fine views across the water to **St Mary's Church** (*see BATTERSEA)* on the south bank.

Retrace your steps, turn left into Beaufort St., right along the King's Road and left on Sydney St.

St Luke's

To view, contact the Parish Office: *open Mon–Fri 9am–12.30pm.* *020 7351 7365. www.chelseaparish.org.*

The Bath stone church of 1820 is an early example of the Gothic Revival. The pinnacled west tower *(242ft/74m)* is pierced at the base to provide a porch extending the full width of the west front.

Back on the King's Road, note the **Pheasantry** *(No. 152, now a restaurant)* erected in 1881 by the Jouberts to sell French wallpapers and furniture; alas, today only the façade and portico survive.

ADDITIONAL SIGHTS

National Army Museum★

Open daily 10am–5.30pm; free. *Closed 25–26 Dec, 1 Jan.* *020 7881 6606 (info line);* *020 7730 0717.* *www.nam.ac.uk.*

Visit the National Army Museum and find out how Britain's past has helped to shape its present and future. Discover the impact the British Army has had on the story of Britain, Europe and the rest of the world, and see how the actions of a few can affect the futures of many.

Exhibitions – There are a number of permanent exhibitions, including "Con-

Houseboats

Moored on the river are several permanent houseboats: larger and more spacious than a canal barge, these would once have accommodated watermen and river pilots. Today they provide homes for a more bohemian set of Chelsea residents.

flicts of Interest", which examines over three decades of action on the world stage by the modern British Army. The exhibit explores the dichotomies of enforcing peace through violent means, balancing global security with the needs of vulnerable communities and offsetting the impact of the job on the personal lives of our troops.

For the family – Win the battle against boredom at the museum's Kids' Zone. There are activities for all ages to enjoy; comfortable seated areas are provided with easy access to the café.

For Kids – Children will enjoy the "Action Zones", featuring quizzes, games and hands-on activities.

What's On – Complementing these permanent gallery displays, the museum also offers an inspiring programme of exhibitions, celebrity speakers, lectures and events.

Carlyle's House

Open Mar–Oct Wed–Sun and bank holiday Mon 11am–5pm (last admission 4.30pm). £5.10, free to National Trust members. 020 7352 7087. www.nationaltrust.org.uk.

The Scottish historian Thomas Carlyle *(1795–1881)*, famous for his *History of the French Revolution*, lived in this modest Queen Anne brick house with his wife Jane Welsh and had the garret-room at the top of the house soundproofed in order to write his biography of Frederick the Great. The four-storeyed house contains a wealth of memorabilia reflecting the couple's unpretentious lifestyle. The "Sage of Chelsea" is commemorated in a statue by Boehm in Cheyne Walk gardens facing onto the river.

Saatchi Gallery

Duke of York's HQ, King's Road.

Open daily 10am–6pm; last entry 5.30pm; free. Café/Bar. Bookshop. 020 7811 3070. www.saatchi-gallery.co.uk.

Opened at its new location in 2008, this cutting-edge interactive art gallery in the former Duke of York's barracks HQ showcases contemporary art works by largely unseen young British artists or established International artists unknown in Britain.

The vast 70,000sq ft/6,503sq m space with its abundance of natural light holds temporary curated exhibitions; the **Project Room** is a space for exhibitions of artists featured in the collection, but not in the main exhibition programme. There is also a space, the **New Gallery**, where Saatchi Online artists can exhibit their works free of charge and sell them, as well as a pleasant café/bar and a bookshop on site.

The gallery operates a free entry policy to all shows and exhibitions, thanks to a corporate partnership with contemporary art auction house Phillips de Pury, as part of its aim to bring contemporary art to the widest possible audience.

EXCURSION

Fulham

These fine residential areas linked by a bridge enjoy a pleasant riverside location. Fulham has become an offshoot of fashionable Chelsea, while Putney, with its leafy common land, has a rural atmosphere and is popular with young families. It is worth taking a stroll to visit the picturesque pubs and enjoy the scenery.

Fulham, Parsons Green and Walham Green were once riverside villages with the odd large mansion in its own grounds running down to the water's edge. Market gardens covered the fertile marshlands. Urbanisation came within 50 years: in 1851 the population numbered 12,000; in 1901, 137,000.

Downstream from the bridgehead, **Hurlingham House**, an 18C mansion in its own wooded grounds, is the last of the big houses which once lined the river bank. It is now a private club with extensive tennis courts.

Brompton Cemetery and Earl's Court

Brompton Cemetery *(www.royalparks.org.uk)* is a vast 19C necropolis containing more than 35,000 neo-Gothic, Egyptian and Baroque-style tombs. Covering 16.5 hectares/40 acres, it opened in 1840 and is one of Britain's finest cemeteries. It has a formal layout with a central avenue leading to a chapel based on St Peter's Basilica in Rome. People from all walks of life are buried here, including 13 holders of the Victoria Cross and numerous Chelsea Pensioners. The cemetery is also a haven for wildlife including butterflies, foxes and squirrels. v

Earl's Court, to the North of the cemetery, was once a rural area of green fields and market gardens but today is best known as the home of Earls Court Exhibition Centre *(www.eco.co.uk)*, one of Britain's largest indoor arenas. Everything from music concerts (the Rolling Stones, Led Zeppelin and Kylie Minogue have all performed here) to corporate conferences are held in its halls and throughout the year, large shows catering to all tastes take place, including the Ideal Home Show, the National Wedding Show and Destinations travel show. This area has plenty of places to eat to suit all budgets. For affordable Indian food, head to Masala Zone *(147 Earl's Court Road; 020 7373 0220; www.masalazone.com)*, while authentic Thai cuisine can be found at Siam Garden *(5a Hogarth Place; 020 7370 4371)*, a small family restaurant discreetly tucked away off the main road. Good-quality food is also served in many of the local pubs: **The Atlas** *(see Addresses)* has a tiny terrace and the traditional **Kings Head** *(17 Hogarth Place; 020 7244 5931)* serves decent food.

Walk up Fulham Palace Rd. and turn left into Bishop's Ave.

Fulham Palace

The **Palace**, which retains the appearance of a modest Tudor manor, was the official summer residence of the Bishop of London from 704 to 1973. The gateway, a low 16C arch with massive beamed doors, leads through to the courtyard *(1480–1525)*, graced by a large central fountain *(1885)*. The chapel *(1866)*, added on the south side, was designed by **William Butterfield** in Mock Tudor style (*see Sight*).

The first magnolia to be grown in Europe and several other exotic species were planted in the grounds by Bishop Compton. The old walled kitchen garden contains some beech hedge screens, a fragrant herb garden and a pretty **wisteria walk**. *Open daily.*

At 210 New King's Road one disused bottle kiln still stands on the site of the former **Fulham Pottery** established by John Dwight in 1671.

Return to the bridge and turn right into Church Gate.

All Saints Church

Open Mon–Sat 10am–4pm. Guide book. 020 7736 3264. www.allsaints-fulham.org.uk.

Fulham parish church has been a landmark at this bridging point of the river since the 14C, its square Kentish stone tower a twin to Putney church on the south bank. Inside is a rich collection of monuments and brasses. Fourteen Bishops of London are buried in the yew-shaded churchyard.

Close to the church note the 19C **Powell Almshouses** with steep pitched roofs over a single storey.

Stamford Bridge Stadium Tour

Daily 10am–3pm, every 30min except on home match days. 1hr. 0871 984 1955. www.chelseafc.com.

Chelsea FC is London's most well-known football club and Stamford Bridge has been home to the club since its founding in 1905. The stadium may not be the biggest or most impressive the city has to offer (*see WEMBLEY*) but the guided tour is a rousing experience sure to interest all sports fans. Visitors are led behind the scenes into areas usually only seen by the players, including the dressing rooms and the tunnel onto the pitch. The guides are passionate and entertaining. There's also a museum *(included in tour price; £10, if visited separately).*

ADDRESSES

LIGHT BITE

The Chelsea Farmers' Market, *125 Sydney St. 020 7515 7153. Daily 9.30am–8pm.* The former Chelsea Market is home to several small inexpensive restaurants. **The Market Place** has a pleasant terrace and is ideal for a break at lunchtime.

CAFÉS

Bluebird Chelsea, *350 King's Road. 020 7559 1000.* You can sit out or eat in here, an ideal spot for breakfast, lunch or supper. The bread is from the in-house bakery.

Pâtisserie Valérie, *Duke of York's Square, King's Rd. Mon–Fri 8am–5pm, Sat 8am–7pm, Sun 9am–6pm.* **Maison Blanc**, *303 Fulham Rd. (South Kensington). Mon–Sat 8am–7pm, Sun 9am–7pm.*

PUBS AND BARS

The Atlas, *16 Seagrave Rd., Fulham. West Brompton. 020 7385 9129. Food served: daily noon–2.30pm, 6pm–10pm (Sun 4pm). Pub: daily noon–11pm (Sun 10.30pm).* Charming local pub adjacent to Earls Court Exhibition Centre, with tiny terrace. A cut above your average pub grub.

Troubadour, *263–7 Old Brompton Rd. Earl's Court or West Brompton. 020 7370 1434. www.troubadour.co.uk. Daily 9h–midnight.* High-quality live music (particularly jazz) and simple, tasty food: the daily specials are always reliable. Next door, a grocery of the same name sells takeaway dishes.

SHOPPING

The King's Road is lined with stylish boutiques, often one-offs, and high-end clothing stores. The spiritual home of the 1960s, where Mary Quant started and Vivienne Westwood followed, this stretch of Chelsea is still very cool indeed.

Joseph Outlet, *53 King's Rd., 020 7730 7562. Mon–Sat 10am–6.30pm, Sun noon–6pm.* Factory shop offering Joseph clothing and accessories at up to 80 percent off.

Manolo Blahnik, *49–51 Old Church St., SW3 5BS. Sloane Square. 020 7352 8622. www.manoloblahnik.com. Closed bank holidays.* The source of the most desirable shoes in London. Well-heeled women around the world appreciate the creative and ultra-feminine designs of Blahnik's entirely hand-sewn footwear. Men's shoes also available.

Peter Jones, *Sloane Sq. Sloane Square. 020 7730 3434. www.johnlewis.com. Mon–Sat 9.30am–7pm (Wed 8pm), Sun 11am–5pm.* Although retaining the name of its founder, this department store is now part of the John Lewis chain. Everything from clothing to homeware is available here, all good-quality.

World's End, *430 King's Rd. 020 7352 6551. Mon–Sat 10am–6pm.* This is where Vivienne Westwood, designer and avant-garde punk rock aficiionado, started her fashion career in the 1970s. The building is rickety and has sloping floors, but it's all part of the charm. The clock on the façade is also worth a look – the hands go round backwards.

EVENTS AND FESTIVALS

Chelsea Flower Show, *See Calendar of Events.* *www.rhs.org.uk.* Held in May, this glorious flower show is one of the high points of the London year. The show ground is full of the latest in garden design, products and trends, as well as some of the most perfect – and fragrant – blooms around. A must for anyone with green fingers.

Notting Hill★★

Notting Hill is one of London's most upscale and fashionable areas. Located only slightly outside the centre of the city, this bohemian enclave is a great place to discover the real London. Take the time to soak up the atmosphere in one of the area's quirky cafés or pubs, shop till you drop at the world-famous Portobello Market, and stroll the streets lined with grand 18C and 19C terraced houses, many painted in pastel hues.

- **Location:** Map pp 182–183. ⊖ *Notting Hill Gate.* Just to the West of central London and the West End, Notting Hill sits just north of Kensington.
- **Don't Miss:** Portobello Road antiques market, the annual Notting Hill Carnival (August bank holiday weekend; *see NOTTING HILL CARNIVAL box).*
- **Timing:** Allow half a day, more if you're a keen shopper visiting on market day. Saturdays are exceptionally busy, so allow more time to visit then.

A BIT OF HISTORY

Just 200 years ago Notting Hill was little more than wasteland but in the 19C residential areas began to spring up alongside the pottery works and piggeries *(at one time there were three pigs to every person here)*. During the early 20C the area became a slum, as larger homes were carved up to accommodate more families and cheap lodgings attracted a rather down-at-heel population. After years of decline, however, things turned around quickly, and the 1960s and 1970s saw large-scale redevelopment, which kick-started the gentrification of the area. Notting Hill has now become one of the most desirable parts of the city to live in –with extremely high house prices to match.

The area has also featured in many movies, the best known being, of course, *Notting Hill* (1999), starring Hugh Grant and Julia Roberts. Sadly, the travel bookshop where they met has now closed.

Portobello Road★

This winding road, once a cart-track through the fields from the Notting Hill turnpike, and now lined with attractive 19C townhouses, comes to life with one of London's finest **markets★★** *(open Mon–Wed 8am–6.30pm, Thur 8am–1pm, Sat 8am–6.30pm)*. The best, and busiest, day to visit is Saturday. Different goods are sold each day, with fresh fruit and vegetables available throughout the week, a range of cutting-edge clothes and second-hand goods on Fridays and antiques and bric-a-brac on Saturdays. As you walk down the street away from Notting Hill Gate tube, goods on sale change from Victoriana to jewellery to clothing. Towards the end, under the Westway, are stalls selling funky clothes and second-hand goods *(Fri and Sat only)*.

Notting Hill's main north–south artery, Ladbroke Grove, is the main parade route for the **Notting Hill Carnival**, a three-day Caribbean festival which takes over the area on the last weekend of August and is Europe's largest street carnival *(see p186)*.

© L. Maisant/hemis.fr

Shop on Portbello Road

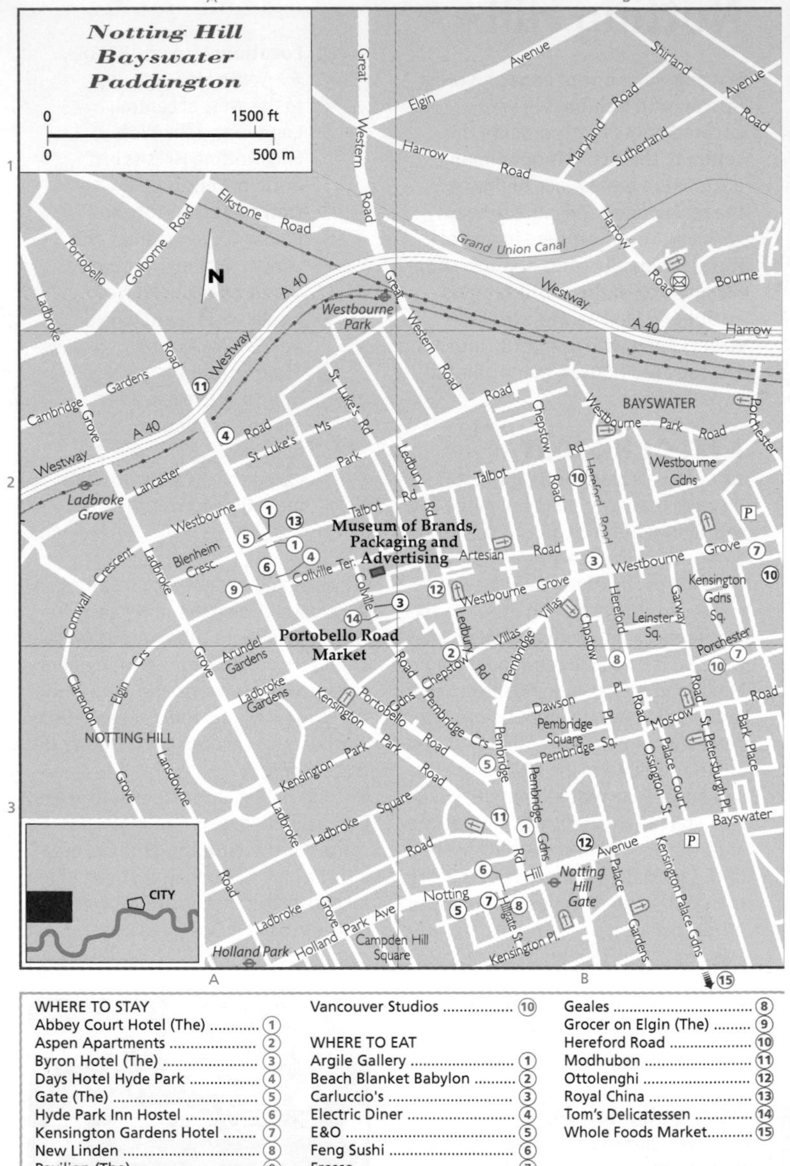

WHERE TO STAY		WHERE TO EAT			
Abbey Court Hotel (The)	1	Argile Gallery	1	Geales	8
Aspen Apartments	2	Beach Blanket Babylon	2	Grocer on Elgin (The)	9
Byron Hotel (The)	3	Carluccio's	3	Hereford Road	10
Days Hotel Hyde Park	4	Electric Diner	4	Modhubon	11
Gate (The)	5	E&O	5	Ottolenghi	12
Hyde Park Inn Hostel	6	Feng Sushi	6	Royal China	13
Kensington Gardens Hotel	7	Fresco	7	Tom's Delicatessen	14
New Linden	8			Whole Foods Market	15
Pavilion (The)	9				
Vancouver Studios	10				

Museum of Brands, Packaging and Advertising

2 Colville Mews, Lonsdale Rd. W11 2AR. Open Tue–Sat 10am–6pm, Sun 11am–5pm. Closed Mon except some bank holidays. £6.50. 020 7908 0880. www.museumofbrands.com. Shop, café.

This treasure trove of memorabilia features more than 12,000 consumer goods, leisure items and domestic devices. It started life as the Robert Opie collection, when Opie decided, at the age of 16, to keep a Munchies wrapper; he then began amassing the sort of items most of us throw away.

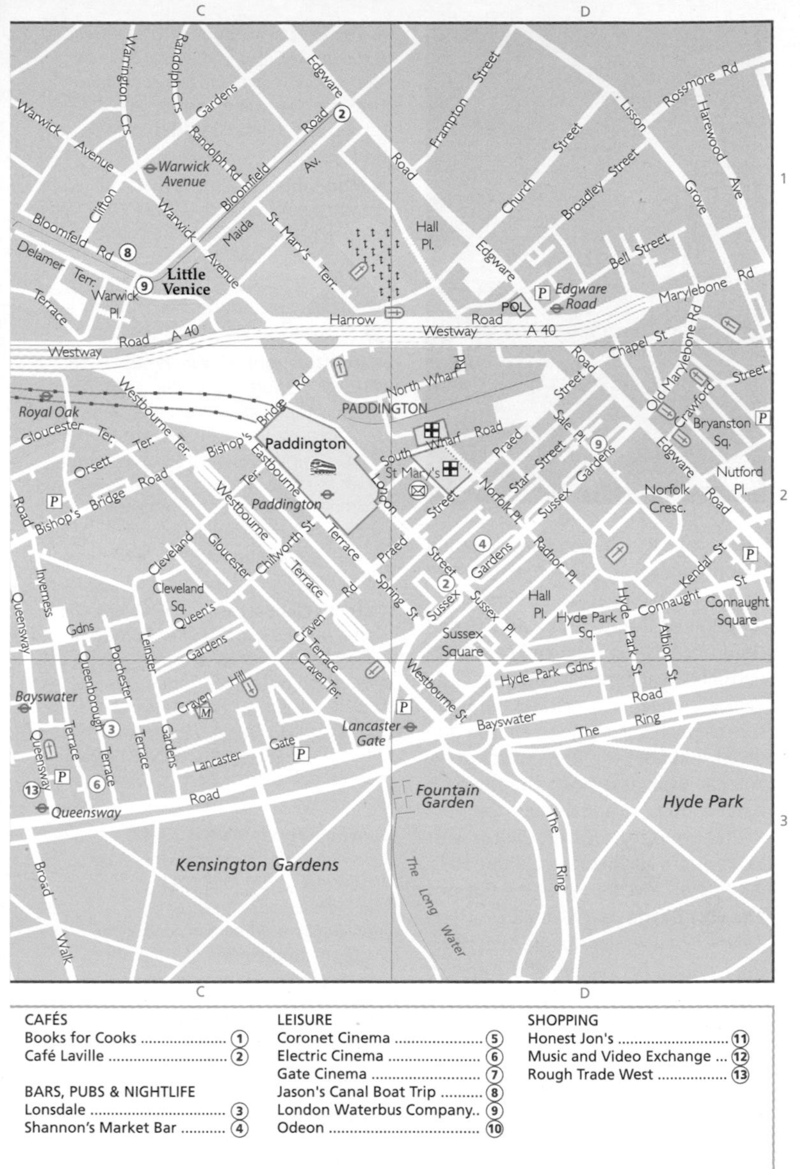

CAFÉS
Books for Cooks 1
Café Laville 2

BARS, PUBS & NIGHTLIFE
Lonsdale 3
Shannon's Market Bar 4

LEISURE
Coronet Cinema 5
Electric Cinema 6
Gate Cinema 7
Jason's Canal Boat Trip 8
London Waterbus Company.. 9
Odeon 10

SHOPPING
Honest Jon's 11
Music and Video Exchange ... 12
Rough Trade West 13

A so-called time tunnel charts consumer history from the Victorian era to the present day, from chocolate bars and laundry powder boxes to ancient TV sets and original branded board games. Together they build to form a picture of life throughout the 19C and 20C, highlighting key trends in domesticity and leisure time and showing how advertising has permeated our lives for many years.

Little Venice

Bloomfield Road. ⊖Warwick Avenue, bus number 6 or 46. www.canalriver trust.org.uk.

Puppet Theatre Barge

© Puppet Theatre Barge

Just beyond Paddington railway station and the elevated section of the A40 known as the Westway, this charming junction of the Regent's and Grand Union Canals is a colourful combination of boats and scenery. Though "Little Venice" somewhat overstates the area's true character, it is a good spot to hop on a canal boat trip *(see Addresses)*. You can walk east along the towpath past London Zoo and through Camden to the Olympic Site *(see p290)* or west to Brentford and in to the Chiltern Hills. Kids will love a show at the **Puppet Theatre Barge** *(£10 or £8.50; 020 7249 6876; www.puppetbarge.com)*, while the Floating Art Gallery and Warwick Castle pub are hits with their parents.

ADDRESSES

LIGHT BITE

Fresco, *25 Westbourne Grove. Bayswater. 020 7221 2355. www.frescojuices.co.uk. Mon–Sat 8am–10.30pm, Sun 9am–10.30pm.* This Lebananese snack bar deserves a visit primarily for its excellent fresh juices, which are made on demand *(£1.50 and £2.25)*, but the pitta sandwiches, falafel and mezze do not disappoint either. Take away or eat on site in the small bright dining room.

The Grocer on Elgin, *6 Elgin Crescent. Ladbroke Grove. 020 7221 3844. Mon–Fri 8am–8pm, Sat–Sun 8am–6pm.* This very classy grocery-store-cum-café serves fresh, seasonal food cooked on the premises.

Modhubon, *29 Pembridge Rd. Notting Hill Gate. 0871 148 3372 (10p/min plus network charges).* Traditional tandoori restaurant. The décor is uninspiring but its low prices and the high quality of its dishes make this a good place for those on a budget.

Ottolenghi, *63 Ledbury Rd., W11 2AD. Notting Hill Gate. 020 7727 1121. www.ottolenghi.co.uk.* This café, deli and great restaurant serving a mix of fashionable dishes with lots of Asian spices is a favourite hangout for trendy "Notting Hillbillies", as the inhabitants of Notting Hill are generally known. Also on Upper St., Islington, *Angel or Highbury & Islington.*

Tom's Delicatessen, *226 Westbourne Grove, Notting Hill, W11 2RH. Notting Hill. 020 7221 8818.* The eponymous owner, son of Terence Conran, has his father's eye for style and design. Half-deli, half-café with framed vintage posters and an impressive cake display. Popular spot with the fashionable Notting Hill crowd.

Whole Foods Market, *63–97 Kensington High Street. Kensington High Street. 020 7368 4500. www.wholefoodsmarket.com. Mon–Sat 8am–10pm, Sun noon–6pm.* Highly recommended, both for the variety and quality of its produce and for the inviting restaurant area next to the deli. Great selection of salads, sandwiches and ready meals *(allow £1/100g)* and a variety of divine pastries.

CAFÉS

Books for Cooks, *4 Bleinheim Crescent, Notting Hill. Ladbroke Grove. 020 7221 1992. www.booksforcooks.com. Tue–Sat 10am–6pm.* As the name suggests, this bookshop is dedicated to the culinary arts and is jam-packed with cook books to any cuisine you can think of. In keeping with the theme, there's also a café, where you can enjoy light snacks and delicious pastries.

Café Laville, *Little Venice Parade, 453 Edgware Rd. ⊖Warwick Avenue or Edgware Road. ✆020 7706 2620.* Located on the Regent's Canal, this tiny café has a verandah perched on a bridge from which to contemplate the water traffic as you tuck into sandwiches, salads and omelettes.

PUBS

Lonsdale, *48 Lonsdale Rd., Notting Hill. ⊖Notting Hill Gate. ✆020 7727 4080. www.thelonsdale.co.uk. Daily 6pm–midnight (FriSat until 1am).* Despite the rather futuristic décor, this bar retains a certain class and the wide variety of cocktails attract a chic crowd. There is a DJ Thursday to Saturday from 9pm.

Shannon's Market Bar, *240 Portobello Rd., Notting Hill. ⊖Ladbroke Grove. ✆020 7313 6516. www.shannonpubs.co.uk.* This lively bar is always busy, attracting an eclectic happy crowd of mostly locals. DJs take up residence every other Friday night.

SHOPPING

In adddition to **Portobello Road Market** *(fruit and veg Mon–Sat, clothes and second-hand goods Fri, antiques and bric-a-brac Sat)* where you can spend an entire day browsing for antiquities, Victoriana, silver-ware, china, stamps and small items along a two-mile-long winding road, the area boasts a range of shops to suit all needs.

Music – Music and Video Exchange *(38 Notting Hill Gate, ✆020 7243 8573).* Thousands of second-hand records and CDs, great for finding that long-lost music.**Rough Trade West** *(130 Talbot Rd, ✆020 7392 7790).* A classic record shop that opened in 1983, Rough Trade provides the quintessential music retail experience you thought had disappeared. **Honest Jon's** *(278 Portobello Rd, ✆020 8969 9822).* Independent record shop that opened in 1974 selling a vast range of music in all genres.

Clothing – Several high-street retailers have outposts in Notting Hill (Joseph, Jigsaw, etc.), but there are also numerous designer boutiques, including Beatrice von Tresckow *(9 Portobello Rd.)* and Paul Smith *(122 Kensington Park Rd.)* in a gorgeous 19C townhouse typical of the area. Don't miss the vintage shops, such as One of a Kind *(259 Portobello Rd.)* or Retro Clothing *(28 Pembridge Road; www.mgeshops.com)*, with a great selection of retro and vintage clothes for men and women.

ENTERTAINMENT

Coronet Cinema, *103 Notting Hill Gate ⊖Notting Hill Gate. ✆020 7727 6705. www.coronet.org. 3 screens. £7.50 (£3.50 on Tuesdays).* The oldest cinema in London (it opened in 1898 as a theatre), the Coronet runs a programme of both independent and mainstream films. Although badly in need of refurbishment, the building still has plenty of character.

Electric Cinema, *191 Portobello Rd., Notting Hill. ⊖Ladbroke Grove. ✆020 7908 9696. www.electriccinema.co.uk. £12.50 (Mon £7.50).* With leather armchairs and side tables, this cinema makes movie-going a novel experience – there are even sofas in the front row. Julia Roberts and Hugh Grant filmed a scene of their film *Notting Hill* here.

Gate Cinema, *87 Notting Hill Gate. ⊖Notting Hill Gate. ✆0871 902 5731 or 0870 755 0063 (for bookings). www.picturehouses.co.uk. 3 screens. peak £12.50, off-peak £8.50.* Arthouse cinema with some international titles.

Odeon, *Whiteleys Shopping Centre (2nd floor). ⊖Bayswater. ✆0871 2244 007. 8 screens. £9.50.* Mainstream cinema screening mostly American blockbusters.

ACTIVITIES

Boat Trips – Numerous agencies offer boat cruises on Regent's Canal between Little Venice and Camden Lock *(45–50min).*

Jason's Canal Boat Trip, *opposite 42 Bloomfield Rd. ⊖Warwick Avenue. ✆020 7286 3428. www.jasons.co.uk. Apr–Oct: 10.30am, 12.30pm, 2.30pm and 4.30pm. £8 single, £9 return.*

London Waterbus Company, *Bloomfield Rd. ⊖Warwick Avenue. ✆020 7482 2660 (for info) or 020 7482 2550 (to book). www.londonwaterbus.com. Apr–Sep: every hour from 10am to 5pm; Oct: Thur–Fri 11am, 1pm and 3pm, Sat–Sun every hour from 11am to 4pm; Nov–Mar: Sat–Sun 11am, 1pm and 3pm. Closed late Dec to early Jan. £7.20 single, £10.30 return. Including drop off at London Zoo, with ticket: £22.* see CAMDEN for boat trips starting there.

© Jon Arnold/hemis.fr

Notting Hill Carnival

Notting Hill is not only known as one of London's trendiest neighbourhoods – its image is inextricably linked to the event it plays host to every August: Europe's largest street festival, the Notting Hill Carnival.

A Bit of History

After World War II thousands of immigrants from the Caribbean region arrived in London, many of them settling in the Notting Hill area. Racial tension during the 1950s led to the 1958 Notting Hill race riots, a series of riots initiated by white racists against the area's West Indian residents. The following year, in order to celebrate West Indian culture and promote better understanding within the community, Claudia Jones established the Notting Hill Carnival, a Mardi Gras-style festival based on the Caribbean carnivals of the early 19C.

The Festival Today

Taking place over the August Bank Holiday weekend *(the last weekend of the month)*, the Notting Hill Carnival is a three-day free festival attracting millions of visitors from around the globe. On the Saturday events kick off with the steel band competition and on the Sunday a children's carnival lights the way for the dazzling display that is the carnival's main event – the parade on Monday. Dozens of traditional steel bands, pumping sound systems and astonishingly complex decorated floats take to the streets from around 9am, beginning on Great Western Road, winding their way along Chepstow Road on to Westbourne Grove and finally parading along Ladbroke Grove. Performers dress in amazing colourful costumes and traditional and contemporary sounds fill the air for miles around.

Music encompasses everything from soca and calypso to funk, house and reggae, and the live stages have seen everyone from Wyclef Jean to Jamiroquai perform. Numerous food stalls set up around the area, serve up jerk chicken, curries, fried plantain and other Caribbean dishes, washed down with rum punch.The streets around Notting Hill get packed to bursting point during the carnival, so go with the flow of the crowd and be aware of pickpockets.

The best way to reach the carnival is by tube but note that some stations are exit-only or closed altogether during the event.

Liberal and elegant, Bloomsbury has historically been defined by a cultured, creative vibe, which remains evident today. The area has numerous literary connections, having been home to writers such as Virginia Woolf and Charles Dickens, and today is a patchwork of genteel garden squares and elegant Georgian terraces, with the British Museum the principal attraction. It is also home to the University of London and the presence of so many students means pubs and cafés are not in short supply. To the South lies Holborn, a livelier area of offices, restaurants and bars, as well as being the home of the legal profession.

A Bit of Geography

Holborn lies immediately to the North and East of Covent Garden, with the Inns of Court around Chancery Lane located to its East. The main thoroughfare is High Holborn, which runs from the end of New Oxford Street in the West to Holborn Viaduct and the City in the East. Bloomsbury borders Holborn to the North, its large squares and wide streets leading up towards Euston Road and the mainline stations of Euston and King's Cross. The University of London and several of its colleges dominate Bloombury's northern reaches, while the British Museum occupies much of its southeast corner.

Highlights

1 Explore what it means to be human at the **Wellcome Collection** (p191)

2 Discover Dickens at the **Charles Dickens Museum** (p192)

3 Indulge your inner child at the **Toy Museum** (p192)

4 Give thanks to poet John Betjeman at **St Pancras Station**, who helped save it from demolition (p193)

5 Join thousands of others in the pursuit of knowledge at the **British Library** (p193)

A Bit of History

Bloomsbury's reputation as a bohemian enclave was inspired in the 19C and 20C by the Bloomsbury Group *(sometimes referred to as the Bloomsbury Set)*, which included Virginia Woolf, Aldous Huxley, EM Forster and John Maynard Keynes, who all lived here, meeting in the area's private homes to discuss and further their work.

The British Museum opened to the public here on 15 January 1759 in a 17C mansion building called Montagu House, which is located on the site of the current museum building, a vast quadrangle designed in the mid-19C by Sir Robert Smirke.

Holborn is first mentioned in a charter of Westminster Abbey dated 969. Its name is thought to have come from the Middle English "hol" for hollow and "bourne" for brook, referring to the river Fleet. At first, Holborn lay outside the City's jurisdiction and was part of the county of Middlesex. In 1394 parts of it were brought into the City and in 1855, the

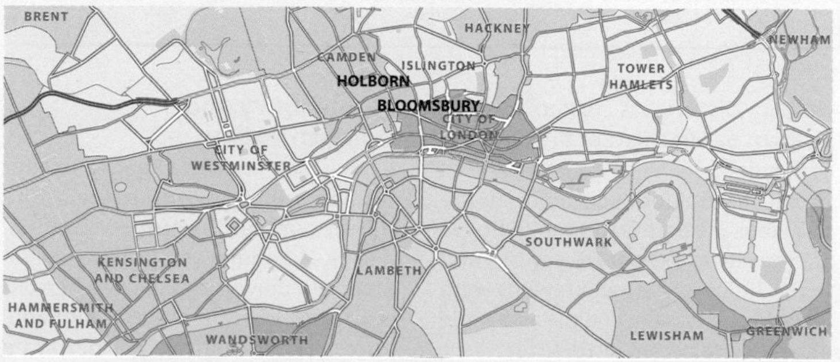

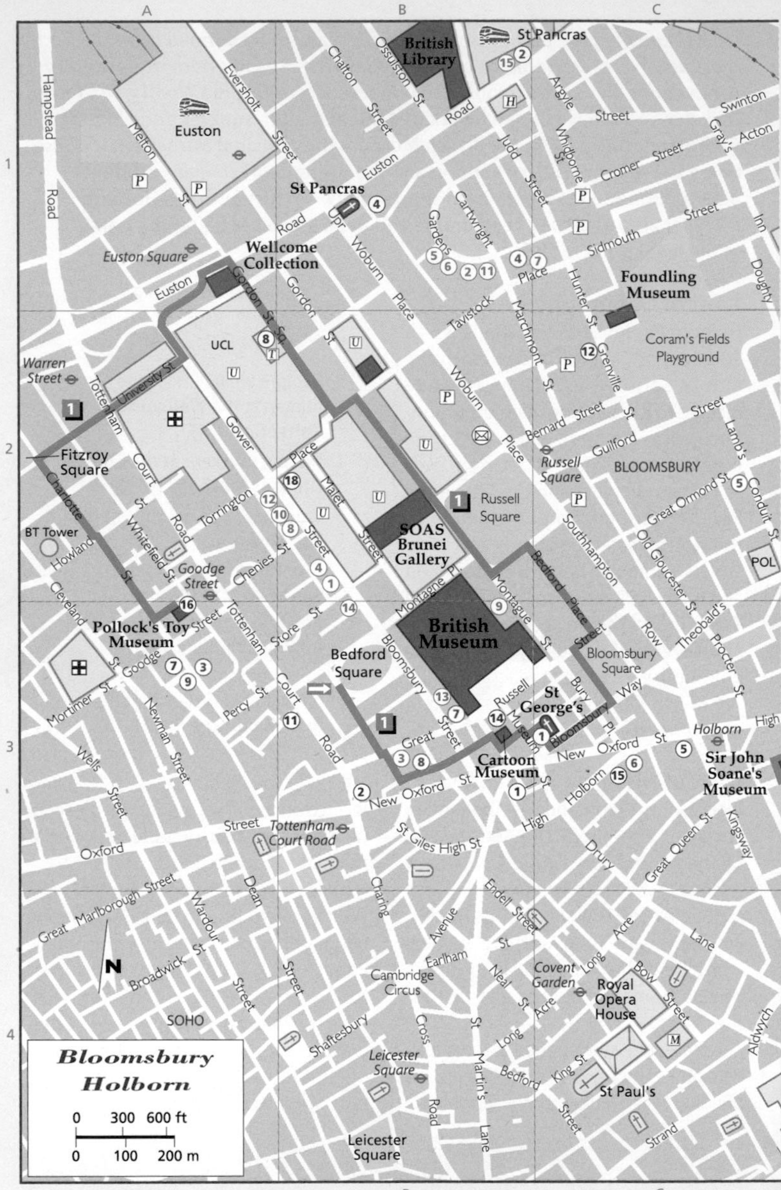

Holborn District was created. In 1965, Holborn became part of the Borough of Camden.

In the 18C Holborn was home to the infamous Mother Clap's molly house *(a precursor to the modern gay bar)* and in the 1860s 22 inns and taverns were recorded here, reflecting the area's role as an entertainment district.

Bloomsbury and Holborn Today

Bloomsbury remains engaged in educational pursuits, with many of the colleges of the University of London, plus the London campuses of several American universities located here. It is also still considered a fashionable place to live, though many of the private

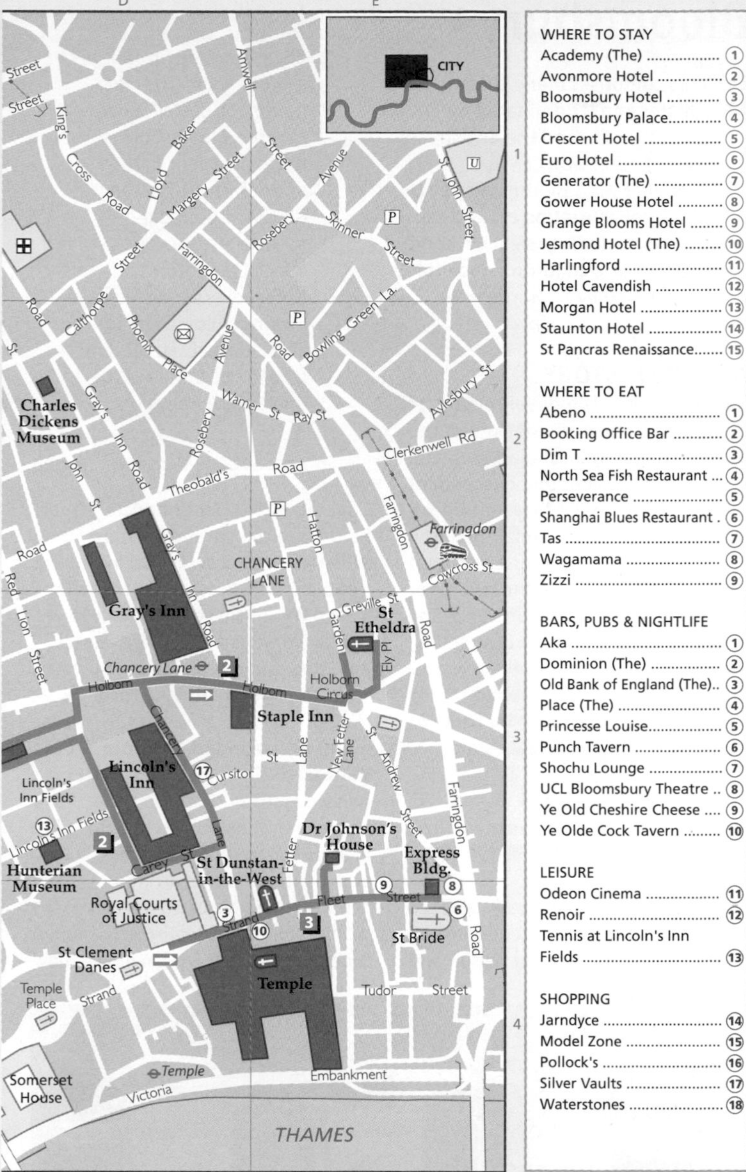

homes in the area have long since been converted into hotels and guest houses. Holborn is now principally a place of work, with the head offices of several large businesses including that of the Sainsburys supermarket chain located here, along with the four vast Inns of Court, the epicentre of the British legal system *(every barrister is aligned to one of them)*, which are situated around Chancery Lane.

However, the area retains its role as a place of leisure too, being home to numerous restaurants and bars, which cater mostly to the after-work social lives of local workers.

Bloomsbury★

This area comprises many 18C and 19C squares and is dominated by London University and the British Museum (*see MAJOR CENTRAL LONDON MUSEUMS***). Bloomsbury also contains a concentration of medical institutions, including Great Ormond Street Hospital, a children's hospital partly endowed by JM Barrie with the royalties of** *Peter Pan***.**

- **Location:** Map pp 188–189. *Tottenham Court Rd.; Goodge St; Russell Square; Holborn.* Bloomsbury is north of Covent Garden and Soho, with Euston Rd. as the boundary to the North, beyond which is Islington.
- **Kids:** Pollocks Toy Museum
- **Timing:** Allow a day to stroll the leafy streets and take in one or two of the area's small museums.

A BIT OF HISTORY

The Squares – The development of **Bloomsbury Square** in 1661 introduced a new concept in local planning. The 4th Earl of Southampton, descendant of the Lord Chancellor to whom **Henry VIII** had granted the feudal manor in 1545, erected grand houses around three sides of a square, a mansion for himself on the fourth (northern) side and an innovative network of streets all around, so ordering, in Evelyn's words, "a little town". His only daughter, Lady Rachel, married the future **1st Duke of Bedford**, uniting two great estates.

Other squares followed in the 19C: **Russell** in 1800, **Tavistock** in 1806–26, **Torrington** in 1825, **Woburn** in 1829, **Gordon** in 1850 (*see INTRODUCTION – Architecture*).

From the late 18C to the early 20C the Bloomsbury district was frequented by artists and writers: Richard Wilson and Constable (**No. 76** Charlotte Street); Ford Madox Brown and **Bernard Shaw**, **Whistler** and **Sickert** in **Fitzroy Square**; Verlaine and Rimbaud in Howland Street; Wyndham Lewis in Percy Street, and David Garnet in Bedford Square.

The most famous residents, however, were the **Bloomsbury Group** (*see INTRODUCTION – Painting*), whose members included **Virginia Woolf**, **Vanessa Bell**, the art critic **Roger Fry** (who organised London's first Post-Impressionist Exhibition in 1910), Clive Bell, EM Forster, Lytton Strachey – friend and mentor of Dora Carrington – Duncan Grant and Maynard Keynes. In the vicinity of Gordon Square resided Rupert Brooke (war poet), DH Lawrence (nov-

No. 29 Fitzroy Square

elist), **Bertrand Russell** (Nobel Prize for Literature) and his mistress, Lady Ottoline Morrell.

WALKING TOUR 1

BLOOMSBURY

Elegant **Bedford Square★★** was developed to designs by Thomas Leverton.

Leave the square via Adeline Pl. and turn left into Great Russell St.

Great Russell Street

The West end of the street is marked by the YMCA.

Turn right opposite the British Museum (*see MAJOR CENTRAL LONDON MUSEUMS*) onto Coptic St. and left onto Little Russell St.

Cartoon Museum

35 Little Russell Street. Open Mon–Sat 10.30am–5.30pm, Sun noon–5.30pm. £5.50. Talks, lectures and events. Shop. 020 7580 8155. www.cartoonmuseum.org.

The **Cartoon Trust** and its museum exhibit humorous and satirical art works, drawings, engravings, adverts, comic strips and films from the time of William Hogarth to the present day.

The collection comprises some 1,500 cartoons and comics, which include evocative names such as Mr Punch, Rupert Bear, *The Beano*, Dan Dare, Andy Capp, Captain Pugwash, Fred Bassett, Heath Robinson, Giles, Calman and Garland. **Heneage Reference Library** *(open Wed 10.30am–1.30pm; ID required)* contains over 4,000 books on cartoons and 2,500 comics.

Continue along Little Russell St.

St George's Bloomsbury

Usually open daily 1pm–4pm. Call up beforehand to check. Closed bank holidays. 020 7242 1979. www.stgeorgesbloomsbury.org.uk.

Designed by the leading architect of English Baroque, **Nicholas Hawksmoor** *(1716–31)*, this thriving parish church and concert venue has a pedimented portico at the top of a flight of steps. Topping the steeple is a statue of the unpopular George I.

Continue to Bloomsbury Sq. and turn left.

Bloomsbury Square

In the southwest corner are two mid-18C houses; one of them is the former residence of **Isaac** and **Benjamin Disraeli** *(1818–26)*.

Leave the Square via Bedford Pl., cross Russell Sq. and continue onto Torrington Sq.

Brunei Gallery SOAS

Thornhaugh Street. Open Tue–Sat 10.30am–5pm, Thur until 8pm; free. 020 7898 4046 (recorded info). www.soas.ac.uk/gallery.

The public face of London's respected **School of Oriental and African Studies** is this fantastic gallery, which hosts a programme of changing contemporary and historical exhibitions from Asia, Africa and the Middle East. It is a student resource as well as a public one, aiming to promote understanding of cultures from these regions. The **Japanese Roof Garden** is especially attractive.

Continue along Torrington Sq. and onto Gordon St.

University College

The college houses the **Flaxman Sculpture Galleries**. There are also a number of excellent **museums** *(www.ucl.ac.uk/museums)* attached to departments such as geology, zoology and archaeology, and the **Petrie Collection** *(Tue–Sat 1pm–5pm; free)* of Egyptian and Sudanese artefacts consists of 80,000 objects housed in galleries so dark you need a torch!

Continue along Gordon St. and turn left onto Euston Rd.

Charles Dickens (1812–70)

Dickens drew generously on his fertile imagination as well as on his own experiences for his serialised novels: characters were modelled on friends, close relations and acquaintances made in connection with the theatre and the amateur dramatics he so enjoyed, and the philanthropic works he undertook.

An early, happy childhood in Chatham was brought to an abrupt end when his father was sent to Marshalsea Prison for debts and he, aged 12, was put to work blacking shoes. As an office boy he studied shorthand and secured a place on the *Morning Chronicle* reporting on debates in the House of Commons. There, he developed his acute sense of observation and sharp humour.

Close associates and admirers included Thackeray, Wilkie Collins and Hans Christian Andersen. His wife, Catherine Hogarth (1815–79), was a promising young journalist when she married the rising novelist (1835). She bore him 10 children *(Dora died in 1851)*. She was persuaded to accept a Deed of Separation (1858) as Dickens was emotionally involved with Ellen Ternan, a beautiful young actress.

Wellcome Collection

183 Euston Road. Open Tue–Sat 10am–6pm (Thurs 10pm), Sun 11am–6pm. Bank hol noon–6pm. 020 7611 2222. www.wellcomecollection.org.
Located at the northern end of London's **Museum Mile** *(www.museum-mile.org)*, which stretches from the British Library down to Somerset House, the Wellcome Collection features all sorts of weird and wonderful artefacts, from Darwin's walking stick to Napoleon's toothbrush. The museum aims to make people think about what it means to be human and temporary exhibitions examine all dimensions of the human condition. Check the website for details.

Continue along Euston Rd. and turn left onto Conway St.

Fitzroy Square★

Both George Bernard Shaw and Virginia Woolf lived (separately) at **No. 29** of this attractive Georgian square, named after Charles FitzRoy, 1st Baron Southampton, who developed the area in the late 18C and early 19C as residences for aristocratic families.

Leave Fitzroy Sq. on Conway St., turn left on Maple St. and right onto Cleveland Mews.

BT Tower

The landmark, originally known as the Post Office Tower, was erected in 1965 to provide an unimpeded path for London's telecommunications system.

Turn left into Howland St. and right into **Charlotte St.**, famous for its restaurants. **No. 76** was the residence of Richard Wilson and Constable. Turn left onto Scala St.

Pollock's Toy Museum and Shop

1 Scala Street. Open Mon–Sat 10am–5pm, last entry 4.30pm. Closed bank holidays. £3. 020 7636 3452. www.pollockstoymuseum.com.
This eccentric and enchanting museum was founded by Marguerite Fawdry and takes its name from Benjamin Pollock, the last of the Victorian toy theatre printers, whose stock she purchased to make up the initial collection. Here, old toys are displayed in an atmospheric setting of small rooms connected by narrow, winding staircases.

The collection of 19C and 20C toys includes **toy theatres**, wax, tin, porcelain, peg and spoon dolls, **teddy bears**, mechanical and optical toys, carved wooden animals, dolls' houses, puppets and board games. Live toy theatre performances are given during the school holidays and there's a toy shop proper on the ground floor.

ADDITIONAL SIGHTS

Charles Dickens Museum

48 Doughty Street. Open Mon–Sun 10am–5pm (last admission 4pm). Closed 25–26 Dec, 1 Jan. Guided walks. £8. Brochure and gallery cards (10 languages). 020 7405 2127. www.dickensmuseum.com.

The only surviving London home of **Charles Dickens**, who moved into this late 18C house shortly after his marriage to his "pet mouse" Catherine Hogarth. Dickens lived there with his young family from April 1837 to December 1839, during which time he completed *Pickwick Papers* and wrote *Oliver Twist* and *Nicholas Nickleby.*

The house holds letters and manuscripts, copies used for public readings and original illustrations. Original paintings and furniture and authentic décor recreate Dickens' London life here. The museum also holds readings, walks, tours and lectures, as well as special exhibitions about Dickens' life and works.

Foundling Museum

40 Brunswick Square. Open Tue–Sat 10am–5pm, Sun 11pm–5pm. Closed 24–27, 31 Dec, 1–2 Jan. £7.50. 020 7841 3600. www.foundlingmuseum.org.uk.

London's first home for abandoned children was a wholly philanthropic affair, founded by Thomas Coram but backed by artistic luminaries such as Hogarth and Handel, both of whom left substantial bodies of their work (including the original manuscript of Handel's *Messiah*) to the Foundation.

With Hogarth as a fundraiser, the Foundation became London's first art gallery, leading to the creation of the Royal Academy of Arts in 1768. The Foundation looked after 27,000 children until its closure in 1953. Coram, the children's charity, now continues the work.

Reopened as a museum, the Foundling holds an impressive art collection, with works by British artists, notably Hogarth, Gainsborough, Reynolds, Wilson Highmore, Roubiliac and Rysbrack, all of which are displayed in fully restored interiors that aim to provide a similar viewing experience to that enjoyed by visitors to the original Hospital in the 1700s.

The museum also houses a collection of material relating to Handel and his contemporaries.

Major Railway Stations

The area contains three of London's six major railway terminals. To the East stands **King's Cross** *(1852)*; the Great Northern terminus, built by Lewis Cubitt (the clock in the tower was displayed at the 1851 Exhibition *see SOUTH KENSINGTON)*. King's Cross is probably best known for something which doesn't exist; it was from platform 9¾ that Harry Potter set off for Hogwarts. Now it is marked by a Harry Potter shop selling official merchandise, and a discarded luggage trolley.

St Pancras (1864, Medieval Gothic in brick with Italian terracotta; *see below*) was designed by Sir George Gilbert Scott. Beautifully renovated, St Pancras serves the North, but it is also London's Eurostar terminus, from where you catch the train to Paris and Brussels.

Euston *(1837)* was rebuilt in 1968; a statue of Robert Stephenson, chief engineer of the London Birmingham line *(1838)*, stands in front.

St Pancras – This building, with its intricate red-brick Gothic frontage (1868–76), has been consistently voted one of London's favourites. In 1966, plans to amalgamate the station with King's Cross next door threatened St Pancras with demolition or at least extensive redevelopment. However, the demolition of Euston's beloved Doric arch in 1961 sharpened public opinion against such projects and after Sir John Betjeman, later poet laureate, stepped in, the building was subsequently saved and listed as Grade I.

The front part of the building is now the St Pancras Renaissance Hotel (*see YOUR STAY IN LONDON)*.

British Library

British Library★★

96 Euston Road. ♿ Open Mon–Sat, 9.30am–6pm (8pm Tue; 5pm Sat), Sun, 11am–5pm. Reading rooms (pass required). 0843 208 1144. www.bl.uk.

When first built, this red-brick premises for the British Library earned few compliments; it was described by HRH the Prince of Wales as "a dim collection of sheds groping for some symbolic significance". But the public has grown fond of it, and its exhibitions are worth visiting. In the forecourt stands a powerful statue of Sir Isaac Newton by the British sculptor **Eduardo Paolozzi.**

The entrance hall in light Portland stone rises the full height of the building and the eye is drawn to the stacks of the **King George III Library**. The reading rooms are quiet havens. Three exhibition galleries present the Library's treasures **(John Ritblat Gallery)** – technology enables visitors to turn the pages of rare books at the touch of a finger. Learn about the story of book production from the Middle Ages to the present time.

The British Library collections include rare manuscripts, Books of Hours, examples of early printing *(Caxton and Wynkyn de Worde's books)*, famous works (Lindisfarne Gospel, **Codex Sinaiticus**, Gutenberg Bible), handmade books, children's books, postage stamps, George III's library and Henry Davis' Gift *(fine bindings)*. Among the broad range of historical documents *(early maps, musical scores, modern calligraphy)* are copies of the **Magna Carta**, Essex's death warrant, Nelson's last letter, Shakespeare's signature and first folio *(1623)*. The core collection is stored on site, with the remainder stored elsewhere.

The new precincts now also accommodate the **National Sound Archive** for discs and tape recordings of music, oral history, documentary material, spoken literature, language and dialect.

St Pancras Parish Church

Upper Woburn Place, Euston Road. Open Sun 7.45am–11.30am, 5pm–7pm, usually Mon–Fri 8am– 6pm (phone ahead to check). Brochure (6 languages). Concert: Thu at 1.15pm; no charge. 020 7388 1461. www.stpancraschurch.org.

The church was built in 1819–22 at the time of the Greek Revival and William Inwood's design, selected from 30 submitted in response to an advertisement, echoes the Erechtheon on the Acropolis in Athens in the caryatids supporting the roofs of the square vestries, north and south. The columned two-stage elevation of the octagonal steeple and front Classical colonnade are modelled on the Tower of the Winds in Athens. Too tall to fit, the caryatid figures had to have their trunks shortened – hence their air of malaise.

ADDRESSES

LIGHT BITES

Bloomsbury has no shortage of pleasant but affordable places to eat. If you can't quite make up your mind, head to Charlotte St. *(parallel to Tottenham Court Rd.)*, and see what takes your fancy from the international range of outlets there. Among the restaurant chains *(see p410)* are:

Wagamama (4 Streatham St. Mon–Thur 11.30am–10pm, Fri, Sat 11.30am–11pm, Sun 11.30am–10pm; and Italian chain **Zizzi** (33–41 Charlotte St; Mon–Sat 11.30am–11pm, Sun noon–10.30pm).

PUB

Princesse Louise, *208 High Holborn ⊖Holborn. ✆ 020 7405 8816. Mon–Fri 11.30am–11pm, Sat noon–11pm, Sun noon–10.30pm.* Superb 19C pub with magnificent original Victorian decoration.

NIGHTLIFE

Aka, *18 West Central St. ⊖Tottenham Court Road. ✆020 7836 0110. www.akalondon.com. Tue 6.45pm–5am, Thur 8pm–3am, Fri 6pm–3am, Sat 8pm–5am, Sun 11pm–5am. Admission fee (£5–10) some nights, after a certain time (usually 10 or 11pm).* Housed in a former warehouse, this stylish bar serves a range of cocktails and hosts DJs nightly from 10pm.

Shanghai Blues Bar, *193–197 High Holborn. ⊖Holborn. ✆020 7404 1668. www.shanghaiblues.co.uk. Daily noon–11.30pm.* *See Where to Eat.* Jazz concerts Fridays and Saturdays *(8pm–10pm).*

Shochu Lounge, *37 Charlotte St. (underneath Roka). ⊖Goodge Street. ✆020 7580 6464. www.shochulounge.com. Mon–Fri noon–midnight, Sat 5.30pm–midnight, Sun and bank holidays 5.30pm–10.30pm.* Housed in the basement of stylish restaurant Roka, this cosy lounge bar with contemporary décor and a touch of the exotic offers cocktails made with *shochu*, a Japanese liquor distilled from rice, sweet potato, wheat or corn.

ENTERTAINMENT

The Dominion, *268 Tottenham Court Rd. ⊖Tottenham Court Rd. ✆020 7927 0900, box office 0844 847 1775. www.dominiontheatre.co.uk.* Large theatre, which has been home to the Queen musical *We Will Rock You*, since 2002.

Odeon Cinema, *30 Tottenham Court Rd. ⊖Tottenham Court Road. ✆ 0871 22 44 007. www.odeon.co.uk. £11.30 (prices cheaper Mon–Fri before 2pm).* All the latest blockbusters.

The Place, *17 Duke's Rd. ⊖Euston. ✆020 7121 1100. www.theplace.org.uk.* Home of the London Contemporary Dance School, this venue is dedicated to contemporary dance, with great shows at the Robin Howard Dance Theatre.

Renoir, *Brunswick Sq. ⊖Russell Square. ✆0330 500 1331 (recorded information line). Ticket £7–10, depending on day and time.* Arthouse cinema showing international titles.

UCL Bloomsbury Theatre, *15 Gordon St. ⊖Euston. ✆020 7388 8822. www.thebloomsbury.com. Box office: Mon–Fri 10am–6pm, Sat noon–6pm.* Varied programme, year-round; good venue for stand-up comedy.

SHOPPING

Bloomsbury is known for its **bookshops.**

Jarndyce – *46 Great Russell St. ⊖Tottenham Court Rd. or Holborn. ✆020 7631 4220. www.jarndyce.co.uk. Mon–Fri 11am–5.30pm* Situated opposite the British Museum, this antiquarian bookseller specialises in 18C and 19C English literature and history.

Pollock's, *1 Scala St. ⊖Goodge Street. ✆020 7636 3452. www.pollockstoymuseum.com. Mon–Sat 10am–5pm.* The quaint shop attached to **Pollock's Toy Museum** *(see p192)* sells vintage and modern toys.

Waterstones – *82 Gower St. ⊖Goodge Street. ✆020 7636 1577. www.waterstones.co.uk. Mon, Wed–Sat 9.30am–8pm (Sat 7pm), Tue 9.45am – 8pm, Sun noon–6pm).* Located at the heart of the University of London, this is Europe's largest academic bookshop. It also has a good selection of fiction and non-fiction, and a café, stationer's and music and DVD store in the basement.

Chancery Lane★

The character of the area bounded by High Holborn and Fleet Street is defined by the ancient traditions of the Inns of Court. Take the time to wander through the hidden alleyways to discover the fascinating history that underlies modern sites and stresses continuity through the ages. Leafy squares provide a haven from the bustling crowds. During the Middle Ages, the area around the palace of the Bishop of Ely was surrounded by open fields. By the late 16C the four Inns of Court and dependent *(now defunct)* Inns of Chancery had been established for nearly 300 years as the country's great law societies. Litigation was a serious business; there were disputes on land entitlement and inheritance, while actions for slurs and insults were also a fashionable pastime. From the 16C there were some 2,000 students dining in the halls.

Location: Map pp 188–189. *Holborn; Chancery Lane* This area lies to the North of Fleet St. and to the East of Covent Garden. It sits on the western boundary of the City of London.

Timing: Allow half a day to walk around the area, including a pause at Ye Old Mitre pub, off Hatton Garden.

Don't miss: Sir John Soane's museum when open late and illuminated by candlelight.

WALKING TOUR 2

CHANCERY LANE

From Chancery Lane Station turn left along High Holborn and left again to Lincoln's Inn Fields.

Sir John Soane's Museum★★

13 Lincoln's Inn Fields, WC2. Open Tue–Sat 10am–5pm (first Tue of each month candlelit tour 6pm–9pm). Closed bank holidays, 24 Dec. Free (£10 late-night opening). Guided tour Sat 11am (£5; no booking). Library and drawings collection available to scholars by appointment. 020 7405 2107. www.soane.org.

On the north side of Lincoln's Inn Fields is Sir John Soane's Museum. In 1833, Soane obtained a private Act of Parliament to ensure the perpetuation of the museum after his death. His house and collections now offer an insight into the mind of a British collector of that period. Soane acquired **No. 12** in 1792 as his town house, **No. 13** in 1805 *(as his museum)* and he built **No. 14** in 1824.

Interior – The rooms are small and passages narrow, but mirrors, skylights, windows on inner courts and domes give an illusion of space and perspective. Fragments, casts and models are displayed throughout the galleries, while below ground are the Crypt, the **Gothic Monk's Parlour** and the Sepulchral Chamber containing the **sarcophagus** of the Egyptian pharaoh Seti I *(c.1392 BC)*. On the first floor are architectural drawings *(8,000 by Robert and James Adam, 12,000 by Soane)*. Note the painting by **Turner** in the south drawing room.

On the ground floor is Soane's **collection of pictures★★**, assembled on folding planes in the picture room; it includes drawings by Piranesi and 12 of **Hogarth**'s paintings of the *Election* and the *Rake's Progress*. Elsewhere are **Canaletto**, **Reynolds** and **Turner**.

Lincoln's Inn Fields

By 1650 a developer, who had purchased the common fields to the West of Lincoln's Inn 20 years before, had surrounded them on three sides with houses. Of that period, one, **Lindsey House**, remains, and was probably designed by Inigo Jones. 18C houses in

Sir John Soane (1753–1837)

Born the son of a country builder, Soane was one of Britain's most influential architects: he worked under **George Dance Junior** and **Henry Holland**; he won prizes and a travelling scholarship to Italy *(1777–80)* while at the Royal Academy where, in later years, he was Professor of Architecture. He held the important office of Surveyor to the Bank of England *(1788–1833)*, for which he executed the most original designs ever made for a bank.

Sir John Soane's Museum

the square include the Palladian style (**Nos. 57–58**, from 1730), and **No. 66**, **Powis House** of 1777, with a pediment marking the centre window. On the north side **Nos. 1–2** are early 18C, **Nos. 5–9** Georgian, and **No. 15** mid-18C. The square's south side is occupied by the neo-Jacobean **Land Registry**, neo-Georgian **Nuffield College of Surgical Sciences** (1956–58), 19C–20C **Royal College of Surgeons**, housing the **Hunterian Museum** dedicated to the study of pathology and anatomy *(♿ open Tue–Sat 10am–5pm; ☎ 020 7869 6560; www.rcseng.ac.uk/museums)*.

▶ Walk through the square and turn right to the porter's lodge.

Lincoln's Inn★★

Grounds: *Open Mon–Fri 7am–7pm. Closed Sat–Sun and bank holidays.* ***Chapel:*** *Open Mon–Fri noon–2.30pm.* ***Old Hall, New Hall and Library:*** *Guided tour (min. 15 people, four different tours from £5–£45 per head with refreshments). See website for email contacts to book tour. Tours at 10.30am and 2.30pm. ☎ 020 7405 1393. www.lincolnsinn.org.uk.*

Dick Whittington

The third son of a Gloucestershire squire, Whittington came to London, entered the mercers' trade, married well and rose rapidly both in trade, from which he amassed a fortune, and in the Corporation, where he progressed from ward member to four-times Lord Mayor *(in 1397, 1397–8, 1406–7 and 1419–20)*. He was not knighted, though an important part of his contact with the Crown seems to have been the provision of loans; according to legend he gave a banquet for Henry V at which he burned bonds discharged for the King worth £60,000.

His great wealth continued after his death, as in his lifetime, to be devoted to the public cause: permanent buildings for Leadenhall Market, the construction of Greyfriars Library, half the cost of founding the Guildhall Library, the foundation of a college and almshouses at St Michael Paternoster Royal.

In 1605, licence was granted for performances of a play (now lost): *The History of Richard Whittington, of his lowe byrth, his great fortune.* When an engraver, Renold Elstrack, portrayed him in classic pose with his hand upon a skull, popular protest was so loud that the engraver altered the plate, replacing the skull with a cat (which may have given rise to the legend of Dick Whittington and his cat). He died in 1423, in his early sixties.

New Hall and Library, Lincoln's Inn

© Y. Kanazawa/Michelin

The site belonged to the Dominicans until 1276 before being acquired by the Earl of Lincoln, who built a large mansion, which he bequeathed as a residential college, or inn, for young lawyers. The brick buildings with stone decoration date from the late 15C. The main gateway leads to several intercommunating courts and beautiful gardens with an ornate Gothic toolshed.

New Square, surrounded by 17C four-storey buildings, features an archway leading south to Carey Street.

The **Stone Buildings** date from 1775–80. The red-brick mid-19C **New Hall** and **Library** are diapered in the Tudor manner.

The **Old Hall** dates from 1490. The Gothic-style **Chapel** was rebuilt in 1619–23. In the windows, benchers and treasurers are commemorated by their arms and names: Thomas More, Thomas Cromwell, Pitt, Walpole, Newman, Canning, Disraeli, Gladstone, Asquith and others.

The gabled brick buildings immediately south of the court, known as the **Old Buildings**, are Tudor in style *(redone in 1609)*.

The **gatehouse** on Chancery Lane, with its corner towers and original massive oak doors, dates from 1518. Above the arch are the arms of Henry VIII, the Earl of Lincoln and Sir Thomas Lovell.

Pass through the gate and walk north along Chancery Lane.

At **No. 53** the **London Silver Vaults** present a dazzling array of Georgian, Victorian and modern silver and silverplate. *Open Mon–Fri 9am–5.30pm (1pm Sat). Closed bank holidays. 020 7242 3844. www.thesilvervaults.com*

Continue north to High Holborn, turn right, cross the road and pass under a wide arch onto Gray's Inn Sq.

Gray's Inn★

Gardens: *Open Mon–Fri noon–2.30pm. Closed bank holidays.* ***Squares:*** *Open daily. 020 7458 7800. www.graysinn.info.*

Gray's Inn, founded in the 14C and extended in the 16C, was largely rebuilt after the war. The main entrance is through the **Gatehouse** of 1688. **South Square** has at its centre an elegant bronze statue of **Sir Francis Bacon**, the Inn's most illustrious member.

The gardens that so delighted **Samuel Pepys** and **Joseph Addison** are enclosed by 18C wrought-iron railings. The **hall**, which was burnt out, was rebuilt in its 16C style.

Staple Inn★

Lying just inside the limits of the City, Staple Inn was one of the Inns of Chancery, where law students spent their first year studying. The half-timbered houses, built in 1586–96, survived the Great Fire and have retained their overall character. An arched entrance leads to the Inn surrounding a central courtyard.

Once an inn of Chancery, **Barnard's Inn** is now home to **Gresham College** *(see The CITY – Guildhall)*, an institution that dates back over 400 years.

Across Holborn stands the **Prudential Assurance Building**, a red building designed by Alfred Waterhouse at the turn of the century. On the east side of Barnard's Inn, the former **Daily Mirror Building** is marked by a curtain wall of stone *(170ft/52m high)*, elbowed by taller buildings of glass that extend south between Fetter and New Fetter Lanes *(1957–60)*.

Holborn Circus is now punctuated by a traffic island with a statue of Prince Albert, mounted and with hat aloft.

Just south is **St Andrew Holborn** *(open Mon–Fri 9am–5pm; 020 7583 7394; www.standrewholborn.co.uk)*, a church designed by Wren.

At the west end, in a recess is the tomb of **Thomas Coram** *(d.1751)*, sea captain and parishioner *(see BLOOMSBURY – The Foundling Museum)*. The font *(1804)*, pulpit *(1752)* and the case and organ presented to Coram by **Handel** in 1750 are of particular interest.

Cross the Circus.

Hatton Garden

Ely Place recalls the Bishop of Ely's town house in Holborn, alluded to by Richard, Duke of Gloucester: "My lord of Ely, when I was last in Holborn, I saw good strawberries in your garden there, I do beseech you send for some of them" *(Richard III;* 3 iv). In 1576 the property was given at Queen Elizabeth's command to **Sir Christopher Hatton**, her "dancing Chancellor" for a yearly rent of 10 pounds, a red rose and 10 hayloads. Today, the Garden, which was built up in the 1680s, is the centre of diamond merchants and jewellery craftsmen. Early history is recalled in the name of **Ye Olde Mitre** in Ely Court, a narrow alley off Hatton Garden.

St Etheldreda

Open Mon–Sat 8am–5pm, Sun 8am–12.30pm. 020 7405 1061.

The church was built as a chapel attached to the Bishop of Ely's house. Subjected to neglect and wartime bombing, the 13C building underwent extensive restoration work. New stained-glass windows depict the five English martyrs beneath Tyburn gallows and against the east wall is a carved medieval wood reliquary. The **crypt**, which houses a café, has bare masonry walls and blackened Medieval roof timbers.

ADDRESSES

PUBS

The Old Bank of England, *194 Fleet St. Temple. 020 7430 2255. Mon–Fri 11am–11pm.* This pub, built in 1995, in the building which used to house the Bank of England, is a beautiful, though busy place for a drink.

The Punch Tavern, *99 Fleet St. Blackfriars. 020 7353 6658. Mon–Wed 7.30am–11pm, Thur, Fri 7.30am–noon, Sat, Sun 11am–7pm.* Fleet Street was once synonymous with newspapers and drawings on the walls recall that this place saw the birth of famous satirical magazine *Punch*.

Ye Olde Cheshire Cheese, *145 Fleet St. Blackfriars. 020 7353 6170. Mon–Fri 11am–11pm, Sat noon–11pm.* Nestled in a narrow passage, this historic 17C pub has no shortage of atmosphere, thanks to its many small rooms dressed in dark wood.

Ye Olde Cock Tavern, *22 Fleet St. Blackfriars. 020 7353 8570. Mon–Wed 7am–midnight, Thur 7am–1am, Fri 7am–2am, Sat noon–9pm.* The narrow front now rising on Fleet St. is home to a pub dating back to 1549, renovated from the 17C original after a fire destroyed its interior. It was the preferred watering hole of many famous people, such as Samuel Pepys, Charles Dickens and Dr Johnson.

SHOPPING

London Silver Vaults, *53 Chancery Lane. Chancery Lane. 020 7242 3844. www.thesilvervaults.com. Mon–Fri 9am–5.30pm, Sat 9am–1pm. Closed bank holidays.* Lovers of gold and silver should not miss this underground gallery, which brings together around 40 shops, offering objects from different eras.

Model Zone, *202 High Holborn. Holborn. 020 7405 6285. Mon–Sat 9.30am–6pm, Sun 11am–5pm.* A haven for model enthusiasts, selling everything from Action Men to *Star Wars* figures.

ACTIVITIES

Tennis, *Lincoln's Inn Fields. Chancery Lane. 07525 278 647. Daily 8am–dusk. Three courts open to all. £7/hr. Reservations necessary.*

Temple★★

The Order of the Knights Templar was founded in 1118 to protect pilgrims on the road to the Holy City of Jerusalem and welcomed to England by Henry I. They settled by the river, where they began building their church in 1185. In 1312 the Templars were suppressed and their property assigned to the Hospitallers, who in turn were dispossessed by Henry VIII. The church reverted to the Crown; the outlying property was granted to the lawyers, together with the safekeeping of the church, by James I in 1608. The lawyers formed themselves into three Societies: the Inner Temple (being within the City; emblem, a Pegasus), the Middle Temple (emblem, a Pascal lamb) and the Outer Temple, which was on the site of Essex Street but has long since disappeared. Today the area is abuzz with lawyers during the week and a haven of peace at weekends. At night, it is lit by gaslight.

Location: Map pp 188–189. *⊖Temple; Chancery Lane* On the north bank of the river adjacent to Somerset House, this area marks the western edge of the City of London and sits just south of Chancery Lane.

Timing: Allow a couple of hours to walk around the area and explore the Temple itself.

WALKING TOUR 3

TEMPLE BAR TO LUDGATE CIRCUS

Named after the **River Fleet**, which flows south from Hampstead to drain into the Thames at Blackfriars, **Fleet Street** links the City with Westminster. Once synonymous with the press, the street has changed in character since the newspapers moved elsewhere. It is lined with imposing buildings in a variety of styles, such as **Child & Co** (**No. 1**), one of the country's oldest banks *(now Royal Bank of Scotland)* "at the sign of the Marigold" *(see OSTERLEY PARK)*.

Pass through Inner Temple Gateway (between Nos. 16 and 17 Fleet Street).

Temple★★

Inner Temple – The three-storeyed **Inner Temple Gateway**, dating from 1610 *(reconstructed 1906)*, leads into the lane, past 19C buildings and the house *(right)* where Dr Johnson lived from 1760 to 1765, to the church.

Temple Church★★ – *For visiting hours, see the website. £4. 020 7353 8559. www.templechurch.com.*
This special church is one of the most historic and beautiful in London, with over 800 years of history.
The round church, originally built in 1160–85, was modelled on the Church of the Holy Sepulchre in Jerusalem. In 1185 it was consecrated by Heraclius, Patriarch of Jerusalem, in the presence of King Henry II and from then on, it acted as the headquarters of the Knights Templar in Britain. Today it remains a private chapel under the jurisdiction of the Sovereign as Head of the Church, who appoints the Master of the Temple.
Architecturally, a sense of clarity and order is enhanced by the stylised capital decoration and polished ringed shafts of Purbeck marble, the first freestanding Purbeck columns ever cut, that soar up to the conical roof.
On the stone floor lie 10 10C–13C effigies of knights in armour. To be buried in the Temple Church was highly desirable for the knights, as to be "buried in the Round" was to be buried "in Jerusalem". These effigies were created not as memorials, but as symbols of what was to come. The knights' eyes are open, ever-alert and ready for battle, and all are portrayed in their early 30s, the age at which Christ died and which the dead will rise on his return. The traditional

flexed posture of some of the effigies may indicate these knights took part in the crusades.

In the chancel *(1220–40)*, slender Purbeck columns rise to form the ribs of the quadripartite vaulting. Behind the 16C monument of Edmund Plowden on the north side a door leads to the penitential cell dating back to Templar times. The oak reredos designed by Wren was carved by **William Emmett** in 1682.

In the graveyard *(north side)* lies **Oliver Goldsmith**, a contemporary of Dr Johnson. To the northeast of the church stands the **Master's House**, rebuilt in 17C style. The Temple Church survived the Great Fire but was badly damaged in the Blitz *(1941)*. The **Inner Temple Hall**, **Treasury** and **Library** were all rebuilt after the war. The northern of the two ranges overlooking **King's Bench Walk** *(accessible through a passageway to the East)* dates from 1678 and is by **Christopher Wren** (**No. 1** rebuilt).

Middle Temple lies on the west side. The cloisters between Church Court and Pump Court and the south side of Pump Court have been rebuilt *(Edward Maufe)*; the north *(except for the 19C Farrar's Building)* is late 17C.

Middle Temple Hall★★

Open for guided tours Mon–Fri 9.30am–noon. £5 Closed bank holidays and law vacations. 020 7427 4820. www.middletemple.org.uk.

The Elizabethan great hall has a double hammerbeam roof *(1574)*, arguably the finest of the period. Medieval law students not only ate here, but attended lectures and even slept in the Hall. According to tradition, **Queen Elizabeth I** watched the first performance of Shakespeare's play *Twelfth Night* (1602) here. When the spectacular 16C carved screen at the Hall's east end was shattered by a World War II bomb, the splintered pieces were painstakingly reassembled.

Up the steps from **Fountain Court** (immortalised by Dickens in *Martin Chuzzlewit)* is **New Court**, with its Wren building of 1676.

Middle Temple Gateway and Lane

The pedimented gateway with giant pilasters was erected only in 1684, although the Lane is referred to as early as 1330 since it used to end in stairs on the river, affording a short cut by water to Westminster.

Return to Fleet St. and proceed East.

On the south side of Fleet Street stands the **Cock Tavern (Ye Olde Cocke Tavern)** (*see Addresses*). At **No. 17** is **Prince Henry's Room**. It's one of the few houses which survive from before the Great Fire of London in 1666. It's currently closed to the public. Contact www.cityoflondon.gov.uk for details.

St Dunstan-in-the-West

Usually Mon–Fri 9.30am–5pm. 020 7405 1929. www.stdunstaninthewest.org.

Built in 1833 by John Shaw within the City boundary, this church was badly bombed in 1944. The exterior, apart from the neo-Gothic tower and openwork octagonal lantern, is chiefly remarkable for the additions that associ-

Temple Bar

It has been the City's western barrier since the Middle Ages; the Sovereign pauses here to receive and return the Pearl Sword from the Lord Mayor on entering the City. The present memorial pillar, with statues of Queen Victoria and the future Edward VII surmounted by the City griffin, dates from 1880. It replaced the "bars" that had developed from 13C posts and chains, and at various times constituted a high, arched building, a prison *(thrown down by* **Wat Tyler** *in 1381)* and finally, an arch of Portland stone designed by Wren in 1672 and used in the days of public execution as a spike for heads and quarters. It was finally dismantled in 1870 and removed to Theobald's Park, near Waltham Cross.

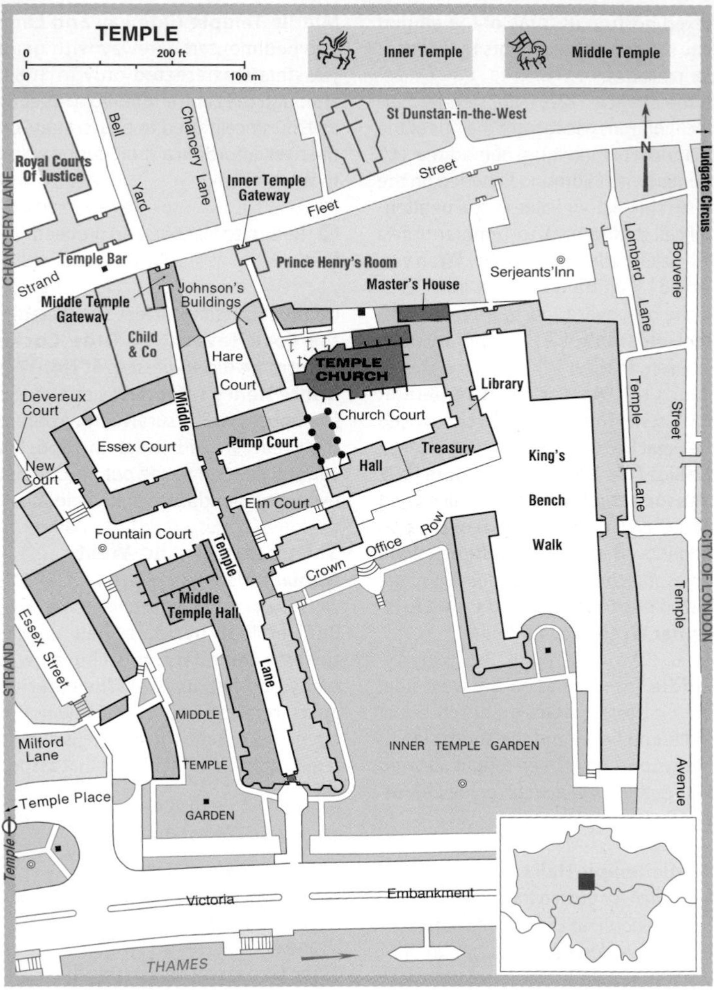

ate the church with Fleet Street: the bust of **Lord Northcliffe** *(1930)*, the public **clock** complete with its giant oak jacks; the **statues** from the 1586 **Lud Gate** include that of Queen Elizabeth I, while to the right stand figures of the mythical King Lud and his two sons *(1586)*. Corbels at the main door are carved with the likenesses of Tyndale *(west)* and John Donne *(east)*, both associated with St Dunstan's. St Dunstan's, dedicated to the patron of goldsmiths, jewellers and locksmiths, is octagonal with a high, star vault.

▶ Turn into Hind Court to Gough Sq.

Dr Johnson's House★

17 Gough Square. Open Mon–Sat 11am–5.30pm (5pm Oct–Apr). Closed bank holidays. £4.50 (cash only). Guide book (4 languages). Guided tour by appointment (50min) . 020 7353 3745. www.drjohnsonshouse.org

This unremarkable house, so typical of the late 17C, was home to the great scholar and lexicographer between 1748 and 1759. Modest in both size and proportion, it was chosen by **Johnson** *(1709–84)* almost certainly for its large, well-lit garret, where he worked with five secretaries to complete his *Dictionary*, published in 1755. The small rooms on each floor are sparsely furnished with 18C oak gate-leg tables and chairs, period prints, mementoes and a collection of books on the impecunious essayist's life and times.

The work completed, he moved to chambers in the Temple, in 1765 to **No. 7 Fleet Street** (known purely coincidentally as Johnson's Court), and finally to Bolt Court, where he died in 1784.

Return to Fleet St., past Shoe Lane, then cross to the south side.

In Wine Office Court is the **Cheshire Cheese** pub and restaurant. The **Express Group** building at Nos. 121–8 remains a landmark, its bold 1931 black-and-clear glass panels set in chromium; at No. 135 stands the **Daily Telegraph** building (1928), boasting a ponderous mixture of styles. The *Express* and the *Telegraph* have both now moved out.

St Bride's★

Open Mon–Fri 8am–6pm, Sun 10am–6.30pm. Closed bank holidays. Recitals: Thur, Fri at 1.15pm except for Lent, Aug and Dec. 020 7427 0133. www.stbrides.com.

The famous white **spire**★★of St Bride's, Wren's tallest and most floating steeple, rises by four open octagonal stages to a final open pedestal and tapering obelisk that terminates in a vane *(226ft/69m above ground)*. When the spire was newly erected, a baker used it as a model for wedding cakes; he made a fortune and inaugurated a lasting tradition.

In 1940 Wren's church was gutted by a fire that left only the steeple and calcined outer walls standing. During rebuilding, the crypt was opened; subsequent excavations revealed a Roman ditch, walls, a pavement and the outlines of church buildings on the site dating to Saxon times at least. Inside, Wren's design of a barrel-vaulted nave and groined aisles has been retained. The decoration is 17C.

The **St Bride Printing Library** and Bridewell Theatre are located nearby, as is the **Punch Tavern** (*see Addresses*), named after the magazine, which had premises there.

St Bride's Associations

It is St Bride's associations rather than its architecture that makes it unique to many: **Thomas Becket** was born close by; **King John** held a parliament in the church in 1210; **Henry VIII**, advised by **Thomas Wolsey**, built Bridewell Palace nearby between the church and the river, and received Charles V there in 1522; high-ranking churchmen unable to pay for lodgings within the City walls built town houses in the neighbourhood *(Salisbury Square)* and since the clergy were the largest literate group in the land it was only natural that when **Wynkyn de Worde** acquired his master's press in 1491, he should remove it from Westminster to St Bride's and Fleet Street (Caxton had been wealthy enough not to have to depend upon the press for his livelihood, unlike his apprentice). By the time de Worde died in 1535 *(he was buried in St Bride's)*, the parish boasted several printers, including Richard Grafton, who printed the first English-language Bible in 1539. The church was the first to use the Book of Common Prayer, while its neighbouring taverns and coffeehouses were frequented by Chaucer, Shakespeare, Milton, Lovelace, Evelyn, Pepys *(born nearby and like all his family, christened in the church)*, Dryden, Izaac Walton, Edmund Waller (poet), Aubrey, Ashmole, John Ogilby (mapmaker), Thomas Tompion (father of English clock and watchmaking), Addison; in the 18C by Johnson and Boswell, Joshua Reynolds, Goldsmith, Garrick, Burke, Pope, Richardson *(coffin in the crypt)* and Hogarth; in the 19C by Charles Lamb, Hazlitt, Wordsworth, Keats, Hood, Leigh Hunt, Dickens. Today modern pew backs are labelled with the names of contemporaries, for St Bride's remains the printers' church, the Cathedral of Fleet Street.

CAMDEN AND ISLINGTON

The north London boroughs of Camden and Islington are two of the capital's most desirable, featuring fashionable homes, leafy streets and some of the city's best nightlife. Once an industrial area, Camden is now at the cutting edge of alternative culture, with quirky markets and an edgy music and clubbing scene, while upmarket Islington retains the village vibe it has cultivated for centuries.

Highlights

1 Watch contemporary dance at **Sadler's Wells** (p208)
2 Enjoy dinner and drinks on trendy **Upper Street** (p211)
3 Unearth bargains at **Camden Markets** (p214)
4 Take a boat trip on the **Regent's Canal** (p215)
5 Dance to the alternative beat of Camden's **live music** scene (p215)

A Bit of Geography

Camden stretches out behind Euston and King's Cross along the eastern and northern sides of Regent's Park. Chalk Farm marks the northern extension of Camden proper, beyond which is Belsize Park, though the borough extends up to Hampstead and Highgate *(see pp 342–348)*.

Islington's main thoroughfare is Upper Street, which begins at Angel station in the South, just north of Clerkenwell and East of King's Cross, and extends north to Highbury Corner and Highbury and Islington station. The borough continues north into Holloway and towards Finsbury Park to the East, as well as South to Farringdon.

A Bit of History

Camden is named after Charles Pratt, the 1st Earl of Camden, so-called for his estate Camden Place, near Chislehurst, Kent. Camden Town was once part of Kentish Town manor acquired by Pratt in the 18C. In 1791 he started to grant leases for residences to be built on the site and in 1816, the Regent's Canal was built, giving the area an industrial character. It was not considered a nice place to live until well into the 20C, after the Camden Markets began in 1973.

Islington's name comes from an Old English name meaning Gisla's hill *(dun meaning hill)*, eventually mutating into Isledon, from which the area gets its current name. During the medieval period Islington was a small manor. It later became a rural village and was just close enough to London to become a popular residence for the rich. Its good water supply meant the area was used for growing vegetables and the turnpike built here to connect the City with Highgate Hill meant that several taverns and inns opened up along what is now

Regent's Canal at Camden Lock

© C. Eymenier/Michelin

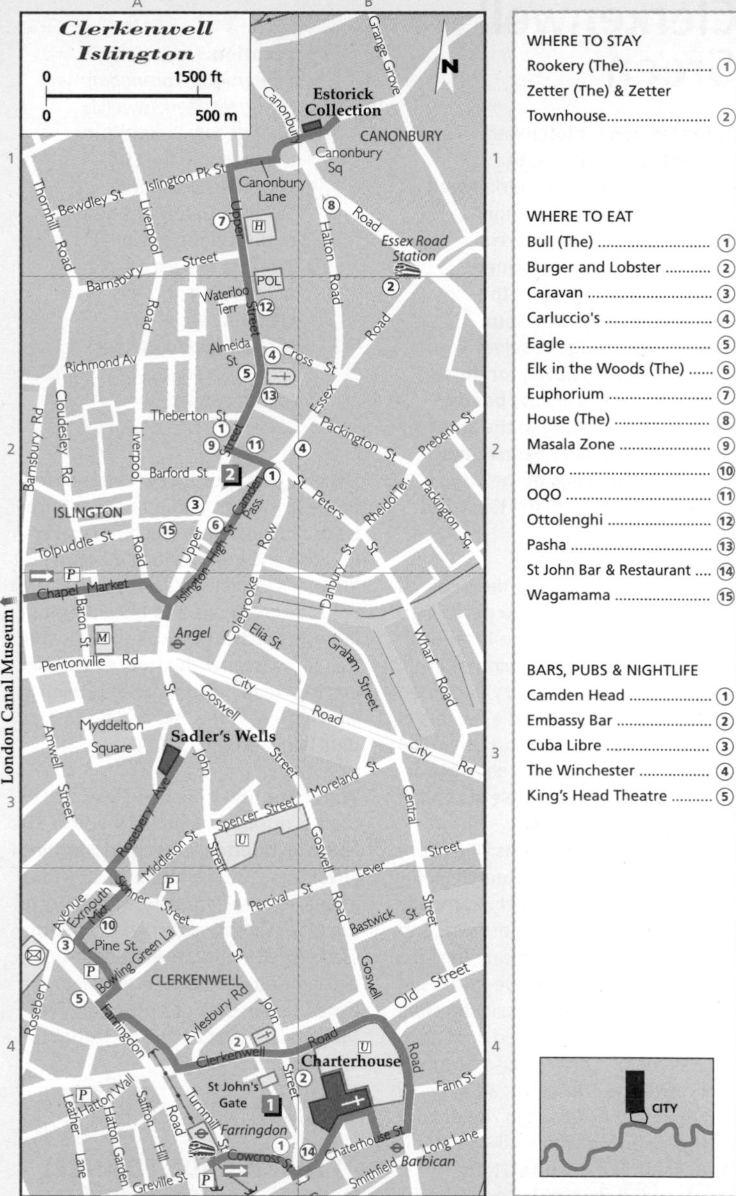

Upper Street. In 1862 the Royal Agricultural Hall was built on Liverpool Road and was London's principal exhibition site until the 20C.

During WWII it was requisitioned for use by Mount Pleasant Sorting Office and never reopened.

Camden and Islington Today

Both neighbourhoods are fashionable places to live and known for their nightlife; Camden for its alternative culture and lively music scene, and Islington for its more upmarket range of bars and restaurants, particularly along Upper Street.

Clerkenwell Green

Location: Map p 205. ⊖*Barbican; Farringdon; Old Street.* Clerkenwell is bounded by Bloomsbury, Islington and the City.
Don't Miss: The 16C St John's Gate, once home to the Knights Hospitaller.
Timing: Allow a couple of hours to enjoy this charming area – and stick around for dinner. Weekdays are best for atmosphere.

As the fashion for loft living took hold in the 1990s, the secluded character of Clerkenwell underwent a radical change. Warehouses and commercial properties were transformed with glass frontages and the trendsetters moved in, soon followed by a range of select eating places. However, for those in the know it has always been a desirable area, owing to the air of faded gentility and its convenient location on the edge of the City and a short hop from the West End.

A BIT OF HISTORY

Clerkenwell recalls in name the Medieval parish clerks, who each year performed plays outside the City at a local well-head *(viewed through a window at 14–16 Farringdon Lane)*. Finsbury is named after the Fiennes family, the owners of the local manor (bury/burh/burg in Old English) who, in the 14C, gave **Moorfields**, a marsh, to the people of London as its first free open space.

Some open land remains: Finsbury Square, Finsbury Circus, Bunhill Fields and the Honourable Artillery Company Fields, but the outflow of artisans and cottage industry workers from the City, particularly after the Plague *(1665)* and Fire *(1666)*, caused poor quality housing and tenements to be erected right up to the walls of the Charterhouse, St John's Priory, Bethlem *(in what is now City Road)* and the other hospitals in the district – the only one of which now extant is **Moorfields Eye Hospital** (1805).

The crowded days of home industry in the early 19C are recalled by the Eagle Pub *(see p414)* and the rhyme:

Half a pound of twopenny rice,
Half a pound of Treacle,
Up and down the City Road,
In and out the Eagle,
That's the way the money goes,
Pop goes the Weasel.

Over the centuries, Clerkenwell became home to groups holding nonconformist or radical beliefs, such as Quakers, Chartists and other militant movements. St Peter's Church in Clerkenwell Road, colourful festivals and excellent Italian grocery stores recall the sizeable Italian quarter with street entertainers, ice-cream vendors and craftsmen, which grew in the 19C and flourished until fairly recently.

Water Supply – The New River undertaking originated in 1609 when **Sir Hugh Myddelton**, a City goldsmith and jeweller, put up the capital to construct a canal from springs in Hertfordshire to the City. Water was carried down from Clerkenwell to the City in wooden pipes and individual subscribers supplied with water on tap; the enterprise was eventually taken over by the Metropolitan Water Board (1904–74).

WALKING TOUR

1 FARRINGDON TO ANGEL

From Farringdon Station turn left on Cowcross St., left into Charterhouse St. and left again onto Charterhouse Sq.

Charterhouse★

Guided tours Apr–Sept, £10 per person. To book, email or write to: Clerk of the Brothers (Tours), Charterhouse,

Tudor Great Hall of Charterhouse

Sutton's Hospital, London EC1M 6AN. Payment by cheque. Guide book. www.thecharterhouse.org. ✆020 7253 9503.
At every stage of its history – 14C priory, Tudor mansion, 17C hospital and boys' school, 20C residence for aged Brothers – the buildings of the Charterhouse have been replaced or altered in a variety of materials and architectural styles.

The building comprises the 15C gateway, with its original massive gates and the adjoining house, now the Master's lodging, dated 1716.

On the north side of Master's Court the Tudor **Great Hall**, with hammerbeam roof and 16C screen and gallery remains intact. The Elizabethan **Great Chamber** is hung with Flemish tapestries. In the tower, to which the belfry and cupola were added in 1614, is the treasury, vaulted in the Tudor period.

The present **chapel** was created in 1614 out of the monks' Chapter House with the addition of a north aisle and further enlarged to the North in 1824.

View Florin Court, the Art Deco mansion block where fictional character Poirot lived, before returning to Charterhouse St. Turn right up St John St and fork left onto St John's Lane.

St John's Gate

The Order of the Grand Priory, which developed from the First Crusade as a religious order to look after pilgrims visiting the Holy Land, became a military order during the 12C. It left the Holy Land on the fall of Acre in 1291. In 1540 **Henry VIII** dissolved the **Hospitallers** and in 1546 issued a warrant *(in the museum)* for the buildings to be dismantled, but the gate survived. St John's was re-established as a Protestant Order by Royal Charter in 1888.

Gatehouse and Museum of the Order of St John – The 16C gatehouse was the Priory's south entrance. In the 20C Tudor-style Chapter Hall, where the Maltese banners hang in the lantern, in the Council Chamber and the Library are displayed pharmacy jars and a rare collection of beaten silver Maltese glove trays and the illuminated **Rhodes Missal**, on which the knights took their vows. *Open Mon–Sat, 10am–5pm (4pm Sat). Closed Sun and Bank Holiday Sat–Mon. Guided tours (1hr) Tue, Fri, Sat at 11am and 2.30pm. Donation. ✆020 7324 4005. www.museumstjohn.org.uk.*

St John's Church and Crypt – The Grand Priory Church of St John once extended further west into the square, where setts in the road mark the site of the round nave. The crypt is 12C, the only original Priory building to survive.

Turn left along Clerkenwell Rd.

Clerkenwell Green

Clerkenwell Green, the rallying point in the 18C and 19C for workers protest-

ing against the social and industrial injustices of the period, is an appropriate site for the **Karl Marx Memorial Library**, an 18C house (*No. 37a*). Cheerful pavement cafés and artists' studios now surround the Green and the area has become a trendy place to live, especially among media professionals. St James Walk even featured as Will Freeman's (Hugh Grant's) bachelor pad in 2002 film, *About a Boy*, based on Nick Hornby's novel.

Continue along Clerkenwell Rd. to Farringdon Rd.; turn right and right again onto Exmouth Market.

Surrounded by the modern buildings of **City University** *(St John St.)* is the original Northampton Institute (1894–96), designed by E Mountford in an eclectic baroque style. **Finsbury Health Centre** *(17 Pine St.)* was designed to bring moderm, hygienic healthcare to a borough blighted by tuberculosis and slum clearances. Constructed between 1935–38, it is truly modern in spirit and style.

Exmouth Market

A market place since the 1890s, Exmouth Market hosts a daily street food market (Mon–Fri noon–3pm approx.) selling everything from olives and cheese to crêpes and Ghanaian dishes. Both sides of this pedestrianised street are lined with trendy bars and restaurants, and numerous independent design shops. At the junction of Exmouth Market and Roseberry Avenue is **Mount Pleasant**, now one of the main Post Office inland mail sorting offices and centre of the now-defunct Post Office railway.

Turn left along Rosoman St. and right on Rosebery Ave.

Sadler's Wells Theatre

Rosebery Avenue. ☎0844 412 4300. www.sadlerswells.com.

The UK's leading dance theatre is named after Richard Sadler, who opened a music house in 1683 and rediscovered medicinal wells. The theatre was renovated very successfully a few years ago; it specialises in all kinds of dance, from contemporary dance to tango, hip hop to flamenco *(see YOUR STAY IN THE CITY)*.

Also on Rosebery Avenue is the **New River Head** *(Thames Water Authority)*; the neo-Georgian building (now flats) contains a fireplace that is attributed to Grinling Gibbons and pretty plaster ceilings c.1693.

Take Arlington Way behind the theatre and turn left onto Myddelton Passage to Myddleton Sq.

The elegant terraces of **Myddelton Square** were built in the late 1700s on part of the New River Company's estate.

ADDRESSES

LIGHT BITE

Moro, *34–36 Exmouth Market. ⊖Farringdon. ☎020 7833 8336. www.moro.co.uk. Mon–Sat noon–2.30pm & 6–10.30pm, Sun 12.30pm–2.45pm Tapas served all day.* Award-winning Moorish restaurant serving innovative cuisine, taking the flavours of the southern Mediterranean and Morocco.

BARS *see map p216.*

Bleeding Heart Tavern, *19 Greville St. ⊖Farringdon. ☎020 7242 2056. www.bleedingheart.co.uk. Mon–Fri 7am–10.30pm.* No fewer than 450 different wines are served at this stylish restaurant/bar.

Cellar Gascon, *59 West Smithfield. ⊖Farringdon. ☎020 7600 7561, www.clubgascon.com. Mon–Fri noon–midnight.* The stylish bar attached to Club Gascon *(see Where to Eat)* is a pleasant place for a glass of wine.

Smiths of Smithfield, *67–77 Charterhouse St., EC1M 6HJ. ⊖Farringdon. ☎020 7251 7950. www.smithsofsmithfield.co.uk. Mon–Fri 7am–late, Sat and Sun 9.30am–late.* The clever renovation of this former meat warehouse has been an undisputed success since opening. A great place for a quiet brunch on Sundays.

Angel and Canonbury

Islington's elegant Georgian squares, its Victorian terraces, and the proximity to the West End and City of London ensure its popularity as a residential area. It is a curious mix of gentrification and dilapidation; this is reflected in its smart restaurants, bustling bars, antique shops, an art cinema and avant-garde theatres, which do a roaring trade right next to the street market and social housing schemes. There are plenty of pleasant discoveries to be made as one strolls around the district.

Location: Map p 205. *Angel; Highbury & Islington*. Islington is to the North of the City of London, with the mainline stations King's Cross, St Pancras and Euston to the West. It merges with the East End.

Kids: Traditional Italian ice cream at the London Canal Museum.

Timing: A leisurely morning for the walking tour, then lunch and a little afternoon shopping on Upper St.

A BIT OF HISTORY

Islington became a fashionable suburb in the 17C when people fled the City after the Plague *(1665)* and the Great Fire *(1666)*. Taverns marked the stages on the centuries-old roads from the North, well-trodden by those driving cattle, sheep and swine south to Smithfield (until the coming of the railways). In the 19C, new builder-developers moved into the area, soon inhabited by workers from the new light industries. By the 20C Islington and Angel in particular had become a synonym for slums, grime, grinding poverty, the Caledonian Market *(Cally Market)* and the gas-lit glories of Collins Music Hall.

Since World War II restoration and repainting have returned terraces and squares to their precise, well-groomed lines – notably **Duncan Terrace**, **Colebrooke Row**, built in 1761, and **Charlton Place**, with their Tuscan column framed front doors and lanterns, or rounded doorways; slums have been largely replaced by four- to eight-storey blocks of brick, reminders of the locality's past as a major London brickfield.

WALKING TOUR

2 ANGEL TO CANONBURY

From King's Cross take York Way.

London Canal Museum

12–13 New Wharf Road. Open Tue–Sun and Bank Holiday Mon 10am–4.30pm (4pm last admission), late opening on first Thu of each month until 7.30pm. Closed 24–26 Dec. £4. 020 7713 0836. www.canalmuseum.org.uk.

The museum is housed in an old ice house beside the Battlebridge basin on the Regent's Canal, which once supplied Carlo Gatti, Victorian London's leading ice-cream maker, with natural ice from Norway. An old film, *Barging through London*, illustrates canal life in 1924. The display records the building of canals in England, the construction of the Regent's Canal, the various methods of towing or propelling the barges (horsepower, legging, poling, steam tug, towpath tractors), 20C decline and conversion to leisure use: towpath walk *(1970)*; boating, canoeing, fishing.

Take Wharfdale Rd. to Killick St. Turn right and left onto Collier St. Continue onto Donegal St., left up Penton St. and right along Chapel Market to Angel.

Angel

Five main thoroughfares converge on this ancient crossroads – named after the Angel Inn that once stood here.

New River Walk

To really get to grips with this area, follow the New River Walk *(www.london-footprints.co.uk/wknewriverroute.htm)* from Highbury and Islington station back to Angel, winding through the streets between Upper St. and Essex Rd.

Walk north up Upper St.

The former **Royal Agricultural Hall** *(1861–62)* is now the Business Design Centre, a venue for trade exhibitions *(52 Upper Street; 020 7288 6272; www.businessdesigncentre.co.uk)*. It was used successively for cattle shows, military tournaments, revivalist meetings, bull-fighting *(1888)* and Cruft's Dog Show *(1891–1939)*.

Turn off Upper St. onto Charlton Pl. and right onto Camden Passage.

Camden Passage

Upper Street. Open Wed and Sat. www.camdenpassageislington.co.uk.
The quaint old alley, on the east side of Upper Street, is lined with small shops, arcades, restaurants, two Victorian pubs and the newly built "Georgian Village". *See YOUR STAY IN THE CITY – Shopping.* Returning to Upper St. and turning right will bring you to **Islington Green**. The triangular green has a statue of Sir Hugh Myddelton at its centre.
A plaque marks the site *(north side)* where, from 1862 until the middle of the last century, **Collins Music Hall** was boisterous with song.

Continue along bustling Upper St., lined with boutiques and places to eat and drink, in the direction of Highbury and Islington station. Take Canonbury Lane to Canonbury Sq.

Canonbury

Canonbury is a network of streets and squares lined by early 19C terraced houses, of which **Canonbury Square★**, once home to George Orwell and Sir Francis Bacon, is the prime example. Minor connecting roads, such as Canonbury Grove with small country cottages overlooking a New River backwater, and others, like Alwynne Road in which later-19C villas and semi-detached houses stand in the shade of plane trees, add to the atmosphere.

Continue along Canonbury Pl.

Canonbury Tower

A square dark-red brick tower *(60ft/18m high)* is all that remains of the 16C manor, once the country residence of Sir John Spencer, Lord Mayor and owner of Crosby House in Bishopsgate.

Return to Canonbury Sq.

Estorick Collection of Modern Italian Art

39a Canonbury Square. Open Wed–Sat 10am–6pm, Sun noon–5pm. Library: by appointment. £5. Café. Shop. Garden. 020 7704 9522. www.estorickcollection.com.
Eric Estorick, an American sociologist and writer, collected works of art after World War II. Estorick was fascinated with Italian art, in particular, the notion of "universal dynamism" put forward by the Futurists.
In the words of the Futurist manifesto of 1910, "a clean sweep should be made of all stale and threadbare subject-matter in order to express the vortex of modern life... of steel, fever, pitch and headlong speed." Besides the **Italian Futurists**, Estorick collected works by De Chirico (*The Revolt of the Sage*, 1916), Rosso, Modigliani, Morandi and Marini.

ADDITIONAL SIGHT

Highbury

By the 19C Highbury had fallen into the hands of undistinguished developers except for **Highbury Place** *(1774–79)*, Highbury Terrace *(1789)* and Highbury Crescent *(1830s)*, where detached and semi-detached villas had been erected for the more affluent.

Emirates Stadium Tour

Ashburton Grove. Open daily; tour times vary. £17.50, museum only £7. Shop. 020 7619 5000. www.arsenal.com.

In 2006 Arsenal, one of London's biggest and most successful football clubs, unveiled its new stadium: the Emirates. The Stadium took over three years to build, at a cost of £390 million, and can seat 60,000 spectators. Tours run daily, allowing visitors to get behind the scenes, sitting in the players' dressing room and walking down the tunnel onto the pitch. Tours led by a range of "Arsenal legends" are also available *(£35)*. All tours include the interactive museum, home to numerous articles of footballing memorabilia.

ADDRESSES

LIGHT BITE

The Bull, *100 Upper St. Angel. 020 7354 9174. www.thebullislington.co.uk.* Warm and friendly pub/bar with dim lights, cool music and comfy sofas. A simple menu of light snacks, homemade burgers, cakes and pies is served and there's brunch and roasts on weekends.

The Elk in the Woods, *37 Camden Passage. Angel. 020 7226 3535. www.the-elk-in-the-woods.co.uk.* A chic bar/pub with minimalist décor and a traditional British menu for all-day dining.

Euphorium, *202 Upper St. Highbury & Islington. 020 7704 6905. www.euphoriumbakery.com.* The original location of this expanding bakery chain has recently been refurbished and now boasts a table service area in addition to the takeaway counter. Serves great pastries and all manner of breads. It's a good place to recharge your batteries during an Upper Street shopping trip.

Masala Zone, *80 Upper St. Angel. 020 7359 3399. www.masalazone.com.* This outpost of the popular Indian chain serves its menu of affordable curries and thalis in either the contemporary interior or outside on the terrace overlooking Islington Green.

OQO, *4–6 Islington Green. Angel. 020 7704 2332.* This avant-garde bar serves Chinese-style tapas and is best visited in the evenings. Good cocktails.

PUBS

Camden Head, *2 Camden Walk, Camden Passage. Angel. 020 7359 0851.* A large, traditional pub with rich mahogany panelling, etched glass and a decent selection of real ales. Pleasant terrace for sunny days.

The House, *63–69 Canonbury Rd. Highbury & Islington. 020 7704 7410. www.thehouseislington.com. Mon–Wed 4–10pm, Thur–Fri 11.30am–10pm, Sat–Sun 9.30am–10pm. See Where to Eat.* Interesting wine list and cocktails *(£6–8)*.

The Winchester, *2 Essex Road. Angel. 020 7288 2493.* Modern gastropub serving upmarket pub grub, such as homemade burgers, and featuring a good wine list and extensive, interesting cocktail menu. DJs play later on and the atmosphere gets pretty lively.

NIGHTLIFE

Cuba Libre, *72 Upper St. Angel. 020 7354 9998. www.cubalibrelondon.co.uk.* Great tapas and Cuban-themed cocktails are served both inside this lively bar/restaurant and at pavement tables outside. After 9pm the tables nearest the bar are cleared away to make room for a dance floor.

Embassy Bar, *119 Essex Rd. Angel or Highbury & Islington. 020 7226 7901. Sun–Wed 2pm–midnight, Thur 2pm–1am, Fri 2pm–2am. Free during the week, Fri–Sat £3–5 after 9pm.* One of the first DJ bars in the neighbourhood remains one of the most popular. There's a dance floor in the basement, where a DJ spins the tunes *(soul, funk, hip hop, electro, house)*.

King's Head Theatre, *115 Upper St. Angel or Highbury & Islington. 020 7478 0160. www.kingsheadtheatrepub.com.* There's been a King's Head Pub on this site since the 1500s. It was the first pub theatre to be founded in England and today features live music *(from jazz to blues)*, while the theatre hosts performances of everything from opera and musicals to childrens' theatre. Check website for listings.

Camden Town

Once an industrial heartland, linked to the rest of the city by both rail and canal, Camden Town is now strongly associated with counterculture. The ever-popular markets, pubs and clubs here have a Bohemian atmosphere, especially at weekends, and all manner of streetlife can be seen along the main thoroughfare, Chalk Farm Road. This is a heartland for music and hosts an annual festival, the Camden Crawl, each spring.

Location: Map opposite. *Camden Town, Chalk Farm.* Camden is located north of Regent's Park and west of Islington in inner North London. Most of the action happens along Chalk Farm Road, which runs north from Camden Town tube station to Chalk Farm.

Kids: Children will love poking around the markets.

Timing: Allow at least half a day to explore this lively part of the city; longer if you're a keen market shopper.

CAMDEN TOWN

From the tube station, walk up Chalk Farm Rd past the markets (*see YOUR STAY IN THE CITY – Shopping*).

Close to Regent's Park and Primrose Hill, Camden Town, with its delightful village atmosphere, has pockets of elegant houses much sought after by artists, writers, actors and media people. In stark contrast to the local terraced houses, the Post-Modernist **TV-AM building**, in Hawley Crescent *(near Camden Lock)*, designed by T Farrell, is of some interest. From Camden Lock it is possible to take a boat trip upstream to London Zoo and Little Venice or downstream to Limehouse in the Docklands.

Roundhouse

Chalk Farm Road. 020 7424 9991. www.roundhouse.org.uk

This 1840s former locomotive shed, a Grade II listed building, has been converted into a lively cultural and performance venue with a bold programme of live music, theatre, dance, circus and new media, and an attractive modern bar/café. Young people are the focus, helping to plan events and taking part in creative projects in the 24 state-of-the-art TV, radio and music studios.

Shops on Camden High Street

© D. Chapuis/Michelin

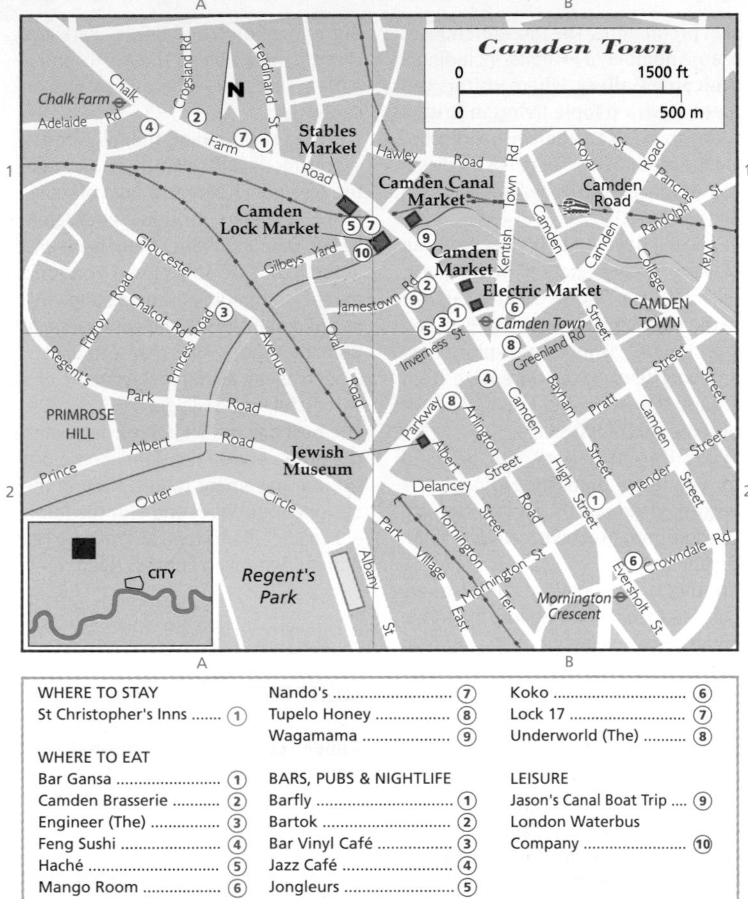

Camden Lock Market

Facing onto the canal, the former timber wharf here was renovated in the late 1980s and offered at low rents to young artisans for use as workshops. Once very trendy and upmarket, this has now become the centre of street style, and cutting-edge fashion designers come here seeking inspiration. On weekends, endless ethnic food stalls open up to cater to the crowds of browsers.

The **Regent's Canal Information Centre**, housed in an old lock-keeper's cottage, presents historical displays relating to the canal's development. Plans are in place to open up a coffee shop here.

Stables Antique Market

The Stables, as their name suggests, were built in the 1840s to accommodate the horses that hauled the barges along the Regent's Canal. The present buildings house a large market (*see Addresses*): Art Deco artefacts, 1950s and 1960s clothing, period fixtures and fittings and antiques. There are more stalls in the cobbled yard.

Jewish Museum

129–131 Albert St. Open Mon–Thur 10am–5pm, Fri 10am–2pm, Sun 10am–5pm. £7.50. Welcome Gallery, shop and café free. 020 7284 7384. www.jewishmuseum.org.uk.

The exhibition space at Raymond Burton House has undergone a huge expansion programme. The museum houses a large number of exhibits, including a **Welcome Gallery**, where visitors can meet Jewish people living in Britain today through an audiovisual display. On the ground floor there is a medieval *mikveh*, uncovered by archaeologists in London in 2002.

In an area devoted to history, you can play the "Great Migration" board game, take part in a Yiddish theatre karaoke session or wander down a 19C East End street. Here, visitors can explore how and why Jews have come here from around the world and how they have become part of British life.

In a different gallery, not advised for young children, the Holocaust is uncovered through the eyes of one man, London-born Auschwitz survivor Leon Greenman.

Another gallery explores Judaism, its beliefs and traditions. Explore the Torah, try on a prayershawl, or build your own synagogue. An emphasis is also put on the Jewish Faith today, and to what extent it is practised in different areas of Britain, from the occasional bowl of chicken soup to the full Shabbat.

Finally, special exhibitions space houses changing exhibitions, throwing new light on Jewish culture, heritage and identity over the last 4,000 years.

Camley Street Natural Park

Camley Street; www.wildlondon.org.uk

A wildlife haven has been created in a 2-acre/0.8ha park on the banks of the Regent's Canal, including ponds, a marsh and reed beds, with the aim of attracting insects, butterflies and birds.

Primrose Hill

On the north side of Regent's Park, Primrose Hill *(256ft/78m)* has given its name to the surrounding district just west of Camden. Like Regent's Park, it was once part of Henry VIII's Great Chase and became Crown property in 1841. In 1842 an act of Parliament returned the land to the public, securing it as an open space. The hill itself affords some of the best views in London, with the city stretched out to the South and Belsize Park and Hampstead visible to the North, and is a great place for walks and picnics on sunny days.

The area surrounding the hill is today synonymous with celebrity, its Victorian terraces now home to a host of music and media stars, including chef Jamie Oliver, Damon Albarn of Blur fame and actor Jude Law. It is one of London's most fashionable addresses and with its affluent residents and wide range of upmarket shops, bars and restaurants, is seen as the archetypal example of a successful urban village.

The best day to visit is Saturday, when the area's stylish residents come out to sit at pavement tables, shop in the designer boutiques and visit the farmers' market *(9am–1pm)* at Primrose Hill Primary School on Princess Road.

ADDRESSES

LIGHT BITE

Weekends are a great time to go to **Camden Lock** and **Stables Antique Markets** to sample a wide variety of international food from the stalls: African, Indian, Chinese and Mexican cuisines are all represented.

Haché, *24 Inverness St. Camden Town. 020 7485 9100. www.hacheburgers.com. Daily noon–10.30pm.* Pleasantly located down from the hustle and bustle of Camden High Street, this charming little room is often packed. And for good reason: the place offers the best burgers in the city, served in ciabatta with a range of delicious sides. There are also à la carte salads, fish and vegetarian dishes.

Tupelo Honey, *27 Parkway. Camden Town. 020 7284 2989. Mon 9am–6pm, Tue–Sat 9am–11pm, Sun noon–8pm.* Located off Camden High Street close to the Jewish Museum, this café is a pleasant place for a lunch break. Make your selection at the counter on the ground floor, then take a seat in one of the cosy rooms arranged over three floors, or better yet, on the roof terrace. Sandwiches, salads, hot dishes and above all, delicious cake are served.

BARS AND NIGHTLIFE

Barfly, *49 Chalk Farm Rd. ⊖Chalk Farm. ✆020 7688 8994 or 0844 477 1000 (reservations). www.barflyclub.com.* One of Camden's most famous venues, this indie bar and gig venue has seen the likes of Oasis and Blur perform. Call in to spot the stars of tomorrow.

Bar Vinyl, *6 Inverness St. ⊖Camden Town. ✆020 7485 9318. www.barvinyl.com. 11.30am–11pm.* Simultaneously record store and retro café, this discreet place attracts a hip 20- to 30-something crowd and features edgy music.

Bartok, *78-79 Chalk Farm Rd. ⊖Chalk Farm. ✆020 7916 0595. Mon–Thur 5pm–1am, Fri 5pm–2am, Sat noon–2am, Sun noon–midnight.* An unexpected delight, this very un-Camden bar has opulent red décor, sophisticated drinks and a playlist which features Stravinski and Strauss.

Electric Ballroom, *184 Camden High St. ⊖Camden Town. ✆020 7485 9006. www.electricballroom.co.uk. Fri (£5–7) and Sat (£7–10); 10.30pm–3am.* A key part of the Camden scene, this busy club has seen everyone from Sid Vicious and The Clash to The Killers and Paul McCartney grace its stage over the years. Expect a lively night.

Jongleurs, *38 Middle Yard, Camden Lock. ⊖Camden Town. ✆08700 111 960. www.jongleurs.com. Fri–Sat 7pm–2am. £15.* Popular comedy club featuring a line-up of established and emerging comedians.

Lock 17, *38 Middle Yard, Camden Lock. ⊖Camden Town. ✆020 7428 5929. www.lock17-camden.co.uk. Daily 7.30pm–midnight (2am Fri–Sat).* At the heart of Camden Lock, above Jongleurs, this trendy bar has a nice loft and a beautiful terrace overlooking the canal.

The Underworld, *174 Camden High St. (under the World's End pub). ⊖Camden Town. ✆020 7482 1932. www.theunderworldcamden.co.uk.* This club and live music venue continues to host big-name gigs and provides a party atmosphere on club nights. Fridays *(11pm–3am, £6 or £4 with flyer)* see Pop It! play pop and party tunes from the past three decades, while Saturday's Silver indie club night *(11pm–3am, £6 or £5 with flyer)* features new alternative sounds and is run by people with a true passion for music.

MARKETS

Camden Lock Market – *Chalk Farm Rd. ⊖Camden Town or Chalk Farm. ✆020 7485 7963. Open daily.* Camden's famous markets attract thousands of visitors every weekend. This is the original arts and crafts market, celebrating 40 years.

Camden Market – *Corner of Camden High St. and Buck St. ⊖Camden Town. Thu–Sun.*

Electric Market – *184 Camden High St. ⊖Camden Town. www.electricballroom.co.uk. Sat–Sun 9.30am–5.30pm.* Film, CD and record fair on alternate Saturdays, streetwear, vintage and leather jackets for sale on Sundays.

Stables Market – *off Chalk Farm Rd. ⊖Camden Town or Chalk Farm. Sat–Sun.* The biggest market in Camden, an endless maze of cobbled alleyways, converted warehouses and outdoor eating areas, selling everything from secondhand clothes and CDs to food and furniture. The antiques are tucked away at the back of the market.

ACTIVITIES

Boat Trips Several providers offer boat trips along the Regent's Canal between Camden and Little Venice *(45–50min each way).*

Jason's Canal Boat Trip, *Café Crema, Walker's Quay, Camden Lock. ✆020 7286 3428. www.jasons.co.uk. Apr–Oct: 11.15am, 1.15pm, 3.15pm and 5.15pm (weekends Jun to Sep). £8 one way, £9 return.* Boats calling at London Zoo, 35min from Little Venice *(in the direction of Camden)* and 15min from Camden *(in the direction of Little Venice).*

London Waterbus Company, *58 West Yard, Camden Lock. ✆020 7482 2660 (info) or 020 7482 2550 (reservations). www.londonwaterbus.com. Apr–Sep: departs every hour from 10am to 5pm (1.15pm in place of 1pm); Oct: Thur–Fri noon, 2pm and 4pm; weekends every hour from 11am to 4pm; Nov–Mar: weekends noon, 2.15pm and 4pm. Closed 22 Dec–4 Jan. £7.20 one way, £10.30 return.* Boat trips dropping off at London Zoo. Tickets to the Zoo are included in the £22 ticket price.

THE CITY

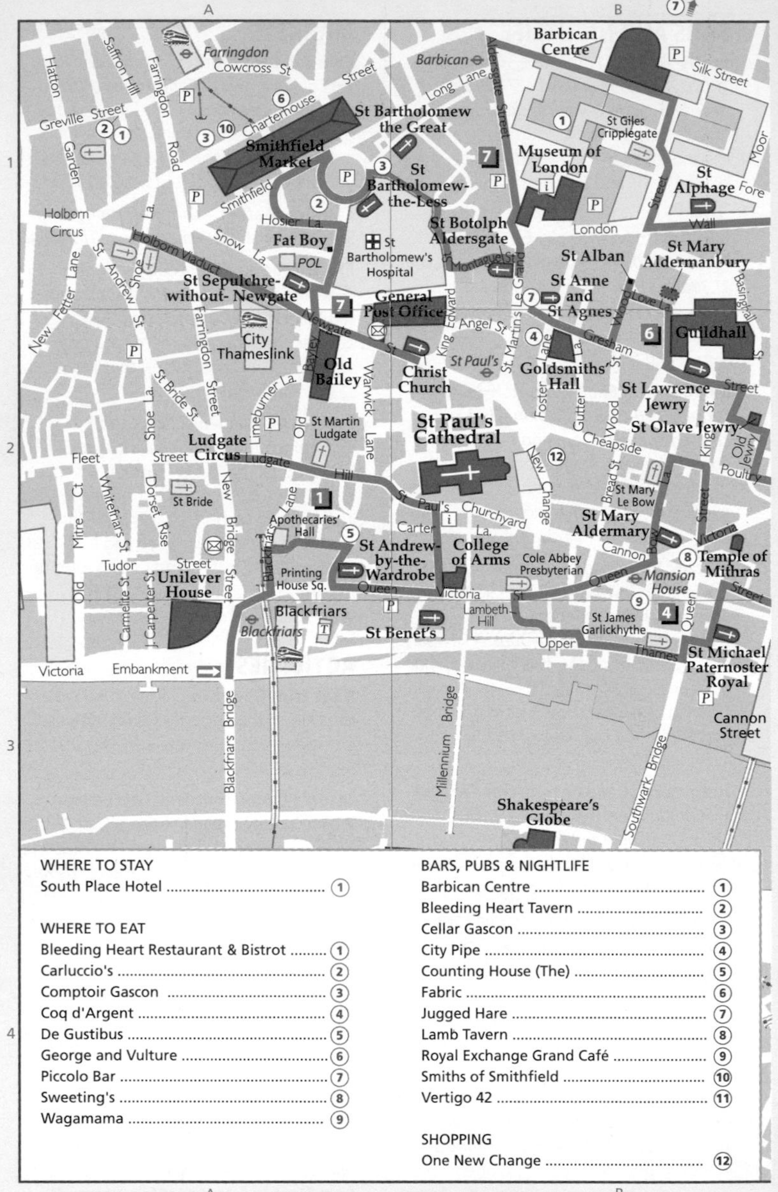

The City of London, also known as the "Square Mile", is a compact area on the north bank of the Thames, now identified with finance. Animated by a commuting workforce on weekdays, at night and weekends many streets are almost eerrily quiet. As Docklands to the East makes its mark as a potential rival in the business world, the City continues to expand and reinvent itself, with a skyline of high-rise buildings in modern architectural styles that have attracted nicknames such as "The Gherkin", "The Cheesegrater" or "The Walkie-Talkie", all set between historic architecture and a plethora of churches.

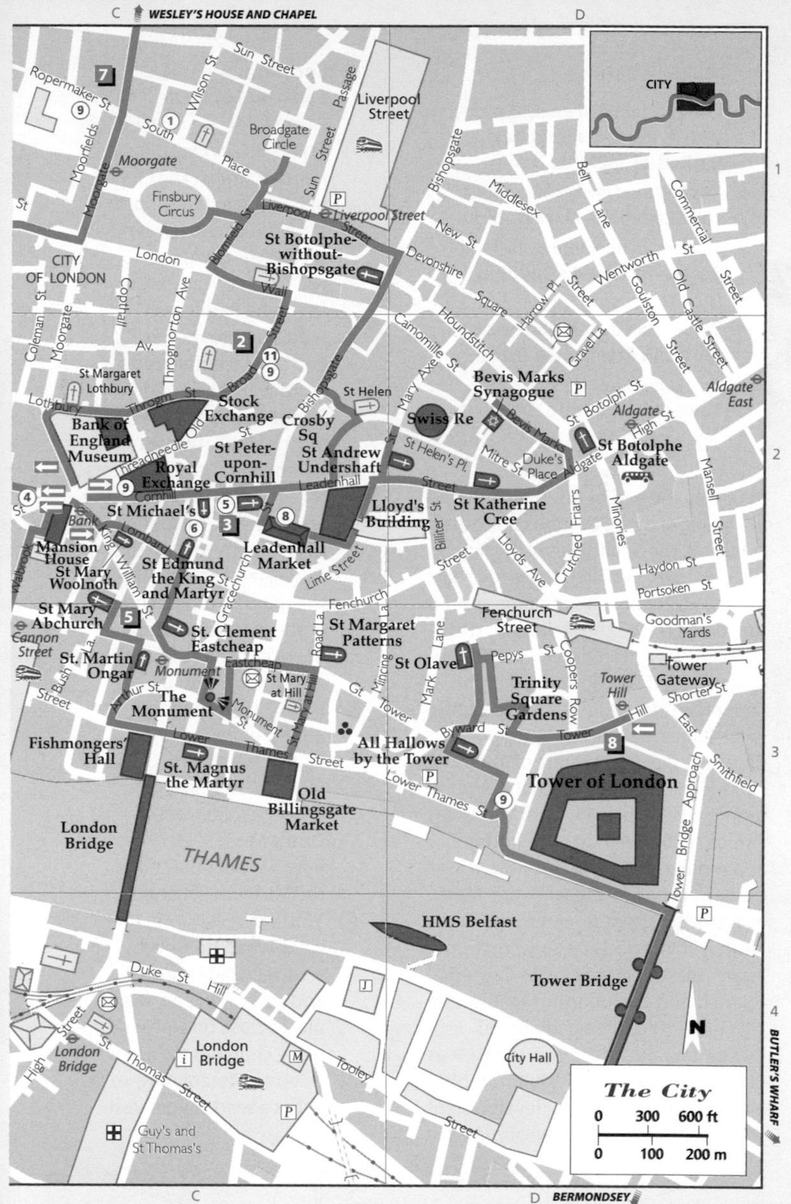

A Bit of Geography

The boundaries of the City of London have remained largely unchanged since the Middle Ages and still cover the eponymous "Square Mile". The City is now surrounded by trendy districts: Holborn to the West, Clerkenwell and Shoreditch to the North and Whitechapel to the East.

A Bit of History

The City is the oldest part of London and the original city has a history stretching back to Roman times. It is believed that London was first established on the Thames in about 47AD, and later moved to its present location after being sacked by the Iceni and their queen Boudica. It was the largest settlement in Roman

Highlights

1 Christopher Wren's masterpiece, with its iconic dome: **St Paul's Cathedral** (p219–222)
2 Bustling food market in a historic hall: **Leadenhall Market** (p230)
3 Modern architecture by Richard Rogers: The **Lloyd's Building** (p231)
4 World-class theatre and music at **Barbican Arts Centre** (p245)
5 Sparkling Crown Jewels at the **Tower of London** (p252)

Britain by the end of the 1C and by the beginning of the 2C overtook Colchester as capital. The boundaries of the Roman city were very similar to those of today; the city wall was built sometime around the turn of the 3C and included gates at Ludgate, Newgate, Cripplegate, Bishopsgate and Aldgate.

London's fortunes fell with the demise of the Roman empire but by the 16C, the City was a significant centre of trade and commerce, the Royal Exchange being founded here in 1565. After the Great Fire of 1666, a plan to rebuild the City as a renaissance-style settlement was drawn up but in the end the Medieval street pattern re-emerged almost entirely intact. In 1708 Sir Christopher Wren's masterpiece St Paul's Cathedral opened and throughout the 18C and 19C, growth continued unabated.

By the late 19C the population was falling sharply; heavy WWII bombing allowed greater modern development than might otherwise have occurred.

Location: *⊖Bank; Barbican; Moorgate; Liverpool St; Mansion House; St Paul's; Cannon St; Tower Hill; Blackfriars.* The City of London extends north from the river between Blackfriars Bridge and the Tower of London as far as the Barbican. It is adjacent to the East End and faces Bankside, Southwark and London Bridge across the river. Most of the City institutions do not admit casual visitors for security reasons and the whole area is surrounded by a security system that can instantly close off all the roads to protect one of the world's greatest financial centres from the threat of car bombs.

Info: City of London Information Centre, St Paul's Churchyard, EC4M 8BX. 020 7332 1456. www.cityoflondon.gov.uk.

Don't Miss: St Mary-le-Bow, St Paul's Cathedral, the Museum of London.

Timing: Visit during the week when the streets are lively and churches and pubs are open. Many places close on weekends; some churches are open by appointment only, so check ahead of your visit.

St Paul's Cathedral★★★

The imposing dome of St Paul's has dominated London's skyline for centuries and is one of the city's most enduring sights. The grandeur of the edifice, combined with its harmonious proportions and sheer size, inspires a sense of wonder. There are many surprises in store: discover the Whispering Gallery and its amazing acoustics; climb up to the dome for a close-up view of the frescoes, wonderful perspectives of the interior and a bird's-eye view of the city; explore the crypt with its remarkable monuments to famous men and women; or simply pause for refreshment in the café and restaurant.

- **Michelin Map:** p 220.
- **Location:** ⊖*St Paul's.* *For the sights outside the immediate vicinity, see pp 222–223.* St Paul's is a focal point in the City of London from which to explore the surrounding area; the Barbican and the Tower of London are within easy access and it's a short walk to the South Bank over the Millennium Bridge.
- **Kids:** A climb up to the dome to discover the fascinating acoustics of the Whispering Gallery and the view from one of the higher galleries.
- **Don't Miss:** The view from the Stone Gallery *(378 steps)*, or if you're ready for even more stairs, the view from the higher Golden Gallery *(530 steps)*.
- **Timing:** Guided tours last an hour-and-a-half to two hours. Allow time to enjoy the garden and for a sit-down break, have a snack or sandwich in the Crypt Café.

A BIT OF HISTORY

St Paul's is the cathedral of the Diocese of London. It was here on 19 July 1981 that the marriage of HRH Prince Charles to Lady Diana Spencer was celebrated with pomp and glory. It has also seen the funerals of Lord Nelson, the Duke of Wellington and Sir Winston Churchill; and the peace services marking the end of the World Wars I and II – among many other great occasions.

Ever since the dome of St Paul's first rose out of the ashes of the Great Fire *(1666)*, it has been a talisman for Londoners. In December 1940, when the whole City and docks were set ablaze, the dome soared above the smoke and flames as a symbol of hope and in August 1944, the bells, silent since the start of the war, rang out to celebrate Paris' liberation. After nearly three centuries the glorious dome has lost none of its majesty. Neighbouring **Paternoster Square** *(now home to the London Stock Exchange)* was recently redeveloped to open up views of the Cathedral, while the creation of the Millennium Bridge offers an uninterrupted view from the river.

Old St Paul's – The present cathedral of St Paul is probably the fifth to stand on the site. Records document a church founded here in AD 604. After the 1087 fire destroyed the third building, the next cathedral, planned on a grand scale, featured a massive tower above the central crossing, embellished with a lead-covered 514ft/156m steeple *(in 1561, this was struck by lightning and never replaced)*. In 1258–1314 the chancel was replaced by a longer decorated choir so that the building measured 620ft/189m from east to west.

During the next three centuries, Old St Paul's was neglected and gradually decayed. In the early 17C, it was partly repaired and **Inigo Jones** added an outstanding **Classical portico**★.

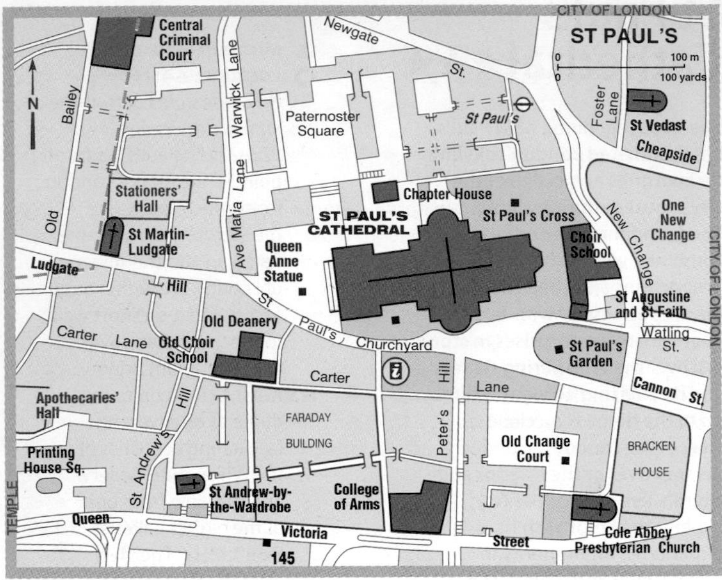

Unfortunately, the Civil War brought, in Carlyle's words, "horses stamping in the canons' stalls" and "mean shops squatting in the portico". A commission, which included **Christopher Wren**, then 31 and untried as an architect, was appointed in 1663 "to survey the general decays". Before it had time to report, the Great Fire swept through the Cathedral, leading Wren to write, "St Paul's is now a sad ruin and that beautiful portico now rent in pieces".

Wren's Cathedral – Wren's first two designs were rejected by the church authorities. However, having been appointed Surveyor General to the King's Works in 1669, he resolved to go ahead "as ordered by his Majesty".

In 1708, after 32 years of unceasing work, Wren saw the final stone, the topmost in the lantern, set in place by his son; he himself was 75. Fifteen years later *(1723)*, he died and was buried within the Cathedral walls.

In 2008, on its 300th anniversary, the Cathedral underwent a multi-million- pound cleaning and restoration project, both inside and out, which included improving access and facilities for those with disabilities, increasing educational facilities, the relighting of the Nelson and Wellington Chambers and the opening of the **Triforium Gallery** to the public.

VISIT

Open for visitors Mon–Sat 8.30am–4pm, Sun for services only. ***Galleries:*** *Mon–Sat 9.30am–4.15pm (last admission). £15. Guided tours (15–90min) 10am, 11am, 1pm, 2pm. Regular organ recitals. Audio guide (12 languages). Leaflets (8 languages). Guide book (6 languages). 020 7246 8357. www.stpauls.co.uk.*

Exterior

The building is dominated by its **dome ★★**, which rises from a drum to a stone lantern crowned by a golden ball and cross. The exterior of the drum is divided into two tiers, the upper tier being recessed so as to provide a circular viewing gallery, the **Stone Gallery★**. Unlike the dome of St Peter's Basilica in Rome, which influenced Wren, the dome of St Paul's is not a true hemisphere. In fact, it consists of three structures (*see illustration*): the outer lead-covered timber superstructure designed to satisfy purely aesthetic considerations, an invisible inner brick cone that supports the weight of the lantern *(850 tons)*; and the inner brick dome that opens at the apex *(20ft/6m diameter)* into the space beneath the lantern.

At the **west end**, the two-tier portico is flanked by the west towers, Wren's most Baroque spires. The shallow **transepts** terminate in semicircular, columned porticoes surmounted by triangular pediments crowned by statues.

The carving and texture of many features are emphasised by floodlighting:statues, reliefs, figures by **Caius Cibber** and Francis Bird; garlands, swags, panels and innocent cherub heads in stone by **Grinling Gibbons**.

Interior

The greatest impact is the size and scale of the building, its almost-luminescent stone flattered by gold and mosaic. After 1790, when the figures of four national benefactors – Joshua Reynolds, the penal reformer John Howard, **Dr Johnson** and the orientalist Sir William Jones – were placed by the dome piers, marble statuary proliferated.

Nave – At the west end of the aisles are the chapels of St Dunstan *(left)* and St Michael and St George *(right)*, each preceded by a finely carved wooden screen *(17C–18C)*.

The **Wellington** monument **(1)**, completed in 1912 and featuring a full-size equestrian statue of the Duke, occupies the entire space between two piers in the north aisle.

In the pavement are the Night Watch memorial stone *(cathedral guardians 1939–45)* and the inscription commemorating the resting of **Sir Winston Churchill**'s coffin in the Cathedral during the state funeral on 30 January 1965. Beneath the dome is Wren's own epitaph in Latin: "Reader, if you seek his monument, look around you".

Crossing and Transepts – The space beneath the dome is emphasised by giant supporting piers that flank the entrances to the shallow transepts. The north transept features a dish-shaped font *(carved in 1727 by Francis Bird)* and a statue of Sir Joshua Reynolds **(4)**. The south transept includes the exceptional portrait statue of **Nelson** by **Flaxman (3)★** and the beautiful wooden doorcase with fluted columns made up in the 19C from a wooden screen designed by Wren and decked with garlands carved by Grinling Gibbons.

Dome – *Entrance in the south transept.* From the **Whispering Gallery★★** *(259 steps)* there is an impressive perspective of the choir, arches and clerestory far below and a closer view of the dome frescoes painted by **Thornhill**. A hushed word uttered next to the wall can be heard quite clearly by a person standing diametrically opposite.

The **Stone Gallery** *(378 steps)* provides a good, but less extensive **view★★★** of the City rooftops than the one from the **Golden Gallery** *(530 steps)* at the top of the dome.

Choir and Ambulatory – In the east end, the marble high altar is set below a massive post-war baldachin carved and gilded from Wren's drawings. Note the Christ in Majesty in the domed apse.

Facts and Figures

The cost of the Cathedral, recorded as £736,752 3s 3¼d, was met, together with the cost of rebuilding the City churches, by a tax levied on all sea coal imported into the Port of London. Wren was paid £200 a year during the construction of the Cathedral.

The Cathedral's overall length is 500ft/152m; height to the summit of the cross 365ft/111m; height of the portico columns 40ft/12m; height of the statue on the apex of the pediment 12ft/3.7m; length of the nave 180ft/55m; width of the nave, including the aisles, 121ft/37m; width across the transept 242ft/74m; internal diameter of the dome 110ft/33.5m; height of the nave 92½ft/28m; height to the Whispering Gallery 100ft/30.5m; height to the apex of the internal dome 218ft/66.5m; total surface area approximately 78,000 sq ft/7,200sq m.

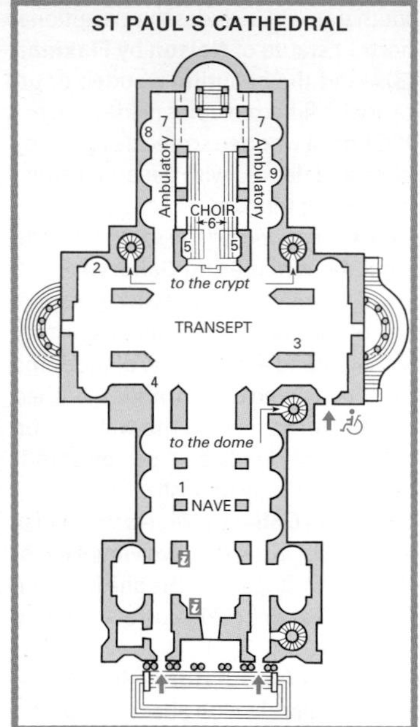

The dark oak **choir stalls★★(6)** are the exquisite work of **Grinling Gibbons** and his craftsmen. Each stall is different from the next; even the stall backs are carved, forming a screen between the choir and the chancel aisles.

The **organ (5)**, a late-17C Smith instrument, together with its Gibbons' case, has been divided and now towers on either side of the choir opening.

The iron railing, the gates to the chancel aisles and the gilded screens **(7)** enclosing the sanctuary are by **Jean Tijou**, wrought-iron smith extraordinaire.

In the north ambulatory, the graceful marble sculpture of the Virgin and Child **(8)** is by **Henry Moore** (1984). In the south ambulatory, against the first outer west pillar, is a statue by **Nicholas Stone** of **John Donne (9)**, the metaphysical poet and Dean of St Paul's *(1621–31)*.

Crypt – *Entrance in the south transept.* At the east end is the Chapel of the Order of the British Empire (OBE). Grouped in bays, formed by the massive piers which support the low-groined and tunnel vaulting are the tombs, memorials and busts of men and women of all talents of the 18C, 19C and 20C of British, Commonwealth or foreign origin, who contributed to the national life; not all those commemorated are buried here.

In the south aisle, east of the staircase, is an area known as **Artists' Corner** honouring, among others, Christopher Wren *(beneath a plain black marble stone)*, William Blake, Ivor Novello, Sir John Everett Millais, **JMW Turner**, Sir Joshua Reynolds and Holman Hunt.

In the north aisle are commemorations of Sir Arthur Sullivan, Sir Hubert Parry, William Boyce *(on the floor)*, John Constable and Sir Alexander Fleming.

Down the steps, **Wellington** occupies the Cornish porphyry and granite sarcophagus; memorials to 10 of the great soldiers of World War II are a more recent addition; beyond, to the south, is a plaque to Florence Nightingale. Below the dome, at the centre of a circle of Tuscan columns lies **Nelson** beneath a curving black marble sarcophagus (originally intended for Cardinal Wolsey and subsequently proposed, but rejected, for Henry VIII).

Only a handful of effigies were rescued from Old St Paul's, in which Sir Philip Sidney and Sir Anthony van Dyck were buried *(modern plaque)*.

North transept: the **Treasury** displays plate and embroidered vestments.

West end: models showing the construction of the Cathedral and dome.

Around the Cathedral

A perfectly proportioned red-brick building, the **Chapter House** was built by Wren *(1710–14)*. The iron hand pump *(west)* was erected in 1819 by the parishioners of St Faith's.

St Paul's Cross *(site marked on the pavement north of the apse)*, used as a preaching cross in 1256, became the symbol of free speech and so was removed by the Long Parliament in 1643.

The modern buildings of the **Choir School** abut the tower of the church of **St Augustine and St Faith** *(1680–87)*, built by Wren and destroyed during World War II. The square tower, tulip-shaped dome and lead spire were rebuilt after the war to Wren's original design.

Under the dome, St Paul's Cathedral

St Paul's Garden is complemented by George Ehrlich's sculpture, *The Young Lovers*.

Cheapside, a wide commercial street, takes its name from the Anglo-Saxon *ceap*, meaning to barter. The names of the side streets, **Milk Street**, **Bread Street**, **Honey Lane**, indicate the commodities sold there; other streets were inhabited by craft and tradesmen.

The street was also the setting for many a Medieval tournament, with contests watched from the upper windows by householders and royalty alike; the Lord Mayor and aldermen watched from a balcony in the tower of St Mary-le-Bow, rebuilt after the Fire.

The Wren-designed **St Vedast's** church *(1670–73)* is dedicated to the beatified Bishop of Arras *(open Mon–Fri 8am–6pm; closed bank holidays; sung Mass Sun 11am, Mon–Fri 12.15pm; guide book (3 languages); 020 7606 3998; www.vedast.net)*.

The **tower and spire★** consist of a square stone tower on which Wren later *(1697)* set a lantern below the ribbed stone spire surmounted by a ball and vane. The exterior is almost unnoticeable from Foster Lane. The interior is entirely new: the black-and-white marble floor; pews aligned collegiate style beneath the **ceiling★**, reinstalled to Wren's design.

ADDRESSES

LIGHT BITE

De Gustibus, *53-55 Carter Lane. St Paul's. 020 7236 0056. www.degustibus.co.uk. Mon–Fri 6am–5pm.* This chain of bakeries is renowned for the variety and quality of its breads. Queue up with the City workers at lunchtime to choose your bread and a filling for a delicious sandwich, to eat in or takeaway. Also soups and salads.

PUB

City Pipe, *31–33 Foster Lane. St Paul's or Blackfriars. 020 7606 2110. www.davy.co.uk. Mon 11am–9pm, Tue 11am–10pm, Wed–Fri 11am–11pm.* A Davy's wine bar, two minutes walk from St Paul's, with a wide selection of wines by the glass and good British food.

SHOPPING

One New Change, *EC4M 9AF. St Paul's, Mansion House. www.onenewchange.com.* This new shopping and dining destination featuring big-name brands and flagship restaurants opened on Cheapside in 2010. Unusually for this area, it is open late into the evening and at weekends.

WALKING TOUR

1 BLACKFRIARS

Blackfriars

The name **Blackfriars** commemorates Blackfriars Monastery, dissolved in 1538 and abandoned until 1576, when a theatre was founded in the cloisters. Here, a professional children's company would rehearse before performing at court. Twenty years later **James Burbage** converted another part of the monastery into the Blackfriars Theatre for the performance of Shakespeare's later plays and those of Beaumont and Fletcher. The theatre, demolished in 1655, is commemorated in Playhouse Yard.

Begin the walking tour on the north bank of the Thames at the end of **Blackfriars Bridge**. It was built during the prosperous last years of the 19C. The latest redevelopment and refurbishment makes it the first railway station to span the Thames; the Millennium footbridge, built a century later, leads directly to the piazza of the Tate Modern on the South Bank (*see pp 325–328*). The striking structure marks a technical achievement combining sculpture and architecture. On your left is the vast stone building of **Unilever House** *(1931)*, with its rusticated ground floor, pillars and large sculptures in typical 1930s style. **The Black Friar**, a wedge-shaped pub *(1896)*, is fronted by a fat friar.

Turn right onto Queen Victoria St.

Queen Victoria Street

The street, the first City street to be lit by electricity, was created in 1867–71 by cutting through a maze of alleys and buildings. Stretching from Bank to Blackfriars, it is lined by a number of widely contrasting ancient and modern institutions.

Continue along Queen Victoria St.

Printing House Square

The Square acquired its name after the Great Fire, when the King's Printer set up presses and began to publish acts, the King James Bible, proclamations and the *London Gazette* (1666 – as *Oxford Gazette* 1665). The name remained after the printer moved nearer to Fleet Street in 1770. In 1784, John Walter purchased a house in the Square and the following year, began publication of the *Daily Universal Register*, altering its title on 1 January 1788 to *The Times*. In 1964, a new slate- and-glass building was constructed for the broadsheet's offices with the old square as the forecourt; 10 years later, they moved to Gray's Inn Road before finally transferring in 1986 to Wapping (*see p 285*).

The Square's history is recounted on a plaque situated on what is now the Continental Bank house.

Turn left up Blackfriars Lane.

Up Blackfriars Lane stands **Apothecaries' Hall** *(1632, rebuilt c.1670)*; in the courtyard a pillared lamp stands over the old monastic well.

Turn right on Playhouse Yard and on into Ireland Yard.

St Andrew-by-the-Wardrobe

Open Mon–Fri 8.15am–4pm. Services: Wed 12.15pm, Thu Catholic mass 12.30pm, Sun Indian Orthodox service 9am. 020 7329 3632. www.standrewbythewardrobe.net

Wren's last city church, St Andrew takes its name from the Great Wardrobe or royal storehouse, which stood nearby (*plaque in Wardrobe Place*). Shakespeare would have known the church as he lived in the parish; a memorial is in the west gallery. Church and Wardrobe were destroyed in the Great Fire; only St Andrew was rebuilt. On 29/30 December 1940, fire again gutted the church, leaving just the tower and the outer walls. It was rebuilt in 1959–61. The galleried church has attractive vaulting and plaster work.

Go down St Andrews Hill and left along Queen Victoria St.

College of Arms

Open Mon–Fri 10am–4pm. Closed bank holidays, State and special occasions. Brochure. Shop. 020 7248 2762. www.college-of-arms.gov.uk.

The college, overlooking a forecourt behind splendid wrought-iron gates, dates from 1671–88, when it was rebuilt after the Fire. The compact red-brick building was truncated when Queen Victoria Street was created.

The interior woodwork is by **William Emmett**, a contemporary of Grinling Gibbons. The Earl Marshal's Court, the main room, is panelled and furnished with a throne and gallery.

The College is responsible for granting coats of arms and monitoring their application; it also organises State ceremonies and undertakes genealogical research.

Cross Queen Victoria St.

St Benet's Metropolitan Welsh Church

Open Thu 11am–3pm or by appointment. Services (in Welsh) Sun at 11am and 3.30pm. 020 7489 8754. www.stbenetwelshchurch.org.uk.

Rebuilt by **Wren** after the original was destroyed by the Great Fire in 1666, this is a small brick church with a hipped roof, rounded windows with carved stone festoons and a general country, Dutch air. There's been a church here since the 12C, and Shakespeare refers to it in *Twelfth Night*. The interior is lined with galleries supported on panelled Corinthian columns, which rise above the base of the galleries. The great architect Inigo Jones is buried here (1652).

Walk up Peter's Hill, turn left past St Paul's Cathedral to Ludgate Hill.

Ludgate Hill

A plaque on the south abutment of the 19C railway states "In a house near the site was published in 1702 the *Daily Courant* first London daily newspaper". Above the bridge stood **Lud Gate**, demolished in 1760 *(plaque on the wall of St Martin-within-Ludgate)*. It was the first curfew gate to be closed at night and was named after the legendary King Lud (66 BC), who is said to have built the first gate on the site. Statues from the 1586 gate were removed to St Dunstan-in-the-West (*see p 201*).

Continue on Ludgate Hill.

St-Martin-within-Ludgate

Open Mon, Fri 11am–3pm, Tue, Wed, Thu 9.30am–3pm. Music recitals: Mon (except Aug) 1.05pm. Donations welcome. 020 7248 6054. www.stmartin-within-ludgate.org.uk.

In 1643 William Penn, whose son founded Pennsylvania, was married in the original church, which stood by the Great Medieval Lud Gate. After it was burnt down in the Great Fire (1666), **Wren** rebuilt the church; he cut off the hill frontage inside by means of stout pillars, on which he rested a gallery and thick coffered arches. At ground level, the area is laid out as a square within a square by means of four inner columns on which the groined vault rests, formed by the intersection of barrel vaulting above the nave, chancel and transepts *(the woodwork is 17C)*. The churchwardens' double chair dating from 1690 is unique. Look out for the 17C bread shelves, where the wealthy would leave bread for the poor to take. From a lead-covered cupola and lantern, ringed by a balcony, rises a black needle **spire**★, the perfect foil to the green dome of St Paul's Cathedral.

Continue on Ludgate Hill to its junction with Farringdon St.

Ludgate Circus

The Circus, built in 1875 on the site of the Fleet Bridge to Ludgate Hill, includes a plaque to **Edgar Wallace** *(1875–1932)*, a Greenwich foundling, who became a successful writer of crime novels.

With your back to the river, gaze up **Farringdon Road** to see the red wrought-ironwork of **Holborn Viaduct**, constructed in the mid-1860s to span the steep-sided Holborn Hill and over the River Fleet Valley.

Bank and Bishopsgate★★★

The beating heart of one of the world's leading financial centres, this area is mostly a place of work, with thousands of Londoners commuting in daily to the offices here. During the week the place has a real buzz about it, while weekends see many places close and the streets empty.

- **Location:** Map pp 216–217. *Bank*. The heart of the City and the national economy is the Bank of England **(Bank)** from which radiate principal thoroughfares.
- **Don't Miss:** Watching a summer lawn bowls match in Finsbury Circus.
- **Timing:** The area is liveliest during weekdays. Take a detailed map to explore the area as the Medieval street layout can be confusing
- **Kids:** Attending a Christmas Carol concert in December in one of the churches is a magical experience.

WALKING TOUR

2 BANK – BISHOPSGATE

Bank: Cornhill exit.

Bank of England

Seven floors of offices are housed in the Bank – a massive, undistinguished building, designed and erected by **Sir Herbert Baker**, an associate of Lutyens *(1924–39)*. His version of the Bank of England replaced an earlier building by **Sir John Soane**. The façade sculptures representing Britannia served by six bearers and guardians of wealth are by Sir Charles Wheeler.

The Bank was incorporated under royal charter in 1694 to finance the continuation of the wars against Louis XIV. It acquired its nickname a century later when the institution was forced to suspend cash payments: Gillray drew a caricature captioned "The Old Lady of Threadneedle Street in Danger". The Bank supervises note issue and national debt, and acts as the central reserve. The Governor is appointed by the Crown.

Follow Princes St. and turn right into Lothbury for the Bank of England Museum.

Bank of England Museum★

Threadneedle Street. Open Mon–Fri 10am–5pm. Free. Closed bank holidays. Guide (9 languages). 020 7601 5545. www.bankofengland.co.uk.

The museum opens with a description of the history of the building in a reconstruction of Sir John Soane's Bank Stock Office. Chronological displays illustrate early banking using goldsmiths' notes; the Charter dated 27 July 1694; Letters Patent under the Great Seal of William and Mary; a £1 million note used for accounting purposes only; a display of gold bars; paper money and forgeries; the gold standard; silver vessels; minted coins. Interactive touch screens explain modern banking while a modern dealing desk with telephone and screen provides an insight into money dealing.

Return to Lothbury.

St Margaret Lothbury★

Open Mon–Fri 7am–5.15pm. Closed bank holidays. Organ recitals Thu 1.10pm. Guide book. 020 7726 4878. www.stml.org.uk.

The present building, designed by Wren in 1686–1701, features a slender obelisk **spire★** balancing a gilded ball and vane. The church is renowned for its magnificent interior.

The remarkable **woodwork★** includes an exquisitely carved **pulpit★** with massive sounding board, dancing cherubs and a reredos with balustered rails; a wonderful oak **screen★** *(dated c.1689 and one of only two made to Wren's*

Broadgate

© Ming Tang Evans/Apa Publications

design); at the centre pierced pilasters are surmounted by three broken pediments, the central one supported by a great carved eagle.

The dividing screen and the reredos from St Olave Jewry are particularly noteworthy in the south aisle. The **font★** is attributed to Grinling Gibbons.

Head E to Throgmorton St.

Old Stock Exchange

8 Throgmorton Street.

Trading in stocks and shares originated in this country in the 17C: it took place in the coffeehouses of **Change Alley** until the first Stock Exchange was inaugurated in Threadneedle Street *(1773)*. In 1801 and 1971, ever-larger buildings rose on the site. In 2004, the Stock Exchange moved to a new home in Paternoster Square, beside St Paul's Cathedral.

Continue along Broad St. past Tower 42 and turn left onto London Wall.

On your right is **All Hallows London Wall**, now the home of a youth-work charity (XLP). Its Portland-stone tower is topped by a pilastered lantern cupola. Inside, note the fine, snowflake-patterned barrel vault *(open Wed 11am–3pm; 020 7256 6240; www.allhallowsonthewall.org)*.

Finsbury Circus

Mid-19C–20C buildings surround the only bowling green in the City. Popular in summer with office workers.

Continue along Blomfield St.

Broadgate

This redeveloped area features a variety of architectural styles, open spaces, fountains, monumental modern sculpture and as its focal point, a circular Arena for open-air entertainment, which turns into an ice rink in winter *(020 7505 4120; www.broadgate.co.uk)*.

Liverpool Street Station, erected in 1875, looks like a vast iron Gothic cathedral with soaring arches. Adjoining it is the **Great Eastern Hotel**, designed by Charles Barry, son of the Houses of Parliament's architect, Sir Giles Gilbert Scott. Following renovations, the hotel reopened in 2000.

Off Bishopsgate to the right is Middlesex Street, known as **Petticoat Lane** and famous for its **market** *(see YOUR STAY IN THE CITY – Shopping)*.

Retrace your steps to Bishopsgate.

St Botolph-without-Bishopsgate

Open Mon–Fri 8am–5.30pm. 020 7588 3388. www.botolph.org.uk.

The church was rebuilt in 1725–29 on a 13C site. The square brick tower, unusu-

City Churches

There have been churches in the Square Mile since Saxon times. By 1666, there were 100, of which 87 were destroyed by the **Great Fire** and 51 rebuilt under the supervision of Wren; more were constructed by Hawksmoor.

The City churches are usually symmetrical and rectangular in plan, orientated as far as possible in the cramped and awkward sites available. The choir played a reduced part in the new Protestant service, which hinged on long sermons: large galleries were provided to accommodate extra seating; side chapels and side aisles were eliminated. The prototype for these light and airy hall-churches derived partly from Dutch Calvinist models and partly from Jesuit churches. Exceptions are centrally planned as a cross in a square *(St Martin Ludgate; St Anne and St Agnes; St Mary at Hill)*, as a vaulted octagon or a domed square *(St Mary Abchurch)*. Perhaps the most original is St Stephen Walbrook, which achieves a truly Baroque spirit hitherto unknown in Puritan England.

By 1939 the construction of new roads had drastically reduced the number of churches here. Nearly all were damaged and several totally destroyed during World War II, but as the floor plans survived, it was possible for some to be reconstructed. Today there are 40 Anglican churches in the City: 11 pre-Fire; 23 by Wren, as well as six of the nine freestanding towers; the remaining 6 are post-Wren (18C–19C). Twenty-four are parish churches; 12 guild churches; one leased to the Lutherans; one a centre for religious education; one a "Centre for Peace and Reconciliation". There are also five non-Anglican churches.

Apply to the City Information Centre (St Paul's Churchyard, The City, London, EC4M 8AE; 020 7332 1456) or enquire at the churches for more information.

ally at the east end, rises directly from the Bishopsgate pavement to support a balustrade, clock tower, turret, cupola and crowning urn. Inside, note the wide coffered ceiling and drum-shaped glass dome, added in 1821. The poet **Keats** was baptised in the font in 1795.

In Bishopsgate Churchyard, the **Old Turkish Bath** *(1895)* faced with decorative glazed tiling is now a restaurant and bar (*see YOUR STAY*). Nearby is the site of the Saxon gate, demolished in 1760. Note the gilded mitres from the old Bishop's Gate on the walls of **Nos. 105** and **108**.

Continue south on Bishopsgate

St Helen Bishopsgate★

Usually open Mon–Fri 9.30am–12.30pm. Call the office to visit. 020 7283 2231. www.st-helens.org.uk.

Behind a patch of grass and plane trees stands the late-Gothic church *(Entrance on the south side)*, which incorporates a small 12C parish church and a 13C conventual church; both were extensively remodelled to give the double-fronted stone façade surmounted by a 17C white belfry turret. Restoration following damage inflicted by a terrorist bomb has returned the church to pre-Reformation airiness and lightness.

Inside, note the small **Night Staircase** *(built c.1500)*, in the middle of the north wall for nuns attending night services; also noteworthy are the **Processional Entrance**, originally 13C, the canopied carved **pulpit** and the 17C **font**.

Monuments★★ – In 1874, when St Martin Outwich was demolished, 18 major monuments and brasses were transferred here, including those of Sir John Crosby *(d. 1475)* and his first wife *(d. 1460)*, owner of the great City mansion Crosby Hall (*see CHELSEA*) and the black marble slabbed tomb chest of **Sir Thomas Gresham** *(d. 1579)*.

Bank of England (left) and Royal Exchange

© J. Malburet/MICHELIN

Crosby Square records the original site of **Crosby Hall**, which now stands on Chelsea Embankment.

Turn left into Threadneedle St. past the ornate façades of buildings housing banks and the Merchant Taylors' Guild.

Royal Exchange★

The Exchange was first built with brick at the sole charge of a merchant, **Sir Thomas Gresham**.

On 27 January 1571 **Queen Elizabeth** came to view and caused it to be proclaimed the Royal Exchange. Rebuilt after the Great Fire of 1666, it burned down again in 1838 and afterwards a third, larger building was constructed. The wide steps, monumental Corinthian portico and pediment with allegorical figures *(10ft/3m tall)* provide an impressive entrance to an edifice that was once the very hub of the City.

in front of the Royal Exchange is a large equestrian bronze statue of **Wellington**; against the north wall are statues of Whittington and Myddelton, while at the rear, Gresham, whose personal emblem – a gilded bronze grasshopper – acts as an unusual weathervane.

St Ethelburga

The early-15C church, which stood on this site until destroyed by a terrorist bomb on 24 April 1993, was the City's smallest church and one of the few medieval buildings to escape the Great Fire (1666) and survive World War II with only slight damage. The church has been rebuilt to its original plan as three walls and much of the timber, stone mouldings and fittings have survived; it serves as a Centre for Reconciliation and Peace.

ADDRESSES

BARS

Royal Exchange Grand Café, *Royal Exchange. ⊖Bank. ✆020 7618 2480. www.royalexchange-grandcafe.co.uk. Mon–Fri 8am–11pm.* The atrium of the Royal Exchange is a magnificent setting for this café with its stylish bar.

Vertigo 42, *Tower 42, 25 Old Broad St. ⊖Liverpool Street. ✆020 7877 7842. www.vertigo42.co.uk. By reservation only.* Situated atop one of the highest towers in the City, this champagne bar is worth a visit for its superb views.

Cornhill and Aldgate

Marking the eastern edge of the City of London, Aldgate gets its name from the gate which used to stand here, marking the road to Colchester. Today the area is dominated by financial companies and the insurance industry.

3 CORNHILL – ALDGATE

CORNHILL

⊖Bank: Cornhill exit or start from ⊖Aldgate and do the tour in reverse.
Cornhill, named after a Medieval corn market, is one of the two hills upon which London was first built.

Turn right onto St Michael's Alley.

St Michael's

Open Mon–Fri 8am–5.30pm. Organ recital: Mon (except bank holidays) at 1pm. 07976 363 480. www.st-michaels.org.uk.
The four-tiered tower *(1718–24)* was designed by **Hawksmoor** to replace the one that had survived the Fire but had since become unsafe.
The church was extensively remodelled by **Giles Gilbert Scott** *(1857–60)*, but Wren's vault resting on tall Tuscan columns *(1670–77)* has survived; don't miss the large **18C wooden pelican**.
Walk along the alleys south of St Michael's and discover **former coffeehouses**: the **Jamaica Wine House**, dating from 1652, and the 600-year-old **George and Vulture**, twice destroyed by fire.

St Peter-upon-Cornhill claims to stand on the highest ground and on the oldest church site in the City. The present building *(1677–87)* was designed by Wren *(Entrance from St Peter's Alley; open by appointment; 020 7283 2231; St Helen's Bishopsgate Church Office)*.

Location: This eastern part of the City of London runs from Bank in the West towards Whitechapel and the start of the East End.
Don't Miss: the Lloyd's Building, the Swiss Re.
Timing: Allow a couple of hours to admire this area's superb modern architecture. Visiting during the week is advisable as many places close at weekends.

The unusual vane in the form of a key, flying at the top of the spire, is visible only from the churchyard *(south)* and Gracechurch Street *(east)*.
Inside, one's eyes are drawn to the oak **screen★**, one of only two to survive in Wren's churches *(see INTRODUCTION – Architecture)*. The **organ gallery**, which is meant to have accommodated Mendelssohn on at least two occasions, is original, as are other furnishings, including the pulpit and the font.

Continue along Cornhill, turn right onto Gracechurch St. and left onto Leadenhall Market.

Leadenhall Market

Gracechurch Street.
Leadenhall, a bustling food market specialising in game, is at its most spectacular at the start of the shooting season and at Christmas. The glass and ironwork market hall is an architectural delight. The **Lamb Tavern**, with its early-20C décor, is frequented by market traders. There has been a market on this site since Roman times. The market takes its name from the house's lead-covered roof; burned down in the Fire, the market buildings were re-erected then, and again to their present form in 1881.

Turn left up Lime St. and pass round to the front of the Lloyd's Building.

Lloyd's Institutions

The **Lutine Bell** was retrieved from *HMS Lutine*, a captured French frigate sunk off the Netherlands in 1799 with gold and specie valued at nearly £1.5 million and insured by Lloyd's. Its bullion was partly salvaged in 1857–61.
The bell is struck to mark the end of a crisis involving an overdue vessel: once for a loss, twice for a safe arrival. A reminder of coffeehouse origins is provided by the **liveried doormen**, resplendent in red frock coats with black velvet collars and gilt-buckled top hats.
The Lloyd's Marine Intelligence Unit *(www.lloydsmiu.com)* keeps details of some 117,000 vessels, 163,500 shipping companies and 3.6 million shipping movements a year.

Lloyd's★★

Open once a year as part of London's Open House day; call for details. *020 7327 1000. www.lloyds.com.*
The trading activities of Lloyd's, the biggest insurance corporation in the world, are conducted in a striking steel and glass building *(1986)* designed by **Sir Richard Rogers**, one of the architects of the Pompidou Centre in Paris, with which it bears striking similarities.
Six towers enclose a central atrium that rises 200ft/61m to a glass barrel vault. Great long escalators link the storeys with the ground level featuring an open-plan environment; glass lifts travel up the exterior of the building. Ventilation shafts, power ducting and water conduits are also streamlined along the outside.
The company's **history** goes back to 1691, when Edward Lloyd took over Pontaq's at 16 Lombard Street *(plaque on Coutts' Bank)*, a French-owned eating house. The house became the favourite meeting place of merchants, shippers, bankers, underwriters, agents and newsmen. Lloyd inaugurated the still-current system of posting notices and lists of port agents, transport vessels, cargo shipments, agents and other such shipping intelligence. He died in 1713 *(plaque in St Mary Woolnoth)* and in 1774, Lloyd's transferred to more spacious quarters at Cornhill, where it remained until 1928, when the first insurance offices opened in Lime Street.

Cross Leadenhall St. and turn left up St Mary Axe.

The Swiss Re Building

The 40-storey Swiss Re Building, better known as "the Gherkin", was designed by the UK's other architectural superstars, **Sir Norman Foster and Partners**. Now a much loved feature of the London skyline, the Gherkin is circular, bulging in the middle and tapering as it soars into the sky. It is Britain's first environmentally sustainable high-rise, making maximum use of recycled materials, natural air and light.

The Swiss Re Building – "the Gherkin"

© C. Hebard/Michelin

Continue along St Mary Axe.

St Andrew Undershaft

The 16C church of **St Andrew Undershaft** is named after the maypole shaft that stood in front of it until 1517 *(open by appointment; 020 7283 2231; St Helen's Bishopsgate Church Office;*

www.st-helens.org.uk). A staircase turret breaks the square outline of the ancient stone tower, part of which is probably early 14C. The interior boasts a late 16C–17C west window depicting Tudor and Stuart sovereigns, a Renatus Harris organ and altar rails fashioned by **Tijou** *(1704)*.The most famous of St Andrew's **monuments★** is **Nicholas Stone**'s half-length carved alabaster ruffed figure of **John Stow** *(1525–1605)*, the antiquarian whose *Survey of London and Westminster* was published in 1598. The quill pen poised to "write something worth reading about" is renewed annually by the Lord Mayor.

Return to Leadenhall St. and turn left.

St Katharine Cree

Open Mon–Fri 10.30am–4pm. 020 7283 5733.

A rare example of a church built (1628–30) during the reign of Charles I, it is one of the few which survived the Great Fire of 1666, and much of its 17C character is retained.

The ragstone corner tower rises to a parapet and small white-pillared turret. Inside the nave, giant Corinthian columns support a series of decorative round arches below the clerestory. High up, above the plain reredos, is a traceried rose window glazed with 17C glass; the central ridge of the lierne vault is decorated with a row of brightly coloured bosses bearing the badges of 17 City Companies. Note the early-17C alabaster font, 18C pulpit and altar table.

Continue on Leadenhall St.

Aldgate

The name derives from the Anglo-Saxon *aelgate* meaning free or open to all. The Romans built a gate here on the road to Colchester. In the 14C, **Chaucer** leased the dwelling over the gate and in the 16C Mary Tudor rode through after being proclaimed Queen.

The gate was demolished in 1761. The **Aldgate Pump** still stands at the west end of the street.

Continue on Aldgate to Aldgate High St.

St Botolph Aldgate

Open Mon–Thu 10am–3pm. Lunchtime recitals Wed 1.05pm. 020 7283 1670. www.stbotolphs.org.uk.

The site on the outer side of the gate had been occupied by a church for over 1,000 years when **George Dance the Elder** came to rebuild it *(1741–44)*. The stone steeple stands on a four-tier brick tower trimmed with stone quoins. Dance's interior was remodelled in the 19C: note in particular the **plasterwork frieze** decorating the coved ceiling.

Walk up Duke's Place to Bevis Marks.

The street name, a corruption of Buries Marks, recalls the site of the 12C mansion of the abbots of Bury St Edmunds.

Bevis Marks Synagogue

Open Sun 10.30am–12.30pm, Mon, Wed, Thu 10.30am–2pm, Tue, Fri 10.30am–1pm. £4. Guided tour Wed and Fri 11.15am, Sun 10.45pm. 020 7626 1274. www.bevismarks.org.uk

The synagogue, built for Spanish and Portuguese Jews, is the oldest in England *(1701)* and the only one in the City of London. Set back from the street, the Grade I listed building is plainly functional except for seven splendid **brass chandeliers**, which hang down low and are lit for all festive occasions. Also noteworthy is the Ark containing the handwritten Scrolls and the raised Tebah surrounded by twisted balusters.

ADDRESSES

PUB

The Counting House, *50 Cornhill. Bank. 020 7283 7123. Mon noon–9pm, Tue–Fri noon–10pm.* Set in the sumptuous lobby of an old counting house built in 1893, this large pub has retained its 19C grandeur, with its rich décor, glass dome and beautiful wooden staircase.

Mansion House

Until the mid-18C, Lord Mayors remained in their own residences during the years of their mayoralty. The Palladian-style mansion in Portland stone *(1739–52)*, designed by George Dance the Elder, features a raised portico of six giant Corinthian columns, surmounted by a pediment decorated with an allegory of the splendour of London. The Lord Mayor is Chief Magistrate of the City and on the ground floor on the east side is a Court of Justice, with cells below.

Location: *⊖Mansion House, Cannon St.* This most southerly part of the City of London runs down to the north bank of the Thames between Blackfriars and Tower Bridge. Immediately to the North are Bank and St Pauls

Guided tour for groups only of the Mansion House *(15–40min)* on written application to the Principal Assistant-Diary, Mansion House, London EC4N 8BH.

Timing: Allow half a day and visit on a weekday to avoid weekend church closures.

VISIT

Mansion House

City Guide tour: Tues 2pm, 1hr. £7. Meet at the A-board near the porch entrance at 1.45pm. Closed Easter, Aug and 24–25 Dec. 020 7626 2500.

The interior is designed as a suite of magnificent state rooms from the portico leading to the dining or Egyptian Hall. In the hall, giant **Corinthian columns** forming an ambulatory support the cornice on which the decorated ceiling rests; the walled niches are filled with Victorian statuary on subjects taken from English literature from Chaucer to Byron. The Ball Room is on the second floor.

London Stone

A block of limestone *(set into the wall of 111 Cannon Street)*, "its origin and purpose are unknown," may have been a milestone or milliary, or according to legend, may be a fragment of an altar erected in 800 BC by Trojan, the mythical founder of Britain.

4 AROUND MANSION HOUSE

From outside the Mansion House, proceed along Walbrook Ct.

St Stephen Walbrook★

Open Mon–Fri 10am–4pm. Services Thu 12.45pm (Sung Eucharist – Monteverdi, Lassus, Byrd, Palestrina). Organ recital: Fri 12.30pm–1.30pm. 020 7626 9000. www.stephenwalbrook.net.

The most striking feature is Wren's **dome★**; it undoubtedly served as a model for St Paul's, which it pre-dates. The slightly off-centre cupola rests on eight circular arches; the bays delineated by freestanding Corinthian columns grouped to produce unexpected perspectives. Below the dome and raised on two communion steps sits **Henry Moore's** monumental altar of golden travertine *(1986)*.

Cannon Street

In the Middle Ages Candelwriteystrete was the home of candlemakers and wick chandlers – hence the presence on Dowgate Hill of the **Tallow Chandlers' Hall**, rebuilt in 1670–72 and Italianised in 1880, and **Skinners' Hall**, a late-18C building accommodating a fine staircase and a hall decorated by **Frank Brangwyn** *(1904–10)*.

All that remains of the mid-Victorian **Cannon Street Station** building are two monumental towers, adorned with

gilded weathervanes, flanking the viaduct high above the riverbank.

Continue along Cannon St. west and turn left into College Hill.

St Michael Paternoster Royal

Open Mon–Fri 9am–5pm. 020 7248 5202. www.missiontoseafarers.org.

The "fair parish church", as Stow described it, "new built by Richard Whittington," was destroyed in the Fire, rebuilt by Wren and again, badly damaged in July 1944. The **spire★** *(added in 1715)* takes the form of a three-tier octagonal lantern, marked at each angle by an Ionic column and urn.

Inside, the most remarkable features are the post-war stained-glass windows, which include *(south-west corner)* young Dick Whittington with his cat. **Whittington** (*see p 197*), who lived in an adjoining house, founded an almshouse, also adjoining, and on his death in 1423, was buried in the church.

At the end of College Hill turn right into College St.

St James Garlickhythe

Open usually Mon–Fri 10.30am–4pm. Closed Bank Holiday Mon. Services Sun 10am (Sung Eucharist), Wed 1.15pm. 020 7248 7546. www.stjamesgarlickhythe.org.uk.

The church, which owes its name to a flourishing garlic trade during the Middle Ages, is dedicated to St James of Compostella *(look out for the saint's emblem, a scallop shell)*.

It was built to a perfectly symmetrical plan, on an isolated site, and christened "Wren's Lantern" owing to its many windows. The woodwork is principally 17C: note the dowel peg for the preacher's wig. **Sword rests★**, complete with unicorn supporters, recall six Medieval Lord Mayors and others.

On the other side of Upper Thames Street stands the **Vintners' Hall**; built in 1671, restored in 1948 and boasting a majestic hall with late-17C panelling. **Queenhithe Dock**, once London's main dock above London Bridge, is beyond.

After the footbridge, but before the tunnel, on the north side of Upper Thames Street stands all that survives of **St Mary Somerset**: a slim, square tower *(1695)*, built by Wren and adorned with masks, rises from its garden setting.

Walk along Upper Thames St., up Lambeth Hill and cross Queen Victoria St. (*see WALK No* 5).

The square stone tower of **Cole Abbey Presbyterian Church** supports an octagonal lead **spire★** that rises to a gilded three-masted ship weathervane. The church was burned out in 1666 and again in 1941. The stone exterior is

N M Rothschild and Sons Ltd

The merchant bank Rothschild's earned its status in this country in its early years, under the London branch founder Nathan Mayer Rothschild (1777–1836). It acquired at low cost the drafts issued by Wellington, which the government was unable to meet, and renewed them. Ultimately, they were redeemed at par. NMR increased his fortune and the Government appointed him chief negotiator of future Allied war loans!

His confidence in victory against Napoleon and in his own intelligence service again increased NMR's wealth, it is said, on the occasion of Waterloo, fought throughout Sunday 18 June. On the Monday, when only rumour was circulating, Nathan bought; the market rose, he sold; the market plunged, he bought again and made a fortune as his personal messenger arrived from the battle scene confirming victory. Wellington's despatches only arrived by messenger the following Wednesday and a report was published in *The Times* on Thursday (22nd). Other business included negotiating lucrative textile deals.

Spire of St Mary-le-Bow

The Great Bell of Bow

In 1334 the Great Bell of Bow called people from bed at 5.45am and rang the curfew at 9pm; the practice continued for over 400 years, ceasing only in 1874. This sound came to define the limits of the City, giving rise to the saying that "a true Londoner, a Cockney, must be born within the sound of Bow Bells". According to legend it was these bells that chimed out "Turn again Whittington, Lord Mayor of London". During World War I, the 12-bell chime was used as a recognition signal by the BBC and came to mean hope and freedom to millions all over the world, thus deserving the title "the most famous peal in Christendom".

pierced by rounded windows beneath corbelled hoods and circled by an open balustrade. Its woodwork is 17C (*open by appointment; www.londonfreechurch.org.uk*).

At the crossroads, cross over to join Bow Lane.

Stow tells how the area was once occupied by shoemakers and the narrow and winding **Bow Lane** was previously known as Hosiers' Lane.

Turn right into Watling St.

St Mary Aldermary

Open Mon–Fri 8.30am–6pm. Guided tours by appointment, Fri. 020 7248 9902. www.stmaryaldermary.co.uk.

Corner buttresses, robust pinnacles and gilded finials adorn the tower of St Mary, rebuilt by Wren in the Gothic style at the request of a benefactor.

The beautiful interior retains its fan vaulting and central rosettes, as well as a **Grinling Gibbons**' pulpit and rich west doorcase *(with a peapod)* and against the third south pillar, an oak **sword rest** from 1682, carved with fruit and flowers by Gibbons.

Return to Bow Lane.

Williamson's Tavern *(Groveland Court)* is accommodated in a 17C house with a contemporary wrought-iron gate and once served as a Lord Mayor's residence *(1666–1753)*.

St Mary-le-Bow★★

Open Mon–Wed 7.30am–6pm (Thu 6.30pm, Fri 4pm). Closed bank holidays. Concerts: Thu in term time at 1.05pm. Brochure (2 languages). 020 7248 5139. www.stmarylebow.co.uk.

The tower contains the famous **Bow Bells** and supports Wren's most notable **spire★★***(1671–80)*, in which he used all five Classical orders and the bow *(the mason's term for a stone arch)* from which the church takes its name.

The **weather vane**, a winged dragon *(8ft 10in/2.5m long)* is poised at the top *(239ft/72.8m)* with a rope dancer riding on its back.

Built in Portland stone in 1673 and modelled on the Basilica of Constantine in Rome, the church was the most expensive of Wren's Churches. The Norman **crypt** dates from 1087.

In May 1941 the church was bombed. The exterior was restored to Wren's design, while the interior layout was redesigned. The unique carved rood

Lord Mayor's Show

The Lord Mayor's Show marks the Lord Mayor's progress from the City to his swearing-in before the Lord Chief Justice in Westminster, an observance that dates back to the charter of 1215, which required the Mayor to be presented to the Monarch or his Justices at the Palace of Westminster.

Running for almost 800 years, the route has changed but survived plague, fire and countless wars to remain a unique part of City life. For years while the Mayor owned a civic barge *(15C)*, the procession was partly undertaken over water. In 1553, full pageantry became the order of the day with men parading their best liveries, trumpets sounding and poems recited along the route.

Golden carriage carrying Lord Mayor of the City of London

© Xie Xiudong/Xinhua/Photoshot

Today, with the Judges removed from Westminster, the oath is taken at the **Royal Courts of Justice** in the Strand; the route running over three miles to reach its destination from Mansion House. After a decline in the 19C, the pageantry has returned and the 21C show sees floats, and the new and old Mayors progressing in the golden state and other horse-drawn coaches accompanied by outriders.

The spectacular show takes place on the second Saturday in November and commences with the march from Mansion House at 11am. The return journey begins at 1pm from Victoria Embankment, returning to Mansion House around 2.30pm. It is followed by a huge fireworks display at 5pm and on the Monday evening by the Lord Mavyor's Banquet in Guildhall, which by tradition began with turtle soup, and at which the principal speakers are the new Lord Mayor and the Prime Minister. www.lordmayorsshow.org.

is a gift from the people of Germany. The bronze sculpture was given by the Norwegians in memory of those who died in the Resistance.

The twin pulpits are used for the famous dialogues where two public figures of opposing views debate moral points.

Turn right into Cheapside (see *ST PAUL'S*), take Bucklersbury Passage and walk down Queen Victoria St.

Temple of Mithras

The stone temple was erected in the 2C AD when Roman legions were stationed in the City. In 1954, excavations revealed walls laid in the outline of a basilica.

The head of the god Mithras in a Phrygian cap, those of Minerva and Serapis, the Egyptian god of the Underworld with a corn measure on his head, together with other retrieved artefacts are now in the **Museum of London**. The temple itself, removed to enable an office block to rise as planned, was then reconstructed in the forecourt.

Monument

This area marks the location of the start of the Great Fire *(1666)*, which began in a baker's on Pudding Lane. Today, Monument lies at the centre of the City and is home to numerous office buildings.

Location: ⊖*Bank, Monument.* Located just back from the Thames, this area is at the City's heart.

Kids: Climb the Monument.

Timing: As almost the only City attraction to be open daily, the Monument is a good place to visit on weekends. Allow at least 30mins for the climb, plus time to look around at street level.

5 MONUMENT AND AROUND

From Bank take King William St. and fork left onto Lombard St.

St Mary Woolnoth of the Nativity

Open Mon–Fri 9am–5pm.
Closed bank holidays.
020 7626 9701.

The church, built in stone by **William the Conqueror**, was damaged in the Great Fire and replaced by the present English Baroque structure *(1716–27)* designed by **Nicholas Hawksmoor**. The rusticated stone tower rises to Corinthian columns and twin turrets, linked and crowned by open balustrades. Inside, massive fluted Corinthian columns in threes mark each corner of the square nave and support a heavily ornamented cornice, with semi-circular clerestory windows above. The reredos is also by Hawksmoor, with its twisted columns and inlaid pulpit.

Continue along Lombard St.

Lombard Street

The name derives from the late-13C Lombard merchants, moneychangers and pawnbrokers who settled there. The street, now synonymous with City banking, is lined with 19C and 20C buildings. Note the brightly painted bank signs overhanging the pavement, including Lloyd's horse of 1677, a grasshopper *(1563, formerly Martins)*, a cat and fiddle *(by Nicholas Lane)* and a massive Barclays eagle in stone.

The Clearing House *(10 Lombard Street)* has its origins in the 18C, when bank clerks – known as "clearers" – met in the street to exchange and settle for cheques payable at their respective banks. The first Clearing House was built on the site in 1833; the present building is post-war. Further on, **St Edmund the King and Martyr** is another of Wren's churches, its distinctive black *(lead-covered)* octagonal lantern and stout **spire★** ending in a bulb and vane, rising from a square stone belfry. The interior was altered in the 19C but is remarkable for its woodwork *(open Mon–Fri 10am–6pm; closed bank holidays; 020 7621 1391; www.spiritualitycentre.org)*.

Monument: engraving of 1680

The Great Fire

The Monument was erected near to the point where the Great Fire began in the King's baker's house in Pudding Lane, near London Bridge. It ended at Pie Corner, near Smithfield. The flames, fanned by a strong easterly wind, raged throughout Monday and part of Tuesday; on Wednesday the fire slackened and on Thursday, it was thought to be extinguished. When it burst out again that evening at the Temple adjoining houses were demolished with gunpowder to prevent it from spreading further. People escaped with what they could carry by boat or on foot to Moorfields or the hills of Hampstead and Highgate. The most vivid account is told in the Diary of **Samuel Pepys** (2 September 1666):

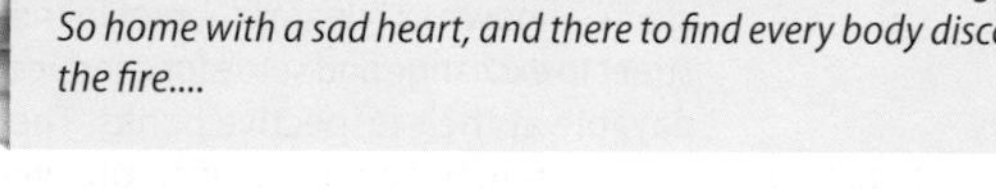

So near the fire as we could for smoke; and all over the Thames, with one's face in the wind, you were almost burned with a shower of fire-drops... When we could endure it no more upon the water, we to a little ale-house on the Bankside... and there staid till dark almost, and saw the fire grow; and as it grew darker, appeared more and more; and in corners and upon steeples, and between churches and houses, as far as we could see up the hill of the City, in a most horrid, malicious, bloody flame, not like the fine flame of an ordinary fire... The churches, houses, and all on fire, and flaming at once; and a horrid noise the flames made, and the cracking of houses at their ruine. So home with a sad heart, and there to find every body discoursing and lamenting the fire....

▶ Turn right along St Clements Lane.

St Clement Eastcheap

Open Mon–Fri 8.30am–5.30pm.
020 7623 5454.

Rebuilt to Wren's design, the church features a brick tower with stone quoins and a balustrade. Inside, note the very ornate **pulpit★★**, the finely carved organ cases *(Purcell played on the organ)* and the gilded altarpiece showing the Virgin and an angel with St Martin and St Clement.

▶ Continue to the crossroads at Monument station and proceed along Eastcheap. Take the first right into Fish St Hill.

Monument★

Open daily 9.30am–5.30pm.
Closed 24–26 Dec and 1 Jan.
£3, combined ticket with Tower Bridge Exhibition £9. Children under 13 must be accompanied by an adult.
020 7626 2717.
www.themonument.info.

The fluted Doric column of Portland stone, surmounted by a square viewing platform and gilded, flaming urn, was erected in 1671–77 in commemoration of the Great Fire and was designed by **Sir Christopher Wren**. It is the tallest free-standing stone column in the world. The hollow shaft stands 202ft/62m tall and 202ft/62m from the baker's in Pudding Lane where the Fire began, right on the route between London and Southwark until the construction of Blackfriars Bridge *(1769)*. The relief of Charles II on the west face of the pedestal is by Caius Cibber.

A later inscription blaming the papists for the Fire was finally effaced in 1831. The **view★** from the platform *(up 311 steps)* is now partially obscured by the towering office blocks that also mask the column at ground level but is still more than worth the leg-stretching climb.

▶ Return to Eastcheap and turn right.

Off Eastcheap to the left is yet another Wren church, **St Margaret Pattens**, its slender hexagonal lead-covered **spire★** sharpening to a needlepoint, on which a gilded vane balances (*open Mon–Fri 7am–6pm; closed bank holidays; 020 7623 6630*). The outstanding **woodwork★** includes the 17C reredos, framing a contemporary Italian painting, carved with fruit, a pea pod and flowers; in front, turned balusters support the communion rail; note a finely carved

eagle lectern and the only two **canopied pews** in London.

Walk down St Mary-at-Hill opposite.

St Mary-at-Hill★★

Entrance located between 6 and 7 St Mary-at-Hill. Open Tue–Thu 10am–5pm. 020 7626 4184 (office).

The Wren **plan**★ *(1670–76)*, almost square, is divided into three x three bays beneath a shallow central dome, and supported on freestanding Corinthian columns.

The interior was damaged by fire in 1988 and not all the **woodwork**, for which St Mary's was known, was restored: note the font cover *(late 17C)*; great oak reredos, communion table, altar rails *(early 18C)*; organ gallery *(musical trophies)*, lectern and turned balustrade, pulpit garlanded with fruit and flowers beneath a massive sounding board and approached by a beautiful curved staircase by **William Gibbs Rogers** *(19C)*; box pews. Turn left to admire the ruins of **St Dunstan-in-the-East**★ with its four-tier **tower**★ surmounted by an elegant Portland stone steeple.

In the early Middle Ages, **Thames Street** ran the length of the river wall; by the 17C, it would have been lined by eight churches and provided rear access to castles and mansions, quays, warehouses and markets. Today Upper and Lower Thames Street are separated by London Bridge.

The present **Custom House** *(1813–17)*, with five lanterns as sole decoration, is the sixth to stand on this site.

Across Lower Thames and up St Mary-at-Hill on the left *(No. 18)* is the small **Watermen and Lightermen's Hall** *(1780)*, which belongs to an ancient City Guild dating back to Tudor times.

Cross Lower Thames St. towards the river.

Old Billingsgate Market

There was a market on this site from 1297 to 1982, when the wholesale fish market moved to new premises in the West India Docks on the Isle of Dogs. The building *(1876)* with Britannia presiding over two dolphins on its decorative roof, was converted into offices in 1990.

Return to Lower Thames St. and turn left.

St Magnus-the-Martyr

Lower Thames Street. Open Tue–Fri 10am–4pm, Sun 10am–1pm. Brochures. Guide sheets. 020 7623 8022.

The massive square stone **tower**★ rises to an octagonal belfry, a leaded cupola, lantern and obelisk spire surmounted by a golden vane. St Magnus stood as a stone sentinel on an ancient Roman wharf at the foot of London Bridge from 1176 *(Wren rebuilt it on the same site)*. The interior, remodelled in the late 18C features a barrel-vaulted nave supported by fluted Ionic columns and oval clerestory windows.

However, much remains from the 17C. Note the iron **sword rest**★dated 1708, 16C–17C shrine *(right of the altar)*, altarpiece and rails, font *(1683)* and pulpit.

Continue along Lower Thames St.

London Bridge★

London Bridge was the only crossing over the lower Thames until 1750, when Westminster was constructed. The Romans probably built the first bridge; the Saxons later erected a wooden structure that had to be repeatedly rebuilt. Between 1176 and 1209 a stone bridge was constructed on 19 pointed arches rising from slender piles anchored onto wood and rubble piers, which considerably reduced river flow.

In winter, ice would form so that when at last the river froze over, great **Frost Fairs** could be held *(the most famous being between 1683 and 1684)*. The bridge itself was lined with houses, shops and even a chapel; it was here that traitors' heads were exposed: Jack Cade *(1450)*, Thomas More *(1535)*.

In 1831 John Rennie constructed a robust granite bridge *(60yd/55m)* upstream. In 1973, it was replaced by the existing sleek crossing; Rennie's bridge was sold

A City Within a City

The City is governed by the City of London Corporation and has a city status – and a police force – of its own. It has a markedly different air to the city surrounding it and within its maze of ancient streets you'll find a multitude of centuries-old pubs, chic wine bars, high-quality restaurants and elegant designer shops. The City remains primarily a place of work and most areas are far busier during the week than they are at weekends. However, in recent years the area has seen new developments aimed at enticing people into the City for leisure. In 2010 One New Change, a new shopping and dining destination featuring big-name brands and flagship restaurants, opened on Cheapside – crucially it is open at weekends.

Though the epicentre of the UK's high-tech banking and finance system, the area is alive to the traditions of the past: the royal carriage still halts at Temple Bar when the Sovereign enters the City; the Prime Minister makes an annual major policy speech at the Lord Mayor's Banquet and on 20 June each year, the Guild of Watermen and Lightermen pays a "fine" of one red rose to the Lord Mayor, imposed on Lady Knollys in 1381 for building a bridge across Seething Lane without permission.

for £1 million and removed to Arizona, USA. London legend has it that the American purchaser thought he was buying Tower Bridge!

On the west side of London Bridge sits **Fishmongers' Hall**, a neo-Greek building *(1831–34)* with a rich interior gold leaf decoration *(restored post-war)*.

Cross to Arthur St. and Martin Lane.

Ye Olde Wine Shades is a colourful double-fronted pub *(1663)* with painted boards outside. It claims to be the oldest wine house in London. Presently, it is surrounded by the spiky marble and glass buildings of Minster Court.

The tower *(19C)* marks the site of the medieval church of **St Martin Orgar**.

Proceed west along Cannon St. and cross to the north side.

St Mary Abchurch★

Open Mon 11am–3pm, Tue, Thu, Fri 11am–4pm. 020 7626 0306

The Fire consumed "a fair church", last of a line dating back to the 12C. The site was minute, some 80ft/24m square, and Wren decided to cover the new church with a painted **dome★**, approximately 40ft/12m in diameter. Inside, it rises from arches springing directly from the outer walls. There are no buttresses and only one interior column.

Note Robert Bird's original gilded copper pelican weather vane *(removed as unsafe in 1764)* over the west door and the pulpit with garlands and cherubs' heads. Authenticated by bills and a personal letter from **Grinling Gibbons** himself is the **reredos★★**, massive in size, magnificent in detail and delicacy. The **tower and spire★** are on the same small scale as the church: red brick with stone quoins, surmounted by a cupola, lantern and slender lead spire.

Cannon Street Station stands on the opposite side of the street *(for description see walk no 4)*. Turn right onto **St Swithin's Lane**. The street is synonymous with the prestigious merchant bank NM Rothschild's. The clean-lined building is post-war; the lane remains old and narrow, and is often blocked from end-to-end with waiting Rolls-Royces and Bentleys.

ADDRESSES

PUB

Lamb Tavern, *10–12 Leadenhall Market. Monument. 020 7626 2454. Mon–Fri 11am–11pm.* At the heart of the City, the oldest pub *(1790)* on Leadenhall Market boasts a magnificent Victorian interior.

Guildhall

The City was granted its first charter by William the Conqueror in 1067 and the first Mayor was installed in a building, probably on the present site, in 1193. For at least 850 years, therefore, Guildhall has been the seat of civic government. "This Guildhall," Stow quoted in 1598, "was begun to be built new in the year 1411;... the same was made of a little cottage, a large and great house... towards the charges whereof the (livery) companies gave large benevolences; also offences of men were pardoned for sums of money, extraordinary fees were raised, fines... during 7 years, with a continuation of 3 years more... Executors to Richard Whittington gave towards the paving of this great hall... with hard stone of Purbeck". All was complete by c.1440, but the site is much changed since then.

Location: Gresham Street, EC2P 2EJ. ⊖*Bank, St Paul's, Moorgate, Liverpool Street*. Guildhall is located in the centre of the City, surrounded by the offices and businesses of Moorgate, Bank and St Paul's.

Kids: Clock Museum.

Timing: Allow a couple of hours, longer if you plan to do the walking tour. Open *(civic functions permitting)* Mon–Sat 10am–4.30pm. Closed Good Fri, Easter Mon, 25–26 Dec, 1 Jan. ℘020 7332 1313. www.guildhall.cityoflondon.gov.uk.

VISIT

Guildhall★

The Great Fire left the outer walls and crypt standing. Rebuilding began immediately and in 1669 **Pepys** noted: "I passed by Guildhall, which is almost finished". In 1940 history repeated itself. Reconstruction was once more complete in 1954. In the course of recent building work, excavations have revealed the site of a Roman amphitheatre, traces of the Medieval Jewish quarter and of the 15C Guildhall chapel.

Architecture – Guildhall's 18C façade, a mixture of Classical and Gothic motifs, extends across nine bays, rises to four storeys and culminates, on the four buttresses which divide the face into equal parts, in large and peculiar pinnacles. Crowning the central area are the City arms, which are composed of the Cross of St George, the sword of the patron saint, St Paul, on a shield supported by winged griffins, probably incorporated in the 16C. The **porch** *(at the centre)* however, is still covered by two bays of Medieval tierceron vaulting.

Inside, the **Hall** also is in part Medieval: the walls date back to the 15C and the chamber in which today's banquets are held is the same in dimension *(152 x 49 ft/46 x 15m)* as that in which **Lady Jane Grey** and others were tried.

A cornice at clerestory level bears the arms of England, the City and the 12 Great Livery Companies whose banners hang in front; below, the bays between the piers contain memorial statues, notably *(north wall)* a seated bronze of **Churchill** by Oscar Nemon; Nelson; Wellington; Pitt the Elder by John Bacon. East of the entrance porch in the south wall, behind where the Lord Mayor sits at banquets, is a canopied oak buffet on which are displayed the City sword and mace and plate; to the West beneath the only remaining 15C window are the Imperial Standards of Length *(1878)*, with the Metric measures *(1973)* on the right.

Crypt – *Guided tours by appointment Mon–Fri. ℘020 7332 1313.*

The crypt comprises two parts: the western pre-15C section with its four pairs of stone columns was vaulted by Wren after the earlier hall above collapsed in the Great Fire.

The 15C eastern section below the present Guildhall – the largest Medieval

Gog and Magog

Guarding the Musicians' Gallery are the post-war replica giants carved in limewood by David Evans after the figures set up in Guildhall in 1708. They themselves are descendants of 15C and 16C midsummer pageant figures, who were said to have originated in a legendary conflict between ancient Britons and Trojans in 1000 BC.

Both images, © J. Malburet/MICHELIN

crypt in London – survived both 17C and 20C fires: it remains notable for its size and the six blue Purbeck marble clustered piers supporting the vaulting.

Guildhall Library – *Open Mon–Sat 9.30am–5pm. Closed bank holidays and Sat preceding bank holiday Mon. 020 7332 1868.*

The library, founded c.1423, despoiled in the 16C and refounded in 1824, possesses a unique collection of books on the history and development of the City and London.

Clock Museum★ – *Open Mon–Sat 9.30am–4.45pm. Closed bank holidays. 020 7332 1868 (Guildhall Library).*

The 700 timepieces that make up the Museum of the Worshipful Company of Clockmakers range in size from long case (grandfather) clocks to minute watches, in date from the 15C to the 20C; in manufacture from all wood composition; in movement from perpetual motion *(with a ball that rolls 2,522 mi/4,058km a year)* and in aesthetic appeal from a silver skull watch, said to have belonged to Mary Queen of Scots, to jewelled confections, enamelled, decorated, engraved and chased. The collection also includes two fine Harrison clocks (*see GREENWICH*).

Guildhall Art Gallery – *Open Mon–Sat 10am–5pm; Sun noon–4pm. Free guided tours of the highlights of the permanent collection at 12.15pm, 1.15pm, 2.15pm and 3.15pm. Closed 25–26 Dec, 1 Jan and special occasions. 020 7332 3700 (recorded information). www.cityoflondon.gov.uk.*

A fine modern building, replacing the original gallery *(which was burned down during an air raid in 1941)* houses the art collection owned by the Corporation of London: displays of the 250 works in the collection are rotated to explore different themes and allow lesser-seen pictures to come out of storage: the collection's highlights include portraits and sculptures of dignitaries from 17C–20C (as well as a marble statue of **Margaret Thatcher**), 18C paintings, a remarkable *Salisbury Cathedral* by Constable and works by Victorian painters *(Pre-Raphaelites)*.

Take a step back into antiquity and visit the Roman amphitheatre, unearthed in 1988 by Museum of London archaeologists, and now subsumed into the Guildhall Art Gallery.

WALKING TOUR

6 AROUND GUILDHALL

From Bank station's Cornhill exit walk west along Poultry.

Poultry

The buildings (HSBC) on the north side were designed by **Lutyens** *(1924–39)* – high on the corners is a sculpture by Dick Reid of a fat boy driving a goose to the Stocks Market *(1282–1737)* that was once located nearby and famous for its herbs and fresh fruit. Rent from the stalls was allocated to the maintenance of London Bridge.

Turn right into Old Jewry.

The two-stage stone tower of **St Olave Jewry** is topped by a beautiful **weather vane**, a three-master fully rigged. The church, rebuilt by Wren *(1670–76)*, was destroyed in 1940.

Turn left into Gresham St.

Gresham Street

The street bears the name of **Sir Thomas Gresham** *(see BANK – BISHOPSGATE)*, who founded **Gresham College** in his will as a kind of free university in his mansion in Bishopsgate, Gresham House, which fronted on Old Broad Street. The house was demolished in 1768 and the institution re-established in 1843 at **No. 91** Gresham Street. The college, an independent institution supported by the Corporation of London and the Mercers' Company, now occupies premises at **Barnard's Inn** *(see CHANCERY LANE Walk)*.

Note the 1956 **Mercers' Hall** in Ironmonger Lane to your left.

Next on Gresham Street is **St Lawrence Jewry** *(open Mon–Fri 8am–6pm; recitals Mon at 1pm (piano), Tue at 1pm (organ), daily in Aug; Guide book; 020 7600 9478)*. The church owes its name to the Jewish community that inhabited the district in Medieval times. The stone tower rises to a balustrade, with corner obelisks enclosing a lantern.

A lead obelisk spire sits above, from which flies the original gridiron weather vane, now also incorporating a replica of the incendiary bomb that caused the almost total destruction of the church in 1940.

Wren designed a building of modest outward appearance squaring up the interior by varying the thickness of the walls. The restored ceiling, coffered and decorated to Wren's original design with **gilded plaster work**, emphasises the rectangular plan. The brilliant windows by Christopher Webb contrast with the plain and unassuming modern woodwork. The modern church is the church of the City Corporation.

Turn right into Aldermanbury.

St Mary Aldermanbury

The 12C site is now a garden, with only bases of the perimeter walls and pillars outlining the bombed Wren church *(1670)*. The stones were numbered and sent to Fulton, USA, where the church has been rebuilt to its 17C plan.

Turn left onto Love Lane.

St Alban

All that remains of Wren's church *(1697–98)* is the Gothic tower with its slim corner buttresses crowned by a balustrade and crocketed pinnacles.

Turn left back to Gresham St.

Goldsmiths' Hall

Open-day tours held during the year, noon–2pm. Call City Information Office for details 020 7332 1456. 020 7606 7010. www.thegoldsmiths.co.uk.

This grand hall in Foster Lane dates from 1835. It is endowed by an exceptional collection of gold and silver plate. Its **Baroque** interior provides a lavish setting for its annual summer exhibition, plus a number of smaller exhibitions and selling fairs throughout the year. Check the website for details.

St Anne and St Agnes

Open Sun all day, Mon, Wed, Thu, Fri 10am–2pm. Concerts: Mon (except bank holidays and Aug) and Fri at 1.10pm. 020 7606 4986. www.stanneslutheranchurch.org.

The church, which was mentioned c.1200, was rebuilt by Wren *(1676–87)* to the ancient domed-cross plan within a square, and again after World War II. The exterior is of rose-red brick with round-headed windows under central pediments. The small, square, stuccoed-stone tower is surmounted by an even smaller square domed turret, with a vane in the shape of the letter "A".

Barbican★

Conceived in the aftermath of World War II, the Barbican Project was established in the City on the bombed sites of Cripplegate. Today, this residential neighbourhood incorporates schools, shops, open spaces and a conference and arts centre. Construction began in 1962, the first residential phase was completed in 1976 and the arts centre opened in 1982. The complex includes 40-storey tower blocks, crescents and mews linked by high- and low-level walkways, interspersed with gardens and sports areas. At its heart stands St Giles, a vestige of Cripplegate and the only tangible link with the past.

Location: *Barbican, Moorgate.* Barbican marks the northernmost reaches of the City of London and is located between Farringdon and Liverpool Street. London Wall *(the line of the old city wall)* marks its southern boundary.

Timing: Visit in the week if you want to see inside the churches and set aside an evening for a show or event at the Barbican Centre.

WALKING TOUR

7 BEYOND THE CITY WALL

Old Street, City Rd. exit. Walk south down City Rd.

Wesley's House and Chapel

49 City Road. Open Mon–Sat 10am–4pm, Sun 12.30pm–1.45pm. Closed Thu 12.45pm–1.30pm, between Christmas and New Year, and bank holiday Mondays. Audioguides, brochures and guidebook. 020 7253 2262. www.wesleyschapel.org.uk.

The charismatic Methodist minister **John Wesley**, who is buried in the churchyard, laid the foundation stone of the chapel in 1777. The interior is notable for the tribune supported on seven jasper columns and the white-and-gold ceiling by **Robert Adam**. Wesley's mahogany pulpit stands at the centre. A **Museum of Methodism** is housed in the crypt. Opposite is the entrance to **Bunhill Fields**, used as a burial ground until its closure in 1852. Among the tombs are those of: **William Blake** *(1757–1827)*, **John Bunyan** *(1628–88)* and **Daniel Defoe** *(1661–1731)*.

Just south are the 18C barracks of the **Honourable Artillery Company**, the oldest regiment of the British Army.

Continue south on City Rd.

Moorgate

The street is named after a gate cut in the City wall in 1415 *(demolished in 1760)* to provide access to Moorfields, the open common on which people practised archery, dried clothes and flew kites. Two and a half centuries later, it was one of the main exits for thousands fleeing the Great Plague.

The street is today overlooked by modern office buildings and the **City of London College**, which dates from the rebuilding of London Bridge in 1831.

Continue south to London Wall.

St Alphage

14C pointed stone arches in black flint walls mark the west tower of the chapel of Elsing Spital Priory, dissolved by Henry VIII, but revealed by 1940 bombs.

Turn right along London Wall and right onto Wood St.

St Giles Cripplegate★

Open Mon–Fri 11am–4pm. 020 7638 1997. www.stgilescripplegate.com.

Dwarfed but in no way overpowered by the Barbican, St Giles' tower is built of stone and brick; corner pinnacles guard an open cupola merry-go-round-shaped turret sporting a weather vane.

During its 900-year history, St Giles has been scarred by regular acts of destruction and rebuilding – the most recent in 1940. Signatures recorded in the registers confirm associations with the poet **John Milton** *(buried in the chancel, 1674)*, the navigator **Martin Frobisher** *(buried in south aisle, 1594)*, the author of the *Book of Martyrs* **John Foxe** *(buried 1587)*, the mapmaker **John Speed** *(buried 1629 below his monument on the south wall)*, **Oliver Cromwell** *(married 22 August 1620)*, **Sir Thomas More, Ben Jonson** and **Shakespeare**.

Walk along Fore St, to Moor Lane, turn left and left again on Silk St.

The Barbican

Silk Street. Open Mon–Sat 9am – 11pm, Sun and public holidays noon–11pm. 020 7638 8891 (box office, Mon–Sat 10am–8pm, Sun, bank holidays 11am–8pm). www.barbican.org.uk.

The centre, of which five out of 10 storeys are below ground, contains a concert hall *(the permanent home of the London Symphony Orchestra)*, two theatres, three cinemas, a library, art gallery, sculpture court *(on the roof of the concert hall)*, exhibition halls, meeting rooms and restaurants.

Also incorporated into the concrete maze is the **Guildhall School of Music and Drama** *(1977)*, which is endowed with a canted façade.

Follow the signs to the Museum of London (*see p303*).

Aldersgate

The original gate was said to have been built by a Saxon named Aldred. As James I entered the capital at this point on his accession, the gate was rebuilt in 1617 in commemoration of his entry, but demolished in 1761.

St Botolph Aldersgate

Open Tue 1pm–4pm for a lunchtime talk for city workers. 020 7606 0684.

The church *(1788–91)*, built of dark red-brown brick, is lit by conventional rounded windows. Its small square tower is topped by a cupola with a wooden turret and gilded vane. The interior is mainly **Georgian** with elaborate rosettes in high relief on the white plaster ceiling. An inlaid pulpit stands on a carved palm tree.

Given its situation by a gate in the City Wall, the church is dedicated to the 7C Saxon saint and patron of travellers.

Adjacent is Postman's Park, which contains a number of memorials to ordinary members of the public who died saving the lives of others.

Take Little Britain, Bartholomew Close and an alleyway to St Bartholomew-the-Great.

St Bartholomew-the-Great★★

Open Mon–Fri 8.30am–5pm (4pm in winter), Sat 10.30am–4pm, Sun 8.30am–8pm. £4. Guide book. 020 7248 2294. www.greatstbarts.com.

St Bartholomew's was once a great, spacious church of which the present building was only the chancel. It was founded in 1123 by a one-time courtier, **Rahere**, on land granted by **Henry I**. He established both the hospital and an Augustinian priory, of which he became the first prior. By the time of his death in 1143, the Norman chancel had been completed; nearly 400 years later, the church was 280ft/85m long, the west door being where the gateway onto Little Britain now stands. In 1539 **Henry VIII** dissolved the priory, demolished the church nave and ordained that the truncated building be used only as a parish church. The church fell into disrepair over the next 300 years: the Lady Chapel was "squatted in" and became a printers' workshop (**Benjamin Franklin** was employed here in 1724); the north transept was turned into a forge, the remains of the cloister became a stable, earth covered the church floor and limewash obscured the walls. The church was restored between 1863 and 1910.

The Building – The gateway, a 13C arch and the original entrance to the nave, is surmounted by a late-16C half-timbered gatehouse *(restored 1932)*. The path

through the churchyard is at the level of the Medieval church. The square brick castellated **tower**, with a small vaned turret, was erected in 1628 off-centre at the west end of the curtailed church. The porch, west front and other exterior flint and stone refacing date from 1839 *(restoration by Sir Aston Webb)*.

The **choir★** is Norman. An arcade of circular arches springing from massive round piers and plainly scalloped capitals supports a relieving arch and a gallery of arched openings divided into groups of four by slender columns. The late Perpendicular-style clerestory, rebuilt in 1405, has survived intact, save the insertion of an **oriel** window in the south gallery in 1520. The Lady Chapel completed in 1336 was all but rebuilt in 1897, so only the end north and south windows are original. 15C oak doors lead to the east walk of the old cloister *(c.1405, rebuilt early 20C)*.

Rahere, the founder, lies on a 16C decorated tomb chest beneath a crested canopy. The **font**, used at Hogarth's baptism in 1697, dates from the early 15C and is one of the oldest in the City.

Walk south on Giltspur St.

St Bartholomew's Hospital

Guided tour (including St Bartholomew-the-Less, St Bartholomew the Great and Cloth Fair) Fri 2pm. Closed Good Fri, 25 Dec. £5. 020 7837 0546. www.stbartsandthe london.org.uk. Call for details.

Bart's hospital was founded by Rahere in 1123 as part of an Augustinian priory. Modern blocks now supplement the collegiate-style buildings *(1730–66)*, designed by James Gibbs. The north wing includes the staircase decorated with vast murals by **Hogarth** *(1734)* and the Great Hall *(closed to the public)*.

St Bartholomew-the-Less

Open daily 7am–8pm or later. 020 7601 8066.

By the 18C, the 12C hospital church was so derelict as to need repair first in 1789 by **George Dance the Younger** and again in 1823 by **Philip Hardwick**. Monuments date back to the 14C *(vestry pavements)*, while the more modern ones chiefly commemorate hospital personnel. The 15C square tower with a domed corner turret is visible from the market, although the church stands within the walls of the hospital.

Cross the square.

Smithfield London Central Markets

Smithfield was opened as a wholesale and retail dead meat, poultry and provision market in 1868; previously the stock had come in live. Its name is derived from "smooth field". The livestock market was transferred in 1855 to the Caledonian Market, Islington. The listed buildings, erected in 1868 and since enlarged, are of red brick and stone, with domed towers at either end; they extend over 8 acres/3ha, with 15 miles/24km of rails capable of hanging 60,000 sides of beef. A £70 million facelift has restored the building to its former glory and brought standards of efficiency and hygiene up to modern levels; go very early in the morning to see it in action.

Return to Giltspur St.; walk south.

Fat Boy

The gilded oak figure, said to mark where the **Great Fire** stopped, stands on a site then known as Pie Corner.

Continue south on Giltspur St.

St Sepulchre-without-Newgate

Open Mon–Fri 11am–3pm. Recitals Wed 1pm, other times various programmes including evening events. 020 7236 1145. www.st-sepulchre. org.uk.

The **Church of the Holy Sepulchre** that stands "without the city wall" was of an earlier foundation, renamed at the time of the crusades after the Jerusalem church. The square stone tower *(restored)* surmounted by four heavy crocketed pinnacles dates from 1450,

as does the fan-vaulted porch decorated with carved bosses. St Sepulchre is "the Musicians' Church", its choir central to the emergence of the Royal School of Church Music. Along the north side is the Musicians' Chapel, which contains the ashes of **Sir Henry Wood** *(1869–1944)*, founder of The Proms. The organ *(1670)* has a superb case that includes the monogram of Charles II and is reputed to have been played by **Handel** and **Mendelssohn**.

Other mementoes include a stone from the Church of the Holy Sepulchre in Jerusalem, the hand bell rung outside condemned men's cells at midnight in the old Newgate Prison and the colours of the Royal Fusiliers City of London Regiment.

Cross Newgate St. and continue south on to Old Bailey.

Central Criminal Court, the Old Bailey

Open to the public when the Courts are sitting, Mon–Fri approx. 10am–1pm, 2pm–5pm. Guided tours of the complex are offered by **Old Bailey Insight**. *www.old-bailey.com.*

This is the third Criminal Court to occupy the site. The original trial halls, erected in 1539, were built to protect judges from "much peril and danger" in the form of sickness and infestation so rife in the gaols that the Common Council passed a resolution "that a convenient place be made upon the common ground of this City in the old bailey of London". The site chosen was located by **New Gate**, a gate in the wall built by the Romans for the main road west enlarged in the early Middle Ages, near which a City gaol had been constructed *(1180)*.

Remains of a triumphal arch *(c.AD 200)* marking the city's western entrance have been excavated in Newgate Street.

The Building – The granite structure is dressed in Portland stone, its dramatic entrance emphasised with a broken pediment and allegories of Truth, Justice and the Recording Angel, while the Lady of Justice, a gold figure *(12ft/3.5m tall)* holding scales and a sword *(3ft 3in/1m)* stands high above, perched on a green copper dome *(1907)*. This dominant feature of the City skyline is cast in bronze and covered in gold leaf – unusually, she is neither blindfolded nor blind.

Inside all is marble, a grand staircase sweeping up to halls on two floors with painted murals. The complex also has cells to accommodate prisoners brought from Brixton and Holloway Prisons.

Walk eastwards along Newgate St.

General Post Office

Plaques on the turn-of-the-19C building indicate the site of Greyfriars *(f.1225)* and Christ's Hospital, which occupied the buildings from 1552 to 1902. Outside the main building stands the statue of **Sir Rowland Hill**, who in 1840 introduced the Penny Post, the uniform rate for a letter sent anywhere in the kingdom.

Christ Church★

The slender square stone tower rises in stages to a slim, decorated turret and vane. Christ Church was founded by Henry VIII on the site occupied by the Greyfriars monastery *(1225–1538)*, possibly to serve Christ's Hospital, the second royal foundation nearby, and also known as the Bluecoat School *(1552–1902)*. The church, destroyed in the **Fire**, was redesigned by **Wren** *(1667–91)*.

Return to the crossroads.

Holborn Viaduct

The viaduct was built in 1863–69 to connect the City and West End. The bridge is an example of Victorian cast-iron work, strongly constructed and ornate with uplifting statues and lions.

Alongside the viaduct stands the **City Temple** marked by its high square and pillared tower surmounted by a square lantern, lead dome and cross. Wartime bombing gutted the sanctuary so that the building now presents the contrast of a Victorian/Palladian exterior and modern interior.

Tower of London★★★

The romantic outline of the Tower of London is evocative of scenes of horror, royal pageantry and of the sometimes brutal politics of Great Britain's past. The Tower is an essential experience, for its fraught history, dazzling Crown Jewels and the dramatic tales of its entertaining Yeoman Warders in their traditional attire. A visit to Tower Bridge is also a fascinating experience, with a memorable bird's-eye view of the City enjoyed from its regal elevated walkway.

Location: Map pp 216–217 and opposite. ⊖*Tower Hill; DLR Tower Gateway*. The tower marks the boundary between the City and Wapping; it is well served by buses. Boats call at Tower Pier on the way from Westminster to Greenwich.

Don't Miss: the Jewel House, where the Crown Jewels are on display.

Timing: Start in the morning: allow three hours to visit the Tower, then cross Tower Bridge, taking in the views from the high-level footbridges. On the South Bank, east of Tower Bridge, is the riverside Design Museum and the restaurants of Bermondsey, where you can enjoy a well-deserved meal.

Kids: The Royal Armouries Collection, as well as the reconstructions, activities and events scheduled at the Tower; the top of Tower Bridge.

A BIT OF HISTORY

Tower of London – This royal residence, now a UNESCO World Heritage Site, was established by William I *(the Conqueror)* primarily to deter Londoners from revolt in the immediate aftermath of the Norman Conquest; additionally its vantage point beside the river gave immediate sighting of any hostile force approaching up the Thames. The first fortress of wood *(1067)* was replaced by a stone building *(c.1077–97)* within the Roman City Wall, of which a piece still stands *(A on map)*. Norman, Plantagenet and Tudor monarchs extended the fortress until it occupied 18 acres/7ha. Excavations have revealed part of a 13C perimeter wall and the Coldharbour Gate *(B on map)*; St Peter's Church was incorporated within the Tower, a second fortified perimeter wall was built, the moat excavated and barracks erected. The last sovereign in residence was **James I**. The palatial buildings were demolished under Cromwell. The Tower was opened to the public in Victorian times, drawing large crowds who were intrigued by lurid tales from Romantic literature.

Royal Stronghold – The reputation of the Tower rests mainly on its role as a prison and place of execution for traitors. Among unwilling inmates were individuals captured in battle or suspected of intrigue: **King John of France** *(1356–60)* captured at Poitiers; **Richard II** *(1399)*; **Charles Duke of Orleans** *(1415–37)* captured at Agincourt; **Henry VI** *(1465–71)*; the **Little Princes** *(1483–85)*, Edward V and Richard of York, who, according to legend, were murdered in the Bloody Tower; **Thomas More** *(1534–35)*; **Anne Boleyn** *(1536)*; **Lady Jane Grey** *(1554)*; **Sir Walter Raleigh** *(1603–16)*; **Guy Fawkes** *(1605)*; **Roger Casement** *(1916)* and **Rudolf Hess** *(1941)*.

Following the restoration of the monarchy in 1660, when **Charles II** returned from exile, the Tower was remodelled and a permanent garrison posted within the precincts equipped with a battery of weaponry. From 1300 to 1812 the Tower housed the **Royal Mint**. Because of its impregnability it became the **Royal Jewel House**. From the 13C, the **Royal**

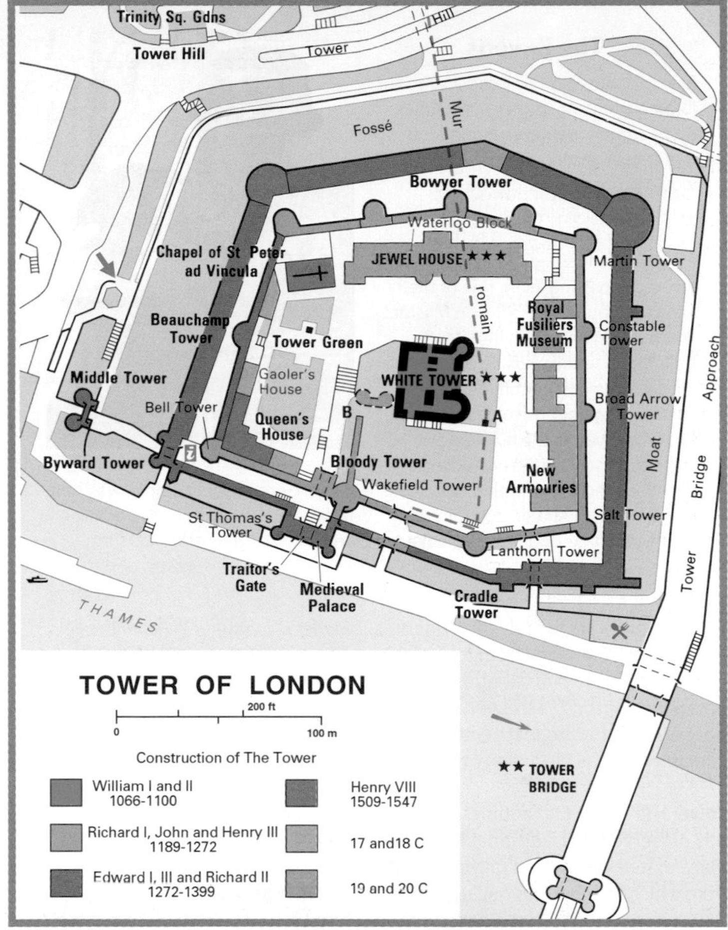

Menagerie was kept in the Lion Tower *(demolished)*; it was closed in 1834 by the Duke of Wellington.

The **Royal Armouries** collection, started by **Henry VIII**, was redistributed by **Charles II** between Windsor Castle and the Tower. A considerable part is now housed in the purpose-built Royal Armoury Museum in Leeds *(see Michelin Green Guide GREAT BRITAIN)*.

Ceremony and Tradition – The 40 **Yeoman Warders** *(including Gaoler and Chief Warder)* are former long-serving non-commissioned officers from the Army, Royal Marines or Royal Air Force holding the Long Service or Good Conduct Medal. They wear Tudor uniform *(dark blue and red "undress" for every day; scarlet for ceremony)*, embroidered with the Sovereign's monogram and may be seen on parade in the Inner Ward *(daily at 11am)*.

The **Ceremony of the Keys**, the ceremonial closing of the Main Gates, takes place every night *(at 10.05pm; admission on written application only)*. After the curfew a password *(changed daily)*, is required to gain admission.

Every third year at Rogationtide *(the three days before Ascension Day)* the 31 boundary stones of the Tower Liberty are beaten by the choirboys of St Peter ad Vincula, armed with long white wands, the Governor and Warders in procession *(2014, 2017)*.

The Ravens

© Historic Royal Palaces/newsteam.co.uk

Ravens are usually regarded as birds of ill-omen, feeding as they sometimes do on carrion. However, legend has it that their absence from the Tower would portend disaster. The practice of having six ravens at all times was decreed by Charles II; today there are seven (one spare). To prevent the ravens from flying away, one of their wings is clipped by the Raven Master. This painless operation imbalances their flight, so the birds do not stray far. Each raven is identified by a coloured leg ring. The oldest resident, Jim Crow, lived to the great age of 44, and occasionally ravens have been dismissed for "unbecoming behaviour" – Raven George, for example, was sent to the Welsh Mountain Zoo for eating TV aerials. The ravens eat 170g of raw meat a day, plus bird biscuits soaked in blood.

Royal Salutes are fired by the Honourable Artillery Company from four guns on the wharf *(at 1pm)*, 62 guns for the Sovereign's birthday, accession, coronation; 41 guns for the State Opening of Parliament or the birth of a royal child.

Tower Hill – Over the centuries the area has preserved its traditional role as a place of free speech and rallying point from which marchers set out, usually to Westminster. In 1380 **Wat Tyler** and the Kentish rebels summarily executed the Lord Chancellor and other prisoners.

VISIT

Open Mar–Oct Tue–Sat 9am–5.30pm, Sun–Mon 10am–5.30pm; Nov–Feb Tue–Sat 9am–4.30pm, Sun–Mon 10am–4.30pm; last admission 30min before closing. Closed 24–26 Dec, 1 Jan. £20.90, discounts for tickets booked online or for joint tickets with Hampton Court and Kensington Palace. Advance booking recommended in high season. **Guided tour (1hr) by Yeoman Warders** *from the Middle Tower (exteriors only) included. Twilight tours Nov–Mar Weds 7pm–8.30pm. £25. Audio guide (Prisoners' Trail – 5 languages) £4. Guide book and leaflet (7 languages). Royal Fusiliers Regimental Museum: free with entry to the Tower. 0844 482 7777. www.hrp.org.uk/toweroflondon. There are regular special exhibitions, costumed re-enactments, concerts and other activities, together with children's events at half-term and during the school holidays.*

Landward Entrance

The Lion Tower *(demolished; position marked by stones in the pavement)* took its name from the Royal Menagerie introduced by Henry III *(1216–72)*, which included an elephant donated by Louis IX of France in 1255, three leopards given by the German Emperor and a polar bear from the King of Norway. The **Middle Tower** *(13C; rebuilt in the 18C)* stood between the second and third drawbridges. The moat was drained and grassed over in the 19C.

Pass through the **Byward Tower** *(13C)* and continue straight on before turning left through the **Bloody Tower** uphill into the main enclave.

On your left is the **Bell Tower**, where **Elizabeth I**, among others, was confined by her sister Mary; she took exercise on the ramparts beyond.

Traitor's Gate

The gateway *(13C)* served as the main entrance to the Tower when the Thames was London's principal thoroughfare. Later on, it was used for delivering prisoners unseen by prying eyes, hence its name.

The Medieval Palace

St Thomas' Tower contains the Great Chamber where **King Edward I** slept. Meticulous archaeological research has allowed this Magna Camera to be re-created. He ruled as an absolute monarch and extended English power across to France. The end room *(or Aula)* was where the King played chess and took his meals.

The octagonal Throne Room in the **Wakefield Tower** *(1240)* served as the main official government chamber. Its furniture includes a reproduction of the Coronation Chair in Westminster Abbey. The corner turret accommodates a small oratory, where **Henry VI** is thought to have been murdered while at prayer on the orders of **Edward IV**.

Bloody Tower

The former Garden Tower acquired its lurid name in the 16C, probably because the **Little Princes** were last seen alive there or after the suicide of Henry Percy, 8th Earl of Northumberland. It was once the main watergate and the portcullis can be seen in the lower storey. The study, which is paved with the original tiles *(protected by matting)*, is furnished as in the time of **Sir Walter Raleigh**, the longest and most famous "resident", who wrote his *History of the World* while imprisoned there *(1603–16)*.

White Tower★★★

The White Tower was begun by **William I** in 1078 and completed 20 years later by **William Rufus**. The high walls *(100ft/30m)* of Kentish rag stone *(Blue stone)* dressed with Portland stone form an uneven quadrilateral, defended at the corners by one circular and three square towers. It became known as the White Tower in 1241 when **Henry III** had the royal apartments and exterior whitewashed.

Chapel of St John the Evangelist★★ – *Entrance from south side.*

The second-floor Caen stone chapel is little changed since its completion in 1080, although the interior painted decoration and rood screen have gone. The nave is divided from the aisles and ambulatory by an arcade of 12 great round piers *(known as the 12 Apostles)*, with simply carved capitals rising to typical Norman round-headed arches, a tribune gallery and tunnel vault.

Swiss Re Building and the White Tower

Royal Armour

Henry VIII had one suit of armour made in 1520, when the Tudor king was 29; it weighed 49lb. A larger suit was made in 1540, silvered and engraved for the King and his horse. Some suits were made in Greenwich, including examples tailored to Robert Dudley *(c.1575)* and for Worcester *(110lb)*. Note also the armour made in France in 1598 for the Earl of Southampton *(1573–1624)*, the only acknowledged patron of Shakespeare; a three-quarter gilt suit with helmet and cuirass, probably made for **Charles I** as a boy *(c.1610)*; the ornate Stuart royal armours *(c.1625–30)*.

The Royal Armouries Collection – The early organisation of a Royal Armoury begins with **Henry VIII**, his personal armours and private arsenal. Between the 15C and 19C, the nation's arsenal depended upon the Office of Ordnance, which supervised the design, manufacture and trial of arms for service on land and sea, while maintaining fortifications of the realm and its garrisons. A large number of paintings, engravings and documentation are used to complete the exhibitions. Smaller arms, several more gruesome weapons allegedly captured from the Armada *(1588)* and larger trophies retrieved from various battlefields are also on display. The **Line of Kings** reunites a series of 17C life-size portraits of the kings of England dressed in personal attire or suits of armour.

Tower Green

The square was the site of the scaffold, where executions took place. A plaque bears the names of the seven noble victims privileged to be beheaded within the Tower *(the last was the Earl of Essex in 1601)*, with an axe except Anne Boleyn, who was executed by the sword. Commoners, on the other hand, were publicly hanged on Tower Hill.

Chapel Royal of St Peter ad Vincula

The chapel takes its name from the day of its consecration in the 12C: the feast of St Peter in Chains. It is the burial place of "two dukes between the queens, to wit, the Duke of Somerset and the **Duke of Northumberland** between Queen Anne and Queen Catherine, all four beheaded," to whom Stow might have added Lady Jane Grey, Guildford Dudley, her husband, Monmouth and hundreds more. Note the Tudor font and carvings by **Grinling Gibbons**.

Beauchamp Tower

The three-storey tower *(pronounced Beecham)*, which served from the 14C as a place of confinement large enough to accommodate a nobleman's household, is probably named after Thomas Beauchamp, 3rd Earl of Warwick *(imprisoned 1397–99)*. The main chamber *(first floor)* contains many graffiti carved by the prisoners.

The timber-framed **Queen's House** *(⊶ closed to the public)* was built by Henry VIII on the south side of Tower Green as lodgings for Anne Boleyn before her coronation in 1533.

Jewel House★★★

The antechamber, bearing the armorials of every ruling monarch from **William the Conqueror** to **Queen Elizabeth II**, serves as a rightful reminder of the long tradition associated with the Crown Jewels. For the most part, the priceless gems are real and the Coronation regalia is still used on formal occasions, such as the State Opening of Parliament.

Visitors pass in front of the sparkling displays on **moving walkways** that allow just a few seconds' viewing.

The engraved **Anointing Spoon** is the oldest piece of regalia, having been made for Henry II or Richard I (**the Lionheart**). Otherwise, most of the **Crown Jewels,** which consist of crowns, orbs and rings, in fact date from the Restoration *(1660)* as the earlier regalia was sold or melted down on the orders of Cromwell.

St Edward's Crown, so named because it may have belonged to Edward the Confessor, was remodelled for the coronation of Charles II and is worn at every coronation. The **Imperial State Crown**, made for **Queen Victoria** in 1838, is worn on state occasions such as the State Opening of Parliament. It contains a total of 3,733 precious jewels, including a ruby said to have been given to the Black Prince by Pedro the Cruel after the Battle of Najera in 1367 and a diamond, the second-largest of the Stars of Africa cut from the **Cullinan diamond** and presented to Edward VII in 1907. The famous **Koh-i-Noor diamond** *(Mountain of Light)* is incorporated in the crown made for Queen Elizabeth the Queen Mother for the coronation in 1937. The **Royal Sceptre** contains the **Star of Africa**, the biggest diamond *(530 carats)* in the world.

On a more modest scale note **Queen Victoria's small crown**, familiar to every stamp collector. To the right of Jewel House is the **Royal Fusiliers Regimental Museum** *(separate entrance charge)*, which presents the history of the regiment from its formation in 1685 to the present day.

Cradle Tower – A watergate, was created here *(1348–55)* as a private entrance for the King.

East Wall Walk

The walk starts in the **Salt Tower** *(1240)*, passes through the **Broad Arrow Tower** *(1240)* furnished as a knight's lodging in the 13C, through the **Constable Tower** *(1240, rebuilt in the 19C)* and ends in the **Martin Tower,** which houses the exhibition entitled "**Crowns and Diamonds**" presenting additional royal crown frames that would have been temporarily fitted with cut diamonds and precious stones.

WALKING TOUR

8 AROUND THE TOWER

Start at Tower Hill Station.

Trinity Square Gardens

The gardens include the site *(railed area)* of the permanent **scaffold and gallows** erected in 1455; the last execution took place in 1747.

On the north side stands **Trinity House**, seat of the Corporation, founded in the 13C, responsible for the maintenance of automatic lighthouses, lightships, navigation buoys and beacons.

On the south side are the **Mercantile Marine Memorials** *(1914–18)* designed by **Edwin Lutyens** and *(1939–45)* by Edward Maufe.

Farther east are a section of the **City Wall**, part-Medieval and part-Roman, a monumental Roman inscription *(original in the British Museum)* and the remains of a 13C gate tower.

Walk up Cooper's Row and turn left into Pepys St.

St Olave's★

Open Mon–Fri 9am–5pm.Closed week after Christmas and week after Easter, and month of August.
Concerts: *Wed and Thu at 1.05pm.*
020 7488 4318. www.sanctuaryin thecity.net

The church was restored in 1953 after severe bomb damage in 1941. The dedication to **St Olaf**, who in 1013 helped **Ethelred** against the Danes, remains vivid in the new Norwegian flag. A bust *(19C)* of **Samuel Pepys**, diarist and founder of the modern Navy, blocks the former south doorway.

The churchyard gateway on Seething Lane, decorated exclusively with **skulls**, is dated 1658.

The church porch, into which one descends, is 15C, like the major part of the church. The interior is divided into a nave and aisle of three bays by quatrefoil marble pillars, probably from a former, 13C, church. The monuments,

which, incredibly, survived the Fire, include tablets, brasses, natural and polychrome stone effigies. Note, in an oval niche high on the sanctuary north wall, the 17C bust of **Elizabeth Pepys**, who married at 15 and died aged 29. The **crypt** *(steps at west end)* of two chambers with ribbed vaulting, is built over a well and is a survival of the early 13C church.

Take Hart St. west, walk down Mark Lane to Tower St. and cross the busy main road.

All Hallows-by-the-Tower

Open Mon–Fri 8am–5pm (Wed 6pm), Sat 10am–4pm, Sun 10am–1pm depending on service. Undercroft museum. Organ recital: Thu 1.10pm. Guide book. Guided tours Apr–Oct. 020 7481 2928. www.allhallowsbythetower.org.uk.

Four churches have stood on the site since the late 7C, the last rebuilding dating from 1957. The square brick tower was built in the 17C. The lantern, encircled by a balustrade and supporting a tapering green copper **spire**, was added after World War II, making it the only shaped spire to be added to a City Church since Wren. The tower is the one climbed by Pepys on 5 September 1666, when he "saw the saddest sight of desolation that I ever saw" during the Great Fire of London.

Inside, the south wall of the tower is pierced by the only Anglo-Saxon arch still standing in the City *(AD 675)*; in the baptistery is an exquisite wooden **font cover★★**, attributed to Grinling Gibbons. Note also 18 exceptional **brasses★** dating from 1389–1591 (of which eight may be rubbed – *by appointment only)*.

Walk down Tower Hill towards Tower Bridge and across the river to Bermondsey.

Bermondsey

Until the Reformation, Bermondsey was known for its famous Cluniac monastery, Bermondsey Abbey, founded in 1082. In the 18C the area became fashionable as a spa famous for its spring water.

Situated on the South Bank of the Thames extending east of Tower Bridge, the area has undergone extensive redevelopment and the riverfront is alive with people enjoying the restaurants, bars and wonderful river views.

For details of the Friday Bermondsey or New Caledonian Market, see YOUR STAY IN THE CITY – Shopping.

Butler's Wharf

Presently listed as a conservation area, this part of London is slowly developing its own resident population and commercial interests; fine restaurants and designer bars line the waterfront and there are interesting specialist shops.

TOWER BRIDGE★★

Open daily Apr–Sept 10am–6pm; Oct–Mar 9.30am–5.30pm. Last admission 1hr before closing. Closed 24–26 Dec. Opens noon 1 Jan. £8, £9 with Monument. Guide book (5 languages). 020 7403 3761. www.towerbridge.org.uk.

The Bridge was designed by Sir John Wolfe Barry and Horace Jones to harmonise with the Tower of London and was built between 1886 and 1894. The familiar Gothic towers are linked by high-level footbridges, encased in steel lattice-work, which provide **panoramic views★★★** of London and a display entitled the **Tower Bridge Experience**.

The Bridge had to allow for the passage of road traffic without impeding the river traffic, hence the bascules *(1,100 tonnes)* raised by hydraulic pumps powered by electricity since 1976.

New displays include a simulation in the Engine Room of how the opening of the bridge looks if you are underneath it.

Design Museum

Shad Thames. Open daily 10am–5.45pm (last entry 5.15pm) Closed 25–26 Dec. £11.85. Café. 020 7403 6933. www.designmuseum.org.

The museum opened in 1989 to popularise, explain, analyse and criticise past

China Wharf

Beyond the Design Museum, **Cinnamon Wharf** *(the first residential warehouse conversion on Butler's Wharf)* and **St Saviour's Wharf**, stands China Wharf facing conspicuously onto the river. Completed in 1988, this striking, orange-red, scalloped building sitting in the river has won its architects CZWG several awards. The unit consists of 17 two-bedroom apartments designed to fill a gap between the existing **New Concordia** and **Reed Wharves**. Note the front entrance balcony named **The Great Harry**.

Other inventive warehouse conversions include the glazed design-studio-cum-residential **David Mellor Building** *(22–24 Shad Thames)*, the modernist **Saffron Wharf** *(18)* and the untreated Iroko timber-clad **Camera Press** *(21/23 Queen Elizabeth St.)*. The four gently curving blocks that make up **The Circle** *(Queen Elizabeth St.)*, faced with glazed cobalt-blue tiles, replace the Courage Brewery stables; its balconies swirl in a great spiralling sweep – a far cry from Jacob's Island, the inspiration for Bill Sykes' abject den of vice and poverty described in Charles Dickens' *Oliver Twist*.

and present design, and speculate about design in the future. True to the Conran empire ethic, the complex has been summed up as "modest, clean, spacious and white."

The **Review Gallery** on the first floor displays a selection of state-of-the-art products from around the world.

The main space is dedicated to temporary *(six-monthly)* exhibitions of product or graphic design and architecture. Early designs and manufacture are compared and contrasted with current fads and fashions produced by different industrial processes.

The airy top-floor space is reserved for the museum's collection of household appliances, television sets, cameras, spectacles, furniture, cars and bicycles.

Church of St Mary Magdalen

Junction of Tower Bridge Rd. and Long Lane. ♿ *Open Mon–Fri 9.30am –noon. 020 7357 0984.*

The parish church founded in 1290 retains 12C carved capitals *(from Bermondsey Abbey, once on the same site)*, 17C woodwork, three hatchments vividly painted with armorial bearings and tombstones in the aisle pavements, giving a sobering insight into 18C infant mortality.

ADDRESSES

LIGHT BITE

M Manze's, *87 Tower Bridge Rd, SE1 4TW. Tower Hill. 020 7407 2985. www.manze.co.uk.* You'll get a real taste of old London at this great pie 'n' mash and eel shop, which has been serving the residents and workers of the area since 1902. The décor is beautiful and harks back to yesteryear, and the owners provide a warm welcome.

Piccolo Bar *7 Gresham St., EC2V 7BX. London Bridge. 020 7606 1492.* Local good-value café especially popular with cabbies for its excellent fry-ups. There's a good range of dishes (chicken curry, jacket potatoes, lasagne, bacon butties) and a wide selection of food to take away.

PUB

Jugged Hare, *49 Chiswell Street, EC1Y 4SA. Moorgate, Barbican or Liverpool Street. 020 7614 0134. www.thejuggedhare.com. Mon–Wed 7am–11pm, Thu–Sat 7am–12pm, Sun 7am–10.30pm* This is a classic gastropub favoured by the city workers in the area, serving wonderful burgers, jugged hare – of course – and a wide range of game dishes. It's located in the Grade II listed former Whitbread Brewery (now a hotel).

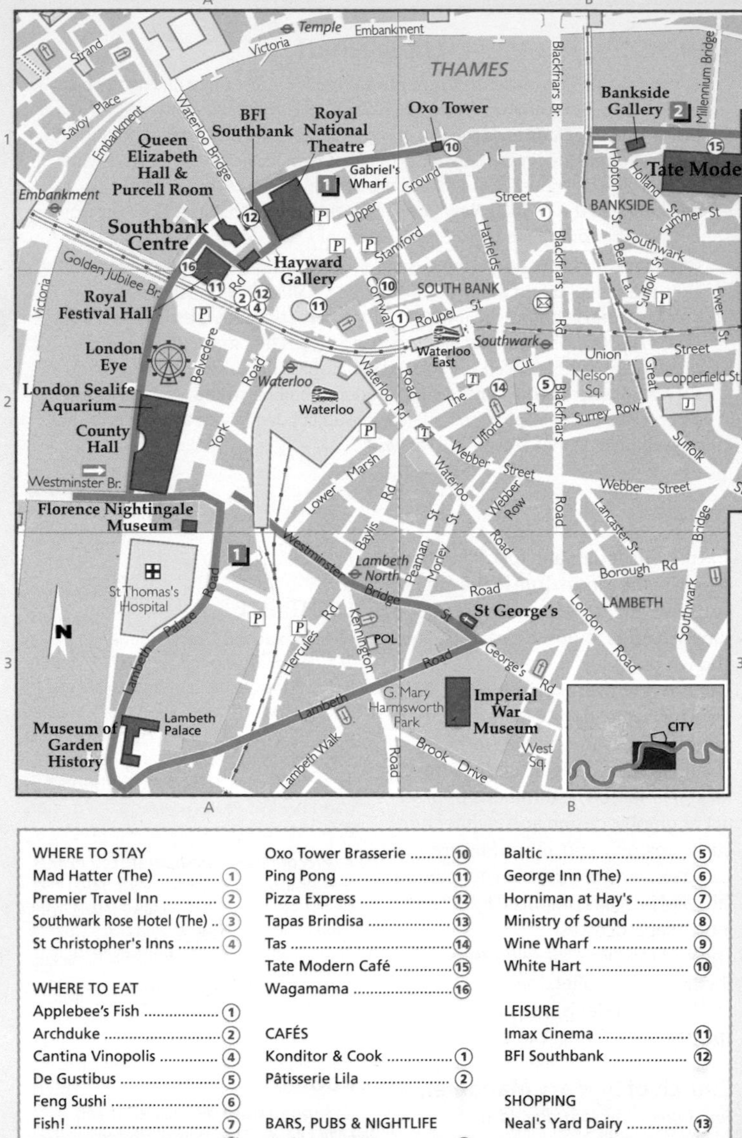

WHERE TO STAY
Mad Hatter (The) 1
Premier Travel Inn 2
Southwark Rose Hotel (The) .. 3
St Christopher's Inns 4

WHERE TO EAT
Applebee's Fish 1
Archduke 2
Cantina Vinopolis 4
De Gustibus 5
Feng Sushi 6
Fish! 7
M. Manze's 8
Nando's 9
Oxo Tower Brasserie 10
Ping Pong 11
Pizza Express 12
Tapas Brindisa 13
Tas 14
Tate Modern Café 15
Wagamama 16

CAFÉS
Konditor & Cook 1
Pâtisserie Lila 2

BARS, PUBS & NIGHTLIFE
Anchor Bankside................. 3
Archduke Wine Bar 4
Baltic 5
George Inn (The) 6
Horniman at Hay's 7
Ministry of Sound 8
Wine Wharf 9
White Hart 10

LEISURE
Imax Cinema 11
BFI Southbank 12

SHOPPING
Neal's Yard Dairy 13

Stretching along the South Bank of the River Thames as it loops through central London, Southwark and Lambeth bustle with vibrancy and creative innovation. This is the perfect day out for culture vultures, whether to enjoy a play at the National Theatre or Shakespeare's Globe or an exhibition at Tate Modern, to browse through the second-hand bookstalls during a riverside walk or to shop for gastronomic treats at Borough Market. Further upstream, Battersea Park in leafy Wandsworth is a hidden gem with open-air jazz evenings, festivals and a children's zoo.

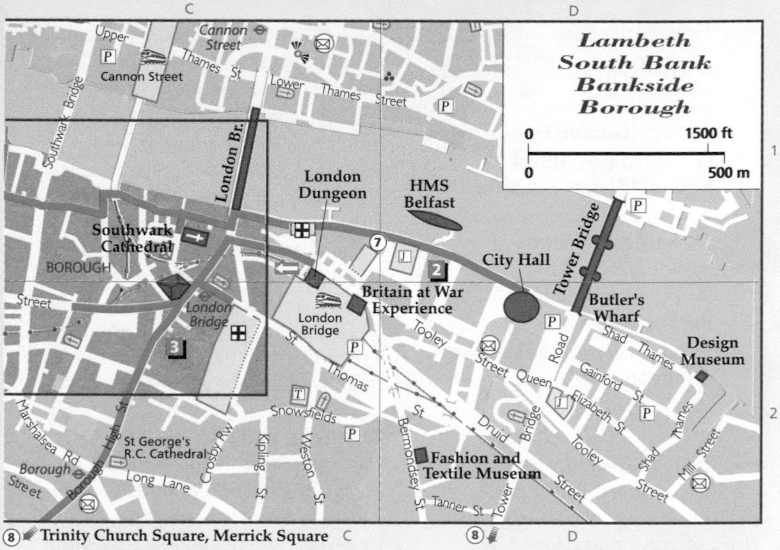

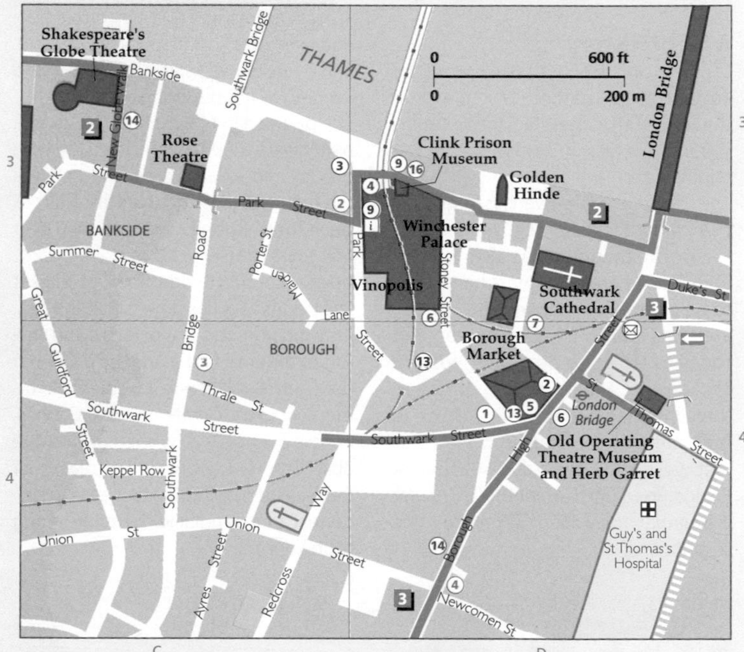

A Bit of Geography

The three boroughs of Southwark, Lambeth and Wandsworth sit immediately to the South of the meandering Thames, looking back across the river towards Westminster and the City. Furthest east, Blackfriars Bridge and London Bridge, with Bankside in between them, are in Southwark. At Waterloo, Southwark gives way to Lambeth, home to the London Eye and National Theatre, and just past Vauxhall Bridge, the Borough of Wandsworth begins. The South Bank stretches 2sq mi/5sq km along the Thames, straddling both Southwark and Lambeth, and is the

Highlights

1 Get a feel for the city from the top of the **London Eye** (p260)
2 Be inspired at the **Royal National Theatre** (p261)
3 Watch plays in the open air at **Shakespeare's Globe** theatre (p265)
4 Browse the stalls at historic **Borough Market** (p268)
5 Test your nerves at the **London Dungeon** (p269)

area where the majority of attractions are found. The area is not particularly well served by public transport but is pleasant to explore on foot.

A Bit of History

Lambeth and the South Bank sit on the ancient site of Lambeth Marsh, where the horse ferry operated to Westminster and the City of London during the Middle Ages.

The area south of the river has frequently been regarded as somehow inferior to the North, though it has always been the place where Londoners have gone to be entertained. During the 16C the area was known for bear-baiting and theatres. The site on which William Shakespeare and his playing company, the Lord Chamberlain's Men, chose to build their Globe Theatre in 1599 was just west of modern-day Southwark Bridge Road *(the current Globe Theatre is approximately 750ft/ 230m from the original site)*.

Urban post-war regeneration began here in 1951 with the Festival of Britain, for which the Royal Festival Hall was built. Additions in the 1960s and 70s resulted in the opening of the iconic concrete South Bank Centre complex, echoing neighbouring Bankside's history as an entertainment district.

Around London Bridge, Southwark has been known as "The Borough" since the 1550s, in order to distinguish it from the City of London. Southwark Cathedral is a reminder that much of this area for centuries belonged to the Church.

The Area Today

The South Bank and Bankside are London's cultural crucible, with numerous theatres, concert halls and galleries located along here. The area buzzes with visitors enjoying al fresco coffee, outdoor performances of music and theatre, and riverside walks; it is as lively in the evening as it is during the day.

The pedestrian Millennium Bridge was built here in 2000 to link Bankside with the City and St Paul's Cathedral, and was the first new crossing over the Thames since Tower Bridge, which opened over 100 years earlier *(1894)*.

Up near London Bridge, Borough Market still trades as it has done since the 13C, drawing huge crowds of locals and visitors to the area. East along the river from the South Bank Centre, County Hall, former seat of the Greater London Council, is now overlooked by the London Eye observation wheel, while upstream past Chelsea Bridge, Battersea is a leafy residential area popular with trendy young professionals.

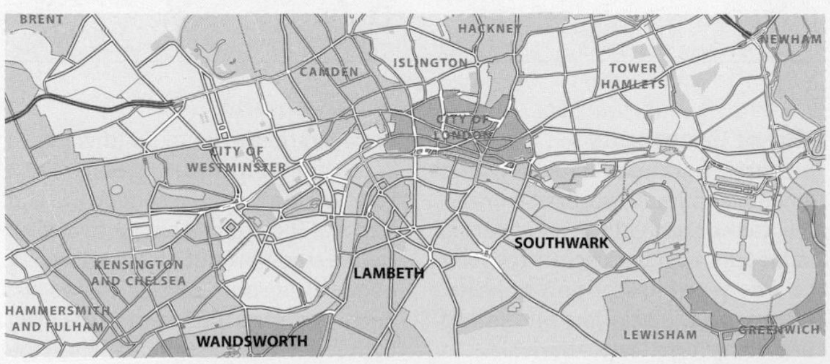

South Bank★★★

Amble along the riverside for classic views of Westminster and live music, then stop for a drink in one of the many restaurants or bars in the modernist environs. Next, browse the second-hand book stalls under Waterloo Bridge, take in a show at the National Theatre, enjoy a concert at the Royal Festival Hall, settle down to some classic cinema at the BFI Southbank or enjoy an exhibition at the Hayward – the choice is yours! The new image of the South Bank as a tourist hot spot is borne out by the crowds of visitors thronging to the attractions built to mark the third millennium. It's a success story that has been enhanced by the complete transformation of the Hungerford Bridge *(rail and pedestrian access from the Embankment and Charing Cross)* and the ongoing revitalisation of the South Bank complex as London's second home for the arts.

Location: Map pp 256–257. ⊖*Waterloo; Westminster.* The area known as the South Bank lies opposite Westminster and Charing Cross, and past Waterloo Bridge to Blackfriars. The Queen's Walk starting from Westminster Bridge to Southwark, Tower Bridge and Bermondsey, runs past most of the attractions of the South Bank. There are several piers for those arriving by boat.

Timing: Allow an afternoon to stroll along the riverside walk, admiring the views, and take a ride in one of the London Eye's glass pods.

Kids: The London Eye, one of the most popular attractions in the city *(book in advance)* and the London Aquarium in County Hall.

A BIT OF HISTORY

The area on the South Bank remained rural until the construction of Westminster and Blackfriars Bridges, and their approach roads in the mid-18C.

The evolution of public transport developed the area, which finally became a suburb, where squares and terraces were erected by **Thomas Cubitt** and lesser men between the major roads.

Benefiting from an ample workforce and easy transport by river, and later by railway, this area boasts a long list of **industrial works** and plants, including the Vauxhall Plate Glass Works *(1665–1780)*, the Coade Stone Factory *(18C)*, Doultons, lead-shot foundries *(a shot tower stood at the centre of the 1951 Festival of Britain)*, as well as vinegar, basket, brush factories, boat yards, breweries, distillers, specialist workshops and potteries, including one producing Lambeth delft.

Bombing during World War II devastated acres of Victorian streets, slums, the Lambeth Walk and factories, making it possible for the authorities to rebuild on a vast scale.

WALKING TOUR 1

Start from Westminster Bridge (*see description in WESTMINSTER*).

The **South Bank Lion** *(13ft/4m long, 12ft/3.6m high)*, carved out of Coade stone, gazes speculatively from a plinth at the foot of Westminster Bridge. Painted red, it was the mascot of the Lion Brewery in the 19C, until placed at the bridgefoot in 1952.

County Hall★

Belvedere Road.

County Hall was the headquarters of the Greater London Council until 1986. It now houses two hotels, some flats, a few restaurants and tourist attractions, as well as an amusement arcade with the latest electronic games.The hall, a colonnaded arc 700ft/213m in diameter,

London Eye at night

© D. Chapuis/Michelin

built in 1908, is still one of London's most distinctive buildings.

London Sealife Aquarium★

In County Hall, Belvedere Rd. Open Mon–Thu 10am–6pm (5pm last admission), Fri–Sun 10am–7pm. Closed 25 Dec, reduced hours Christmas–New Year period. £20.70 (3–15 yrs £15), discount if booked online. 0871 663 1678. www.visitsealife.co.uk.

"A fish cathedral", this monumental aquarium has been built in the basement of the former County Hall, reaching two floors below the Thames water level. Highlights include sharks, moon jellyfish and friendly rays, which come up to have their chins tickled. Various activities for children are organised during the school holidays, such as behind the scenes tours and feeding the turtles. You can even have a turn at snorkelling with sharks *(charge)*.

Directly opposite the Aquarium, across Westminster Bridge on the north side of the river, is **Westminster Pier**, from which boat trips frequently run down the river to the Thames Barrier at Woolwich *(www.westminsterpier.co.uk)*. The stunning barrier with stainless steel cowls was completed in 1982 to protect Central London from surge tides *(See p 359)*.

London Eye★

Open Jan–Mar 10am–8.30pm; Apr–Jun 10am–9pm; Jul–Aug 10am–9.30pm; Sep–Dec 10am–8.30pm. Closed 25 Dec and 10 days in Jan for maintenance. £19.20 (4–15 yrs £12.30); fast track £29.16 (discounts for booking online). Discounted tickets for a variety of London attractions when bought with a ticket for the Eye. Timed tickets. Advance booking recommended; essential in high season. 0871 781 3000. www.londoneye.com.

The giant wheel, a triumph of engineering, is a spectacular addition to the landscape of the Thames and one of London's favourite tourist attractions. Designed by husband and wife architects David Marks and Julia Barfield, it is 200 times the size of the average racing bike wheel and, at 443ft/135m high (twice the height of the Prater in Vienna), it is the largest observation wheel ever built and the only cantilevered structure of its kind in the world. Criticism that it overshadowed the Houses of Parliament has long since been silenced.

Accommodated in closed pods, sightseers *(trip 30min)* enjoy unparalleled **views**★★★ of London extending 25mi/40km in all directions on a clear day, as the wheel rotates to its apex. The glass pods were specially designed to twist with the wheel and allow a 360 degree view at all times. There are also river trips from the pier at the foot of the Eye and regular photographic exhibitions in the office area.

The **Jubilee Gardens**, on the site of the 1951 Festival, were opened in 1977 to celebrate the 25th anniversary of HM The Queen's accession. The whole area has been redeveloped into a first-class park *(www.jubileegardens.org.uk)*.

Southbank Centre★

This is an extremely popular arts centre on the South Bank of the Thames, where art and activities take place inside and outside. The different parts of the arts complex – the Royal Festival Hall, the Queen Elizabeth Hall and Purcell Room and the Hayward Gallery—are connected by elevated walkways.

After the war, the London County Council cleared bomb-damage debris from the riverside to make way for the 1951 Festival of Britain and a future arts centre.
The riverfront is a lively area for tourists and locals, filled with walkways, shops, bars, restaurants and cafés.

Royal Festival Hall★ – The Royal Festival Hall *(open daily 10am – 11pm)* is at the heart of the Southbank Centre complex. Opened in 1951 as part of the Festival of Britain, the Grade I listed Hall is one of the world's leading performance venues. Architects Sir Leslie Martin and Sir Robert Matthew gave priority to the acoustics, the visibility of the stage (capable of holding a choir of 250), and comfortable seating for an audience of 3,000 – in that order.
They managed the space to avoid crowding and afford views of the river and inner perspectives of the building itself; finally, the whole edifice was insulated against noise from nearby Waterloo Station. Having been refurbished, it now ranks among the greatest concert halls in the world. In 1962–65 the river frontage was redesigned to include the main entrance and faced with Portland stone. There are refreshment facilities, book and record shops in the foyer, and markets are often held in the front of the building.

Queen Elizabeth Hall and Purcell Room – In 1967 a second, smaller concert venue with seating for 1,100 was opened with a third, the **Purcell Room**, providing a recital space for 370. The exterior is in unfaced concrete; the interior acoustics are superb.

Hayward Gallery
Open Mon noon–6pm, Tue, Wed, Sat, Sun 10am–6pm, Thu–Fri 10am–8pm. £8. Café/bar. Shop. 0803 800 400. www.southbank centre.co.uk/venues.
The gallery, purpose-built to house major temporary exhibitions of painting and sculpture, was opened in 1968 and is an outstanding example of sixties Brutalist architecture. A terrace-like structure of concrete, it provides five large gallery spaces and three open-air sculpture courts on two levels.

Exit at the rear onto Belvedere Rd. and turn right on Waterloo Rd.

BFI IMAX – *0870 787 2525. www.bfi.org.uk.*
The circular structure houses a state-of-the-art cinema screening **2D and 3D films**. The auditorium has 485 seats, including premium seats. Here you can watch exciting adventures as the world comes alive in 3D.

Return to the riverbank.

BFI Southbank – *0870 787 2525. www.bfi.org.uk.* Formerly known as the National Film Theatre, the BFI comprises four auditoriums: NFT1 *(450 seats)*, NFT2 *(125 seats)*, NFT3 *(134 seats)* and a studio *(38 seats)*. It is one of the world's leading cinématheques and organises the BFI London Film Festival in November each year.

National Theatre★★

Guided backstage tour daily (75min). £8.50. Booking in advance by telephone or in person at the Lyttelton Information Desk (9.30am–11pm). "Platforms" (early evening discussions, readings, interviews, debates: 45min) as advertised. Bookshop. Restaurant. Cafés. Bars. Free concerts and performances in Lyttelton foyer. 020 7452 3000. www.nationaltheatre.org.uk.
The National Theatre stages more than 20 productions a year in its three theatres: the **Lyttelton**, with proscenium stage and seating for 890; the **Olivier**, with large open stage and audience capacity of 1,150; and the **Cottesloe**, a studio theatre with a maximum of 300 seats. It's fair to say that not everyone was impressed by architect Denys Lasdun's Brutalist concrete monument to the arts when it opened in 1976, but the National Theatre is now a firm favourite amongst the British public. Inside, in addition to the theatres, are free exhibitions and live music, bookshops,

bars and cafés and a beautiful **view** of Somerset House and St Paul's beyond. Founded by Sir Laurence Olivier in 1963, the National Theatre is quite simply magnificent, with the world's greatest theatrical stars regularly on stage in a varied repertoire, including works by Shakespeare, Ibsen, Alan Bennett, Mike Leigh and a host of new writers. In front of the National Theatre stands a statue of Sir Laurence Olivier as Hamlet.

The sleek, five-arched concrete structure of **Waterloo Bridge**, faced in Portland stone, was designed by GG Scott in 1945; it replaced the original by Rennie that was opened on the second anniversary of the **Battle of Waterloo** *(18 June 1817)*.

Continue east along the river.

On the waterfront is lively **Gabriel's Wharf**, a workplace for craftspeople, which has evolved alongside the gardens and low-cost housing of the Coin Street development *(open Tue–Sun 11am–6pm (later bars and restaurants); 020 7021 1600; www.coinstreet.org)*. From **Bernie Spain Gardens**, a pleasant, sunken green space, you can enjoy the ever-changing spectacle on the river and the north bank.

Oxo Tower Wharf is marked by the **OXO Tower**, a former beef-extract factory now housing a selection of restaurants (with great views over the river) and designer studios. The makers of Oxo got round the ban on advertising by having the word OXO spelled out in the windows at the top of the tower. The **Bargehouse** houses temporary off-beat exhibitions.

ADDRESSES

LIGHT BITE

Konditor & Cook, *22 Cornwall Rd., Southwark, SE1 8TW. Southwark. 020 7261 0456. www.konditorandcook.co.uk. Mon–Fri 7.30am–6.30pm, Sat 8.30am–3pm.* Photographs from past performances at the adjacent Young Vic line the walls of this unpretentious café. You can choose homemade cakes and pastries, or soups, salads and vegetarian dishes. There is a branch next to Borough Market at *10 Stoney St., SE1 9AD. London Bridge. 020 7407 5100.*

Ping Pong, *South Bank Centre, Belvedere Rd., SE1 8XX. Waterloo. 020 7960 4160. www.pingpongdimsum.com. Mon–Wed noon–midnight, Thu, Fri, Sat noon–1am, Sun noon–10.30pm.* This outpost of the casual, yet stylish dim-sum chain lives up to its billing of serving "little steamed parcels of deliciousness". The cocktails are good, too.

Pizza Express, *The White House, 9C Belvedere Rd., SE1 8YP. Waterloo. 020 7928 4091. Mon–Sat 11.30am–midnight, Sun 11.30am–11.30pm.* The Pizza Express chain is consistently reliable, with light, thin-based pizzas and a wide choice of toppings. Lively atmosphere and décor in a refurbished space.

Skylon, *Royal Festival Hall, SE1 8XX. Waterloo. 020 7654 7800. www.skylonrestaurant.co.uk. Mon–Sat noon–2.30pm & 5.30pm–10.30pm, Sun noon–4pm.* Amazing panorama of river views and London skyline at this fine-dining restaurant, part of the Royal Festival Hall. Good central cocktail bar for a casual drink.

PUBS AND BARS

Archduke Wine Bar, *Concert Hall Approach, SE1 8XU. Waterloo. 020 7928 9370. www.thearchduke.co.uk. Mon–Thur 11am–midnight, Fri 11am–1am, Sat 10am–1am, Sun 10am–11pm.* Friendly, welcoming wine bar, well placed for the **South Bank Centre**, offering everything from salads and sandwiches to hot dishes. Located under the railway arches, cool jazz in the evenings adds to the atmosphere.

Baltic, *74 Blackfriars Rd. Southwark. 020 7928 1111, www.balticrestaurant.co.uk. Bar daily noon–midnight.* This hip bar attracts a decidedly designer crowd to sip its wide range of cocktails and over 29 varieties of vodka. Free jazz concerts Sundays from 7pm.

White Hart, *29 Cornwall Rd., SE1 8TJ. Waterloo. 020 7928 9190. www.thewhitehartwaterloo.co.uk. Tue–Sat noon–midnight, Sun–Mon noon–11pm.* Transformed from a decrepit backstreet pub to a smart venue, with its comfortable décor of sofas and benches, curtains and candles, this is worth searching out. Good light dishes and a buzzing atmosphere.

Bankside★ – Southwark★

The Globe and Tate Modern are two potent symbols that combine history and modernity on Bankside, while the bustling London Bridge City and Hay's Galleria, east of London Bridge, highlight the vitality of the Borough of Southwark, which extends south from the Thames to Crystal Palace. After years of neglect and dereliction, the area is one of the trendiest in London, full of fashionable loft apartments, theatres, museums, attractive bars and restaurants – and a relaxed atmosphere that invites visitors to stroll and enjoy wonderful views of the river and the City skyline, dominated by the dome of St Paul's on the north bank.

- **Location:** Map pp 256–257. *⊖Southwark; London Bridge; Blackfriars.* Stretching along the southern bank of the Thames, this area winds its way from Blackfriars Bridge in the West to Tower Bridge in the East.
- **Timing:** Allow a full day to explore this lively area and visit the numerous museums located here, plus an evening for Shakespearean theatre at the Globe.

A BIT OF HISTORY

The Roman Invasion to the Dissolution of the Monasteries – The construction by the Romans of a bridge and the convergence at the bridgehead of roads from the South of England attracted settlers to the fishing village already established on one of the few sites relatively free from flooding on the low-lying marshlands of the Thames' South Bank.

By Anglo-Saxon times the bridge had become a defence against ship-borne invaders and the village, the *sud werk* or "south work", against attacking land forces: **Olaf of Norway**'s rescue of Ethelred from the Danes is commemorated locally in Tooley Street; the Conqueror fired Southwark before he took London by encirclement. In the **Domesday Book**, Southwark was described as having a strand where ships could tie up, a street, a herring fishery and a priory. Southwark people were also fishermen and boatmen. Industries developed, such as mortar making, weaving, brewing (by refugees from the Low Countries), glassmaking and leather tanning.

Walking along the river

© London on View

William Shakespeare (1564–1616)

England's greatest poet and playwright *(38 plays)* was born the son of a glovemaker. He married Anne Hathaway in Stratford-upon-Avon before coming to London to find success and fame. The couple had three children. His popularity is rooted in the rich use of colloquial language, humour that sometimes verges on the bawdy, and a timeless portrayal of human nature. Although there are no autographed copies, a total of 18 plays were printed in his own lifetime, 36 followed in a folio, the first collected edition, published in 1623. He also wrote 154 sonnets and four long poems before he died on his 52nd birthday.

The Dissolution to the 20C – Henry VIII rapidly sold off the monastery estates. The City increased its interests in Southwark, but it never acquired jurisdiction over the Clink prison or Paris Garden.

As the Industrial Revolution kicked in, the area close to the river, largely owned by the City and known as the Borough of Southwark (which time has shortened to **Borough**), became heavily industri-alised following the building of the bridges, the 19C expansion of the docks and the coming of the railway.

By the late 19C the last prisons had been demolished: the **Clink** in 1780; the **Marshalsea** (1842); King's Bench (1860) and Horsemonger Lane Jail (1879). World War II caused devastation to the area and Southwark is an amalgam of historical and post-war construction.

Borough Market – The Borough Market, London's oldest *(13C)*, was formally established in 1756 and the profits go to rates relief. The market has excellent restaurants and on Fridays and Saturdays, serves as one of London's best farmers' markets. *See box p 268.*

WALKING TOUR

2 ALONG THE RIVERSIDE

Southwark; Blackfriars (on the north side of the bridge).

From Blackfriars Bridge, take Queen's Walk heading east.

Bankside Gallery

Open daily 11am–6pm, ring in advance as the Gallery closes for a few days between exhibitions. Free. 020 7928 7521. www.banksidegallery.com. This is the gallery of the Royal Watercolour Society and the Royal Society of Painter-Printmakers. Talks and events are held here on the art of watercolours and print-making, and there's a shop specialising in the subjects.

Continue east along the river, past Tate Modern (*see MAJOR MUSEUMS*).

Millennium Bridge

A remarkable architectural and technical achievement, the steel suspension bridge *(960ft/338m long)*, designed by Sir Anthony Caro and Foster & Partners, has curving balustrades that form "a blaze of light" spanning the Thames at night. After initial problems, when its swinging gave it the nickname the "wobbly bridge", it now provides a pedestrian link, with fabulous **views** between St Paul's and the Tate Modern.

Old Houses

Turn right into **Cardinal Cap Alley**. On either side are two 18C houses. The first (**No. 49**), the oldest house on Bankside, was built on the site of the Cardinal's Hatte, some 50 years after the Great Fire *(1666)*. The reference to Catherine of Aragon on the plaque is therefore questionable, as is the belief that Sir Christopher Wren lived there during the building of St Paul's Cathedral.

Return to the river bank.

Shakespeare's Globe

© Y. Kanazawa/Michelin

Shakespeare's Globe★★

21 New Globe Walk. Open Apr–mid-Oct daily 9am–5pm; late Oct–Mar daily 10am–5pm (exhibition and tour on the hour and half hour; may close occasionally for events, rehearsals and performances; call ahead to check.) Theatre season Apr–Oct. Closed 24–25 Dec. £13.50 (tour), theatre tickets from £5 standing, £15 seated. Restaurant and café. 020 7902 1400; box office 020 7401 9919. www.shakespearesglobe.org.

In 1597, the Privy Council threatened all theatres with closure for sedition; the following year, the Chamberlain's Men's lease of the Shoreditch Theatre ran out. The company, which included Richard Burbage and Shakespeare, tore down the theatre and moved the whole thing across the river to Southwark, rebuilding it as the Globe – close to the site of the modern Globe.

The idea for creating a centre dedicated to encouraging the study and dramatic interpretation of Shakespeare's work came from the late American actor-director Sam Wanamaker. Funding such a dream was arduous and included supporters paying for individual bricks. The result is a runaway success.

Globe Theatre – The "Wooden O" *(33ft/10m high, 100ft/30.5m in diameter and 300ft/91.5m in circumference)* has been modelled on surviving documentary evidence of the original theatre, pulled down in 1644, and from archaeological excavations of the original Globe (*see EAST END – Shoreditch*) around the corner. Wherever possible, similar materials and building methods have been used to re-create the half-covered theatre. Performances *(Apr–Oct)* are held during the afternoon, much as in Shakespeare's day, without the use of artificial stage lighting – and subject to fine weather! The audience can sit on hard benches (*use a cushion*) or stand in the pit for the duration of the performance.

The Playground of London

In the 16C permission was accorded by the authorities for two theatres to be set up in the old monastery cloisters north of the river in Blackfriars and the area became known as the playground of London. The reign of the **Rose** *(1587)*, the **Swan** *(1595/6)*, the **Globe** *(1599)* and the **Hope** *(1613)* theatres was, however, brief: those that had not already reverted or become bull and bear baiting rings were finally closed under the Commonwealth by the Puritans in 1642.

Sam Wanamaker Playhouse – A new indoor theatre is being built, named after the Globe's founder Sam Wanamaker. This will be a candlelit venue in keeping with theatre performances in Shakespeare's time.

Turn right into New Globe Walk and left into Park Street.

The Rose Theatre Exhibition

56 Park Street. Guided tour for pre-booked groups only in summer. 020 7261 9565 (Shakespeare's Globe). www.rosetheatre.org.uk

An imaginative light and sound show brings to life the history of the Rose Theatre, the first theatre on Bankside. Excavations have revealed the remains of the building, now covered by a pool of water, partly due to lack of funds and partly because this is the best way to preserve the foundations.

Southwark Bridge

Rennie's bridge *(1815–19)*, referred to by Dickens in *Little Dorrit* as the "Cast Iron Bridge", was replaced in 1919 with the iron structure by Ernest George. **Excavations** in the Park Street area have revealed Roman warehouse ruins.

Cross the street to view the ground plan of the original Globe theatre clearly marked on the site of a former brewery. Continue to the end of the street and turn left to the riverfront.

The **Anchor Bankside** (*see Addresses*) is an historical tavern erected in 1770–75 on the site of earlier inns.

Continue east along the river.

Winchester Palace

At the heart of a modern development stands the old ruin comprising the screen wall of the 12C **great hall** of Winchester Palace; it is pierced by a **rose window** *(14C)* of Reigate stone and three archways that once would have led to the servery and kitchens.

The Bishops of Winchester took rent from the numerous brothels in the area, and the precinct of the palace contained a prison for errant clergy and nuns, which lay below water level at high tide. From the 15C it was known as the **Clink Prison** *(see below)*, from which is derived the expression "to be in the clink"; between 1630 until its closure in 1780 it was used for poor debtors.

Clink Prison Museum

1 Clink Street. Open Oct–June Mon–Fri 10am–6pm & Sat–Sun 10am–7.30pm, Jul–Sep daily 10am–9pm. Closed 25 Dec. £7.50. Guided tour, telephone for details. 020 7403 0900. www.clink.co.uk.

In an alleyway near the river, stairs lead down to a basement on the site of the old Clink jail, which dates back to 1144. The exhibition traces the history of imprisonment and torture, and of the Bankside brothels.

The Golden Hinde

Open daily 10am–5pm/5.30pm, telephone ahead to confirm availability. Self-guided tour with leaflet. £6. Overnight stays, pirate parties, weddings, corporate functions. Discounted joint ticket with Clink Prison Museum available. 020 7403 0123. www.golden hinde.com

The full-scale galleon replica of Sir Francis Drake's **Golden Hinde** *(see box, right)* stands dramatically just back from the river. Her cabins and quarters,

Replica of Golden Hinde, St Mary Overie Dock

© C. Eymenier/Michelin

People relaxing in the Southwark Cathedral yard

galley and hold can be explored, giving an insight into the life of Tudor sailors during Drake's circumnavigation of the globe *(1577–1580)*.

A riverside **viewing panel** identifies the buildings on the north bank: the twin pavilions at the north end of **Cannon Street Railway Bridge** were built at the same time as the bridge *(1866)* by J W Barry and J Hawkshaw.

Southwark Cathedral★★ (St Saviour and St Mary Overie)

Open daily 8am (Sat, Sun 8.30am)–6pm. Donation £4. Audio tours £5. Exhibition. £3. 020 7367 6700. www.southwark.anglican.org.

The site's history is a progression from Roman building to Saxon minster, from Augustinian priory *(1106)* to parish Church of St Saviour *(1540)* and, finally, to Cathedral *(1905)*.

The name, it is thought, derived from the convent being endowed with "the profits of a cross-ferry", from which the church came to be known as "over the river" or St Mary Overie.

Interior – Immediately to the left is the Gothic arcading of the church, rebuilt after a fire in 1206. Against the west wall at the end of the north aisle are 12 **ceiling bosses** rescued from the 15C wooden roof when it collapsed in 1830: the pelican, heraldic sunflowers and roses, malice, gluttony, falsehood, Judas being swallowed by the Devil. The **nave** was rebuilt in neo-Gothic style in 1890–97 to harmonise with the 13C chancel. There are fragments of a Norman arch in the north wall.

A Great Adventure

In 1577 Francis Drake *(c.1540–96)* set sail on the *Pelican* into the unknown. He returned three years later from the Pacific having laid claim to Nova Albion (California) and the Port of Sir Francis Drake (San Francisco) on the *Golden Hinde,* his ship having been renamed as she approached the Straits of Magellan. Drake chose the name after the symbol of a golden passant hind representing the armorial of the expedition's sponsor, Sir Christopher Hatton (*see INTRODUCTION – History*). On arrival, the vessel was moored at Deptford (*see GREENWICH*) and visited by Queen Elizabeth I, who took the opportunity to knight Drake there and then.

The **north transept**, with 13C Purbeck marble shafts set against 12C base walls, includes the allegorical Austin monument of 1633, showing a standing figure, Agriculture, between girls in sun hats asleep in the harvest field; also the reclining figure, with gaunt face of the quack doctor Lionel Lockyer *(1672)*.

From the nave near the transept crossing is an uninterrupted **view** of the intimately proportioned 13C chancel.

The Gothic **altar screen** *(1520, the statues added in 1905)* is sumptuous. Funeral pavement stones commemorate the church burial of Edmund *(d. 1607)*, brother of William Shakespeare, and the Jacobean dramatists, John Fletcher *(d. 1625)* and Philip Massinger *(d. 1640)*.

Adjoining the arch is the **Harvard Chapel**, dedicated to the founder of Harvard University in the USA. **John Harvard** was born on Borough High Street and baptised in the church in 1607 (emigrated 1638).

The 13C retrochoir is divided into four chapels by piers; from 1540–1617 it served as prison, billet, sty and bakery.

In the **south chancel aisle** near the altar is the freestanding tomb of Lancelot Andrewes *(d. 1626)*, Bishop of Winchester. In the **south transept**, mainly 14C and early 15C, with early Perpendicular tracery in the three windows, are to the left, the red painted arms and hat of Cardinal Beaufort, 15C Bishop of Winchester, and on the right, a recumbent effigy of William Emerson *(d. 1575)*, above, John Bingham *(d. 1625)*, saddler to Queen Elizabeth. Note the tessellated paving from a Roman villa at the chancel step. Against the wall of the south aisle is a memorial to Shakespeare.

Visitor Centre – *Access from the north aisle or from the north door into Lancelot's Link.*

Discover the history of the Cathedral through artefacts uncovered during excavations and using interactive cameras. A 360-degree view is reflected in a smooth dish.

A **1C Roman road**, vestiges of the Norman church, the Medieval priory and 17C–18C pottery kilns can be viewed from the glazed link.

Pass under London Bridge (*see The CITY*).

London Bridge

The sleek granite surfaces of **No. 1 London Bridge** are in sharp contrast to **St Olaf House** *(Hay's Wharf)*.

The latter is built in Portland stone in Art Deco style; fine gilded faience relief panels designed by Frank Dobson provide a central motif on the Thames front.

The Shard

Dominating this area is the Shard, a 72-storey glass-panelled skyscraper, which redefined the London city-

Borough Market

8 Stoney St., Borough High St. London Bridge. 020 7407 1002. www.boroughmarket.org.uk. Open Thu 11am–5pm, Fri noon–6pm, Sat 8am–5pm.

Specialising in food from around the world, this huge, traditional market is full of the best organic and farm produce, and is reputedly London's oldest market. The place teems with people, fresh fruit and veg, hot takeaway dishes made in front of you, fresh fish, wheatgrass drinks, ciders, coffee and lots more! Perfect for a snack or to prepare for a picnic before a stroll along the Thames.

© Y. Kanazawa/Michelin

scape when completed in spring 2012. Designed by Renzo Piano, it is a truly mixed-use building, comprising offices, a five-star hotel *(the Shangri-La)*, bars, restaurants, luxury apartments and the top-floor observatory, where **views** extend for more than 40 miles across the city.

Continue east along the river.

Hay's Galleria and City Hall

The original Hay's Dock has been sealed over: the Galleria now boasts a 90ft/27m high glass barrel vault.

Pride of place is given to a monumental kinetic sculpture, *The Navigators* by David Kemp. The converted warehouses now house shops, bars and restaurants.

The walk continues along the riverside (Queen's Walk).

HMS *Belfast*

Open Mar–Oct daily 10am–6pm, Nov–Feb daily 10am–5pm (last admission an hour before closing). Closed 24–26 Dec. £14.50. Brochure. 020 7940 6300. www.iwm.org.uk.

The Royal Navy light cruiser saw service with the Arctic convoys and on D-Day. It is painted in the original "Admiralty disruptive camouflage colours".

Nine decks of the ship are on display; you can explore the interactive Operations Room, and get the feel of a battle atmosphere in the Gun Turret Experience. The story of the North Atlantic Convoys in World War II is told on film.

Past HMS *Belfast*, opposite the Tower of London, on a site where archaeological excavation has identified the precincts of **Edward II**'s 14C Rosary Palace, sits London's **City Hall**, home of the Mayor's office and Greater London Assembly. Every aspect of this building, designed by **Sir Norman Foster** and partners in the shape of a 10-storey glass dish around a central spiral corridor, was created to be environmentally friendly *(open to the public Mon–Thu 8.30am–6pm, Fri 8.30am–5.30pm)*.

3 BOROUGH

Start from London Bridge train station.

London Dungeon

34 Tooley Street. Mon, Tue, Wed, Fri 10am–4.30pm Thu 11am–4.30pm. Sat, Sun 10am–5.30pm. Check website in advance. Closed 25 Dec. £24.60 on the door (£18.45 when booked in advance online). Leaflet (3 languages). Refreshments. 0871 423 2240. www.thedungeons.com.

The dungeon holds a gruesome (if rather ham-horror) parade of tableaux relating to scenes of death from disease (leprosy and plague), Medieval torture and various types of execution, as well as early surgery. The museum is not suitable for young children or anyone with a nervous disposition (the exhibits have a way of "coming alive"!).

Continue along Tooley St.

Winston Churchill's Britain at War

64 Tooley Street. Open daily 10am–5pm (4.30pm Nov–Mar). Closed 24–26 Dec. £14.50. 020 7403 3171. www.britainatwar.co.uk.

An old London Underground lift provides Tardis-like time travel for visitors to an Underground station fitted with bunks, a canteen and tea urn and a WVS lending library. The exhibition continues with displays of **war-time fashion**, mementoes of rationing, air raids, an Anderson shelter, a refuge room, evacuation, women at work in factories, the life of Sir Winston Churchill and a reconstruction of simulated air raid damage.

Retrace your steps along Tooley St., past the station and turn left.

Borough High Street

The Borough, kernel of London south of the Thames, is a vibrant area, full of historic street and inn names. This is Dickens' old stamping ground, and home to the last remaining galleried

pub in London, The George Inn *(see Addresses)*.

The focus is the vibrant **Borough Market** *(see box)*.

Turn left into St Thomas Street.

Old Operating Theatre, Museum and Herb Garret

9A St Thomas's St. Open early Jan–mid-Dec daily 10.30am–5pm. £6. 020 7188 2679. www.thegarret.org.uk

The attic of St Thomas's Parish Church was already in use as a herb garret when, in 1821, it was converted into a women's operating theatre for St Thomas's Hospital *(see LAMBETH)*.

The theatre pre-dates the advent of anaesthetics and antiseptic surgery. Its semicircular amphitheatre is ringed by five rows of "standings" for students. Below the operating table was a box of sawdust that could "be kicked to the place where most blood was running".

Guy's Hospital

The complex retains its 18C railings, gateway and forecourt. The court is flanked by brick wings leading to the centre range with a frontispiece decorated with allegorical figures by Bacon. In the court stands a bronze statue by Scheemakers of Thomas Guy *(1644–1724)*, son of a Southwark lighterman and coal dealer, who began as a bookseller (Bibles), gambled successfully on the South Sea Bubble and eventually became a patron of medical institutions. In the chapel *(centre of the West Wing)* is a full-size memorial of Guy by **John Bacon**. In the rear quadrangles are a statue of Lord Nuffield, a 20C philanthropist, and a mid-18C alcove from old London Bridge.

Return to Borough High St.

The Yards and the Inns of Southwark

Several narrow streets and yards off Borough High Street, south of St Thomas Street, mark the entrances to the old inns, the overnight stops of those arriving too late at night to cross the bridge into the capital. These inns were also the starting point for coach services to the southern counties and the ports.

King's Head Yard: the King's Head, known as the Pope's Head before the Reformation, and now a 19C building, sports a coloured effigy of Henry VIII.

White Hart Yard: the pub *(no longer in existence)* was the headquarters of Jack Cade in 1450 and where **Mr Pickwick** first met Sam Weller.

The George Inn★ *(see Addresses)*: when rebuilt in 1676 after a fire, the George Inn had galleries on three sides but only part of the south range remains. There are tables in the cobbled yard in summer and open fires in winter. Note the Act of Parliament clock constructed in 1797 when a tax of five shillings *(25 pence)* made people sell their timepieces and rely on clocks in public places; the Act was repealed within the year.

Talbot Yard: recalled by **Chaucer** in the Prologue to *The Canterbury Tales*: "At the Tabbard as I lay, At night was come into that hostelrie Wel nyne and twenty in a compagnye of sondrye folk and pilgrims were they alle That toward Canterbury wolden ryde."

Queen's Head Yard: site of the Queen's Head *(demolished 1900)* sold by John Harvard before he set out for America; Newcomen Street: the **King's Arms** *(1890)* takes its name from the lion and unicorn supporting the arms of George II *(not George III, as inscribed)*, a massive emblem that originally decorated the south gatehouse of old London Bridge.

Return to Borough High St.

A plaque at **No. 163** indicates the first site of **Marshalsea Prison** *(1376–1811)*, the notorious penitentiary of which only one high wall remains on the later site *(No. 211)*. **No. 116** marks the location of the 16C palace of the Duke of Suffolk, who married a daughter of Henry VII.

St George the Martyr

Open Sun 10am–4pm, Wed noon–1.30pm, Thu (except holiday periods) 12.30pm–2pm. Induction loop.

℘020 7357 7331. www.stgeorge-the martyr.co.uk.
The spire and square tower of the 1736 church on a 12C site mark the end of the first section of the High Street. **Dickens** features the church in *Little Dorrit*, who is commemorated in the east window. The pulpit is the highest in London.

Continue to the next crossroads and turn left into Trinity St.

Trinity Church Square★
The early-19C square is an unbroken quadrilateral of three-storey houses, punctuated by round-arched doorways. The statue in the central garden is known as **King Alfred** and believed to be the oldest in London.
The church *(1824)* was converted in 1975 into a studio for use by major orchestras.

Merrick Square★
The early-19C square with elegant lamp standards and modest houses is named after the merchant who left the property to the Corporation of Trinity House.

ADDITIONAL SIGHT
Fashion and Textile Museum
83 Bermondsey Street. Open Tue–Sat 11am–6pm (last admission 5.15pm). £7. Café. ℘020 7407 8664. www.ftmlondon.org.
Founded and run by flamboyant designer Zandra Rhodes at her Bermondsey studio, this museum to fashion has various temporary exhibitions.

ADDRESSES

LIGHT BITE
Applebee's Fish, *5 Stoney St. Borough Market. ⊖London Bridge.* Delicious fresh fish, served simply. Menu changes daily to incorporate the catch from the day before.

De Gustibus, *4 Southwark St. Borough Market. ⊖London Bridge. ℘ 020 7407 3625. www.degustibus.co.uk. Mon–Fri 7am–5pm, Sat 7am–4pm.* This small chain of bakeries is renowned for the variety and the excellent quality of its breads. Sandwiches made to order plus hot dishes, salads and soups, to eat in or takeaway.

Pâtisserie Lila, *1 Bedale St., Borough Market. ⊖London Bridge. ℘020 7403 6304. Mon–Sat 8am–7pm, Sun 9am–6pm.* Located in the heart of Borough Market, this charming tea room on two levels offers delicious pastries, served with tea or coffee.

Tate Modern Café, *Tate Modern Museum (2nd floor), Bankside. ⊖Southwark or Blackfriars. ℘020 7401 5014. www.tate.org.uk. Mon–Thu 10am–6pm, Fri 10am–9pm, Sat 9am–7pm, Sun 9am–6pm.* *See p 328.*

PUBS AND BARS
Anchor Bankside, *34 Park St. ⊖London Bridge. ℘020 7407 1577. Mon–Wed 11am–11pm, Thur–Sat 11am–midnight, Sun noon–11pm.* Rebuilt in 1676 after the Great Fire of London, this historic pub situated at the foot of Southwark bridge is a labyrinth of small dark rooms. There's also a pleasant terrace overlooking the Thames. Food is served, although service is very slow.

The George Inn, *77 Borough High St. ⊖London Bridge. ℘020 7407 2056. Mon–Fri 11am–11pm, Sun noon–10.30pm.* Nestled in a narrow alley off Borough High St., this old coaching inn is the last remaining galleried inn in London. You can sit in the courtyard or in one of several rooms; serves good classic British fare.

Horniman at Hay's, *Hay's Galleria, Tooley St. ⊖London Bridge. ℘020 7407 1991. Mon–Tue 10am–11.30pm, Wed 10am–midnight, Thu–Sat 10am–12.30am, Sun 10am–11pm.* Touristy pub, but with cracking views of Tower Bridge.

Wine Wharf, *Stoney St., Borough Market. ⊖London Bridge. ℘020 7940 8335. www.winewharf.co.uk. Mon–Fri noon–3pm, 5.30pm–11pm, Sat noon–11pm, Sun noon–8pm.* Oenphiles will appreciate the bar at Vinopolis, where more than 300 varieties of wine from around the world are served in a relaxed atmosphere under the brick vaulting of the railway arches.

Lambeth

At the start of the 21C, the property boom has made the South Bank highly desirable and as young professionals move in, the signs of change are evident all over the district. With its convenient location, a world-class museum, the London Eye and the South Bank Centre *(see SOUTH BANK)*, **the future is bright as the regeneration of the neighbourhood progresses apace.**

- **Location:** Map pp 256–257. *Lambeth North.* This district, wedged between Southwark and Battersea, is the gateway to the southern suburbs as well as the outlying counties of Kent and Surrey.
- **Don't Miss:** The view of the Palace of Westminster from across the river.
- **Timing:** Allow 3hr, including a tour of the Imperial War Museum.

A BIT OF HISTORY

In the Middle Ages the public horse-ferry from Westminster landed at Lambeth, and it was here that the Archbishop of Canterbury obtained a parcel of land on which he built himself a London seat: **Lambeth Palace**. In the mid-18C the building of Westminster Bridge and of new roads brought about industrial development such as timber yards, dye works, potteries and lime kilns, and the Coade Stone factory.

The population increased and in the early 19C there arose prisons, welfare institutions and asylums. There were also louche taverns and pleasure gardens, which gave the area a dubious reputation. In the late 19C and early 20C St Thomas's Hospital and the **Imperial War Museum** *(see MAJOR CENTRAL LONDON MUSEUMS)* were established and changed the character of this proletarian area.

To the South the streets of Kennington are lined with elegant Georgian houses and terraces, as well as Victorian houses and bay window cottages.

Lambeth Walk, formerly the centre of Old Lambeth, is now lined by grass verges and modern flats. **The Oval**, a famous cricket ground, was a former market garden.

WALKING TOUR 4

From Westminster Bridge (*see WESTMINSTER*) take Lambeth Palace Rd.

Florence Nightingale Museum

St Thomas's Hospital, 2 Lambeth Palace Road. Open daily 10am–5pm (last admission 4pm). Closed Good Fri, Dec 25–26. £5.80. Film (20min). Refreshments. 020 7620 0374. www.florence-nightingale.co.uk.

The work of Florence Nightingale *(1820–1910)*, nicknamed the "Lady of the Lamp" by the British soldiers she nursed in Istanbul during the Crimean War *(1854–56)*, has become legendary in pioneering healthcare. Photographs and written panels are supplemented by various personal exhibits, including her medicine chest and copies of her many publications on nursing.

Continue along Lambeth Palace Rd.

The red and white buildings of **St Thomas's Hospital** have scarcely changed in outward appearance since being built in 1868–71, in spite of a few 7–14 storeyed buildings dating from the 1970s. The **13C Infirmary**, set up in Southwark and dedicated to **St Thomas Becket**, evolved into a hospital endowed by **Dick Whittington** with a lying-in ward for unmarried mothers. In the 16C it was forfeited as a conventual establishment to Henry VIII and closed, only to be rescued in 1552 by the City, which purchased and re-dedicated it to Thomas the Apostle *(Thomas Becket having been decanonised)*.

The story since is one of expansion, of removal to Lambeth in the 19C, of research and development, of the foundation of the Nightingale Fund Training School for Nurses and of 10 aerial attacks between September 1940 and July 1944, when at least one operating theatre was always open.

Just south of the hospital is **Lambeth Palace**, the London residence of the Archbishop of Canterbury, head of the Anglican *(Episcopalian)* church worldwide. The Medieval red-brick building boasts an impressive **Great Hall** with hammerbeam roof. The magnificent gateway dates from 1490. Archbishop's Park to the northeast, formerly part of the palace grounds, provides a good **view** of the palace.

Continue along Lambeth Palace Rd.

The Garden Museum

Lambeth Palace Road. Open Sun–Fri 10.30am–5pm, Sat 10.30am–4pm. Exhibitions, lectures, courses, outings. £7.50. Café. Shop. 020 7401 8865. www.gardenmuseum.org.uk

The Garden Museum *(formerly the Museum of Garden History)* was founded by the **Tradescant Trust** *(1977)* in the redundant church of St Mary-at-Lambeth. The church's graveyard contains the graves of the two John Tradescants, father and son, royal gardeners and importers of exotic plants, who planted the first physic garden in 1628 at their house in Lambeth. The centrepiece in the churchyard is a garden, including a **knot garden**, created with **17C plants**.

There is an exhibition of historic garden tools. Lawrence Lee designed the window depicting Adam and Eve and the Tradescants. At their house they also exhibited a collection of "all things strange and rare", which later, under their neighbour, Elias Ashmole, formed the nucleus of the Ashmolean Museum in Oxford.

Turn left into Lambeth Rd. passing the Imperial War Museum (see p 299).

The Garden Museum

©Gavin Kingcome/The Garden Museum

St George's Roman Catholic Cathedral

St George's Road. Open daily, 7.30am–7pm. Guided tour by appointment. Brochure. 020 7928 5256. www.southwark-rc-cathedral.org.uk.

The mid-19C cathedral was designed by **AW Pugin** *(1812–52)*, the impassioned advocate of the Gothic Revival. Destroyed by incendiary bombs during World War II, it was rebuilt and reopened in 1958. The **interior** of the new Cathedral with an added clerestory is much lighter than the original: fluted columns of white Painswick stone support high pointed arches; plain glass lights the aisles, the only elaborate windows being those at the East and West ends. The new building's sole ornate feature is the high altar with its carved and gilded reredos; statues are modern in uncoloured stone.

Westminster Bridge Road was developed in 1750 when the bridge was built. Note the white spire encircled by red brick bands of Christchurch, built in 1874 with funds from the USA.

On the right is **Waterloo International**, designed by Grimshaw Architects and winner of the prestigious Royal Institute of British Architects' Building of the Year award. In November 2007, after 13 years, it gave up its role as the Eurostar Terminal in favour of St Pancras International.

Battersea

Battersea has changed beyond measure from a sedate backwater to a desirable residential area for the overspill from Chelsea. The park hosts funfairs, concerts and the colourful Easter parade. Development of the riverside is well underway, lining the South Bank with glamorous and extremely expensive apartment blocks, while the eventual long-delayed redevelopment of the massive power station, a famous riverside landmark, will give a further boost to the district.

- **Location:** Overground rail: Battersea Park from Victoria; Queenstown Road from Waterloo. Battersea is located over the river from Chelsea and is just west of Chelsea Bridge.
- **Timing:** Spend a couple of hours walking in Battersea Park and around the surrounding area.

A BIT OF HISTORY

Battersea's transformation from a rural to an industrial town took just 100 years. In 1782, 2,160 locals were engaged in cultivating strawberries, asparagus and vegetables for seed; they sent their produce to Westminster. By 1845 the railway had extended to Clapham *(originally Battersea)* Junction and the population explosion began.

WALKING TOUR

Start from Battersea Bridge and turn right into Battersea Church Rd.

Battersea Bridge

The present construction was designed by Joseph Bazalgette in 1890. Its predecessor, a wooden bridge *(1771)* lit first by oil lamps *(1799)* and then by gas *(1824)*, was the inspiration for Whistler's painting entitled *Nocturne*.

Battersea Old Church, St Mary's

Open Tue–Wed 11am–3pm (ask at the Parish Office), or by appointment. Services: Sun 8.30am, 11am, 6.30pm. Guide book (English). 020 7228 9648. www.stmarysbattersea.org.uk.

Since Saxon times there has been a church well forward at the river bend. The current building with a conical green copper spire dates from 1775 *(portico 1823)*; the 14C east window encloses 17C tracery and painted heraldic glass. Famous people with local connections include **William Blake**, who married here, and **Turner**, who sketched the river from the vestry window and whose chair now stands in the chancel.

Continue along Vicarage Cres.

Devonshire House is an early-18C stucco house of three storeys with a Doric porch and small curved iron balconies and **St Mary's House**, a late-17C mansion. **Old Battersea House** (**No. 30**) is a two-storey brick mansion built by Sir Walter St John in 1699.

At the end of Vicarage Cres, turn left into Battersea High St.

The Raven, with curving Dutch gables, has dominated the crossroads since the 17C. **Sir Walter St John School**, founded in 1700, was rebuilt in the 19C–20C on the original site in Tudor-Gothic style. Note the St John motto surmounted by helm and falcon at the entrance.

Continue along Battersea High St., turn right into Westbridge Rd. and continue on Parkgate Rd. to Albert Bridge Rd.

Albert Bridge★

The cantilever suspension bridge, which is most attractive when lit up at night, was designed by RW Ordish in 1873; it was modified by Joseph Bazalgette and reinforced with a central support in the

Battersea Power Station

1970s; spare bulbs are stored in the twin tollmen's huts at either end.

Take a walk through the park.

Battersea Park

The marshy waste of Battersea Fields, popular in the 16C for pigeon shooting, fairs, donkey racing and duels, had become ill-famed by the beginning of the 19C. In 1843 **Thomas Cubitt** proposed that a park be laid out; a bill was passed in 1846 and the site built up with land excavated from Victoria Docks.

Today the park is one of London's most charming and interesting, with a boating lake, a garden *(accessible to wheelchair users)*, sculptures by **Henry Moore** and Barbara Hepworth, an **adventure playground** and **children's zoo**, a deer enclosure, cafés and many sports facilities. It has a busy programme of events and is the nesting ground of various birds.

The **Japanese Peace Pagoda** *(1985)* is one of several instituted by a world peace organisation.

The present **Chelsea Bridge** is a suspension bridge dating from 1934.

Marco Polo House, on Queenstown Road, is a bold building that is clad in hi-tech Japanese panels of Neo-Paries and Pilkington glass.

Continue south to Battersea Park Rd. and turn left.

Battersea Power Station

Battersea Pk Rd.

This iconic industrial landmark, with its four white chimneys overlooking the river, was largely built in 1932–34 and completed by Giles Gilbert Scott after WWII. The power station was shut down in 1983 and it has lain dormant ever since, in increasing stages of dereliction. Proposals of what to do with it are periodically put forward – at present there are plans to convert the massive structure and its 31 acre/12ha site into a shopping and entertainment centre, but as yet, nothing has been put in motion.

ADDITIONAL SIGHTS

De Morgan Foundation

38 West Hill. Open Tue–Fri 1pm –5pm (9pm on last Thu of the month), Sat 11am–5pm. 020 8871 1144. www.demorgan.org.uk.

An imposing white brick building houses a collection of ceramics by **William de Morgan,** who was associated with the Arts and Crafts movement; and paintings and drawings by Evelyn de Morgan Spencer Stanhope, JM Strudwick and Cadogan Cowper.

Battersea Dogs and Cats Home

4 Battersea Park Rd. Open daily 10.30am–5pm. 0843 509 4444. www.battersea.org.uk.

The UK's premier rescue centre for dogs and cats, established in 1860.

EAST LONDON

From its graphic depiction in the novels of Charles Dickens to the Spirit of the Blitz and the modern television soap, *Eastenders*, the East End of London has always had a special place in the story of the capital. For centuries it has been an area marked by immigration and that remains as true today as ever. It is also a place of new hope and renegeration following the London 2012 Olympic Games. There is great wealth and great poverty, great diversity and yet still a sense that this is as much 'London' as any other part of the capital.

Highlights

1. Drink with the hip crowd on a night out in **Shoreditch** (p278)
2. Discover East End life at **Dennis Severs' House** (p279)
3. Revisit simpler times at the **V&A Museum of Childhood** (p280)
4. Explore the decorative arts at the **William Morris Gallery** (p281)
5. Browse for unique goods at **Columbia Road** and **Brick Lane** Markets (p283)

A Bit of Geography

The East End stretches east from the City to Stratford, West Ham and as far as the River Lee, and includes the riverside communities on the north bank, such as Wapping. The Docklands Light Railway and the Jubilee Line opened up many areas of the East End during the 1990s; more recently, the East London Overground line connects these areas to surrounding neighbourhoods.

A Bit of History

There have been 'Eastenders' for centuries but a collection of disparate settlements began to come together and grow from the time of the Norman Conquest onwards (1066), as London became a major centre for trade, and the City and its docks attracted workers from around the nation and abroad. It was not long before the area became synonymous with immigration, overcrowding and the kind of grinding poverty described by Charles Dickens. People from all over the world crowded into its narrow streets and tenements: Dutch and French Huguenots, Irish, eastern European Jews and Chinese, to name but a few. Conditions were appalling, with Spitalfields, Whitechapel (the scene of Jack the Rippers' infamous murders), Stepney, Mile End and Bethnal Green among the worst. The area was badly damaged during World War II, and afterwards, many people moved out of the East End for good, while others were resettled into high rise blocks of flats built on the scene of post-war slum clearances.

East London Today

The East End today is still a heady mix of cultures and faiths, wealth and poverty. The development of Canary Wharf has brought into the area some of the biggest names in world banking, while nearby are some of the poorest areas of London. The impact of immigration can still be seen in the bustling Muslim

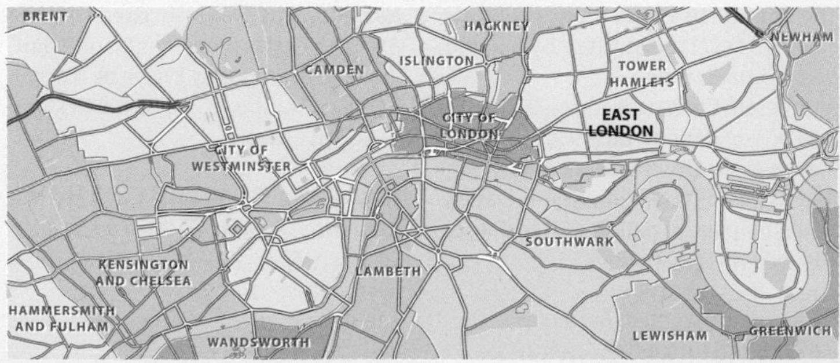

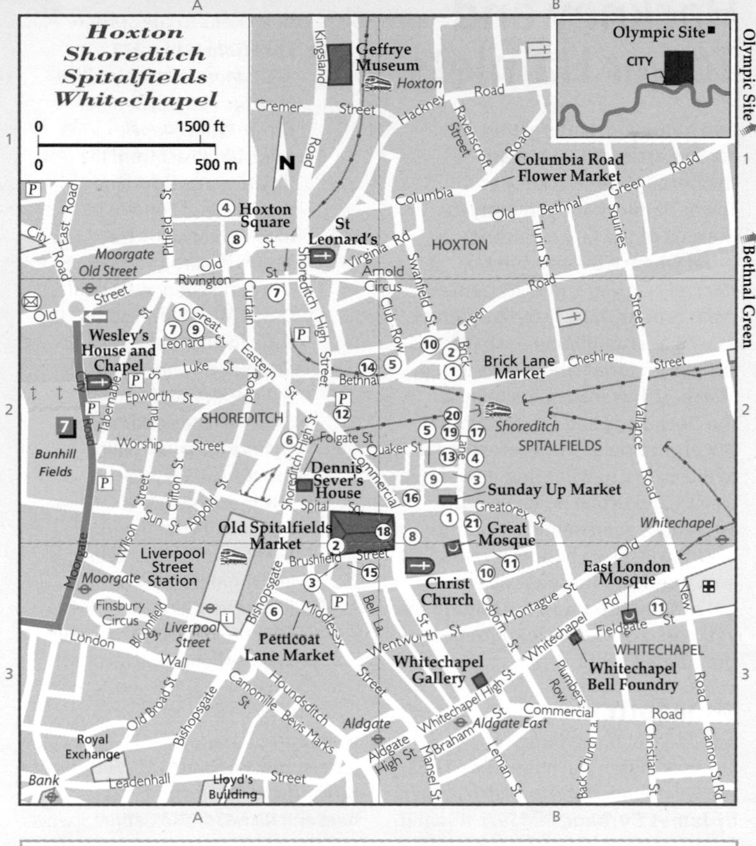

WHERE TO STAY
Hoxton Hotel .... (1)

WHERE TO EAT
Bengal Village .... (1)
Brick Lane Beigel Bake ...... (2)
Café 1001 .... (3)
Hoxton Apprentice .... (4)
Les Trois Garçons .... (5)
Light (The) .... (6)
Princess of Shoreditch .... (7)
St John Bread and Wine .... (8)
Story Deli .... (9)
Sweet & Spicy .... (10)
Tayyabs .... (11)

CAFÉS
Hookah Lounge .... (1)
Pâtisserie Valérie .... (2)
Verde & Co .... (3)

BARS, PUBS & NIGHTLIFE
93 Feet East .... (4)
Big Chill Bar (The) .... (5)
Boisdale .... (6)
Cargo .... (7)
Club 333 .... (8)
East Village.......................... (9)
Loungelover .... (10)
Pride of Spitalfields (The) .. (11)
Public Life .... (12)
Vibe Bar .... (13)

LEISURE
Rich Mix .... (14)

SHOPPING
A. Gold .... (15)
Absolute Vintage .... (16)
Brick Lane Bookshop .... (17)
Queens .... (18)
Laden Showroom (The) .... (19)
Rokit .... (20)
Taj Stores .... (21)

communities along Commercial Road, close to the Roman Catholic churches that testify to Irish immigrants from a previous generation. Whitechapel Gallery and Hoxton are centres of artistic creativity, and there are high hopes that the London 2012 Olympic legacy will bring yet more positive regeneration to the area. There is not much left of the rhyming slang, Pearly Kings and Queens and jellied eels of the past. The East End has changed but it is still in many ways what it always was: a pot-pourri of peoples, languages, styles and cultures. The look may have changed, but the spirit has not.

Hackney and Tower Hamlets

Two of the most interesting yet diverse areas of London are the boroughs of Hackney and Tower Hamlets. Immediately to the east of the City is Hackney (from whence the London taxi, or Hackney carriage, gets its name). It has around 1300 listed buildings as well as stunning open spaces such as Victoria Park and Hackney Marshes. Tower Hamlets takes in the Docklands and Canary Wharf but also some of the poorest areas of London, a bewildering mix of wealth and urban poverty. Both areas have seen immense change over the last two hundred years, and, thanks to the legacy of the 2012 Olympic Games, are hoping for yet more positive development in the coming years.

Location: Map p 277. *Aldgate East, Shoreditch High St., Hoxton, Bethnal Green, Whitechapel.* Stretching east from the City towards Docklands, this is one of London's most vibrant areas, a sprawling urban mélange featuring every walk of life.

Don't Miss: Having a curry in Brick Lane; the revamped William Morris Gallery, devoted to the 19C designer and socialist; the Geffrye Museum, telling the story of the home.

Timing: Visit at the weekend to get the best out of the markets and nightlife.

Kids: The V&A Museum of Childhood runs fun activities in the school holidays.

SHOREDITCH

Old Street, Shoreditch

The first English playhouse, **The Theatre**, was founded in Shoreditch in 1576 by **James Burbage** *(d. 1597)*. A joiner by trade, he also founded the **Little Curtain**, named after the curtain wall of the enclosure. In 1597 The Theatre in Shoreditch was pulled down on the orders of the Privy Council and the materials were used by James's son **Cuthbert** *(d. 1635)* to build the **Globe** *(see BANKSIDE – SOUTHWARK)* on the South Bank in 1599; his other son **Richard Burbage** *(d. 1619)* was the first actor to play Shakespeare's Richard III and Hamlet – all three Burbages are buried in St Leonard's Church.

Proceed east along Old St. to the junction with Kingsland Rd. (*see Geffrye Museum and Hackney Rd.*).

St Leonard's Church

119 Shoreditch High Street. Open by appointment only. 020 7739 2063.

This mid-18C building boasts a 192ft/58.5m spire. Within its precincts were buried one of Henry VIII's court jesters, William Somers *(d. 1560)*; **James Burbage** *(d. 1597)* and his sons **Cuthbert** and **Richard**; also Gabriel Spencer *(d. 1598)*, a player at the Rose Theatre, who was killed in a duel by **Ben Jonson** *(see WESTMINSTER)*.

Hoxton Square

This working-class district gained a certain notoriety as artists, musicians and other creative types moved in and set up their studios. Though many of these trailblazers have since moved up to Dalston and out to Hackney Wick, sleek bars, restaurants and art galleries attract Bohemian and trendy crowds to the small grassy square.

SPITALFIELDS

Shoreditch; Liverpool Street.

In 1991 London's largest wholesale fruit and vegetable market was moved to Leyton. The eastern part of the Victorian structure is all that remains of **Old Spitalfields Market**★ *(along Commercial Street, see YOUR STAY IN THE*

Georgian houses on Fournier Street, Spitalfields

CITY – Shopping). Today, the market is a vibrant and popular destination for tourists and locals browsing fashion, jewellery, antiques and organic produce. It is at its busiest on Sundays when all the stalls and surrounding shops are open.

Across the street stands **Christ Church**, built by Hawksmoor in 1714–30, its spire rising above a Classical west portico; at the east end, a **Venetian window** is framed by paired niches beneath a pediment *(♿ ⏲ open Sun 1–4pm, Tue 10am–4pm; also Mon and Fri 10am–4pm, if church not in use; ☎ 020 7377 2440; www.ccspitalfields.org)*.

The church holds a number of events in the area, including many as part of the **Spitalfields Festival** *(☎ 020 7377 6793; www.spitalfieldsvenue.org)*.

As you walk along **Fournier Street** to Brick Lane, note the handsome Georgian houses *(1718–28)*, once occupied by silk weavers and merchants.

Right next to Spitalfields is **Petticoat Lane Market**: here you can find some of the cheapest items in London as well as touristy souvenirs. *See WELCOME TO LONDON – Shopping.*

Brick Lane

The area is often known as "little Bangladesh", or "Bangla Town". It can be crowded at the weekend and some say it's the victim of its own success, but this is still a great place to go for a curry. The history of the **mosque**, which was built as a Christian chapel in 1743 and later became a synagogue, reflects the successive waves of immigrants who have lived in the district.

The spacious glass-fronted reception area of **Truman's Brewery** *(1666)* reveals older buildings round a cobbled yard.

On Sunday mornings, a bric-a-brac and second-hand clothes **market** spreads through the district around Bethnal Green Road, Cheshire Street. Just north, along **Columbia Road**, the equally lively flower market also takes place on Sundays.

Dennis Severs' House

18 Folgate Street. ⏲ Open Mon 6–9pm and Sun noon–4pm (last admission 3.15pm). Also the Mon following the 1st and 3rd Sunday of the month noon–2pm (last admission 1.30pm). £14. ☎ 020 7247 4013. www.dennisseversh ouse.co.uk

More than merely a museum, Dennis Severs' House takes visitors on a sensory journey, room by room. Beginning in the basement in 1724 and finishing at the top of the house in the mid-19C significantly sparser surrounds (it was a slum then), your visit is designed to immerse you in the life and history of the house. The present is left at the front door and everything set up as if the family living here have just left the room as you enter: floorboards creak, voices are heard outside, clocks tick and on the table food is left half-eaten, the coffee still steaming.

As Severs himself said: "What you hear and smell is as much part of the picture as anything you see."

WHITECHAPEL

Aldgate East. Walk east along Whitechapel Rd.

Whitechapel Gallery

Open Tue–Sat Sat 11am–6pm, Thu till 9pm. No charge. Talks, tours and film screenings, telephone for details. Café. 020 7522 7888. www.whitechapelgallery.org.

Recently redeveloped and expanded, the Whitechapel Gallery was founded in 1901 "to bring art to the people of the East End of London". For over a century, the gallery has premiered world-class artists such as Picasso, Pollock and Rothco, and provided exhibition space for non-established artists; **Barbara Hepworth** and **David Hockney** first showed their work here. The building *(1901)*, designed by **CH Townsend**, is decorated with contemporary Arts and Crafts reliefs.

The former **Passmore Edwards Library**, now part of the gallery, was built in the Arts and Crafts style and has a panel of decorated tiles depicting the Whitechapel Hay Market.

Whitechapel Bell Foundry

The foundry has been on its present site since 1738. It has cast and recast – owing to the 1666 Great Fire and World War II – the bells of St Mary-le-Bow, St Clement Dane's and Big Ben. Nearby, the **East London Mosque** was built in 1985 by the most recent immigrants, who came from the Indian subcontinent.

Mile End Road

Whitechapel

The Trinity Almshouses *(1695)* form a terrace of basement and ground-floor cottages around three sides of a tree-planted quadrangle.

On Trinity Green, a statue *(1979)* of General **William Booth** marks the site where he began the work that led to the foundation of the Salvation Army.

BETHNAL GREEN

Shoreditch, Bethnal Green

St Matthew parish church *(1743–46)* was built by George Dance the Elder and the interior remodelled *(1859–61)* by Knightly. The **Watch House** *(1826)* stands in the southwest corner of the churchyard.

The west tower of **St John on Bethnal Green** *(1825–28)*, a Grade I listed building, was designed by Sir John Soane. Though not high, it is an easily distinguished landmark as it rises to a vaned cupola. *Open at Mass times and by appointment. 020 8980 1742. www.stjohnonbethnalgreen.org.*

V&A Museum of Childhood

Cambridge Heath Road, Bethnal Green. Bethnal Green. Open daily 10am–5.45pm (last admission 5pm). Free. 020 8983 5200. www.museumofchildhood.org.uk.

The museum houses the Victoria and Albert Museum's enchanting collection of toys, dolls, games, puppets, toy soldiers, as well as children's clothing, furniture, paintings, books and other childhood artefacts. Many of the exhibits are behind glass and may appeal more to adults, but there are plenty of interactive displays to keep the children happy, as well as entertaining special exhibitions. During the school holidays activities and workshops are organised, such as puppet-making and T-shirt printing.

The building, an impressive pre-fabricated iron and glass construction, was originally erected to contain items from the **1851 Exhibition** (*see MAJOR CENTRAL LONDON MUSEUMS – Victoria & Albert Museum*); it was re-erected and opened on the present site in 1872.

WEST HAM

Bromley By Bow

West Ham developed early into a manufacturing town owing to its position near the confluence of the navigable River Lee and the Thames, and its proximity to London. In the 18C Bow Pottery was the largest porcelain factory in England. At the end of the 19C there were about

300 companies in the area engaged in various industries.

Three Mills

Three Mills Island, Three Mills Lane. Guided tours May–Oct Oct Sun 11am–4pm; Mar, Apr, Dec 1st Sun in month 11am–4pm. £3. Leaflet. 020 8980 4626. www.housemill.org.uk.

At the north end of Bow Creek there is an attractive group of early industrial buildings. **The House Mill**, built in 1776, is the largest tide mill known in the country. The original **miller's house** *(demolished in the 1950s)* has been reconstructed as part of the restored Georgian street front.

Granite setts and flagstones mark the path across to the **Clock Mill**, which dates from 1817. The ornate clock tower, which is earlier, is surmounted by an octagonal turret containing a bell and a weather vane. The conical caps of the two **drying kilns** are Victorian.

Abbey Mills Pumping Station

The impressive cruciform building that houses sewage pumping machinery was designed by **Sir Joseph Bazalgette** and Vulliamy *(1865–68)* in the Venetian Gothic style with an octagonal lantern above the crossing.

ADDITIONAL SIGHTS

Geffrye Museum★

Kingsland Road. Old Street, Liverpool St, Hoxton. Open Tue–Sat 10am–5pm, Sun and bank holiday Mon noon–5pm. Closed Good Fri, 24–26 Dec, 1 Jan. No charge. Guided tour for groups only (audio tour available to all). ***Herb garden and period garden rooms:*** *Open Apr–Oct. Restaurant. Shop. 020 7739 9893. www.geffrye-museum.org.uk.*

Housed in almshouses erected in 1712–19, this delightful small museum features period rooms which explore the home from 1600 to the present day, focusing on the living rooms of the English urban middle classes. A series of rooms leads you on a walk through time, from 17C oak furniture and panelling, past understated Georgian elegance, through

Period room: a drawing room in 1830, Geffrye Museum

eclectic Victorian style, and finally to 21C modernity and contemporary living. In tandem you can explore a sequence of period gardens and a walled herb garden, illustrating the role of the garden in home life.

The planned redevelopment project *(completion date 2016)* aims to expand and improve the facilities, opening new gallery spaces and a restaurant.

Sutton House

2, 4 Homerton High St. Bethnal Green. Open Feb–Dec Thu–Sun 12.30–4.30pm. ***Art Gallery:*** *Open early Jan–late Dec Wed–Sun 1.30–5pm. £3.50. No photography. No dogs. Braille Guide. Café. 020 8986 2264. www.nationaltrust.org.uk.*

The house, dating from c.1535, was originally known as the "bryk place" as most buildings then were timber-framed structures. It was modified through the centuries but the interior contains one of the **original Tudor transom windows**, now in the Lobby. The Parlour is entirely lined with 16C **oak linenfold panelling** and has retained its original stone fireplace, surmounted by an overmantel with typical Renaissance fluted pilasters. The **painted staircase** is decorated with coloured oil painting directly on to plaster and the Little Chamber lined with 16C **Baltic oak panelling**.

William Morris Gallery★
Walthamstow Central. Lloyd Park, Forest Road, E17. Open Wed–Sun 10am–5pm. No charge. Leaflet. 020 8496 4390. www.wmgallery.org.uk.
Reopened in 2012 after major redevelopment, this excellent museum is accommodated in the home of **William Morris** *(1834–96)*, where he lived with his family between 1848 and 1856. The house itself dates back to 1750. The life and works of William Morris are explored in separate themes throughout the museum, presenting Morris' varied skills as a designer, craftsman, writer and activist, and the work of the firm Morris & Co. *(1861–1940)*.
The Workshop is a new hands-on space where visitors can find out how products were designed and made, using techniques such as weaving, carpet knotting, dyeing and textile printing. The actual textile printing blocks used by Morris & Co are on display. Upstairs The **Ideal Book gallery** looks at Morris as a storyteller and printer, while the **Arts and Crafts Movement** is explored in another gallery. Due credit is given to **Sir Frank Brangwyn**, who shared Morris' view that art should not exist only for the privileged few. Brangwyn donated most of his private art collection to museums, including Walthamstow.

ADDRESSES

LIGHT BITE

On Sunday, stalls serving world cuisine set up in the markets of Brick Lane and Old Spitalfields.

Bengal Village, *75 Brick Lane. Shoreditch High St. or Liverpool Street. 020 7366 4868. Daily 6pm–11pm.* Neighbourhood restaurant serving quality Bangladeshi cuisine in a fresh contemporary setting.

Brick Lane Beigel Bake, *159 Brick Lane. Shoreditch High St or Liverpool Street. 020 7729 0616. Daily 24hr.* This bakery is famous for its fresh bagels, served at any time of day or night.

Café 1001, *3 Redchurch St. Shoreditch High St. or Liverpool Street. 020 7247 9679.* A café with a relaxed atmosphere, which is frequented by the budget-conscious young and trendy.

Story Deli, *3 Dray Walk. Shoreditch High St. or Liverpool Street. 020 7247 3137. Noon–10.15pm.* Story Deli has moved to new premises but is still as popular as ever. Well-cooked organic food, including delicious pizzas, salads and quiches, is served around large communal tables.

Sweet & Spicy, *40 Brick Lane. Aldgate East or Shoreditch High St. 020 7247 1081.* Delicious affordable Pakistani cuisine served at basic Formica tables.

CAFÉS

Hookah Lounge, *133 Brick Lane. Shoreditch High St. or Liverpool Street. 020 7033 9072.* Amazing selection of coffees and teas served in a Middle Eastern setting; here you can try the eponymous hookah (shisha pipe), something which is becoming increasingly popular around London.

Verde & Co, *40 Brushfield St. Liverpool Street. 020 7247 1924. Mon–Fri 9am–7pm, Sat–Sun 10am–5pm.* Simultaneously a deli, antiques store and tearoom, this charming shop offers a timeless setting in which to escape after a trawl around bustling Spitalfields.

PUBS

The Pride of Spitalfields, *3 Heneage St. Shoreditch High St. or Liverpool Street. 020 7247 8933. Mon–Sat 11am–11pm, Sun noon–10.30pm.* The area is best known for its bars but this country-style pub makes the ideal escape from nearby Brick Lane.

NIGHTLIFE

The Big Chill Bar, *Dray Walk, Old Truman Brewery, 91 Brick Lane. Shoreditch High St. or Liverpool Street. 020 7392 9180. www.bigchill.net. Noon–midnight (Thu–Sat 1am).* This large friendly place has comfortable sofas and big communal tables plus a variety of quality music. Some seats outside.

Boisdale, *Swedeland Court, 202 Bishopsgate. Liverpool Street. 020 7283 1763. www.boisdale.co.uk.*

Mon–Fri 11am–11pm. This opulent piano bar hosts live jazz most evenings.

Cargo, *83 Rivington St. ⊖ Old Street. ☎020 7739 3440. www.cargo-london.com. Mon–Thur noon–1am, Fri noon–3am, Sat 6pm–3am, Sun noon–midnight. £1–12.* Located under the railway arches, Cargo is good value and has a great atmosphere.

Club 333, *333 Old St. ⊖ Old Street. ☎020 7739 5949. www.333mother.com. Fri 10pm–4am. £12 (£8 before 11pm).* On the ground floor of the Mother bar, the 333 is one of the oldest clubs in the area but is still very popular for its club nights.

East Village, *89 Great Eastern St. ⊖ Old Street. ☎020 7739 5173. www.eastvillageclub.co.uk. Wed–Sun. Check website for details of what's on.* This trendy but popular bar has earned its reputation as one of the best nightspots in Shoreditch.

The Light, *233 Shoreditch High St., E1 6PJ. ⊖ Shoreditch High St. or Liverpool Street. ☎020 7247 8989. www.thelighte1.com. Mon–Wed noon–midnight, Thur–Fri noon–2am, Sat 6.30pm–2am, Sun noon–10.30pm.* This converted electricity generating station will surprise you with its sheer size and industrial décor of exposed beams and bricks. It attracts a lively crowd.

Loungelover, *1 Witby St. ⊖ Shoreditch High St. or Liverpool Street. ☎ 020 7012 1234, www.loungelover.uk.com. Mon–Thur and Sun 6pm–midnight, Fri 5.30pm–1am, Sat 6pm–1am.* This former meatpacking plant has been converted into a decadent, designer bar with colourful, kitsch décor. The cocktails are particularly good.

93 Feet East, *150 Brick Lane. ⊖ Shoreditch High St. or Liverpool Street. ☎ 020 7770 6006. www.93feeteast.co.uk. Mon–Thur 5pm–11pm, Fri 5pm–1am, Sat 5pm–1am, Sun 3pm–10.30pm.* A very fashionable place but one which retains a friendly atmosphere. The line-up of DJs who run the eclectic evenings is impressive.

Vibe Bar, *91–95 Brick Lane. ⊖ Shoreditch High St. or Liverpool Street. ☎020 7247 3479. www.vibe-bar.co.uk. Daily 11am–11.30pm (1am Fri–Sat).* Housed in the heart of the old Truman Brewery on Brick Lane, the Vibe Bar was one of the first to set up in the neighbourhood and one of the pioneers of garage music.

ENTERTAINMENT

Several agencies offer a guided tour at night on the trail of **Jack the Ripper**, the serial killer who terrorised the population of Whitechapel and Spitalfields in 1888, brutally murdering five prostitutes.

Rich Mix, *35–47 Bethnal Green Rd. ⊖ Shoreditch High St. or Liverpool Street. ☎020 7613 7498, www.richmix.org.uk. Mon–Fri 9am–11pm, Sat 10am–11pm.* Evidence of the dynamism of the neighbourhood, this cultural centre brings together three cinemas, a theatre, an exhibition space, workshops and recording studios.

SHOPPING

Most boutiques on and around Brick Lane open only around 11am or noon. Food stores observe more conventional hours. The East End retains the most popular markets in London, although the gradual arrival of artists' studios and causes saw more upmarket stores establish themselves. Fleamarket stalls and smaller thrift now rub shoulders with upscale boutiques. For details, visit www.eastlondonmarkets.com.

For independent shops and boutiques head for Cheshire Street, which runs between the top of Brick Lane and Bethnal Green to the East. Here, you'll find charming shops selling everything from wooden-etched jewellery to quirky household products.

Absolute Vintage, *15 Hanbury St. ⊖ Shoreditch High St. or Liverpool Street. ☎020 7247 3883. www.absolutevintage.co.uk. Daily 11am–7pm.* Hundreds of pairs of vintage shoes, sandals, boots and bags.

A. Gold, *42 Brushfield St. ⊖ Liverpool Street. ☎020 7247 2487. Mon–Fri 10am–4pm, Sat–Sun 11am–5pm.* This quaint grocery store is a real contrast to the fashion boutiques which surround it.

Brick Lane Market, *Brick Lane. ⊖ Shoreditch High St. or Liverpool Street. Sun 9am–5pm.* A range of cheap leather clothing stores are concentrated around the part of Brick Lane nearest the tube station *(Sclater St., Cheshire St.)* but quality is often poor. There are, however, some good deals, especially on market day. Nothing particularly interesting is for sale, but it is colourful and the atmosphere is very friendly.

Columbia Road Flower Market

© Ming Tang Evans/Apa Publications

Columbia Road Flower Market, *Columbia Rd. ⊖ Shoreditch High St., Hoxton or Bethnal Green. www.columbia road.info. Sun 8am–3pm.* This colourful flower market is the perfect place to spend a Sunday morning.

Brick Lane Bookshop, *166 Brick Lane. ⊖ Shoreditch High St. or Liverpool Street. ☏020 7247 0216. www.eastsidebooks. co.uk. Daily 11am–6.30pm.* If you are interested in local history, you'll find an interesting range dedicated to the East End here, including historical texts, stories, sociological studies and novels.

The Laden Showroom, *103 Brick Lane. ⊖ Shoreditch High St. or Liverpool Street. ☏020 7247 2431. www.laden.co.uk. Mon–Fri 11am–6.30pm (Sat 7pm), Sun 10.30am–6pm.* More than 40 different young fashion designers share this vast store.

Old Spitalfields Market, *at the junction of Commercial and Brushfield Sts. ⊖ Liverpool Street. www.oldspitalfields market.com. Tues–Fri 10am–4pm, Sat–Sun 9am–5pm.* One of London's best markets sells vintage fashions daily and hosts an antiques market on Thursdays. Sundays are the busiest day.

Petticoat Lane Market, *along Petticoat Lane, Wentworth St. and neighbouring streets. ⊖ Liverpool Street. Mon–Fri 8am–4pm, Sun 9am–2pm. Closed Sat.* Mostly clothes are for sale at this market but quality can be low – though prices are even lower.

Queens, *Old Spitalfields Market. ⊖ Liverpool Street. ☏020 7426 0017. Mon noon–7pm, Tue–Fri 11am–7pm, Sat 11am–6pm, Sun 10am–6.30pm.* A unique range of gifts, which run the gamut from kissing pink poodles to fairy-themed dresses.

Rokit, *101 and 107 Brick Lane. ⊖ Shoreditch High St. or Liverpool Street. ☏020 7375 3864. www.rokit.co.uk. Mon–Fri 11am–7pm, Sat–Sun 10am–7pm.* Two classic vintage stores selling a huge range of clothing and accessories from all eras; this is where you'll pick up that 1950s cocktail dress or vintage suit.

Sunday Up Market, *Old Truman Brewery, 91 Brick Lane. ⊖ Shoreditch High St. ☏020 7770 6028. www.sundayupmarket. co.uk. Sun 10am–5pm.* Located in the courtyard of the former brewery, this vast storehouse is packed with young designers, dealers and secondhand clothes stalls.

Taj Stores, *112 Brick Lane. ⊖ Shoreditch High St. or Liverpool Street. ☏020 7377 0061. www.tajstores.co.uk. 9am–9pm.* Large, cheap grocery store selling all the traditional Indian spices, sauces for tandoori, vindaloo and biryani plus a range of pickles, chutneys, naan and chapati.

Docklands★

The area opposite Greenwich has undergone a radical change since Canary Wharf was built in the 1980s. Set in a series of great bends in the Thames, this shimmering landmark overlooks a host of award-winning architecture. Arrive by the overhead Docklands Light Railway, or by boat to get a sense of the scale of the redevelopment that heralded the extension of London into the East.

- **Location:** Map p 287. ⊖*Tower Bridge; Canary Wharf.* Docklands stretches east of central London from Tower Bridge to the Royal Docks in North Woolwich. The area is served by an overground light train – the Docklands Light Railway (DLR) and the Underground's Jubilee Line.
- **Timing:** This area is fairly spread out so allow plenty of time to get from one place to the next.

A BIT OF HISTORY

Under the London Docklands Development Corporation (LDDC) established in 1981, the redundant London docks have been transformed into a modern annexe to the City, thus regenerating the riverside communities: Wapping, Isle of Dogs and Silvertown – some 4,942 acres/2,000ha extending 5mi/8km east of Tower Bridge on the north bank, and Bermondsey and Rotherhithe on the South Bank.

WAPPING

⊖*Tower Hill. DLR: Tower Gateway; Shadwell.*

Wapping was just a village beside the Thames until the 16C when a continuous riverside sprawl began to develop; there were many stairs *(landing places)* along the densely populated waterfront cut by alleys, steps, stages and docks, where **Charles Dickens** set several of his novels.

Commercial Docks

Built at the beginning of the 19C, the **London Docks** and **St Katharine Docks★** finally closed in 1969. The London Docks were infilled and redeveloped as the offices of News International *(1986)*, responsible for publishing *The Times* and *Sunday Times*. Warehouses on the waterfront have been converted into luxury apartments.

St Katharine Docks

© Eric Nathan/Loop Images/Photononstop

St Katharine Docks★ takes its name from the **Hospital of St Katharine by the Tower**. Founded in 1148 outside the City, it sheltered refugees, among them the English forced to quit Calais in 1558, Flemings, Huguenots and others.
In 1968 the 19C dock basins were converted into a **yacht marina**; Telford's Italianate building, renamed **Ivory house**, was transformed into residential units and arcades of shops; part of a pre-1820 timber brewery was converted into the **Dickens Inn**; the **Coronarium Chapel**, consecrated in June 1977, remembers the Medieval hospice.
New buildings on the dockside accommodate the **World Trade Centre** *(east side)*; the **London Commodity Exchange** *(north side)*, which trades in cocoa, coffee, sugar, etc.; and the **International Petrol Exchange**.

The **Wapping Pierhead** terraces of 18C houses originally flanked the entrance to the docks, housing dock officials.

River Police Boat Yard

The modern building houses the 33 craft of the **Metropolitan Special Constabulary** *(Thames Division)*, which patrols the last 54mi/87km of the River Thames. The attractive old building, which was originally a **pumping station** providing hydraulic power *(1892–1977)*, is now a trendy restaurant and art gallery.

Tobacco Dock★

The beautiful brick vaults and cast-iron superstructure of the Skin Floor *(1811–13)* of the London Docks are of interest. The dock was developed as a chic shopping mall, a sort of East End Covent Garden. Sadly, however, it failed and is largely empty now while decisions are taken on what to do next.
Two historic ships are moored at the rear, on the canal. The *Sea Lark* is an American-built schooner that ran the blockade from 1810–14 and now tells the classic adventure of *Kidnapped* by RL Stevenson. The *Three Sisters*, a replica of the original, which traded from 1788 to 1854, traces the history of piracy.

St George-in-the-East

Cannon Street Road or Cable Street.
Open Mon–Fri 8am–6pm, Sat–Sun 9am–5pm; call for group tours. 020 7481 1345. www.stgite.org.uk.
The church, designed by **Hawksmoor** and consecrated in 1729, was severely damaged in 1941; a modern church *(1964)* was built within the 18C shell. The **tower**, with its two-tier octagonal lantern, is a distinctive feature.

LIMEHOUSE

DLR: Limehouse

Limehouse, named after its lime kilns, was a shipbuilding centre. Its exotic street names and fine Chinese restaurants are a reminder that Chinese immigrants first settled here in the 18C.

Limehouse Basin

From Dunbar Wharf, locally brewed India Pale Ale was shipped to India and Australia. **Regent's Canal Dock**, built in 1820 and subsequently enlarged, used to accommodate barges coming down the Regent's Canal to the Thames or into the Lea Navigation canal system via the Limehouse Cut *(1mi/1.6km long)*.

St Anne's Limehouse

Open Sun 10.30am–12.30pm.
020 7987 1502.
A distinctive square tower marks Hawksmoor's first church in the East End of London *(1712–24)*.

ISLE OF DOGS★

DLR: West India Quay; Canary Wharf; Crossharbour; Island Gardens; Heron Quays; Mudchute; South Quay.
The Isle of Dogs is a tongue of land, around which the Thames makes a huge loop south from Limehouse to Blackwall, characterised today by skyscrapers such as One Canada Square *(also known as the Canary Wharf Tower)*, Citigroup Centre, 8 Canada Square. In the 19C the Island developed into a densely populated industrial district. Since the docks were closed to shipping in 1980, the area has been transformed into a high-tech commercial alternative to the City.

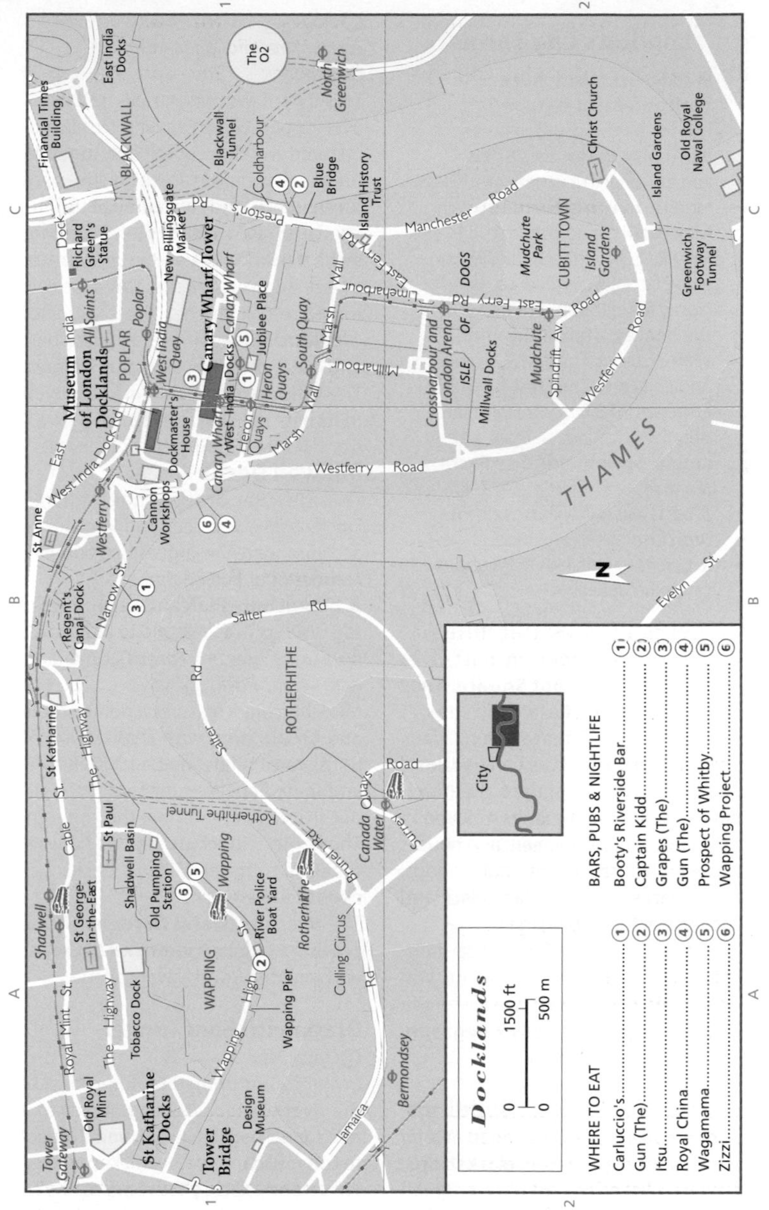

West India Docks

Extensive development of the Island began early in the 19C when the **West India Docks** *(1802–06)* were built to receive rum and sugar from the West Indies. The docks were enclosed by a high brick wall and patrolled by their own police force. The **City Canal** *(1805)* was transformed into a dock in 1870.

Canary Wharf★★ – This ambitious project was sponsored entirely by private funding. Development began with the construction of the seven

London's City Farms

In addition to **Mudchute Park and Farm** *(see right)*, London has other urban farms where visitors can get up close and personal to a variety of farmyard animals. **Hackney City Farm** *(1a Goldsmith's Row, E2 8QA, 020 7729 6381; www.hackneycityfarm.co.uk; closed Mon)* is home to Larry the donkey, a favourite among visitors, as well as goats, sheep and chickens. The Mini-Farmers Club *(Sat 10.30am–12.30pm)* is a great way for kids to learn about nature. **Spitalfields City Farm** *(Buxton St., E1 5AR, 020 7247 8762; www.spitalfieldscityfarm.org; closed Mon)* organises activities to help kids learn about caring for animals.

buildings suspended in part over water, enclosing **Cabot Square**. They are dominated by Cesar Pelli's tower block, **1 Canada Square** *(800ft/244m, 50 floors)*, also known as Canary Wharf Tower. Ships belonging to the **Maritime Trust** are sometimes moored in the docks. The development also houses a concert hall, restaurants, pubs, shops, open spaces and the Canada Place and Jubilee Place shopping malls.

The blue-glass South Quay Plaza shimmers with reflections from the still waters. Peterborough House was the editorial office of the **Daily Telegraph**, until its move to Victoria.

Old West India Dock Buildings

At the west end of the old import *(North)* dock stand the **Cannon Workshops**, now occupied by a number of small businesses. To the North stands the old **Dockmaster's House** *(now an Indian restaurant)*. The north quay of the dock is lined by two large **warehouses** *(1802)*.

Museum of London Docklands★

No. 1 Warehouse, West India Quay, E14 4AL. Open daily 10am–6pm (galleries begin to close 5.40pm). Closed 24–26 Dec. 020 7001 9844. www.museumoflondon.org.uk/docklands.

This award-winning museum covers every aspect of port activity. Displays of restored working equipment, tugs and barges, *Mudlarks* – an interactive area for children – and *London, Sugar & Slavery*, which reveals the city's involvement in the transatlantic slave trade, make for a fascinating experience. There are costumed re-enactments, a re-creation of 19C riverside Wapping called *Sailortown* and guided walks along the Thames. The **Billingsgate fish market** moved to its new building in 1982.

Millwall Docks

The 30ft/9m draft of the Millwall Docks *(1868)* was required in order to accommodate the larger ships bringing cargoes of grain and timber.

Mudchute Park and Farm, *Pier St., Isle of Dogs E14 3HP. 020 7515 5901. www.mudchute.org.* ***Farm:*** *Open daily 8am–4pm.* ***Park:*** *Daily.*

Mudchute Park features a riding stable and urban farm, with a collection of British rare breeds and over 200 animals and fowl. Activities are held throughout the year to entertain the children. The name "Mudchute" recalls how silt dredged from the Millwall docks was deposited here.

The riverside **Island Gardens** *(1895)*, provide a fabulous **view★★★** to Greenwich and the Royal Naval College.

Greenwich Foot Tunnel

Open 24hr.

In the round domed building beside the river a lift *(or 100 steps)* leads to a foot tunnel beneath the Thames *(10min)* to Greenwich.

The **Island History Trust** maintains an extensive archive of photographs and organises bi-annual festivals of local history, recollection and reunion *(Island House, Roserton Street; open Tue–Wed and 1st Sun of each month 1.30–4.30pm; 020 7987 6041; www.islandhistory.org.uk)*. The blue Dutch-design **lifting bridge** *(1969)* marks the eastern entrance to the South Dock. The nearby

Gun pub (see Addresses) dates from the 15C; from time to time Lady Hamilton stayed in the upper room.

BLACKWALL

DLR: All Saints

When Queen Elizabeth granted a charter to the **East India Company** in 1600, it established a shipbuilding and repair yard at **Blackwall**. Houses and inns developed on either side of Poplar High Street. In 1776 the company built **St Mathias Church** *(now a nursery)*, with seven masts supporting the roof, then Brunswick Dock in 1789 *(demolished in 1862)*; in 1806 this dock was incorporated into **East India Docks**.

Early-17C emigrants to America and later, mid-19C emigrants to Australia and New Zealand, sailed from Blackwall. The Blackwall yard made its name with fast clipper ships and later, with iron ships; in 1943 the East India Import Dock was used for the construction of the Phoenix units of the floating Mulberry harbour used in the 1944 D-Day landings. Today, just above the Blackwall Tunnel, impressive modern buildings accommodate the Town Hall, alongside the **Financial Times printworks** by Nicholas Grimshaw of 1988.

The **Old Blackwall Tunnel** *(1897)* carries northbound traffic, the New Tunnel *(1963)* covers the southbound.

The **Reuters Data Centre** *(Blackwall Yard)*, by **Richard Rogers**, features black glass and, as with the Lloyd's Building, coloured service ducts.

Bow Creek is the name given to the estuary of the **River Lea**.

ADDRESSES

PUBS AND BARS

Booty's Riverside Bar, *92a Narrow St., Limehouse. DLR: Westferry. 020 7987 8343. Daily noon–midnight.* This friendly local pub with a flower-decked façade is lit by a beautiful bay window with views onto the Thames. Jazz concert on Saturdays, 9–11.30pm.

Captain Kidd, *108 Wapping High St. Wapping. 020 7480 5759. Mon–Sat 11am–11pm, Sun noon–10.30pm.* An antique placard reminds sunken in the wall of this spot, where Captain Kidd was executed in 1701. The carefully maintained woodwork interior adds charm and the menu offers traditional pub food.

The Grapes, *76 Narrow St., Limehouse-Docklands, E14 8BP. Westferry DLR. 020 7987 4396. www.grapes.co.uk. Mon–Wed noon–3pm & 5.30–11pm, Thu–Sat noon–11pm.* Charles Dickens described this 18C pub under the name of The Six Jolly Fellowship Porters in ***Our Mutual Friend***. Well-kept real ales; fish-led bar meals and snacks. Small speciality fish restaurant; booking essential. Tiny outside deck for spectacular Thames views in a slightly out-of-the-way area near Canary Wharf.

The Gun, *27 Coldharbour, E14 9NS. Blackwall DLR. 020 7515 5222. www.thegundocklands.com. Mon–Sat 11am–midnight, Sun 11am–11pm.* This pub looking onto the Thames is named after the neighbouring foundry that produced canons during Nelson's era.

Prospect of Whitby, *57 Wapping Wall, E1W 3SH. Wapping. 020 7481 1095. Mon–Thu noon–11pm, Fri–Sat noon–midnight, Sat 11am–midnight, Sun noon–10.30pm.* Built in 1520, this is one of the oldest port-side pubs, where mariners came before sailing to the New World. History remains in its original flagstone floor and wonderful pewter bar. It is also one of the most romantic spots, with a balcony terrace beside the Thames. The pub is nevertheless a victim of its own success, with coaches dropping off tourists for lunch and dinner.

Wapping Project, *Wapping Hydrolic Power Station, Wapping Wall. Wapping. 020 7680 2080. www.thewapping project.com. Mon–Sat noon–10.30pm, Sat 10am–11pm, Sun noon–5.30pm.* This former waterworks is now an arts centre with contemporary photos and paintings hung on the old brick walls. A Med-influenced kitchen serves food all day and the wine list is extensive. Visit for brunch, view the artwork and then take a stroll along the river.

Team GB cyclists in London 2012 Velodrome

© Ben Stansall/AFP/Getty Images

London after the Olympic Games

On 6 July 2005, it was announced to a jubilant crowd in Trafalgar Square that London was to be the host city for the 2012 Olympic and Paralympic Games, making it the first city to host the event three times. Preparations were made so that 26 different sports could be staged across the city in the summer of 2012 in a mix of brand new and existing venues. 'Legacy' was the key to London's successful bid, with a promise of large-scale redevelopment of some of the capital's most deprived areas, located in the East of the city.

Once the events were over, the process began of turning the centrepiece of the Games, the Olympic Park in Stratford *(⊖Stratford)*, into the **Queen Elizabeth Olympic Park** *(www.noordinarypark.co.uk)*. Described as a 'brand new piece of the city', the £292m project (completion date 2014) involves dismantling the temporary venues – such as the hockey and basketball arenas – and turning the site into an area of parkland, with walking and cycling routes and recreational facilities. The area will also have thousands of new homes, new businesses, schools, restaurants and shops. Other major venues – the Olympic Stadium, the velodrome and swimming pool – continue to be used for sport. Also open to the public will be the ArcelorMittal Orbit, the giant twisted sculpture at the heart of the Olympic area, designed by Anish Kapoor and Cecil Balmond. **Westfield Stratford City**, Europe's largest urban shopping centre, is the main gateway into the Park itself *(www.westfield.com/stratfordcity)*. For a spectacular aerial view of the whole Olympic site, take a trip on the cable car across the Thames from North Greenwich to the Royal Docks *(www.emiratesairline.co.uk)*.

Stratford was not the only part of London to host Olympic events, and the list of other venues reads like a catalogue of some of the capital's most noted tourist sights: archery at Lord's Cricket Ground *(see p 132)*, tennis at Wimbledon *(see p 380)*, football at Wembley Stadium *(see p 440)*, beach volleyball on Horse Guard's Parade, triathlon in Hyde Park and road cycling in the grounds of Hampton Court Palace *(see pp 382–387)*.

In addition to the familiar eating and drinking options at Stratford City and within the park itself, a number of independently owned cafés in neighbouring Hackney Wick have opened, including **Counter Café** *(great breakfast, home-made pies, all day food and cakes; 7 Roach Rd., E3 2PA; ℘07834 275 920, www.thecountercafe.co.uk)* and **The Hackney Pearl** *(panini and soup for lunch, brunches and evening à la carte; 11 Prince Edward Rd., E9 5LX; ℘020 8510 3605, http://thehackneypearl.com)*.

MAJOR CENTRAL LONDON MUSEUMS

British Museum, Imperial War Museum, Museum of London, National Gallery, Natural History Museum, Science Museum, Tate Britain, Tate Modern, Victoria and Albert Museum and Wallace Collection.

From ancient to innovative, grand to eclectic, London's museum and galleries are world-class. Start with the largest, such as the British, Victoria and Albert, Science, and Natural History museums and the National Gallery for a taste of the sheer scale and quality of the national collections. The contemporary world gets a lively take with Tate Modern's displays of art, while the Science Museum takes a cutting-edge look at the scientific discoveries and questions of our age. The recently refurbished exhibition space at the Museum of London has revived the collection to vividly tell the city's story.

Finding the Museums

South Kensington and Bloomsbury *(www.museum-mile.org.uk)* are both notable for their density of museums and galleries.

South Kensington has the three giants, the **Victoria and Albert Museum** *(popularly known as the V&A)*, the **Science Museum** and the **Natural History Museum**, all within a two-minute walk of each other. Elsewhere, the **National Gallery** and **National Portrait Gallery** are adjacent at Trafalgar Square; the **British Museum** occupies a large site further north in Bloomsbury; the **Museum of London** is in the City; the **Wallace Collection** stands facing a leafy residential square in Marylebone, close to Oxford Street; and **Tate Britain** is located in Pimlico, adjacent to Victoria. South of the river, the **Imperial War Museum** and **Tate Modern** are a 20-minute walk apart in the boroughs of Lambeth and Bankside respectively.

Origins of the Collections

The roots of many of London's collections lie in the bequests of private collections from 18C and 19C figures from the arts, business and politics, including Henry Tate *(Tate Britain)*, Sir Hans Soane *(Natural History Museum and British Museum)* and Richard Wallace *(The Wallace Collection)*. Others have evolved through necessity or resourcefulness; the V&A was originally built to house the works created for the 1851 Great Exhibition, while in the 20C, the Tate turned a former power station in Bankside into the outstandingly successful display space for contemporary art that is the Tate Modern.

Highlights

1. Mummies and ancient Greek marbles at **The British Museum** (p292)
2. The **Museum of London**'s Galleries of Modern London (p303)
3. The Tudor Galleries at the **National Portrait Gallery** (p310)
4. The IMAX at the **Science Museum** (p317)
5. Contemporary installations in the **Tate Modern** (p325)

Visiting

With so many museums and galleries to visit, you'll be hard pressed to see even a fraction of them in a typical visit. The national museums have vast permanent collections, constantly invigorated by innovative temporary exhibitions that often tour internationally, and by exhibitions showcasing a part of cultural or historical achievement, thereby shedding new light and debate on a subject. Most major museums and galleries are subsidised and therefore free to visit *(though donations are much appreciated)*, continuing an ingrained tradition of culture. All of the establishments in this section offer a lively programme of talks and events for adults and children, as well as unique gift shops and places to eat and drink.

For further information on museums in London, www.culture24.org.uk is an excellent source.

The British Museum★★★

The British Museum is undoubtedly one of the finest institutions of the genre, and its treasures represent a vast canvas of the history of civilisation. It is an uplifting experience to view the rare artefacts, which reveal the ingenuity of man from early beginnings to the present day.

A BIT OF HISTORY

Foundation – The final spur to found the British Museum was supplied in 1753 when **Sir Hans Sloane**, the famous naturalist, bequeathed his collection to the nation. Parliament had already stored in vaults in Westminster a priceless collection of medieval manuscripts acquired in 1700. Elsewhere were documents collected by the Earls of Oxford, which were made available, and the old Royal Library was added by George II. A lottery raised the funds for the purchase of Montagu House, which opened in 1759.

Collections – Important acquisitions include: Sir William Hamilton's collection of antique vases *(1772)*; Egyptian antiquities, including the **Rosetta Stone** *(1802,* *see p 298*); the Townley Vase (1805); and the **Parthenon (Elgin) Marbles** *(1816,* *see p 296*).

Location: Map pp188–189. *Tottenham Court Road; Russell Square; Holborn.* The main entrance is on the south side off Great Russell Street; the Montague Place entrance is on the north side of the building.

Don't Miss: The Rosetta Stone; the Egyptian Mummies; the Parthenon frieze; the Portland Vase; the Easter Island Statue; the Lewis Chessmen. Galleries are open till 8.30pm every Friday evening.

Timing: Allow half a day for the must-sees across the entire museum. Obtain a floor plan at the Information desk located in the Great Court. Time permitting, join a 50min guided tour.

Kids: Hands-on desks in 6 galleries; Free Hamlyn family trails; Ford activity backpacks; the Samsung Digital Discovery Centre *(booking required)*; special children's multimedia guide.

Great Court, British Museum

Young visitors looking at Parthenon (Elgin) Marbles

© C. Ochterbeck/MICHELIN

In 1823, George IV presented his father's library of 65,000 volumes, 19,000 pamphlets, maps and charts; in 1824 came the Payne-Knight bequest of Classical antiquities, bronzes and drawings; in 1827 Banks' bequest of books, botanical specimens and ethnography.

Accommodation – In 1824 **Robert Smirke** was appointed to produce plans for a more permanent building that would replace the decayed Montagu House. The new building, with a Greek-inspired colonnaded façade surrounding the Great Court, was completed 20 years later. In 1857 the Reading Room was added at the centre of the Great Court; the Natural History departments were transferred to the new Natural History Museum in South Kensington in 1880–83. The Edward VII Galleries were added in 1914, and the Duveen Galleries opened in 1938. Further extensions were built in 1978 and 1991. In 1991 the British Library was moved to new, purpose-built premises in St Pancras *(See BLOOMSBURY)* prompting a massive redevelopment of the Museum.

VISIT

Great Russell Street. *Open daily 10am–5.30pm (until 8.30pm Fri).* *Closed 1 Jan, 24–26 Dec.* *No charge*

Ground Floor

1	Enlightenment Gallery
2–3	Special Exhibitions 2, 3 *(right of main entrance)*
4	Egypt
6-10	Middle East
34	Middle East (Islamic World)
6, 11–23	Greece and Rome
24	Living and Dying
26–27	Americas
33	Asia
33a	Asia (India)
33b	Asia (Chinese jade)
67	Asia (Korea, up the North stairs)
95	Asia (Chinese ceramics)

Lower Floor

25	Africa *(from Room 24)*
77–78	Greece and Roman architecture *(Room 21)*

Upper Floors

38–41, 45–51	Britain and Europe
52–59	Near East
61–66	Egypt
92–94	Asia (Japan)
68	Money
69–73	Greece and Rome
90	Prints and Drawings
35, 69a, 90–1	Special Exhibitions
34	Middle East (Islamic World)

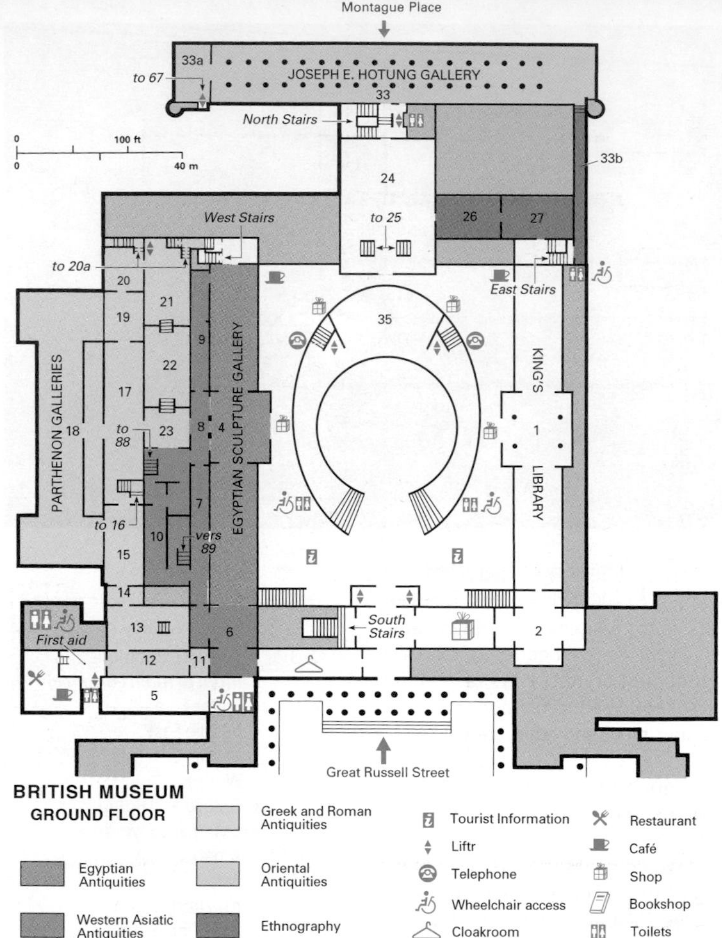

but donation appreciated. Multimedia guides available (10 languages; £5) and free talks. Family events and free activities for children. Restaurant, café, shops. Wheelchairs available for hire. ✆020 7323 8299 (general information). ✆020 7323 8181 (tickets). www.britishmuseum.org.

Great Court

The Great Court was an open, rather gloomy courtyard, filled with a huddle of uninspiring buildings until 2000, when the Museum's Millennium project roofed over the Great Court to create the largest covered square in Europe. Its soaring glass-and-steel roof, spanning the space to the Reading Room, is an architectural marvel, designed by **Sir Norman Foster**. Sculptures displayed in the public areas introduce the great civilisations and the Court has become the hub of the museum with cafés, information desks, several shops and a restaurant.

Reading Room

The circular **Reading Room** *(1857)* was designed to occupy the originally gloomy courtyard at the centre of the building. It was built by the architect **Sydney Smirke**, who used a sketch by librarian Antonio Panizzi. The Reading Room, with its splendid blue-and-gold dome, was restored in 1997. Currently

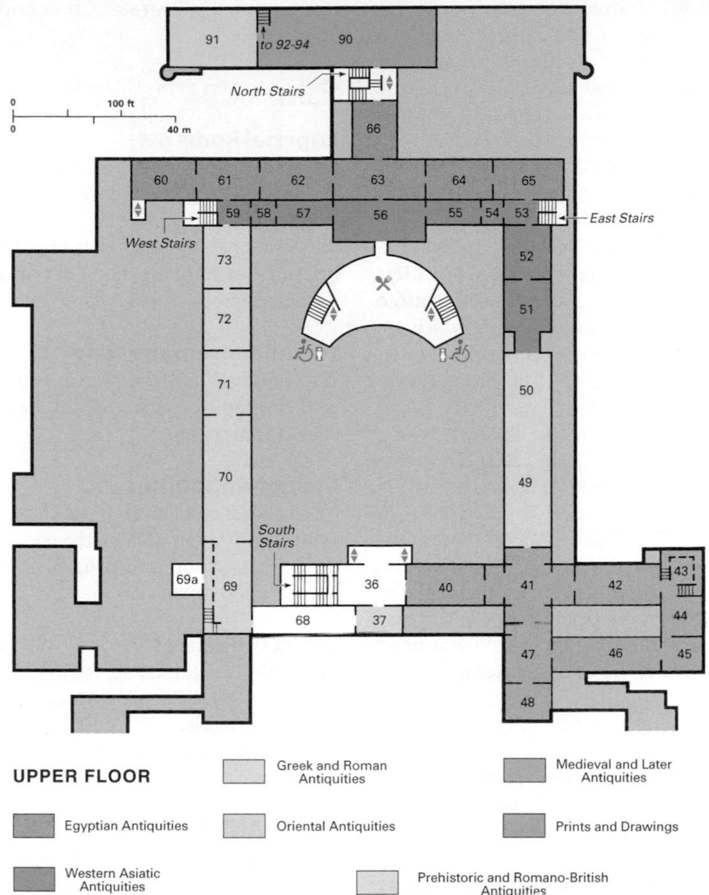

the Reading Room houses world-class temporary exhibitions.

The King's Library

Room 1, on the Great Court's east wall.

Built in 1827 to house the personal library of King George III, the King's Library is now known as the *Enlightenment Gallery*. Works highlight the seven disciplines of the age: natural history, archaeology, decipherment, art history, ethnography, religion and even the surprisingly interesting art of classification.

THE CLASSICAL COLLECTIONS

Ancient Greece and Rome

Prehistoric to Archaic Greece –

A distinctive civilisation flourished in the Cycladic Islands around 3200–1500 BC, which is characterised by marble figurines usually found in graves.

The influence of Minoan Crete spread throughout the Aegean in the Middle Bronze Age *(12)*, including the **Aigina Treasure**, which includes an elaborate gold pendant of a nature god. Early Greek vases *(13)* displayed narrative scenes drawn from mythology with geometric and "orientalising" motifs. Later, red-figured vases *(14)* from Athens depicted daily life and mythology.

5C BC – The bronze head of Apollo *(15)*, known as the **Chatsworth Head**, is a rare Classical statue. The **Temple of Apollo Epikourios** *(16)* depicts a lively battle between the Greeks and Amazons and the Lapiths and Centaurs *(420–400 BC)* and the reconstructed **Nereid Monument** *(17)* from Xantos in south-west Turkey has noted elegance.

The Parthenon Galleries *(18)* display the famous **Parthenon (Elgin) Marbles**, a collection of classical Greek marble sculptures and inscriptions, which are deemed to be the culmination of Hellenic art from the 5C BC and celebrate Athenian power and wealth. The taking of these treasures for display in Britain *(1801–12)* has always been hotly disputed and in mid-2009, days before the opening of the new Acropolis Museum in Athens, a major dispute erupted over "ownership" when the Athens museum asserted its right to house the artefacts, which came from Greece in the first place. A resolution has still not been reached. The **Caryatid Room** *(19)* displays sculptures from the Acropolis in Athens *(430–400 BC)*.

4C BC – The **Payava Tomb** from Lycian Xantos *(c.360 BC) (20)*, on the Mediterranean coast of Turkey, is typical of the local style of funerary monuments. The **Mausoleum of Halikarnassos** *(21)*, one of the Seven Wonders of the World, is the origination of the noun "mausoleum". Admire also the sculpted column *(22)* from the **Temple of Artemis at Ephesos** with striking figured decoration.

Hellenistic art *(23)* is highly theatrical and stresses individual traits; note the sensuous marble statue of Aphrodite.

Greek and Roman architecture and sculpture are displayed in the lower-floor galleries reached from *room 21*.

Fragments of ancient Greek and Roman buildings abound *(77)* and inscriptions *(78)*, while *room 82* is mainly dedicated to fragments of the **Temple of Artemis of Ephesos**.

Rooms 83–84 contain a wealth of Roman sculpture, including the **Townley Vase**. *Room 85* houses Roman portrait sculptures. *Room 69* illustrates Greek and Roman daily life.

South stairs to the Upper floor.

Imperial Rome *(70)*

This room spans over a thousand years of Roman history. The bronze **Head of Augustus** is remarkable. Take note of the intentional mutilation on the **Basalt bust of Germanicus**. The **Portland Vase** is a famous cameo-glass vessel.

Pre-Roman Empire Italy *(71)*

The sophistication of the Etruscan world is illustrated by black lustrous ware known as *bucchero*.

Cypriot Antiquities *(72)*

A rich collection of artefacts illustrates Cypriot civilisation up until the end of the Roman period: **sculptures**, gold jewellery and ceramics.

Greek Influences *(73)*

Greek cities established colonies in southern Italy, evidenced by the fine red-figured bowls, bronze figurines *(fine bronze horseman c.550 BC)* and funerary artefacts.

COINS AND MEDALS

Room 68 illustrates the development of money and its importance from early 3C BC Aes ingots, 4C Raffia cloth currency to today's plastic cards.

PREHISTORY AND ROMAN BRITAIN

Prehistoric to Celtic Britain

In the Early Bronze Age *(51)* fine pottery with geometric patterns contained rich grave goods in burials such as the **Folkton Drums**.

Celtic art flourished in the Iron Age *(50)*. Note the elegant **Basse-Yutz wine-flagons** *(c.400 BC)* from France.

Roman Britain *(49)*

Highlights include the **Mildenhall Treasure** and the **Hoxne Hoard**, which comprises thousands of coins, jewellery and silver plate, two of the finest treasure troves found in Britain.

MEDIEVAL, RENAISSANCE AND MODERN COLLECTIONS FOREIGN INFLUENCES

Among Anglo-Saxon and Norman antiquities *(4C–11C)* found in the British Isles *(41)* is the **Sutton Hoo Ship Burial**, which shows the rich variety of artefacts retrieved from a royal tomb in Suffolk. The mid-12C **Lewis Chessmen** *(40)*, thought to be Scandinavian in origin, consist of 80 pieces carved from walrus ivory; they were found in 1831 in the Outer Hebrides. Clocks, watches and precision regulators *(38–9)* trace the evolution of mechanical timekeeping highlighted by the fascinating Prague-made **Galleon Clock** *(c.1585)* with figures moving to music as the ship pitches and rolls, and a firing gun. The **Waddesdon Bequest** *(45)* includes a reliquary for a thorn from Christ's crown made for the Duc de Berry *(c.1400–10)*.

European Applied Arts

A glittering array *(46)* illustrates the craft of goldsmithing from 1400–1800: the **Armada Service**, a silver dinner set from the Tudor period; Limoges and Battersea enamels; Huguenot silver. The 19C *(47)* is represented by European ceramics such as The **Pegasus Vase**. The Modern Gallery *(48)* is dedicated to decorative arts of the 20C: examples are continuously acquired and include work by **Marianne Brandt** and Eliel Saarinen.

EGYPTIAN ANTIQUITIES

Start on the Ground floor.

Egyptian Sculpture Gallery *(4)*

Pride of place is given to the **Rosetta Stone** (*see box*). The monumental sculptures are of great historical interest, primarily the colossal head of Amenhotep III *(c.1350 BC)*. The granite bust of Ramesses II *(c.1250 BC)* exudes power.

Egyptian Tombs *(62–3, Upper floor)*

Mummies bandaged in cases and coffins, gilded and painted, include the preserved remains of humans and animals, too.

Early Egypt and Ethiopia

(64–66)

These galleries explore Egypt's relationship with neighbouring Nubia and the introduction of Coptic Orthodox Christianity.

ANCIENT NEAR EAST

Turn left from the main entrance.

Assyrian Sculpture *(6–10)*

Fabled kings built splendid palaces lavishly decorated in Nimrud, Khorsabad and Nineveh. Note the five feet of the Colossal stone statues of human-headed **winged lions** *(6)*.

The **friezes of lion hunting** *(10)* from the Northern Palace of Nineveh are striking in their depictions of an ancient royal sport.

Arabic World

Antiquities from the Islamic collections range from decorative pottery, carved and mosaic glass to inlaid and engraved metalwork. Admire the colourful **Damascus** and **Iznik** ceramics *(34)* and the Damascene geomantic instrument. The South Arabian territories *(North and South Yemen)* prospered along an important incense trading route. Alabaster sculptures and calcite incense burners are on display *(53)*.

Ancient Iran *(52)*

The fabulous **Oxus Treasure** *(5C–4C BC)* attests to the wealth and sophistication of the Achaemenid court. The **Cyrus cylinder** from Persepolis *(539–530 BC)* records the declaration of the reforms promised by King Cyrus.

Ancient Turkey and Iraq *(54)*

Antiquities *(5500–300 BC)* of Anatolia reveal Assyrian influence: note in particular the bronze figure of a winged bull from Urartu.

Mesopotamia *(55–56)*

This illustrates the arts and daily life of the Sumerians and Babylonians. The **Flood Tablet** tells a story from the Epic of Gilgamesh.

An Important Find

The **Rosetta Stone** is part of a 6ft/1.8m block of black basalt found at Rashid, or Rosetta, in the western Egyptian Delta region and retrieved by French soldiers on campaign there during the Napoleonic wars. With the Capitulation of Alexandria in 1801, the French were compelled to surrender the stone to the British, and it went on show at the British Museum in 1802. Its significance rests in the parallel transcriptions in Ancient Greek and two written forms of Egyptian of a decree passed on 27 March 196 BC: thereby the French Egyptologist, Champollion, was able to decipher pictorial hieroglyphs in use since the third millennium BC and the linguistics of Demotic texts formalised in 643 BC.

The Ancient Levant *(57–59)*

Syrian civilisation flourished during the third and second millennium BC. An impressive statue of King Idrimi *(16C BC)* is in an austere and simplistic style. Ancient Palestine was an important trading centre and the Phoenicians established themselves in the Mediterranean, exemplified by a fine collection of ivories that includes a delicately carved plaque of a lion killing a boy *(9C–8C BC)*.

ETHNOGRAPHY

The **Wellcome Trust Gallery of Living and Dying** *(24)* explores how humanity handles life and death. The room is dominated by **Hoa Hakananai'a**, a moai from Easter Island. The quartz **crystal skull** *(19C)* is fascinating.

Americas

Exhibits in *room 26* illustrate the life of the Native peoples of North America and the effect of European influence. *Room 27* is devoted to important civilisations of Mesoamerica before the Spanish Conquest.

Africa *(25, lower floor)*

The collections reflect the vitality and diversity of Africa. Highlights include the magnificent 16C **Benin bronzes**, a brass head, masks and carvings from Nigeria; Asante **goldwork** from Ghana and 16C Afro-Portuguese **ivories**.

PRINTS AND DRAWINGS *(90)*

This room hosts special exhibitions from the extensive collection of prints and drawings, including works by Rembrandt, Michelangelo and Raphael.

ASIA

Start on the ground floor.

China, India, South and Southeast Asia *(33, 33a and 33b)*

Chinese bronzes, exquisite jades and ceramics that became mass-produced and diffused throughout Asia to the West are marks of this collection. Early **Buddhist art** from Gandhara *(modern Pakistan)* reflects the prolific generation of followers from the 5C BC.

Korea *(67)*

Korea's arts were marked by the Chinese and Buddhist traditions such as the frontispiece of an **Amitabha Sutra manuscript** *(1341)*. From 15C on, Confucianism is illustrated through portraiture.

Japan *(92–94, Upper floor)*

Society was strictly regulated and its complexity is reflected in the arts. Note the set of splendid **Momoyama period armour** *(late 16C)*.

ADDRESSES

LIGHT BITE

Gallery Café – *Ground floor, past the cloakroom and room 4. Daily 11am–5pm.* Relaxed, family-friendly café serving hearty hot meals and a range of snacks, sweet and savoury.

Imperial War Museum★★★

The Imperial War Museum is fascinating, even for those with no real interest in military history: the social stories are compelling. The galleries are currently undergoing transformation, with brand new exhibition space being created in order to mark the centenary of the outbreak of World War I in 2014.

- **Location:** Map pp 256–257. ⊖*Lambeth North.* The museum is a short walk from the Tube station and well-signposted.
- **Don't Miss:** The sobering Holocaust Exhibition; the Family in Wartime exhibition; and the powerful World War galleries (reopening in 2014).
- **Timing:** Arrive early as there is a lot to see and leave at least an hour to visit the Holocaust Exhibition alone.
- **Kids:** The major new family exhibition **Horrible Histories®: Spies** has plenty to entertain children.

A BIT OF HISTORY

The museum, of what Churchill termed "the Age of Violence", was founded in 1917, principally through the efforts of **Sir Alfred Mond**, who stated in the opening ceremony that the museum "was not a monument of military glory, but a record of toil and sacrifice".

In 1936 the museum was moved to the present building, which stands on the site of a 19C psychiatric hospital known as Bedlam.

The white obelisk milestone at St George's Circus leading to the museum commemorates Brass Crosby, Lord Mayor of London in 1771, who refused to convict a printer for publishing parliamentary debates. Crosby was imprisoned in the Tower, but was freed thanks to the demands of the populace. Thereafter press reporting of Commons' proceedings was inaugurated.

VISIT

Lambeth Road. ⊖Lambeth North. The museum is currently undergoing a refurbishment of all of its galleries. Since completion is scheduled for July 2013 (except World War galleries), after publication of this guide, the description below reflects gallery content before the renovation. Please check the website for the latest information. Open daily 10am–6pm (last admission 5pm). Closed 24–26 Dec. No charge,

Majestic Imperial War Museum

The Sopwith Camel, a World War I single-seat biplane

© Imperial War Museum

except for some special exhibitions. Parking for the disabled. Leaflet (3 languages). Audio-guide. Café. ☎020 7416 5000. www.iwm.org.uk.
The museum in no sense glorifies war, but honours those who served and looks at the social history surrounding British wars from 1914 to the present day. Two British **15-inch naval guns**, used in action during World War II, command the main gate and to the side stands a piece of the **Berlin Wall**.

Military Weapons

(Ground floor)
The wide range of weapons and equipment on display in the **Large Exhibits Gallery** encompass World War I to the present day. Highlights of World War I weapons include a 4-inch gun from the destroyer **HMS Lance**, which fired the first British shot of World War I. The increasing importance of tank development to break the deadlock of trench warfare is exemplified by the **Mark V Tank** *(1918)*.

A **Supermarine Spitfire Mark IA**, which saw action in the Battle of Britain, represents one of the iconic weapons from World War II. The **Tamzine** is the smallest surviving craft used in the Dunkirk evacuation of May 1940. The intensity of bombing raids on the civilian population can be seen by the enormous **V2 rocket**, over 6,500 weapons of this kind which descended on London. The V2 could not be intercepted once launched.

The **M3A3 Grant tank** was famously used by Field Marshal Montgomery during the Battle of El Alamein *(see Lord Monty p 301)*.

The **Submarines** gallery includes interactive displays such as listening to underwater sounds in solar stations and using a periscope.

Of interest to note is the resplendent **Brough Superior Motorcycle**, owned by TE Lawrence of Arabia, in front of the **Cinema**.

First World War Galleries

(Closed until 2014.)
The **Origins and Outbreak of the War** looks at the complex shift of power and colliding national ambitions in Europe that led to the conflict.

The **Western Front** includes equipment and personal belongings of the men in the trenches. There is also a model of the front detailing the battlefront and also road signs that were used to name the trenches themselves.

War in the Air explains the growing importance of air reconnaisance and the pilot aces who made a name for themselves.

The **War on Other Fronts** details the conflicts in the Balkans, Turkey, Russia and Egypt.

The **Home Front** details the effects on civilian life that ensued, such as food rationing and the employment of women in industrial jobs.

The **Inter-War Years**, located in the central corridor of this floor, explores the rise of the Nazi Dictatorship in 1933 and the end of Britain's Appeasement policy in 1939.

Second World War Galleries

(Closed until 2014.)

The Blitz Experience reconstructs an air raid shelter and a blitzed street in 1940s Britain, complete with sights, sounds and atmospheric effects to evoke the sensation of being caught up in a bombing raid.

The Blitzkrieg highlights the German attacks on Scandinavia and Western Europe, and the escape of British and French troops at the Dunkirk evacuation in 1940.

The Battle of Britain details, through archive footage and exhibits, the British victory over the German Luftwaffe which indefinitely postponed Hitler's plans to invade Britain.

The Home Front 1940–45 shows how civilians coped in a world of rationing and bomb shelters through sustained aeriel bombardment. Exhibits include bomb shelter permits, produce such as powdered eggs and evocative photographs showing Londoners using underground platforms to evade the bombs.

The War at Sea 1939–45 describes the conflict between German U-Boats and the Allied merchant shipping they targeted. Britain's dependence on imports underlined the importance of stopping them.

The Mediterranean and the Middle East gallery chronicles the conflict in North Africa, the Montgomery's victory over Rommel at El Alamein and the success of Operation Torch, led by Eisenhower.

The Eastern Front 1941–45 shows how Hitler used a Blitzkreig offensive against the Russians and the comprehensive Russian victory at Stalingrad, which drove the Germans out of Russian territory.

Europe under the Nazis recounts the exploitation of conquered territories and how resistance movements carried out a guerrilla war against Nazi Germany.

Lord Monty

Bernard Montgomery *(1887–1976)*, led the Allies to victory at the Battle of El Alamein *(1942)*, one of the turning points of World War II. He inspired loyalty and great belief in his troops. His documents and medals in the exhibition show how he became one of the great battlefield commanders.

The Bomber Offensive marks out Air Marshal Harris' bombing of German cities to destroy morale and disrupt their production lines. This led to the controversial destruction of Dresden, with thousands of civilian deaths.

North West Europe recounts the D-Day Landings, the assault through Normandy and the Low Countries to the subsequent defeat of Hitler. Exhibits include the signed *Instrument of Surrender* dated 4 May 1945.

The **War in the Far East** outlines the Allied war aginst Japan, which started with the Japanese attack on Pearl Harbor in 1941. The turning point came with their defeat at the Battle of Midway in 1942 before the atomic bombs on Hiroshima *(6 August 1945)* and Nagasaki *(9 August 1945)* brought about the end of the conflict.

Conflicts since 1945

(Lower ground floor)

This is a gallery dedicated to wars since 1945, encompassing Post-war Britain, the Falklands War, the Cold War, right up to the First Gulf War. Displays include firearms and uniforms, along with audiovisual displays to emphasise the key events from each major conflict, including the Suez Crisis and the Vietnam War. There is also a permanent exhibition dedicated to the exploits of Field Marshal Montgomery, entitled **Monty: Master of the Battlefield**, opened to coincide with the 60th anniversary of the Battle of El Alamein *(see Lord Monty p 301)*.

Secret War
(First floor)
This compelling exhibition details the clandestine world of Britain's government agencies, MI5 and MI6, as well as the elite special forces, such as the Special Air Service and the Long Range Desert Group.
Film footage shows reconstructions of operations and training methods undertaken by these groups. Exhibits include SOE sabotage devices and bottles of invisible ink used by Germans during World War I.

VE Day Revellers
© Imperial War Museum

The Lord Ashcroft Gallery

(First floor)
This new gallery is dedicated to winners of the **Victoria Cross** and the **George Cross**, Britain's highest medals for gallantry. These are accompanied by the inspiring stories of the recipients and the sacrifices each individual made in conflicts from the Crimean War to recent battlefields in Iraq and Afghanistan.

Art Galleries
(Second floor)
The **Art Gallery** and the nearby **John Singer Sargent Room** contain paintings and sculptures from the museum's collection of World War I and II art works. The emphasis is on the individual's lot in war: food queues, people sleeping in tube shelters, the wounded, service life and boredom.
The artists covered are some of the most well known from their age: **Percy Wyndham Lewis**, **Paul Nash**, **Henry Moore** and **Graham Sutherland**. One of the most well-known paintings is *Gassed (c.1918)* by **John Singer Sargent**, displayed in the **Sargent Room**. It is a powerful portrayal of war on the front line.
There are also regular special exhibitions covering everything from children at war to 1940s fashion, such as **Legacy**, a film and photography installation about the long-term effects of The Troubles in Northern Ireland.

Holocaust Exhibition
(Third floor. Please note: not recommended for children under 14 years of age.)
The exhibition uses historical material to recall this sombre part of history, from the rise of the Nazi Party and the perversion of Nazi race theory to its full-blown euthanasia policies. Artefacts on display document personal tales of persecution and resistance that are amplified by the silence in the gallery itself. Notable exhibits include a funeral cart from the Warsaw Ghetto, a deportation railcar that visitors can enter and a wagon used to heave labourers in a concentration camp.

ADDRESSES

LIGHT BITE

Museum Café – *Ground floor, left-hand side. Daily 10am–5.30pm.* Fresh, seasonal food cooked on the premises. A good place for afternoon tea and cakes.

Museum of London★★

A city with such a long, varied and vibrant history as London needs a world-class museum to tell its story and the Museum of London more than lives up to this task. Chronicling the tale of the capital's turbulent and never-dull past, the nine permanent galleries here begin in prehistoric times and continue right through to the third millennium, presenting artefacts from all time periods in an engaging way, using both traditional and multi-media displays.

Location: Map pp 216–217. ⊖*Barbican*. The museum is a short walk from the Tube station up Aldersgate Street.

Don't Miss: The recently refurbished Galleries of Modern London.

Timing: Allow at least three hours and visit during the week when the galleries are quieter.

Kids: Childrens' events on Sundays and during school holidays.

A BIT OF HISTORY

The Guildhall Museum first opened in 1826 in the City of London, concerning itself primarily with archaeological artefacts: its first acquisition was a fragment of Roman mosaic from nearby Tower Street. The London Museum, founded in 1912, first opened at Kensington Palace before moving to new premises in Lancaster House.

During World War II both museums were forced to close, not reopening until the 1950s. In 1965 the Museum of London Act amalgamated the two and formed the new museum. The original building, designed by Powell & Moya, opened in 1976. In 2003, a massive redevelopment by award-winning architects Wilkinson Eyre added a new entrance canopy, a special exhibits gallery and a museum shop. In 2010 the museum unveiled the new **Galleries of Modern London** – a multi-million pound transformation of several existing galleries as well as the newly constructed state-of-the-art **Clore Learning Centre**, designed by the same architectural firm.

VISIT

150 London Wall, London EC2Y 5HN. Open daily 10am–6pm. Closed 24–26 Dec. Free gallery tours daily 11am (not Sat), noon, 3pm and 4pm. No charge. 020 7001 9844. www.museumoflondon.org.uk.

This museum comprehensively and entertainingly tells of London's turbulent past from prehistory to today.

The museum operates a team of archaeologists specialising in urban excavation; this allows sites to be dug with the co-operation of building developers – work is undertaken to restricted timeframes before great concrete foundations are irrevocably sunk through the layers of history. Over the long term, digs have revealed a broad range of artefacts which, classified and compared to other flora, fauna, bone, wood, ceramic, glass or metal finds, provide a reliable record of London and its inhabitants through the ages and ravages of war, fire, flood and plague. Many of these form the basis of the collection.

Displays are organised into galleries of bays according to time and theme, from prehistory to the present day. Throughout, impressive interactive technology abounds. There are regular special events, including walking tours of the area, and an excellent branch museum: the **Museum of London Docklands** (*see entry p 288*).

The Galleries

The museum begins with **London Before London**, a gallery which focuses on the prehistoric Thames Valley, from 450,000BC to the arrival of the Romans in AD50. The remains of a 5,000-year-old woman, the skull of a now-extinct

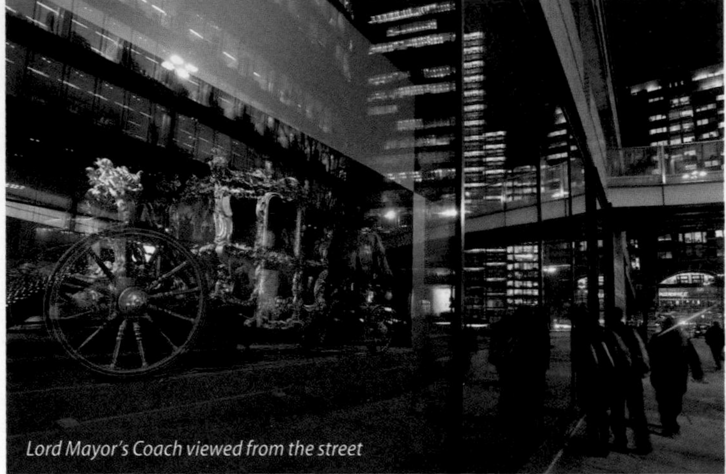
Lord Mayor's Coach viewed from the street

©Museum of London

auroch (wild ox) and a 6,000-year-old ceremonial axehead are all on display here.

Next on the timeline, the **Roman London** gallery explores the foundation and rise of the city they called Londinium. Note the marble sculptures from the temple of Mithras.

The **Medieval** *(410–1558)* galleries are home to items from everyday life, such as beakers, clothing and children's toys, along with a reconstruction of an Anglo-Saxon house.

The turbulent 16C and 17C are brought to life in **War, Plague and Fire**, which features displays on the Black Death and Fire of London; while **Expanding City** *(1666–1850s)* details the rapid growth undergone by the city after the fire. Don't miss the **Wellclose Square prison cell**, an original from the 18C, which visitors can step inside. Note the graffiti.

By the 1850s London was the world's wealthiest city and population growth was out of control. The **People's City** *(1850s–1940s)* gallery explores the issues dogging the city at this time, including poverty, worker's and women's rights; also the approach of war. Highlights include Charles Booth's poverty maps and a stunning Art Deco lift from Selfridge's department store.

The museum brings visitors up to date in **World City: 1950s–today**, a gallery devoted to modern London. Items reflecting domestic and social change such as TVs, computers and miniskirts can be seen here, alongside multi-media displays which question the future and debate the issues affecting London today.

Perhaps the highlight of the museum is the **Lord Mayor's Coach**. Now over 250 years old, it is located in the new **City Gallery**, which opens up the building's ground floor and allows the museum, and the coach, to be seen from the street for the very first time.

ADDRESSES

LIGHT BITE

benugo, *Entrance hall. www.benugo.com. Daily 10am–5.30pm.* Hot and cold lunches, sandwiches, salads and cakes – all made from fresh, locally sourced ingredients – either to eat in or to take away.

London Wall Bar and Kitchen – *150 London Wall. Mon–Fri 11am–11pm, Sun noon–6pm.* Located immediately outside the museum entrance, this stylish, yet relaxed bar and restaurant serves a menu of all-day British classics, plus a good wine list and expertly mixed cocktails. The terrace is a rarity in this part of the city.

National Gallery★★★

The focal point of Trafalgar Square is the popular National Gallery, one of the highlights of the capital. Stand on the portico to enjoy a fine perspective of the Square and a lovely vista along Whitehall to the Houses of Parliament. The collection is one of the finest in the world and represents the best in all European schools.

- **Location:** Map pp 92–93. ⊖*Charing Cross.* The gallery is well served by public transport and is conveniently situated near Leicester Square, Piccadilly Circus and Charing Cross.
- **Don't Miss:** Leonardo da Vinci's *The Burlington House Cartoon*, Rembrandt's self portraits, portraits of *Bathers* by Cézanne and Seurat, Van Gogh's *Sunflowers*, the Impressionist Collection and works saved for the nation with the gallery's help.
- **Timing:** After a visit to the gallery, it is a short walk to the cinemas, theatres, bars and clubs in the West End.
- **Kids:** Interactive story sessions and art workshops on Sundays.

A BIT OF HISTORY

Origins – The collection was founded by parliamentary purchase in 1824, with the intent of offering the wonders of art to all and to inspire young artists. The nucleus was 38 pictures assembled by financier **John Julius Angerstein**, which included works by Rubens, Claude, Rembrandt and Hogarth, displayed at his residence at 100 Pall Mall.

Move to Trafalgar Square – Completed in Trafalgar Square in 1838, the new building designed by **William Wilkins** on the site of the Royal Mews provides an architectural climax to the Square with the great portico composed of Corinthian columns.

During World War II the collection was evacuated to Wales, but every month one painting was exhibited in London.

The **Sainsbury Wing**, designed by Robert Venturi, was opened in 1991. Between 2004 and 2006, the East Wing Project made the building accessible at street level and restored the ceiling decoration in the Staircase Hall.

Collection – There are now more than 2,300 paintings in the collection, hung in

National Gallery

PLANNING YOUR VISIT

Trawling through a large museum can be both exhilarating and exhausting. If you are pressed for time, choose a **favourite period in history**, and focus on that. The Gallery floorplan can recommend highlights to view. Browsing, however, will allow you to discover unfamiliar images and perhaps provide you with some new "favourites".

Gallery Floor Plan – This is available from the entrance foyers for £1.

Books – The National Gallery has an extensive bookshop selling general and specialist publications on the fine arts, cards, slides and posters.

Website – The Gallery's entire collection is described on the website, with background information on both the artists and their subjects.

Audio Guides – The main audio guide has key information on over **1,000 paintings**. Various themed tours covering about 40 paintings each are also available in several languages. There are also special children's trails *(paper and audio)*.

Special Exhibitions – Major exhibitions are held in the **Sainsbury Wing** (Level -2) and are usually ticketed; other temporary exhibitions take place in the Sunley Room and Room 1, usually free of charge.

Special Note – The National Gallery stays **open until 9pm on Friday evenings.**

a loose chronological order from the early Renaissance to French Impressionism. Because individual works are occasionally rehung or on loan, room locations given below cannot be guaranteed.

VISIT

Trafalgar Square. Open Sat–Thu 10am–6pm, Fri 10am–9pm. Closed 1 Jan, 24–26 Dec. No charge, except for special exhibitions. Guided tour (1hr): daily 11.30am, 2.30pm (and 7pm on Fri), from the Sainsbury Wing Information Desk. Themed Audio guides for hire (12 languages).
Children's trails (printed and audio-guides) available. Family activities every Sun. Gallery floor plan. Restaurant (Sainsbury Wing). Café and Espresso Bar (Getty Entrance). Shops.
No photography. 020 7747 2885. www.nationalgallery.org.uk.

13C - 15C PAINTINGS

Sainsbury Wing

Rooms 51–66 present the development of naturalism and show how gilding was used for more stylised depictions.

Giotto is considered the forefather of Renaissance painting. The *Wilton Diptych (Room 53)* was painted for Richard II by an unknown French or English artist, with examples of elaborate sgraffito gilding contrasting with the ultramarine blues of the Virgin and angels. **Masaccio** uses light to cast shadows and mould three-dimensional form (*Virgin and Child)*.

Uccello *(Room 54)* employs linear perspective to create an illusion of depth in his *Battle of San Romano*. Note also **Fra Filippo Lippi**'s masterly *Annunciation*.

Jan van Eyck *(Room 56)* uses light to convey intimacy and space in the *Arnolfini Portrait*. Note the reflections in the mirror.

Rooms 57–59 display the Venetian **Crivelli** *(The Annunciation, with St Emidius)*, a master of perspective in his time, and **Botticelli**, the master of line *(Room 58)*. His *Venus and Mars* is a sensuous portayal of love conquering war. Master of the Umbrian School, **Perugino** *(Room 60)* learned the art of colour from Piero della Francesca and taught **Raphael** *(Portrait of Pope Julius II, Room 8)* to endow his figures with grace and poise. His style evolved into the epitome of the High Renaissance.

Mantegna *(Rooms 61–62)* studied the arts of Antiquity; note the construction in his *Agony in the Garden*. Compare this with his brother-in-law **Bellini**'s more realistic work of the same name. He perfected the use of oil paint, using it

to capture rich tones of colour and light: *The Doge Leonardo Loredan*.
The Baptism of Christ, originally the central section of a polyptych, by **Piero della Francesca** *(Room 66)*, uses composition to emphasise the serenity of the event.

16C PAINTINGS

West Wing
Playful gestures and softness, as in *The Madonna and Child with Saints* by **Parmigianino**, hint at the advent of Mannerism, which eventually develops into elongated forms and contorted positions. *Room 2* houses **Leonardo da Vinci**'s *Virgin of the Rocks (the first version is in the Louvre)* and his fragile preparatory *Burlington House Cartoon*, representing two ageless images of mothers with their young sons.
Holbein's *The Ambassadors (Room 4; stand to the right to view the distorted skull)* is filled with symbolism. In his *Cupid Complaining to Venus*, **Cranach the Elder** aims to convey a moral message: "life's pleasure is mixed with pain". Distinctive styles are represented by **Michelangelo**'s monumental but incomplete *The Entombment* and **Raphael**'s *The Madonna of the Pinks (8)*, a small devotional picture intended for personal contemplation. *Rooms 9–10* are dedicated to the **Venetian School**. **Titian**'s *Bacchus and Ariadne* depicts Bacchus leaping from his chariot. Bacchus raised Ariadne to heaven and turned her into a constellation, represented by the crown of stars.
Lorenzo Lotto's *Portrait of Giovanni della Volta with his Wife and Children* presents an ideal family *(Central Hall)*, while the intricate detail of **Jan Gossaert** 's *Adoration of the Kings (Room 14)*, affirms the message of Christ's birth.

17C PAINTINGS

North Wing
Works by **Claude** and **Turner** are exhibited together *(15)*. This was a special concession for Turner, who specified in his will that his *Sun Rising Through Vapour* and *Dido Building Carthage* should be hung with *Seaport with the Embarkation of the Queen of Sheba* and *Landscape with the Marriage of Isaac and Rebekah* by Claude.
The *Peepshow* by the Dutch painter **Samuel van Hoogstraten** is an interesting curiosity *(Room 25)*.
Claude *(Room 20)* painted peaceful coastal scenes at sunset with mythological subjects. His *Enchanted Castle* is said to have influenced Keats' "Ode to a Nightingale".
Poussin's *(Room 19)* Classical style was inspired by the poets of Antiquity, as seen by *Cephalus and Aurora*.
Cuyp's *River Landscape with Horseman and Peasants* is a beautiful example of a Dutch landscape *(Room 21)*. The **Dutch School** also includes **Hobbema** *(The*

Detail of *Jean de Dinteville and Georges de Selve (The Ambassadors)* (1533) by Hans Holbein

Avenue at Middelharnis) and **Ruysdael** *(River Scene)*, who depict various aspects of the landscape *(Room 16)*. Several of **Rembrandt**'s classics hang in *Rooms 23–24*, such as *Belshazzar's Feast, A Woman Bathing in a Stream, Portrait of Margaretha de Geer, Wife of Jacob Trip* and *Self Portrait at the Age of 34*.
Vermeer *(Room 25)* specialised in tranquil domestic scenes: *A Young Woman Standing at a Virginal (c.1670)* is a particularly fine example.
Rubens *(Room 29)* displayed skill in all genres: *Samson and Delilah, Portrait of Susanna Lunden* and *The Judgement of Paris*. The master of the **Spanish School** *(Room 30)* was **Velázquez**, who evolved a strong portrait style under royal patronage: *The Rokeby Venus* and *Philip IV of Spain in Brown and Silver*.
Van Dyck *(Room 31)* is the supreme master of portraiture in a grand confident style: *Equestrian Portrait of Charles I*.
Intense drama animates pictures of the **Baroque**, none more so than **Caravaggio** *(Room 32)*. Intensity comes alive in his use of highlights and shadows *(chiaroscuro)*. *The Supper at Emmaus* depicts a beardless Jesus. Note how the basket of fruit teeters on the edge, showing off the artist's illusionistic skills.

18C – EARLY-20C PAINTINGS

East Wing

Drouais' portrait of *Madame de Pompadour at her Tambour Frame* depicts the famous patron of the **Rococo** style *(Room 33)*, which emphasised curves and delicate colour. *Pan and Syrinx* by **Boucher** is an example of this. Also note *Self Portrait in a Straw Hat*, **Vigée Le Brun**'s take on Rubens, by the famous female painter of the 18C.
The **British School** *(Room 34)* at its height *(see Introduction to London – Painting)* is exemplified by *Anne, 2nd Countess of Albemarle* **(Reynolds)**; *The Fighting Temeraire* **(Turner)** and *The Hay Wain* **(Constable)**. *Whistlejacket* by **George Stubbs** is a wonderfully realistic portrait of a racehorse.
William Hogarth's moralising series *Marriage A-la-Mode* is displayed in *Room 35*, along with *Mr and Mrs Andrews* by **Gainsborough**, considered the masterpiece of his early years.
Canaletto *(Room 38)* was the Venetian master of sparkling landscape painting *(note the waves)*. *The Stonemason's Yard* is one of his finest paintings.
Guardi and **Goya** *(Room 39)* were two quite distinctive masters. Guardi's paintings are full of atmosphere, while Goya's portraits are character studies.
Neoclassicism *(Room 41)* was a counter-reaction to the *ancien régime*. **Delaroche**'s *The Execution of Lady Jane Grey* dominates the room.
Wagner's German Romanticism is transposed into paint, as exemplified by *Winter Landscape* by **Friedrich** *(Room 42)*. Depictions of modern life and atmospheric effects are the trademarks

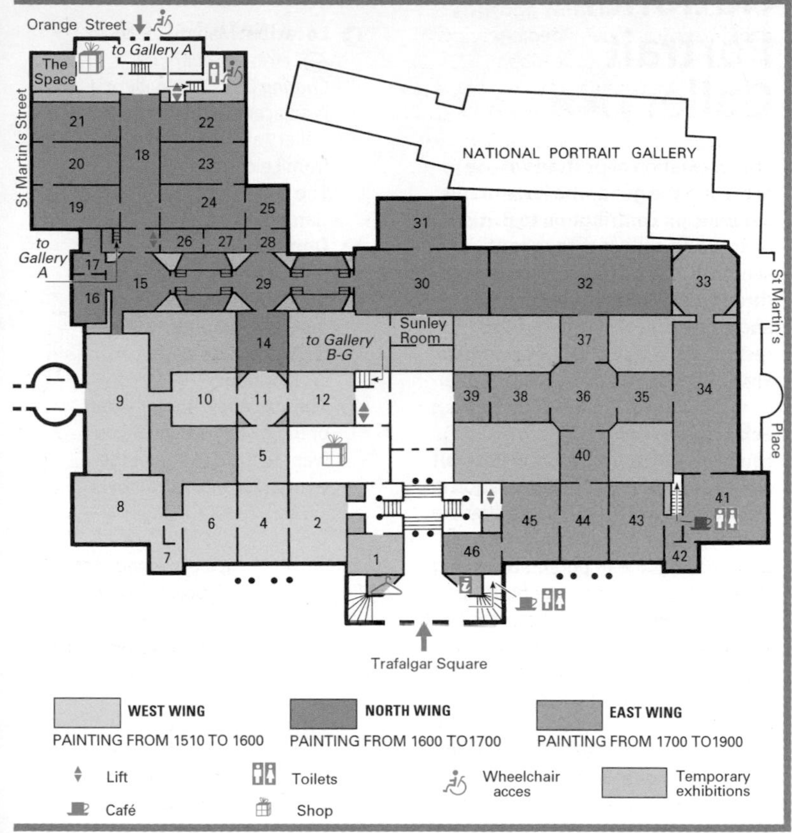

of **Impressionism** and beyond *(Rooms 43–44)*. The transient quality of light is carefully explored and captured in outdoor scenes by **Renoir** *(The Skiff)*, **Seurat** *(Bathers at Asnières*; radiant with his pointillist technique*)* and **Monet** *(Bathers at La Grenouillère*, a sketch he produced possibly for a larger canvas, now lost), or in a celebration of industrialisation by **Pissarro** *(The Boulevard Montmartre at Night)*.

In *Room 45*, **Rousseau**'s *Surprised!* combines elaborate patterns with the exotic; **Cézanne**'s *Bathers (Les Grandes Baigneuses)* inspired Cubism; and **Van Gogh**'s famous *Sunflowers* captivates the room with its thick yellow brush-strokes. In *Room 46* enjoy the fiery reds of *La Coiffure* by **Degas**.

ADDRESSES

LIGHT BITE

Espresso Bar – *Level 0. Sat–Thur 10am–5.30pm, Fri 10am–8.45pm.* Self-service coffee bar serving a full range of hot drinks plus a selection of baguettes, pastries and cakes. The ArtStart touchscreen system means you can browse the collection while you relax.

National Café – *St Martin's Place. Mon–Fri 8am–11pm, Sat 9am–11pm, Sun 9am–6pm.* Breakfast, lunch and dinner are served at this modern café, which has its own entrance, separate from the museum. The grab-and-go self-service area is great for picking up a sandwich while sightseeing; the European menu features soups, salads and hearty main meals.

National Portrait Gallery★★

The fascination of portraits of the great and the good who have made a significant contribution to British history and culture throughout the centuries is irresistible. Wander through the gallery at leisure and enjoy a meal in the roof-top restaurant, which offers a wonderful vista over the West End.

- **Location:** Map pp 92–93. *⊖Leicester Square; Charing Cross.* The gallery is adjacent to the National Gallery and a short walk from Leicester Square, The Strand and Covent Garden Piazza.
- **Don't Miss:** Elizabeth I and her favourites, Shakespeare, the Romantics, Prince Albert, the Brontë Sisters, Sir Alexander Fleming in his laboratory *(1944)*.
- **Timing:** Allow 3hr for a tour of the gallery, longer if you want to include one of the temporary shows *(charge)*.

A BIT OF HISTORY

Founded in 1856, the **National Portrait Gallery** moved to its present location in 1896. Today, over 5,000 personalities are portrayed in various media, from painting and sculpture to photography and digital works. To complement the permanent collection, the Gallery stages a diverse and ever-changing programme of exhibitions, talks and events that explore the nature of portraiture.

The permanent collection is presented in chronological order from the top down. The Digital Space *(located inside the Main Hall)* makes the gallery's collections accessible to all.

VISIT

St Martin's Place, WC2H OHE. Open Sat–Wed 10am–6pm, Thu–Fri 10am–9pm. Closed 24–26 Dec. No charge, except for special exhibitions. Audio guide (6 languages) £3. Restaurant (third floor; booking recommended: 020 7312 2490), Portrait Café. 020 7312 2463 (recorded information). www.npg.org.uk.

Take the escalator to the Second Floor from the Main Hall.

TUDORS TO THE REGENCY

Second Floor

The Tudor Galleries *(Rooms 1–3)*

Holbein's fragment of a larger sketch shows **Henry VIII** (1491–1547; *Room 1*) with his father, Henry VII, the founder of the Tudor dynasty; the distorted, anamorphorphic portrait of Henry's

National Portrait Gallery

son, **Edward VI**, painted by William Scrots *(1546)*, may be viewed in correct perspective from the right.

The statesman and Humanist author **Sir Thomas More** is portrayed with his family: he was executed for opposing Henry VIII's self-appointment as Head of the Church. **Mary I** *(1516–58)*, known as Bloody Mary, sent almost 300 Protestants to their deaths before marrying King Philip of Spain. The long gallery *(Room 2)* displays several portraits of **Elizabeth I** *(1533–1603)*. She was an intelligent monarch who saw the Spanish defeated and a flowering of literature. **Sir Francis Drake**, who sailed round the world, was a favourite at Elizabeth's court. **James I** (1566–1625; *Room 3*) was crowned King of England in 1603 following the death of Elizabeth I.

The 17C *(Rooms 4–8)*

The *Chandos Portrait (Room 4)* is arguably the most famous of **William Shakespeare** *(1564–1616)*, painted at the apogee of his career. The portrait of **Charles I** *(1600–49)* is by Daniel Mytens *(Room 5)*. The King attracted to his court the diplomat and painter Peter Paul Rubens *(Thomas Howard)* and Sir Anthony van Dyck *(several portraits hang in Room 5)*. **Oliver Cromwell** *(1599–1658)* promoted the King's execution and was appointed Protector of the Commonwealth in 1653. **The Restoration** *(Room 7)* is illustrated by **Charles II** *(1630–85)*, portrayed by Thomas Hawker, who emphasises his libertine reputation.

The portrait of **Nell Gwyn**, Charles II's most famous mistress, is by Simon Verelst. **Samuel Pepys** witnessed the Great Plague of 1665, followed in 1666 by the Great Fire, which devastated the City. Charles' younger brother **James II** (1633–1701*; Room 8*), painted by Sir Peter Lely *(see box opposite)*, was forced to flee in 1688.

William III (1650–1702*; Room 8*), the grandson of Charles I and **Mary II** *(1662–94)*, daughter of James II, acceded to the throne in 1688. Their joint rule brought tolerance to the kingdom. **Queen Anne** *(1665–1714)* succeeded her brother-in-law William in 1702.

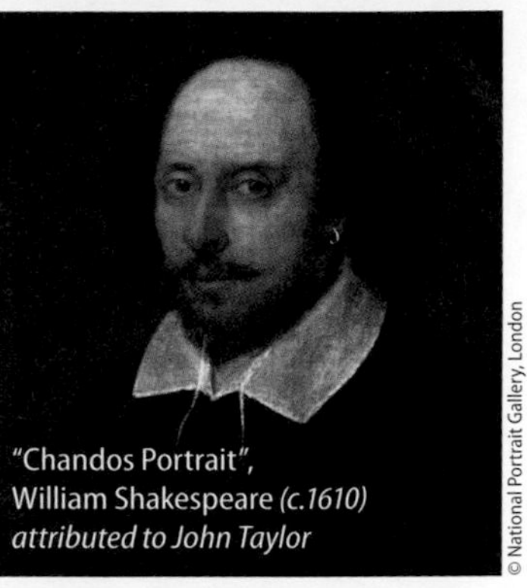

"Chandos Portrait", William Shakespeare *(c.1610)* *attributed to John Taylor*

Others pictured include **Isaac Newton**, who established the concept of gravitation, and soldier **John Churchill**, victor at the Battle of Blenheim and ancestor of Winston Churchill.

Georgian and Regency *(Rooms 9–20)*

The **Kit-Cat Club** *(Room 9)* attracted its distinguished members from political and literary circles. The throne passed to the Hanoverian **George I** *(1660–1727)*. The Arts and Sciences flourished throughout the 18C: **Sir Christopher Wren** *(Room 10)* achieved fame with rebuilding St Paul's Cathedral; **Sir Joshua Reynolds**, depicted in a famous self-portrait *(Room 12)*, promoted the ideal of the imperfect in art and **Sir**

Sir Peter Lely (1618–80)

Pieter van der Faes was born in Germany of Dutch parentage. He served his apprenticeship in Haarlem and moved to London in the 1640s. During the Commonwealth he produced noncontroversial history pictures, tailoring his grand and influential manner for the Restoration, succeeding Van Dyck as Principal Painter to Charles II in 1661. His paintings presented ladies of the Court endowed with languid beauty *(Nell Gwynne, the King's favourite)* and victorious military leaders with masculine dignity.

Hans Sloane *(Room 13)* provided the foundation for the British Museum.

Among those who contributed to British expansion during the 18C *(Room 14)* are **Captain James Cook**, who made the first European contact with Australia; and **Robert Clive** of India, who laid the foundations of British power in India.

Britain in the late 18C was shaped by **William Pitt the Younger** *(Room 20)*; **Horatio Nelson** *(Room 17)*, the victor of Trafalgar, who is portrayed next to his mistress **Lady Hamilton**; the **Duke of Wellington**, who defeated Napoleon at Waterloo *(1815)* and later became Prime Minister. There are several portraits by Sir Thomas Lawrence of **George IV** *(1762–1830)*, painted while he ruled by proxy as Prince Regent.

The Romantic generation of writers *(Room 18)* includes **William Wordsworth** and **Samuel Coleridge**; Scotland's favourite son **Robert Burns** and **Lord Byron** in his Greco-Albanian costume.

George Stephenson *(Room 19)* built the first public railway line.

THE VICTORIANS TO TODAY

First Floor

The Victorians *(Rooms 21–29)*

The display starts with portraits of **Queen Victoria** *(1819–1901)* and **Prince Albert** *(Room 21)*.

The Statesmen's Gallery *(Room 22)* has portraits and busts of political figures such as **Randolph Churchill** and **Robert Peel**, who created the police force.

Zaha Hadid (2008) by Michael Craig-Martin

The personalities who secured Britain's interests in the world *(Room 23)* include **Sir Richard Burton**, the African explorer; and **Florence Nightingale**, the pioneering nurse.

The Victorian Age *(Room 24)* is epitomised by the Poet Laureate **Alfred Tennyson**, **Charles Dickens** and the engineer **Isambard K Brunel** *(Room 27)*.

The world of politics *(Room 25)* is illustrated by portraits of the two great statesmen, **Gladstone** and **Disraeli**.

The late Victorians *(Room 28)* include **RL Stevenson** and **Rudyard Kipling**.

The 20C *(Rooms 30–33)*

General Officers and *Statesmen of the Great War (Room 30)* by **John Singer Sargent** and James Guthrie respectively encapsulate the great figures of the time. *Room 31* deals with Britain between 1919–59, exemplified by **Winston Churchill** and **Viscount Montgomery**.

The artistic environment reflected new ideas in painting, literature and music. Highlights include the writers **Virginia Woolf**, **EM Forster**, **DH Lawrence** and **TS Eliot**; the actor **Laurence Olivier** and the scientist **Alexander Fleming**.

The Balcony Gallery *(Room 32)* is devoted to Britain 1960–90: iconic figures from all walks of life illustrate social and political change, such as **Her Majesty the Queen** and the **Royal Family**, **Alec Guinness**, **Paul McCartney** and **Margaret Thatcher**.

Britain Since 1990 – *Ground Floor*. Portraits of people in the public eye from all walks of life include **Sir Ian McKellan**, **Camila Batmanghelidjh**, **VS Naipul** and **HRH The Duchess of Cambridge**.

ADDRESSES

LIGHT BITE

Portrait Café – *Basement. Sat–Wed 10am–5pm, Thur–Fri 10am–8pm*. Stylish, informal café serving light meals with an emphasis on British produce.

Portrait Restaurant – (*See WHERE TO EAT*)

Natural History Museum★★

A BIT OF HISTORY

The Natural History Museum is housed in London's famous Waterhouse building *(1873–81)*, an example of neo-Romanesque architecture designed by Alfred Waterhouse. Dominating the Cromwell Road, it is the centrepiece of Prince Albert's vision for a new learning district in London. The foundation for the collection began as the natural history department of the British Museum in Bloomsbury; the separate museum was opened to the public in 1881. After more than a century, the museum remains one of the most renowned centres for biological study in the world, not to mention one of London's finest museums.

Location: Map pp 160–161. *South Kensington.* The museum is a 5min walk from the Tube station by subway tunnel.

Don't Miss: The fascinating Earth Galleries, the vast blue whale in the Mammals Gallery and the interactive displays in the Human Biology area.

Timing: Get to the museum as early as you can – queues can be long. Expect to spend around 2–3hr on a visit.

Kids: The Dinosaur galleries with their skeletons and animatronics, Creepy Crawlies and **Investigate**, the hands-on education centre.

VISIT

Exhibition Rd./Cromwell Rd. South Kensington. Open daily 10am–5.50pm (5.30pm last admission). Closed 24–26 Dec. No charge except for some exhibitions. Map and guide. Tours at different times of the day; enquire at reception. Changing programme of special events and children's activities, with additional events during school holidays. Bookshop; shop. Restaurant, café, snack bar and picnic area. 020 7942 5000. www.nhm.ac.uk.

The vast neo-Romanesque building expresses the solemn reverence and sense of mission in public education in the 19C. The detail in the exterior decoration is stunning, and includes lifelike mouldings of living and extinct species to the west and east wings respectively. The museum is divided into **different coloured zones**: Blue and Green *(the Life Galleries)*; Red *(the Earth Galleries)* and Orange *(the Darwin Centre and the Wildlife Garden)*.

The Blue Zone

On the left of the Central Hall, home to an impressive Diplodocus skeleton, is the **Dinosaurs** gallery, which traces the development and extinction of these creatures, including a Triceratops skeleton. A set of animatronic dinosaurs is on display, featuring a Tyrannosaurus rex in a dramatic desert scene.

The **Human Biology** interactive displays explain how our senses, memories and organs work together in the human body, including interactive experiences on cells, genetics and what a baby experiences in the womb.

An enormous blue whale suspended from the ceiling dominates the **Mammals gallery**, where there are also audio-visual programmes *(3min)*, films, sounds, written panels, illustrations and stuffed originals; whales and their relatives are described in the gallery *(upstairs)*, including exhibits on how to make whale noises and the truth about unicorns.

The **Marine Invertebrates** gallery displays corals, urchins, crabs, starfish, sponges, molluscs, squid and shells, and shows how pollution effects their environment. Note the black webbed vampire squid with its red eyes and the wonderful display of sea fans.

The **Fishes, Amphibians and Reptiles** gallery includes exhibits about snakes, turtles and lizards. Of particular interest is the sword of a swordfish, the prehistoric-looking komodo dragons and examples of a football fish, which has a light-emitting lure that lights up the depths of the ocean.

The Green Zone

On the mezzanine floor above the Central Hall is **Treasures**, a new permanent gallery whose artefacts and specimens showcase the diversity of natural and man-made creations. Items on view include a lion's skull, an elephant's tooth, a moon rock and a first edition of Darwin's *Origin of Species*.

On the right side of the Central Hall, **Creepy Crawlies** illustrates the nature and diversity of insects and arthropods, including Chan's Megastick, the world's longest insect.

The **Investigate Centre** down the stairs on the Lower Ground Floor offers families the chance to handle special exhibits of animals and plants (*open Mon–Fri 2.30pm–5pm (11am–5pm during school holidays), Sat–Sun 11am–5pm; no charge*).

Alongside on the Ground Floor is the **Fossil Marine Reptile Gallery**, containing one of the most complete collections of fossilised sea dinosaurs such as the ichthyosaur.

The **Birds** gallery displays an array of specimens, from tiny hummingbirds to a giant ostrich. It also contains a specimen of the extinct Mauritius dodo and the rarest parrot in the world, the kakapo.

The **Waterhouse Gallery** displays temporary exhibitions such as the Wildlife Photographer of the Year exhibition.

The **Ecology** Gallery traces the impact of man's activities on our living planet, including a dazzling video quadrasphere display on the importance of water. It also shows an educational guide to conserving our planet's ecology through everyday actions.

At the top of the grand staircase in the Central Hall is a slice through the trunk of a **Giant Sequoia** felled in 1892 in San Francisco. Note the TREE artwork on the ceiling of the mezzanine gallery by Tania Kovats.

The **Minerals** gallery displays a whole host of raw and cut gemstones, including the reptilianesque snake stone. **The Vault** at the end displays the museum's most valuable treasures, such as the Nakhla Martian meteorite and the Devonshire Emerald, which has a mass of 1,383 carats.

The Red Zone

Access via the Ground Floor Birds Gallery or through the Exhibition Rd. entrance.

The **Earth Hall** contains an elevator rising from the "molten magma core" to the core of the Earth leading to the second floor, where, with sound, vibration and light effects, **Volcanoes and Earthquakes** (formerly **The Power**

Central Hall

The World's Largest Cocoon

The **Darwin Centre** is a 213ft/65m, eight-storey cocoon in a glass atrium. It is the largest sprayed concrete, curved structure in Europe and the largest extension to the museum since it opened in 1881. Inside, the building houses over 20 million insect and plant specimens, and offers wonderful views of West London. Visitors are able to watch scientists working on research in modern laboratories and partake in interactive exhibitions. The David Attenborough Studio within incorporates interactive films and discussions with leading naturalists about the natural world.

©Natural History Museum

Within) demonstrates how these geological phenomena wreak havoc.

The **Restless Surface Gallery** examines how rock formations shape our planet and explains the formation of a stalagmite as well as how the Himalayas were formed.

On the first floor, the **Earth's Treasury** gallery displays specimens of gemstones, rocks and minerals. Particular highlights are the fluorescent minerals, the organic shaped hematite minerals and displays of rare platinum nuggets.

From the Beginning displays a time rail that runs through the gallery, detailing 25 million years of planet life. The fearsome skeleton of a gigantic crocodile is a worthy exhibit.

The **Earth Lab** on the mezzanine level offers users computer and interactive exhibits to compare over 2,000 specimens of fossil, mineral and rock.

Returning to the Ground Floor, the **Lasting Impressions** gallery contains exhibits such as the footprints of a Triassic period dinosaur and explains how to calculate a whale's age from its teeth.

The **Earth Today and Tomorrow** looks at the importance of sustainable development to man and the planet.

The Orange Zone

This zone incorporates the **Darwin Centre** *(open 10am–5.50pm; no charge)* – with a fascinating Cocoon Experience, Climate Change Wall and more – and the **Wildlife Garden** *(open Apr–Oct)*, located on the West lawn outside the museum. It re-creates over an acre of British woods, heaths and meadowlands in a living exhibition.

The Spirit Collection Tour

This tour *(suitable only for adults and children over 8 years old; times vary; ask at reception)* allows a fascinating glimpse into the building's 27 kilometres (17mi) of shelves and some of the 22 million specimens held here, including hidden treasures such as the giant squid and specimens collected by Charles Darwin.

ADDRESSES

LIGHT BITE

Central Hall Café – *Blue zone, behind the main staircase. Daily 10am–5.30pm.* Newly refurbished café serving a range of healthy snacks and sandwiches.

Science Museum★★★

Location: Map pp 160–161. ⊖*South Kensington*. The museum is a 5min walk from the Tube station by subway tunnel.

Don't Miss: The Secret Life of the Home, Making the Modern World, Exploring Space, Flight, and the Motionride Simulators.

Timing: There's a lot to see and do, so split your day between the lower and upper floors, stopping for a picnic or restaurant lunch midway.

Kids: The Garden, Pattern Pod, IMAX cinema, Antenna, Who Am I?, Energy and Launchpad City.

A BIT OF HISTORY

The museum was founded as part of the South Kensington Museum in 1857 under the guiding hand of Bennet Woodcroft, a major figure in the development of textile machinery, with exhibits composed from the Royal Society of Arts and items from the Great Exhibition of 1851.

In its present location the museum was opened to the public from 1919–28. The Central Block galleries were redeveloped in the 1960s to form the backbone of the present layout. Further expansion was undertaken at the end of the century and the resulting Wellcome Wing, with its futuristic décor, was opened in 2000 to exhibit technologies of the future.

VISIT

Exhibition Road. ⊖South Kensington. Open daily 10am–6pm. Closed 24–26 Dec. No charge except for special exhibitions; IMAX cinema £10. Brochure (4 languages). Bookshop; shop. Restaurant; picnic area. Guided tours run daily; themes are Flight, Challenge of Materials and Making the Modern World. Last Wed of the month adults-only late nights with special shows and exhibitions. 0870 870 4868; www.sciencemuseum.org.uk.

As the public face of human ingenuity, the Science Museum's world-class collection forms an enduring record of scientific, technological and medical achievements from across the globe. Spread over seven floors, the Museum aims to make sense of the science that shapes our lives, inspiring visitors with

Making the Modern World

PLANNING YOUR VISIT

Touch-screen Information terminals around the museum display details of exhibitions, events and visitor facilities in six languages, as well as floor plans.

Highlights – For a quick tour consider visiting the sections entitled The Secret Life of the Home ***(basement)***; Exploring Space, Making the Modern World *(Ground Floor)*; The Challenge of Materials *(First Floor)*; Motionride Simulators; and Flight *(Third Floor)*.

Children – Recommended sections include those entitled The Garden *(basement)*; Pattern Pod, IMAX cinema, Antenna *(Ground Floor)*; Who am I? *(First Floor)*; Energy *(Second Floor)* and Launchpad City *(Third floor)*.

Interactive learning – Demonstrations are given in Launchpad and Flight sections ***(enquire at the information desk for times)***. Excellent programme of talks, workshops and children's events with additional events during half-term and school holidays ***(see website)***.

Overcrowding – Timed ticketing stops the galleries from being over-run with schoolchildren.

Science Museum Library – The Reference library is now based at two sites, in London and Swindon. The archives collection is housed in the Swindon facility, where readers can consult original scientific journals and books dating from 1486 onwards. *℘020 7942 4242*.

Books – The well-stocked bookshop has technical manuals, documentation, teaching packs and souvenirs.

Shop – An ethical, retro and inventive products shopping haven – one of the best places in the UK to buy presents, including games and gadgets for children ***(also mail order)***.

Imax – One of two IMAX screens in London; wide variety of films. ***℘0870 870 4868.***

iconic objects, award-winning exhibitions and incredible stories of scientific achievement. There are innumerable objects displayed, constantly updated "Science Boxes", countless working models and interactive computer terminals, while Explainers *(in red T-shirts)* are on hand throughout the galleries to advise and inform.

The museum galleries are divided into six floors but with constant reinvention of the exhibition space, expect displays to vary from those below.

Basement

Children can enjoy the interactive exhibits of **The Garden**, which make science fun in a multi-sensory environment, turning play into learning such principles as floating, sinking, shadows and reflections. **The Secret Life of the Home** explains the development of household appliances that we take for granted, from CD players to washing machines. It also shows how applied robotics will develop gadgets for the future.

Ground Floor

Energy Hall celebrates how steam has been the driving force of industry for more than 300 years with displays such as the large *Mill engine by Burnley Ironworks Company* (1903), which exemplifies how steam engines became Britain's main power source.

Rockets, satellites and space exploration are the exciting themes of **Exploring Space** with a full-size replica of the *Eagle lander*, which took Armstrong and Aldrin to the Moon in 1969.

Above the gallery are suspended two real space rockets, a *British Black Arrow* and a *United States Scout*.

In **Making the Modern World**, some 150 exhibits including *Stephenson's "Rocket"* locomotive *(1829)* and the *Apollo 10 command module (1969)* mark the development of the modern industrial world from 1750 and show how these iconic items have framed modern history.

The Ground Floor also has a **Theatre** room, which hosts educational and fun scientific shows *(30min; no charge)*, investigating the science of heat and temperature, changes of state and the transfer of energy.

First Floor

The **Challenge of Materials** gallery explains the various uses of state-of-the-art materials in the modern world. Note the *Steel wedding dress* (1995), made from stainless-steel wire. A spectacular glass bridge spans the gallery above the main hall, responding to the visitor with light and sound effects. Original artefacts and interactive exhibits, such as the Three-ring Enigma cypher machine *(c.1930s)*, illustrate the development of **Telecommunications**.

Special exhibitions present artefacts from the museum's collection to explore changes in science, technology, industry and medicine. A *Massey-Ferguson combine harvester (1953–62)* contrasts with the ancient Chinese ploughs illustrating the changing world of **Agriculture**.

The **Time Measurement** gallery explores how people have kept time over the centuries: sundials, sandglasses, water clocks and early Rolex designs.

Note the beautiful *Early balance spring watch* by Thomas Tompion *(1675–79)*.

Second Floor

The innovative **Energy Gallery** allows children to think critically about energy through interactive displays, including touch-sensitive screens, giant spinning drums and dance-floor footpads. The *Energy Ring*, a huge interactive sculpture suspended in the air, displays the thoughts of visitors who enter answers in the touch-screen terminals.

In **Computing and Mathematics** are Babbage's *Difference Engine No 2* and *DEC PDP-8 minicomputer* (1965), the forerunners of the modern computer. Another fascinating object on show is the *1956 Ferranti Pegasus*, the oldest working computer in the world, which is run regularly for visitors.

Human identity and the effects of biomedical sciences are the themes explored in **Who am I?** Visitors can morph their face to any age and search the geneaology of their surname.

Third Floor

From young to old, everyone will delight in the world of aviation, which is brought expertly to life on the Third Floor. Learn about the principles of flight in the exciting **Motionride simulators** *(£2.50; child £2)*, a highlight of any visit to this museum. Follow the progress of aviation in **Flight**, which

Kids playing in the Launchpad gallery

Science Museum Lates

On the last Wednesday of every month, the Science Museum offers an evening of entertainment (adults only), where guests can explore all the most enjoyable aspects of the museum, including interactive science exhibits, pub quizzes and the Launchpad exhibition, accompanied by live music and a fully licensed bar *(6.45pm–10pm; no charge)*.

Science Nights for children feature hands-on workshops, science shows and a sleepover at the museum, camping out amongst the exhibits, followed by breakfast and a film in the IMAX *(on various weekend nights; £45; reservations: 020 7942 4777)*.

displays an extraordinary collection of aircraft, engines and models: a replica of the *Wright brothers' plane*, which made the first controlled flight in 1903; Alcock and Brown's *Vickers Vimy biplane*, which made the first non-stop Atlantic crossing in 1919 and a *Gloster-Whittle jet aeroplane* (1941), the first successful British jet aircraft.

Launchpad City, the most popular gallery in the museum, allows children to explore and ask questions about their environment through over 50 interactive exhibits. Kids will see carbon dioxide turn from a solid into a gas and light rays breaking into rainbow patterns.

Health Matters relates the history of medicine in the second half of the 20C and uses interactive exhibits to explore the prevention of ill health. George III's collection of scientific apparatus forms the nucleus of **Science in the 18C.**

Take part in issue-raising games focused on various themes relating to technological developments in **In Future**.

Fourth Floor

Glimpses of Medical History illustrates the history of practical medicine from the Neolithic to the Modern Age with reconstructions and dioramas such as a warship's surgery during the Age of Nelson. The adjacent **Psychology** exhibition explores the mind's inner workings.

Fifth Floor

The Science and Art of Medicine presents a social and scientific history of medicine in cultures around the world with over 5,000 objects including the wonderfully painted Giustiniani medicine chest *(c.1565)* and a mummified Egyptian cat *(c.2 000–100 BC)*.

Veterinary History illustrates the treatment of animals: a stunning anatomical model of a horse by Louis Auzoux *(c.1850–80)* dominates the centre of the gallery.

Wellcome Wing

This modern annexe is devoted to innovative displays on contemporary science, technology and medicine.

Antenna *(Ground Floor of Wellcome Wing)* is a space devoted entirely to contemporary science, featuring constantly changing exhibitions and thought-provoking **Topic Zone** displays questioning the influence of modern science on our way of life.

An **IMAX cinema** presents spectacular shows on a screen higher than four stacked double-decker buses. Journey through space in *Hubble 3D*, join astronauts as they float to the International Space Station in *Space Station 3D* and dive with some of the planet's most colourful creatures in *Deep Sea 3D*.

Pattern Pod is a hands-on gallery that invites children *(aged 5–8)* to study patterns in recurring events through a series of multi-sensory exhibits.

ADDRESSES

LIGHT BITE

Deep Blue – *Ground floor. Same hours as museum.* Family restaurant serving hot meals. Activity boxes for children.

Tate Britain★★★

On a superb waterfront setting overlooking the riverside, this bright, imposing building is a splendid showcase for British Art from 1540 to the present day, with modern facilities for innovative displays of its fine collections. The gallery has a strong tradition of well-presented special exhibitions and public events; it also sponsors The Turner Prize, a prestigious, if controversial, award for the visual arts.

- **Location:** Map pp 134–135. ⊖*Pimlico*. The gallery is situated along the embankment running from Westminster to Chelsea and near Vauxhall Bridge. Victoria Station is to the West.
- **Don't Miss:** The paintings of John Constable; the works of the Pre-Raphaelites, in particular Millais; those of the American-born Whistler and John Singer Sargent; the Clore Gallery entirely devoted to Turner.
- **Timing:** Allow 3–4hr for a good overall view of what is on display. Obtain a gallery plan from the information desk; the galleries are regularly re-hung as only a small part of the Tate's collection is on show at any given time. If you intend to visit the collection to see a particular work, contact the gallery first to check if it is on display.
- **Kids:** The Tate organises several family activities for children and adults to enjoy together.

A BIT OF HISTORY

National Gallery of British Art – Fifty years after the founding of the National Gallery *(1824)*, the nation had acquired a large number of works that were shuffled between the National Gallery, the Victoria and Albert Museum and Marlborough House. In 1889, the sugar broker **Henry Tate**, an astute collector of British art, offered his collection of 67 paintings (including JE Millais' *Ophelia*) to the nation, together with £80,000 for a purpose-built gallery dedicated to British art post-1790 on condition that the Government provide a site for it. In 1897, the Tate opened on the site of the former Millbank Prison.

National Collection of Modern Foreign Art – In 1915, Sir Hugh Lane died when the *Lusitania* was torpedoed off the south coast of Ireland, leaving 39 paintings, including some superb Impressionists, "to found a collection of Modern Continental Art in London". Extensions to the original building were endowed by the son of Sir Joseph Duveen in 1926 and in 1937 to accommodate sculpture. In 1954 the Tate Gallery became legally independent of the National Gallery. Further building was completed in 1979; the Tate then took over the former Queen Alexandra Hospital before the **Clore Wing** was designed by James Stirling (1987) to accommodate the Turner collection.
Today, Tate Britain is devoted exclusively to **British Art from 1540 to the Present Day**.

VISIT

Milbank. ⊖Pimlico. At the time of writing, the main displays at Tate Britain were in the process of being re-hung. The new, chronological order of the collection, called Walk Through British Art, *presents famous artworks alongside work by less familiar artists. The following description represents the gallery before the re-hang. Check the website for up-to-date information. Open daily 10am–6pm, last entry 45min before closing. Restaurant open daily 10am–5pm. Café. No charge except for some special exhibitions. Guided tours daily 11am, noon, 2pm, 3pm. Multimedia*

Tate Britain

guide (4 languages) £3.50. ☎020 7887 8888 (booking & information); ☎020 7887 8687 (minicom). www.tate.org.uk/britain.

PAINTING IN BRITAIN 1500–1900

Rooms 2–15.

Image and Allegory: English Renaissance

John Bettes painted the earliest English work in the collection. His *A Man in a Black Cap* betrays the influence of Holbein, highlighting the face against a background of mottled brown wall and fur collar, black cap and robe.

Nicholas Hilliard, the famous Elizabethan miniaturist, encapsulates an idealised vision of his gracious queen: flat, stylised, linear, exquisite and fragile. *Queen Elizabeth I* is shown holding a rose, a Tudor emblem *(red for the House of Lancaster)*, thornless like that borne by the Virgin Mary, "the rose without thorn": a powerful image full of political allegory.

The prolific **Van Dyck** introduced a change from simple austerity to a celebration of status, painting his figures standing comfortably in space, poised in movement or gesture *(A Lady of the Spencer Family)*.

William Dobson's portrait of *Endymion Porter*, executed in Oxford during the exile of Charles I in the Civil War, shows the artist's concern for capturing the personality of his sitters.

Peter Lely adapted to the delicate political climate. His sitters are shown with elegant informality in uncontroversial poses *(Two Ladies of the Lake Family)*. His biblical and mythological subjects, meanwhile, verge on the erotic, hitherto unprecedented in the Puritan age.

Hogarth and Modern Life

Hogarth was a perceptive portraitist *(Thomas Herring, Archbishop of Canterbury)* and versatile painter, the patriotic author of "modern moral subjects" and humorous satires that make him the first great commentator of his era *(O The Roast Beef of Old England* and *A Scene from "The Beggar's Opera" VI)*.

The fashion for "conversation pieces", usually representing a domestic interior, proved popular with his successors **Francis Hayman** and Joseph Highmore, who exploited the illustrative quality of the genre. Hayman was among the first painters to draw inspiration from Shakespeare *(The Wrestling Scene from "As You Like It")*.

18C: Courtly Portraiture

The term "Grand Style" alluded to art in the manner of the great Italian Renaissance masters *(Michelangelo, Raphael,*

A Moral Dilemma

The delicate moral question of infidelity and prostitution was topical at a time when abandoned mistresses and high-society prostitutes would flaunt themselves on horseback in Hyde Park. In literature the subject was treated by Abbé Prévost *(Manon Lescaut)*, Marquis de Sade *(Justine, ou les Malheurs de la Vertu)*, Laclos *(Liaisons Dangereuses)*, Dumas *(La Dame aux Camélias)* and Flaubert *(Madame Bovary)*. It was also explored in music by Mozart *(Don Giovanni)*, Verdi *(La Traviata)*, Rossini and Massenet. In painting, the cause was publicised with realism by Frith, Millais, Tissot or condoned by the Aesthetes and Decadents with idealisations of exotic beauty *(Leighton, Alma Tadema, Russell Flint)*.

Titian). Subjects were usually drawn from the Bible, classical mythology or literature and thus qualified as "high art". **Joshua Reynolds** was quick to recognise that English "history" pictures found little favour with English patrons and therefore fashioned his own style of portraiture. Sitters were flattered *(Lady Charlotte Hill, Countess Talbot)* and often posed as Classical gods *(Three Ladies Adorning a Term of Hymen)*. In contrast, **Gainsborough**'s portraits are full of movement and gesture, colour, light and space *(Giovanna Baccelli)*. His patrons were largely country gentry and his sitters are often depicted in Arcadian landscapes.

Landscape and Empire: Aspects of Naturalism, Sporting Art and Genre Painting

The man who most successfully painted landscape in the Grand Manner was **Richard Wilson**, having travelled in Italy for seven years. His topographical landscapes suggest admiration for Claude *(Meleager and Atalanta)* and the Venetians.

George Stubbs adapted the Grand Manner to equestrian pictures *(Horse Frightened By a Lion)*, as did **Joseph Wright of Derby** to modern genre painting and portraiture, such as *An Iron Forge*, where industry is seen as intense and poetic.

Watercolour became the favourite medium of travellers to the Continent for recording impressions of lofty mountains, avalanches, sun-baked plains and erupting volcanoes.

One room, as well as temporary exhibitions, is usually devoted to the great British landscape painter **John Constable** *(Flatford Mill, A Bank on Hampstead Heath, East Bergholt House)*.

Works on Paper: Watercolours and Prints 1680–1900

The exhibit on **William Blake** and his followers includes the visionary painters Samuel Palmer, Edward Calvert, George Richmond, known as the "Ancients". Blake *(1757–1827)* pioneered monotype printing methods for his limited edition illustrations of the Creation. Pigment was applied to a hard board upon which sheets of paper were laid, each taking a different impression before the colour dried; this image was then separately worked up with pen, ink and watercolour. Romantic subjects were chosen from great literature (*Illustrations to Thornton's "Pastorals of Virgil"*).

Samuel Palmer *(1805–81)* was profoundly impressed by Blake, not only in the use of woodcut and tempera on a relatively small scale, but also in his mystical view of the English landscape *(A Hilly Scene)*. He was followed by **Richard Dadd** *(1817–86)*, who produced highly individual illustrations (*The Fairy Feller's Master-Stroke)*. In 1843, Dadd murdered his father and was condemned to Bethlem Hospital and Broadmoor Prison, where he was able to explore his hallucinatory world of fantasy, visions, fairies and hobgoblins.

Girtin's *The White House at Chelsea* marks a new departure in watercolour painting from the stained, monochrome drawings of the 18C to the luminous, atmospheric "impressions" of the

19C. Great swathes of delicate wash are applied to the absorbent white paper which he favoured, the low horizon a homage to the watercolours and etchings of Rembrandt.

Art and Victorian Society

The Royal Academy School taught technique and its gallery displayed current artistic trends: **Wilkie** *(The Village Holiday)*, **Frith** and **Edwin Landseer** *(A Scene at Abbotsford)* – Queen Victoria's favourite painter, who had been an infant prodigy, exhibiting his work at the RA from the age of 12, and who learnt to endow his animal subjects with human-like expressions.

Pre-Raphaelites and Symbolists – JE Millais encapsulated the ethic of the Pre-Raphaelite Brotherhood in his painting *Christ in the House of His Parents*, exhibited in 1849, and full of meticulous realism and elaborate iconography. The carpenter's shop was based on premises in Oxford Street. Joseph's figure and hands are modelled upon those of a real carpenter; his head is a portrait of Millais' father. The sheep were drawn from two heads obtained by the painter from a local butcher's; the still life on the back wall is charged with the symbolism of the Crucifixion *(Dove of the Holy Spirit, the triangle of the Trinity, the tools that represent the Passion)*. The overall effect was new and precipitated controversy.

Rossetti was the son of an Italian political refugee living in London. From an early age he showed a fascination for Dante and the dreamy world of Romance, legend, pure love and chivalry that would also to inspire him to write poetry. In 1850 he met Elizabeth Siddal. She became his muse and eventually his wife *(1860)*, only to die two years later from an overdose of laudanum, a derivative of opium. Bereft of her, Rossetti became a virtual recluse and eventually died a chloral addict. In *Ecce Ancilla Domini*, Rossetti beautifully combines realism with religious fervour.

Holman Hunt's *The Ship* shows a moonlit voyage, which symbolises his life and religious self doubts; the man at the wheel with his back turned possibly represents Hunt himself.

William Frith's *Derby Day* was much admired when exhibited in 1858. It is a prize piece of Victorian genre, complete with accurate portraits of recognisable people (young and old, rich and poor). Realistic vignettes of occasions such as gambling, entertainment and lavish picnics are all set against a meticulously rendered view of Epsom Racecourse painted from specially commissioned photographs.

Edward Burne-Jones *(1833–98)* is closely associated with William Morris. His idealised young subjects are bathed in a dreamy soft light *(Sidonia von Bork)*; profiles and textures are carefully contrasted one with another (flesh tones, stone carving, embroidered fabric, metal armour, flora and foliage). A preference for tall compositions may reflect the contemporary use of paintings as decorative panels integrated into more complex interior schemes.

Aestheticism

The movement's call for "art for art's sake" evolved during the 1870s and found its manifesto in Walter Hamilton's *The Aesthetic Movement in England,* published in 1882. Whistler and Albert Moore imported their own ideas from Paris; at home, the handsome, intellectual, well-travelled and charismatic **Lord Leighton** *(The Bath of Psyche)*, elected President of the Royal Academy in 1879, assumed the mantle. Alma-Tadema, Watts and Poynter, otherwise known as the **Olympians**, drew inspiration from Hellenistic Greece and the images evoked by the Elgin Marbles. Composition is simplified, colour carefully blended into harmonious arrangements, form precisely outlined and defined by texture or surface decoration, the fall of drapery or perspective of a tiled floor.

British Art and France

The most original painter to digest the current influence and instigate Continental modernism was **James Abbott McNeil Whistler** *(1834–1903)*. Receptive to all the prevailing artistic movements in Paris, Whistler assimilated influences from the Impressionists (overall composition), imported Japanese prints (unusual perspective and muted colour), the writings of established art critics such as the Romantic poets Baudelaire and Gautier, as well as the spirit of his middle-class Parisian contemporaries Gustave Moreau, Marcel Proust, George Sand, Chopin, Gounod and Berlioz, among others. *Symphony in White, No. 2: The Little White Girl* is a wonderfully composed, dreamlike portrait of his lover, enriched with Japanese objects.

John Singer Sargent *(1856–1925)*, an American painter who had worked outdoors with Claude Monet and Camille Pissarro, moved to London in 1885 *(Carnation, Lily, Lily, Rose)*.

THE MODERN AGE

British artists reacted to the events of the early 20C in a particular way. The impact of World War I is illustrated in the works of the futurist **Nevinson** *(A Star Shell)* and **Matthew Smith** *(Nude, Fitzroy Street, No. 1)*. In the 1930s **Henry Moore** *(Mask)*, **Barbara Hepworth** *(Figure of a Woman)* and **Ben Nicholson** (*Le Quotidien*, 1932) were pioneers of modernism. The destructiveness of World War II was seen through the haunting works of **Paul Nash** *(Flight of the Magnolia)*, **John Piper** *(All Saints Chapel, Bath)* and **Graham Sutherland** *(Devastation, 1941: East End, Wrecked Public House)*.

The period from 1960 to the present day is illustrated by changing displays. **David Hockney** and **Peter Blake** are leading exponents of Pop Art; abstract painting *(***Bernard Cohen**, **Richard Smith***)* and sculpture *(***Anthony Caro**, **Phillip King***)* flourished.

Conceptual art, which is exemplified by artists such as **Gilbert and George, the Living Sculptors** and **Richard Long**, was rejected by the School of London formed by **Howard Hodgkin**, **Lucian Freud** and **Kitaj**. Sculpture became symbolic and allusive, as in the works of **Stephen Cox**, **Bill Woodrow** and **Richard Deacon**.

Contemporary art is marked by the YBAs *(Young British Artists)*, whose leading figures are **Damian Hirst**, **Tracey Emin** and **Marc Quinn**. Other artists such as **Tacita Dean**, **Steve McQueen** and the **Wilson twins** explore different media including film and video.

CLORE GALLERY: TURNER COLLECTION

JMW Turner bequeathed a large portion *(100)* of his finished paintings to the nation with the request that they be hung in their own separate gallery. The will was subsequently challenged by his heirs and the Tate received some 300 oil paintings, together with 19,000 watercolours and drawings. The Turner Bequest is presently displayed in its purpose-built three temporary and six permanent galleries.

Much research has been undertaken to analyse Turner's genius. Influences include Poussin, Claude, 17C Dutch masters and Salvator Rosa, as he switches from historical subjects *(Hannibal and his Army Crossing the Alps)* to Classical *(The Decline of the Carthaginian Empire)* and topographical ones *(London from Greenwich)*. Perhaps it is sufficient to admire them for their evocation of wind and sunshine *(Shipwreck)*, reality or imagination *(Norham Castle, Sunrise)*, artistic talent and technique, and enjoy them for their colour, light, movement and poetic spirit.

Studies and Projects: *Self-Portrait* (1800). The Classical Ideal: works produced in admiration of Claude before Turner's first visit to Italy in 1819. Italy and Venice: *Bridge of Sighs, Ducal Palace and Custom House*. Seascapes: *(Ship and Cutter)*.

ADDRESSES

LIGHT BITE

Millbank Café and Bar – *Basement. Daily 10am–5.30pm.* The café has relocated while visitor areas are being renovated. In October 2013 new dining facilities will open.

Tate Modern★★

Now one of London's headline attractions, this thoroughly modern temple to contemporary art wasn't here until the beginning of the 21C. The newest of the family of four Tate galleries, the vast Tate Modern displays the national collection of international modern art *(defined as art since 1900)* and represents all major movements from Fauvism onwards. The permanent collection is arranged over four wings on levels 3 and 5; at the centre of each wing is a "hub", which focuses on a key period in the development of 20C art.

Location: Map pp 256–257. ⊖*Southwark; St Paul's.* Tate Modern is a 10min walk from the station and well-signposted. Or approach across the Millennium Bridge, which links Tate Modern with St Paul's on the north bank of the Thames.

Don't Miss: The panoramic **views** *(from the top floor)* of the Thames and the city; temporary installations by contemporary artists in the Turbine Hall.

A BIT OF HISTORY

The former **Bankside Power Station**, a massive structure *(1957–60)* known to some as the "cathedral of the age of electricity" with its single chimney *(325ft/99m)* and Aztec-inspired stepped brickwork was designed by Giles Gilbert Scott. The oil-fired power station, which closed in 1981, was converted to house the Tate Gallery's collection of international **20C art** and opened in 2000. The wealth of the Tate Modern Art Collection is largely due to the bequests made by Sir Roland Penrose, friend of Picasso and Ernst, and that of Edward James, a patron of Dalí and Magritte. Works by 20C British artists are also on view at Tate Britain.

VISIT

Open Sun–Thu 10am–6pm, Fri–Sat 10am–10pm (last admission is 45min before closing). Closed 24–26 Dec. Parking for the disabled only; pre-booking essential. Guided tours daily (45min) at 11am, noon, 2pm, 3pm. No charge. Multimedia tours £3. Touch tours for the visually impaired. Events for children and families. Bar/restaurant (level 6) and café (level 1). 020 7887 8888; www.tate.org.uk/modern. **Tate to Tate Boat** *every 40min between Tate Modern and Tate Britain, daily 10.10am–5.10pm. £5.50 single, £3.70 if you already hold a travelcard. www.thamesclippers.com.*

Tate Modern

The **museum collections** are displayed over four wings on levels two, three and four, each with a 'hub' gallery. **Special exhibitions** are on levels two and three. On level 0 is the **Turbine Hall**, which hosts vast commissions by different artists every six months.

As the exhibits are rotated according to various themes, the texts below traces the general evolution of genres for a better understanding of the displays.

France – Primitive Art inspired the "Sunday" painters **Rousseau** *(1844–1910)* and **Gauguin** *(1848–1903)*, who stylised form and used patches of flat colour for space within a composition and pattern to provide texture and relief. The **Nabis** group *(1889–99)*, including Edouard Vuillard, Bonnard, Maurice Denis and Maillol, rejected realism, instead drawing on symbolism and the Japanese prints they so admired to create representational works in a variety of media.
Post-Impressionist, **Vincent van Gogh** *(1853–90)* used pure colour and painted out of doors with strong brushstrokes and impasto technique, and although highly regarded now, was little appreciated during his lifetime.
The Neo-Impressionist **Georges Seurat** *(1859–91)* suggests luminosity by juxtaposed coloured dashes. His pointillist technique has scientific precision.

Henri Matisse *(1869–1954)* was versatile and prolific: he collaborated with the Nabis, Cézanne, Signac and Picasso, and was a major exponent of the **Fauves** group *(along with André Derain)*, which emphasised strong, strident colours and were characterised by seemingly wild brushstrokes.

Paul Cézanne *(1839–1906)* conceived landscape in terms of geometric volumes in which perspective is determined by colour. His portraiture *(The Gardener Vallier, c.1906)* and still-life paintings are also conceived as studies of mass, textured by pattern and moulded by shadow.

Pablo Picasso *(1881–1973)* drew on the Symbolist use of colour to suggest mood *(Nude Woman with Necklace*, 1968*)* and experimented with non-naturalistic blue, violet and green tones. Picasso, Braque, Modigliani and Brancusi were all greatly impressed by stylised Iberian sculpture and Oceanic carvings. From this artform, each explored eroticism or abstraction.

Cubism *(1906–14)* was the first truly abstract movement, which evolved as a counter-reaction to the visual appeal of Impressionism and Fauvism. It attempted to capture the volume or essence of the subject (form, shape, texture, purpose) as a series of fractured details. In a *Clarinet and Bottle of Rum on a Mantelpiece*, **Braque** presents the instrument as something associated with music (represented here by symbols for the clefs). **Léger** *(Leaves and Shell*, 1927*)*, meanwhile, forged his interpretation by highlighting with geometric patterning.

Dada and Surrealism – Dada *(1915–22)* originated in Zurich during World War I and was a deliberately nihilistic, anti-artform that was intended to shock. It was politically motivated by anti-war sentiment. Breton, Tzara, **Duchamp** *(The Large Glass, Fountain)*, Arp and Picabia all explored the fundamental nature of art by contradicting any established classification or justification with humour. Later, a more intellectual approach was pioneered by the Surrealist writers Apollinaire and Eluard.
They were joined in Paris by a wave of foreign artists: **Ernst** *(Dadaville, c. 1924)*, De Chirico, **Magritte** *(The Reckless Sleeper, 1928)*, **Salvador Dalí** (*Mountain Lake* and *Forgotten Horizon*) and **Joan Miro** *(Painting*, 1927*)*.

Futurism – "A new art for a new century" was formulated by a group of Italians such as **Balla** *(Abstract Speed – The Car has Passed)*, Boccioni, Carra, Severini and **Dottori** (*Expolsion of Red on Green*, 1910*)* to celebrate modern civilisation. Several main protagonists died during

Inside the gallery

© London on View

World War I, by which time the movement had fired the **Vorticists**.

German Expressionism – The Expressionists were happy to compromise naturalism by exaggerating form and colour if the end result had a more powerful impact. **Die Brücke** *(1905–13)* meaning "The Bridge" united Kirchner, Heckel, **Schmidt-Rottluff** (*Male Head, 1917)* and Bleyl in Dresden; soon it included Nolde, Pechstein, **Edvard Munch** and Der Blaue Reiter, a group started in 1911 in Munich by Marc, Kandinsky, Macke, Campendonk and Klee. **George Grosz** *(Drawing for "The Mirror of the Bourgeoisie", c.1925)* admitted his "profound disgust for life" before the outbreak of war. This was intensified by personal experience and his work focuses on such themes as prostitutes, bloated businessmen and death. **Max Beckmann** evolved a brave new style of realism *(Prunier, 1944)*, which went against the introverted, emotional motivations of Expressionism and is known for the numerous self-portraits he produced throughout his life.

Abstraction – If form is whittled down to its purest outline and most perfect surface, then the subject has forsaken its personality and become abstract. In pursuing abstraction, an artist must necessarily pare away his character to explore his inner spirituality or religion: Theosophy is the mystical rationale contained in the work of **Kandinsky** *(Lake Starnberg* and *Cossacks)*. **Suprematism** was pioneered by **Malevich** *(Composition, 1912–3)*, who rejected the "weight of the real world" in favour of a black square suspended in a void. **Constructivism** originated in Russia out of collages via reliefs and mobiles into abstract compositions of diverse materials. By 1921 the movement was dead, its concepts transposed to architecture and furniture design.

De Stijl was a Dutch magazine that promoted **Mondrian** *(The Tree A, c.1913)* and Neo-Plasticism. Borne out of a graphic medium, the De Stiljl movement had a huge impact on packaging and commercial art, but it also left its mark on Gropius and the Bauhaus ideals.

British Abstraction – In Britain, an interest in abstraction can be dated to the conservative Seven and Five Society in 1919, which soon attracted artists such as **Barbara Hepworth** *(Orpheus, Maquette 2)* and **Henry Moore** (*Three Points, 1939–40)*; it reformed in 1926 as the Seven and Five Abstract Group and enlisted John Piper.
Realism and traditional values returned after the War, when it was recognised that art had splintered into fractured groups. **Stanley Spencer** *(The Centurion's Servant)* excelled at figurative

painting, much of his work depicting Biblican scenes. **Lucian Freud** evolved his own realism by painting from life, and in the 1950s began to paint nudes to the almost total exclusion of any other subject. He was so focused, it is said that he cleaned his brush after each stroke. The **Kitchen Sink School**, which emphasises the domestic and, some would say, the banality of daily life, emerged from the Royal College in the 1950s and was so-named because of a painting by expressionist John Bratby, which included a kitchen sink. More violent are the styles of Dubuffet and **Giacometti** *(Venice Woman IX,* 1956*)*, who preceded the trio **Francis Bacon** *(Study for Portrait on Folding Bed* and *Seated Figure)*, Sutherland and **Henry Moore**.

Repercussions – **The Euston Road School** was founded in 1937 as a counter-reaction to the avant-garde, with artists such as **Bell**, Coldstream, and Rogers. The prospectus stated: "In teaching, particular emphasis will be laid on training the observation ... No attempt, however, will be made to impose a style and students will be left with maximum freedom of expression." Many of its exponents were politically left-leaning and to some naturalism was seen as a more relevant, and therefore more accessible, form of art.

Abstract Expressionism *(1942–52)* originated in New York, where Ernst and Mondrian sought refuge during the war, with De Kooning , **Newman** (*Adam*, 1951–2), **Jackson Pollock** (*Naked Man with Knife* and *Summertime: Number 9A*) and **Mark Rothko** (*Untitled*, c.1950–2) all exploring similar concepts in different media and styles, often on a large scale: "The familiar identity of things has to be pulverised in order to destroy the finite associations with which our society increasingly enshrouds every aspect of our environment" (Rothko, 1947).

Op and Kinetic Art, which explores the distinction between reality and the nature of illusion, was developed by the Hungarian Vasarely and Bridget Riley. **Pop Art and New Realism** is drawn as its title suggests from popular culture and graphic art. In the 1950s at the ICA, the likes of Paolozzi and Hamilton used collages of mundane objects to capture the spirit of the period. The second phase *(1961)* emerged from the Royal College with **Hockney**, Peter Blake, Jones, Boshier, Phillips, **Roy Lichtenstein** *(Whaam!,* 1963*)*, **Claes Oldenburg** *(Counter and Plates with Potato and Ham,* 1961*)*, **Andy Warhol** *(Self-Portrait,* 1967*)* and Jasper Johns.

Contemporary Art – Auerback, Francis Bacon, Lucian Freud and David Hockney today continue an historic British preoccupation with the representation of contemporary figures in their social context. Artists such as Hirst, Emin and **Cornelia Parker** *(Thirty Pieces of Silver,* 1988–9) are stars of the **Young British Artists** or "YBAs" working in conceptual media, from paint to installations.

ADDRESSES

LIGHT BITE

Tate Café – *Level 1. Mon–Thur 10am–6pm, Fri 10am–9pm, Sat 9am–7pm, Sun 9am–6pm.* Bright, modern café with a relaxed atmosphere. The menu focuses on fresh, seasonal ingredients, and there are homemade smoothies, Illy coffee and views across the river.

Tate Modern Restaurant – *Level 6. Sun–Thur 10am–5.30pm, Fri–Sat 10am–9.30pm.* Taking full advantage of one of the best views in London *(across to St Paul's)*, this bustling restaurant and bar serves high-quality seasonal produce and has an extensive wine list. Great cocktails too. Either book a table in advance or sharpen those elbows for a seat in the bar facing the window – this is no hidden gem!

Victoria and Albert Museum★★★

The Victoria and Albert Museum, Britain's national museum of art and design, is a treasure trove of art objects. Masterpieces from around the world representing a period of more than 3,000 years are on display here, creating a wonderful hub of decorative arts.

Location: Map pp 160–161. *South Kensington.* The museum is close to Knightsbridge.

Don't Miss: *Tipu's Tiger*; the **British Collections** *(Levels 2 and 4)*, particularly silver and furniture *(the Great Bed of Ware)*; **Constable and Turner** *(Level 3, Room 87)*, the lively **Fashion Collection** *(Level 1, Room 40)*; the **Furniture Gallery** *(Level 6);* the tranquil Italianate courtyard and reflecting pool of the **John Madejski Garden**, and the wonderfully decorated café housed in the **Morris, Gamble and Poynter Rooms**.

Timing: For the one-time visitor, it's best to go to the departments of personal interest first and then meander back through the other sections.

Kids: Hands-on exhibits, activities, family trails, events and backpacks.

A BIT OF HISTORY

The museum was created to accommodate the contemporary works manufactured for the 1851 Exhibition (*See KENSINGTON*). In 1857, the collection was moved from Marlborough House to South Kensington, and in 1899, it was renamed in honour of Queen Victoria and Prince Albert.

The museum is divided into four broad themes: **Asia**, **Europe**, **Materials and Techniques** and **Modern**.

VISIT

Cromwell Road. Open Sat–Thu 10am–5.45pm, Fri 10am–10pm. Closed 24–26 Dec. No charge except for some special exhibitions. Free walks and tours from the Grand Entrance; lunchtime talks Wed 1pm–2pm. Check website for details. Photography permitted (no flash, no tripods). Café. Shops. Entrances in Cromwell Road and Exhibition Road. 020 7942 2000. www.vam.ac.uk.

ASIA

The museum's Asian collections include objects from East Asia, South and South-East Asia and the Middle East, and are located on Level 1.

Rooms 17–20 explore Buddhist sculpture, detailing Asian conventions in contrast to the adjacent European sculpture. In Room 41, **Hindu**, **Buddhist** and **Jain India** are represented by stylised figurative works. Note the refined gilt bronze Buddha, with his handsome head crowned like a monarch.

The **Mughal Empire** produced fabulous illuminated manuscripts such as *The Akbarnma* and Jahangir's *Memoirs,* as well as carpet weaving.

Many of the museum's South-East Asian artefacts are collected in Rooms 47a–c and show how the Himalayan regions blended Indian, Chinese, Kashmiri, Nepalese and Central Asian designs with Buddhist art.

Nepal was sustained more directly by eastern India, exemplified by the **Newar** community *(Bhairava* sculpture*)*. The legacy of Angkor in Cambodia, Pagan in Burma, Sukhothai in Thailand and the complex temple communities of central and east Java can also be seen here.

In Room 42 you'll find the museum's **Islamic Middle East** collections. From Spain to Central Asia, the area was

Ardabil Carpet (c.1539), Jameel Gallery

united under Islam and art subjugated to rigorous rules that encouraged alternative embellishment in the form of superlative calligraphy. The *Ardabil Carpet (c.1539)* is the oldest in the world.

The fascinating **China** gallery *(Rooms 44 and 47e)* takes in the Bronze Age **Shang** state *(1700 BC)*, when metal signified the greatest wealth and luxury; the **Han dynasty** *(206 BC–AD 220)* with its naturalistic tomb paintings; the **Tang dynasty** *(618–906)*, which produced lavish white porcelain; the **Song period**, witnessing the development of new forms of ceramic and detailed sculpture *(Bodhisattva Guanyin,* c.1200*)*; the **Yuan** dynasty of the Mongols *(1279–1368)*, which exude political ambition in their art; and finally, the **Ming dynasty** *(1368–1644)*, whose exotic textiles evoke the Forbidden City in Beijing.

Just next door the **Japan** gallery *(Room 45)* displays how the **Nara dynasty** *(645–794)* assimilated Chinese Tang influences into ceramic designs. The **Heian court** *(794–1185)* patronised the arts and culture; this was continued by the **Kamakura rule** *(1185–1333)*, during which time paintings and sculptures of Buddha become more refined.

The **Edo period** *(1615–1868)* is noted for the production of porcelain and woodblock printing. The Momoyama period *(early 17C)* six-fold screen depicts the arrival of European traders in Japan.

Finally, the **Korea** Room *(Room 47g)* exhibits the museum's main Korean collection, which dates from the Koryo dynasty *(918–1392)*, when the Arts strived for perfection, shown in simple and restrained ceramics with harmonious colours.

EUROPE

The museum's European collection is extensive and divided into geographical and chronological galleries, allowing visitors to focus on a specific period or theme.

The **Medieval 3C–15C** gallery *(Level 0, Rooms 8–10)* is home to numerous small objects from this time period, the highlights of which are the rich ivory carvings and metalwork. The **Medieval and Renaissance** galleries *(spread over three levels in the east wing)* illustrate Medieval and Renaissance Art from 300 to 1600. Look out for marvels such as Michelangelo's *Slave,* a wax preparatory model for a figure for the tomb of Pope Julius II.

The **Religious Sculptures in Europe 1300–1600** Rooms *(Level 1, Rooms 16a, 26–27)* feature important artworks from France, Germany, Holland, Spain, Italy and England, including stained glass and sculptures in wood and stone.

The **Raphael Cartoons** *(Room 48a)* were commissioned in 1515 by Pope Leo X for the Sistine Chapel and illustrate incidents from the lives of the Apostles St Peter and St Paul.

The **Europe 1600–1800 Gallery** *(Level 0, Rooms 1–7)* display sumptuous objects which reflect ideas of European empires, courts and cities.

The **Europe and America 19C Room** *(Level 3, Room 101)* houses the 19C Collection, which includes an impressive Gothic- Revival bookcase by Carl Leistler and Sons and wonderful Art Nouveau objects.

The **20th Century Rooms** *(Level 3, Rooms 74, 76)* show the influence of Modernism and Functionalism throughout the 20C on the design of furniture and objects.

British Collections 1500–1900

Level 2, Rooms 52–58; Level 4, Rooms 118–125.

The most remarkable single piece from this period is the *Great Bed of Ware*, made of carved oak *(Room 57)*. Mentioned by Shakespeare, the bed has become legendary since it was made as a tourist attraction for the White Hart Inn, a popular hostelry on the way from London to Cambridge.

Of particular interest is the **18C** collection, with pieces by the great furniture designers **Chippendale** (*see INTRODUCTION – Furniture*). Recreated interiors include the Glass Drawing Room from Northumberland House *(1700s)*.

The **19C** section is one of the strongest of the furniture collection, many of which were purely ornamental, demonstrating the eclectic tastes of the Victorian Age. Notable pieces include **Pugin**'s armoire and a painted screen by **Vanessa Bell**, reflecting the influence of Matisse.

William Morris (1834–96)

Morris epitomises the Victorian age as a well-educated, middle-class, talented and successful designer, craftsman, poet, conservator and political theorist endowed with enormous vision, imagination and energy.

He attended Oxford to study theology; there he met members of the Pre-Raphaelite Brotherhood (DG Rossetti, Burne-Jones, Ford Madox Brown) and commissioned his friend Philip Webb to design a house in Bexleyheath. When trying to furnish The Red House, Morris discovered how "all the minor arts were in a state of complete degradation" and set about improving the situation. Morris, Marshall, Faulkner & Co. quickly proved successful; major projects included reception rooms at St James's Palace and a new refreshment room for the South Kensington Museum *(V & A)*; in 1875 the company was re-formed as **Morris & Co** and manufacturing continued until 1940.

Morris employed the services of other like-minded talented technicians and draughtsmen: Webb, Burne-Jones (figurative tapestries and stained glass), George Jack (furniture, including the famous Morris chair) and William de Morgan; from embroideries he moved on to wallpapers, stained glass, printed and woven textiles, carpets, rugs, tapestries, furniture, light fittings and ceramics. In 1890 he founded the **Kelmscott Press** for the specialist production of exquisitely printed books modelled on Medieval manuscripts.

William Morris upheld the importance of good craftsmanship in the face of mechanisation and industrial processes, the use of the most appropriate materials for functional objects and the need for good design in even the most lowly, domestic things. His lasting reputation and example have inspired the ethic of 20C industrial design.

MATERIALS AND TECHNIQUES

To gain a greater understanding of both art and design, explore the museum's well-presented rooms, which focus on specific materials or disciplines.

For **Sculpture**, head to Level 1, Rooms 21–24, for 17C to 20C British, French and Italian sculptures, specifically **Rodin** *(Metamorphosis of Ovid)*, **Bernini** *(Neptune and Triton)*, **Canova** *(Theseus and the Minotaur)* and impressive British portraits and memorial sculptures. The open arcade of *Gilbert Bayes Sculpture Gallery (Level 3, Room 111)* is devoted to the making of sculpture from idea to finished object, ranging from early medieval ivories to modern bronzes. It also affords extensive **views** over the superb **Cast Courts** below, home to the museum's most important plaster cast and electrotype reproductions.

The history of **photography** *(Level 3, Room 100 and Level 1, Room 38a)* is explored through displays detailing the museum's half a million strong collection of photographs.

Also on Level 1 the **fashion collection** *(Room 40)* charts developments in men's, ladies' and children's wear from the 16C onwards. Displays start with the complicated trimmings and contrivances of the eclectic 18C, which contrast with the late-19C and early-20C artefacts. Designers represented here include Dior, Chanel, Karl Lagerfeld, **Vivienne Westwood** *(Evening Dress, 1994)* and Cristóbal Balenciaga *(Evening ensemble 1967)*.

On Level 3, the **Jewellery Rooms** *(Rooms 91–93)* illustrate the history of jewellery from Antiquity to the present and include exquisite Prussian iron jewellery, pieces designed by Paris, London and New York jewellers and Oriental jewellery.

Also on Level 3 the **silver collection** *(Rooms 65–70a)* exhibits the important British silver tradition, exemplified by the Worshipful Company of Goldsmiths *(See THE CITY)*. Also note the wonderful panelling of the **Ceramic Staircase**. The **Gilbert Collection** *(Rooms 70–73)* has also been relocated here from Somerset House and includes **gold**, silver and micro-mosaics.

The diverse collection of **Metalware** *(Room 116)* ranges from the 16C to the present day, encompassing a broad selection of brass items and displays highlighting the history of pewters.

In the **Ironwork Rooms** *(Rooms 113–114e)* ranges of wrought-iron grilles and railings illustrate the skill of the blacksmith through the ages, while the **Sacred Silver and Stained Glass Rooms** *(Rooms 83–84)* exhibit glass from the 12C to today, illuminated by the museum's tall windows.

The museum's **paintings** are displayed nearby *(Rooms 81, 82, 87, 88)*, and a highlight of any visit is *The Mill – Girls Dancing to Music by a River* by Edward Burne-Jones. Works by Delacroix, Redgrave, Courbet, Etty and Ingres adorn the walls of Room 82. Landscape painting in Britain is displayed through works by Constable and Turner.

The **Prints and Drawings gallery** *(Rooms 88a and 90)* features changing displays. In Room 90a, the **portrait Miniatures** gallery traces the artform's history from the court of Henry VIII to its heyday in the 19C.

Room 94 is dominated by the detailed *Hunting Tapestries (c.1425)* made in Arras, Flanders.

The **Theatre and Performance** gallery *(Rooms 103–106)* focuses on the process of performance and includes highlights such as Kylie Minogue's Dressing Room (2007), Adam Ant's "Prince Charming" uniform and *Lion King* costumes.

On Level 4, the **Architecture Rooms** *(127–128)* form a unique guide to architecture from different ages and areas of the world, and include a huge isometric drawing of St Paul's Cathedral.

The **Glass** gallery *(Rooms 129, 131)* illustrates the history of glass-making from the impact of Venetian blown glass in the 16C to the most famous of the English glassmakers.

The **Ceramics Galleries** on Level 6 *(Rooms 183–139; 140–145)* chart the evolution of pottery, ranging from Greek and Roman; tin-glazed earth-

Pottery

Iznik, in Turkey, produced the finest-quality pottery of the Islamic world.
Hispano-Moresque was made in Islamic Spain *(8C–1492)*: colours include green, yellow, white, black and manganese; shapes include albarello drug or water jars.
Delftware or Dutch tin-glazed earthenware was inspired by Italian maiolica *(Antwerp, c.1584)*. The commonplace use of underglaze blue was a direct response to Chinese wares imported through the Dutch East India Company founded in 1609.
Lustre is the name given to the iridescent metallic finish: silver oxide provides a brassy yellow colour, copper for a rich red. Pioneered in Baghdad, developed in Spain (Malaga, Valencia) and Italy (Deruta, Gubbio), revived by William de Morgan *(19C)*. Other, less durable gilding methods adopted by Wedgwood included the use of platinum salts for silver, gold for pink, purple lustre.
Cream ware consists of lead glazed stoneware with a cream-coloured body containing flint (silica). Cheap to produce, hardwearing and a lighter alternative to porcelain, it also facilitated intricate open basket work. Its colour was ideally suited to transfer printing.
Slipware suggests the use of diluted clay (slip) for trailed or dripped decoration, sealed with clear glaze.

enware such as **maiolica** from Italy; stoneware, including pieces by **Josiah Wedgwood** *(1730–95)* and enamels from **Limoges**.

The **Furniture Gallery 14C–21C** *(Level 6, Rooms 133–136)* tells the story of furniture design and production, and includes outstanding pieces by Thomas Chippendale, Frank Lloyd Wright, Eileen Gray, Thonet Brothers, Marcel Breuer, Ray Eames and more.

ADDRESSES

LIGHT BITE

The V&A Café – *Sat–Thur 10am–5.15pm, Fri 10am–9.30pm.* In the V&A's original refreshment rooms, lined with beautiful tiling, the café serves food prepared on site, including salads, sandwiches and cakes. These three rooms, called the Morris, Gamble and Poynter Rooms, were intended as a showpiece of modern design and craftsmanship.

A Gory Image

Tipu's painted wood tiger represents an Indian tiger mauling a British officer. The tiger's body contains a miniature (possibly French) organ, which ingeniously simulates its roar as well as the groans of its victim. Captured in 1799 at the fall of Seringapatam, during which Tipu the ruler of Mysore was killed, it became a favourite exhibit in the East India Company's London museum. The statue is mentioned in Keats' satirical poem, *The Cap and Bells*.

Tipu's Tiger

Wallace Collection★★★

Location: Map pp 120–121 *Bond Street.* The Wallace Collection is a few minutes' walk from the Tube Station and 15 minutes from Oxford Circus.

Don't Miss: The famous *Laughing Cavalier* by Frans Hals, the display of exquisite gold snuffboxes and portraits by Velázquez, Gainsborough and Rembrandt.

Timing: The Wallace Collection is a detailed experience and you will need at least 2–3hr to see all of it properly.

A BIT OF HISTORY

On the north side of Manchester Square stands **Hertford House**, an imposing mansion built between 1776–88 for the 4th Duke of Manchester. After being used to house the Spanish Embassy, the mansion was leased by the Second Marquess of Hertford as his principal residence to entertain the great and good of London society. In 1900, the Office of Works opened the residence as a public museum. An ingenious remodelling in 2000 has created an airy, glass-roofed courtyard, home to an excellent restaurant and more exhibition space.

Noble patronage – The family art collection was started by the **1st Marquess of Hertford** *(1719–94)*, Ambassador to Paris and Lord Lieutenant of Ireland. The reclusive **4th Marquess of Hertford** *(1800–70)* transformed it into one of the world's finest collections of French 18C art. Living most of his life in Paris, he collected Old Masters and 18C paintings (by **Watteau**, **Boucher** and **Fragonard**), tapestries, Sèvres porcelain and the finest French furniture of the 17C and 18C (by **Boulle**, **Cressent** and **Riesener**). **Sir Richard Wallace**, the 4th Marquess' son *(1818–90)*, moved the collection to Britain for safety from the Commune uprisings and made substantial additions, specialising in the decorative arts. The collection was bequeathed to the nation by his widow **Lady Wallace** *(1897)* on condition that the Government provide premises in central London for it and that objects never be loaned or sold. Hertford House was therefore purchased from the Wallace family heir and transformed into a museum.

VISIT

Open daily 10am–5pm. The Great Gallery is undergoing refurbishment and is due to reopen in autumn 2014; all other galleries remain open. Check website for information. Closed 24–26 Dec. Free highlights tour of the Collection Mon and Fri 1pm, Tue and Thu 1pm and 2.30pm, Wed, Sat–Sun 11.30pm and 2.30pm. Max 25 people per tour, first come first served. Audiovisual tours. Free floorplans from front desk. No charge. Wheelchairs are available on request from the cloakroom. ✆ *020 7563 9500. www.wallacecollection.org.*

An Introduction to the Collection

This opulent yet intimate national museum reveals a unique collection of treasures. In 25 galleries are unsurpassed displays of 18C French painting, furniture and porcelain; Old Master painting; Renaissance art; 19C oils and watercolours; sculpture; and a world-class armoury.

Although the **Great Gallery** will be closed for refurbishment until autumn 2014, most of the paintings usually hung in this room will be on display in interesting groupings in the more intimate state rooms; it is worth seeking out these stunning works by Old Masters. Of particular note is the Venetian great **Titian**'s *Perseus and Andromeda (c.1554–6)*; portraits by **Velázquez** such as *The Lady with a Fan, (c.1640)*, an intense and sober portrait that exemplifies the style of the artist; and the world-famous enigmatic portrait by **Frans Hals**, *The Laughing Cavalier (1624)*.

Among the masterpieces of English 18C painting are **Gainsborough**'s *Mrs Mary Robinson Perdita, (1781)* (who became mistress of the Prince of Wales, later George IV), and **Joshua Reynolds**' *Mrs Elizabeth Carnac (c.1775)*. The room guide below presents the highlights of the other splendid collections in the museum.

Ground Floor

Hanging in the **Entrance Hall** is *The Arab Tent (c.1865–6)* by Sir Edwin Henry Landseer, author of the four lions in Trafalgar Square. Below is a selection of some of the Wallace Collection's most striking exhibits, as well as portrait busts of the founders.

The **Billiard Room** *(Room 2)* is furnished with Louis XIV *(1643–1715)* and Régence *(1715–23)* period furniture, including a wardrobe and inkstand by Boulle.

The former **Dining Room** *(Room 3)* displays the fine and applied arts of the Louis XV *(1723–74)* and Louis XVI *(1774–92)* periods, including two Venetian paintings by Canaletto. The *Mantel Clock (1781)* by Jean-Baptiste Lepaute is adorned with winged sphinxes based on the Neo-classical style. Note the portrait bust of *Madame de Sérilly* by the renowned French sculptor, Jean Antoine Houdon.

The **Back State Room** *(Room 4)* contains, among other treasures, a magnificent Sèvres porcelain inkstand *(1758)* and an oak Gaudreaus and Caffiéri commode, which belonged to Louis XV of France.

The **Front State Room** *(Room 5)* is hung with English 18C and 19C portraits by Joshua Reynolds *("Old Q" as Earl of March)* and Thomas Lawrence *(Margaret, Countess of Blessington, 1822)* and a gilt bronze vase by Robert Joseph Auguste *(c.1760–65)*. Note also the lovely miniature by Henry Bone *(after Vigée Le Brun)* depicting *Lady Hamilton as a Bacchante* (the famous lover of Admiral Nelson and a renowned beauty of the 18C).

The **Sixteenth Century Gallery** *(Room 6)* contains Medieval and Renaissance works of art *(St. Catherine of Alexandria,* c.1502*)*, curiosities from the 15C and 16C Italian and Northern School, sculpted figures *(bronze, boxwood, ivory)*, wax miniatures to Limoges enamels and Venetian glass.

The former **Smoking Room** *(Room 7)* offers displays of Renaissance jewellery, ceramics by the French potter **Bernard Palissy** *(c.1510–89)* and Italian maiolica, a highlight of which is the wine cooler from 1574 made for Cosimo de' Medici. The *hand bell of St Mura* from Ireland was said in legend to have descended from heaven ringing loudly.

The Armories

The **Armories Corridor**, with its collection of 16C earthenware plates, leads on to the **European Armories Collection** *(Rooms 8, 9, 10)*, which is one of the best of its kind in the world. On display is a mêlée of weapons and armour from 10C–16C. Two impressive sets of Gothic-style armour depicting knights mounted on horses dominate **European Armoury II** *(Room 9)*, while **European Armoury I** *(Room 10)* holds a rare visored helmet *(c.1390–1410)* from

Oval Drawing Room

Milan, which evokes the great battles of the Hundred Years War in Europe, such as the Battle of Agincourt in 1415.

The Oriental Armoury *(Room 11)* is devoted to arms set with gemstones, armour and 19C French Orientalist paintings. The 17C Sword of Tipu Sultan, which belonged to the Sultan of Southern India *(1782–99)*, has a hilt decorated with diamonds, rubies and emeralds, and inlaid gold inscriptions.

What were formerly the **Housekeeper's Room** *(Room 12)* and **Breakfast Room** now host the museum shop *(art books, gallery catalogues, cards and gifts on sale)* and cloakroom.

First Floor

Accessible from the Ground Floor via the Grand Staircase in the Entrance Hall. Lift available.

The walls of the **Grand Staircase** and the first-floor **Landing** are hung with canvases by **François Boucher** depicting the epitome of the rococo style: *An Autumn Pastoral*, *The Rape of Europa*, *The Rising of the Sun*, *The Setting of the Sun*, *Mercury confiding the Infant Bacchus to the Nymphs* and a *Summer Pastoral*.

Lady Wallace's **Boudoir** *(Room 13)* features genre pictures and marble decorations, such as the gilt bronze chimneypiece *(c.1769–75)*.

In the **Boudoir Cabinet** is a magnificent collection of gold **snuffboxes★** painted with enamels or lacquered and set with gems.

The **Study** *(Room 14)* houses the largest collection of Marie-Antoinette's belongings in any single room in the world, including splendid marquetry furniture created for her by Riesener and portraits by Greuze *(Portrait of a Lady)* and Vigée Le Brun *(Madame Perregaux, 1789)*.

The **Oval Drawing-Room** *(Room 15)* features 18C portraits such as Fragonard's charming *A Boy as Pierrot (c.1785)* and a portrait by Boucher of *Madame de Pompadour*, the mistress of Louis XV and illustrious patroness of the artist. The most famous painting in this room is **Fragonard**'s masterpiece, *The Happy Accidents of the Swing*, symbolising hedonism and the loss of virginity in the rococo era.

The **Large Drawing Room** *(Room 16)* is hung with striking green wall silk and decorated with an oak wardrobe *(c.1700)* resplendent with brass and tortoiseshell, and a pedestal clock attributed to Boulle.

The **Small Drawing Room** *(Room 17)* contains French 18C furniture and Fête Galante genre paintings (a sub-genre of rococo depicting scenes of idyllic charm in outdoor settings) by Lancret, Pater and **Jean-Antoine Watteau**, including his *Harlequin and Columbine (c. 1716–18)*.

The Flemish **East Drawing Room** houses **Rubens**' magisterial *The Rain-*

bow Landscape (c.1636) and **Jacob Jordaens**' *An Allegory of Fruitfulness (1620-29)*, which explores the theme of cornucopia in striking colours.

The East Galleries

These galleries benefit from the raised ceiling and skylights that were installed during the recent refurbishment, which have returned the rooms to the way Sir Richard Wallace originally conceived them in the 1870s.

In **East Gallery I** is **Rembrandt**'s sensitive portrait of his son, *Titus, the Artist's Son (c.1657)* hangs opposite his *Self-Portrait in a Black Cap (1637)*. **East Gallery II** features genre scenes and portraits of the Dutch Golden Age, including **Caspar Netscher**'s undisputed masterpiece, *The Lace Maker (1662)*, while the final gallery in this wing focuses on Italianate landscapes and seascapes of this period, such as atmospheric works by **Nicolaes Berchem** and **Willem van de Velde the Younger**.

The West Galleries

The west wing of the first floor holds an equally impressive collection of 18C and 19C paintings. The **Nineteenth Century Gallery** (Room 23) displays 19C French painting and miniatures, including works by **Delacroix**, **Géricault**, **Scheffer** and **Meissonier** (one of the favourite artists of Lord Hertford). The *Temptation of Saint Hilarion* by **Dominique Papety** *(c.1843–4)*, is a vivid work on the theme of sexual temptation.

The **West Gallery** *(Room 24)* was a former dressing room of Sir Richard and Lady Wallace. The room is furnished with fine 18C French furniture by **René Dubois**, and impressive 18C Venetian landscapes line the walls, including works by **Francesco Guardi** and **Canaletto**.

The **West Room** *(Room 25)*, which was the bedroom of Lady Wallace, is decorated in an elegant feminine 18C style, with the works of art on display complemented by this intimate setting.

Laughing Cavalier *(1624) by Frans Hals*

Lower Ground Floor

Accessible from the Ground Floor via staircases adjacent to the Entrance Hall and European Armoury I. Lift available.

The **Porphyry Court** is the central atrium of this floor and displays French and Italian sculptures *(17–18C)* and porphyry vases.

The Lower Ground Floor also contains the Goodison Theatre *(which holds special lectures throughout the year)*; the Mary Weston Education Studio, which hosts workshops and school parties *(information and booking available by phoning ✆020 7563 9551)*; the **Eranda Visitors' Library** *(open by appointment only: ✆020 7563 9528)*; and the special exhibition and **Ritblat conservation galleries** *(check website for details)*.

ADDRESSES

LIGHT BITE

The Wallace Restaurant – *The Wallace Collection, Hertford House, Manchester Sq., W1U 3BN. ⊖Bond Street. ✆ 020 7563 9505. Sun–Thur 10am–5pm, Fri–Sat 10am–11pm.* The glazed courtyard of Hertford House provides a stunning setting for lunch or afternoon tea. The menu is all-day brasserie in style – simple and delicious. For the latest menus and booking details, see the restaurant website: *www.peytonandbyrne.co.uk/the-wallace-restaurant.*

H_2O FLOATING RESTAURANT
020
VIOLET

Riverside path along the Thames, Richmond
© London on View

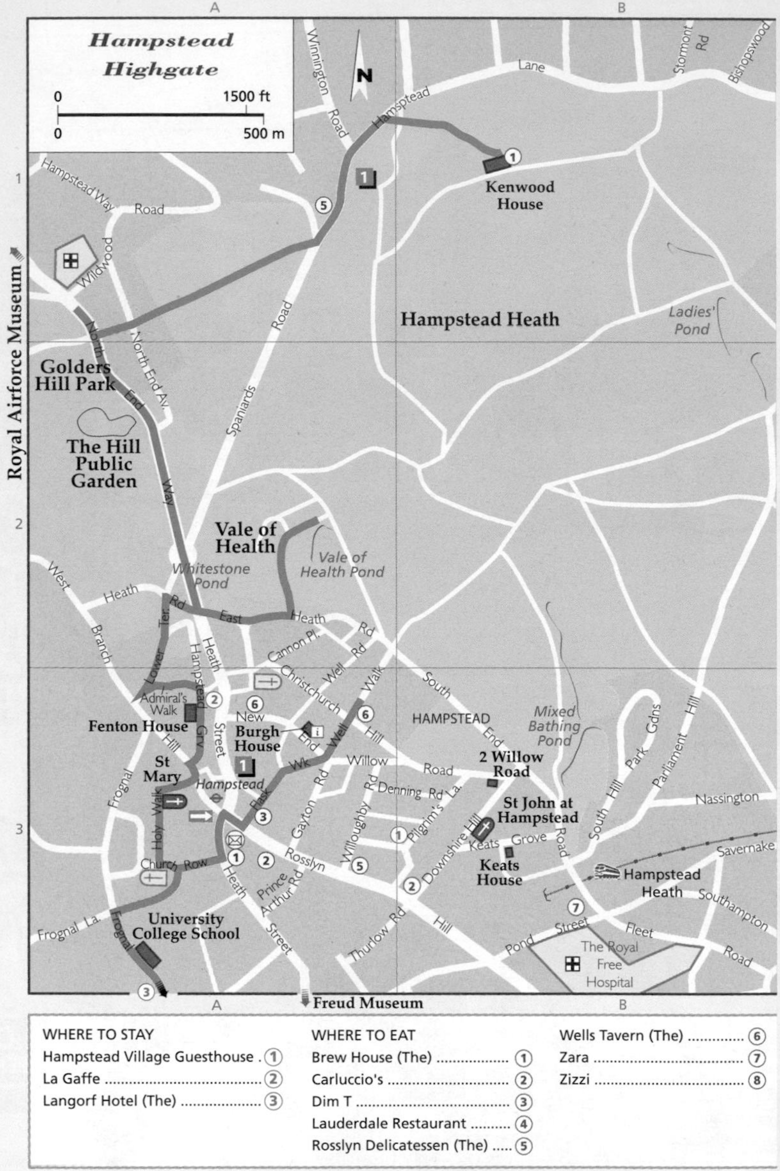

Hampstead and Highgate are two of London's most affluent suburbs, offering an easy escape from the hustle and bustle of the city centre.

A Bit of Geography

Hampstead is located to the northwest of Camden and Regent's Park. Hampstead village is to the South of the vast Heath, one of London's much-loved wide open spaces; Highgate lies to the Northeast.

History

Hampstead's name comes from the Anglo Saxon words "ham" and "stede", together meaning homestead. The area was referred to in the Domesday Book but only started to develop after it became popular as a spa in the 18C.

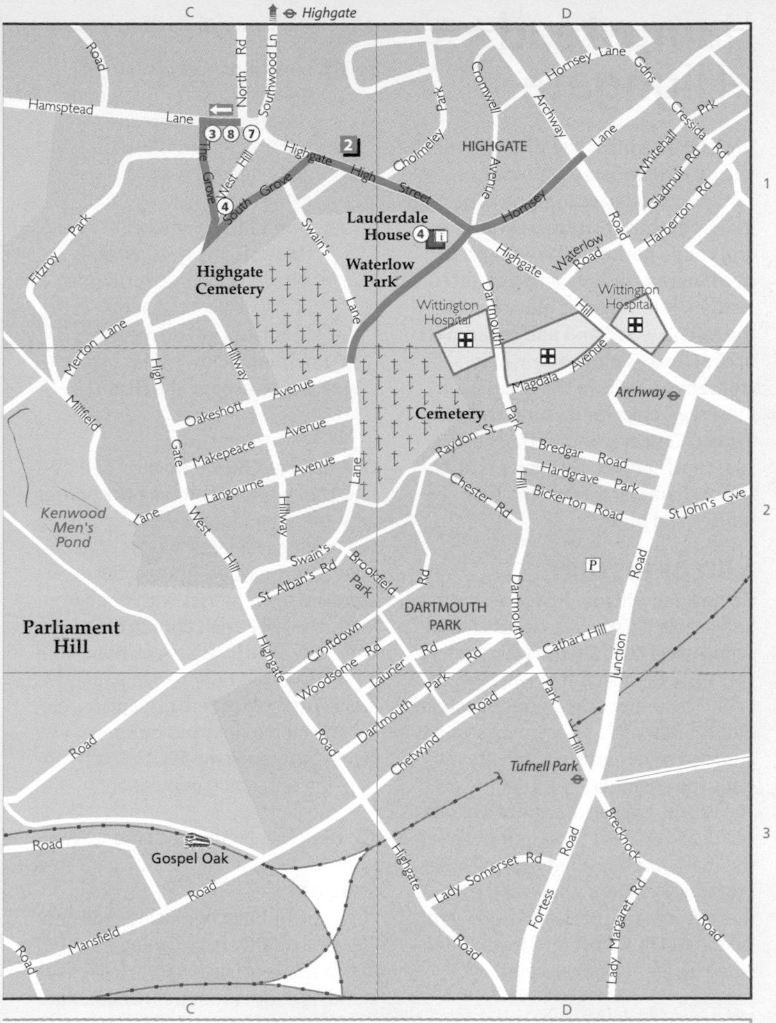

CAFÉS

Louis .... ①
Maison Blanc .... ②

BARS, PUBS & NIGHTLIFE

Flask (The) .... ③
Flask Tavern (The) .... ④
New End Theatre .... ⑤
Spaniard's Inn .... ⑥
The Gatehouse .... ⑦

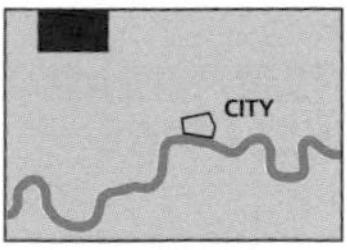

Highgate adjoined the Bishop of London's hunting estate and was home to a tollhouse. Europe's first cable car operated up Highgate Hill from 1884–1909. Home to more millionaires than almost anywhere else in Britain, Hampstead and Highgate remain two of London's most sought-after places to live, with a pleasant village atmosphere and established café culture.

Highlights

1 Take a stroll on **Hampstead Heath** (p342)
2 **Highgate Cemetery** (p345)
3 Enjoy live music at a **Kenwood House** concert (p348)

Hampstead★★ –Highgate

High up on a hill is the picturesque village of Hampstead, a maze of alleyways and passages, historic buildings, smart shops, restaurants and coffee houses, all frequented by affluent residents and delighted visitors. Hampstead's glory lies in the rolling woodland and meadows of the Heath, enjoyed by walkers (some even swim in the ponds) and film crews alike for its rural London aspect. Concerts and funfairs are seasonal features. Highgate is also full of character, with some fine houses and pubs.

- **Location:** Map pp 340–341. *⊖Hampstead or Hampstead Heath rail.* Hampstead is North of Regent's Park, and Highgate is slightly to the Northeast.
- **Don't Miss:** Fenton House, Hampstead Village, Kenwood, on the North side of the Heath; stop at the Spaniard's Inn on the way.
- **Timing:** Allow at least half a day to explore the Heath.

A BIT OF HISTORY

Hampstead Village developed into a fashionable 18C spa when the chalybeate springs were discovered in what became Well Walk. Grand houses were built, and in 1907 came the Underground. Throughout its history this pleasant district has attracted writers, artists, architects, musicians and scientists.

The village, built on the side of a hill, has kept its original street pattern; between the main roads is a network of lanes, groves, alleys, steps, courts and rises. At the foot of the hill lie Hampstead Ponds. On the North side of the Heath is Kenwood *(see Additional Sights)*.

WALKING TOUR

1 HAMPSTEAD VILLAGE – WEST SIDE

Flask Walk, which begins as a pedestrian street with a Victorian pub and tea merchant, continues east past Gardnor House, built in 1736, to New End Square and Well Walk beyond.

John Constable lived at No. 40 Well Walk from 1826 to his death in 1834.

Christchurch Hill, with its Georgian cottages, leads to the mid-19C church with a soaring spire that's visible for miles.

Walk back and up Fitzjohn's Ave.

One flank of **Church Row** is lined by a fine 1720 terrace of brown brick houses with Georgian doors. The range along the north pavement includes cottages, a weatherboarded house and three-storeyed town houses with good ironwork. The 18C **Parish Church of St John** at the row's end boasts a spire rising from a battlemented brick tower, banded in stone. The interior, with giant pillars, galleries on three sides and box pews, was twice enlarged in the 19C to accommodate the expanding population.

Detour to Frognal via Frognal Way.

Frognal

Noteworthy buildings include the neo-Georgian University College School with a statue of Edward VII in full regalia standing above the entrance door; **Kate Greenaway**'s house (No. 39) designed in 1885 by **Norman Shaw** in story book style, with rambling gables and balconies; and the Sun House *(No. 9 Frognal Way)* by **Maxwell Fry** at his 1935 best.

Return and turn into Holly Walk.

Holly Walk

The path north from the church, bordered by the 1810 cemetery extension crowded with funeral monuments, rises to the green- and pink-washed, three-storey houses of Prospect Place *(1814)* and delightful cottages of Benham's Place *(1813)*. Holly Place *(1816)* is another short terrace flanking **St Mary's**, one of

the earliest RC churches to be built in London, founded by Abbé Morel, refugee from the French Revolution, who came to Hampstead in 1796. From the top of the hill a maze of steps and alleys leads down to Heath Street.
Overlooking **Mount Vernon Junction** is **Romney's House** *(plaque)*, built of brick and weatherboarding in 1797.

Walk up Hampstead Grove past Fenton House (*see Additional Sights*) and turn left.

Admiral's Walk

The road leads to Admiral's House, an early-18C mansion with nautical superstructure, named after the colourful Admiral Matthew Burton *(1715–95)*. It was the home of **Sir George Gilbert Scott** from 1854 to 1864.
The adjoining Grove Lodge was **Galsworthy**'s home from 1918 until his death in 1933, where he wrote all but the first part of the *Forsyte Saga*. Lower Terrace, at the end of Admiral's Walk, is where **Constable** lived from 1821 to 1825 before moving to Well Walk.

Continue up Lower Terrace to Heath St. and the Whitestone Pond.

Hampstead Heath

Hampstead Heath was the common of Hampstead Manor; this is the place where laundresses once laid out washing to bleach in the 18C. With its rambling paths, ancient woodlands and ponds, it's a popular place to come for a walk and a breath of fresh air.
To the South East is **Parliament Hill**, with fabulous views (protected by Parliament) of the whole of London. In the South West corner of the Heath are three swimming ponds *(ladies', men's and mixed)*, which are open daily throughout the year *(020 7485 3873)*.
Whitestone Pond and the milestone *("Holborn Bars 4½" in the bushes at the base of the aerial)* from which it takes its name are on London's highest ground *(437ft/133m)*.

Short detour down East Heath Rd.

Old Brewery Mews

Off Hampstead High Street on the East side, the former brewery is well protected by a wrought-iron cage and has been converted into offices and a row of modern town houses.

Vale of Health

The Vale, a cluster of 18C–19C cottages, mid-Victorian, and now a few modern houses and blocks, connected by a maze of narrow roads and paths, has at various times been the home of Leigh Hunt, DH Lawrence, **Edgar Wallace** and Compton Mackenzie. The origin of the Vale's name is said to derive from the fact that the area was unaffected by the Plague in 1665.

Return and proceed to North End Way.

At the crossroads stands **Jack Straw's Castle**, a former inn *(now flats)* first mentioned in local records in 1713. Almost opposite is **Heath House**, a plain early-18C mansion of brown brick, chiefly remarkable for its commanding position and the visitors received by its 18C–19C owner, the Quaker abolitionist, **Samuel Hoare**: **William Wilberforce**,

Hampstead Garden Suburb

The Suburb was conceived by **Dame Henrietta Barnett**, living in what is now Heath End House, as a scheme for rehousing London slum dwellers in the early 20C. Raymond Unwin, the principal architect, designed an irregular pattern of tree-lined streets and closes converging on a central square with its Institute and two churches *(one Anglican and one Nonconformist)* by **Sir Edwin Lutyens**. The houses are in varied architectural styles. It is now a very affluent area.

An Ancient Land

Highgate Wood *(north of Archway and Muswell Hill junction)* comprises 70 acres/28ha and is classified an ancient woodland, a remnant of the larger Ancient Forest of Middlesex, mentioned in the **Domesday Book**. Archaeological surveys have revealed that potteries were active in the area around the time of the Roman conquest (AD 43). Between the 16C and 18C hornbeam would have been coppiced, while oak would have been grown to provide the Crown with timber for shipbuilding. In 1885, under threat of development, the wood was acquired by the Corporation of London. Today it is protected by an active conservation policy and equipped with children's recreation facilities.

Elizabeth Fry and the leading politicians of the day.

Further up North End Way stands Inverforth House, rebuilt in 1914 and now a residential development. Lord Leverhulme's extensive pergola, sweet with wisteria, rambling roses, clematis and honeysuckle, now forms part of **The Hill Public Garden**, formally laid out on a steeply sloping site and framed by the natural beauty of the trees of the West Heath.

Nearby on the northern edge of the West Heath lies **Golders Hill Park**, its landscaped lawns sweeping down to two ponds, past animal enclosures.

On the east side of North End Way stands the Bull and Bush, an old pub once patronised by **Joshua Reynolds**, **Gainsborough**, **Constable** and **John Romney**.

▶ A path runs east across the Heath to Spaniards Rd., which leads north to Kenwood House, past the 18C Tollhouse and the Spaniards Inn.

2 HIGHGATE

⊖ *Archway; Highgate*

The area began to be developed in the 17C when rich merchants decided it was the place to build their country seats. Today Highgate remains a village in character, centred on pretty Pond Square and the High Street.

▶ Start from the top of Highgate High St., walk west along Hampstead Lane and turn left into The Grove.

The Grove

This wide, tree-planted road presents late 17C to early 18C rose-brick terrace housing. The poet and critic **Samuel Taylor Coleridge** lived at No. 3 from 1823 until his death in 1834 and is buried in **St Michael's Church**, discernable by its tapering octagonal spire *(1830)* overlooking Highgate Cemetery.

The Flask *(1721)* on Highgate West Hill corner is a period country pub with outdoor courtyard *(see Addresses)*.

South Grove is lined with various houses: the early 18C Church House *(No. 10)*, the Highgate Literary and Scientific Society *(No. 11)*, Moreton House *(No. 14)*, a brick mansion of 1715, and the late 17C **Old Hall**, with its great bow window.

Bacon's Lane honours the philosopher Francis Bacon, who was a frequent guest (and died) at Arundel House, which used to be where Old Hall now stands.

Pond Square

Small houses and cottages line three sides of the irregularly shaped Pond Square. On the south side **Rock House** *(No. 6)* retains its overhanging wooden bay windows *(18C)*.

▶ Left into South Grove, then continue down the High St.

Highgate High Street

The **Gatehouse Tavern** *(see Addresses)* stands on the site of a 1386 gatehouse to the Bishop of London's park; **No. 23** opposite, with its straight-headed windows and modillion frieze, and **Nos. 17, 19** and **21** are all early 18C.

Highgate Hill

Just inside **Waterlow Park** stands **Lauderdale House**, 16C in origin but remodelled in the 18C in small country- house style *(now a cultural centre)*.

Highgate Cemetery★★

Swains Lane. Open Mon–Fri 10am–4pm, Sat–Sun 11am–4pm. Closed funerals and 25–26 Dec. East Cemetery. £4; cash only. West Cemetery accessible by guided tour only. £12; cash only (includes entrance to East Cemetery within a month). 020 8340 1834. www.highgate-cemetery.org.

Perhaps an eccentric thing to do, but a guided tour of Highgate Cemetery can be one of the most fascinating days out in London, with a story behind every tombstone and an enormous cast of the great, the good and the howlingly eccentric.

The Eastern Cemetery is still in use; here lie **George Eliot** *(1819–80)* and **Karl Marx** *(d.1883)* – bust *(1956)* by Laurence Bradshaw. The Western Cemetery *(opened 1838)* contains some remarkable 19C monumental masonry and the tombs of **Michael Faraday** *(1791–1867)*, Charles Cruft, who started the dog shows in 1886, and **Dante Gabriel** and **Christina Rossetti** *(see MAJOR CENTRAL LONDON MUSEUMS –Tate Britain)*.

Walk back to Highgate Hill.

Opposite, high above the road, is **The Bank**, a row of brick houses; **Nos. 110, 108** and **106** are early 18C; **No. 104**, of now mellow red brick with a solid parapet, is 16C and has an octagonal domed turret *(1638)*.

A short detour along Hornsey Lane leads to the **Archway**, a viaduct built to allow the road north *(A1)* to pass through the hill 80ft/24m below Hornsey Lane.

The original structure by John Nash was replaced in 1897 by a metal construction designed by Alexander Binnie.

The **Whittington Stone** *(1821)*, a marble cat sitting on a stone, marks the spot where, according to tradition, **Dick Whittington** heard Bow bells telling him to "turn again".

Spas

In the 18C a number of **London spas** developed around mineral springs, where people could take the waters in rural surroundings. They were frequented by the less wealthy, who could not afford the elegance of Bath. Among the most popular were Hampstead and Islington, and also Sadler's Wells, which offered dancing, pantomimes and rope dancing, accompanied by the consumption of cold meat and wine.

ADDITIONAL SIGHTS

Fenton House★★

Open Mar–Oct Wed–Sun and bank holidays 11am–5pm. £6.50; joint ticket with 2 Willow Road £9. Free to NT members. Guidebook (4 languages). Braille guide. No photography. 020 7435 3471. www.nationaltrust.org.uk/fenton-house.

An iron gate *(1707)* by **Tijou** gives access to a red-brick house, built in 1693; it is Hampstead's finest, besides being one of its earliest and largest. The original main pine staircase, with its twisted balusters and wide handrail, has survived, as well as some doorcases, panelling and chimney-pieces.

In 1793 the house was bought by a Riga merchant, Philip Fenton, after whom it is still named; in 1952 it was bequeathed to the National Trust.

Collection

The furniture and pictures form a background to 18C porcelain – English, German and French – and the Benton-Fletcher collection of early **keyboard instruments**, some 18 in number, ranging in date from 1540–1805. The instruments are for the most part kept in good playing order and are accessible to students. There are frequent concerts. On the ground floor are harpsichords *(1770 English; 1612 Flemish)*, as well as the most important part of the English porcelain collection *(Bristol, Plymouth, Chelsea, Bow, Worcester)*.

On the first floor are German figurines, teapots, Worcester apple green porcelain in satinwood cabinets and the most important piece of English porcelain in the collection, a **Worcester pink-scale vase** and cover, probably decorated in London. *(Drawing Room)*: 17–18C Chinese blue-and-white porcelain, 18C English harpsichords, a 16C Italian and early 18C English **spinet**, and a 17C virginal. On the *Top Floor*: 18C square pianos, 17C and 18C harpischords, 17C and 20C clavichords, and a 17C spinet and virginal. The 17C needlework pictures *(Rockingham Room)*, the bird and flower pictures by the 18C artist Samuel Dixon *(Porcelain Room)* and the works of Sir William Nicholson *(Dining Room)* are all noteworthy.

Kenwood House★★

Access by bus 210 from Golders Green or Archway. ***House:*** *The house is due to reopen in autumn 2013 following extensive refurbishment; check the website for details. Closed 24–26 Dec. Group tours. Events and activities all year round.* ***Grounds:*** *Open daily 7am–dusk. Parking; picnic area. 020 8348 1286. www.english-heritage.org.uk.*

"A great 18C gentleman's country house with pictures such as an 18C collector might have assembled" – William Murray, younger son of a Scottish peer, acquired Kenwood in 1754, two years before he was appointed Lord Chief Justice and created Earl of Mansfield. In 1764 he invited his fellow Scot **Robert Adam** to enlarge the house.

Kenwood was purchased by **Lord Iveagh** in 1925. He filled it with the remarkable collection of pictures he had formed at the end of the 19C and bequeathed to the nation in 1927. The original furnishings which were sold in 1922 are slowly returning to the house (including the Adam side table, pedestals and wine cistern in the Hall). The **Suffolk Collection** of portraits is also on display on the First Floor.

Exterior – The pedimented portico with giant fluted columns, frieze and medallion was Adam's typical contribution to the *North front*; on the *South front*, from which there is a splendid **view** down to the lake, Adam raised the central block to three floors, refaced the existing Orangery and designed the Library to the East to balance the façade.

Interior – Of the rooms on either side of the hall, the most remarkable are the Music and Dining Rooms *(cornice and doorcase related in motif to the preceding enriched columns and entablatures)*, the Adam Library and Orangery.

Adam Library★★ – The "room for receiving company," as Adam described it, is richly decorated with Adam motifs and painted predominantly in pale blues and pinks, with white mouldings. The oblong room, beneath a curved ceiling, leads into two apsidal ends, each lined with bookcases and screened off by a horizontal beam supported on fluted Corinthian columns. Arched recesses, fitted with triple mirrors, flank the fireplace and reflect the three tall windows opposite.

Paintings★★ – In the Dining Room wing hang *Portrait of the Artist* by **Rembrandt**, *Pieter van den Broecke* by **Frans Hals**, the ringletted young girl *Guitar Player* by **Vermeer**, and works by Bol, Snyders, Cuyp and Crome. Also here are seascapes by **Van de Velde** and **Turner**. Portraits by the English School fill the South Front rooms and Music Room wing: beautiful Gainsborough women, including *Mary, Lady Howe* in pink silk, *Lady Hamilton* by Romney, children's portraits by **Reynolds** *(The Brummell Children)* and **Lawrence** *(Miss Murray)*.

Gainsboroughs of unusual character hang in the South Front rooms and up the staircase: *Going to Market, Two Shepherd Boys with Dogs Fighting* and the dramatic *Hounds Coursing a Fox*.

Burgh House

New End Square, Hampstead. House and Museum: Open Wed–Fri, Sun noon–5pm. Closed Good Fri, Easter Mon, 25 Dec–1 Jan. Licensed Buttery Open Tue–Fri 11am–5.30pm, Sat–Sun 9.30am–5pm. 020 7431 0144 or 020 7794 2905 (Buttery). www.burghhouse.org.uk.

A Romantic Poet

John Keats (1795–1821) was the eldest of three sons. From an early age he showed a keen talent for poetry by translating Virgil's *Aeneid* into prose while still at school. In 1810, after losing both his parents (his father in a riding accident and his mother to consumption), he was apprenticed to a surgeon; four years later he transferred to St Thomas' and Guy's Hospitals in Southwark. By 1817, then living in the City, Keats decided to devote himself to the study of Elizabethan literature and to writing poetry, adopting the free form of the heroic couplet. When his brother and sister-in-law resolved to sail for America, he travelled to Liverpool to see them off and onwards on an extensive tour of the north (Lancaster, Lake District, Carlisle, Dumfries, Ireland, Ayr, Glasgow). Spent by the exertion and exposure, Keats began to display the symptoms of his fatal malady. His other brother died that December and Keats returned to Hampstead, where he met Fanny Brawne not long before he, too, was to die in Rome.

This dignified, Grade I listed house, with its south-facing terrace, was built in 1703 when Hampstead was becoming popular as a spa. The house takes its name from the Revd Allatson Burgh, vicar of St Lawrence Jewry in the City, who was so unpopular that his parishioners petitioned Queen Victoria to have him removed.

The panelled rooms are now used for poetry and music recitals, exhibitions by local artists and the Hampstead Museum; one room is devoted to the artist **John Constable**; while another is licensed for civil marriages.

2 Willow Road

Open Mar–Oct, Guided tours (1hr) by timed ticket Wed–Sun at 11am, noon, 1pm and 2pm; self-guided visits 3pm–5pm. £6; joint ticket with Fenton House £9. 020 7435 6166. www.nationaltrust.org.uk.

This striking Modernist home was designed by architect **Erno Goldfinger** *(1902–87)* in 1939. Born in Hungary, Goldfinger went to Paris in 1920, where he studied architecture at the École des Beaux-Arts; five years later, he and a number of fellow students persuaded Auguste Perret, a pioneer in the use of reinforced concrete and "structural rationalism", to set up a studio. In Paris he met and married the striking Ursula Blackwell (of the Crosse & Blackwell family), who then began painting under Amédée Ozenfant, a former collaborator of Le Corbusier. The three houses they built replaced a run-down terrace. Despite causing early controversy, their discreet, modern, functional design is sympathetic to the Georgian brick houses around. Inside, the central block is spacious, airy, light and full of individual mementoes, as well as art collected by the couple *(Ernst, Penrose, Miller, Picasso)*.

St John-at-Hampstead

Downshire Hill. Open Mon–Sat 9am–5.30pm, Sun 8am–7pm. 020 7794 5808. www.hampsteadparish church.org.uk.

This church marks the Keats Grove fork, white and upright with a domed bell turret. It has a Classical pediment, large name plaque and square portico, and is a chapel of ease dating from 1818.

Keats House

Open Mar–Oct Tue–Sun 1pm–5pm, Nov–Feb Fri–Sun 1pm–5pm (Tue–Thu pre-booked groups only). Closed Good Friday, 25–26 Dec, 1 Jan. £5. 020 7332 3868. www.cityoflondon.gov.uk/keats.

Two small semi-detached Regency houses with a common garden, known as Wentworth Place, were erected in 1815–16 by two friends, with whom Keats and his brother became acquainted. In 1818, Keats came to live with his friend Brown in the left-hand house; shortly afterwards Mrs Brawne and her children became tenants of the other. He wrote poems, including *Ode to a Nightingale*, in the garden.

Freud Museum

20 Maresfield Gardens. ⊖ Swiss Cottage ♿ Open Wed–Sun noon–5pm. Closed Easter bank holidays, 24–26 Dec, 1 Jan (call for details). £6. Brochure (5 languages). Limited parking. Shop. 020 7435 2002. www.freud.org.uk.

The house to which **Sigmund Freud** escaped from Nazi persecution in Vienna in 1938 has been turned into a museum devoted to his life and work, and to the history and development of psychoanalysis. On the ground floor are his study and working library, with his famous couch and collection of books, pictures and **antiquities★★**.

ADDRESSES

CAFÉS

Louis, *32 Heath St., Hampstead. ⊖ Hampstead. 020 7435 9908. Daily 9am–6pm.* Hungarian patisserie serving a wide range of sweets and a few Eastern European dishes.

Maison Blanc, *76 High St., Hampstead. ⊖ Hampstead. 020 872 148 1811. Mon–Fri 7am–7pm, Sat 8am–7pm, Sun 8am–8pm.* Top-notch French bakery.

LIGHT BITE

The Brew House, *Kenwood House, Hampstead Lane. ⊖ Hampstead. 020 8341 5384. Daily Apr–Oct 9am–6pm, Nov–Mar 9am–4pm.* In the former servants' wing of Kenwood House, this pleasant café serves sandwiches, salads, hot dishes and a good variety of tasty desserts. On sunny days, there's a comfortable terrace.

Lauderdale Restaurant, *Lauderdale House, Waterlow Park. ⊖ Archway. 020 8341 4807. www.lauderdalehouse.co.uk. Tue–Sun 9am–6pm (5pm winter).* Lauderdale House is home to a nice tearoom, where you can also have a quick lunch (salads, quiches, pies, fish & chips). Pleasant garden.

The Rosslyn Delicatessen, *56 Rosslyn Hill. ⊖ Hampstead. 020 7794 9210. Mon–Sat 8am–8.30pm, Sun 8.30am–8pm).* This delightful deli has no tables of its own but is in an ideal spot for putting together a picnic to eat on the Heath.

PUBS AND BARS

The Flask, *14 Flask Walk, Hampstead, NW3 1HE. ⊖ Highgate. 020 7435 4580. www.theflaskhampstead.co.uk.* A quaint pub with a roaring fire in winter, where Karl Marx was a frequent visitor. Large outdoor space that can get very crowded on sunny days. Good pub food.

The Flask Tavern, *77 Highgate West Hill, N6 6BU. ⊖ Highgate; Archway. 020 8348 7346.* Delightful, historic pub with a warren of rooms and an outside courtyard. Decent pub food.

Gatehouse, *1 North Rd., Highgate, N6 4BD. ⊖ Highgate or Archway. 020 8340 8054 and 020 8340 3488 (box office). www.upstairsatthegatehouse.com.* A busy pub, with elaborate décor and historic associations. The theatre upstairs showcases young writers and actors in a regularly changing rep programme.

Spaniard's Inn, *Spaniards Rd., NW3 7JJ. ⊖ Hampstead. 020 8731 8406.* One of London's oldest pubs, founded in 1585 as a tollgate inn – the tollgate still stands opposite. Highwaymen frequented the area, and Dick Turpin is said to have been a regular. Dickens mentions the inn in *The Pickwick Papers*.

The Wells, *30 Well Walk, Hampstead NW3 1BX. ⊖ Hampstead. 020 7794 3785. www.thewellshampstead.co.uk.* Attractive 18C pub on the edge of Hampstead Heath, with leather sofas and good food.

ENTERTAINMENT

Music on a Summer Evening, *Kenwood Lakeside. ⊖ Hampstead or Highgate. 020 8233 5000 or 020 7413 1443 (reservations). www.picnicconcerts.com.* In summer, concerts are held in the extensive grounds of Kenwood House.

New End Theatre, *27 New End, Hampstead. ⊖ Hampstead. 020 7472 5800 or 0870 033 2733 (reservations), www.offwestendtheatres.co.uk. Box office: Mon–Sat 10am–8pm, Sun noon–6pm.* Small theatre with bold programming.

Royal Air Force Museum★★

Magnificent flying machines and simulators inform and entertain enthusiasts and laymen alike at this well-presented museum with over 200 aircraft, as well as many smaller exhibits. Interactive exhibits and a 3D cinema help bring it all alive.

Location: Grahame Park Way, NW9 5LL. Buses: 226 along Edgware Road; 204 towards Edgware. *Colindale (Edgware branch of the Northern Line)*. Colindale is to the Northwest of London, off the A5 or A41.

A BIT OF HISTORY

Affiliated with the Imperial War Museum (*see MAJOR CENTRAL LONDON MUSEUMS*), this museum is dedicated to the history of aviation and of the RAF, and is presented in several hangars on the historic site of Old Hendon Airfield, where Grahame-White established his flying school before World War I.

VISIT

(licensed) **P** ***Museum:*** *Open daily 10am–6pm (last admission 5.30pm).* ***Grahame White Factory:*** *Closed noon–1.30pm. Closed 24–26 Dec, 1 Jan; one week in Jan. No charge. Guided tours. Picnic area. Shop. 020 8205 2266. www.rafmuseum.org.uk.*

This is Britain's only museum dedicated wholly to aviation; with its world-class aircraft collection, as well as engines, weapons and smaller items, from logbooks and uniforms to medals, and its innovative approach, the museum is an exciting place to visit.

The Aeronauts Interactive Centre has plenty of hands-on experiments to help visitors learn how an aeroplane flies, and regular special events.

Milestones of Flight

Opened to celebrate the 100th anniversary of powered flight, this fascinating exhibit traces the history of aviation from its earliest beginnings to the present day.

Historic Hangars

World War I halls present a unique collection of aircraft in chronological order, from a Blériot monoplane through a Supermarine Stranraer flying boat, and a Sikorsky hoverfly to a Lightning Mach 2. The **Flight Simulator** enables visitors to experience the thrill of a flight with the Red Arrows and others.

Bomber Hall

This hall relates the history of aerial bombing from World War I to the present day. Bombers displayed include an **Avro Lancaster**, a Heinkel He 162A-2, a B17 Flying Fortress and a **Vulcan**. Note also a replica of the office of Sir Barnes Wallis, who invented the bouncing bomb.

Battle of Britain Collection

A special hall is dedicated to the battle that was fought in the skies of Southeast England during the summer of 1940. The Forces involved are represented by an impressive array of aircraft: Junkers 87 and 88, **Heinkel 111**, Messerschmitt against Gloster Gladiators, Tiger Moths, Spitfires and Hurricanes. In addition to the machines, you'll find an operations room, uniforms, **medals**, documents, relics and other memorabilia. There is also a 30min sound and light show.

Eurofighter, Royal Air Force Museum

Southeast London is a sprawling suburban area which encompasses the gritty residential streets of Peckham and Lewisham, the upmarket villages of Dulwich and Blackheath, and the area's crowning glory: Greenwich. Attractions here may be few and far between, but well worth travelling out from the city to see – from former palaces to important maritime sites, ancient scientific buildings to sweeping areas of parkland.

Highlights

1. Explore the **National Maritime Museum** (p353)
2. Catch a concert at the **O2** (p354)
3. Board the ***Cutty Sark*** (p355)
4. Straddle the Greenwich Meridian up at the **Royal Observatory** (p358)
5. Immerse yourself in Art Deco luxury at **Eltham Palace** (p360)

A Bit of Geography

Southeast London stretches away from the city centre on the southern side of the Thames towards the county of Kent. Greenwich, the main attraction, sits on the banks of the river opposite Docklands, with Greenwich Park stretching back to the village of Blackheath. Further east is Eltham and its eponymous Palace, while Dulwich is located to the West.

A Bit of History

The name "Greenwich" comes from the Saxon word "Grenewic" meaning green village. The Domesday Book records Bishop Odo of Bayeaux as owner of the manor sited here, and a royal palace or hunting lodge has been located in the area since before 1300. The royal connections continued for many years: Henry IV made his will here; the Palace of Placentia (or Greenwich Palace), created here in 1447, became Henry VII's principal residence and Henry VIII, his son, was born here.

Henry VIII's daughters, Mary and Elizabeth, both lived at the Palace during the 16C, but by the reign of James I in the 17C, it had fallen from favour and the Queens House, designed by Inigo Jones, was commissioned by his wife Anne in 1616. It was the first fully Classical building to be seen in England.

During the Civil War the Palace was used as a POW camp and during the Interregnum seized to become a mansion for Cromwell. It was demolished in the 17C and replaced with the Greenwich Hospital, later the Royal Naval College.

In 1675 Charles II commissioned the Royal Observatory and the original section of the structure, Flamsteed House designed by Sir Christopher Wren, was built. It was the first purpose-built scientific research building ever to be constructed in Britain and, as it was used for measurement, became home to the

Royal Observatory Greenwich

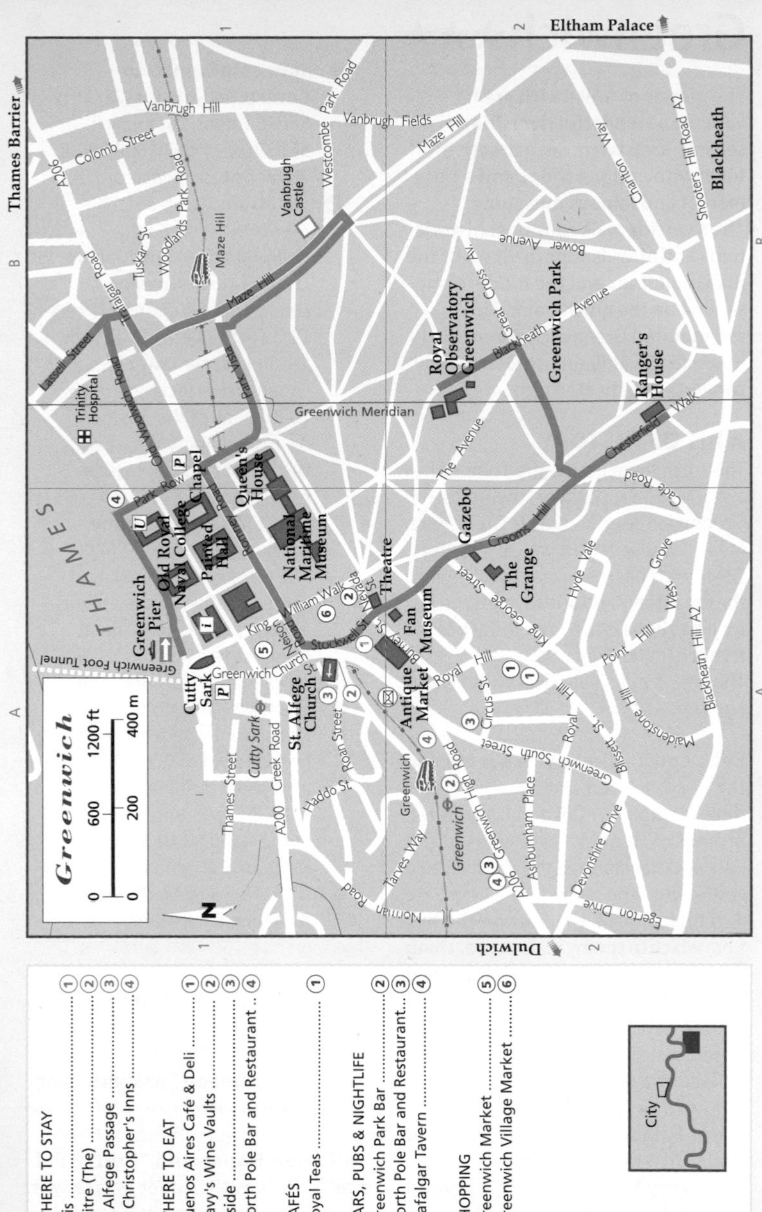

Prime Meridian, the basis for all longitudinal measurements, in 1851.

Southeast London Today

The major buildings of Greenwich and the grounds in which they sit became a World Heritage Site in 1997. Today, this is a popular tourist destination, as well as a much-loved place of leisure for Londoners, who come to stroll through the town, sit or play games in the park, wander around the markets, and eat or drink in the many restaurants and pubs. It is also a sought-after residential area.

Greenwich★★★

The glories of Greenwich are various: a wonderful riverside setting, a vast park, an attractive town with antique shops and a busy market and famous museums. The riverside walk runs past historic pubs and affords superb views of the royal buildings and the modernistic skyline on the north bank. The regenerated Greenwich Peninsula is home to the Millennium Dome, now converted to the 02 Arena.

Tourist Information Centre: Pepys House, 2 Cutty Sark Gardens, Greenwich, SE10 9LW. ℘0870 608 2000; www.visitgreenwich.org.uk.

Location: Map p 351. *⊖North Greenwich; Overground: Greenwich from Charing Cross; Waterloo; London Bridge; Cannon Street; DLR: Cutty Sark; by boat from Westminster or Tower Bridge.* Greenwich is located on the south bank of the Thames opposite Canary Wharf and the Isle of Dogs. Access by road is via the A206 or A2.

Don't Miss: The **antique market** *(see YOUR STAY IN THE CITY)* is well known and there are other shops selling antiques and second-hand books. A footway tunnel *(lift or 100 steps)* leads under the Thames *(10min)* to the Isle of Dogs, from where there is a fine **view★★** of Greenwich, as painted by Canaletto in 1750. The painting is now in the National Maritime Museum Collection.

Kids: National Maritime Museum; *Cutty Sark*.

A BIT OF HISTORY

The small town beside the Thames has a worldwide reputation owing to the Greenwich Meridian and Greenwich Mean Time at The Royal Observatory. Greenwich has many associations with the Royal Navy and British maritime history, and its days as a royal residence are recalled in the Queen's House.
The area is now a UNESCO World Heritage Site.

Bella Court – Greenwich has been in the royal domain since King Alfred's time. Humphrey, Duke of Gloucester, brother of Henry V first enclosed the park and transformed the manor into a castle, which he named Bella Court. He also built a fortified tower on the hill, from which to spy invaders approaching up the Thames or along the Roman road from Dover. On Duke Humphrey's death in 1447, Henry VI's queen, **Margaret of Anjou**, annexed the castle and renamed it **Placentia** or Pleasaunce.

Tudor Palace – The Tudors preferred Greenwich to their other residences, and **Henry VIII**, born there, enlarged the castle into a vast palace with a royal armoury, where craftsmen produced armour to rival the Italian and German suits *(see TOWER OF LONDON)*.
Henry also founded naval dockyards upstream at Deptford and downstream at Woolwich. The docks were also accessible by a road skirting the wall, which divided the extensive royal gardens from the park.

Overlooking the thoroughfare was a gatehouse in front of which, legend has it, **Walter Raleigh** threw down his cloak so that **Queen Elizabeth** might cross a mire dryshod.

Palladian House and "Pretty Palace" – Rich as the Tudor palace was, in 1615 **James I** commissioned **Inigo Jones** *(see INTRODUCTION– Architecture)* to build a house for his queen **(Anne of Denmark)** on the exact site of the gatehouse, straddling the busy Woolwich-Deptford road. Based on the principles of the Italian architect, **Palladio** *(1508–80)*, it is a compact and well-proportioned house despite its "bridge room" over the road.

Work stopped on Anne's death and was resumed only when **Charles I** offered the house to his queen, **Henrietta Maria**. During the Commonwealth the Tudor palace was cleared for use as a barracks and prison. At the Restoration, the Queen's House alone emerged relatively unscathed. In 1665 Charles II commissioned a King's House to be built by **John Webb**, a student of Inigo Jones – now the King Charles Block of the Old Royal Naval College. With the exception of the Observatory, however, construction ceased due to lack of funds before Charles' "pretty palace" was complete.

Royal Hospital to Royal Naval College – Work at Greenwich was resumed in 1694 when **William and Mary**, who preferred Hampton Court as a royal residence, granted a charter for a Royal Hospital for Seamen at Greenwich, founded on the lines of the Royal Military Hospital in Chelsea, appointing **Sir Christoper Wren** as Surveyor of Works. Wren submitted numerous plans before proposing the one we know today.

At Queen Mary's insistence, this incorporated the Queen's House and its 150ft/46m wide river vista, the King Charles Block alongside the construction of three additional blocks, the King William (SW), Queen Mary (SE) and Queen Anne (NE, below which exists a crypt, sole remnant of the Tudor palace *(closed to the public)*.

To complete the scheme emphasis was focused by projecting cupolas before the refectory and chapel, and the course of the Thames was modified and embanked – the only major vista design by Wren to be properly realised. The project took more than half a century to complete and involved **Vanbrugh**, **Hawksmoor** and **Colen Campbell**.

In 1873 the buildings were transformed into the Royal Naval College and remained so until 1998. Most are now part of the University of Greenwich. The Queen's House became part of the National Maritime Museum in 1937.

SIGHTS

National Maritime Museum★★★

Open daily 10am–5pm; some galleries open Thu till 8pm (last admission 30min before closing); 31 Dec closes 3pm, 1 Jan opens noon. See website for details. Highlights guided tours (2hr). Closed 24–26 Dec. No charge except for some temporary exhibitions. Licensed café-restaurant. Play area. 020 8312 6565 (24hr recorded information); 020 8858 4422 (administration). www.rmg.co.uk.

A fabulous collection of all things maritime *(fine art, rare instruments, treasures and mementoes)* is displayed in this beautifully organised museum.

The development of Britain as a sea power is traced from Henry VIII's Tudor

National Maritime Museum, Queen's House, Old Royal Naval Collage and Canary Wharf viewed from Greenwich Park

Maritime London Gallery, National Maritime Museum

fleet through **Captain Cook**'s travels in the South Seas and Pacific Islands to Sir John Franklin's Polar exploration.

The theme of **Explorers** is the quest of early navigators and explorers. **Atlantic Worlds** examines the settlement in America, the development of the trans-Atlantic slave trade and its abolition, unrest in the colonies and the move to independence. **Traders** explores Britain's maritime trade with Asia, focusing on the role played by the East India Company. The museum illustrates the importance of London's proximity to the sea; **Maritime London** has held a prominent place in international economic and social development, and the city's history and growth is bound with the thriving docks and related industries.

The newly opened Sammy Ofer Wing provides exhibition space and houses archives, a brasserie and shop, and has an entrance on to the park.

Voyagers is the permanent gallery here that highlights the contemporary significance of maritime history. Younger visitors can explore maritime skills from deep-sea diving to steering a ship into port in the **Children's Gallery** and **The Bridge** interactive gallery.

Nelson, Navy, Nation, a new permanent gallery housing the museum's unrivalled collections relating to the celebrated naval hero Horatio Nelson, opens in October 2013.

Queen's House★★

Open daily 10am–5pm (last admission 30min before closing), 31 Dec, 1 Jan. See website for temporary closures. Closed 24–26 Dec. 020 8312 6565 (24hr recorded information). 020 8858 4422 (administration). www.rmg.co.uk.

This Palladian villa *(1616)*, England's first Classical building, was designed by **Inigo Jones** for the wives of James I and Charles I. The ground-floor rooms display portraits of the Tudor and Stuart kings and queens, and historical paintings of the old Greenwich Palace of Placentia.

On the first floor **Art for the Nation** displays 200 paintings, including works by Gainsborough, Lely, Hogarth, Reynolds and **Canaletto**.

Old Royal Naval College★★

Enter from Cutty Sark Gardens, College Approach, Romney Road Gate, Royal Gate and on Park Row. Painted Hall & Chapel and Greenwich Gateway Visitor Centre (Pepys Building, beside Cutty Sark entrance): Open daily 10am–5pm. Grounds: Open daily 8am–6pm. 020 8269 4799. www.ornc.org.

The college accommodates the University of Greenwich's Maritime Campus.

The Painted Hall★
Wren's domed refectory was completed in 1703. In 1805 Nelson lay in state here before his burial in St Paul's.
The hall and upper hall were painted in exuberant Baroque by **Sir James Thornhill** *(1708–27)*: William and Mary, Anne, George I and his descendants celebrate Britain's maritime power in a wealth of involved allegory. The artist was paid £3 a sq yd/0.8sq m for the ceilings, £1 for the walls.

Chapel★
After a fire in 1779, Wren's chapel was redecorated by "Athenian" Stuart and William Newton in Wedgwood pastel colours. Across the apse is *The Preservation of St Paul after the Shipwreck at Malta* by Benjamin West (1738–1820).

GREENWICH

Start at Greenwich Pier, where a foot tunnel runs to the Isle of Dogs.

Cutty Sark★★
Open daily 10am–5pm (last admission 4pm). Closed 24–26 Dec. 020 8312 6608. www.rmg.co.uk.
Standing proud near the river, the *Cutty Sark* makes a handsome sight. Launched at Dumbarton in 1869 for the China tea trade, the *Cutty Sark* became famous as being the fastest tea clipper afloat. Her best day's run with all 32,000 sq ft/ 2,975sq m or 0.5 acre/0.2ha of canvas fully spread was 363mi/584km. In her heyday she brought tea from China and later, wool from Australia. Her name refers to the the cutty sark, or short chemise, of the witch Nannie, "a winsome wench" in Robert Burns' poem *Tam O'Shanter*, hence the ship's distinctive figurehead. In 1922 she was converted into a nautical training school and transferred to dry dock at Greenwich in 1954. Despite a terrible fire in 2007, the *Cutty Sark* has been meticulously restored to her former glory, using only materials and techniques contemporary to the 19C. You can now walk beneath the iron hull, explore the cargo and lower decks, and try out the cabins.

Walk east along the river past the Old Royal Naval College (*see Sights*) and left into Park Row.

Riverside Downstream

This area is full of historical heritage and elegance.
The **Trafalgar Tavern** (*see Addresses*), of 1837, recollects the personalities and events of Nelson's time. In the early 19C it was the setting for the Liberal ministers' "**whitebait dinners**" . **Dickens** used to meet there with Thackeray and Cruikshank. Backing onto Crane Street is **The Yacht**, a century older.
The **Cutty Sark Tavern** was rebuilt with a great bow window in 1804 on the site of earlier inns, while at the end stands the four-square Harbourmaster's Office *(No. 21)* which for 50 years, until the 1890s, controlled colliers entering the Pool of London.

Return to Trafalgar Rd. and turn right into Maze Hill.

A Famous Name

Cutty Sark is also the name of a pale, delicate Scotch whisky branded by **Berry Bros & Rudd** of St James's. The name was suggested by the clipper, which had just returned to British waters having traded under the Portuguese flag. The whisky, meanwhile, was especially blended for the export market – destined for America and supplied throughout Prohibition (1920–33) via Nassau in the Bahamas – "the real McCoy", a certain Captain William McCoy, was one such bootlegger there. Between 1973 and 2003, the annual *Cutty Sark* Tall Ships' Races *(now the Tall Ships' Races)* were sponsored by wine and spirit merchants.

Vanbrugh Castle

This caricature of a Medieval fortress stands on Maze Hill. It was built and occupied by the architect and playwright, Sir John Vanbrugh, from 1717–26.

Cross into the park.

Greenwich Park

Palisaded in 1433 and surrounded by a wall in Stuart times, Greenwich Park is the oldest enclosed royal domain. It extends for 180 acres/73ha in a sweep of chestnut avenues and grass to a point 155ft/47m above the river crowned by the Royal Observatory and the **General Wolfe** monument. On the slope below the Observatory are traces of the 17C giant grass steps by Le Nôtre. In the Park west of the castle, beyond the Roman Villa, is a wilderness with a small herd of fallow deer.

Leave the Park in its northwest corner onto Greenwich High Rd.

St Alfege Church

Open Mon–Wed, Fri 11am–4pm, Thu 11am–2pm, Sat 10am–4pm, Sun noon–4pm. Lunchtime recitals Thu at 1pm. www.st-alfege.org.

This gaunt church *(1718)* with its Doric portico is by **Nicholas Hawksmoor**, the tower is by John James. Inside the murals *(east end)* are by Thornhill and the carving is by **Grinling Gibbons**.

Take Stockwell St. to Croom's Hill.

Croom's Hill

This winding lane was a thoroughfare in the 15C, when the park was enclosed, and became its western boundary.

At the bottom of Crooms Hill is the **Greenwich Theatre** *(www.greenwich theatre.org.uk)*, built in 1968 in the shell of a Victorian music hall.

The Georgian terrace *(Nos. 6–12)* dates from 1721–23. Poet Laureate, Cecil Day Lewis, lived at No. 6 from 1968 to 1972.

Continue to the Fan Museum.

Fan Museum★

Crooms Hill. Open Tue–Sat 11am–5pm, Sun noon–5pm. Closed Yom Kippur, 24–26 Dec, 1 Jan. £3 (no charge for senior citizens Tue after 2pm). Fan-making workshop 1st Sat of every month. Audio-guide. Brochure. 020 8305 1441. www.thefanmuseum.org.uk.

This delightful museum owns 3,500 fans from the 11C to the present day, with strong reference to the 18C and 19C. *(Regular demonstrations on fan-making, conservation and restoration.)*

Turn right onto Gloucester Circus.

Gloucester Circus, designed by Michael Searle in the 1700s, has retained original houses on the East and South sides. **The Grange,** an early 17C building with 18C additions, stands on a site recorded as having been given to Ghent Abbey in 818 by a daughter of Alfred the Great; overlooking the park is a 17C **gazebo**. **Heath Gate House** is a relatively low brick mansion with gabled dormers and pilasters supporting the upper floor. The red-brick **Manor House** is typical of 1697, even down to the hooded porch with a carved shell motif.

Return to Croom's Hill, turn right and then left onto Chesterfield Walkleads to the Ranger's House.

Ranger's House★

Chesterfield Walk, Blackheath. Open Apr–Sept Sun–Wed 10am–5pm, Oct–Mar group access only, Thu (pre-book). £6.50. Audio-tour. Parking. 020 8294 2548. www.english-heritage.org.uk.

Originally a small brick villa with a stone balustrade, the house had rounded wings added by Philip, 4th Earl of Chesterfield *(1694–1733)*.

The ground and first floors provide a splendid setting for the **Wernher Collection** of European Art, which reflects the eclectic taste of Sir Julius Wernher *(1850–1912)*, the mining magnate and philanthropist instrumental in founding Imperial College *(see KENSINGTON)*.

J Harrison's Marine Timekeeper No 1

A Pioneering Clockmaker

John Harrison *(1693–1776)* was born the son of a carpenter; little otherwise is known of his early life until 1713, when he completed his first pendulum clock made entirely of wood: oak for the wheels and box for the axles (Worshipful Company of Clockmakers Museum. *See CITY – Guildhall*).

In 1722 Harrison installed a unique clock at Brocklesby Park made from lignum vitae, a tropical hardwood; this continues to keep accurate "mean" time today. His next important invention was the bi-metallic gridiron-grasshopper pendulum *(1725–27)*; the grasshopper mechanism provided a friction-free means of clocking the units of time.

At an age of increasing maritime activity, it was critical for sailors to determine longitude in order to accurately chart the oceans that divided land masses. In 1730 Harrison journeyed to London with drawings and calculations for a reliable clock that would be seaworthy: pendulumless, resistant to corrosion or rust and resilient to extremes in weather. There, he met the astronomer Dr Edmund Halley. Harrison's No. 1 *(H-1)* was tried on a journey to Lisbon in 1737; the clock proved itself accurate and the Board of Longitude convened for the first time. Described by **Hogarth** in his *Analysis of Beauty* as "one of the most exquisite movements ever made" *(1753)*, H-1 helped the English roll out colonisation of foreign shores.

The Collection includes rare early religious paintings *(Filippo Lippi, Hans Memling)*, paintings by Dutch painters *(Metsu, Van Ostade, de Hooch)*, Renaissance jewellery and Medieval silverware. Also on view are Majolica ceramics, Limoges plates, Sèvres porcelain and Meissen pottery, plus tapestries and portraits by Joshua Reynolds and George Romney.

Continue to the Park's centre.

Royal Observatory Greenwich★★

Tour 45min. Open daily 10am–5pm (6pm summer, last admission 30min before closing, last Planetarium show 4pm), 31 Dec, 1 Jan. Flamsteed House and Meridian Courtyard: £7; entrance to the Astronomy Centre is free. Closed 24–26 Dec. Leaflet (6 languages). Café and restaurant. 020 8312 6565 (24hr recorded information), 020 8858 4422. www.rmg.co.uk.

In 1675 **Charles II** directed **Sir Christopher Wren** to "build a small observatory within our park at Greenwich" for "the finding out of the longitude of places for perfecting navigation and astronomy." Wren, a former astronomer as well as an architect, designed a house of red brick; it is named Flamsteed House after John Flamsteed, the first Astronomer Royal, appointed in 1675.

The **Meridian Building**, a mid-18C addition, was built to house the observatory's **collection★★** of instruments. At the main gate is the 24-hour dial of the Shepherd Gate Clock *(1851)* clock and British Standard Measures. The **tour** begins in the Meridian courtyard, where visitors may record the exact time they stand on the Greenwich Meridian, the brass meridian of zero longitude linked in a line to the North and South Poles.

The Millennium Dome

© Christopher Steer/iStockphoto.com

Riverside walks, parkland and lakes to attract wildlife have transformed the Greenwich Peninsula, where the site of a former gasworks has been redeveloped to include roads, housing, stores and other amenities for the local population. However, the focal point of the regenerated area is the Millennium Dome, with its domed glass-fibre roof designed by **Lord Richard Rogers** to mark the third millennium. After the rather disappointing Millennium Experience and years of wrangling over its fate, this controversial structure has now been transformed into the successful **02 Arena**, a concert venue and exhibition space.

On the south face of Flamsteed House are sundials. The red time ball on the roof, erected in 1833, served as a time check for ships on the Thames; the ball rises to the top of the mast and drops at exactly 13: 00 hours GMT.

Within **Flamsteed House** the first rooms trace the Observatory's foundation and the evolution of man's understanding of the heavens. Other displays trace the discovery of latitude and longitude, including the standardisation of the Greenwich meridian in 1884 at the Meridian Conference in Washington.

The **Meridian Building** contains the **Quadrant Room**, the Airy Transit Circle through which the meridian passes *(video)* and the Telescope Dome, with Britain's largest *(28in/50cm)* refracting telescope *(video of the moon landing)*.

At the **Astronomy Centre** you can touch a 4.5 billion year-old meteorite, learn about how our solar system was formed, and explore the cosmos in the state of the art **Peter Harrison Planetarium**.

ADDITIONAL SIGHTS

Blackheath★

Overground: Blackheath from Cannon Street or London Bridge.

The course of the Roman Watling Street between the South Coast and London is marked by Blackheath Road, Blackheath Hill and Shooters Hill, notorious for highwaymen in the 18C. Rebel forces have used the heath as a rallying ground: **Wat Tyler** *(1381)*; the Kentishmen under **Jack Cade** *(1450)*; the Cornishmen under Audley *(1497)*. In more joyful mood, in 1415, the people greeted **Henry V** on his victorious return from Agincourt; in 1660, **Charles II** was welcomed by the Restoration Army and in 1608, it is said, **James I** taught the English to play golf on Blackheath.

The heath is ringed by stately 18C and 19C **terraces** and **houses★**, when merchants, newly rich from the expanding docks, began to build in the vicinity.

Overlooking the heath from the **South side** are buildings including **Colonnade House** *(South Row)* and **The Paragon**, a late-18C crescent by Michael Searles.

On the **West side** are the early-18C Spencer House and Perceval House.

Blackheath Village's main street and Tranquil Vale – in reality full of traffic – lead off the heath southwards to modern estates.

DEPTFORD

Overground: Deptford from London Bridge.

The riverside village expanded during the reign of **Henry VIII** as a shipbuilding yard. It was in Deptford Creek that **Queen Elizabeth** boarded the *Golden Hinde* in 1581 to dub **Francis Drake** knight for his globe circumnavigation and where **Christopher Marlowe** was stabbed in a tavern brawl *(1593)*. In the 17C, diarist **John Evelyn** lived at Sayes

Court, which he briefly leased to **Peter the Great** in 1698, while the latter learned the art of shipbuilding in the yards. The dockyard closed in 1869.

St Paul's Church

East of Deptford High Street. Open for services or by appointment only. 020 8692 7449.

One of London's finest Baroque parish churches, St Paul's was built by Thomas Archer *(1712–30)*. It has a stone portico and Corinthian columns upholding a sculpted plaster ceiling.

St Nicholas' Church

Corner of Deptford Green and Stowage Lane. Open Mon–Fri 9.15am–2pm, Sat–Sun by arrangement. Guided tours by appointment. 020 8692 2749.

Of particular interest are the reredos by the church's 17C parishioner **Grinling Gibbons**. There is also an odd carved relief by Gibbons, known as the *Valley of Dry Bones*. The Jacobean pulpit is supported on a ship's figurehead.

The skulls on the gateposts were originally above crossed bones and since so many privateers sailed from Deptford, it is claimed they inspired the skull and crossbones flag. More honourably, the church, associated with **Sir Francis Drake**, has the privilege of flying the White Ensign. **Christopher Marlowe** is buried here.

Thames Barrier★

1 Unity Way, Woolwich. Open Thur–Sun 10.30am–5pm. £3.50. Parking (fee applies). 020 8305 4188. www.environment-agency.gov.uk.

Thames Barrier
© K. Brett/MICHELIN

The stunning, futuristic barrier, with its distinctive stainless steel cowls, is London's main flood defence. The information centre has an exhibition, which explains how it was designed and built, and how it all works. There's also a café overlooking the river.

ADDRESSES

CAFÉS

Buenos Aires Café & Deli, *86 Royal Hill. Blackheath rail. 020 8488 6764. www.buenosairesltd.com. Mon–Fri 8am–6pm, Sat–Sun 9am–6pm.* This coffee-shop has fresh, organic vegetables, meats, cheeses and rustic breads.

Royal Teas, *76 Royal Hill. Greenwich. 020 8691 7240. www.royalteascafe.co.uk. Mon–Sat 9.30am–5.30pm, Sun 10.30am–5.30pm.* This cosy café serves homemade cakes and good tea and coffee.

PUBS AND BARS

Greenwich Park Bar, *1 King William Walk. Greenwich. 020 8858 8791. www.thegreenwichpark.com. Sun–Thu noon–midnight, Fri–Sat noon–1am.* A lovely location by the park entrance. There's a lounge upstairs for more intimate drinks.

North Pole Bar, *131 Greenwich High Rd. Greenwich. 020 8853 3020, www.northpolegreenwich.com. Mon–Sat noon–midnight, Sun noon–10pm.* Modern bar with a friendly, relaxed atmosphere. In the basement the **South Pole Bar** is a good place for a dance.

Trafalgar Tavern, *6 Park Row. Greenwich. 020 8858 2909. www.trafalgartavern.co.uk. Mon–Thur noon–11pm, Fri–Sat noon–midnight, Sun noon–10.30pm.* This historic pub *(1837)* was visited and immortalised by Dickens in his novel, *Our Mutual Friend.*

SHOPPING

Greenwich Market, *Greenwich High Rd. Greenwich. Tue–Sun and bank holidays 10am–5.30pm. 020 8269 5096.* Very popular market packed full of stalls selling original arts and crafts, antiques, local designer and vintage clothing and produce. Arrive early as it gets packed.

Eltham Palace★

The vision of discerning art lovers has preserved the remains of Eltham Palace, while creating a refined residence. The wonderful Art Deco interior has been lavishly restored.

Location: Court Yard, Eltham SE9 5QE. *Rail: Eltham or Mottingham from London Bridge.*

A BIT OF HISTORY

South of Eltham High Street, nestles Eltham Palace, a historical country retreat documented as being in the possession of Odo, Bishop of Bayeux and half-brother of William the Conqueror in 1086. **Edward II** was the first of several monarchs to live there, preferring it to Windsor. **Edward IV** added the Great Hall in 1479–80; **Henry VIII** met **Erasmus** there, happy to live there until an interest in ships spurred him to move to Greenwich.

The Palace gradually fell into ruins and was abandoned during the late 18C and 19C – painted as a Romantic folly by **Turner** and **Girtin**. In 1931, it was leased to **Sir Stephen Courtauld**, who restored the lovely Great Hall and built his own country residence.

VISIT

Open Mar–Oct Mon–Wed and Sun 10am–5pm, Nov–Feb Sun 10am–4pm. Check website as may close at short notice. Closed 21 Dec–31 Jan. House and gardens £9.60; gardens only £6. Guidebook. No dogs. 020 8294 2548. www.english-heritage.org.uk.

Entrance Hall, Eltham Palace

The house is approached over a fine stone bridge straddling the moat. The **Great Hall** is built of brick, faced with stone. Its chief glory is the sweet-chestnut hammerbeam roof with a central hexagonal louvred section that would once have served to expel smoke from the large open hearth.

The windows are placed high in the wall, allowing for heavy tapestry hangings to insulate the lower sections. The wooden reredos was installed in the 1930s. Beyond the dais, reached via the oriels or bay windows, once lay the King's and Queen's apartments.

Courtauld House

Architects **John Seely** and **Paul Paget** redeveloped the site. The five entertainment rooms with the bedrooms above are in the south wing, extending in line with the Great Hall. All "mod cons" pervade the house, including a centralised vacuum cleaner in the basement and underfloor heating. It is, however, the unique quality of the 1930s internal decoration that is particularly remarkable: wooden veneer *(flexwood)* panelling is fitted in all the main bedrooms.

Notable features include the entrance-hall inlaid panels of Venice and Sweden (Roman gladiator and Scandinavian Viking) and **Alice in Wonderland** reliefs set between the windows; Lady Courtauld's bathroom with its onyx basin, gold-plated taps and mosaic alcove; the dining room with a square-coffered silver-leafed ceiling and 1930s black marble fireplace set with mother-of-pearl ribbons and polished Art Deco grate.

The house has been lovingly furnished in Art Deco style based on a detailed inventory and on photographs.

The landscaped **gardens** have mature trees and beds of fragrant flowers.

Dulwich★

The highlights of Dulwich are its fine museums, handsome weather-boarded buildings and elegant houses. The area is also home to a vast park of magnificent oak trees.

Location: ⊖Rail: *West Dulwich from Victoria, North Dulwich from London Bridge.* Dulwich lies to the South of Southwark.

A BIT OF HISTORY

Dulwich Manor, owned by **Bermondsey Abbey** until the Reformation, was acquired in the 17C by Edward Alleyn. The houses reflect the transition from 17C village to small country town, where 18C–19C city merchants resided.

Nos. 60 and 62 Dulwich Village date from 1767. In the 18C the ironwork canopy on pillars over the pavement shaded the village butcher. **Nos. 97–105** form an 18C terrace; the last two houses date from the mid-1700s.

Dulwich College★

Edward Alleyn, one of the greatest actors of the late 16C, bought Dulwich manor and founded the Chapel and College of God's Gift *(1619)* to serve as almshouses and a school for poor children. The buildings at the top of College Road include the chapel where Alleyn is buried.

College Road

The house at No. 31, Pickwick Cottage, is said to be where **Dickens** envisaged Mr Pickwick retiring. Bell Cottage (No. 23) is a rare example of the once-common weatherboarded local cottages.

Pond Cottages *(beyond the main road, Dulwich Common)* is an 18C group overlooking the Mill Pond, several wholly or partly weatherboarded. The **Toll Gate** is the last in use in the London area.

Dulwich Picture Gallery★

Open Tue–Fri and public holidays 10am–5pm, Sat–Sun 11am–5pm. Closed 24–26 Dec, 31 Dec–1 Jan. Free tours Sat and Sun 3pm. £6 permanent collection (£11 temporary and permanent). 020 8693 5254. www.dulwichpicturegallery.org.uk.

Dulwich Gallery, opened in 1814, is the oldest public picture gallery in the country. It was designed by **Sir John Soane** to house a collection of 400 paintings donated by a Frenchman, **Noel Joseph Desenfans**. Facing the central entrance is the small domed mausoleum of the founders, Sir Francis Bourgeois, Noel Desenfans and his wife. An extension *(1999)* comprises an elegant cloister in glass and bronze.

The Collection – Several landscapes by **Aelbert Cuyp**, three **Rembrandts** including *The Girl at a Window* and *Titus*, 17C and 18C landscapes and pastorals by **Poussin**; **Gainsborough** portraits of the Linley family, a **Reynolds** self-portrait and portrait of *Mrs Siddons* are among the collection highlights, which also includes works by **Van Dyck**, Raphael, Canaletto, **Rubens**, Murillo and Reni.

Horniman Museum★★★

100 London Road, Forest Hill.
Museum: *Open daily 10.30am–5.30pm.* ***Gardens:*** *Open Mon–Sat 7.15am–dusk, Sun and public holidays 8am–dusk. No charge except for temporary exhibitions and the Aquarium. 020 8699 1872. www.horniman.ac.uk.*

In 1901, Victorian tea trader Frederick Horniman left his house and collection of curiosities to the people. The resulting museum is one of London's most original. The **African Worlds and Centenary Galleries** includes displays from **Africa** *(archaeological material, masks)*, **America** *(Inuit exhibits, Navajo textiles)* and **Asia** *(masks and puppets)*. The **European** collection concentrates on folk art; the **Pacific** area collection includes material from Polynesia.

Children love the **Musical Instruments Collection** *(7,000 items)*, the Aquarium and the petting zoo. The gardens include formal rose gardens, and concerts are hosted in summer.

SOUTHWEST LONDON

Southwest London has a very different character to any other part of the city. This is an area of vast parks, sweeping gardens and river views. There are castles, palaces and stately homes, and almost every community has a village feel and a unique character. Although each suburb has its own identity, they can easily be imagined together as London's back garden, a place where visitors come to escape the bustle and crowds of the city.

Highlights

1 Stroll along the **Thames** (p364)
2 Watch wildlife at the **London Wetland Centre** (p369)
3 Visit Kew's **Royal Botanic Gardens** (p370)
4 Wander around **Hampton Court Palace** (p382)
5 Explore **Windsor Castle** (p390)

A Bit of Geography

Southwest London ranges along the banks of the river Thames west of the city centre. Hammersmith and Chiswick are located on the north bank just to the West of Kensington and Earls Court above a bend in the river. The bulbous section of land created by the snaking river here is home to Barnes and the London Wetland Centre. Putney is just to the East. Further west, Richmond and Kew, home to the Royal Botanic Gardens, occupy the south bank of the Thames, with Richmond Park stretching out behind them to the South. Wimbledon is just beyond here.

Facing Kew and its gardens across the Thames is Syon Park and further south, Twickenham and Hampton Court Palace. The M4 motorway makes its way out of London from just north of Kew, passing through Osterley Park and, 13mi/21km further on, reaching Windsor and the famous castle.

Transport connections to this part of the city are not quite so good as to other suburban areas, with limited tube coverage, but there are useful rail routes criss-crossing the area and calling at most of the main sites of interest.

A Bit of History

Much of the area west of London remained undeveloped until relatively recently and in comparison with other parts of the city, very little industrial activity has taken place here. Richmond's history began in the 16C with the building of Richmond Palace within what was then the royal manor of Sheen. It was commissioned by Henry VII, formerly known as the Earl of Richmond, who not only named the Palace after himself but also forced the surrounding community of Sheen to change its name to Richmond to match.

Chiswick Mall

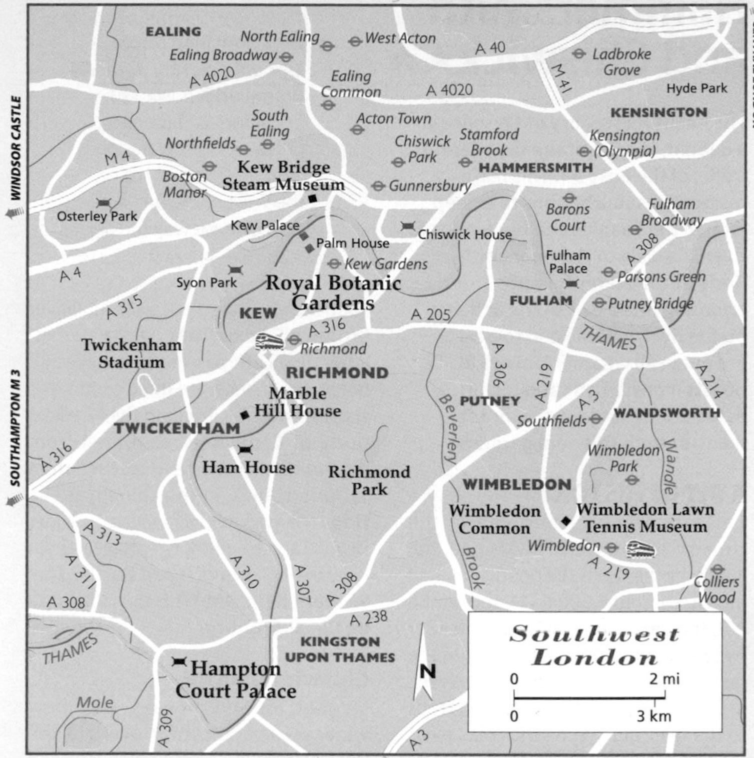

Both Putney and Barnes appear in the Domesday book *(as Putelei and Berne respectively)* and were reasonably significant communities, Putney because of its ferry. Barnes is home to some of the oldest riverside housing in London, dating from the 18C, signifying its long-running desirability as a place to live.

Kew's history begins with the creation of the Royal Botanic Gardens in 1759. Before this, little development had taken place here.

Windsor has a long and illustrious history as a royal residence and was recorded as Windsor Castle even in the Domesday book *(1086)*. During the Middle Ages this was one of the 50th wealthiest towns in England, a significant and prosperous community thanks to the presence of the Castle. The town began to decline after the Reformation but returned to favour in the 19C when Queen Victoria began holding state visits at the Castle, thereby placing it at the centre of the British Empire. Much of southwest London benefited greatly from the coming of the railways in the 19C, developing into more significant communities. Once these leafy areas became more accessible from London, the city's wealthy residents began to move into the area, a trend which continues today.

Southwest London Today

Despite the city's sprawl, southwest London remains a surprisingly green area and as a result, is an extremely desirable place to live. Many of London's wealthiest residents have their homes here, commuting daily into the city for work. The villagey atmosphere of many of the communities in this area *(Richmond, Wimbledon, Kew)* means that café culture is thriving and there are enough upmarket restaurants, classy pubs and boutique shops to keep visitors busy for days.

Hammersmith and Chiswick★★

The beautiful scenery of Chiswick is a delight, in spite of the thundering traffic of the busy A4. This leafy residential suburb clings to a deep loop of the Thames and has a pretty riverside walk to Hammersmith Bridge past delightful pubs affording fine views of the activity on the river, where keen rowers are out in all weather. Chiswick boasts many artistic and historic associations, and a magnificent mansion with splendid gardens.

Location: Map p 365. ⊖*Hammersmith; Turnham Green* and Bus No. 190 or overground train to Chiswick from Waterloo Station. Chiswick is to the West of the A4 dual carriageway.

A BIT OF HISTORY

Chiswick retains something of the country village, which it was until the 1860s; by the 1880s the population had increased from 6,500 to 15,600; in the 20C the motorway *(M4)* and its feeder flyover divided the riverside from the rest. Georgian houses survive, however, in Church Street and other parallel roads to the river, and in Chiswick Mall overlooking the river and the Eyot.

WALKING TOUR

From the station walk to Chiswick House and Hogarth's House (see Additional Sights), then cross Burlington Lane and proceed to Church St.

Chiswick Square

Burlington Lane.

Low, two-storey houses *(1680)* flank a forecourt in front of the three-storey **Boston House** *(1740)* where, in **Thackeray**'s *Vanity Fair*, Becky Sharp threw away her dictionary.

St Nicholas Parish Church

Open for services and by appointment. 020 8995 4717. www.stnicholaschiswick.org

This site was mentioned as far back as 1181. The deceptively broad church has a buttressed and battlemented west tower *(1436)*; the rest dates from the 1880s. Lady Mary Fauconberg, Oliver Cromwell's daughter, was a parishioner of St Nicholas. In the family vault below the chancel are three coffins, the shortest possibly holding the headless body of **Cromwell**, exhumed from Westminster Abbey and rescued from Tyburn in 1661. In the churchyard lie **Hogarth** *(enclosed with railings)* – under David Garrick's epitaph "Farewell, Great Painter of Mankind"; **Lord Burlington**; **William Kent**; **JM Whistler**; **Philippe de Loutherbourg**.

Chiswick Mall★★

Elegant 18C–19C houses, with bow windows and balconies, overlook the river. Particularly noteworthy are the three-storeyed **Morton House** *(1730)*, **Strawberry House** *(1735)* with its six bays and attic dormers, and **Walpole House** *(16C–17C)* boasting a fine iron gate and railings, once the residence of Barbara Villiers, Duchess of Cleveland (and mistress of Charles II).

Hammersmith Riverside

The most attractive part of Hammersmith is along the waterfront. Upstream from the bridge the embankment developed gradually from the early 18C with modest houses built singly or in terraces, adorned with balconies or festooned with purple wisteria; in the past the view included sailing barges making for harbour; now there are yachts or oarsmen in training. This is at the centre of the annual **Boat Race** course, a cut-throat rowing race between Oxford and Cambridge Universities, which started in 1829 (*see PLANNING YOUR TRIP – Calendar of Events*). It is rowed along a 4.25mi/6.84km stretch of the Thames

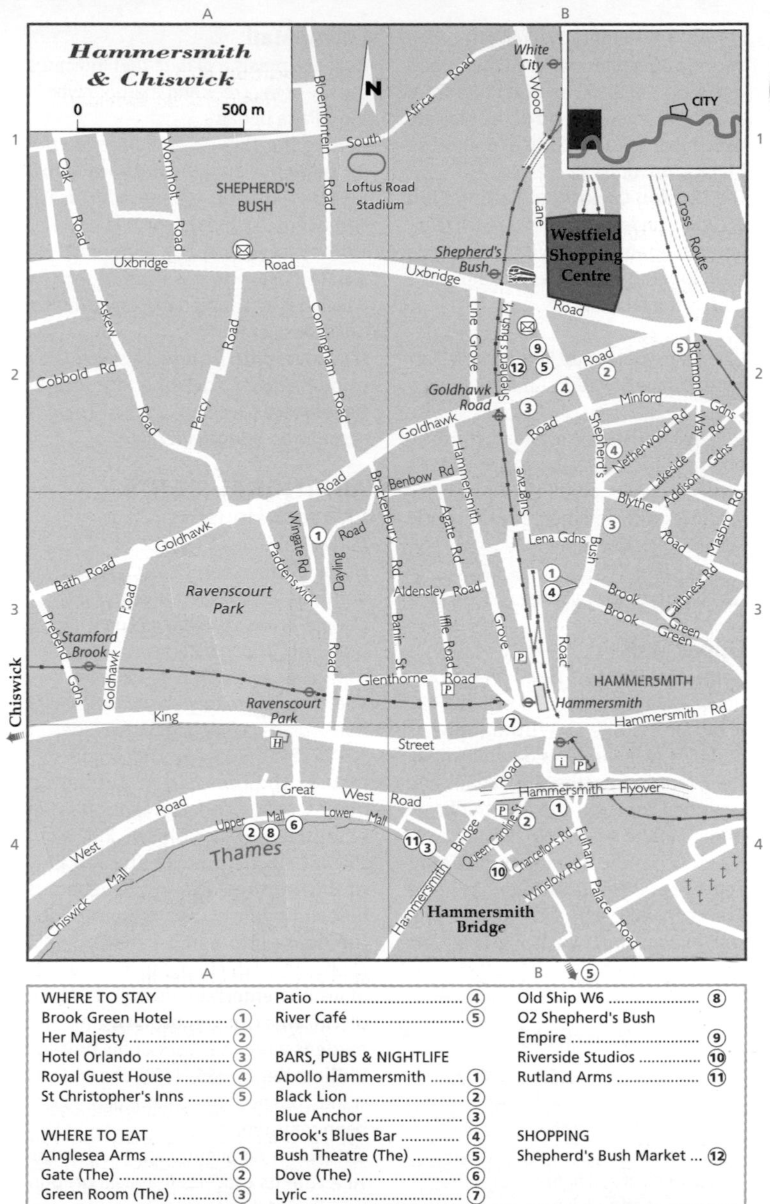

from Putney to Mortlake. In September, the **Great River Race** *(www.greatriver-race.co.uk)*, which began in 1988, is a longer and jollier affair, with up to 150 craft, from Celtic curricles to Viking longboats and Chinese dragon boats taking to the water for 22mi/35.4km from Richmond to London Docklands.

Hammersmith Terrace

The urban terrace of 17 almost identical brick houses of three and four storeys, built as a single unit facing the river, dates from the mid-18C. In the 18C, **Philippe de Loutherbourg**, artist and scenic designer at the Drury Lane Theatre *(see COVENT GARDEN)*, once lived

at No. 13; Sir Emery Walker, antiquary and typographer, who collaborated with Morris at the Kelmscott Press, lived at No. 7. At the west end of the Mall are two pubs: the **Old Ship W6** and the **Black Lion** *(see Addresses)*.
The **London Corinthian Sailing Club** occupies Linden House *(18C, much refurbished)*; opposite, above the riverside wall, looking like a glassed-in crow's nest, is the race officers' box.

Make a detour up South Black Lion Lane to view St Peter's Church.

North of the Great West Road, the focal point of St Peter's Square is **St Peter's Church** *(1829)*, a yellow stock-brick landmark with pedimented portico and square clock tower.

Return to the riverside.

Upper Mall

Kelmscott House, a plain three-storey house, dates from the 1780s. In the 19C it became home to **William Morris** and his family until his death in 1896. Here, Morris drew the illustrations and designed fonts for the fine books he printed in the nearby **No. 14** and published under the imprint of the **Kelmscott Press**. The **Dove** pub has had a licence for 400 years, although the present building goes back only 200 years *(see Addresses)*.

Westfield

Westfield London *(uk.westfield.com/london)* in Shepherds Bush *(Shepherd's Bush)* is an upmarket shopping mall, housing upwards of 250 high-street brands and a "village" of designer stores such as Gucci, Prada and Dior. There's also a selection of mid-range restaurants and a large cinema. For an alternative shopping experience, visit Shepherd's Bush Market *(Mon–Sat)* off Uxbridge Road.

Lower Mall

Near the pier is a plaque that indicates the site of the creek and "harbour where the village began".
Among the 18C–19C buildings are the **Blue Anchor** pub; the **Rutland Arms**, a Victorian pub *(see Addresses)*; Kent House *(No. 10)*, which is late 18C with symmetrical bay windows; the Amateur Rowing Association *(No. 6)*, which has a canopied balcony over the boathouse entrance.
Hammersmith Bridge is a suspension bridge *(1884–7)* designed by Joseph **Bazalgette** to replace the first Thames suspension bridge *(1827)*.

ADDITIONAL SIGHTS

Chiswick House★

Burlington Lane.
House: Open Apr–Oct Sun–Wed and bank holidays 10am–5pm; Nov–Dec pre-booked group tours only. Gardens: Open daily year round 7am–dusk. £5.70 house; gardens free. Guided tours by appointment. Audio-guide (3 languages). Tea room. 020 8995 0508. www.chgt.org.uk.
In 1682 the first Earl of Burlington purchased a Jacobean mansion set in extensive acres at Chiswick. During the 18C, Richard Boyle, the **3rd Earl of Burlington** *(1695–1753)*, generous host and patron of the arts, transformed the house into a neo-Palladian villa *(1725–29)* in which to display his works of art and entertain his friends. Much of the interior decoration and the gardens were the work of his protégé **William Kent** *(1686–1748)*. The villa still stands, but nothing remains of the Jacobean mansion.
Exterior – An avenue approaches the villa with its graceful Classical proportion. Paired dog-leg staircases are overlooked by statues of Palladio *(left)* and Inigo Jones (*right*).
Interior – The lower floor octagon hall, lobbies and library now display material about the design and restoration of the house and garden. From the library, the pillared link building leads to the Summer Parlour *(1717)*, originally connected to the Jacobean mansion.

On the first floor, rooms are arranged around a central octagon. The **Dome Saloon** has a coffered cupola rising from an ochre-coloured entablature to a windowed drum. The Red, Green and Blue Velvet Rooms have richly gilded coffered ceilings and Venetian windows. The roundels in the Blue Room are of Inigo Jones *(by Dobson)* and Pope *(by Kent)*. The **gallery** runs along the west front, and consists of three rooms: the apsed, oblong central room communicates through arches to circular and octagonal end rooms. From the octagonal room a passage leads into the upper storey of the link building.

The **gardens** were mostly landscaped by Kent, who planted the giant cedars; temples, obelisks and statues were strategically placed so as to catch the stroller unawares. The greenhouse was probably the work of Joseph Paxton from Chatsworth. The Inigo Jones Gateway *(northeast of the house)* was a gift from **Sir Hans Sloane** in 1736. The gardens have recently benefited from a £12.1m restoration, involving regenerating statues, paths, monuments and the planting of 1,600 trees.

Hogarth's House★

Open Tue–Sun noon–5pm. Closed 25–26 Dec, Good Friday and Easter Monday. 020 8994 6757. www.hounslow.info.

This is the delightful country home, built in 1700, of the great painter, engraver and satirist William Hogarth; he called the house his "little country box by the Thames". The mulberry tree in the small garden grew there in his day. He entertained such contemporaries as **David Garrick** here. Hogarth found fame as a commentator on 18C London life; note in particular: *The Election, London Scenes, The Harlot's Progress and Marriage à la Mode*. The museum was beautifully refurbished in 2011.

The **Fuller's Brewery** stands across the Hogarth roundabout (*book ahead for guided tours. £10 in advance, £12 on the day – including tasting session; no children under 16 yrs; 020 8996 2063; www.fullers.co.uk*).

ADDRESSES

LIGHT BITE

Hummingbird Café, *1C Oaklands Grove. Shepherds Bush Market. 020 8746 2333. Tue–Sat 7.30am–10pm, Sun–Mon 7.30am–7pm.* A quiet spot just off the Uxbridge Road serving fabulous full breakfasts, light lunches and delicious cakes and pastries. There are plenty of tables outside too which catch the sun – or you can use the blankets provided.

PUBS AND BARS

Black Lion, *2 South Black Lion Lane. Ravenscourt Park or Stamford Brook. 020 8748 2639.* This attractive pub is set back from the river, with plenty of tables outside for eating alfresco in summer.

Blue Anchor, *13 Lower Mall. Ravenscourt Park or Hammersmith. 020 8748 5774.* A bustling pub with a lovely riverside location, which attracts a lively crowd.

The Dove, *19 Upper Mall. Ravenscourt Park. 020 8748 9474.* In the 18C this was a coffee house where James Thomson is said to have written the words of "Rule Britannia!". It is now a quintessential English pub, with wooden beams and what is claimed to be the smallest bar in the country

Old Ship W6, *25 Upper Mall. Ravenscourt Park. 020 8748 2593. www.oldshipW6.co.uk.* A smart, sleekly refurbished pub by the river dating back to 1722. This is a great place to sit and watch the world go by.

Rutland Arms, *15 Lower Mall. Ravenscourt Park; Hammersmith 020 8748 5586.* A Victorian pub in an attractive riverside location.

ENTERTAINMENT

Brooks Blues Bar, *238–246 King St. Hammersmith. 020 8741 1940. www.brooksbluesbar.co.uk. First Sat of month 8pm–11.30pm. £8–15.* Live blues concerts at the Jazz Cafe Posk in the Polish cultural centre. See website for details.

Riverside Studios *Crisp Rd., Hammersmith. Hammersmith. 020 8237 1000. www.riversidestudios.co.uk. Box office: noon–9pm.* Cinema, theatre, music, dance and exhibitions.

Putney and Barnes

These fine residential areas linked by a bridge enjoy a pleasant riverside location. Fulham has become an offshoot of fashionable Chelsea, while Putney, with its leafy common land, has a rural atmosphere and is popular with young families.
It is worth taking a leisurely stroll to visit the pubs and enjoy the picturesque scenery.

Location: *⊖Putney Bridge.* Fulham and Putney lie to the Southwest and are bisected by the A308 and A219, which merge and lead to the A3 and M25.

A BIT OF HISTORY

Fulham, Parsons Green and Walham Green were once riverside villages with the odd large mansion in its own grounds running down to the water's edge. Market gardens covered the fertile marshlands. Urbanisation came within 50 years: in 1851 the population numbered 12,000; in 1901, 137,000.

PUTNEY

The area's transformation was precipitated by the arrival of the railway in the mid-19C. However, the early association with the river remains: rowing clubs still line the Surrey bank.
Putney Bridge, which marks the beginning *(just upstream in line with the Universities' Stone by the Star and Garter pub)* of the **Oxford and Cambridge Boat Race** *(4.5mi/7km to Mortlake)*, was designed in Cornish granite by **Joseph Bazalgette** in 1884.

St Mary's Parish Church

Open daily 9am–6pm. Leaflet. 020 8394 6062.
The church at the approach to Putney bridge, burnt out in 1973, reopened after restoration in 1982. The 16C chantry chapel and 15C tower were preserved when it was rebuilt in 1836.

Take Lower Richmond Rd. west.

Lower Richmond Road winds upriver past a line of village and antique shops and small Victorian houses, punctuated by pubs *(late 18C–19C)*, including the **Dukes Head**, overlooking the river and just before the common, the Georgian **Boat and Dragon** and the gabled **Spencer Arms**.
On the Lower Common is **All Saints Church** *(1874)*, notable for its Burne-Jones windows *(open for services)*.

Return to the bridge and walk south.

The bustling **Putney High Street** has a Tudor-style, gargoyle-decorated pub, the **Old Spotted Horse** *(www.spottedhorse.co.uk)*, halfway along and still includes tall 19C house-fronts.
At the start of **Putney Hill**, near the crossroads, are to left and right, No. 11, The Pines, a foreboding, tall grey Victorian House where **Swinburne** lived, and No. 28A, a pink-washed Georgian villa with a firemark set on its pale wall.

Fulham Palace

Grounds: *Open daily, dawn till dusk.* ***Museum:*** *Open Sat–Wed 1pm–4pm (last admission 3.45pm). Café daily 10am–4pm. Guided tours Mon–Fri, Sun; call to book. £8. 020 7736 3233. www.fulhampalace.org.*
Housed in the east wing, in the Dining Room and Library *(formerly a chapel)*, the museum traces the history of the site, the buildings and the gardens, including archaeological finds such as Roman coins and pottery, ecclesiastical vestments and stained glass. The riverside grounds are a pleasant place for a stroll, followed by tea at the café.

BARNES

Barnes Bridge or Barnes rail from London Waterloo or Vauxhall.
Barnes is located on the south bank of the Thames opposite Chiswick, in

London Wetland Centre

a loop which stretches south from Hammersmith Bridge. Its southern reaches are dominated by **Barnes Common**, a local nature reserve, while the historic village area centred on an attractive pond to its north is a conservation area and noted for its exceptional 18C and 19C buildings.

The Terrace around Barnes Bridge railway station is believed to contain some of London's oldest riverside housing: a line of Georgian mansions constructed from around 1720. English composer **Gustav Holst** once lived at No. 10 and is commemorated with a blue plaque.

LONDON WETLAND CENTRE

Queen Elizabeth's Walk, SW13 9WT. Open daily 9.30am–5pm (6pm in summer), last admission 1hr before closing. £11.65. Guided tours (free) daily at 11.30am and 2.30pm. Activites for children. Café. 020 8409 4400. www.wwt.org.uk.

The 105-acre/42ha §network of large lakes, small pools, reed beds, seasonally flooded wetlands, fen meadows and wet woodland is considered by many to be the best urban wildlife site in Europe. Located next to the Thames, around 6mi/10km southwest of central London, it is a haven for numerous species, including more than 180 varieties of bird, amphibian and butterfly.

In spring and summer hundreds of wetland birds, including lapwings, terns, grebes, warblers and blackcaps, come to the Centre to nest, while autumn sees an exciting mix of migrating birds, including osprey, spoonbills and herons passing through to feed. The warmer months are also a good time to spot the Centre's three native reptile species: the common lizard, grass snake and slow worm. The Centre is also home to a thriving water vole colony, otters, and dozens of smaller species such as dragonflies, slow worms, moths and water fleas. You can watch the otters and birds of prey being fed or take a personal birding tour.

ADDRESSES

PUBS

The Brown Dog, *28 Cross St., SW13 0AP. Barnes Bridge. 020 8392 2200. www.thebrowndog.co.uk.* There is a pleasant blend of original features and design elements in this popular local. Concise menu of hearty dishes, such as 28-day aged sirloin and fresh fruit crumble.

Dukes Head, *8 Lower Richmond Rd., SW15 1JN . Putney Bridge. 020 8788 2552. www.dukesheadputney.com.* This pub, set in a large traditional building, combines cocktails with real ales and does a cracking Sunday roast.

Spencer Arms, *237 Lower Richmond Rd., SW15 1HJ. Putney Bridge. 020 8788 0640. www.thespencerarms.co.uk.* Sleek gastropub with plain wooden fittings in its dining rooms, which are flooded with natural light.

Kew★★★

The Thames draws a great loop around Kew, an affluent residential area with a village atmosphere. A day excursion out of town brings much enjoyment as one strolls through the splendid gardens with their rare and exotic species, great glasshouses and picturesque dells.

Location: *Kew Gardens.* Exit the station through the row of shops and walk down Lichfield Road to reach Victoria Gate. Access to Kew is by the A4 or A315 and the A205 *(South Circular).*

A BIT OF HISTORY

Royal Residence

In 1721 the future **George II** bought **Richmond Lodge** around which his consort, Queen Caroline, laid out elaborate gardens featuring typical 18C ornamental statues and follies. In 1730, Frederick, Prince of Wales, although on unfriendly terms with George II, leased the **White House**, only a mile away. Frederick and his wife Augusta rebuilt the house *(known also as Kew House)* on a site now marked by a sundial, in which the Princess continued to reside after Frederick's death in 1751, devoting herself particularly to the garden.

With a growing family of 15 children **King George III** *(1760–1820)* and Queen Charlotte found both Richmond Lodge and the White House too small and in 1773, the **Dutch House** was leased for the young Prince of Wales (the future George IV) and his brother. A new palace, designed by **James Wyatt**, was never completed, but like the White House was demolished, leaving alone of all the cousinhood of royal residences, just the Dutch House or Kew Palace, which was then opened as a museum in 1899.

ROYAL BOTANIC GARDENS★★★

Kew Green. **Gardens:** *Open Apr–Oct Mon–Fri 9.30am–6.30pm, Sat–Sun and bank holidays 9.30am–7.30pm (last admission 45min before closing); Sept–Mar earlier closing; check website for details. Closed 24–25 Dec. Glasshouses, museum and galleries close earlier. £14.50. Visitor Centre at Victoria Gate. Guided tours from Victoria Plaza daily at 11am, noon and 1.30pm. Maps (5 languages). Restaurants. Shops. There are regular exhibitions, festivals and events throughout the year, including an orchid festival in spring, summer open-air concerts and a Christmas festival with an atmospheric open-air ice rink. 020 8332 5655. www.kew.org.*

Kew Gardens are pure pleasure. The colour and architecture of the trees, singly like the weeping willow and the stone pine, or in groups, delight in all seasons. The layman will spot commonplace flowers and shrubs and gaze on delicate exotics; gardeners check their knowledge against the labels, for this 300 acre/120ha garden is the superb offshoot of laboratories engaged in the

Palm House, Kew

identification of plants and plant material from all parts of the world.

The curatorship of the biggest herbarium in the world, a wood museum, a botanical library of more than 100,000 volumes and the training of student gardeners are also within the establishment's province. Declared a UNESCO World Heritage Site in 2003, these are probably the most important botanical gardens in the world.

Princess Augusta was personally responsible for the inauguration of a botanic garden south of the Orangery and the enlargement of the gardens from seven to more than 100 acres/40ha. **William Kent** rebuilt the White House and landscaped the garden. In 1751, the Dowager Princess of Wales, guided by the Earl of Bute *(a considerable botanist)*, appointed William Aiton head gardener *(1759–93)* and **William Chambers** as architect *(1760)*.

Under Aiton, a Scot who had worked at the Chelsea Physic Garden, his son who succeeded him *(1793–1841)* and **Sir Joseph Banks** *(d.1820)*, voyager, distinguished botanist, naturalist, biologist and finally director, plants began to be collected from all parts of the world for research and cultivation. By 1789, 5,500 species were growing in the gardens.

In 1772 on the death of Princess Augusta, George III combined the Kew and Richmond Lodge gardens and had them landscaped by **Capability Brown**. A 200yd/200m tree walkway allows you to climb high above the treetops and walk among the lime, sweet chestnut and oak trees.

Greenhouses

Palm House★★ – The iron-and-glass structure designed by **Decimus Burton** and the engineer Richard Turner, as a purely functional building *(362ft/110m long, 33ft/10m high in the wings and 62ft/19m at the centre)* took four years to erect *(1844–48)*. Inside are tropical plants, both useful *(coffee, cocoa)* and ornamental. The Chilean runner lizards in residence were given to Kew by the then Customs and Excise after having been smuggled into Britain.

Outside *(west)* a semicircular rose garden; the pond *(east)* is watched over by the Queen's Beasts (stone replicas of those designed by James Woodward to stand outside Westminster Abbey at the Coronation in 1953).

Temperate House★– The house, again by Burton but 20 years later, epitomises Victorian conservatory construction.

The **Evolution House** re-creates the climate of change affecting the Earth.

Alpine House – Beneath a glass pyramid, built in 1981, from which rainwater drains into the surrounding moat, is a rock landscape including a refrigerated bed.

Princess of Wales Tropical Conservatory – In this modern steel-and-glass diamond-shaped structure 10 different tropical habitats are recreated, ranging from the extremes of mangrove swamp to desert – from ferns and orchids to carnivorous and stone plants (*Lithops*), cacti and succulents set against a Mohave desert diorama. In 1996, a titan arum or "corpse flower" (which blooms every 30-odd years), attracted great attention: the Sumatran native has flowered at Kew in 1889, 1926 and 1963.

Marianne North Gallery

Varies; call first. 020 8332 5655.

In a building *(1882)* designed by her architect friend James Ferguson is an exhibition of paintings by Victorian artist North, showing plants, insects and general scenes from the many countries she visited between 1871 and 1884.

Shirley Sherwood Gallery

Open daily 9.30am–5.30pm.

Opened in 2008, this gallery is dedicated to botanical art – both from Kew's historic collection and the contemporary collection of Dr Sherwood.

Kew Palace★★ (Dutch House)

The terra-cotta brick building was built by Samuel Fortrey, a London Merchant of Dutch parentage, who commemorated his house's construction in a monogram and the date 1631 over the front door. At the rear is the **Queen's Garden**, a formal arrangement of pleached alleys of laburnum and hornbeam, parterres (formal symmetrical beds), a gazebo and plants popular in the 17C. The 17C nosegay garden has been replanted with contemporary herbs.

The rooms downstairs are all panelled: the **King's Dining Room** in white 18C style, the Breakfast Room in early-17C style and the Library Ante-Room in re-set 16C linenfold. The Pages' Waiting Room houses an exhibition of minor royal possessions. Upstairs, apart from the white-and-gold Queen's Drawing Room, formally set out with lyre-back chairs, the rooms are wallpapered and intimate with family portraits by **Gainsborough** and **Zoffany**. In the King's rooms note the embossed terra-cotta paper in the Ante-room.

Queen Charlotte's Cottage

The two-storey thatched house, typical of "rustic" buildings of the period *(1772)* was designed by Queen Charlotte as a picnic house.

Other Buildings and Monuments

Under Princess Augusta, **William Chambers** set about constructing typical 18C garden follies: temples, a ruined arch, an **Orangery**★*(1761)* and a **Pagoda**★*(1761)*; also a garden ornament 163ft/49m and 10 storeys high. Now alas without its gilded dragon finials, this folly had its floors pierced by the RAF during World War II to give them a 100ft/30m vertical drop to test model bombs. The **Main Gates** are by Decimus Burton *(1848, the lion and unicorn on the original gate are now above gates in Kew Road)*. The **Japanese Gateway**★ was imported for the Anglo-Japanese Exhibition of 1912.

SIGHTS

Kew Green

The most attractive houses on the green are those by the main gates to the gardens. Dominating the north *(river)* side are Kew Herbarium: 5 million dried plants and library (*open to specialists)*, a three-storey Georgian house and extensive annexe, followed by an irregular line of 18–19C brick houses *(Nos. 61–83)*. On the far side of the gates backing onto the gardens is a line of one-time royal "cottages", including, at No. 37, Cambridge Cottage, now the **Wood Museum** and **Kew Gardens Gallery** *(enter from inside the Gardens)*.

The nave and chancel of **St Anne's Church** were constructed in 1710–14 on the site of a 16C chapel. In 1770 a north aisle was built and George III added the Royal Gallery in 1805. **Gainsborough** *(d.1788)* and Zoffany *(d.1810)* both lie in the churchyard.

National Archives

Kew. Open Tue, Thu 9am–7pm, Wed, Fri, Sat 9am–5pm. Closed Sun, public holidays, bank holiday weekends, Christmas, New Year and Easter. ID required for admission. 020 8876 3444. www.nationalarchives.gov.uk.

The **Domesday Book**, the Magna Carta, **Shakespeare**'s will, **Guy Fawkes**'s confessions, **Captain Cook**'s charts and Bligh's accounts of the mutiny on the

Kew's Breathing Planet Programme

Plants are essential to help humanity deal with the environmental challenges we are facing – biodiversity loss, food and water scarcity, disease and changing climate to name a few – and Kew's Breathing Planet Programme aims to help find a way forward. One example is Kew's work to save some of the world's rarest orchids; scientists have evolved a way of germinating plants from seed without the symbiotic fungus required in natural habitats. Some 5,000 species (about 20 percent of the total known number) are now propagated at Kew, having been accumulated over the last 200 years. At Kew's Wakehurst Place site, in West Sussex, the **Millennium Seed Bank** is another crucial conservation project aimed at safeguarding the world's most endangered plants.

The Domesday Book

The famous register of lands of England, named after *Domus dei* – where the volumes were originally preserved in Winchester Cathedral – was commissioned by William the Conqueror so that he might ascertain the dues owed him by his subjects, thereby setting the rules by which the Monarch, later the Government, might levy tax nationwide. As a result we have a comprehensive idea of how the kingdom was divided in 1085–86, both in terms of land holding and popular employment. Lords of the manor held the bulk of the land on a freehold basis, which they tenanted or leased to a complex hierarchy of dependents, villeins or freemen. Land was allocated to agricultural functions (meadow, pasture) in proportion to hunting (woodland) and fishing (ponds, rivers). The **Little Domesday** *(384 pages)* records estates throughout latter-day Essex, Norfolk and Suffolk, while the **Great Domesday** *(450 pages)* surveys the rest of the kingdom with the exception of Northumberland, Cumberland, Durham, parts of Lancashire and Westmorland, which lay outside the King's jurisdiction. The City of London is also omitted as the conquering king could not have been certain of brokering his rights over the shrewd and powerful business community. A facsimile is displayed at the **National Archives** in Kew.

Bounty are just a few of the precious historic charters, accounts, maps, seals, reports, registers, government papers and old chests stored at the National Archive, founded in 1838. Fragile papers are kept in controlled environments but there are fascinating regular exhibitions too.

ADDITIONAL SIGHTS

Kew Bridge Steam Museum

Brentford. Entrance in Green Dragon Lane. ♿ Open Tue–Sun 11am–4pm. Closed 20–28 Dec, 31 Dec–2 Jan. £10 (annual ticket). Children under 16 must be accompanied by an adult. Guidebook and brochure (6 languages). Parking. Café. ☎ 020 8568 4757. www.kbsm.org.

This museum of water supply demonstrates the development of James Watt's basic idea through over a century of improved efficiency and increased scale. There are six Cornish Beam Engines and the Waddon Engine, the last steam-powered water pumping engine used commercially until 1983.

Smaller steam engines, traction engines and steam lorries, a narrow-gauge railway, a water-wheel *(1702)*, a forge, machine shop and relics connected with London's water supply complete the display. The standpipe tower outside is a local landmark nearly 200ft/61m high.

Musical Museum

399 High St., Brentford. ♿ Open Tue–Sun 11am–5.30pm (last admission 4.30pm). £8. Guidebook, recordings available. ☎ 020 8560 8108. www.musicalmuseum.co.uk.

The museum's fascinating collection of some 200 mechanical music-makers – pianolas, organs and a Wurlitzer – is displayed in modern brightly painted premises.

Boston Manor

*⊖ Boston Manor. **Grounds:** Open daily. **House:** Open Apr–Oct, Sat–Sun and bank holidays noon–5pm. No charge. Guidebook. ☎ 0845 456 2800. www.hounslow.info/parks/boston.*

The three-storey red-brick house was built in 1623 for Lady Mary Read, a young widow who remarried soon after into the Spencer family (ancestors of the late Diana, Princess of Wales).

The magnificent 17C state rooms can be visited; in the Drawing Room is a beautiful Jacobean plaster ceiling. In 1670, East India merchant **James Clitherow** bought the property for £5,136, extended it and landscaped the grounds with cedars and a lake. It remained in the family until 1924, when it was taken over by the borough of Hounslow.

Syon Park★★

The prospect of this splendid mansion, set in a vast park by the Thames and opposite Kew Gardens, is enchanting. It has been the seat of an aristocratic family since the 16C and is a prime example of the Robert Adam style. Take a stroll through the fragrant rose garden, admire the great conservatory and enjoy the many other attractions in the grounds.

Location: ⊖*Overground: Syon Lane from Waterloo Station; bus 237 or 267 to Brent Lea bus stop, or E2 or E8 to Brentford, then signposted walk.* Syon Park is south of the A4 and near the M4 *(Exit 2)*.

A BIT OF HISTORY

Artistic Patronage – On the walls inside are portraits of the men and women who built up the house and their royal patrons by **Gainsborough**, **Reynolds**, **Van Dyck**, **Mytens**, **Lely** and by unknown artists of the English 16C school. Two men were principally responsible for the construction: the **Lord Protector**, **Duke of Somerset**, brother of Henry's Queen Jane Seymour in the 16C, and Hugh Percy, **1st Duke of Northumberland**, in the 18C. Somerset was given the former monastery site in 1547 by his nephew **Edward VI** and erected a Tudor mansion in the plan of a hollow square. He dined his monarch there in 1550 and laid out gardens, including the first Physic garden in England, but in 1552 he was charged with conspiracy and duly executed.

In 1594, the estate was acquired by the Percy family, who still own it and live there. Moreover, with the marriage in 1682 of Elizabeth Percy to Charles, 6th Duke of Somerset, Syon returned to a descendant of its earlier owner, who also held office under the Crown. In the 18C the new heirs, the Duke and Duchess of Northumberland, considered the house and grounds in urgent need of remodelling and commissioned **Robert Adam** and **Capability Brown** to produce designs.

HIGHLIGHTS

Gardens: *Open daily Mar–Oct 10.30am–5pm (last admission 4pm).* ***House:*** *Open Mar–Oct Wed, Thu, Sun and bank holidays 11am–5pm (last admission 4pm). Guide book. Leaflet. House and gardens £11; gardens only £6. 020 8560 0882. www.syonpark.co.uk.*

Great Conservatory, Syon Park

© K. Brett/MICHELIN

The House

The colonnaded east front of Syon House is visible across the river from Kew Gardens, the **Northumberland Lion** with outstretched tail silhouetted against the sky; a second beast, also from the model by **Michelangelo**, crowns the Lion Gate and graceful Adam screen on the London Road *(A315)*.

In the **Great Hall**, Adam is at his most formal: the high ceiling echoes the patterns laid into the black-and-white marble pavement; in the apses at either end nestle copies of Classical statues – the *Apollo Belvedere*, the *Dying Gladiator*.

The **Ante-room**, in contrast, gleams darkly with heavy gilding, reds, blues, yellows in the patterned *scagliola* floor, and green marble and *scagliola* pillars *(dredged from the Tiber)*.

The long **State Dining Room** with column-screened apses at either end was first to be remodelled by Adam: deep niches with copies of antique statues along the left wall were reflected in pier mirrors; frieze, cornice, ceiling, decorated half-domes, beautiful doorcases and doors afforded a perfect setting for the banquets given by the Duke and Duchess in the late 18C.

The rich decoration of the **Red Drawing Room** includes scarlet Spitalfields silk, blooming with intricate pale gold roses, on the walls and at the windows; a carpet, signed and dated 1769, woven at Moorfields; door pilasters with ivory panels covered with **ormolu**; gilded ceiling studded with Cipriani painted medallions. The room is, however, dominated by its commanding Stuart portraits by Lely, Van Dyck, Van Honthorst, Mignard, and Huysmans. Note the elegant, mosaic-topped side tables.

The **Long Gallery** of the Tudor house was transformed by Adam into a ladies' withdrawing room *(136ft/42m long, 14ft/4m wide)*, lined with grouped pilasters, wall niches and pier mirrors, arranged so as to disguise the length. Much of the furniture was designed by Adam, notably the veneered chest of drawers made by Chippendale.

The furniture in the **Print Room** includes two remarkable walnut, marquetry inlaid cabinets that date to the late 17C; the walls are hung with family portraits, most notably by Gainsborough and Reynolds.

A huge Sèvres vase stands at the foot of the main staircase leading to the **bedrooms**, two of which were refurbished in 1832 for the Duchess of Kent and her daughter, the future Queen Victoria: note the canopied beds, sofa and chairs, all enhanced by the same blue silk.

Gardens★

Capability Brown assisted in designing the gardens, which extend all the way to the river. In 1837, the gardens were world famous for their botanical specimens and subsequently opened to the public. A vast fragrant **rose garden** *(separate entrance south of the house)* is in bloom from May to August.

The **Great Conservatory**, a beautiful semicircular building with a central cupola and end pavilions, was designed by Charles Fowler in 1820–27. Inside the graceful space are an abundance of cacti and a small aquarium.

Other Attractions

The extensive grounds contain a number of other attractions. Ideal for children is the large indoor adventure playground **Snakes and Ladders** *(020 8847 0946; www.snakes-and-ladders.co.uk)* which also has a playground outside; for keen anglers, there is **Syon Park Trout Fishery** *(020 8568 6354 or 07956 378138; www.alburyestatefisheries.com)*; and a well-stocked **garden centre** *(020 8568 0134; www.thegardencentre-group.co.uk)* is ideal for gardeners.

ADDRESSES

PUBS

London Apprentice, *62 Church St., Isleworth, TW7 6BG. Isleworth Rail or Richmond. 020 8560 1915.* Said to be named after one of the apprentices who, from the 16C to 19C, rowed up the river on their annual holiday and made the inn their own for a day. A very pleasant pub on the river serving good food.

Richmond★★

In an attractive riverside location, the vibrant town of Richmond has smart shops and riverside pubs. Fine mansions recall past aristocratic associations when Richmond Palace was a favourite residence of the Tudor monarchs. Together with neighbouring Twickenham, Richmond is a highly desirable area and has all the amenities of an affluent town.

Information: www.visitrichmond.co.uk or email: info@visitrichmond.co.uk. You can visit or write to: Civic Centre, 44 York Street, Twickenham TW1 3BZ.

Location: ⊖*Richmond; Overground: Richmond from Waterloo Station and by London Overground.* Richmond lies southwest of London between the main axes to the A3 and M3. It is also accessible by boat from Westminster Pier.

A BIT OF HISTORY

Richmond, possessing what has been called the most beautiful urban green in England, grew to importance between the 12C and 17C as a royal seat and, after the Restoration, as the residential area of members of the Court. In the courtiers' wake followed diplomats, politicians, professionals, dames and schools, and with the coming of the railway in 1840, prosperous Victorian commuters.

Richmond Palace: Royal Residence Through Six Reigns – The 12C manor house was extended and embellished by **Edward III**, who died in it in 1377, and favoured by **Richard II**, his grandson, while his Queen was alive but demolished upon her death in 1394. A new palace, the second, was begun by **Henry V** but completed only 40 years after his death in the reign of **Edward IV**, who gave it with the royal manor of Shene to his Queen, Elizabeth Woodville, from whom it was confiscated by Henry VII; in 1499 it burned to the ground.

Henry VII, parsimonious where his son was prodigal, nevertheless, "rebuilded [the Palace] again sumptuously and costly and changed the name of Shene and called it Richmond because his father and he were Earls of Rychmonde" [in Yorkshire]. This palace, the third on the site, was to be the last. **Henry VII**, **Henry VIII**, **Queen Elizabeth** and **Charles I** all resided here. The new Tudor palace conformed to standard design: service buildings of red brick, preserved today in the gateway, enclosed an outer or Base Court *(now Old Palace Yard)*, from which a second gateway led to an inner or Middle Court, lined along one side by a Great Hall of stone with a lead roof. **The Privy Lodging**, which included the state rooms, surrounded another court. Domed towers and turrets crowned the construction, which covered 10 acres/4ha and was by far the most splendid in the kingdom, favoured by several monarchs. At Charles I's execution the Palace was stripped and the contents sold. By the 18C little remained and private houses were built from the ruins.

WALKING TOUR

Take a stroll through the town.

Town Centre

On the east side of the main road are reminders of the growing village in the parish **Church of St Mary Magdalene**, with its 16C square flint and stone tower, 18C houses, 19C cottages, the Vineyard dating back in name to the 16–17C when local vines were famous and the rebuilt almshouses of 17C foundation. In Paradise Road stands Hogarth House, built in 1748, where **Leonard** and **Virginia Woolf** *(who lived there from 1915 to 1924)* founded the **Hogarth Press**.

Cross the High St. and pass through charming alleyways to Richmond Green.

Richmond Green

The Green, once the scene of Tudor jousting, has been a cricket pitch since the middle of the 17C.

Richmond Theatre, which overlooks the Little Green, was refurbished in 1991 in accordance with its late-19C appearance. The east side of the Green is lined with 17C and 18C houses.

Along the west side is **Old Palace Terrace** *(1692–1700)*, six two-storey brick houses with straight hooded doorways, built by John Powell *(who lived in No. 32)*.

Oak House and **Old Palace Place** date back to 1700. **Old Friars** *(1687)* stands on part of the site of a monastery founded by Henry VII in 1500; the house was extended in the 18C to include a concert room.

Maids of Honour Row★★★ – The three-storey brick-built houses, adorned with pilasters and friezes, were erected in 1724, "to serve as lodgings for the Maids of Honour attending the Princess of Wales."

Old Palace and Gatehouse – To the South are two houses: the first boasts a central doorway incorporating brickwork from Henry VII's palace; the second is the Palace's original outer gateway.

The Wardrobe – *Old Palace Yard.* Note the blue diapered Tudor walls incorporated in the early-18C building and the fine 18C ironwork.

Trumpeters' House★ – *Old Palace Yard.* The main front of this house *(converted c.1701 from the Middle Gate of Richmond Palace)*, overlooks the garden and can be seen through the trees from the riverside path. The pedimented portico of paired columns was guarded by stone statues, after which the house is named.

▶ Walk down Old Palace Lane.

Richmond Riverside

Old Palace Lane, lined by modest, wistaria-covered 19C houses and cottages, leads from the southwest corner of Richmond Green to the river.

Asgill House★ – The house at the end of the lane was built c.1760 as a weekend and summer residence for the City banker and sometime Lord Mayor, Sir Charles Asgill. In pale golden stone with strong horizontal lines and a tall central bay, it was one of the last of its type to be built overlooking the Thames. Take the towpath upstream to Whittaker Avenue.

View of the Thames from Richmond Hill

The Old Town Hall houses the **Museum of Richmond**, with its displays on local history and a model of Richmond Palace in 1562 *(open Tue–Sat 11am–5pm; 020 8332 1141; www.museumofrichmond.com)*.

Richmond Bridge★★ – The classical, stone structure designed by James Paine was built in 1774 and widened in 1937; tolls were levied until the 19C. There is a milestone-obelisk at the north end.

▶ Walk up Richmond Hill.

Richmond Hill

The **view★★**– Immortalised by many artists, including Turner and **Reynolds**, the view gets better as you climb the road, which is lined by balconied terraces. At the top stands **Ancaster House**, a brick mansion built in 1722 to designs by **Robert Adam**. The house is now part of the **Star and Garter Home** for disabled sailors, soldiers and airmen. The gates at the hilltop *(1700)* are by **Capability Brown**.

Richmond Park★★

The countryside had been a royal chase for centuries when **Charles I** enclosed 2,470 acres/4,94ha as a park in 1637. It is the largest of the royal parks and famous for its varied **fauna and flora** – most notably herds of almost tame red and fallow deer, majestic **oak trees**, **spring flowers**, and increasingly large numbers of parakeets.

On a fine day from the top of the Henry VIII mound there is a dramatic **panoramic view★★★** extending from Windsor Castle to the dome of St Paul's.

Among the houses in the park are **Pembroke Lodge** *(cafeteria)* adapted by **John Soane** from a molecatcher's cottage and later used by the philosopher **Bertrand Russell**; and **White Lodge**, built by George II in 1727 as a hunting lodge and since 1955, the junior section of the **Royal Ballet School**.

TWICKENHAM

Overground: Twickenham; St Margaret's from Waterloo.

Twickenham nowadays draws visitors to its rugby matches, rather than to the riverside. In the 19C, **Louis-Philippe**, cousin of Louis XVI and future King of France *(1830–48)*, lived with his family in as many as nine houses in Twickenham. Of these, three remain: **Bushy House** was the home of the future William IV; it is now leased by the Crown Estates to the National Physical Laboratory *(Teddington)*. The other two are **Morgan House** on Ham Common, now part of the Cassel Hospital, and **York House**. In the grounds of Upper Lodge is the most complete 18C water garden in London.

See Marble Hill House.

Twickenham Stadium Tour

Rugby Road Tours Tue–Sat 10.30am, noon, 1.30pm and 3pm, Sun 1pm and 3pm. £15 020 8892 8877. www.twickenhamstadiumtoursguide.co.uk.

The home of English rugby runs tours, giving a behind-the-scenes look at everything from the Royal box to the players' changing rooms. There are breathtaking **views** from the top of the stand and the pitchside walk is a fitting finale.

York House

Richmond Road.

The Yorke family lived and worked a farm on the site in the 15C and 16C; successors altered and rebuilt the house, including (in the 19C) members of the exiled French royal family.

Sion Road

The road to the river is joined halfway down by Ferry Road, a close of "two down, two up" cottages. At the end is a line of houses of all periods.

ADDITIONAL SIGHTS

Ham House★★

Overground: Twickenham from Waterloo. ***House:*** *Open Mar–early Nov Sat–Thu and Good Friday noon–4pm. House may close at other times; check website.* ***Garden:*** *Open Sat–Wed 11am–5pm/dusk. Closed 25–26 Dec, 1 Jan. £10, garden only £4. Parking. Refreshments. 020 8940 1950. www.nationaltrust.org.uk.*

Ham House was at its prime under Elizabeth Dysart, **Duchess of Lauderdale**. Her father – William Murray, first Earl of Dysart – had literally been youthful "whipping boy" for Prince Charles, future Charles I. Elizabeth, it was said, became for a time the Protector's mistress.

The Lauderdales enlarged the house, which had been built to the conventional Jacobean plan in 1610, and modified the front. A family idiosyncrasy for making inventories has enabled the house to be returned to its 1678 appearance. The gardens have been relaid to the 17C plan.

Exterior – The fabric is brick with stone dressings; the building, three storeys beneath a hipped roof with a five-bay centre *(north side)* recessed between square bays and typical Jacobean outer bays. Iron gates and piers date from 1671. The present forecourt, with the **Coade stone** figure of **Father Thames** by John Bacon, was laid out in 1800.

Interior – Paintings bring to life the period of Charles II and furniture, doors and fireplaces display the craftsmanship of the period. The remarkable ceilings show the progress from geometrical plasterwork to garlands and spandrels.

Ground Floor – The Great Hall boasts a Round Gallery with a decorated plaster ceiling by Kinsman *(1637)*. **Lely** portraits adorn the gallery.

Notable features of other rooms include the gilt leather wall hangings, the 1679 cedar side tables, the gilded panelling and the silver chimney furniture in the **Marble Dining Room**. In the **Duchess's Bedchamber** are damask hangings; in the **Yellow Bedroom** or Volury Room the bed is hung with purple and yellow; in the **White Closet** are an oysterwork veneered writing desk and picture of the south front of the house *(1683)*. The altar cloth of "crimson velvet & gould & silver stuff" in the chapel is original.

The **Great Staircase** of 1637, built of oak round a square well and gilded, has a singularly beautiful balustrade.

Upper Floor – Lady Maynard's suite contains 17C Flemish tapestries below a wooden frieze and family portraits.

The **Museum Room** displays examples of the original upholstery and contains the 1679 inventory. The **North Drawing Room** is sumptuous with its plaster frieze and rich ceiling *(1637)* above walls hung with English silk tapestries, carved and gilded wainscoting, doorcases and doors; furniture is also carved, gilded and richly upholstered; the fireplace exuberantly Baroque.

Equally opulent is the **Queen's Suite**, rich with late-17C garlanded plaster ceilings; the furniture includes Oriental screens, English japanned chairs, a small Chinese cabinet and 18C tapestries.

Marble Hill House★

Across the river from Ham House (foot ferry). Open Apr–Oct Sat 10am–2pm, Sun and bank holidays 10am–5pm. £5.50. Guided tour (1hr) by appointment. 020 8892 5115. www.english-heritage.org.uk.

The last of the Palladian mansions that once lined this stretch of the Thames, Marble Hill House was built in 1729 by Henrietta Howard (a mistress of the future George II), with monies from her royal lover. It was 1731, however, before Henrietta, now **Countess of Suffolk** and Mistress of the Robes, could "often visit Marble Hill" and several years more before she took up residence here with her second husband, George Berkeley. She was an active hostess and received politicians, lawyers and Men of Letters, including **Alexander Pope** and **Horace Walpole**. The Palladian-style, stucco house is three storeys high, with the centre advanced beneath a pediment. The square mahogany staircase leads directly to the Great Room, richly decorated in white and gold, with carvings and copies of Van Dyck paintings. Lady Suffolk's bedchamber, divided by Ionic pillars and pilasters to form a bed alcove, is completed by a rich cornice and ceiling decoration. An almost-exact reconstruction has been achieved.

Orleans House Gallery

Riverside; Twickenham. ***Garden:*** *Open Apr–Sept Tue–Sat 1pm–5.30pm, Sun and bank holidays 2pm–5.30pm.* ***House:*** *Open Apr–Sept Tue–Sat 1pm–5.30pm, Sun and bank holidays 2pm–5.30pm; Oct–Mar Tue–Sat 1pm–4.30pm, Sun and bank holidays 2pm–4.30pm. 020 8831 6000. www.richmond.gov.uk.*

The remains of this 18C house serves as Richmond's principal art gallery. Only the **Octagon**, added in 1720, 10 years after the house was built, remains. Designed by **James Gibbs**, it has a brick exterior and splendid plasterwork.

ADDRESSES

LIGHT BITE

Pembroke Lodge, *Richmond Park. Richmond. 020 8940 8207. www.pembroke-lodge.co.uk. Summer: 9am–5.30pm; winter: 9am–sunset.* This Georgian house in Richmond Park serves light lunches and snacks. The terrace has gorgeous views of the Thames Valley.

PUBS

The White Cross, *Riverside Richmond. Richmond. 020 8940 6844. Mon–Sat 10am–11pm, Sun noon–10.30pm.* This local pub serves good-quality meals and has a lovely terrace for sunny days.

Wimbledon

In addition to its thriving village perched on a hilltop and vast common land, Wimbledon takes great pride in its acclaimed tennis championship, which draws international stars every summer. Two theatres and a stadium offer other entertainment.

Location: *Wimbledon; Southfields; Wimbledon Park; Wimbledon rail. Also served by Croydon Tramlink* Accessible via the A3.

A BIT OF HISTORY

The village first came to prominence in 1588, when Thomas Cecil, **Lord Burghley**, then Lord of the Manor, built a mansion with turrets and gables on a slope northeast of the church. It was destroyed in 1720 and the only surviving building from this period is Eagle House *(1613)* in the High Street, which was built by Robert Bell, a founder of the **East India Company**. The Manor eventually passed to **Sarah, Duchess of Marlborough**, who built a new house linked to detached servants' quarters by an underground passage.

VISIT

Wimbledon Common

In 1871, after seven years of legal dispute with Earl Spencer, Lord of the Manor, who wanted to develop it for housing, Wimbledon Common was transferred to the conservators for posterity.

The horse racing, duelling and drilling of soldiers of earlier days have given way to horse riding, cricket, rugby and golf. The 18C saw several large mansions rise around the Common, including **King's College School** *(1750)* with adjoining Great Hall in Gothic Revival style; **Southside House** *(1776)*, Woodhayes Rd. *(open Easter Sat–late Sept Wed, Sat, Sun and bank holiday afternoons; 1hr15min guided tours Wed, Sat–Sun 2pm and 4pm, additional tour Sat–Sun 3pm. £9; 020 8946 7643; http://southsidehouse.com; access by bus 93 to Wimbledon War Memorial)*; **Crooked Billet** and **Hand-in-Hand** are 17C public houses *(see Addresses)*; **Chester House** *(1670)* was owned by the Revd John Horne Tooke, whose election to Parliament in 1801 provoked the Act which made the clergy ineligible; **Cannizaro** *(1727, rebuilt in 1900)* was owned from 1887 by Viscount Melville, who laid out the gardens and entertained **William Pitt**, **Edmund Burke** and **Richard Sheridan** *(open Mon–Fri 8am, Sat–Sun and bank holidays 9am, to dusk or 9.30pm at the latest)*.

Also of interest is the **Round** or **Old Central School** *(Camp Rd.)*, an octagonal building *(1760)*, now part of a primary school. Wimbledon Village Stage Coaches set out from the **Rose and Crown** and later from the **Dog and Fox** in the High Street, although the road over Putney Heath was infested with highwaymen *(see Addresses)*.

St Mary's Church

Church Rd. Open Mon–Tue, Thu–Fri 9am–1pm, 2.30pm–4pm, Wed 2.30pm–4pm. 020 8946 2605. www.stmaryswimbledon.org.

Wimbledon church was mentioned in the **Domesday Book**; parts of a 13C rebuilding remain in the chancel. The present 19C nave, tower and spire were designed by Sir George Gilbert Scott. **William Wilberforce**, leader of the movement to abolish slavery, and **JW Bazalgette**, a Victorian engineer who created London's sewer network, are buried in the churchyard. To the north stands the **Old Rectory** *(1500)*, the oldest house in Wimbledon.

ADDITIONAL SIGHTS

Wimbledon Lawn Tennis Museum

Church Rd. Open daily 10am–5pm (8pm during the Championships, but to tournament ticket holders only). Guided tours daily 4–8 times a day. No tours during the Championship. Closed Sun before and during the Championship and the Mon and Tue following, 24–26 Dec, 1 Jan. Tour £22,

Attending the Championship

The annual Wimbledon Tennis Championship takes place over two weeks in late June and early July, and is attended by thousands of spectators. The so-called "show courts" *(Centre Court and courts 1, 2, 3, 12 and 18)* host the most significant games. The finals all take place on Centre Court.

Tickets are hotly contested, beginning with a public ballot which closes in the preceeding December. Applications are made by post, randomly selected by computer and awarded tickets for a specific date and court.

Additionally, a number of on-the-day tickets *(cash only)* are available: 500 a day for No.1 Court; 500 each of the first nine days for Centre Court and No.2 Court. Eager tennis fans queue for hours in advance, often overnight, and the queue has become such an institution that it is seen by many as part of the event itself. Camping is permitted and both toilets and water are available. There are also left luggage facilities on entering the ground. Several hundred tickets for Centre Court and No.3 Court are also made available online through Ticketmaster (www.ticketmaster.com) one day in advance of play.

Ticket prices range from £35–£100, depending on the day and court.

Visit www.wimbledon.com or call 020 8971 2473 for further information.

museum only £12. Leaflet (6 languages). Restricted parking. Café. ✆020 8946 6131. www.wimbledon.com.
Home to the world's premier tennis tournament, Wimbledon is actually a private members' club: the All England Lawn Tennis and Croquet Club. The museum features interactive displays charting the history of tennis and Wimbledon, with good facilities for the disabled. Among the displays, a section on **fashion** looks at tennis outfits back to 1884. Tours take place in the museum, courts, players' facilities and broadcast studios.

Museum of Wimbledon

Ridgway. Open Sat–Sun 2.30pm–5pm. ✆020 8296 9914. www.wimbledonmuseum.org.uk.
The local history museum is housed in the **Village Club**, built in 1858 to provide enjoyment and improvement through a reading room, library and lectures.

Wimbledon Windmill Museum

Windmill Rd. Open Apr–Oct Sat 2pm–5pm, Sun and bank holiday Mondays 11am–5pm. £2. Parking. Café. ✆020 8947 2825. www.wimbledonwindmill.org.uk.
The windmill, a hollow post mill built on the Common in 1817, has been converted into a museum illustrating the story of windmills.

ADDRESSES

PUBS

Crooked Billet, *14 Crooked Billet Rd., SW19 4RQ. Wimbledon. ✆ 020 8946 4942.* A country pub with oak beams and an open fire. Good real ales.

Dog and Fox, *24 High St., SW19 5EA. Wimbledon. ✆020 8946 6565. www.thedogandfox.com.* Large landmark pub in Wimbledon Village. Good food.

Hand-in-Hand, *6 Crooked Billet Rd., SW19 4RG. Wimbledon. ✆020 8946 5720.* Historic, low-ceilinged 19C cottage pub with bags of charm.

Rose and Crown, *55 High St., SW19 5BA. Wimbledon. ✆020 8947 4713. www.roseandcrownwimbledon.co.uk.* Traditional pub with a nice beer garden.

ENTERTAINMENT

Polka Theatre for Children, *240 The Broadway, SW19 1SB. Wimbledon. ✆020 8543 4888. www.polkatheatre.com. Check website for box office opening times and events.* A full programme of performances and workshops for children; also a playground, shop and café.

Hampton Court★★★

One of King Henry VIII's favourite palaces, Hampton Court was the perfect rural retreat for many a sovereign, with its romantic setting by the Thames. The glorious buildings in contrasting styles and the splendid gardens are enduring symbols of royal power and wealth.

Location: ⊖*Overground rail: Hampton Court from Waterloo. Boat: Hampton Court.* Hampton Court is to the Southwest of London at the junction of the A308 and A309.

A BIT OF HISTORY

Hampton Court Palace was begun in the 16C, an age of splendour and display, which is reflected in the magnificent Tudor buildings. It was extended in the late 17C with two ranges of handsome state apartments designed by **Sir Christopher Wren** for **William** and **Mary**.

Wolsey's Mansion – **Thomas Wolsey**, the son of an Ipswich butcher, rose under **Henry VIII** to become Archbishop of York *(1514)*, Lord Chancellor *(1515)*, Cardinal *(1515)* and Papal Legate *(1518)*. Eager to celebrate his wealth and position, he bought the manor of Hampton, enclosed the estate *(1,800 acres/728ha)* and began to construct a fine mansion according to the usual Tudor plan of consecutive courts bordered by buildings: Base Court, Clock Court, Carpenter's Court, hall and chapel *(300 x 550ft/91 x 168m overall)*.

The mansion was richly furnished throughout and contained some 1,000 rooms. The magnificence of Wolsey's mansion outshone the royal palaces and attracted the eye and envy of the King. After 15 years Wolsey fell from power and later died *(1530)*. Henry annexed Hampton Court.

Tudor Palace – Despite its magnificence, **Henry VIII** enlarged and rebuilt much of the palace. Major additions included the Great Hall, the Great Watching Chamber, the annexes around the Kitchen Court, the Fountain Court and the tennis court wing. He also planted a flower garden, kitchen garden and two orchards.

Edward VI, who was born *(1537)* at Hampton Court, his two sisters, Mary and Elizabeth, and the early Stuarts resided at the palace in fine weather or when the Plague was rife in London. Hampton Court was reserved for **Cromwell** and therefore preserved with its

Hampton Court Palace

© C. Ochterbeck/Michelin

contents. At the Restoration, the buildings remained largely unaltered and unmaintained until the late 17C.

Renaissance Reconstruction – Hampton Court entered its third and last phase of construction during the reign of **William and Mary**, who wished to make Hampton Court their main residence outside London. Initial schemes for the total demolition of the Tudor palace were discarded. Instead **Wren** rebuilt the East and South ranges of the Fountain Court to provide two suites of State Apartments.

The King's Side was in the South range overlooking the Privy Garden; the Queen's Side in the East overlooking the Fountain Garden. Wren also rebuilt the smaller, informal royal apartments facing into the **Fountain Court★** and added a colonnade and a new South range to the Clock Court. The buildings were executed in brick in the classic Renaissance style of the 17C. The rooms were decorated by **Grinling Gibbons** *(sculptures)* and **Antonio Verrio** *(painted ceilings)*. The Banqueting House overlooking the river was built in the last years of William's reign after the death of Mary.

The decoration and furnishing of the State Apartments continued under **Queen Anne** and was completed under **George II**, the last monarch to reside at the palace, who also commissioned **William Kent** to decorate the Cumberland Suite. When the Great Gatehouse was rebuilt *(1771–73)*, it was reduced in height by two storeys.

In 1838 **Queen Victoria** opened the State Apartments, the gardens and Bushy Park to the public.

VISIT

House: *Open daily Apr–Sept 10am–6pm (last admission 5pm), Oct–Mar 10am–4.30pm (last admission 3.30pm).* ***Gardens:*** *1hr later than house. Closed 24–26 Dec. Orientation leaflet (7 languages). Guided tours. Family trails. Audio guide. £17.60 (£16.50 online); gardens only £5.72 (Apr–Sep). Maze £4.40. Parking £1.50/hr. Summer: Hampton Court Flower Show, open-air concerts and theatre. Winter: open-air ice rink, Christmas evenings. 0844 482 7777. www.hrp.org.uk.*

A Curiosity

The **Astronomical Clock** was made for Henry VIII in 1540 by Nicholas Oursian; on the dial *(8ft/2.5m)* the hour, month, date, signs of the zodiac, year and phase of the moon are indicated. It predates the publication of the theories of Copernicus and Galileo and the sun therefore revolves round the earth. In the 19C it was transferred from St James's Palace to its present site in the Clock Court, which was the main Court of Wolsey's house.

HIGHLIGHTS

PALACE★★★

The **Trophy Gates** were built as the main gates in the reign of George II with lion and unicorn supporters.

The **moat and bridge** were constructed by Henry VIII; the bridge is fronted by the King's Beasts.

The **Great Gatehouse** built by Wolsey was flanked with wings in the reign of Henry VIII. **Stone weasels** on the battlements are the same period.

The **Arms of Henry VIII** appear in a panel *(renewed)* beneath the central oriel in the Great Gatehouse and also on Anne Boleyn's Gateway. The **terracotta roundels** depicting Roman emperors, which appear on the turrets and elsewhere, were bought by Wolsey for Hampton Court in 1521. **Anne Boleyn's Gateway** is so called because it was embellished by Henry VIII during her brief period as Queen. The Base Court side bears Elizabeth I's badges and initials; on the other side are Wolsey's arms and his cardinal's hat.

Clock Court is named after the **astronomical clock** made for Henry VIII in 1540.

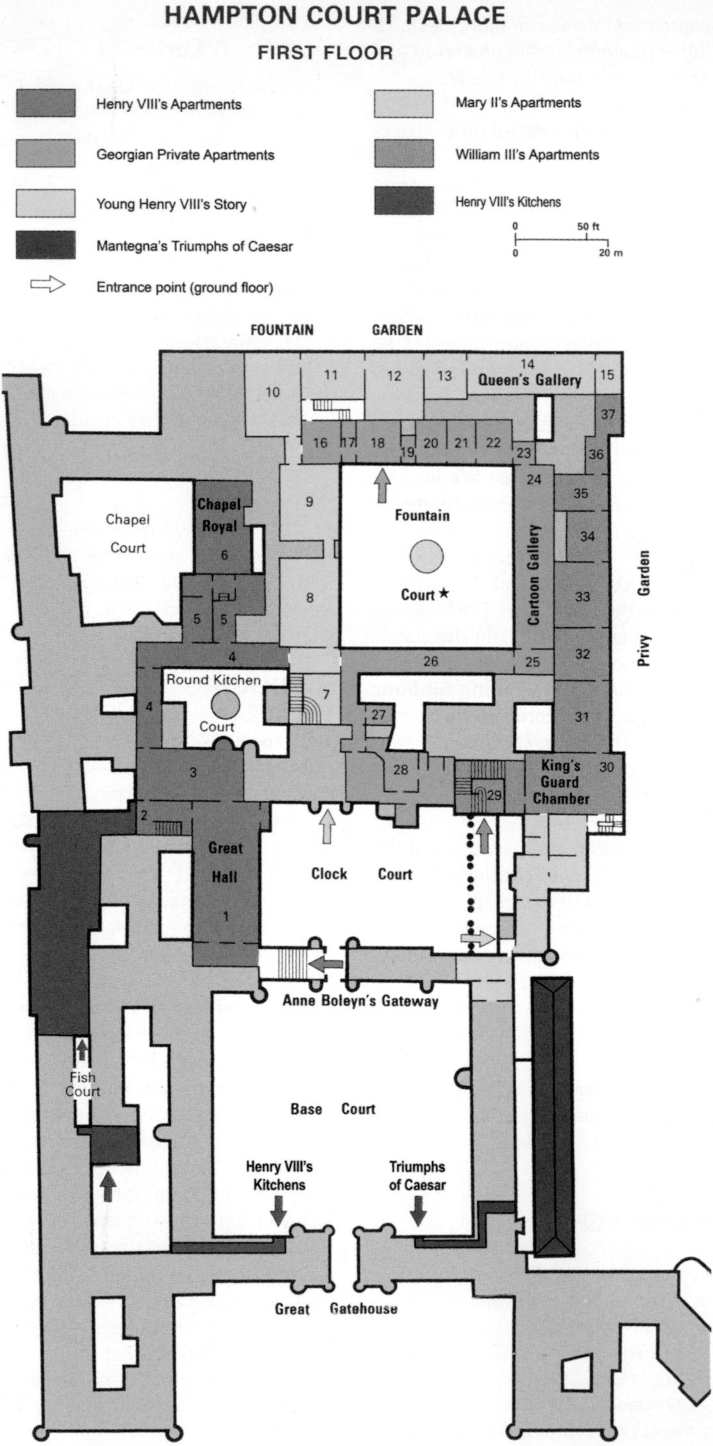

HAMPTON COURT PALACE
FIRST FLOOR

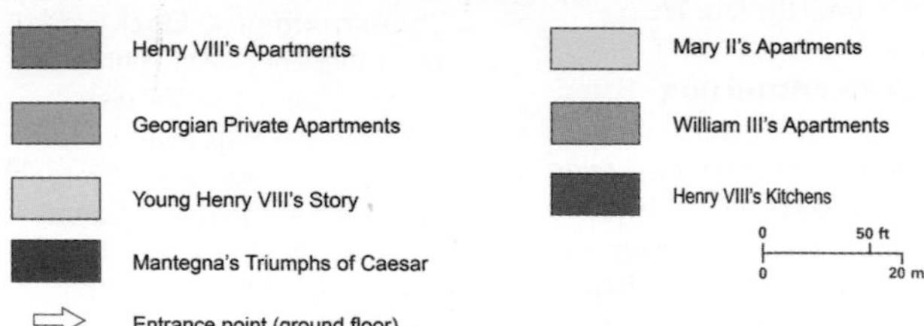

FOUNTAIN GARDEN

14 Queen's Gallery

Chapel Court

Chapel Royal 6

Fountain Court ★

Cartoon Gallery

Privy Garden

Round Kitchen Court

King's Guard Chamber 30

Great Hall 1

Clock Court

Anne Boleyn's Gateway

Fish Court

Base Court

Henry VIII's Kitchens

Triumphs of Caesar

Great Gatehouse

Tudor Royal Lodgings

Entrance in Anne Boleyn's Gateway.

The **Great Hall (1)** (106 x 40 x 60ft/32 x 12 x 18m), used by Henry's men for dining and sleeping, was built in 1531–36. The magnificent roof is ornamented with mouldings, tracery, carving and pendants relieved with gilding and colours. The walls are hung with 16C Flemish tapestries made by Van Orley to illustrate the *Story of Abraham*. At the West end is the Minstrels' Gallery.

The **Horn Room (2)**, from which stairs led down to the kitchens, was the serving place for the upper end of the hall.

The **Great Watching Chamber (3)** was built in 1535–36 at the entrance to the Tudor State Rooms *(demolished)* with a panelled ceiling set with coloured bosses.

The **Haunted Gallery (4)**, said to be haunted by the ghost of Catherine Howard *(condemned for her infidelity)*, looks onto the Round Kitchen Court.

The **Royal Pew (5)** was designed for Queen Anne with a ceiling by Sir James Thornhill.

The **Chapel Royal (6)** was built by Wolsey but lavishly transformed by Henry VIII. The reredos is by **Gibbons**; it is framed by Corinthian pillars and a segmental pediment by **Wren**.

Queen's State Apartments

Entrance in Clock Court.

The beautiful wrought-iron balustrade of the **Queen's Staircase (7)** is by **Tijou** and the lantern by Benjamin Goodison *(1731)*. The walls and ceiling were decorated by Kent *(1735)*. The **Queen's Guard Chamber (8)** contains a monumental chimney-piece carved by Grinling Gibbons.

The **Queen's Presence Chamber (9)** contains a bed and furniture made for Queen Anne *(1714)*. The elaborate plaster ceiling is by Sir John Vanbrugh, the carvings by Gibbons and the paintings by **Tintoretto**, Gentileschi and Vasari.

The **Public Dining Room (10)** was decorated by **Sir John Vanbrugh** c.1716–18 for the future George II and Queen Caroline.

The **Queen's Audience Chamber (11)** is hung with a 16C tapestry illustrating the *Story of Abraham* and contains the canopied Chair of State.

The **Queen's Drawing Room (12)** is decorated with wall and ceiling paintings by Verrio *(1703–05)*, commissioned by Queen Anne. From the central window there is a splendid **view★** of the **Fountain Garden**.

The **Queen's Bedroom (13)** contains a state bed, chair and stools *(1715–16)* in crimson damask and a portrait of *Queen Anne as a child* by **Sir Peter Lely**. The ceiling is **Sir James Thornhill**'s *(1715)*.

In the **Queen's Gallery (14)** the mantelpiece was designed by John Nost; the carvings are by Grinling Gibbons. The adjoining chamber **(15)** is decorated with embroidered wall coverings.

Georgian Rooms

Entrance in Fountain Court.

In contrast with the public state rooms, these private apartments are more intimate and comfortable. Most have been restored to recreate interiors from 1737.

The **Queen's Private Chapel (16)** has a domed ceiling with a lantern. Religious paintings by Fetti surmount the doors.

The **Bathing Closet (17)** leads to the **Private Dining Room (18)** hung with works by Pellegrini. The next room is a second **Closet (19)**.

The **Queen's Private Chamber (20)** is hung with paintings by Ruysdael, Brueghel and Van de Velde.

The **King's Private Dressing Room (21)** contains a small early 18C bed.

George II's Private Chamber (22) is notable for its 1730 flock wallpaper and a portrait of Cardinal Richelieu by Philippe de Champaigne. A small **lobby (23)** leads to the **Cartoon Gallery (24)** designed by **Wren** *(1699)* to display seven of the 10 tapestry cartoons drawn by **Raphael** *(1515)* and depicting scenes from the lives of St Peter and St Paul.

The **lobby (25)** is hung with a view of Hampton Court in George I's reign and a 17C hunting scene.

The **Communication Gallery (26)**, which links the King's and Queen's

Apartments, is hung with the **Windsor Beauties** of Charles II's court by Lely.
Wolsey's Closet (27) contains its original furnishings: linenfold panelling *(restored)*, painted wall panels and Wolsey's motto as a running motif.
The **Cumberland Suite (28)** was designed by **William Kent** *(1732)* for George II's third son and features elaborate plasterwork and portraits of some of the royal children.

King's Apartments

Entrance in Clock Court.

The **King's Staircase (29)** is decorated with allegorical scenes by Verrio *(c.1700)* and a stylised wrought-iron balustrade by Tijou; in the **King's Guard Chamber (30)** the walls are decorated with some 3,000 **arms** arranged by John Harris, William III's gunsmith.
The **First Presence Chamber (31)** contains William III's canopied chair of state. A picture of the King by Kneller *(1701)* hangs in its original place. The smaller **Second Presence Chamber (32)** sometimes served as a dining room.
The **King's Audience Chamber (33)**, which contains the state canopy and 17C chair, offers a **view** of the Privy Garden.
In the **King's Drawing Room (34)** note, above the fireplace, the elaborate carved frame by Grinling **Gibbons**.
In the **King's State Bedroom (35)** the ceiling was painted by Verrio. The state bed was used only for the formal *lever* and *coucher*. The King slept in the **King's Dressing Room (36)**, which is furnished in yellow taffeta; the ceiling by Verrio depicts *Mars in the Lap of Venus*.
The **King's Writing Closet (37)** was used for formal business.
The **King's Private Apartments** on the ground floor display architectural drawings of the Palace and a silver-gilt toilet service *(c.1670)* by Pierre Prévost.
The **Orangery** provided winter shelter for the orange trees.
The **Oak Room** is furnished with bookcases and a writing table.
The **King's Private Dining Room** is hung with portraits of the **Hampton Court Beauties** by Kneller.

Wolsey Rooms and Renaissance Picture Gallery

Entrance in Clock Court.

The Wolsey rooms were probably used by guests. They are currently home to a permanent exhibition exploring the lives of Henry VIII, Katherine of Aragon and Cardinal Wolsey using historic paintings from the Royal Collection together with audiovisual and hands-on displays.
The two **Victorian Rooms** are furnished in the style of the 1840s.

Tudor Kitchens

Entrance in Clock Court. Audio guide.

The 16C kitchens are the largest and most complete to survive from this period. When the Court was in residence, they served two meals a day to some 600 people and employed about 230 staff. They are laid out as for the preparation of the feast served on Midsummer's Day in 1542. The tour begins in the cellar beneath the Great Hall (**model** of the kitchens), proceeds to the main gates, where the produce entered the palace, and passes through the **Butchery**, the **Boiling House**, the **Flesh Larder** and the **Fish Court** to the **Great Kitchens**, where the meat was cooked on spits and sauces prepared over charcoal stoves; the dishes were then transferred to the **Servery**. The Wine Cellar is one of three in which home-brewed ale and imported wine were stored.

GARDENS★★★

The gardens *(50 acres/20ha)* bear the imprint of their creators: the Tudor, Stuart and Orange monarchs. Over the years features have changed with fashions.
The **Privy Garden** began as squares of grass, dotted with heraldic beasts on poles and topiary, and there was a watergate to welcome visitors, who usually travelled by river.
Between 1599 and 1659 the heraldic garden was replaced with four simple grass plots containing fine statuary and the terraces which now flank the Privy Garden were constructed.
Under Charles II the land overlooked by the east front was laid out in the fashion-

able French style practised by Le Nôtre; a vast semicircle of lime trees enclosed three radiating avenues, laid out in a giant goosefoot; the central claw was represented by a canal, known as the Long Water.

The layout of the gardens today has been restored to that of 1702, designed largely by **William III** and **Mary**.

South Side

The **Knot Garden**, a velvety conceit of interlaced ribands of dwarf box or thyme, with infillings of flowers, was replanted this century within its walled Elizabethan site. The royal cipher **ER 1568** appears on the stonework of the bay window in the **South Front** overlooking the Knot Garden; the lead cupola and octagonal turret date from the 16C.

The **Lower Orangery**, a plain building by Wren, now houses the **Mantegna Cartoons** *(c.1431–1506)*, nine giant paintings depicting *the Triumph of Caesar*.

The **Great Vine★**, planted in 1768 by **Capability Brown** for **George III**, produces an annual crop of 500–600 bunches of Black Hamburg grapes. The massive wisteria dates from 1840.

The **Banqueting House** has an important Baroque interior: the *Painted Room* by Verrio.

The **Privy Garden** was reserved for the Monarch and his guests. The last major redesign took place under William and Mary when **Queen Mary's Bower**, a hornbeam alley and the Queen's Terrace were built; the Tudor Water Gallery was demolished and the garden extended to the river; it was screened from the towpath by 12 wrought-iron panels with English, Welsh, Scottish and Irish emblems designed by **Jean Tijou**. The gardens have now been restored.

East Side

The **Broad Walk** was planned by **Wren** and Queen Caroline to separate the Privy Garden from the Fountain Garden. The **Fountain Garden** was created under William III by retaining the radiating avenues created by Charles II and reducing the Long Water to its present length *(0.75mi/1.2km)*; 13 fountains were installed in a formal setting of dwarf box hedges, obelisk-shaped yews and globes of white holly. Under Queen Anne eight fountains at the circumference were removed, the box hedge arabesques replaced by grass and gravel; in Queen Caroline's time the fountains were reduced to the present singleton. In the late 20C, the yews, which grew as they would in the 19C, were trimmed to their present conical shape to make room for flower beds and to reveal spectacular **vistas** from the east front. The double semicircle of lime trees was replanted in the 1980s.

The **Tudor Tennis Court** was built by Henry VIII; the windows are 18C.

North Side

The **Tudor tiltyards**, surrounded by six observation towers, of which one remains, are now walled rose gardens.

The **Wilderness**, now an area of natural woodland, includes a triangular **maze** that dates from 1714. The site, originally occupied by Henry VIII's orchard, was formally laid out by William III.

The **Lion Gates** were part of Wren's grand design for a new north entrance and front to the palace; the **Chestnut Avenue** in Bushy Park is another feature of his plan. Four rows of lime trees flank the double row of chestnut trees extending for over a mile/2km. The **Diana Fountain** was commissioned by Charles II from Francisco Fenelli for the Privy Garden. Northwest of the fountain is a **Woodland Garden** (100 acres/40.5ha), where rhododendrons and azaleas flourish.

HAMPTON COURT GREEN

Opposite the palace gates are houses associated with the Court, particularly in the late 17C and 18C, including **Old Court House**, the home *(1706–23)* of Sir Christopher Wren, and **Faraday House** *(18C)*, where **Michael Faraday** lived in retirement *(1858–67)*. Hidden behind the last two houses is small, square **King's Store Studio**, with white weatherboarding. Facing the Green are the Tudor **Royal Mews**.

Osterley Park★★

This magnificent country mansion, surrounded by parkland on the outskirts of London, is well worth a visit. The rooms are elegantly furnished and decorated to reflect the tastes of wealthy and discerning owners. Osterley Park is the place to see Robert Adam interior decoration at its most complete. Room after room is as he designed it: ceilings, walls, doorcases, doors, handles, carpets, mirrors and furniture down to chairs standing in the exact positions for which they were designed. This is an easy excursion by public transport.

Location: *Osterley.* West of London by the A4 *(North side)* and near the M4 *(Exit 2).*

A BIT OF HISTORY

A Country Seat for City Gentlemen – **Sir Thomas Gresham** bought Osterley Manor in 1562 and began an adjoining country house. When Gresham's mansion was complete, **Queen Elizabeth** honoured her financier with a visit *(1576).* In 1711 the mansion was purchased by another City grandee **Francis Child**, whose grandchild began transforming the place in 1756, work that continued for more than 20 years.

In 1773 **Horace Walpole**, visiting from nearby **Strawberry Hill**, wrote: "The old house is so improved and enriched that all the Percies and Seymours of Sion must die of envy..." Osterley was presented to the nation by the 9th Earl of Jersey in 1949.

VISIT

House: *Open Mar–Oct daily noon–4.30pm, Nov–Dec Sat–Sun noon–3.30pm, Feb–Mar Wed–Sun noon–3.30pm. Closed 25–26 Dec.* ***Garden:*** *Open Mar–Oct Wed–Sun 11am–5pm, Nov–Feb Sat–Sun noon–3.30pm. £8.25; Garden-only £3.60. No photography. Dogs on lead. Car park £3.50. Tearoom. 020 8232 5050 (visitor services); 01494 755 566 (infoline). www.nationaltrust.org.uk/osterley.*

Exterior

The square form with corner towers of Sir Thomas Gresham's house remains, though enlarged and encased by new bricks and stone quoins in the 18C by **Sir William Chambers**, who reduced the courtyard to provide a hall and completed the Gallery and Breakfast Room.

Osterley Park

Robert Adam then added the grand, six-columned portico at the front and at the rear, a horseshoe staircase with wrought-iron and brass work *(1770)*.

Interior

The wide **Hall** is apsed at either end, the fine ceiling filled with floral scrolls is echoed in the two-tone marble pavement. Classical statues nestle in niches on either side of the curved fireplaces and grisaille paintings, each detail designed by **Adam**.

Leave the Hall by the North door and walk to the far end of the passage.

The **Breakfast Room** is painted in a strong lemon yellow contrasted with touches of blue that highlight the ornamental detailing. The ceiling is by Chambers; tables and pier glasses, however, were designed by Adam and the lyre-back mahogany armchairs are probably by Linnell. The **staircase**, begun by Chambers, has a fine iron balustrade and delicate stucco decoration added by Adam, who also designed the three lamps that hang between the Corinthian columns. The sumptuous ceiling painting is particularly Rubensesque.

At the top, turn right.

The **State Bedroom** or Yellow Taffeta Bedchamber is furnished with painted taffeta curtains and bed hangings, and ornate gilded mirrors. The bed, surmounted by cupped acorns, was designed by Adam *(1779)*.
Beyond the stairhead is the suite of less extravagant rooms designed by Chambers for the Childs: his **dressing room**, the **bedchamber** *(note the lacquer dressing-table and French ebony cabinet on a stand)* and her **dressing room** *(chimney-piece and mirror by Linnell)*.

Return downstairs; turn right.

The **Eating Room** is an all-Adam interior: motifs from the pink-and-green ceiling decoration are most typical. According to 18C custom the beautifully carved mahogany lyre-back chairs are set against the wall.
The light and airy **gallery**, boasting a fine **view** of the garden, was designed by Chambers. Marble chimney-pieces, Classical doorcases, 18C Chinese pieces and lacquered furniture are contrasted by the delicate Rococo-style frieze. Other fixtures are by Adam.
The somewhat overgilded **Drawing Room** is dominated by the low, heavy coffered ceiling. Serpentine sofas and chairs are after the early French neo-Classical style. The pier glasses and perfume burners are French in origin.
In the **Tapestry Room**, one's attention is drawn to the richness of the Gobelins' tapestries, signed and dated by (Jacques) Neilson, 1775, an artist of Scottish origin in charge of the works in Paris from 1751 to 1788.
The **State Bed Chamber** is decked in cool green. The Child crest above the chimney glass features an eagle with an adder in its beak. Gilded chairs, their oval backs supported on reclining sphinxes, are one of Adam's most graceful designs *(1777)*.
The **Etruscan Dressing Room**, which helped to launch a fashion for the style of antiquity, boasts ancient Greek decorative themes that Adam took to be Etruscan. According to surviving inventories from 1782, it was here that the japanned **Chippendale** 1773 lady's writing desk was situated.
The **Stables**, built in 1577 by Sir Thomas Gresham, were refitted in the 18C.
The **Pleasure Grounds** *(west of the house)*, which have been restored according to old maps and prints, contain Chambers' Doric temple to Pan and Adam's semicircular garden house *(c.1780)*. Between June and September the grounds erupt in fragrant, colourful blooms – a perfect time to visit.
The cedar trees on the south lawn were planted in the 1760s, as was the large oriental plane tree. The chain of lakes was created in the 1750s; at the head of the **Garden Lake** is a brick bridge leading over to a secluded island.

Windsor Castle★★★

On a steep bluff and in a beautiful park setting, the romantic turrets and massive tower of Windsor Castle rise above the bustling town in the Thames valley. It is a fascinating example of a medieval castle that has evolved into a sumptuous royal residence. The royal association gives great cachet to the pretty town, which boasts a thriving theatre, fine shops, restaurants and tearooms. Over the bridge are the handsome buildings of Eton College, which are of great interest.

Location: 24 High St. 020 7766 7304. www.royalcollection.org.uk. *Overground from London Waterloo or Paddington.* Windsor is to the West of London and easily accessible by the M4. Leave the motorway at Junction 6.

Timing: Allow at least half a day to visit the Castle, then stroll through the town and across the Thames to Eton.

A BIT OF HISTORY

Windsor Castle is the oldest royal residence to have remained in continuous use by the reigning monarchs and the largest castle in England. It was originally intended by **William the Conqueror** *(c.1080)* as one of several defensive strongholds built around London and as such was constructed on the only elevated point in that stretch of the Thames Valley.

Norman castles conformed to a standard plan, with a large tower or keep dominating the complex from an artificially raised earthen mound or *motte*; at Windsor this is flanked by the Upper and Lower Wards. The Castle covers an area of 13 acres/5ha.

The Castle was used from 1110 onwards by successive monarchs. **Henry II** began building the stone castle as a royal residence with state apartments in the Lower Ward and private lodgings on the north side of the Upper Ward *(1165–79)*. Further expansion was undertaken by **Henry III** *(r.1216–72)* and by **Edward III** *(r.1327–77)*.

Used by the Parliamentarians during the Civil War as a prison for Royalist supporters, it became **Charles II**'s favourite (defensible) home outside London. In 1673 the architect **Hugh May** was appointed to manage a series of ambitious renovations mainly concerning the interior: walls were insulated with oak wainscoting and festooned in **Grinling Gibbons** carvings, the ceilings decorated by the Italian painter **Verrio** and

St George's Chapel

©Philip Coblentz/Brand X Pictures

gilded by a French master-craftsman René Coussin.

George III had the Queen's Lodge *(1777)* designed by **William Chambers**; he modernised Frogmore in Home Park as a retreat for Queen Charlotte. Alterations to provide ever-greater comfort were begun by **George IV**. Mock Gothic renovations included the addition of turrets, chimney-stacks and battlements, and the heightening of the Round Tower by 33ft/10m, while extensions were remodelled to accommodate the large and complicated extension of the royal family. For this reason, Windsor was popular with **Queen Victoria**, who received endless visits from her extended family in Europe and chose to receive heads of state there *(King Louis Philippe in 1844; Emperor Napoleon III in 1855; King Victor Emanuel I of Italy; Emperor William I of Germany)*. She started the "dine and sleep" practice maintained by **Queen Elizabeth II**, where guests might be invited to spend an evening and stay overnight. The principal change made by Victoria was the creation of a private chapel in honour of **Prince Albert**, who died at Windsor on 14 December 1861. With the turn of the century came a change in spirit. **George V**'s Queen Mary began careful restoration of the Castle, which became the childhood home of **HRH The Princesses Elizabeth** and **Margaret** during the War; since then it has remained the Royal Family's principal home. The Court is in official residence throughout April and for Ascot Week in June, when the annual Garter Day celebrations are held.

VISIT

Open daily 9.45am–5.15pm (4.15pm Nov–Feb); last admission 1hr 15min before closing. Closed some bank holidays and dates signficant to the Royal Family. ***St George's Chapel:*** *Open (functions permitting) Mon–Sat 10am–4.15pm (4pm last admission). £17.75 (Queen Mary's Dolls' House, State Apartments and St George's Chapel), reduced rate (£9.70) when the State Apartments are closed. Call in advance to check. Audiotour. Guidebook (8 languages).* **Changing of the Guard★★★** *takes place Apr–Jul Mon–Sat 11am.* ***Frogmore House and Gardens:*** *Open May and Aug, certain days. 020 7766 7304 (tickets); 01753 831 118 (information); 01753 865 538 (St George's Chapel). www.royalcollection.org.uk.*

20 November 1992

The fire which broke out in the Queen's Private Chapel at the northeast angle of the Upper Ward is thought to have been caused by a spotlight on a curtain high above the altar. Major losses included the wooden ceiling of the St George Hall and Grand Reception room. Restoration work was completed in November 1997, six months ahead of schedule, to coincide with the Queen's 50th wedding anniversary. It was the largest project of its kind in the 20C, costing over £37 million and calling on the skills of some of the finest craftspeople.

PRECINCTS

Enter from Castle Hill and proceed into the Upper Ward.

Round Tower

Henry II built this impressive section as a main defence feature surrounded by a dry (chalk) moat in c.1170; it was heightened in the 19C. The Tower, which is in fact oval, now houses the Royal Archives *(closed to the public)*. From the North Terrace there is a fine **view** over Eton and the River Thames.

Queen Mary's Dolls' House

Conceived by **Sir Edwin Lutyens** on a scale of 12:1, it was presented to Queen Mary in 1924. The miniature contents include standard amenities, all in working order *(water system, electric lights and two lifts)*, a gramophone, vintage bottles of wine, original paintings and leather-bound books. Wall cases also display a remarkable travelling "trousseau" of designer fashion-wear provided by the French and presented to the Princesses Elizabeth and Margaret after King George VI's official visit to France *(1938)*.

State Apartments★★

When the apartments were remodelled by George IV, Gothic was used for processional spaces *(lobbies, halls, staircases)* and an eclectic form of Classicism for the main reception rooms.

The **Gallery**, designed to serve as the principal entrance hall to the State Apartments, was cut off when the Grand Staircase was remodelled during the reign of Queen Victoria. Today it accommodates temporary exhibitions of prints, drawings and books. The **China Museum** displays fabulous pieces from services in the Royal Collection: Sèvres, Meissen, Copenhagen, Worcester... still used occasionally at banquets.

The **Grand Staircase** leads up to the first floor. The full-size statue is of King George IV. In the fan-vaulted **Grand Vestibule** various 18C and 19C trophies are displayed, acquired after the Battle of Seringapatam *(1799)* and the Napoleonic Wars *(the lead shot that killed Lord Nelson in the Battle of Trafalgar)*.

The **Waterloo Chamber**, used to celebrate the anniversary of the **Battle of Waterloo** on 18 June, is hung with a series of portraits by Sir Thomas Lawrence, depicting political and military leaders who assisted in defeating Napoleon. Today the Chamber is used for the annual luncheon given by HM The Queen for her Knights of the Garter and their consorts, and for balls, receptions and concerts.

The **Garter Throne Room** and the **Ante-Throne Room** are used by the Queen to confer upon her newly chosen knights the Order of the Garter. The **Grand Reception Room** style particularly reflects George IV's personal francophile taste.

Public Rooms – The **King's Drawing Room** was once used by Queen Victoria for private theatrical performances. Note the finely carved dado rail and **Grinling Gibbons** cornice; the five paintings by **Rubens** and his followers; the beautiful boulle kneehole desk reputedly acquired by William III; the carpet presented to Edward VII by the Shah of Persia in 1903. The porcelain is all Chinese.

The **King's Bedchamber** has been considerably altered through history. The grandiose *"polonaise"* bed is attributed to the French furniture designer George Jacob and given its furnishings for the occasion of a visit from Emperor Napoleon III and his wife Eugénie in 1855, whose initials appear at the foot of the bed. The early-19C Aubusson carpet was presented to HM The Queen by President de Gaulle in 1960. Note the Canaletto views of Venice.

The **King's Dressing Room** is lined in red damask, as intended by George III. On the walls hang a number of **masterpieces★★**: works by Dürer *(Portrait of a Young Man)*, Hans Memlinc, Jean Clouet, Hans Holbein, Andrea del Sarto, **Rembrandt** *(The Artist's Mother)*, Rubens *(Portrait of the Artist)*, Jan Steen, Van Dyck *(Charles I in Three Positions)*.

The **King's Closet** is furnished with exquisite pieces, mainly French and made of exotic woods *(mahogany or satinwood)* set with Japanese lacquer panels and bronze mounts.

The **Queen's Drawing Room** was substantially altered by Wyatville in 1834. The room is adorned with early 16C and 17C paintings (Holbein: *Sir Henry Guildford*, Mytens, Van Somer, Dobson: *Charles II*, Lely: *Mary II*) and furniture.

The **Octagon Lobby** is panelled in oak with splendid oval garlands by Gibbons. The **King's Dining Room** retains much of the character imparted to it by Charles II. Verrio's ceiling depicts a banquet enjoyed by the gods, while below, lovely still-life panels illustrate fruit, fish *(lobster)* and fowl; intricate limewood garlands of fruit and flowers carved by Grinling Gibbons and Henry Phillips tumble down the oak panelling. The **Queen's Ballroom** or Queen's Gallery serves as a meeting room in which visiting heads of state may greet members of their diplomatic staff. Note the three

Order of the Garter

The highest order of chivalry in the land is also the oldest to survive in the world. It was established by Edward III in 1348 when England was engaged in the Hundred Years' War with France and may have been modelled on the legendary story of the 5C King Arthur and his Knights of the Round Table. Not only was the order to reward men who had shown valour on the battlefield, but also to honour those who manifested the idealistic and romantic concept of Christian chivalry. Tradition relates how at a ball fêting the conquest of Calais in 1347, the King retrieved a fallen garter and returned it to its rightful owner, the young and beautiful Joan of Kent, Countess of Salisbury, with the words *"Honi soit qui mal y pense"* ("Shame on him who thinks evil of it") – the emblem and motto of the Order. A more likely derivation is a strap or sword-belt from a suit of armour to denote the bond of loyalty and concord. At its initiation, Edward III nominated 25 **English Companion Knights**, including the Heir Apparent *(the Black Prince)*, thereby providing himself with his own jousting team and one with which to do battle! Today there are still 25 Companion Knights, including the Prince of Wales and at least one representative of each force *(Navy, Army, Air Force)*. Additional **"Royal Knights"** may also be appointed by the Sovereign following amendments made to the statutes by George I. Stranger, Foreign or **"Extra Knights"** may also be appointed; since 1905 this has been conferred upon regents or monarchs only (including two Sultans of Turkey, two Shahs of Persia and four Emperors of Japan).

English cut-glass chandeliers made for George III and the 17C silver pieces of furniture between the windows. On the walls hang portraits by **Sir Anthony van Dyck** – the most notable being *Charles I in Robes of State*.

The **Queen's Audience Chamber**, together with the **Queen's Presence Chamber** next door, preserve the skilled artistry of craftsmen employed by Hugh May during the reign of Charles II, in particular **Verrio** and Gibbons. Note the Gobelins tapestries acquired by George IV in Paris in 1825 and the busts by Roubiliac *(Handel)* and Coysevox.

The **Queen's Guard Chamber** was remodelled as a museum of British military achievement: replica French banners, the tricolour and the gold fleur-de-lys are presented each year to HM The Queen by the current Duke of Wellington and the Duke of Marlborough as quit-rents for their estates at Stratfield-Saye and Blenheim, granted to their ancestors on perpetual leases by the grateful nation.

St George's Hall – This long room *(180ft/55m)* formed by remodelling Charles II's chapel and hall, was decorated by Wyatville in the neo-Gothic style inspired by the novels of Sir Walter Scott, so admired by George IV. Completely gutted in the fire, the Hall has been magnificently restored with a hammerbeam oak roof (instead of previous painted plaster ceiling), complete with the 700 coats of arms of past Knights of the Garter.

Quadrangle

The equestrian statue is of Charles II. In the south-east corner is the **Sovereign's Entrance**, which leads directly to the private royal apartments.

Lower Ward

Much of this section of the Castle precincts is given to the **College of St George** founded on 6 August 1348 by Edward III and comprising a dean, 12 canons, 13 vicars and 26 "Poor Knights", on whom was conferred the Order of the Garter. On the left are the mid-16C lodgings of the Military Knights built by Queen Mary. At the bottom stands the Guard House *(1862)*.

To the right sits St George's Chapel and beyond, a maze of cloisters and buildings attached to the chapel and choir school; the brick and timber-framed Horseshoe Cloister is reserved for the lay clerks *(adult choristers)*.

St George's Chapel★★★

The spiritual headquarters of England's prime order of chivalry, the Most Noble Order of the Garter, is also the final resting place of 10 sovereigns, including **Charles I**, brought here after his execution at Whitehall in 1649.

The building, initiated by Edward IV *(1475)* and completed in 1528 in the reign of Henry VIII, is a glorious expression of Perpendicular Gothic architecture. Note the **Royal Beasts** *(modern replacements)* above the flying buttresses of the West end.

Interior – The 1790 Gothic-style Coade stone **organ screen** by Henry Emlyn was installed at the same time as the Samuel Green organ presented by George III. The splendid 75-light **west window** *(36ft/11m high and 29ft/9m wide)* survives in part from 1479, 1503, 1509 and 1842.

George VI Memorial Chapel was built in 1969, the first structural addition to the Chapel since 1504. The windows were designed by John Piper.

Quire – So called at Windsor to differentiate it from the body of choristers or choir, the Quire is separated from the nave by John Tresilien's magnificent set of wrought-iron gates *(1478)*. The glorious east window *(30ft/9m high, 29ft/8.5m wide; 52-lights)* commemorates Prince Albert with incidents from his life illustrated in the lower tier, below the *Resurrection (painted by Benjamin West)* and the *Adoration of the Kings*. The carved alabaster reredos was also given by the Dean and Canons in memory of Prince Albert. The woodwork, executed largely by English and Flemish craftsmen, dates from 1478–85.

Garter Stalls – On installation each knight is granted a stall marked with a numbered enamel nameplate *(North 1 marks the Prince of Wales' stall)*, over which he/she will display their banner *(5ft/1.5m square of heavy silk bearing the arms approved by the College of Arms in the City of London)*, crest, helm, mantling and sword *(made of cloth or wood and depicted half drawn in readiness to defend the Sovereign)* and which they will keep until death when the accoutrements are all removed.Other stalls are reserved for the Military Knights of Windsor *(formerly the 24 Poor Knights appointed by Edward III, impoverished by ransoms paid to the French for their freedom)*.

Memorials – **Emperor Napoleon III** and his wife Eugénie of France, the close friends of Queen Victoria who died at Chislehurst in 1873. Statue of **Leopold I**, King of the Belgians, the uncle of both Queen Victoria and Prince Albert – his first wife, **Princess Charlotte Augusta**, who would have succeeded her father George IV had she not died in childbirth, is commemorated by a sculptural group in the Urswick Chapel, where the tomb of **George V** *(d.1936)* and **Queen Mary** *(d.1953)* by Lutyens is situated. In the north aisle, but despoiled of its effigy and jewels during the Commonwealth, is the tomb of **Edward IV** and Queen Elizabeth Woodville.

The **Royal Vault** extends from the High Altar to the Albert Memorial Chapel; in it rest **George III**, **George IV**, **William IV** and many of their direct descendants. In a second vault lie **Henry VIII**, Jane Seymour and **Charles I**. In the South aisle are the tombs of Edward VII *(d.1910)* and Queen Alexandra *(d.1925)* with their dog Caesar; Henry VI, founder of Eton College and King's College, Cambridge.

Albert Memorial Chapel

This was the original chapel of the Order of the Garter; left to decay, it was renovated by Henry VII as a mausoleum for Henry VI and intended by **Cardinal Wolsey** as his ultimate resting place. It was given its magnificent Victorian embellishment by **Sir George Gilbert Scott** after the death of Albert, the **Prince Consort**, at the age of 42; it stands as a supreme expression of the 19C revivalist age complete with Venetian mosaics, inlaid marble panels and statuary. Prince Albert's tomb was later removed to Frogmore.

Home Park

This section outside the Castle precincts but within the private grounds of Windsor Castle includes **Frogmore House**, which was built in 1684 and used by various members of the Royal household, most notably by **Queen Charlotte** and her unmarried daughters. Today it is furnished with possessions accumulated by Queen Mary.

Other buildings nearby consist of follies *(Gothic ruin, Queen Victoria's Tea House and an Indian kiosk built of white marble)* and the **Royal Mausoleum**, built *(1862)* by Queen Victoria after the untimely death of her husband, Prince Albert. In the **Royal Burial Ground** *(closed to the public)* at Frogmore rest the Duke (**Edward VIII**) and **Duchess of Windsor**.

WINDSOR GREAT PARK★

Open daily dawn till dusk. 01753 860 222. www.theroyallandscape.co.uk.

This 4,800 acre/1,942ha park, once the hunting ground of Saxon leaders and medieval knights, is today linked to the castle by the **Long Walk** *(3mi/5km)* planted by Charles II. At the top of the hill stands the **Copper Horse**, an equestrian statue of George III *(1831)*.

Nestling in the park are two additional secluded former royal residences: **Royal Lodge** and **Cumberland Lodge**.

Smith's Lawn is a stretch of lawn reserved for polo matches, while beyond stretch the **Valley Gardens**, planted by the Duke of Cumberland with shrubs and trees that extend to **Virginia Water**, an area of 130 acres/53ha arranged around an artificial lake *(open daily 10am–6pm (4.30pm/dusk in winter) via local car park (fee); 01753 435 544)*. On the far side of the lake stand the **Ruins**, which consist of fragments brought in 1817 from Leptis Magna in Libya.

The Savill Garden *(open daily Mar–Oct 10am–6pm, Nov–Feb 10am–4.30pm; closed 25–26 Dec; £9 Mar–Oct, £6.25 Nov–Feb; 01784 435 544)* is another, independent landscaped wooded garden laid out in 1932 and endowed with a fine Temperate House. The garden is a glorious show in the spring, when rhododendrons, azaleas, camellias and magnolias burst into symphonies of colour; highlights include many varieties of lily and rose in summer.

ETON COLLEGE★★

School Yard, Chapel, Cloister and Museum of Eton Life: Open daily 10.30am–4.30pm in school holidays and Wed, Fri, Sat–Sun 1.30pm–4.30pm in term time. Tours at 2pm and 3.15pm. Closed occasionally; check website for details. 01753 671 1177. www.etoncollege.com.

Royal Antecedent

"The King's College of Our Lady of Eton beside Windsor" was founded by **Henry VI** in 1440; a year later he founded King's College Cambridge, where the young men might continue their studies. Along the North side of the **School Yard** (now dominated by a statue of the founder and the 16C **Lupton's Tower**) stands the 15C brick building of **Lower School**. Upper School on the West side was added in the 17C.

Chapel★★

At the heart of the college is the chapel, which was completed in 1482 and endowed with many beautiful and significant works of art.

The oldest are the Flemish-style wall paintings *(1479–87)*, executed by at least four masters, considered to be the finest 15C English murals. On the North side are scenes associated with the chapel's patron the Virgin Mary; the South side ones depict the Medieval story of a mythical empress. In 1940 a bomb landed on the Upper School thereby destroying all the glass in the chapel, save that above the organ. The East window was designed by Evie Hone in 1952 to complement panels by John Piper. Famous pupils have included several kings, including **George III**, statesmen *(of whom 19 became prime ministers)*, including **Walpole**, **Gladstone, Pitt the Elder**, Charles James Fox, **Wellington**, Macmillan and Douglas-Home, and the writers **Fielding**, **Shelley**, Thomas Gray, **Aldous Huxley** and **George Orwell**.

Leadenhall Market
©Monica Wells/Pictures Colour Library

YOUR STAY IN LONDON

Where To Stay

London is an expensive place to stay and finding a suitable room in a metropolis with over 27 million visitors annually and an average hotel occupancy rate of 80 percent, often requires patience. Fortunately, the choice of accommodation is surprising and with proper preparation prior to your trip, you will undoubtedly find pleasant accommodation within your price range and in your favourite area. *Bear in mind that advance reservation is a must in any season, especially over Christmas, Easter and during the summer.*
Whether you are looking for a luxury hotel in Mayfair or a modest but pleasant family-run guest house away from the bustle of central London, you should find something to suit in the following listing of hotels, guest houses, B&Bs and youth accommodation that have been carefully chosen for their unique character, convenient location, quality of comfort and value for money. They are grouped in areas covering districts that should be familiar to visitors.

ADDRESSES

SELECTING A DISTRICT

As London is such a large city, it is advisable to decide where to stay according to your budget or what you plan to visit.
The **most elegant central districts** – Mayfair, St James's, the Strand – are home to world-renowned luxury hotels. In the Kensington, Notting Hill and Bayswater areas, many attractive 19C terrace houses have been converted into small, often charming, **moderate-to-expensively priced hotels**. Centrally located Bloomsbury is packed with **small, inexpensive-to-moderate family-run establishments**. Those travelling on a budget will find **no-frills hotels** and B&Bs in Earl's Court and Victoria. **Young travellers** will be surprised at the choice of decent **youth accommodation** in the city centre. Lodging in the suburbs is usually less expensive than in the centre. The suburbs' hotels listed in this guide are located near tourist attractions. Particularly well-connected areas to stay include **Baker Street**, **Liverpool Street** *(for The City)* and **Victoria**, all of which are major bus, Underground and overground rail hubs. Centrally, Covent Garden, Soho, Kensington and Knightsbridge are well served by bus and Tube lines, although most hotels in Central London will be within a 5min walk of an Underground station.

COSTS AND PRICES

Budget accommodation ( ) includes small, simple but well-maintained establishments charging £90 or less for a double room in high season. Expect basic service and shared bathrooms for the least expensive rooms. In the **moderate** range (–) you'll find doubles from £90 to £250 in hotels of greater comfort or tastefully converted houses located in attractive neighbourhoods. For the smaller establishments, booking in advance is recommended. For those in search of a memorable stay, **luxury** accommodation ( ) tends to be priced at more than £250 for double occupancy. There are a limited number of centrally located upmarket establishments that guarantee a truly unforgettable London experience. Stylistically, these hotels run the gamut from traditional British to minimalist contemporary and, as to be expected, the rates reflect the outstanding quality of the comfort and service. One person staying in a double room (*indeed, singles in Central London are often pocket-sized)* will generally be given a reduction on the double rate, except during major events. Note that prices vary widely according to the time of year and whether it is a weekend or weekday. You may be able to negotiate a good rate if you are coming for a long time, or at a low time of year. Booking via the Internet is also usually cheaper, or try the various agencies on the Internet. It is advisable to confirm all details, including the inclusion of VAT and breakfast, before making the reservation. Many hotels offer special prices for short breaks – weekends or stays of at least three days. A credit card number will be requested for all reservations.

A note for light sleepers: Central London is quite noisy, both by day and night. Enquire about noise levels and remember that in small hotels, rooms at the rear are often quieter.

P Parking in Central London is expensive, frustrating and almost impossible – it's best to leave the car at home. A limited number of luxury hotels offer on-site parking for a fee. Chain hotels are often situated near NCP car parks.

Breakfast – As well as the Continental-style breakfast of bread and pastries served with tea and coffee, most establishments offer the traditional cooked full English breakfast of bacon, sausages and eggs with some or all of the following: hash browns, tomatoes, mushrooms, black pudding and baked beans.

TYPES OF ACCOMMODATION

The terms "hotel", "guest house" and "Bed & Breakfast" are used loosely – often according to the proprietor's preference – to apply to a wide variety of accommodation. However, hotels traditionally tend to be medium-to-large establishments, with ensuite rooms and a full range of services. The term "guest house" denotes a smaller operation with fewer facilities and will be generally more appealing to tourists than business visitors; bed and breakfasts tend to be small places run by a local couple or family. Information on bed and breakfast accommodation is available from:

- **At Home in London**
  70 Black Lion Ln., W6 9BE
  ℘020 8748 1943
  www.athomeinlondon.co.uk
- **London Home-to-Home**
  42 Dahomey Rd., London
  SW16 6ND ℘020 8769 3500
  www.londonhometohome.com

DON'T FORGET THE MICHELIN GUIDE

If you are unable to find suitable accommodation among the selected establishments described below, consult the red-cover *Michelin Guide London*, an extract from the annually revised *Michelin Guide Great Britain & Ireland*. This reputed guide lists over 250 hotels throughout Greater London.

- **London Bed and Breakfast Agency Ltd**
  71 Fellows Rd.,
  London NW3 3JY
  ℘020 7586 2768
  www.londonbb.com
- **Uptown Reservations**
  8 Kelso Pl., London W8 5QD
  ℘020 7937 2001
  www.uptownres.co.uk

YOUTH ACCOMMODATION

University Residences and **Youth Hostels**, as well as small hotels, guest houses and B&B accommodation in the budget price bracket, are worthwhile options for young travellers. University Residences are often available during the vacations and offer good cheap places to stay in a central location *(usually Bloomsbury)*.

Some useful addresses:

- **International Students House (ISH)**
  229 Great Portland St.,
  W1N 5HD. ℘020 7631 8310
  www.ish.org.uk
  Short stay accommodation for students in a building in Great Portland Street or in Regent's Park; mostly bunk beds in dormitories, and stays are for a maximum of 21 nights.
- **Venuemasters**
  ℘0114 249 3090
  www.venuemasters.co.uk
  Group accommodation.
- **YMCA, National Council**
  ℘020 8520 5599
  www.ymca.org.uk
  Good value accommodation for young people.

The UK branch of the **International Youth Hostel Federation** *(℘01629 592700; www.yha.org.uk)* can provide information on youth hostels in the UK and take bookings for the seven YHA hostels located in London: Central *(near Regent Street)*, Earl's Court, Holland Park, Oxford Street, St Pancras, St Pauls and Thameside *(Docklands)*. The **Hostelling International /American Youth Hostel Assocation** in the US can be contacted via www.hiusa.org.

CAMPSITES

There are several campsites within reasonable distance of Central London but try to book in advance. Prices vary according to the season:

- **Abbey Wood**
  Federation Rd., Abbey Wood, London SE2 0LS. 12mi/19.3km from Central London. Open all year. ℘020 8311 7708. www.caravanclub.co.uk
- **Crystal Palace Caravan Club Site**
  Crystal Palace Parade, London SE19 1UF. 8mi/12.8km from Central London. Open all year. ℘020 8778 7155 www.caravanclub.co.uk
- **Lee Valley Camping and Caravan Park**
  Meridian Way, Edmonton, London N9 0AR. 10mi/16km from Central London. Open all year. ℘020 8803 6900. www.leevalleypark.org.uk

CHAIN HOTELS

If you are willing to forego charm and personalised service and your budget is limited, London's various chain hotels are a good option.

For descriptions of areas described in the Chain Hotels section, see the Index.

Holiday Inn Express
Comfortable rooms at moderate rates *(from £90)* in more than 50 locations in and around London. *Central booking ℘0871 423 4896. www.hiexpress.com*
Locations: Hotels can be found more or less everywhere. Central properties include Oxford Circus, Mayfair, Bloomsbury, Regent's Park, the City, Victoria and Southwark.

Premier Inn
Simple but comfortable rooms, with rates starting from £49 per night. The cheapest rates are found online. *Service, VAT inc. Central booking ℘0871 527 9222. www.premierinn.com*
Locations: King's Cross, Euston, County Hall *(behind London Eye)*, Southwark, Tower Bridge, Tower Hill, Greenwich, Docklands, Victoria, Kensington, Putney, Kew, Hampstead, Wembley.

Travelodge
Basic rooms starting from £50–80 a night. *VAT inc. Central booking ℘08700 850 950. www.travelodge.co.uk*
Locations: King's Cross, Euston, Marylebone, Covent Garden, Waterloo, Southwark, Tower Bridge, Aldgate, Liverpool Street, Docklands, City, Battersea, Fulham.

HOTEL INFORMATION AND RESERVATION SERVICES

Among the numerous websites worth consulting:

www.bhrc.co.uk
British Hotel Reservation Centre; centres throughout London to help you find somewhere to stay. ℘020 7592 3055.

www.londontown.com
Hotel information and online reservations for moderate and luxury accommodation in London. Special discounted rates for selected hotels.

www.visitbritain.com
Official website of **Visit Britain**, the national tourist agency, with pages specially adapted according to visitors' country of origin.

www.visitlondon.com
Official website of **Visit London**, the capital's tourist agency. Lists all types of accommodation, all bookable online.

Although the lodgings described here have been selected with care, changes may have occurred since our last visit, so please send us your comments, favourable or unfavourable. The properties which follow were selected for their ambience, location and/or value for money.

INNER LONDON

BLOOMSBURY

● **Avonmore Hotel**, *57 Cartwright Gdns., WC1H 9EL. ⊖ Russell Square. ✆020 7387 1939. www.avonmorehotel.net. 15 rooms.* ☕. Located close to transport links on a charming Georgian crescent, this small hotel has basic, but pleasant rooms and Wi-Fi.

● **Crescent Hotel**, *49–50 Cartwright Gdns., WC1H 9EL. ⊖ Russell Square. ✆020 7387 1515. www.crescenthotelof london.com. 27 rooms. 3 floors/no lift.* ☕. Charming hotel occuping two Georgian houses. Pleasant features include a cosy sitting room, a large communal garden and access to tennis courts. Some single rooms have shared bathrooms.

● **The Generator**, *37 Tavistock Pl., WC1H 9SE. ⊖ Russell Square. ✆020 7388 7666. www.generatorhostels.com. 870 beds.* This industrial-complex-turned-youth-hostel with chrome décor comprises a games room, Internet space and a bar, open late. The spartan dormitories vary in size; the more people you're willing to share with, the less you'll pay.

● **Gower House Hotel**, *57 Gower St., WC1E 6HJ. ⊖ Goodge Street. ✆020 7636 4685. www.gowerhousehotel.co.uk. 13 rooms. 3 floors/no lift.* ☕. Pleasant, family-run guest house located in a Georgian terrace. Small garden.

● **Hotel Cavendish**, *75 Gower St., WC1E 6HJ. ⊖ Goodge Street. ✆020 7636 9079. www.hotelcavendish.com. 33 rooms. 3 floors/no lift.* ☕. DH Lawrence once stayed at this Georgian house and guests today enjoy refurbished rooms and a small walled garden.

●● **Bloomsbury Palace Hotel**, *29–31 Gower St., WC1E 6HG. ⊖ Goodge Street. ✆020 7636 5801. www.bloomsbury palacehotel.co.uk. 29 rooms. 3 floors/no lift.* ☕. Comfortably furnished rooms in a Georgian terrace house. Small paved garden and traditional breakfasts. Wi-Fi.

●● **Euro Hotel**, *53 Cartwright Gdns., WC1H 9EL. ⊖ Russell Square. ✆020 7387 4321. www.eurohotel.co.uk. 31 rooms. 3 floors/no lift.* ☕. Set in a beautiful Georgian crescent, this basic but comfortable hotel features an all-you-can-eat breakfast and access to tennis courts. Some rooms have shared bathrooms. Free Wi-Fi.

Coin Ranges Explained

Prices reflect the average cost for a standard double room (for two people), not including taxes.
The ☕ symbol indicates breakfast (continental or full English) is included in the rate.
For other symbols used below, see the Legend on the cover flap.

●	**less than £90**
●●	**£90 to £140**
●●●	**£140 to £250**
●●●●	**more than £250**

●● **Harlingford**, *61–63 Cartwright Gdns., WC1H 9EL. ⊖Russell Square. ✆020 7387 1551. www.harlingfordhotel. com. 43 rooms. 3 floors/no lift.* ☕. Contemporary décor mixed with original Georgian features. Light and airy breakfast room, comfortable lounge and access to tennis courts. Free Wi-Fi.

● **The Jesmond Hotel**, *63 Gower St., WC1E 6HJ. ⊖Goodge Street. ✆020 7636 3199. www.jesmondhotel.org.uk. 15 rooms. 4 floors/no lift.* ☕. A family-run budget B&B with clean, comfortable rooms, some with original fireplaces. Some rooms have shared baths; all guests enjoy hearty breakfasts and free Wi-Fi.

●● **Morgan Hotel**, *24 Bloomsbury St., WC1B 3QJ. ⊖ Tottenham Court Road. ✆020 7636 3735. www.morganhotel. co.uk. 21 rooms. 3 floors/no lift.* Friendly family-owned hotel, close to the British Museum. Rooms are homely and all are en suite; most have Wi-Fi.

●●● **The Academy**, *21 Gower St., WC1E 6HG. ⊖Goodge Street. ✆020 7631 4115. www.theacademyhotel.co.uk. 49 rooms. 3 floors/no lift.* This elegant boutique hotel is located in a restored Georgian town house and features luxurious rooms with upmarket facilities such as 24hr room service, iPod docking stations and free Wi-Fi.

●●● **Bloomsbury Hotel**, *16–22 Great Russell St., WC1B 3NN. ⊖ Russell Square. ✆020 7347 1000.*

www.doylecollection.com. 153 rooms. Stylish grand hotel with a thoroughly British ambience located on a quiet street away from the bustle of nearby Covent Garden, yet only a stone's throw from the action. The rooms are stylish and contemporary with every modern amenity. The fabulous Landseer restaurant and bar *(great cocktails)* are also located within the hotel.

Grange Blooms Hotel, *7 Montague St., WC1B 5BP. ⊖ Russell Square. ℘020 7323 1717. www.grangehotels.com. 26 rooms.* Located in a row of Georgian houses flanking the British Museum, Blooms exudes a good deal of charm and intimacy. Individually designed "themed" rooms and a small rear garden.

Staunton Hotel, *13–15 Gower St. ⊖ Goodge Street. ℘020 7580 2740. www.stauntonhotel.com. 17 rooms. 3 floors/no lift.* ☕. The spacious and tastefully decorated rooms of this upmarket hotel are equipped with every possible facility, including marble bathrooms, while the welcoming atmosphere makes this a real home from home.

KENSINGTON, CHELSEA, EARL'S COURT

Barmy Badger Backpackers, *17 Longridge Rd., SW5 9SB. ⊖ Earl's Court. ℘ 020 7370 5213. www.barmybadger.com. 42 beds. 5 floors/no lift.* ☕. A mix of dorms *(sleeping 6)* and private double and twin rooms with sinks. There's also a sunny kitchen, cosy TV room, laundry and small garden and BBQ area.

Maranton House Hotel, *14 Barkston Gdns., SW5 0EN. ⊖ Earl's Court. ℘020 7373 5782. www.marantonhousehotel.com. 16 rooms. 3 floors/no lift.* ☕. Boutique hotel in an attractive garden square. The warmly decorated rooms all have marble bathrooms, digital freeview TV and daily maid service. Buffet breakfast; free Wi-Fi.

Youth Hostel Earl's Court, *38 Bolton Gdns, SW5 0AQ. ⊖ Earl's Court. ℘0845 371 9114. www.yha.org.uk. 186 beds.* ☕. Buzzy hostel close to the action. Facilities include a TV lounge, garden, well-equipped kitchen, on-site café and Wi-Fi. The single-sex dorms sleep up to 10 people and there are some private rooms.

Amsterdam Hotel, *7 Trebovir Rd., Earl's Court, SW5 9LS. ⊖ Earl's Court. ℘020 7370 5084. www.amsterdam-hotel.com. 19 rooms.* ☕. This small hotel has refurbished bedrooms in soothing, modern colours, a pretty breakfast room and a pleasant garden. Suites and apartments also available. Free Wi-Fi.

Citadines, *35A Gloucester Rd., SW7 4PL. ⊖ Gloucester Road. ℘020 7543 7878. www.citadines.com. 92 apartments.* This aparthotel has a range of newly refurbished studio apartments and one-bedroom duplexes, all with fully equipped kitchens, flatscreen TVs and free Wi-Fi. Breakfast can be delivered and there's a 24hr reception. Also at *94–99 High Holborn, ⊖ Holborn, ℘020 7395 8800; 18–21 Northumberland Ave, ⊖ Charing Cross. ℘ 020 7766 3700* and *7–21 Goswell Rd. ⊖ Barbican, ℘020 7566 8000.*

Henley House, *30 Barkston Gdns., Earl's Court, SW5 0EN. ⊖ Earl's Court. ℘020 7370 4111. www.henleyhousehotel.com. 21 rooms.* ☕. Nestling in a pleasant redbrick square close to Earl's Court Road, this small, friendly hotel is good for well-priced and reliable accommodation close to the museums of South Ken.

London Town Hotel, *15 Penywern Rd., Earl's Court, SW5 9TY. ⊖ Earl's Court. ℘020 7370 4356. www.londontownhotel.co.uk. 30 rooms.* Behind the porticoed Georgian exterior, you'll find a modern hotel, cheerily decorated and with thoughtfully equipped and relatively spacious bedrooms. Rooms to the rear are quieter.

The Mayflower Hotel, *26–28 Trebovir Rd., SW5 9NJ. ⊖ Earl's Court. ℘020 7370 0991. www.themayflowerhotel.co.uk. 48 rooms.* ☕. Located on a quiet street, this stylish town house hotel features elegant, light bedrooms with high ceilings and hand-carved wooden beds. Breakfast is taken in the spacious dining room or outside in the garden; there's also a lounge for drinks. Wi-Fi.

Twenty Nevern Square, *20 Nevern Sq., SW5 9PD. Earl's Court. 020 7565 9555. www.20nevernsquare.com. 20 rooms.* . Newly restored Victorian town house overlooking a garden square. The bedrooms are individually styled, all with en suite bathrooms and hand-carved furniture; some have four-poster beds. A luxury buffet breakfast is served in Café Twenty, complimentary hot drinks are served all day and there's free Wi-Fi in all rooms.

The Rembrandt, *11 Thuloe Pl., SW7 2RS. South Kensington. 020 7589 8100. www.sarova-rembrandthotel.com. 193 rooms.* Set in a handsome Edwardian building, this pleasant hotel boasts a great location opposite the Victoria and Albert Museum and not far from Harrods. Rooms have an en suite bathroom, fridge and flatscreen TV. There's an on-site restaurant/bar, and, for a fee, guests may use the pool and fitness centre at the adjacent spa.

THE CITY

Hoxton Hotel, *81 Great Eastern S., EC2A 3HU. Old Street. 020 7550 1000. www.hoxtonhotels.com. 208 rooms.* . *Restaurant*. This trendy, upmarket hotel opened in 2006 and was an instant hit. Touches such as flat-screen TVs, sleek décor in neutral tones, roaring fires in the lobby and fine linens make this feel far more of an expensive stay than it is. Room prices vary wildly throughout the year; keep an eye on the website for details. Free Wi-Fi.

South Place Hotel, *3 South Pl., EC2M 2AF. Moorgate. 020 3503 0000. www.southplacehotel.com. 80 rooms.* . *Restaurant*. This sleek boutique hotel is within walking distance of the Museum of London and Barbican Centre. Its stylish interior includes commissioned artworks, a fitness center and an on-site spa. The **Angler** restaurant serves up seafood and floor-to-ceiling views, while the **Rooftop Terrace** invites warm-weather dining.

CAMDEN, ISLINGTON, FARRINGDON, KING'S CROSS

St Christopher's Inns, *48–50 Camden High St., NW1 OLT. Camden Town. 020 8600 7500 (central booking line). www.st-christophers.co.uk. 70 beds.* . Directly above Belushi's Bar, this vibrant youth hostel's heart-of-Camden location is ideal for night owls. There's also a common room, laundry and Internet access. Also at *161–165 Borough High St., London Bridge; 28 Hammersmith Broadway, Hammersmith; 189 Greenwich High Rd., Greenwich and 13–15 Shepherd's Bush Green, Shepherd's Bush.*

The Zetter, *St John's Square, 86–88 Clerkenwell Rd., EC1M 5RJ. Farringdon. 020 7324 4444. www.thezetter.com. 59 rooms.* Modern, with clean lines and happy staff, The Zetter is youthful and very much in the spirit of the area. Nice touches in rooms include old Penguin paperbacks and hot water bottles; free fresh coffee and tea is available all day. There's a Mediterranean restaurant downstairs *()*. Free Wi-Fi. Slightly reduced weekend rates.

The Zetter Townhouse, *49–50 St John's Square, EC1V 4JJ. Farringdon. 020 7324 4545. www.thezetter.com. 13 rooms.* Across the cobbles from the Zetter proper is its quirky, so-called "great Aunt" – a boutique hotel set in two Georgian town houses. Individually decorated rooms befit the era of the building and feature huge beds and luxurious bathrooms. The lounge is one of the most relaxed bar and restaurant spaces in London. The humorous décor includes mismatched furniture; the cocktail list is based on old recipes for tinctures and bitters.

The Rookery, *Peters La., Cowcross St., Islington, EC1M 6DS. Farringdon. 020 7336 0931. www.rookeryhotel.com. 33 rooms.* This charming restored 18C house, with wood-panelling, period furniture and open fires, is located in the vibrant area of Farringdon, close to Smithfield market and Fabric nightclub. Bathrooms have Victorian fittings and the suite has a retracting roof over the bedroom.

St Pancras Renaissance, *Euston Rd. NW1 2QR. King's Cross St Pancras. 020 7841 3540. www.marriott.co.uk. 245 rooms.* Situated near the British Library, this hotel is housed in the iconic

Grade I listed former St Pancras railway station. Packed with original features, including ornate ironwork ceiling arches, the wooden ticket office and some of the most beautiful brickwork in Europe, this is no run-of-the-mill hotel – the building makes the hotel feel like a palace. Rooms are effortlessly stylish and the atmosphere is high-class, but very friendly. Don't miss breakfast in the gorgeous Booking Office Bar.

COVENT GARDEN, SOHO, TRAFALGAR SQUARE

Piccadilly Backpackers, *12 Sherwood St. (4th floor) W1F 7BR. ⊖ Piccadilly Circus. 020 7434 9009. www.piccadillyhotel.net. 700 beds.* Extremely central hostel (not for light sleepers!) featuring a newly refurbished common room with TV lounge, Internet and table football. Female-only and mixed dorms plus private doubles and twins. 24hr reception.

YHA Oxford Street, *14 Noel St. (3rd floor), W1F 8GJ. ⊖ Oxford Circus. 0845 371 9133. www.yha.org.uk. 75 beds.* In the heart of Soho, this newly refubished hostel has a TV lounge, laundry and shop, plus Internet access and luggage storage. Dorms and private rooms available. 24hr reception.

Strand Palace Hotel, *372 Strand, WC2R 0JJ. ⊖ Charing Cross or Covent Garden. 020 7379 4737. www.strandpalacehotel.co.uk. 786 rooms.* Good-value central hotel offering contemporary rooms just moments from Covent Garden and the river. Rooms are attractively furnished and there are two restaurants and three bars on-site. Wi-Fi is available in all guest rooms, though a fee applies.

W London, *10 Wardour St., W1D 6QF. ⊖ Leicester Square or Piccadilly Circus. 020 7758 1000. www.wlondon.co.uk. 192 rooms.* The hottest, hippest new hotel on the London scene opened on Valentine's Day 2011 and has hosted all manner of celebrities and A-list events ever since. Located at the heart of the West End, just off Leicester Square itself, the location of this stylish young player cannot be faulted and rooms are equipped with everything necessary for an utterly indulgent stay. The Lounge bar is frequented by the city's beautiful people – dress to impress.

Chancery Court, *252 High Holborn, WC1V 7EN. ⊖ Holborn. 020 7829 9888. www.chancerycourthotel.com. 246 rooms.* Housed in a Grade II listed building, this glamorous hotel features a soaring grand staircase of rare marble, opulent rooms and a warm and friendly cocktail bar. The spa here is one of the best in London and on-site restaurant Pearl is a destination in itself. The location is unbeatable, too, between the West End and the City in lively Holborn.

St Martins Lane, *45 St Martin's La., Covent Garden, WC2N 4HX. ⊖ Charing Cross. 020 7300 5500. www.stmartinslane.com. 204 rooms.* Bearing the signature of French designer Philippe Starck, the St Martins Lane is one of London's most spectacular designer hotels: from the state-of-the-art bedrooms to stylish bars and restaurants.

Savoy, *Strand, WC2R 0EU. ⊖ Charing Cross or Covent Garden. 020 7836 4343. www.savoy-london.com. 268 rooms.* Arguably London's most famous hotel, the Savoy reopened in 2010 after extensive refurbishment. The aura remains the same, though and this is still one of the city's very best places to stay, featuring opulent rooms with soothing décor, butler service and river views. A drink in the iconic American Bar is a must.

NOTTING HILL, BAYSWATER, PADDINGTON

Pavilion Hotel, *34–36 Sussex Gdns., W2 1UL. ⊖ Paddington. 020 7262 0905. www.pavilionhoteluk.com. 30 rooms. 3 floors/no lift.* This quirky, intimate Victorian house brims with antiques gleaned from auctions and flea markets. Choose from themed bedrooms *("Enter the Dragon," "Honky Tonk")*. Free Wi-fi.

Smart Hyde Park Inn Hostel, *48–50 Inverness Terrace, W2 3JA. ⊖ Bayswater or Queensway. 020 7229 0000. www.smartbackpackers.com. 274 beds. 4 floors/no lift.* Located just off Portobello Road, this simple hostel has dorms sleeping up to 16 people plus 6 private rooms. Wi-Fi and linens included. 24hr reception.

Abbey Court, *20 Pembridge Gdns., W2 4DU. Notting Hill Gate. 020 7221 7518. http://abbeycourthotel.co.uk. 22 rooms. 3 floors/no lift.* An ideal base for antique hunters roaming Portobello Road. This elegant town house features individually appointed bedrooms and friendly service. Some rooms have four-poster beds.

Aspen Apartments, *168–172 Sussex Gdns., W2 1TP. Paddington. 020 7402 0202. www.aspenhydepark.com. 15 apartments.* Well-equipped, modern studios and apartments with spacious kitchen, lounge area and free Internet. Limited parking *(small charge).*

Byron Hotel, *36–38 Queensborough Terrace, W2 3SH. Bayswater. 020 7243 0987. www.capricornhotels.co.uk. 45 rooms.* Reasonably priced accommodation in the heart of Bayswater, just steps away from Kensington Gardens. Bedrooms are bright and spacious, and all have en suite showers.

Days Hotel Hyde Park, *148–152 Sussex Gdns., W2 1QT. Paddington. 020 7723 2939. www.daysinnhydepark.com. 57 beds.* More stylish than your average Days Inn, this newly renovated hotel offers functional rooms and a good buffet breakfast. Wi-Fi available.

The Gate, *6 Portobello Rd., W11 3DG. Notting Hill Gate. 020 7221 0707. www.gatehotel.co.uk. 7 rooms. 3 floors/no lift.* In the heart of Notting Hill, this 19th-century town house has a homely atmosphere and comfortable rooms. Breakfast is served in your own room.

Kensington Gardens Hotel, *9 Kensington Gardens Sq., W2 4BH. Bayswater. 020 7243 7600. www.kensingtongardenshotel.co.uk. 16 rooms. 4 floors/no lift.* Restored Victorian town house located just off Queensway. Rooms have a traditional feel and feature Sky TV and room service. Laundry facilities.

New Linden, *58–60 Leinster Sq., W2 4PS. Bayswater. 020 7221 4321. www.lindenhotellondon.co.uk. 50 rooms.* The individually designed rooms in this attractive town house are stylish and equipped with marble bathrooms, flatscreen TVs and free Wi-Fi.

Vancouver Studios, *30 Prince's Sq., W2 4NJ. Bayswater. 020 7243 1270. www.vancouverstudios.co.uk. 45 studios.* Simple, yet stylish studios with fully equipped modern mini-kitchens and luxury bathrooms. The three-bedroom garden apartment sleeps up to 6 and is accessed through the lovely garden.

WESTMINSTER, VICTORIA, PIMLICO

Belgrave House Hotel, *28–32 Belgrave Rd., SW1V 1RG. Victoria. 020 7828 1563. www.belgravehousehotel.com. 39 rooms. 3 floors/no lift.* Great value, no-frills accommodation near Victoria station. Rooms have modern décor, kettle and TV; most have Wi-Fi.

Luna Simone Hotel, *47–49 Belgrave Rd., SW1V 2BB. Pimlico. 020 7834 5897. www.lunasimonehotel.com. 36 rooms. 4 floors/no lift.* You'll receive a warm welcome in this family-run hotel, with its porticoed façade. The house has vibrantly decorated bedrooms with thoughtful extras and a well-equipped computer room.

B+B Belgravia, *64–66 Ebury St., SW1W 9QD. Victoria. 020 7259 8570. www.bb-belgravia.com. 17 rooms. 3 floors/no lift.* These three Grade II listed Georgian town houses are home to 17 contemporary rooms decorated in modern style. A full English breakfast is served overlooking the garden.

Georgian House, *35–39 St George's Dr., SW1V 4DG. Victoria. 020 7834 1438. www.georgianhousehotel.co.uk. 60 rooms. 4 floors/no lift.* This family-run guest house located in a lovely Georgian building has light, spacious rooms with complimentary wine on check-in. Some rooms have shared baths. A few apartments also available.

Melita House Hotel, *35 Charlwood St., SW1V 2DU. Pimlico. 020 7828 0471. www.melitahotel.com. 22 rooms.*

3 floors/no lift. ☕. In a fairly quiet residential street off Belgrave Rd., Melita House offers spacious,modern rooms with fridges and modem points.

££ **Morgan Guest House**, *120 Ebury St., SW1W 9QQ.* ⊖ *Victoria.* ✆ *020 7730 2384. www.morganhouse.co.uk. 11 rooms. 4 floors/no lift.* ☕. The slightly dated rooms feature all mod cons and come with a hearty breakfast.

££ **New England Hotel**, *20 St George's Dr., SW1W 4BN.* ⊖ *Victoria.* ✆ *020 7834 1595. www.newenglandhotel.com. 23 rooms.* ☕. Beautiful 19C–Georgian building with simply furnished en suite accommodation. Family-run. Wi-Fi available.

£££ **Windermere Hotel**, *142–144 Warwick Way, SW1V 4JE.* ⊖ *Victoria.* ✆ *020 7834 5163. www.windermere-hotel.co.uk. 19 rooms.* ☕. This small, friendly hotel has individually decorated (slightly chintzy) rooms with satellite TV and free Wi-Fi. Airport transfers are available.

KNIGHTSBRIDGE, BELGRAVIA

££ **The Diplomat**, *2 Chesham St., Belgravia, SW1X 8DT.* ⊖ *Sloane Square.* ✆ *020 7235 1544. www.thediplomathotel.co.uk. 26 rooms.* This reasonably priced hotel occupies an imposing late-19C corner house in the heart of Belgravia. A sweeping staircase leads to the large, well-decorated rooms; all are en suite.

£££ **Draycott Hotel**, *26 Cadogan Gdns., SW3 2RP.* ⊖ *Sloane Square.* ✆ *020 7730 6466. www.draycotthotel.co.uk. 35 rooms.* This is country-house living, minutes away from Harrods. The charming Victorian house is set in a smart residential street and many of the luxuriously appointed bedrooms overlook a tranquil communal garden. Room service.

£££ **Knightsbridge Green**, *159 Knightsbridge, SW1X 7PD.* ⊖ *Knightsbridge.* ✆ *020 7584 6274. www.knightsbridgegreenhotel.com. 30 rooms.* Discreet, small hotel located in the heart of the famous shopping district. Spacious rooms and reasonable rates for central London. Breakfast served in bedrooms. Suites also available.

££££ **The Berkeley**, *Wilton Pl., Knightsbridge, SW1X 7RL.* ⊖ *Knightsbridge.* ✆ *020 7235 6000. www.the-berkeley.co.uk. 214 rooms.* The Berkeley's discreet charm is evident throughout: in the panelled drawing room, roof-top pool with retracting roof and opulently decorated bedrooms. Restaurants include **Marcus Wareing** *(££££)*.

££££ **The Cadogan**, *75 Sloane St., SW1X 9SG.* ⊖ *Sloane Sq.* ✆ *020 7235 7141. www.cadogan.com. 65 rooms.* This classic English hotel has welcomed such celebrities as Oscar Wilde and Lillie Langtry. The still-charming Cadogan remains a haven of peace, with a wood-panelled lounge that is a favourite afternoon tea spot.

££££ **Knightsbridge**, *10 Beaufort Gdns., Knightsbridge, SW3 1PT.* ⊖ *Knightsbridge.* ✆ *020 7584 6300. www.firmdalehotels.com. 44 rooms.* A porticoed town house tucked away in a quiet, tree-lined street behind Knightsbridge. The rooms vary in size but all have Wi-Fi, iPod docking stations and flatscreen TVs. Guests can use the drawing room and library, both of which have open fires in winter.

££££ **The Levin Hotel**, *28 Basil St., SW3 1AS.* ⊖ *Knightsbridge.* ✆ *020 7589 6286. www.thelevinhotel.co.uk. 12 rooms.* ☕. Sophisticated boutique hotel, a stone's throw from Harrods. The stylish interior features wow-factor works of art and bedrooms are serenely chic. The on-site Le Metro Bar and Brasserie serves an all-day menu of classic British dishes and a wide range of quality wines.

££££ **Mandarin Oriental**, *66 Knightsbridge, SW1X 7LA.* ⊖ *Knightsbridge.* ✆ *020 7235 2000. www.mandarinoriental.com. 198 rooms.* Right in the heart of Knightbridge opposite Harvey Nichols, this opulent hotel more than lives up to its exalted location, with first-class amenities and service to match. The spa in particular is justly famous, while the plush Mandarin Bar is a favourite haunt of London's rich, famous or wannabes and serves great cocktails.

MAYFAIR, MARYLEBONE, REGENT'S PARK

⊖ **Lincoln House**, *33 Gloucester Pl., W1U 8HY. ⊖ Marble Arch. ☎020 7486 7630. www.lincoln-house-hotel.co.uk. 27 rooms. 4 floors/no lift.* A family-run hotel in a convenient location, housed in a late-18C town house. Rooms on the 1st floor are more spacious.

⊖ **London Continental Hotel**, *88 Gloucester Pl., W1U 6HR. ⊖ Baker Street. ☎020 7486 8670. www.londons-continental.com. 24 rooms.* ☕. This fairly basic hotel is located in an accessible part of town and features simple, but comfortable rooms. Some rooms have shared bathrooms.

⊖⊖ **22 York Street**, *22 York St., W1U 6PX. ⊖ Baker Street. ☎020 7224 2990. www.22yorkstreet.co.uk. 10 rooms. 4 floors/no lift.* ☕. This elegant five-storey Georgian terraced house has a variety of traditional homely rooms with wooden floors, French antiques and charming quilts. Guests can relax in the lounge, equipped with Sky TV.

⊖⊖ **Hart House**, *51 Gloucester Pl., Marylebone, W1U 8JF. ⊖ Marble Arch. ☎020 7935 2288. www. harthouse.co.uk. 16 rooms. 3 floors/no lift.* ☕. On a busy road north of Portman Sq., this Georgian house once provided refuge to French nobility fleeing the Revolution. It is now a welcoming, well-maintained hotel. Rear rooms are quieter.

⊖⊖ **St George Hotel**, *49 Gloucester Pl., W1U 8JE. ⊖ Marble Arch. ☎020 7486 8586. www.stgeorge-hotel.net. 18 rooms. 4 floors/no lift.* ☕. Grade II listed town house, a short walk from Oxford Street. The en suite bedrooms are decorated in traditional style and come equipped with king-size bed, tea and coffee facilities and TV.

⊖⊖⊖ **The Blandford**, *80 Chiltern St., W1U 5AF. ⊖ Baker Street. ☎020 7486 3103. www.capricornhotels.co.uk. 33 rooms.* ☕. Close to Regent's Park, this privately owned and newly refurbished hotel has a friendly atmosphere, well-kept rooms and an adjacent car park.

⊖⊖⊖ **Durrants Hotel**, *26–32 George St., Marylebone, W1H 5BJ. ⊖ Bond Street. ☎020 7935 8131. www. durrantshotel. co.uk. 92 rooms.* This elegant, quintessentially English hotel is around the corner from the Wallace Collection. Enjoy afternoon tea in the fire-lit lounges or traditional British fare in the wood-panelled dining room.

⊖⊖⊖ **Flemings**, *13 Half Moon St., W1Y 7RA. ⊖ Green Park. ☎020 7499 0000. www.flemings-mayfair.co.uk. 129 rooms. Restaurant⊖ – ⊖⊖.* The noted polymath Henry Wagner once resided at this address, close to Green Park. The Georgian architecture is complemented by a traditional interior featuring oil paintings and antique English furniture.

⊖⊖⊖ **Park Plaza Sherlock Holmes Hotel**, *108 Baker St., W1U 6LJ. ⊖Baker Street. ☎020 7486 6161. www. parkplazasherlockholmes.com. 119 rooms.* ☕. Rejuvenated from a chintzy hotel to an altogether slicker number by the Park Plaza chain, this central hotel is now full of neutral décor and comfortable touches, such as scatter cushions, sauna, bar and organic restaurant. Regular events are hosted here, including Sherlock Holmes-themed murder mystery nights.

⊖⊖⊖⊖ **Claridge's**, *Brook St., W1K 4HR. ⊖ Bond Street. ☎020 7629 8860. www.claridges.co.uk. 203 rooms.* This hotel has enjoyed Royal patronage to such an extent that a telephone request to speak to the King once required the response: "Which one?" Claridge's continues to epitomise English grandeur and is celebrated for its Art Deco design and luxury. It's home to one of Gordon Ramsay's restaurants, too.

⊖⊖⊖⊖ **The Dorchester**, *Park La, W1K 1QA. ⊖ Hyde Park Corner. ☎020 7629 8888. www.thedorchester.com. 250 rooms.* One of London's finest hotels in one of its greatest locations – opposite Hyde Park. The graceful rooms have the feel of a country house and all overlook either the Park or the hotel's landscaped terraces. Design throughout echoes the hotel's 1930s origins and service is of the highest standard.

Executive Room, The Cavendish London

© The Cavendish London

The Metropolitan by COMO, *Old Park La., W1K 1LB. ⊖ Green Park. ✆020 7447 1000. www.comohotels.com. 144 rooms.* The ultra-minimalist design and hip reputation have made this the favoured haunt of celebrities. The chic **Met Bar** proves hotel bars need not be dull, being open till late, serving cocktails and snacks. Rooms on the higher floors offer views of Hyde Park. Trendy restaurant **Nobu** *(see Where to Eat)* is also located within the hotel.

PICCADILLY, ST JAMES'S

The Stafford, *16–18 St James's Pl., SW1A 1NJ. ⊖ Green Park. ✆020 7493 0111. www.kempinski.com. 105 rooms.* Tucked away in a street beside Green Park, the genteel Stafford is one of London's quietest hotels, with tastefully appointed rooms. Have a drink in the famed 1930s-style **American bar**, where past patrons have left historical memorabilia.

The Cavendish London, *81 Jermyn St., SW1Y 6JF. ⊖ Piccadilly Circus. ✆020 7930 2111. www.thecavendish-london.co.uk. 230 rooms.* Across the street from Fortnum & Mason, this large corporate hotel offers well-appointed rooms with every possible amenity, from movies on demand to turndown service. For great views, ask for a room on one of the top five floors. Wi-Fi available.

Dukes, *St James's Pl., SW1A 1NY. ⊖ Green Park. ✆020 7491 4840. www.dukeshotel.com. 90 rooms.* Located on a quiet courtyard in St James's, this established hotel is full of quintessential English charm. Many rooms have views over Green Park, and the Penthouse looks directly onto royal residence Clarence House. There are numerous comfy nooks and crannies in which to relax, including the Perrier-Jouet Lounge, where champagne and champagne cocktails are served. Ian Fleming allegedly wrote James Bond's line "shaken not stirred" in the martini bar, which serves one of the best martinis in town.

SOUTH BANK, WATERLOO

The Mad Hatter, *3–7 Stamford St., SE1 9NY. ⊖ Southwark. ✆020 7401 9222. www.madhatterhotel.co.uk. 30 rooms.* Hotel above a pub, featuring comfortable modern rooms with en suite bathrooms. Classic pub dishes are served in the downstairs bar.

The Southwark Rose Hotel, *43–47 Southwark Bridge Rd., SE1 9HH. ⊖ London Bridge. ✆020 7015 1480. www.southwarkrosehotel.co.uk. 114 rooms.* This Ibis Styles hotel has modern rooms with contemporary décor. All rooms have flatscreen TV and Wi-Fi.

THE SUBURBS

NORTHWEST: HAMPSTEAD, FINSBURY PARK

Mountview, *31 Mountview Rd., N4 4SS. ⊖ Finsbury Park. ✆020 8340 9222. www.mountviewguesthouse.com. 3 rooms, all on 1st floor/no lift.* This friendly, family-run B&B is housed in an attractively furnished Victorian house in a quiet residential tree-lined street. Bedrooms are individually decorated and two overlook the rear garden. Good transport links into central London *(and out to Cambridge)* from nearby Finsbury Park station.

Hampstead Village Guesthouse, *2 Kemplay Rd., Hampstead, NW3 1SY. Hampstead. 020 7435 8679. www.hampsteadguesthouse.com. 9 rooms.* This Victorian house, close to Hampstead Heath, evokes images of writers and thinkers who have settled in the area. Not every room is en suite, but all are decorated with antiques.

La Gaffe, *107–111 Heath St., NW3 6SS. Hampstead. 020 7435 8965. www.lagaffe.co.uk. 18 rooms. 3 floors/ no lift.* . This small hotel stands on the site of five former shepherds' cottages, and is only a short walk from Hampstead High Street. Ask for one of the bedrooms at the back overlooking a tranquil Georgian Square. The adjoining restaurant, also run by the owners, has a menu of traditional Italian cooking.

Langorf, *20 Frognal, Hampstead, NW3 6AG. Finchley Road. 020 7794 4483. www.langorfhotel.com. 30 rooms.* . This Edwardian house has spacious bedrooms and a breakfast room that overlooks a walled garden. Studios and apartments are available too. Its location is convenient for transport links to central London.

SOUTHEAST: GREENWICH

Ibis, *30 Stockwell St., SE10 9JN Cutty Sark DLR. 020 8305 1177. www.ibis.com. 120 rooms.* Basic chain hotel with simple but fairly stylish rooms featuring satellite TV and Wi-Fi *(charge applies)*. Good central Greenwich location.

The Mitre, *291 Greenwich High Rd., SE10 8NA. Cutty Sark DLR. 020 8293 0037. www.mitregreenwich.com. 24 rooms.* This Grade II listed traditional English pub has simply furnished rooms with flatscreen TVs and en suite bathrooms. There are three bars and a beer garden to relax in, too.

St Alfege Passage, *16 St Alfege Passage (behind the church), SE10 9JS. Cutty Sark DLR. 020 8853 4337. www.st-alfeges.co.uk. 3 rooms, all on 1st floor/no lift.* . Warm and inviting B&B with one four-poster double, one double and one single room. Some rooms offer lovely views of the park and church. The tastefully furnished drawing room features free Wi-Fi.

WEST: RICHMOND, HAMMERSMITH AND SHEPHERDS BUSH

Chase Lodge Hotel, *10 Park Rd., Hampton Wick, KT1 4AS. Richmond. 020 8943 1862. www.chaselodgehotel.com. 13 rooms. 3 floors/no lift.* . A warm welcome is guaranteed at this Victorian property located not far from the Thames. Furnishings and decoration vary, but all rooms are comfortable.

Her Majesty, *49 Shepherd's Bush Green, W12 8PS. Goldhawk Road or Shepherd's Bush. 020 8746 2191. www.hermajestyhotel.com. 16 rooms. 3 floors/ no lift.* . Traditional B&B hotel with simple en suite rooms. Excellent for shoppers – Westfield is just a five-minute walk away.

Hotel Orlando, *83 Shepherd's Bush Rd., W6 7LR. Goldhawk Road or Hammersmith. 020 7603 4890. www.hotelorlando.co.uk. 14 rooms. 3 floors/no lift.* . This small, family-run B&B has well-maintained traditional rooms with en suite showers and free Wi-Fi.

Royal Guest House, *105 Shepherd's Bush Rd., W6 7LP. Shepherd's Bush or Hammersmith. 020 7603 0457. www.royalguesthouse.co.uk. 15 rooms. 4 floors/ no lift.* . Relaxed and friendly family-run B&B with simple, unpretentious rooms equipped with en suite shower, Sky TV and free Wi-Fi. A healthy continental breakfast is served daily.

Brook Green Hotel, *170 Shepherd's Bush Rd., W6 7PB. Hammersmith. 020 7603 2516. www.brookgreenhotel.co.uk. 14 rooms. 3 floors/no lift.* . Welcoming Victorian pub with 14 stylish en suite bedrooms. Wonderfully comfortable beds, plasma TVs with Sky channels and free Wi-Fi make for a luxurious retreat away from the bustle of the city. Breakfast can be delivered to your room.

Where To Eat

London has become a gourmet's paradise and the capital occupies a prominent role on the international culinary scene.
The number and variety of eating places reflect the multitude of current cooking styles, ranging from traditional British (including fish and chips) and classic French, to popular Mediterranean-style and world cuisine inspired by far-flung places across the globe. Indeed, a tasty legacy of the British Empire's former worldwide ties is the abundance of dishes hailing from South Asia, Africa, the Caribbean and the Near and Far East. The term "Modern British", coined in the late 1980s, is loosely applied to the wave of innovative cooking that borrows freely from various international sources, highlighting fresh home-grown and locally sourced products and eye-pleasing presentation. In the 1990s, the unofficial ambassador of British style, Sir Terence Conran, further enhanced London's culinary reputation by launching several spectacular "gastrodomes" *(Bluebird in Chelsea, for example)*. In these sprawling "designer restaurants", eating becomes a multi-sensory experience, stimulating all senses.

Coin Ranges Explained

Prices indicate the average cost of a starter, main course and dessert, not including beverage, tax or tip.

◓ **less than £10**
◓◓ **£10 to £25**
◓◓◓ **£25 to £45**
◓◓◓◓ **more than £45**

ADDRESSES

FOR ALL BUDGETS

Budget eateries (◓) are generally simple, unpretentious places where you can expect to spend less than £10. In the **moderate** range (◓◓–◓◓◓), dining spots are slightly more formal, with a meal costing from £10 to £45. The **expensive** restaurants (◓◓◓◓ – more than £45) are upmarket establishments with a high culinary standard and distinctive ambience. Prices indicate the average cost of a starter, main course and dessert.
If you are tempted to try a noted pricey restaurant but your budget is limited, consider the value lunch menus proposed by many of these establishments. Remember, wine can be an expensive item and consequently the cost of a meal will be substantially higher.

Budget-friendly chain restaurants

One of the cheapest ways to eat out in London is at the high street chain restaurants found throughout the city. Booking is generally not required and dining atmospheres are informal, with families more than welcome *(especially at Giraffe, www.giraffe.net; Nando's, www.nandos.co.uk and Leon, www.leonrestaurants.co.uk)*. For good value Italian staples such as pizza and pasta, try Pizza Express *(www.pizzaexpress.com)*, Strada *(www.strada.co.uk)* or Zizzi *(www.zizzi.co.uk)*, or head to Prezzo (www.prezzorestaurants.co.uk) or Carluccio's *(www.carluccios.com)* for slightly more upmarket Italian fare. The best budget French food is found at Café Rouge *(www.caferouge.co.uk)* or Côte *(www.cote-restaurants.co.uk)*, while Bistro 1 *(bistro1.co.uk)* has unbeatable value set menus. The Diner *(www.goodlifediner.com)* serves up hearty American staples all day long. For Asian cuisine, take a seat at one of Wagamama's *(www.wagamama.com)* communal tables for tasty fusion dishes such as noodles and stir fry, or try the dim sum at Ping Pong *(www.pingpongdimsum.com)* or Japanese favourites at Itsu *(www.itsu.com)*, Feng Sushi *(www.fengsushi.co.uk)* and Yo! Sushi *(www.yosushi.com)*.

Tax is always included in the restaurant bill. Tipping for service is optional, but it is in fact not uncommon for a 12.5 percent service charge to be included in the bill when it is brought to your table. Some restaurants will leave the total open on a credit card slip so that the customer can add their own tip to the bill – in this instance it pays to check whether service has already been added. Most restaurants, particularly those at the budget end of the scale, are now open throughout the day and dining at all hours is generally possible. Standard meal times tend to be approximately noon–2.30pm for lunch and 6.30pm–10pm for dinner. It is advisable to book in the evenings, particularly at weekends, though often not essential unless you are in a group. In almost all restaurants it is quite acceptable to eat only a main course, if you wish to. Most restaurants offer bottled water but tap water will be provided, if requested.

LIGHTER FARE

Cafés and informal eating places and pubs, which keep flexible hours and can provide a light meal in the middle of the day, are listed under *Pubs* and *Light Bites* in the *DISCOVERING LONDON* section of the guide. An average meal in these places will cost under £15. Church refectories are another good place for light meals; those at Southwark Cathedral and St Martin-the-Fields are particularly notable.

AFTERNOON TEA

Tearooms, cafés and hotels providing afternoon tea appear in the *DISCOVERING LONDON* section of the guide. The traditional time for the celebrated institution of afternoon tea is 4 o'clock but in most establishments, it is served between 3pm and 5pm.

Order a selection of sandwiches – cucumber is the traditional filling – or a cream tea *(scones and jam and clotted cream)* or crumpets or muffins with butter, cakes and fruit tarts. Choose from a variety of teas – Indian *(Darjeeling)* or China *(green or perfumed like Lapsang Souchong or Earl Grey)*.

For the authentic atmosphere of an English tearoom, try the Fountain Restaurant in **Fortnum & Mason**, the Ritz Hotel, Brown's Hotel or the Langham Hotel at the top of Regent Street, as well as other well-known places such as the **Dorchester Hotel** *(dress smartly)* and the Winter Garden in the **Landmark London Hotel**. Less select but also very good are the tearooms in the Richoux chain.

The venues listed below were selected for their ambience, location and/or value for money. Rates indicate the average cost of an appetizer, entrée and dessert for one person (not including tax, tip or beverage). Most restaurants are open daily for lunch and dinner, except where noted, and accept major credit cards. Phone or check the website for information on opening hours and reservations.

INNER LONDON

BLOOMSBURY, FITZROVIA

North Sea Fish Restaurant, *7–8 Leigh St. ⊖ Russell Square. 020 7387 5892. www.northseafishrestaurant.co.uk. Closed Sun.* **Fish and chips.** Drop in to this friendly eatery for genuine fish and chips. Dover sole, halibut, cod and haddock are among the many types of fish on the menu. Only ground nut or vegetable oil is used; egg and matzo coating also available. Jumbo sizes, fried or grilled.

Tas, *22 Bloomsbury St. ⊖ Holborn. 020 7637 4555. www.tasrestaurants.co.uk.* **Turkish.** With its colourful flowers cascading outside in large pots, this family-friendly restaurant close to the British Museum is incredibly inviting. Menus include mezze and great lamb kebabs. Also at *33 The Cut, ⊖Southwark; 37 Farringdon Road, ⊖Farringdon and 72 Borough High Street, ⊖London Bridge.*

Dim T, *32 Charlotte St. ⊖ Goodge Street. 020 7637 1122. www.dimtco.uk.* **Asian.** This popular restaurant has built a reputation on its delicious dim sum and range of tasty noodle dishes and curries. Good, hearty food at an affordable price. Also at *56–62 Wilton Road, ⊖ Victoria and 2 More London Place, ⊖ London Bridge.*

DON'T FORGET THE MICHELIN GUIDE

For a more extensive listing of restaurants in the London area, consult the *Michelin Guide London*, an extract from the annually revised *Michelin Guide Great Britain & Ireland*. This respected gastronomical guide lists over 450 restaurants throughout Greater London.

Abeno, *47 Museum St. Holborn. 020 7405 3211. www.abeno.co.uk.* **Japanese.** This eatery, close to the British Museum, was one of the first Japanese restaurants to open in London. On your first visit try the delicious house speciality, which comes from Osaka: Okonomi-yaki *(pancakes cooked on a hotplate at your table)*.

Riding House Café, *43–51 Great Titchfield St. Oxford Circus. 020 7927 0840. www.ridinghousecafe.co.uk.* **British-American.** It's less a café, more of a large, quirkily designed all-day New York-style brasserie and cocktail bar. An appealing selection of small plates designed for sharing. Great atmosphere and cocktails.

The Perseverance, *63 Lamb's Conduit St. Russell Square. 020 7405 8278. www.the-perseverance.moonfruit.com. Closes 8.30pm Sun.* **Pub food.** Homemade gastropub favourites served up alongside a range of premium drinks. The pub's popularity with locals makes it a lively place for dinner; find a table upstairs for more intimacy.

Rasa W1, *6 Dering St. Oxford Circus. 020 7629 1346. www.rasarestaurants.com. No lunch Sun.* **Indian.** Instantly recognisable, thanks to its hot pink façade, this friendly restaurant serves up authentic southern Indian cuisine, including a range of Keralan seafood specialities. Part of the Rasa restaurants chain.

Shanghai Blues Restaurant, *193–197 High Holborn. Holborn. 020 7404 1668. www.shanghaiblues.co.uk.* **Chinese.** This is no ordinary Chinese restaurant: the décor is darkly opulent and there's a feeling of luxury throughout. The menu features a range of traditional and more modern Chinese dishes; the tasting menu is a good introduction.

THE CITY

Le Coq d'Argent, *No. 1 Poultry. Bank. 020 7395 5000. www.coqdargent.co.uk. No lunch Sat, no dinner Sun.* **French.** This spectacular restaurant on top of one of the City's modern buildings also boasts a terrace. The crustacea bar is terrific and the modern European cooking sophisticated. Breakfast is good, too.

George and Vulture, *3 Castle Court. Bank or Monument. 0844 567 2319. Mon–Fri lunch only; closed weekends.* **British.** Located down a narrow passageway, this traditional olde English inn serves up unpretentious traditional pub fare.

Bleeding Heart Restaurant and Bistrot, *Bleeding Heart Yard, off Greville St. Farringdon. 020 7242 8238. www.bleedingheart.co.uk. Closed weekends.* **French.** Located in a quiet courtyard, this French establishment is divided into three areas: the tavern for cheap, light meals, the bar for good food at reasonable prices and the more formal traditional restaurant. Good selection of wines, too.

Comptoir Gascon, *63 Charterhouse St. Farringdon. 020 7608 0851. www.comptoirgascon.com. Closed Sun.* **French.** Refined cuisine from the southwest of France, including foie gras, cassoulet and duck confit, served in a bistro setting. For the same type of cuisine in a more formal setting, try **Club Gascon** *(57A West Smithfield; 020 7600 6144)*.

Sweetings, *39 Queen Victoria St. Mansion House. 020 7248 3062. www.sweetingsrestaurant.com. Mon–Fri lunch.* **Seafood.** This veritable institution has been treating City workers to excellent fish and seafood dishes since 1889 . There are only a few tables, so most customers sit on high stools at the counter. Get here early – no bookings are taken.

EAST LONDON AND DOCKLANDS

The Princess of Shoreditch, *76 Paul St. Old Street. 020 7729 9270. Restaurant closes 9pm Sun.* **Pub food.** Located in trendy Shoreditch, this contemporary gastropub serves up inventive international cuisine and has a generous wine list, too.

Royal China, *30 Westferry Circus. West Ferry DLR or Canary Wharf. 020 7719 0888. www.royalchinagroup.co.uk.* **Chinese.** This upmarket restaurant has a beautiful terrace overlooking the Thames and serves up delectable Chinese specialities including fantastic dim sum *(until 4.30pm only).*

St John Bread and Wine, *94–96 Commercial St. Shoreditch High Street or Liverpool Street. 020 3301 8069. www.stjohnbreadandwine.com.* **British.** Little brother of St John of Smithfield, this bakery and restaurant uses the same concept: a room decorated with unassuming whitewashed walls, a kitchen specialising in offal and the rediscovery of national dishes.

Tayyabs, *83–89 Fieldgate St. Whitechapel or Aldgate East. 020 7247 6400. www.tayyabs.co.uk.* **Pakistani.** Mohammed Tayyab opened his long-running restaurant in a forgotten corner of Whitechapel in 1974. And the key to his success? Pakistani cuisine spiced to perfection, friendly service and rock-bottom prices.

Les Trois Garçons, *1 Club Row. Shoreditch High Street or Liverpool Street. 020 7613 1924. www.lestroisgarcons.com. Mon–Sat dinner only.* **French.** This eccentrically decorated restaurant features chandeliers, huge mirrors, antiques and stuffed animals. Things are less fancy kitchen-side, but the well-controlled French recipes are sprinkled with a pinch of creativity.

CLERKENWELL, ISLINGTON

Caravan, *11–13 Exmouth Market. Farringdon or Angel. 020 7833 8115. www.caravanonexmouth.co.uk. Brunch only at weekends.* **Mediterranean.** Laid-back café-bar and roastery *(superb coffee)*, serving delicious breakfasts and small plus large plates for tapas-style mixing and matching throughout the day.

The Eagle, *159 Farringdon Rd. Farringdon or Chancery Lane. 020 7837 1353. No dinner Sun.* **Pub food.** A large eagle stands sentinel over the green façade of one of London's original gastropubs. The regular clientele enjoys a menu of simple cuisine and a lively vibe.

Ottolenghi, *287 Upper St. Angel or Highbury & Islington. 020 7288 1454. www.ottolenghi.co.uk. Closes at 7pm Sun.* **Mediterranean.** Choose from a range of delicious dishes with colourful Mediterranean flavours *(salads, casseroles, breads, cakes and pastries)* in a sleek space with mostly communal tables.

Pasha, *301 Upper St. Angel. 020 7226 1454. www.pashaislington.co.uk.* **Turkish.** This restaurant is much-loved thanks to its delicious cuisine and elegant setting. It offers a variety of competively priced set menus.

Burger and Lobster, *40 St John St. Farringdon. 020 7490 9230. www.burgerandlobster.com. No lunch Sat. Closed Sun and bank holidays.* **British-American.** The clue's in the title. There are only three items on the menu: burgers, lobster (steamed or grilled) and lobster rolls served with brioche. Very popular with City workers and tourists, who love the cool, casual vibe. This is a great place to come for a cocktail and a simple (though not cheap) meal.

The House, *63–69 Canonbury Rd. Highbury & Islington. 020 7704 7410. www.thehouseislington.com. No lunch Mon–Wed.* **Pub food.** Located in a residential part of Islington, this elegant pub is favoured by local residents, who appreciate its courtyard on sunny days. Serves à la carte French or British recipes.

St John, *26 St John St. Farringdon. 020 7251 0848. www.stjohngroup.uk.com. Dinner only Sat, lunch only Sun.* **British.** This busy, unpretentious restaurant is housed within a former 19C smokehouse. The bar is a popular afterwork meeting place, while the menu specialises in offal and a mix of traditional and rediscovered English dishes.

CAMDEN

Bar Gansa, *2 Inverness St. Mornington Crescent or Camden Town. 020 7267 8909. www.bargansa.co.uk.* **Spanish.** This tapas bar is one of the most popular places in Camden. More than a restaurant, it's a lively and friendly place to nibble some tapas with friends over a drink. Flamenco show Mon and Wed at 8pm.

Camden Brasserie, *9–11 Jamestown Rd. Camden Town. 020 7482 2114. www.camdenbrasserie.co.uk. No lunch Mon.* **Mediterranean.** In a neighbourhood more known for its bars, this modern brasserie is great value. The bright room with elegant décor is a welcoming spot and the European cuisine with Mediterranean influences is tasty.

The Engineer, *65 Gloucester Ave. Chalk Farm or Camden Town. 020 7483 1890. www.theengineerprimrosehill.co.uk.* **Pub food.** Isolated in a quiet street of Primrose Hill, this former Victorian pub, now more "gastro" than "pub", has transformed into a stylish bar and restaurant. International dishes, a friendly atmosphere and the pleasant garden at the rear of the building make this a convivial spot for lunch or dinner.

Mango Room, *10–12 Kentish Town Rd. Camden Town. 020 7482 5065. www.mangoroom.co.uk.* **Caribbean.** As suggested by the large colourful paintings that adorn the walls, this neighbourhood restaurant is all about the Caribbean. Classic West Indian dishes such as curry goat with pimento and spices or chargrilled jerk chicken are favourites, and the service is attentive but unobtrusive. Great cocktails too.

COVENT GARDEN, SOHO, CHINATOWN

Bali Bali, *150 Shaftesbury Ave. Leicester Square or Covent Garden. 020 7836 2644. www.balibalirestaurant.com. No lunch Sun.* **Indonesian.** This affordable authentic restaurant serves up a delicious menu of fiery curries and spicy meat dishes. Vegetarians are well catered for, too and all meat is halal. Service can be slow but the food is worth the wait. Lunch specials are a good deal.

Barrafina, *54 Frith St. Leicester Square or Piccadilly Circus. 020 7813 8016. www.barrafina.co.uk.* **Spanish.** Delicious tapas served as you sit at a counter in stylish surroundings. All dishes are designed to be shared and the produce used is of the highest quality. Extensive list of Spanish wines; no reservations.

Busaba Eathai, *106–110 Wardour St., W1F 0TR. Oxford Circus or Tottenham Court Road. 020 7255 8686. http://busaba.com.* **Thai.** Great ambience, sharing tables and good-value Thai food in a buzzing atmosphere. No booking, so you may have to queue. Also at *22 Store St., Goodge Street; and 8–13 Bird St., Bond Street.*

Golden Dragon, *28–29 Gerrard St. Leicester Square or Piccadilly Circus. 020 7734 2763.* **Chinese.** This spacious restaurant with classic décor remains very popular among the Chinese community and fans of dim sum. There are also various à la carte specialities.

Imperial China, *White Bear Yard, 25a Lisle St. Leicester Square. 020 7734 3388. www.imperial-china.co.uk.* **Chinese.** Particularly pleasant because of the bright room lit by a skylight and its inner courtyard, where a fountain gurgles, this restaurant (one of the largest in Chinatown) offers Cantonese cuisine and an interesting variety of dim sum.

Portrait Restaurant, *National Portrait Gallery, St Martin's Place. Leicester Square or Charing Cross. 020 7312 2490 . www.searcys.co.uk/national-portrait-gallery.* **British.** On the third floor of the National Portrait Gallery, this is a fabulous spot in the heart of London; the views over Trafalgar Square and Nelson's Column, down to Big Ben, the Houses of Parliament and the London Eye, are hard to beat. The pre-theatre menus (two courses for £17.50, three courses for £20.50) are handy if you've got tickets for a show nearby.

Ten Ten Tei, *56 Brewer St. Piccadilly Circus. 020 7287 1738. Closed Sun.* **Japanese.** This small restaurant treats its customers to a wide variety of incredibly tasty Japanese dishes at affordable prices. The place has a somewhat thrown-together feel, but everything is delicious and the lunch menus are great value.

Andrew Edmunds, *46 Lexington St. Oxford Circus or Piccadilly Circus. 020 7437 5708.* **European.** Far from trying to be yet another trendy Soho restaurant, this friendly place is truly authentic. A dozen tables huddle around the bar in a small, dark-wood room and honest European food is served. The atmosphere is casual yet charming – a bit like dining at a friend's home.

Café des Amis, *11–14 Hanover Pl. Covent Garden. 020 7379 3444. www.cafedesamis.co.uk. Closes Sun at 8pm.* **French.** Nestled in a narrow alley behind the Royal Opera House, this restaurant serves modern, refined French cuisine at reasonable prices. The lunch and pre-and post-theatre menus *(before 7pm or after 10pm)* offer excellent value for money *(£16.50–18.50)*. There are a few tables outside on sunny days.

Carom at Meza, *100 Wardour St. Tottenham Court Road. 020 7314 4002, www.meza-soho.co.uk. Closed Sun.* **Indian.** On one side of this venue is Carom, a restaurant serving classic Indian regional dishes with a twist, often using seasonal British ingredients. On the other side is Meza, a popular bar with a late license serving great cocktails.

Endurance, *90 Berwick St. Piccadilly Circus. 020 7437 2944. www.theendurance.co.uk. No dinner Sat, closed Sun.* **Pub food.** At the heart of Berwick Street Market, this gastropub has dark, panelled walls hung with tapestries and serves eclectic, international cuisine.

Les Deux Salons, *40–42 William IV St. Charing Cross or Leicester Square. 020 7420 2050. www.lesdeuxsalons.co.uk. Closes Sun at 6pm.* **French.** Spacious, traditional Parisian brasserie serving simple but delicious food in a large site just off Trafalgar Square. Great atmosphere and super wine list.

Patara, *15 Greek St. Tottenham Court Road. 020 7437 1071. www.pataralondon.com. No lunch Sat or Sun.* **Thai.** Classic dishes with a modern twist, such as do-it-yourself Thai tacos, makes this a more interesting place for dinner than most Thai restaurants. Service is attentive and the surroundings stylish.

Pearl, *252 High Holborn. Holborn. 020 7829 7000. www.pearl-restaurant.com.* **French.** This stylish yet understated restaurant serves exquisite modern French cuisine and has an award-winning wine list of more than 200 varieties. The menu, put together by leading chef Jun Tanaka, changes seasonally and is served as complete menus only – either two or three courses. Prices are surprisingly affordable given the extremely high standard of food and the central location within the opulent Chancery Court hotel.

Rules, *35 Maiden La. Covent Garden. 020 7836 5314. www.rules.co.uk.* **British.** Grouse, partridge and woodcock are some of the game on the menu at London's reputedly oldest restaurant – and all from its own estate! Antique cartoons and drawings adorn the walls, while upstairs, the cocktail bar serves what many believe to be the finest Bloody Mary in town.

Sarastro, *126 Drury La. Covent Garden. 020 7836 0101. www.sarastro-restaurant.com. Closed Sun 4pm–6pm.* **Turkish/Mediterranean.** This flamboyant restaurant serves a range of broadly Mediterranean dishes in uniquely "old curiosity shop"-style surroundings. Ideally located for pre- and post-theatre dining.

Simpson's in The Strand, *100 Strand. Charing Cross. 020 7836 9112. www.simpsonsinthestrand.co.uk.* **British.** An institution since 1828, Simpsons is the place for splendid traditional breakfasts *(try the Ten Deadly Sins)* and classic British cooking. **The Grand Divan** upstairs is the more casual option.

J. Sheekey, *28–32 St Martin's Ct. ⊖ Leicester Square. ✆020 7240 2565. www.j-sheekey.co.uk.* **British.** A well-known address for lovers of fish and seafood, thanks to the freshness and quality of its produce. The cosy atmosphere is ideal for romantic dinners. Lunch menu £26.50.Oyster bar next door.

Souk Medina, *1a Shorts Gdns. ⊖ Covent Garden or Leicester Square. ✆020 7240 1796. www.soukrestaurant.com.* **Moroccan.** Themed as an idealised but rather successful reproduction of a Moroccan interior on two levels, with low tables, large cushions and shisha. Sip tea here by day or enjoy a delicous tajine or cous cous for dinner.

Yauatcha, *15–17 Broadwick St. ⊖ Piccadilly Circus. ✆020 7494 8888. www.yauatcha.com.* **Chinese.** Yauatcha is a Chinese tea house and restaurant known for its tasty dim sum. Especially delicious are the puffs and steamed buns. The ground floor is brighter; downstairs is moodier; service is professional and attentive throughout.

KENSINGTON AND CHELSEA

Bibendum Oyster Bar, *81 Fulham Rd., South Kensington. ⊖ South Kensington. ✆020 7581 5817. www.bibendum.co.uk.* **French.** The foyer of London's beloved Art Nouveau gem, Michelin House, provides the setting for an informal meal of light seafood and shellfish specialities.

Chutney Mary, *535 King's Rd., Chelsea. ⊖ Fulham Broadway. ✆020 7351 3113. www.realindianfood.com.* **Indian.** One of London's leading Indian restaurants, Chutney Mary has been serving high-quality Indian food since 1990. Dishes reflect both the traditions of India's diverse regional cuisines and the food trends of modern India. Stylish setting with extensive wine list.

Gessler at Daquise, *20 Thuloe St. ⊖ South Kensington. ✆020 7589 6117. www.gessleratdaquise.co.uk.* **Polish.** Daquise opened in 1947 and for 63 years it seemed to stay the same – charming but spartan, very much of its Cold War era. Now it's been taken over by a successful Polish catering family from Warsaw and given a shiny new look. Specials include roast goose carved at the table and *pierogi* (dumplings) made to order.

Harrods, *87–136 Brompton Rd. ⊖ Knightsbridge. ✆020 7730 1234. www.harrods.com. Closes at 6pm on Sun.* **International.** Shopping aficionados will be delighted to learn that they need not leave the store, even for lunch. In the famous foodhall, a wide selection of stands and concessions serve up fresh produce to satisfy all tastes, including sushi, oysters, pizza, pancakes, doughnuts and even gourmet Lebanese cuisine.

Maggie Jones, *6 Old Court Pl., Kensington Church Street. ⊖ High Street Kensington. ✆020 7937 6462. www.maggie-jones.co.uk.* **British.** Pass through the gate and you become immersed in the ambience of a 19C country inn. The décor of bouquets of wheat and dried flowers, wicker baskets, buckets and pots, which hang over diners' heads, adds to the atmosphere. The simple home cooking is served by candlelight in antique dishes around long tables. The pies and puddings are particularly recommended.

Zia Teresa, *6 Hans Rd. ⊖ Knightsbridge. ✆020 7589 7634. www.ziateresa.co.uk. Closes at 7pm on Sun.* **Italian.** Far from being intimidated by the proximity of luxury store Harrods, this friendly neighbourhood restaurant is proud to offer a rustic haven for tired shoppers. Zia Teresa serves up all the classics of Italian cuisine in large portions at very reasonable prices.

Amaya, *Halkin Arcade, 19 Motcomb St. ⊖ Knightsbridge. ✆020 7823 1166. www.amaya.biz.* **Indian.** This stylish restaurant in the Masala World family is as remarkable for its sophisticated design as it is for the impeccable quality of its Indian cuisine – praised by critics and awarded a Michelin star in 2006. The focus is on Indian grills, cooked in the theatrical show kitchen.

Bluebird, *350 King's Rd. South Kensington. 020 7559 1000. www.bluebird-restaurant.co.uk.* **British.** This place comprises a foodshop, flower market, café, Bluebird Dining Room and Bluebird – a skylit restaurant and bar. The emphasis here is on seasonal ingredients. This is a very cool spot to be, especially for the weekend brunch.

Launceston Place, *1a Launceston Pl. Gloucester Road. 020 7937 6912. www.launcestonplace-restaurant.co.uk.* **British.** Re-launched and reinvigorated, with dark walls and moody lighting, Launceston Place still has that local feel, and is very handy for the Royal Albert Hall and High Street Kensington. The cooking is original and deflty executed and uses ingredients largely from the British Isles.

Racine, *239 Brompton Rd. Knightsbridge. 020 7584 4477. www.racine-restaurant.com.* **French.** Dark leather banquettes and large mirrors create a Parisian brasserie atmosphere in this award-winning London favourite. Signature dishes include 28-day aged fillet steaks and a divine côte de boeuf.

Cambio de Tercio, *163 Old Brompton Rd. Gloucester Road. 020 7244 8970. www.cambiodetercio.co.uk.* **Spanish.** Warm and friendly restaurant offering modern, refined Spanish cuisine. The bright colours and large canvases that adorn the room create a warm atmosphere. It's always busy – arrive early or book ahead. The less formal tapas bar, Tendido Cero, across the street *(174 Old Brompton Rd.; 020 7370 3685)* serves fabulous tapas in a lively atmosphere.

The Pig's Ear, *35 Old Church St. South Kensington or Sloane Square. 020 7352 2908. www.thepigsear.info. Closes at 9pm on Sun.* **Pub food.** This award-winning gastropub has a traditional, timeless feel. The place is fairly quiet at lunch, but becomes more lively in the evenings, when the restaurant is packed with regulars.

Zaika, *1 Kensington High St. Sloane Square or Fulham Broadway. 020 7795 6533. www.zaika-restaurant.co.uk. No lunch on Mon.* **Indian.** Ideally located opposite Kensington Gardens, this colourful Indian restaurant is housed in a building that used to be a bank. It serves a selection of traditional Indian dishes, as well as more inventive recipes. Various menus are available, such as the five-course tasting menu *(£55; £82 with wine)* and the three-course weekend lunch menu *(£34).*

Zuma, *5 Raphael St. Knightsbridge. 020 7584 1010. www.zumarestaurant.com.* **Japanese.** The ultimate in modern Japanese cuisine, served to an ultra-trendy crowd of London's beautiful people. The mix of materials (wood, glass, steel and granite) that adorn the restaurant are a precursor to the marriage of flavours to be found on every plate. Booking essential.

Gordon Ramsay, *68 Royal Hospital Rd. Sloane Square. 020 7352 4441. www.gordonramsay.com. Closed Sat and Sun.* **British.** One of only two London restaurants to be crowned with three Michelin stars, it goes without saying that the cuisine and service are both impeccable at Gordon Ramsay's most stylish outpost. Head chef Clare Smyth has brought a lighter, more instinctive style to the cooking while still delivering on the Gordon Ramsay classics. Completely refurbished in 2013, the room retains its elegant simplicity, exuding calm and class; service is equally composed and well-organised. Booking *(far in advance)* essential.

NOTTING HILL AND BAYSWATER

Geales, *2 Farmer St. Notting Hill Gate. 020 7727 7528. www.geales.com. Closed Mon lunch; closes at 9.30pm on Sun.* **Fish and chips.** Established in 1939 in a street behind Notting Hill Gate, this local favourite is still going strong. There's a seaside atmosphere to the place, and a handful of tables outside for when the weather's fine. The good quality fish is fresh and charged by weight.

Hereford Road, *3 Hereford Rd. Notting Hill Gate, Royal Oak or Westbourne Park. 020 7727 1144. www.herefordroad.org.* **British.** Splendid British cooking enthusiastically served at this former butcher's. Try duck hearts, calf's brains and braised rabbits, or a whole oxtail to share between two.

Royal China, *13 Queensway. Bayswater or Queensway. 020 7221 2535. www.royalchinagroup.co.uk.* **Chinese.** Luxurious yet authentic Chinese restaurant serving up all the usuals, but with an inventive twist. This was the first Royal China to be opened in London, and has recently been refurbished, with ornate Chinese murals and golf leaf on the ceiling. Best of all, the dim sum still lives up to its reputation.

Ya Hala, *26 London St. Paddington. 020 7262 1111. www.levant.co.uk.* **Lebanese.** This restaurant is a pleasant surprise in a neighbourhood where dining options are limited. There are plenty of tasty appetisers like hummous and falafels, and it's very good value for money. No alcohol is served.

Beach Blanket Babylon, *45 Ledbury Rd., W11 2AA. Notting Hill Gate. 020 7229 2907. www.beachblanket.co.uk.* **European.** Occupying a Georgian mansion, this atmospheric place is a restaurant, bar and club rolled into one. Very popular with the hip Notting Hill set, it was inspired by Spanish architect Antonio Gaudí and has a Baroque feel to it. The restaurant in the vaulted cellars serves delicious à la carte dishes and set menus by candlelight. Also at *19–23 Bethnal Green Rd., Shoreditch High Street, 020 7749 3540.*

Electric Diner, *191 Portobello Rd. Notting Hill. 020 7908 9696.www.electricdiner.com.* **French-American.** The decor is classic diner style, with booth and bar seating, and the service is fast and friendly. You can opt for traditional diner food, like the cheeseburgers, or try something different, like the roasted bone marrow with beef cheek marmalade. Next door is the Electric Cinema, one of the oldest cinemas in London.

E & O, *14 Blenheim Crescent, Notting Hill. Ladbroke Grove. 020 7229 5454. www.rickerrestaurants.com.* **Pan-Asian.** Uncluttered Art Deco design and funky lounge music: there's no doubt that you're in one of Notting Hill's typically trendy bars and restaurants. The Asian fusion cuisine is inventive, and delicious dim sum is served all day at the bar.

WESTMINSTER, VICTORIA, PIMLICO

Seafresh Restaurant, *80–81 Wilton Rd. Victoria. 020 7828 0747. www.seafresh-dining.com. Closed Sun.* **Seafood.** Open since 1965 and now revamped, Seafresh Fish is almost always full for both lunch and dinner, so the place can be quite noisy. Fish and seafood, grilled or fried to perfection are served in more than generous portions and if you can't decide, there's always the Seafresh Platter.

Chimes, *26 Churton St. Victoria or Pimlico. 020 7821 7456. www.chimes-of-pimlico.co.uk.* **British.** Those with any remaining reservations about British cooking should book a table here and enjoy the delicious pies served in earthenware pots. Other British classics include poacher's pie, calves liver and bacon and bangers and mash. A large selection of beers, ciders and wines is served by the glass.

The Vincent Rooms, *Vincent Square. Victoria. 020 7802 8391. www.thevincentrooms.com. Open Mon–Fri lunch and selected evenings. Closed school holidays.* **European.** Want the upmarket London dining experience, but not got the budget for it? This restaurant is attached to the prestigious hotel school at Westminster College, where the great chefs of tomorrow are educated. The "Brasserie" menu changes daily. Reservation essential.

Kazan, *93–94 Wilton Rd. Victoria. 020 7233 7100. www.kazan-restaurant.com.* **Turkish.** A popular place to come for a good range of hot and cold mezze, plus tea and shisha in the afternoon. The decor is stylishly Middle Eastern.

Ken Lo's Memories of China, *65–69 Ebury St. ⊖ Victoria. ✆020 7730 7734. www.atozrestaurants.com.* **Chinese.** This airy, elegant restaurant serves up some of the best Chinese cuisine in town, influenced by the great chef Ken Lo. Service is attentive and unobtrusive.

La Poule au Pot, *231 Ebury St., SW1W 8UT. ⊖ Sloane Square or Victoria. ✆020 7730 7763. www.lapouleaupot.co.uk.* **French.** This restaurant is justly acclaimed for its hearty food, but more especially for the romantic setting. A few tables outside make it a popular spot for dining alfresco in summer. Lunch menus £19.75 (2 courses) and £23.50 (3 courses). Handy for the King's Road.

Quilon, *41 Buckingham Gate. ⊖ St James's Park. ✆ 020 7821 1899. www.quilon.co.uk.* **Indian.** Since its opening in 1999, the London outpost of India's Taj group has served Southwest coastal Indian cuisine in a modern, refined setting with attentive service. Seafood dishes stand out, spicing is judicious and the ingredients first-rate.

The Cinnamon Club, *30–32 Great Smith St. ⊖ Westminster. ✆020 7222 2555. www.cinnamonclub.com. Closed Sun. Closes occasionally; check the website.* **Indian.** Housed in the old Westminster Library, this select address attracts local politicians and businessmen for breakfast, lunch and dinner. The setting is superb and the Indian cuisine deliciously inventive. The menu changes regularly and there's a stylish bar in the basement.

MAYFAIR, MARYLEBONE, REGENT'S PARK

Levant, *Jason Court, 76 Wigmore St. ⊖ Bond Street. ✆020 7224 1111. www.levant.co.uk.* **Middle Eastern.** This exotic restaurant serves a wide range of tempting dishes packed with flavour, from mezze and fresh salads to grilled fish and meat, in glamorous, exotic surroundings. Belly dancing some nights, and DJs Friday and Saturday nights from 10.30pm to 2am.

Maroush I, *21 Edgware Rd. ⊖ Marble Arch. ✆020 7723 0773. www.maroush.com.* **Lebanese.** One of the oldest Lebanese restaurants in London, Maroush gave birth to an empire of a dozen different institutions around the Edgware Road area, including restaurants *(Maroush I to V)*, snack bars, juice bars *(Ranoush Juice Bar, 43 Edgware Rd.)*, fast food *(Beirut Express 112–114 Edgware Rd.)* and a deli *(Maroush Deli, 45–49 Edgware Rd.)*. Whatever your choice, the food is absolutely delicious.

Momo, *25 Heddon St. ⊖ Piccadilly Circus. ✆020 7434 4040. www.momoresto.com. Closed Sun lunch.* **Moroccan.** The "in" crowd loves this colourful restaurant, with its traditional rugs and atmospheric Arabic music. Staff will guide the uninitiated through the comprehensive menu. The more informal Mocafé offers all-day dining and is open on Sunday.

The Providores and Tapa Room, *109 Marylebone High St. ⊖ Baker Street. ✆020 7935 6175. www.theprovidores.co.uk.* **International.** Sit in the buzzing Tapa Room, open all day, for great breakfasts and tapas. You may have to wait for a seat, and when you get one it may be a squeeze, but the heavenly fusion food is worth it. The New Zealand chef uses unusual ingredients to great effect. Upstairs the restaurant is calmer but the food as good.

Queen's Head and Artichoke, *30–32 Albany St. ⊖ Great Portland Street or Regent's Park. ✆020 7916 6206. www.theartichoke.net.* **Pub food.** This gastropub serves modern English dishes with a touch of creativity. Tapas is available during the day in the beautiful panelled bar and roasts are served on Sundays. Food is served in both the lively ground-floor bar and the more relaxed first-floor dining room. There are a few tables outside.

Royal China, *24–26 Baker St. ⊖ Baker Street, Bond Street or Regent's Park. ✆020 7487 4688. www.royalchinagroup.co.uk.* **Chinese.** This restaurant, the largest of the Royal China chain, serves traditional Hong-Kong Chinese cuisine, such as crispy duck with spring onion and pancakes, in a stylish setting just minutes from the shops of Oxford Street.

Galvin Bistro de Luxe, *66 Baker St. ⊖ Baker Street. ✆020 7935 4007. www.galvinrestaurants.com.* **French.** Rightly hailed by critics, brothers Chris and Jeff Galvin offer remarkable regional French cuisine at affordable prices here, the first restaurant they opened. Simple recipes are crafted with the finest seasonal produce, the wine list is superb and the service relaxed and unobtrusive. Two-course set menus available at both lunch (£19.50)and dinner (£21.50).

Maze, *10–13 Grosvenor Sq. ⊖ Bond Street. ✆020 7107 0000. www.gordonramsay.com.* **French-Asian.** This jewel in the crown of celebrity chef Gordon Ramsay is perfect in every way: the cuisine is delightfully inventive, the service gracious and attentive, the décor stylish. Despite being one of London's most acclaimed restaurants, the place also manages to retain a warm and friendly atmosphere. Dishes are offered in small portions *(tapas style)*, or you can opt for the tasting menu. The new sushi bar offers authentic sushi and sashimi dishes prepared in front of you at the counter.

Nobu, *19 Old Park La., W1K 1LB. ⊖Hyde Park Corner. ✆020 7447 4747. www.noburestaurants.com/london.* **Japanese.** The first European venture for eponymous chef Nobu Matsuhisa was this outrageously stylish restaurant on the first floor of Park Lane hotel: the Metropolitan. The restaurant overlooks Hyde Park and features a menu that draws heavily on Matsuhisa's training as a Tokyo sushi chef; it also incorporates numerous South American influences from his travels there. The restaurant was awarded a Michelin star in 1997 which it retains today. There's also a separate sushi bar.

KING'S CROSS, ST PANCRAS

Booking Office Bar, *Euston Rd., NW1 2AR. ⊖ King's Cross St Pancras. ✆020 7841 3566. www.bookingoffice restaurant.com.* **European.** Having sat empty for years, the stunning Gothic St Pancras building is once again open for business, operating as a Marriott hotel. This laidback bar/restaurant is located in what used to be the station's booking office and many of the original details remain, including some impressive woodwork. Breakfast, lunch and dinner are served daily, plus a range of expertly mixed Victorian and contemporary punches, historic ales, porters and perries. Located right next to the Eurostar platform, it's an ideal place to wait for your train. Live music Thu, Fri and Sat.

The Fellow, *24 York Way, N1 9AA. ⊖ King's Cross St Pancras. ✆020 7837 3001. www.thefellow.co.uk.* **Pub food.** This upmarket gastropub, adjacent to King's Cross station, specialises in modern British cuisine with a European twist. Seasonal, locally sourced produce is used and the menu changes daily, featuring dishes such as pigeon, duck confit and apple tart. There's also an upstairs bar area and roof terrace. Good wine list too.

Smithys, *The Stables, 15–17 Leeke St. ⊖ King's Cross St Pancras. ✆020 7278 5949. www.smithys london.com. Opens at 5pm on Sat; closed Sun and some bank holidays.* **European.** Once stables housing the giant shire horses which pulled London's omnibuses, this characterful building tucked down a side street near King's Cross is now home to a little-known family-run bar and restaurant. To the left, the lively bar serves a good range of real ales, while the room to the right is a more sedate dining area. The modern British/European menu changes with the seasons and all produce used is of the highest quality. There's also an extensive and well-thought-out wine list.

SOUTH BANK, BOROUGH, WATERLOO

⊖⊖ **Tas**, *33 The Cut, SE1 8LF. ⊖ Waterloo. ✆020 7928 3300; www.tasrestaurant.com.* **Turkish.** This chain of warmly decorated Anatolian Turkish restaurants offers tasty cuisine, with lots of fresh flavours, served in more than generous portions. Service is prompt and very friendly; prices are extremely affordable. Also at *72 Borough High St., ⊖ London Bridge, ✆020 7403 7200; 20–22 New Globe Walk, ⊖ London Bridge and 97–99 Isabella St. ⊖ Southwark.*

⊖⊖ **Archduke**, *Concert Hall Approach. ⊖Waterloo. ✆020 7928 9370, www.thearchduke.co.uk.* **Mediterranean.** Housed in the railway arches near Waterloo Station, close to the concert halls and entertainment venues of the South Bank, this hip restaurant serves good food in a great setting. The menu changes monthly and there also are jazz concerts in the evenings.

⊖⊖ **Cantina Vinopolis**, *1 Bank End. ⊖ London Bridge. ✆020 7940 8333. www.cantinavinopolis.com. Closed Sun.* **European.** Located in the cavernous brick arches that support the railway track, this rustic-contemporary restaurant is part of wine museum Vinopolis. The main attraction is the wine list, but the food is decent enough.

⊖⊖ **Fish!**, *Cathedral St., Borough Market, Southwark. ⊖ Southwark. ✆020 7407 3803. www.fishkitchen.com. Closed bank holidays.* **Seafood.** This seafood restaurant, in an impressive glass and steel pavillion reminiscent of a giant fish tank, serves sustainable fish, freshly prepared and at affordable prices. An open kitchen allows diners the opportunity to watch the chefs at work and the large outdoor terrace with its views of Southwark Cathedral is a real sun trap when the weather is good.

⊖⊖ **Tapas Brindisa**, *18–20 Southwark Street. ⊖London Bridge. ✆020 7357 8880. www.brindisa.com.* **Spanish.** This is a cut above your average tapas restaurant, serving superb food in a great location on the edge of Borough Market. Brindisa specialises in importing first-rate authentic Iberian products, so the food is the real thing; simple but packed with flavour and beautifully presented. The outside tables catch the sun in the afternoon.

⊖⊖⊖ **Oxo Tower Brasserie**, *Barge House St. (8th floor), Oxo Tower Wharf, Southwark. ⊖Southwark. ✆020 7803 3888. www.harveynichols.com.* **International.** Sharing the 8th floor of a converted factory with a more formal restaurant, the brasserie offers terrace dining with the same spectacular city view. The open-plan kitchen produces exciting cuisine, fusing flavours from around the world, and there's live music in the evenings.

SUBURBS

NORTHWEST: HAMPSTEAD, HIGHGATE, SWISS COTTAGE

⊖⊖ **Dim T**, *1 Hampstead La. ⊖Archway or Highgate. ✆020 8340 8800. www.dimt.co.uk.* **Asian.** This restaurant *(part of a city-wide chain)* has built a reputation on its delicious dim sum, which is ideal for sharing. Also in Hampstead at *3 Heath St. ✆020 7435 0024. ⊖ Hampstead.*

⊖⊖ **The Wells**, *30 Well Walk. ⊖ Hampstead. ✆020 7794 3785. www.thewellshampstead.co.uk.* **Pub food.** Attractive 18C pub on the edge of Hampstead Heath, with leather sofas to sink into after a walk there. The accessible menu is also served in an upstairs dining room.

⊖⊖ **Zara**, *11 Southend Green. ⊖ Belsize Park or Hampstead, or Hampstead Heath Rail. ✆020 7794 5498.* **Turkish.** An authentic restaurant serving the expected selection of mezze and grills, as well as delicious traditional dishes from Anatolia. The décor is somewhat lacking in character, but the welcome is warm and the food authentic and fragrant. Turkish coffee and Turkish delight are served during the afternoons – the perfect way to revive after a long walk on Hampstead Heath.

SOUTHEAST: GREENWICH

££ **Davy's Wine Vaults**, *161 Greenwich High Rd. ⊖ Greenwich DLR or Rail. ✆020 8858 7204. www.davy.co.uk.* **British.** This well-established *(since 1870)* London wine merchant now manages several bars in the capital. Housed in a cellar, the Greenwich outpost is full of character and retains a rustic, family atmosphere. Good-quality cuisine accompanies the wide selection of wines.

£££ **Inside**, *19 Greenwich South St. ⊖Greenwich DLR or Rail. ✆020 8265 5060. www.insiderestaurant.co.uk. No dinner Sun. Closed Mon.* **European.** One of the best restaurants in Greenwich. The reason for its success lies in its sleek, modern design and well-executed, inventive cooking. The menu changes regularly, but is always of a high standard. Good-value set menus are available at breakfast and dinner.

£ **North Pole Bar and Restaurant**, *131 Greenwich High Rd., Greenwich. ⊖ New Cross. ✆020 8853 3020. www.northpolegreenwich.com. Closed 25 Dec and Mon lunch.* **Pub food.** It's a short stroll from Greenwich centre to this lively, trendy establishment, with two bars (one downstairs for dancing) and an upstairs restaurant serving good food in a casual atmosphere. Good roast dinners on Sundays.

SOUTH: BATTERSEA

£ **Santa Maria del Sur**, *129 Queenstown Rd. ⊖ Clapham Common. ✆020 7622 2088. www.santamariadelsur.co.uk.* **Steakhouse.** This place is for carnivores only, as slabs of meat are served on grills at the table. Kick off with chorizo or black pudding, then tuck into an Argentinian steak accompanied by a full-bodied Argentinian red.

£ **Tom Ilic Restaurant**, *123 Queenstown Rd. ⊖ Clapham Junction. ✆020 7622 0555. www.tomilic.com. No lunch Mon and Tue. No dinner Sun and Mon.* **British.** Delightful restaurant, which serves up great food at reasonable prices in a charming, peaceful room.

SOUTHWEST: RICHMOND, KEW, TWICKENHAM, WIMBLEDON

£ **Light House**, *75–77 Ridgeway, Wimbledon. ⊖ Wimbledon. ✆020 8944 6338. www.lighthousewimbledon.com. No dinner Sun.* **Italian.** Close to Wimbledon tube, this bright restaurant has an open kitchen and a changing menu of Italian and fusion dishes. Try the risotto specialities. Great value set lunch available during the week.

££ **Dog and Fox**, *24 High St., Wimbledon. ⊖ Wimbledon. ✆020 8946 6565. www.thedogandfox.com.* **Pub food.** This historic pub is one of the busiest in the heart of Wimbledon Village. The bar serves well-kept real ales and has an extensive wine list, while the kitchen dishes up modern British cuisine with a Pacific Rim influence. Large beer garden.

££ **The Orangery**, *Kew Gdns. ⊖ Kew Gardens. ✆020 8332 5655. www.kew.org. Closes 3pm in winter.* **British.** Set in the beautiful orangery designed by William Chambers in 1761, this restaurant offers good meals at very reasonable prices. Ideal for a break at lunchtime or a pastry accompanied by tea or coffee during the day. Another cafeteria, the **Pavilion Restaurant** *(closed in winter)*, welcomes visitors to the south of the gardens, near the pagoda.

££ **Petersham Nurseries Café**, *Church Lane (off Petersham Road). ⊖ Richmond. ✆020 8940 5230. www.petershamnurseries.com. Lunch only Tue–Sun. Reservations essential.* **British.** The concise menu changes on a weekly basis to reflect the best of what's in season. The food matches the setting – in delightfully ramshackle nurseries by the river – by being natural, earthy and full of goodness. Many dishes have an Italian accent, such as roasted wild salmon with fennel, spinach and rocket or beetroot with buffalo mozzarella and rainbow chard. Engaging service on the terrace if weather permits, or among plants and flowers in a greenhouse.

River Café
© Matteo Piazza

⊖⊖ **Rose and Crown**, *55 High St., Wimbledon. ⊖ Wimbledon. ✆020 8947 4713. www.roseandcrownwimbledon.co.uk.* **Pub food.** This friendly country pub dating from 1659 has retained, despite numerous renovations, its original woodwork and fireplace. Nice paved garden for drinking on sunny days.

⊖⊖ **The White Swan**, *Riverside, Twickenham. ⊖ Twickenham Rail. ✆020 8744 2951. www.whiteswantwickenham.com.* **Pub food.** This lovely traditional pub dating from the 17C enjoys an exceptional waterfront location. The simple décor includes photos which reflect the ties with Twickenham rugby and there's a very pleasant terrace overlooking the Thames.

WEST: HAMMERSMITH, CHISWICK AND SHEPHERDS BUSH

⊖ – ⊖⊖⊖ **Westfield**, *Shepherds Bush Green. ⊖ Shepherds Bush, Shepherds Bush Market, Wood Lane. ✆020 8743 5194. http://uk.westfield.com.* **International.** With over 60 different places to eat and drink in this shopping centre, there's no shortage of choice – from Indonesian street food to Mexican tapas, from Greek mezze to burgers and pizzas. The Southern Terrace restaurants have plenty of tables outside, and overlook a huge plant-covered wall and water feature, ideal for alfresco dining in summer away from the traffic.

⊖⊖ **101 Thai Kitchen**, *352 King St., Hammersmith. ⊖ Stamford Brook. ✆020 8746 6888. www.101thaikitchen.com.* **Thai.** You can tell this is the real thing as it's usually full of Thais. This family-run restaurant serves delicious dishes mostly from Northeast Thailand. The spicy fish curry and sizzling steak with *jaew* (spicy dip) sauce are recommended, and there are good vegetarian options. Specials on the board are in Thai but you can ask for a translation. Take away service available.

⊖⊖ **La Tarantella**, *4 Elliott Rd. ⊖ Turnham Green. ✆020 8987 8877. www.latarantella.co.uk.* **Italian.** This small, family-run restaurant just off Chiswick High Road serves authentic Italian food in a great atmosphere. The restaurant owners are from Naples and are as passionate about their food as they are about their football. It's a bit of a tight squeeze, but the Italian home-cooking more than compensates for the lack of space.

⊖⊖ **Patio**, *5 Goldhawk Rd., Shepherds Bush. ⊖ Goldhawk Road. ✆020 8743 5194. www.patiolondon.com.* **Polish.** A small and very friendly local restaurant serving delicious meat and fish dishes such as smoked salmon, *pierogi* (dumplings) and goulash at extremely affordable prices and in huge portions. One of London's true hidden gems (hiding behind a bright yellow façade).

Anglesea Arms, *35 Wingate Rd., Shepherds Bush. ⊖ Ravenscourt Park or Goldhawk Road. ✆020 8749 1291. www.anglesea-arms.com.* **British.** Away from the bustle of Shepherds Bush and Hammersmith, this neighbourhood pub is probably one of the best gastropubs in the capital. The kitchen serves up dishes of the highest quality and prices are no higher than in traditional (and often inferior) pubs elsewhere. It gets very busy so booking is advised for the restaurant section of the pub. You can also sit and eat in the bar area, where there's a roaring fire in winter.

The Gate, *51 Queen Caroline St. ⊖ Hammersmith. ✆020 8748 6932. http://thegaterestaurants.com.* **Vegetarian.** Totally refurbished in the summer of 2013, the Gate is still amazing customers by how varied and tasty vegetarian cuisine can be. Inspired by recipes from around the world, the Gate's chef offers an inventive menu of dishes made from fresh seasonal ingredients. The mezze platter is a good option for sampling numerous different flavours, and if you'd like to prolong the pleasure, the culinary secrets of the chef have been compiled into a book. Such is the popularity of the Gate that the owners opened a new branch in Islington.

Rotolo, The Gate
The Gate Vegetarian Restaurant

The Green Room, *45a Goldhawk Rd., Shepherds Bush. ⊖ Goldhawk Road. ✆020 8746 2111. www.bushbar.co.uk.* **American.** Look out for the narrow passageway that leads to this place housed in a former milk bottling factory, where you can play American pool and table football, or watch live sports on large screens. Burgers, steaks and other classic American fare is served with draught beers and wines.

La Trompette, *5–7 Devonshire Rd., Chiswick. ⊖ Turnham Green. ✆020 8747 1836. www.latrompette.co.uk.* **French.** This West London favourite is by far the best restaurant in Chiswick. The recently refurbished dining room is cool and stylish, and the quality of the food matches the top spots in central London. The place is always buzzing – in fact it's very difficult to get a table, so book well ahead. There's an excellent wine list too.

Pissarro, *Corney Reach Way, Chiswick. ⊖ Turnham Green. ✆020 8994 3111. www.pissarro.co.uk. No dinner Sun.* **British.** The highlight of Pissarro is its location, sitting right on the river between Hammersmith and Barnes bridges. The light and airy conservatory means you can enjoy splendid views of the Thames while dining on dishes such as potted smoked trout, slow cooked Cornish lamb shank or pan-fried sea bream. It's very hard to believe you are in London here.

River Café, *Rainville Rd., Thames Wharf. ⊖ Hammersmith. ✆020 7386 4200. www.rivercafe.co.uk. No dinner Sun. Closed some bank holidays.* **Italian.** Owned and operated by Ruth Rogers and, until her death in 2010, Rose Gray, this restaurant in a converted warehouse has young staff, an open kitchen and first-rate Italian cuisine incorporating the best seasonal ingredients. The menu changes twice daily. Many successful chefs have trained in the kitchen here, including Jamie Oliver, Hugh Fearnley-Whittingstall and Sam and Sam Clarke of Moro fame.

Entertainment

London is truly one of the world's top cities for entertainment. From "Theatreland" to the city's diverse nightclubs, the best contemporary music concerts to a belly-aching laugh at The Comedy Store, or a quiet pint of ale at one of the capital's historic pubs – London has it all. A variety of publications – many of them free – offer up-to-date listings for events across the city. *Ask at tourist offices and ticket outlets, or get hold of the* Evening Standard, *distributed at Tube stations (no charge).*

CINEMAS

Catching the latest film releases in a comfortable cinema is a great way to relax. The cinemas in Leicester Square are often used for film premieres and festivals, too.

BFI IMAX

1 Charlie Chaplin Walk, South Bank, SE1 8XR. ⊖ Waterloo. ✆0330 333 7878. www.odeon.co.uk/bfiimax. This special cinema shows 2D and 3D films on a screen the height of five double-decker buses: everything from Antarctic adventure to Walt Disney® films.

BFI SOUTHBANK

Belvedere Rd., South Bank, SE1 8XT. ⊖ Waterloo. ✆020 7928 3232. www.bfi.org.uk/whatson. The London Film Festival is held here every year in November. Varied regular programme, strong on seasons.

ODEON CINEMAS

24–26 Leicester Sq., Soho, WC2H 7JY. ⊖ Leicester Square. ✆0871 224 4007. www.odeon.co.uk. Showings daily 11am–9pm. London's biggest cinema *(1,679 seats)*, where the premieres of prestigious British and Hollywood films are shown. Also at *135 Shaftesbury Ave., 40 Leicester Sq., 11–18 Panton St., 30 Tottenham Court Rd. and 10 Edgware Rd. (Marble Arch), among others.*

Ticketmaster

Bookings line: ✆0844 844 0444. www.ticketmaster.co.uk.

RITZY PICTUREHOUSE

Brixton Oval, Coldharbour La., Brixton, SW2 1JG. ⊖ Brixton. ✆0871 902 5739. www.picturehouses.co.uk. £6.50. This Edwardian cinema shows classics and recent films, and is beloved by English producers such as Ken Loach.

COMEDY CLUBS

THE COMEDY STORE

1a Oxendon St., SW1Y 4EE. ⊖ Picadilly Circus; Leicester Sq. ✆0844 871 7699. www.thecomedystore.co.uk. Contact **Ticketmaster** *for tickets (see above).* Big name acts including comedians Andy Parsons, Paul Merton and Russell Howard have played here. Seating is not the most comfortable, but the atmosphere more than makes up for it.

HAMMERSMITH APOLLO

Queen Caroline St., Hammersmith, W6 9QH. ⊖ Hammersmith. ✆0843 221 0100 (for tickets). www.hammersmith apollo.com. This is *the* place for comedy: some of the best UK comedians take centre stage at this large venue. Hot 21C favourites such as Frankie Boyle, Michael McIntyre and Reginald D Hunter have all played here to packed audiences. The Apollo also hosts popular music concerts; come here to see some of the biggest stars.

NIGHTCLUBS

London's energetic club scene is a major attraction. Venues usually offer special rates in the early evening, but the real action starts later and continues until early morning, sometimes later.

Bar Rumba

36 Shaftesbury Ave., Piccadilly, W1D 7EP. ⊖ Piccadilly. ✆020 7287 6933. www.barrumbadisco.co.uk. Open Mon–Tue 6pm–3am, Wed 10pm–3am, Thu–

Sat 6.30pm–3am, Sun 10pm–3am. Comedy Club Fri and Sat 7pm–10pm. Free–£15. In the heart of Soho, the Rumba is one of London's best clubs, although the size of the dancefloor is far too small given the venue's popularity. The place has recently been refurbished, and there's always a good atmosphere. The music varies from night to night, ranging from jazz and funk to house and drum 'n' bass.

Cargo
83 Rivington St., EC2A 3AY. Old Street. 020 7739 3440. www.cargo-london.com. Bar and venue open Mon–Thu 6pm–1am, Fri–Sat 6pm–3am, Sun 6pm–midnight. £5–£18. Located in a Victorian railway arch, Cargo has a restaurant, a lounge bar furnished with big cushions, and a heaving main room, where live bands play. DJs offer great music, from Asian underground to hip hop.

Chinawhite
6 Winsley St., W1W 8HF. Oxford Circus. 020 7290 0580. www.chinawhite.com. Open Wed–Sat 10pm–3am. £15–20. When its previous premises were taken over for redevelopment, infamous club Chinawhite moved away from Soho to set up in well-to-do Fitzrovia. Now housed in a Grade II listed building, this opulent club features a restaurant, the luxurious Temple Bar, and a main room where you'll find the dancefloor and main bar. An Asian influence is palpable throughout and the music mostly funky house and RnB, with a few fun floor-fillers thrown in.

Fabric
77A Charterhouse St., EC1M 6HJ. Farringdon. 020 7336 8898. www.fabriclondon.com. Open Fri 10pm–5am, Sat–Sun 11pm–5am. £8–£18. Fabric is a gigantic club capable of holding 1,500 revellers in three originally decorated halls. The acoustics are exceptional and attract top DJs *(Fatboy Slim, Rennie Pilgrem, Backspace)* and a mixed 20–30-year-old crowd. The music is predominantly drum'n'bass and techno/house.

Heaven
Under The Arches, Villiers St., Strand, WC2N 6NG. Charing Cross. 020 7930 2020. www.heavennightclub-london.com. Open Mon, Thu–Sat 11pm–6am, plus some gig nights. Free–£15. London's (and some say Europe's) biggest gay night takes place under the railway arches near Charing Cross. There are three dancefloors and three types of music, from disco to techno, plus a stunning laser show and all sorts of camp fun from singalongs to "porn idol". This place is extremely popular, so get there early. All welcome.

koko
1A Camden High St., NW1 7JE. Mornington Crescent. 0870 432 5527. www.koko.uk.com. Open Sun–Thu, usually 7pm–11pm (for gigs), Fri gigs at 7pm and club NME 9.30pm–4am, Sat usually 10pm–4am. Check website for upcoming events and prices. Once a music hall, this fun young club is now a warren of a place with terrific sound. Attracts a student-heavy crowd and is almost always packed to the rafters.

Ministry of Sound
103 Gaunt St., Elephant and Castle, SE1 6DP. Elephant & Castle. 0870 0600 0101. www.ministryofsound.com. Open Fri 10.30pm–6am, Sat 11pm–7am (last entry always 4.30am). Buy tickets online or at the door. London's best-known nightclub has become an institution in the capital and draws a mixed crowd of revellers (20–35 years old) for house, garage and techno music every weekend. The sound is exceptional, the experience stunning, but behave yourself if you want to get through the door – and above all, be patient.

Tkts Discount West End Tickets Booth

Run by the Society of London Theatres (SOLT) and based at Leicester Square, **tkts** is the only official half-price and discount theatre ticket organisation. It offers a limited number of half-price tickets to most West End shows on the day of performance. Tickets are available in person only, on a first-come, first-served basis. Only cash and credit or debit payments are accepted and there is a service charge. No returns are possible and there is a maximum of four tickets per application. Visitors can also book full-price advance tickets to shows here. *Open Mon–Sat 9am–7pm, Sun 10.30am–4.30pm. For more information, contact SOLT, 32 Rose St., WC2E 9ET. 020 7557 6700.*

CABARET AND DINNER SHOWS

Madame Jo Jo's

8–10 Brewer St., Soho, W1F 0SE. Piccadilly Circus. 020 7734 3040 (information). www.madamejojos.com. Usually open Tue–Wed, Fri–Sun; club open 7pm–3am, shows 8pm–10pm. £25–£52.50 (Cabaret tickets). Book tickets online. A warm-hearted cabaret for night owls and a favourite haunt of drag queens. Sometimes a bit of a madhouse, the ambience changes from day to day.

Volupte

9 Norwich St., EC4A 1EJ. Chancery Lane. 020 7831 1622. www.volupte-lounge.com. Open Tue–Wed 4.30pm–1am, Thu–Fri 4.30pm–3am, Sat 2pm–3am. £14–15. This decadent supper club serves up live burlesque, circus, vaudeville and cabaret to a soundtrack of blues, jazz and swing. Attracts the crème de la crème of performers and a fun crowd.

PERFORMING ARTS

THEATRE

At all times of the year London offers everything from top block-buster musicals to serious theatre. Experimental theatre is found in the "fringe" theatres, and, during the summer, open-air venues such as the Globe Theatre, Holland Park and Regent's Park host outdoor performances (weather permitting!). Most of the mid-range theatres are grouped together in the West End, in and around Shaftesbury Avenue. You'll also find a wide range of restaurants here, many of which offer excellent pre- and post-theatre two- and three-course set meals at around £15–£20. The theatres listed below are some of the better-known ones that feature long-running plays and musicals. For a complete listing of current shows, consult www.officiallondon theatre.co.uk.

Tickets for West End theatres and musicals are booked by agents who will charge a fee – either 10 percent or a flat fee of a few pounds.

To avoid paying a surcharge, buy seats directly from the theatre box office. Matinée performances are cheaper, although star casts may be replaced by understudies. Many theatres reserve some tickets to sell at the door on the day of the performance; there will invariably be a queue, so get there early.

Ticket prices vary, but generally range between £15 and £45, though you may pay more for a big musical or a play with top stars performing.

Adelphi

409–412 The Strand, WC2R 0NS. Charing Cross. 0844 579 0094. www.reallyuseful.com. Several of Dickens' novels were adapted for the stage here soon after publication *(1837–45)*. This theatre is fondly remembered for some great musical productions (*Me and My Girl, Sunset Boulevard* and recently, *Chicago*).

Apollo Victoria Theatre
17 Wilton Rd., Victoria, SW1V 1LG. ⊖ Victoria. ✆0844 826 8000. www.apollovictorialondon.org. This former cinema *(built 1930)* converted into a theatre in 1979, has hosted such famous performers as Shirley Bassey, Cliff Richard and Sammy Davis Jr. Among recent productions are *Starlight Express* and *Wicked.*

Barbican
Barbican Centre, Silk St., EC2Y 8DS. ⊖ Barbican. ✆020 7638 8891. www.barbican.org.uk. This vast complex is a performing arts centre, the largest of its type in Europe, housing a concert hall, cinema, exhibition areas and restaurants. The theatre offers a wide range of productions, from experimental cabaret to dance, classical theatre and new plays.

The Bush Theatre
7 Uxbridge Road, W12 8LJ. ⊖ Goldhawk Road or Shepherds Bush. ✆020 8743 5050, www.bushtheatre.co.uk. Housed in the former Shepherds Bush library, this vibrant theatre has built its reputation on a bold programme of young and emerging artists. The bar is a cool place for a pre-theatre drink.

Dominion
268–269 Tottenham Court Rd., W1T 0AG. ⊖ Tottenham Court Road. ✆0844 847 1775. www.dominiontheatre.co.uk. Built as a concert hall in a former leprosarium and brewery, and formerly a cinema, the Dominion is now famous for its musicals, such as *Grease* and *We Will Rock You.*

Duke of York's Theatre
St Martin's La., WC2N 4BG. ⊖ Leicester Square. ✆0845 505 8500. www.dukeofyorkstheatre.co.uk. This theatre's name is synonymous with playwrights such as Shaw, Ibsen, Galsworthy and Noël Coward.

Her Majesty's Theatre
Haymarket, St James's, SW1Y 4QL. ⊖Piccadilly Circus. ✆0844 412 2707. www.reallyuseful.com. Designed in 1896 by architect CJ Phills, this beautiful theatre seats 1,200. Popular musical *Phantom of the Opera* has been running here since 1986 and continues to attract large crowds.

London Palladium
8 Argyll St., Soho, W1F 7TF. ⊖Oxford Circus. ✆0844 412 2957. www.reallyuseful.com. This sumptuous theatre, opened in 1910, is famous for variety shows and has hosted more Royal Variety Performances than any other theatre.

Lyceum
21 Wellington St., Covent Garden, WC2E 7RQ. ⊖Covent Garden. ✆0844 871 3006. www.lyceum-theatre.co.uk. The fourth theatre to be built on the site, the Lyceum resembles a Roman temple. Reopened in 1904, it was for a long time the venue for ballets, musicals and classical plays. Today it produces mega-musicals such as the *The Lion King* – playing here since 1999.

Lyric
Lyric Square, King St.., Hammersmith, W6 0QL. ⊖ Hammersmith. ✆ 020 8741 6850. www.lyric.co.uk. This community theatre hosts an eclectic programme veering from high art to populism. New and cutting-edge performances are encouraged and young talent thrives here. The tickets are good value, and there's a pleasant roof-top garden with a café selling paninis and pizzas.

New London Theatre
167 Drury La., Covent Garden, WC2B 5PW. ⊖ Covent Garden. ✆0844 412 2708. www.reallyuseful.com. Although the present building is modern, previous theatres on this site have included the 1851 Middlesex Music Hall rebuilt by Frank Matcham and renamed the Winter Garden 1919. Long-running

musical *Cats* had its debut here in 1981; today it is the home of the extremely successful show *The War Horse*, transferred here from the National Theatre.

The Old Vic

The Cut, Lambeth, SE1 8NB. ⊖ *Waterloo.* *☎0844 871 7628. www.oldvictheatre.com.* Former home of the National Theatre, the Old Vic opened in 1818 as the Coburg Theatre. Taken over by Emma Cons in 1880, it was renamed the Royal Victoria Music Hall and Coffee Tavern. After Cons died in 1912, the "Old Vic" (as it became known) was taken up by her niece, Lilian Baylis. Since 2003 the theatre has been under the artistic leadership of Kevin Spacey, who has been widely acclaimed as having rejuvenated it.

Open Air Theatre

Inner Circle, Regent's Park, NW1 4NU. ⊖ *Baker Street.* *☎0844 826 4242. www.openairtheatre.com. Performances May–Sept.* In summer the New Shakespeare Company, founded in 1932, stages productions outdoors in Regent's Park, including such favourites as *A Midsummer Night's Dream*. Bring warm clothing, a cushion, an umbrella and a picnic *(barbecue and cold buffet available; pavilion bar serves hot drinks).*

Palace Theatre

109 Shaftesbury Ave., W1D 8AY. ⊖ *Leicester Square.* *☎0844 412 4656. www.palacetheatrelondon.org.* Opened as an opera house by Richard D'Oyly Carte, this grandiose building has retained its Victorian atmosphere. It is now a venue for large-scale musicals, such as *The Entertainer, Jesus Christ Superstar, Les Misérables* and *The Woman in White*.

Queen's Theatre

51 Shaftesbury Ave., W1D 6BA. ⊖ *Piccadilly Circus.* *☎0844 482 5160.* After being partially rebuilt by Sir Hugh Casson after bomb damage in the war, this theatre was refurbished in early 1992, hosting musicals such as *Stop the World – I Want to Get Off!* Now owned by Sir Cameron Mackintosh's company, it is currently home to long-running favourite *Les Misérables*, which transferred here from the Palace Theatre in 2004.

Royal Court Theatre

Sloane Sq., Chelsea, SW1W 8AS. ⊖ *Sloane Square.* *☎020 7565 5000. www.royalcourttheatre.com.* The role of the Royal Court is to promote contemporary plays and new English and international talent.

Royal National Theatre

South Bank, SE1 9PX. ⊖ *Waterloo. Guided tours.* *☎020 7452 3000. www.nationaltheatre.org.uk.* The National Theatre Company, founded by Sir Laurence Olivier in 1962, has been based since 1976 in this modern building, designed by Deny Lasdun. There are three different theatres: the Olivier, the Lyttelton and the Cottesloe, and lots of bars and restaurants. Some tickets are reserved for sale on the day of the performance. In the foyers you can usually hear live music in the evenings.

Shakespeare's Globe

21 New Globe Walk, Bankside, SE1 9DT. ⊖ *Blackfriars; Cannon Sreet; London Bridge; Southwark.* *☎020 7401 9919. www.shakespearesglobe.com. Performances May–Sept.* This handsome white building, with a thatched roof, is identical to the original Elizabethan theatre where many of Shakepeare's plays were presented in his lifetime. It is both a museum to the great Bard and his contemporaries, and a theatre. The main theatre is open to the elements, so plays are performed in summer only, but a new indoor Jacobean theatre opened in 2013, thereby allowing the Globe to present a year-round programme of theatrical events.

Theatre Royal, Drury Lane
Catherine St., Covent Garden, WC2B 5JF. www.reallyuseful.com. ⊖ Covent Garden. ✆0844 871 8810. There has been a theatre on this site since 1663. The present building was designed in 1812 by Benjamin Wyatt. Productions over the years here have featured Nell Gwynne, Mrs Jordan, Edmund Keane and the clown Grimaldi. Nowadays it hosts popular musicals (*Oklahoma!, My Fair Lady,* Mel Brooks' *The Producers* and *Shrek the Musical*).

OPERA AND BALLET

The world-class Royal Opera House in Covent Garden is the home of the Royal Opera, the Royal Ballet and the Orchestra of the Royal Opera House. The Coliseum presents opera in the English language and is home to the English National Opera, or ENO. Prices for performances vary enormously, but tickets for the best seats are generally very expensive.

ENGLISH NATIONAL OPERA

London Coliseum, 33 St Martin's La., WC2N 4ES. ⊖Leicester Square; Charing Cross. ✆020 7845 9300. www.eno.org. This large Edwardian theatre was built in 1904 by Sir Oswald Stoll to rival Drury Lane. The building is spectacular, with marble pillars, a lavish interior and London's widest proscenium arch. Since 1968 it has been home to the English National Opera. Tours can be arranged.

ROYAL OPERA HOUSE

Bow St., Covent Garden, WC2E 9DD. ⊖ Covent Garden. ✆020 7304 4000. www.roh.org.uk. In 1999, after extensive renovation the Opera House re-opened to reveal new splendour. This is one of the world's most prestigious opera houses and, consequently, tickets are quite expensive and difficult to obtain. However, there are special schemes running with various sponsors – you may get tickets on certain days for £10.

SADLER'S WELLS THEATRE

Rosebery Ave., Islington, EC1R 4TN. ⊖ Angel. ✆0844 412 4300 (ticket office), ✆020 7863 8198 (general enquiries). www.sadlerswells.com. Standing on a site occupied for more than 300 years by six different Sadler's Wells theatres, the present building is now the UK's leading dance theatre, presenting new and cutting-edge performances by both British and international artists.

CLASSICAL MUSIC

London offers a great range of classical music performed by world-class artists and orchestras. Prices vary, but if you don't mind restricted viewing, you can hear some of the best music in the world for just a few pounds. Westminster Abbey, Westminster Cathedral and St Paul's Cathedral all boast superb choirs that you can hear for free. City churches that organise lunchtime concerts include St Bride's, St Anne and St Agnes, St Lawrence Jewry, St Margaret Lothbury, St Martin-within-Ludgate, St Mary le Bow and St Michael's Cornhill.

BARBICAN

Silk St., EC2Y 8DS. ⊖ Barbican. ✆020 7638 8891. www.barbican.org.uk. Home to the London Symphony Orchestra, this venue is also used by touring orchestras.

ROYAL ALBERT HALL

Kensington Gore, South Kensington, SW7 2AP. ⊖ South Kensington. ✆0845 401 5045. www.royalalberthall.com. Guided tours daily. Located on the edge of Hyde Park, this gorgeous circular concert hall was built to fulfil the vision of Queen Victoria's husband Albert to promote understanding of the arts. The Grade I listed building is now home to the Promenade Concerts *(the Proms; from mid-July to mid-September)*, and to the Royal Philharmonic Orchestra. It also hosts a wide range of other events.

ROYAL FESTIVAL HALL

Belvedere Rd., South Bank, SE1 8XX. ⊖ Waterloo. ✆0844 875 0073. www.southbankcentre.co.uk. The Royal Festival Hall, built in 1951 as part of the Festival of Britain celebrations, is the home of the London Philharmonic Orchestra. Programmes range from large-scale classical orchestral concerts, ballet, films and staged performances of opera to the London Jazz Festival. The two smaller venues, Queen Elizabeth Hall and Purcell Room, host contemporary dance, music theatre, chamber music, solo recitals, world music, poetry events and live art.

ST JAMES'S CHURCH CONCERTS

197 Piccadilly, W1J 9LL. ⊖ Piccadilly Circus. ✆020 7734 4511. www.sjp.org.uk. Lunchtime recitals *(free)* and evening concerts of classical music.

ST JOHN'S, SMITH SQUARE

Smith Sq., Westminster, SW1P 3HA. ⊖ Westminster. ✆020 7222 1061. www.sjss.org.uk. This church, a Grade I listed building, is considered one of the masterpieces of English Baroque architecture and is the setting for the annual Lufthansa Festival of baroque music. There are also regular lunchtime concerts as well as evening chamber and vocal music events.

ST MARTIN-IN-THE-FIELDS

Trafalgar Sq., WC2N 4JJ. ⊖ Trafalgar Square. ✆020 7766 1100. www.stmartin-in-the-fields.org. One of London's most famous churches, located in the heart of the city, hosts a range of lunchtime and evening concerts, plus one of the best Christmas carol concerts in town.

WIGMORE HALL

36 Wigmore St., Marylebone, W1U 2BP. ⊖ Bond Street; Oxford Circus. ✆020 7935 2141. www.wigmore-hall.org.uk. A lovely intimate hall, ideal for solo recitals and chamber orchestras. Sunday morning coffee-concerts are an institution and many talented young artists make their first professional London appearances here. Each week a concert is broadcast live worldwide on BBC Radio 3.

ROCK, ROOTS AND JAZZ

CENTRAL LONDON

Cecil Sharp House

2 Regent's Park Rd., Camden, NW1 7AY. ⊖ Camden Town. ✆020 7485 2206. www.efdss.org. From £3. Folk music, singing and dancing from the English Folk Dance and Song Society.

Dover Street Restaurant and Bar

8–10 Dover St., W1S 4LQ. ⊖ Green Park. ✆020 7491 7509. www.doverst.co.uk. Mon–Thu 5.30pm–3am, Fri–Sat 7pm–3am. Cover charge £7–£15. Jazz bar-restaurant with live music and dancing nightly from 10.30pm. Dress smartly (no trainers).

Jazz Café

5 Parkway, Camden, NW1 7PG. ⊖ Camden Town. ✆020 7485 6834 (general information), ✆0844 847 2514 (tickets) . www.venues.meanfiddler.com. Performances daily (doors usually 7pm); 1980s and '90s club nights Sat from 10.30pm. £4–£22.50. Jazz, soul, Latin American and African rap music every evening in this intimate, two-storey club. Some of the greatest jazzmen have played here.

Pizza Express Jazz Club

10 Dean St., Soho, W1D 3RW. ⊖ Tottenham Court Road. ✆020 7437 9595. www.pizzaexpresslive.com. Open daily 11.30am–midnight. £12–£25. Excellent modern jazz in the basement, enjoyed over pizza and drinks. None of the tables are far from the stage and the atmosphere is intimate.

Ronnie Scott's★

47 Frith St., Soho, W1D 4HT. ⊖ Leicester Square. ✆020 7439 0747. www.ronniescotts.co.uk. Open Mon–Sat 6pm–3am, Sun 6.30pm–

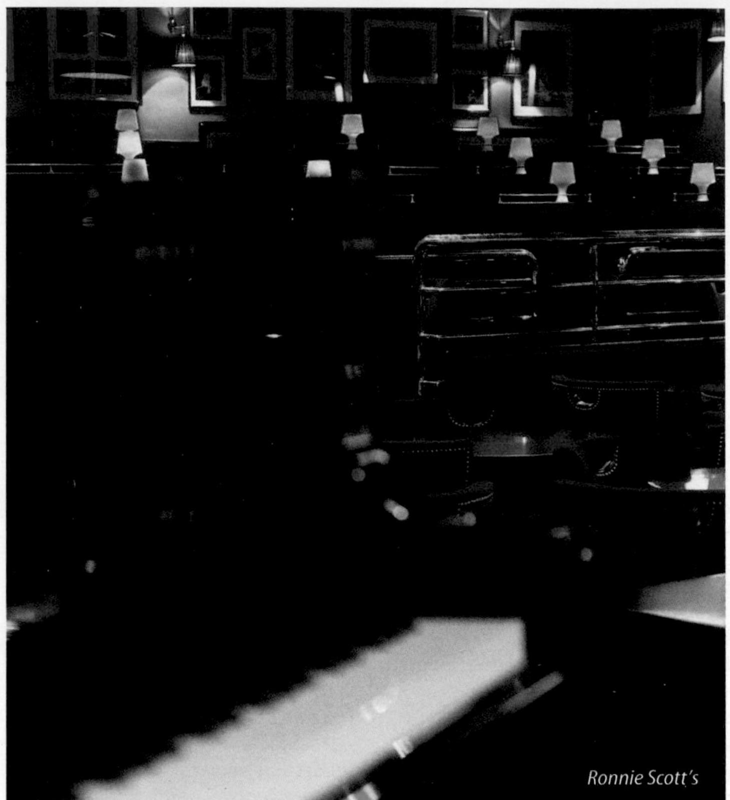
Ronnie Scott's

Ronnie Scott's

midnight, music usually from 7.15pm. ⊜*£15–£47.50.* This legendary Soho jazz club first opened its doors in 1959 and is now famous for its outstanding music and unbeatable atmosphere. Numerous great names have played here and shows are very popular; booking in advance is highly recommended.

O2 Shepherd's Bush Empire

Shepherd's Bush Green, W12 8TT. ⊖ Shepherd's Bush; Goldhawk Road. ☏020 8354 3300 (venue), ☏0844 477 2000 (tickets). www.o2shepherds bushempire.co.uk. ⊜*£10–£30.* Designed by Frank Matcham in the early 20C, "The Empire" was bought by the BBC in 1953 and went on to play a major role in the history of television. Today it's a concert hall with excellent acoustics.

100 Club

100 Oxford St., W1D 1LL. ⊖ Oxford Circus; Tottenham Court Road. ☏020 7636 0933. www.the100club.co.uk. Open daily; doors usually 7.30pm & music 8.30pm. ⊜*£4–£20.* This basement venue, where the Sex Pistols made their debut, now highlights jazz, modern jazz, blues and swing.

606 Club

90 Lots Rd., Chelsea, SW10 0QD. ⊖ Earl's Court. ☏020 7352 5953. www.606club.co.uk. Open daily; doors 7pm/8pm, music from 7.30, 8.30 or 9.30pm. ⊜*Music cover charge £8–£12.* Book for dinner to hear top British jazz musicians play at this atmospheric basement venue.

OUTSIDE THE CENTRE

O2 Academy Brixton

211 Stockwell Rd., Brixton, SW9 9SL. ⊖ Brixton. ✆020 7771 3000 (venue), ✆0844 477 2000 (tickets). www.02academybrixton.co.uk. Open for performances 7pm–11pm (later on club nights). £15–£32.50. Immense hall with Art Deco interior, considered by many to be London's best concert hall. Many greats started out here, including the Rolling Stones, David Bowie, Jamiroquai and UB40. Capacity of 4,700.

The O2 Arena

Peninsula Square, SE10 0DX. ⊖ North Greenwich (Thames Clippers boat service from Waterloo Pier O2 www.thamesclippers.com). ✆020 8463 2000 (venue), ✆0844 856 0202 (tickets). www.theO2.co.uk. Open 9am until late (last admission 1am). Around £40. Huge concert and sports arena in the former Millennium Dome used for big events and big stars. Tickets for some events sell out months in advance, so book early. Also has an Entertainment Avenue of bars and restaurants, a cinema and a gallery space.

The Forum

9–17 Highgate Rd., Kentish Town, NW5 1JY. ⊖ Kentish Town. ✆020 7428 4099. http://mamacolive.com/theforum. Open daily 7–11pm (2am Fri–Sat). £7.50–£39. Originally opened in 1934 as a movie house, this Art Deco building on the edge of Kentish Town has a capacity of 2,000; big bands love its intimate charm. Performers here have included Oasis, Iggy Pop and Macy Gray.

Union Chapel

Compton Terrace, Islington, N1 2XD. ⊖ Highbury & Islington. ✆020 7226 3750. www.unionchapel.org.uk. £10–£35. Using the church as a concert hall was the only way to save Union Chapel from demolition. Music peformed here includes rock, folk, jazz, blues and organ concerts.

TYPES OF BEER	
Pale ale	light and slightly bitter, pale in colour
Bitter beer	less sweet than Pale Ale, pale in colour
Stout	strong and nourishing, dark brown in colour
Porter	a variety of Stout, but less strong
Lager	light and gassy beer or the Continental type, served chilled
Ginger ale	ginger-flavoured drink

GOING OUT FOR A DRINK

PUBS

Pub opening hours are usually Mon–Sat 11am–11pm and Sun noon–10.30pm. Since "24-hour" licensing laws came into effect in 2005, some pubs are now open until midnight or later. **Gastropubs** are ubiquitous across the UK and offer a reasonable standard and variety of dishes, from fish and chips and ham and eggs to burgers, and even Indian and Thai food; some vegetarian options are also available. In more traditional pubs, you can still find classic British dishes (*see below*).

TRADITIONAL PUB GRUB

In older, traditional pubs, you can find staples such as **steak and ale pie** *(pastry pie filled with steak in a thick gravy)*, **lasagne**, **fish and chips**, baked potatoes with a choice of fillings, pasta, burgers, sandwiches and puddings. Most dishes come with chips *(French fries)*. Pubs with atmosphere or historic associations are listed within the Addresses sections in the *Discovering* section of the guide.

The typical drink served in traditional pubs is beer (bitter, lager or stout), sold in pints and half pints on draught, or bottled. A freehouse sells whatever beers it chooses. If the house is tied, it will sell the product of its brewery owner. Many pubs offer guest beers and ales. Most London pubs now have a decent wine list, with at least two or three different reds and whites served by the glass. Of course spirits and soft drinks are always available, too.

WINE BARS AND DJ BARS

These often serve as much beer and spirits as they do wine. Wine is sold by the glass or the bottle and anywhere advertising itself as a "wine bar" should have an extensive list of old and new world varieties. Many places also feature at least a basic cocktail list. The atmosphere is slightly more formal than in pubs and people tend to dress up a bit more. Hours are also different, with many places opening up in the evenings only and often staying open past midnight.

Shopping

London is one of the world's shopping capitals and is home to stores of all shapes and sizes offering the widest range of goods to satisfy even the most demanding shopper. *For business hours and Conversion Tables for sizes, see Basic Information in Planning Your Trip.* **The larger shopping centres and malls, together with bigger stores such as IKEA and Currys, are mostly located on the outskirts of London in easy reach of the North Circular *(Brent Cross)* and South Circular roads *(Croydon, Lakeside and Bluewater)*. Two new shopping centres by retail giant Westfield are also now open in Shepherd's Bush to the West and Stratford to the East.**

WHAT TO BUY LOCALLY

The winter sales at Christmas and New Year and the summer sales in July and August are popular times for shopping in London as prices are reduced on a great range of goods. London is a good place to buy **clothes** and if you know where to go, you can find true one-offs, high-quality designer classics and even some really great bargains. **Classic clothing styles** are sold by well-known brands such as Jaeger, Burberry, Marks & Spencer, John Lewis, Debenhams and House of Fraser. Most of the big brand names can be found in the stores around Oxford and Regent streets and in Kensington and Knightsbridge. **Made-to-measure** clothing for men is available in Savile Row *(tailors)* and Jermyn Street *(shirt-makers)*.
Shops specialising in reasonably priced **ready-to-wear clothing** appeal to a young clientele and are found in areas such as Oxford Street and at the Westfield centres. For **trendy shops** offering styles from established and offbeat designers, visit the King's Road in Chelsea, Carnaby Street in Soho and Covent Garden. Markets selling vintage fashions and more alternative clothing can be found around Portobello Road in the West and Brick Lane in the East. The craft studios at Oxo Tower on the South Bank and in Camden Lock Market are places to explore for a special gift.
Porcelain – The best makes: Wedgwood, Royal Worcester and Royal Doulton are available in London; Harrods sale in January is a good place for bargains.
Food – Smoked salmon, Stilton cheese, pickles, marmalade and drinks such as tea, gin and whisky are favourite items and widely available.

DEPARTMENT STORES AND SHOPS

THE CLASSICS

Harrods
87–135 Brompton Rd., Knightsbridge, SW1X 7XL. ⊖ Knightsbridge. ✆020 7730 1234. www.harrods.com. Open Mon–Sat 10am–8pm, Sun

11.30am–6pm. Harrods boasts that it can supply anything, even a pedigree dog. The foodhalls are particularly impressive (do not miss the displays of fish and cheese). The butcher will even sell you alligator or ostrich steaks. There is also a hairdresser's, a beauty parlour, a travel agency and a shipping service. A world of elegance and comfort, to be visited as you would a museum.

Harvey Nichols
109–125 Knightsbridge, SW1X 7RJ. ⊖Knightsbridge. ✆020 7235 5000. www.harveynichols.com. Open Mon–Sat 10am– 8pm, Sun 11.30am–6pm. This sumptuous store regularly arouses curiosity with its unusual and daring window displays. There is a good range of fashion clothing, especially in smaller sizes, an excellent choice of hats (for Ascot!) and some fine jewellery.

John Lewis
300 Oxford St., W1A 1EX. ⊖ Oxford Circus. ✆020 7629 7711. www.johnlewis.com. Open Mon–Sat 9.30am– 8pm (Thu 9pm), Sun noon–6pm. Suppliers of clothing, household fittings, linen and stationery, this popular high-street store has everything you need for everyday, practical purposes and special occasions. Since its refurbishment, the beauty department on the ground floor is particularly good.

Liberty
Regent St., W1B 5AH. ⊖ Oxford Circus. ✆020 7734 1234. www.liberty.co.uk. Open Mon–Sat 10am–8pm, Sun noon–6pm. This intimate department store has a character all its own, owing to its roots in the East End of London. Goods include Liberty-brand and Indian silks, Chinese ceramics, contemporary glassware and designer clothes. The beautiful half-timbered Mock Tudor façade was built in 1924.

Selfridges
400 Oxford St., W1A 1AB. ⊖ Bond Street. ✆0870 837 7377. www.selfridges.co.uk. Open Mon–Sat 9.30am–9pm, Sun 11.30am–6pm. This well-known department store sells everything from lingerie to household articles, beauty products and stationery, and is an elegant place to browse. It's hard not to get carried

Mock-Tudor façade of Liberty

away in the food halls. The recently added shoe galleries are a special treat and the window displays at Christmas should not be missed.

Westfield London
Westfield London, W12 7SL. ⊖ Shepherds Bush; White City; Wood Lane. ✆020 3371 2300. http://uk.westfield.com/london. Open Mon–Sat 10am–10pm, Sun noon–6pm. This vast shopping mall opened in 2008 and is now home to more than 300 shops *(including a special premium luxury brands area: The Village)*, more than 60 restaurants and bars plus a cinema. Take a day and take a map.

Westfield Stratford City
⊖ Stratford tube and national rail; Stratford. http://uk.westfield.com/stratfordcity. Open Mon–Fri 10am–9pm, Sat 9am–9pm, Sun noon–6pm. The largest urban shopping centre in Europe opened in late 2011 and features more than 300 shops, including large outposts of department store John Lewis and food and clothing retailer Marks & Spencer, a cinema plus numerous cafés and restaurants.

HIGH STREET CHAINS

French Connection
249–251 Regent St., W1B 2EP. ⊖ Oxford Circus. ✆020 7493 3124. www.frenchconnection.com. Open Mon–Sat 9.30am–8.30pm (until 9pm Thu), Sun noon–6pm. Upscale fashion with good tailoring. Also at 99–103 Long Acre *⊖ Covent Garden.*

H & M
234 Regent St., W1B 3BR. ⊖ Oxford Circus. ✆0844 736 9000. www.hm.com. Open Mon–Sat 10am–9pm, Sun noon–6pm. Flagship UK store of this trendy Swedish chain of stores selling moderately priced men's, women's and children's fashion and accessories. Also at *27–29 Long Acre ⊖ Covent Garden.*

Karen Millen
247 Regent St., W1B 2EW. ⊖ Oxford Circus. ✆020 7629 1901. www.karenmillen.com. Open Mon–Fri 10am–8pm, Sat 10am–7.30pm, Sun 11.30am–6.30pm. This British chain offers very feminine and sophisticated fashion and accessories, with an emphasis on structured and gently tailored lines. More expensive than the usual high street stores. Also at *57 South Molton St. ⊖ Bond Street and 33 Brompton Rd. ⊖ Knightsbridge.*

Topshop
36–38 Great Castle St., W1W 8LG. ⊖ Oxford Circus. ✆0844 848 7487. www.topshop.com. Open Mon–Sat 9am–9pm, Sun 11.30am–6pm. Cheap, cheerful and cutting-edge, Topshop is an institution among fashionistas. The stock, much of it channelling the catwalks, changes almost every week – and key pieces featured in magazines sell out almost instantly, so if you see something you like don't "come back for it". Three floors of this flagship store include shoes, vintage, a hairdresser's and nail bar and accessories. Also at *60–64 Strand ⊖ Charing Cross and at 44 Kensington High Street ⊖ High Street Kensington.*

ART AND ANTIQUES

London has always had a buoyant trade in art and antiques.
Fairs are held regularly in London hotels that attract dealers from all over the country: details are available from the **Antiques Trade Gazette**, which comes out on Tuedays. *For details of larger, international fairs, contact the British Antique Dealers Association, 20 Rutland Gate, SW7 1BD. ✆020 7581 5259. www.bada.org.*

BONHAMS

101 New Bond St., W1S 1SR ⊖ Bond Street. ✆020 7447 7447. www.bonhams.com. Founded in 1793, Bonhams is one of the biggest auctioneers of fine art, antiques and collectors' artefacts. It is the fourth-biggest valuers in the world, with expertise in 25 fields, ranging from wine to teddy bears.

CHRISTIE'S

85 Old Brompton Rd., South Kensington, SW7 3LD. ⊖ South Kensington. ✆020 7930 6074. www.christies.com. This internationally renowned institution, founded by James Christie in London *(1766)*, built up its reputation by promoting young artists such as Gainsborough but also by organising the major auctions of the 18C and 19C. The most spectacular auction remains the sale of 198 paintings by Sir Robert Walpole to Catherine the Great, now in the Hermitage Museum. Christie's now has offices in 15 countries and operates in almost 80 fields. Also at *8 King St. ⊖ Green Park.*

SOTHEBY'S

34–35 New Bond St., Mayfair, W1A 2AA. ⊖ Bond Street. ✆020 7293 5000. www.sothebys.com. Sotheby's started out in 1744 as a book valuers. When it moved to its prestigious premises in New Bond Street, the establishment diversified into selling drawings and paintings. The sale of the Goldschmidt collection in 1958 marked a turning point, as did the concurrent opening of the New York office. Particularly memorable was the sale of the Duchess of Windsor's jewellery. Sotheby's, ever forward thinking, launched Internet auctioning in 1999.

MARKETS

Market stall browsing, such as at Spitalfields or on Portobello Road, holds a fascination for lovers of antiques hoping to find that desirable object. The stall holders are often amateurs, but a real find is rare. The earlier you arrive, the greater the choice. Flower stalls are a common sight in the streets of central London: in front of the Danish Embassy in Sloane St., **Gilding the Lily** at South Kensington Underground Station and **Wild at Heart** at 222 Westbourne Grove all have wonderful displays. Camden's markets specialise in clothing.

ANTIQUES AND BRIC-A-BRAC

Alfie's Antiques Market
13–25 Church St., NW8 8DT. ⊖ Edgware Road. ✆020 7723 6066. www.alfiesantiques.com. Open Tue–Sat 10am–6pm. Don't be put off by its slightly scruffy appearance (also known as bohemian chic) – this market in Marylebone sells *everything.*

Bermondsey (New Caledonian) Market
Bermondsey Sq., Southwark, SE1 4QB. ⊖London Bridge. www.bermondsey square.co.uk/antiques. Open Fri 4am–1pm. The market was revived on this site in 1950. Trade in copper and silverware, Victorian jewellery, furniture and other objets d'art begins by torchlight in the early hours.

Camden Passage Antiques Market
Camden Passage, Islington, N1 8EF. ⊖ Angel. www.camdenpassage islington.co.uk. General market Wed and Sat, but many shops open on weekdays or by arrangement. The general Camden Passage area, stretching over several streets, is full of antique shops, selling just about everything. The markets fill the rest of the area, while the Wed and Sat antiques market offers Oriental art, Art Nouveau, Art Deco, silverware and more from around 250 dealers.

Covent Garden Market
Covent Garden Piazza, WC2E 8RF. ⊖Covent Garden. www.covent gardenlondonuk.com. Open Mon–Sat 10am–7pm, Sun 11am–6pm. In the 17C Inigo Jones designed the Piazza to create a trading space for the original market, established by monks before the Reformation, which transferred to Nine Elms in 1974. The current market

buildings, designed by Charles Fowler, were added in 1832. The flower market is now occupied by shops, cafés, restaurants and wine bars, and the Transport Museum. The antiques market features coins, glasses, old tools and silverware.

Grays Antiques Market and Grays in the Mews
58 Davies St. and 1–7 Davies Mews, W1K 5AB. ⊖ Bond Street. ✆020 7629 7034. www.graysantiques.com. Open Mon–Fri 10am–6pm, Sat 11am–5pm. Occupying a split site incorporating 1–7 Davies Mews, the main hall has 170 stands and London's biggest collection of antique jewellery. It's a fascinating place to browse, even if you don't buy anything.

Greenwich Antiques Market
Greenwich High Rd., SE10. ⊖ Cutty Sark. www.greenwich-market.co.uk. Open Tue–Sun 10am–5.30pm. In this flea market expect to find international crafts rather than real antiques, but the atmosphere here is pleasant, more family-orientated and less crowded than Camden Market.

Portobello Road
Portobello Rd., Notting Hill, W11. ⊖ Notting Hill Gate; Ladbroke Grove. ✆020 7229 8354. www.portobelloroad.co.uk. Open Sat 8am–5pm. Browse for antiquities, Victoriana, later silver, chinaware, stamps and other small items.

Old Spitalfields Market
Brushfield St., Commercial St., E1. ⊖ Liverpool Street. ✆020 7247 8556. www.oldspitalfieldsmarket.com. **General market** *Mon–Fri 10am–4pm, Sun 9am–5pm.* **Antiques Fair** *Thu 8am–3.30pm.* **Fashion market** *Fri 10am–4pm.* **Specialist Fair** *Sat 11am–5pm.* This large historic hall is home to a craft market. On weekdays, the second-hand stalls expose their wares, but on Sunday the organic market takes over. The atmosphere is pleasant, with many cafés and restaurants.

CLOTHING

Brick Lane Market
Brick La., E1. ⊖ Aldgate East. Open Sun 8am–2pm. A vast hotchpotch of bric-à-brac and fabrics. Leather and new clothing is sold in the shops at the north end.

Camden Lock Market
Chalk Farm Rd., NW1 8AF. ⊖ Camden Town. ✆020 7284 2084. www.camdenlockmarket.com. Open daily 10am–6pm. Arts and crafts, designer and vintage clothes, jewellery and a wide range of goods are on sale.

Camden Market
Camden High St., Corner of Camden High St. and Buck St., NW1. ⊖ Camden Town. www.camdenlock.net. Open daily 9.30am–6pm. A treasure trove for bargain leather goods and clothing, with more than 200 stands.

Camden Stables Market
Chalk Farm Rd., Camden, NW1 8AH. ⊖ Chalk Farm. ✆020 7485 8355. www.stablesmarket.com. Open daily 10am–6pm. The centre of the alternative fashion scene with 350 shops, selling everything from leather trousers to tie-dye coats.

Leather Lane Market
Leather La., Chancery Lane, EC1. ⊖ Chancery Lane. Open Mon–Fri, 10.30am–2.30pm. The market, dotted with cafés, is always full of bargains. Fashionable clothes for men and women (including sportswear), a tailor and of course, all sorts of leatherwear: shirts, skirts, shoes and bags.

Petticoat Lane Market
Middlesex St., Wentworth St., EC1. ⊖ Liverpool Street. Open Mon–Fri 10am–2.30pm, Sun 9am–2pm. This flea market, just down the road from its original 17C location, is best visited on Sundays.

FOOD AND FLOWERS

Berwick Street
Berwick St., Soho, W1. ⊖ Tottenham Court Road; Oxford Circus. Open Mon–Sat 9am–6pm. Berwick Street is frequented by many nearby restaurateurs. Initially just a fruit and veg market, it now has fish counters, flower stalls and an excellent baker. Atmosphere of bygone times.

Borough Market
Stoney St., Borough High St., Southwark, SE1 1TL. ⊖ London Bridge. ✆020 7407 1002. www.boroughmarket.org.uk. Open Thu 11am–5pm, Fri noon–6pm, Sat 8am–5pm. Probably the oldest food market in London, with archives dating back to 1014. It is known as "the London larder" and is reputed for its organic products and many food stalls.

Brixton Market
Atlantic Rd., SW9 8JX. ⊖ Brixton. http://brixtonmarket.net. Open Mon–Sat 8am–6pm (Wed until 3pm). One of South London's best markets for fresh food. Many exotic products, tropical foods, fabrics and world music.

Columbia Road Market
Columbia Rd., Bethnal Green, E2. ⊖ Shoreditch High Street or Hoxton, buses 26, 48, 55. www.columbiaroad.info. Open Sun 8am–3pm.
This popular flower market is a victim of its own success and crowds can be vast, but the street has a country atmosphere which gives it a charm all of its own. As well as the flowers, there are fashionable boutiques selling clothes and accessories, second-hand stores and a good bakery. Pubs around the market serve good Sunday roasts.

Leadenhall Market
Whittington Ave., EC3. ⊖ Bank. ✆020 7332 1703. www.leadenhallmarket.co.uk. Open Mon–Fri 7am–4pm. A small selection of shops, plus the poultry and fish market. Especially impressive is the huge Hall of Glass designed by Victorian architect Sir Horace Jones *(Smithfields Market, Billingsgate Market).*

Sport and Leisure

London boasts a number of Premier League and First Division football teams and going to games is a popular pasttime for many residents. The city also has the home of cricket *(Lords)* and the world's most famous tennis club, Wimbledon. Rugby matches, especially the Six Nations Cup, are special events.

ALL-ENGLAND LAWN TENNIS CLUB (WIMBLEDON)

Church Rd., Wimbledon SW19 5AE. ⊖ Wimbledon. ✆020 8944 1066. www.wimbledom.com. Home to the world's most prestigious tennis tournament *(June/July)*, Wimbledon is also open year-round for guided tours. *see SUBURBS – WIMBLEDON.*

ARSENAL FC – EMIRATES STADIUM

Avenell Rd., Islington, N5 1BU. ⊖ Arsenal. www.arsenal.com. One of London's more successful clubs has a spectacular home: the Emirates Stadium. Watch a match here to see if they can retain their top-of-table reputation.

THE KIA OVAL

Kennington Oval, Kennington, SE11 5SS. ⊖ Oval. ✆0844 375 1845 (10p/min plus network charges). www.kiaoval.com. London's second cricket ground and home to the Surrey County Cricket Club. Hosts a range of international test matches and county games.

CHELSEA FC – STAMFORD BRIDGE

Stamford Bridge, Fulham Rd., SW6 1HS. ✆0871 984 1955 (10p/min plus network charges). ⊖Fulham Broadway. www.chelseafc.co.uk. One of London's most famous football clubs, Chelsea play their matches at Stamford Bridge in Fulham to a packed stadium. The club vies with Arsenal and Spurs to be London's best. Stadium tours also available.

GUARDS POLO CLUB

Smith's Lawn, Windsor Great Park, TW20 0HP. ⊖ Egham rail (overground). ✆01784 434 212. www.guardspoloclub.com. Matches played every Saturday and Sunday at 3pm. The Cartier International tournament is held here in July. The Ladies' National Polo Championship is held at Ascot Park *(Sunningdale)* in early July.

HARLEQUINS STOOP MEMORIAL GROUND

Langhorn Drive, Twickenham/ Richmond, TW2 7SX. ⊖ Twickenham rail (overground). ✆020 8410 6000 (general enquiries). ✆0871 527 1315 (tickets). www.quins.co.uk. Ground of one of London's premier rugby clubs: The Harlequins.

LORD'S CRICKET GROUND

St John's Wood Rd., NW8 8QN. ⊖ St John's Wood. ✆020 7616 8500. www.lords.org. London's main cricket ground and headquarters of several autonomous bodies: the International Cricket Council that supervises the game at international level; the Marylebone Cricket Club (MCC), founded in 1787, which set up the Test and County Cricket Board to administer international matches and the county game in the United Kingdom; and the Middlesex County Cricket Club, founded in 1877.

TOTTENHAM HOTSPUR FC – WHITE HART LANE

748 High Rd., Tottenham, N17 0AP. ⊖ White Hart Lane. www.tottenhamhotspur.com. One of London's Premier League clubs, "Spurs" play their matches against the other big clubs in Tottenham, North London. Stadium tours also available.

TWICKENHAM

Rugby Rd., TW1 1DZ. ⊖ Twickenham rail. ✆0870 405 2000. www.rfu.com. Britain's finest rugby ground and the headquarters of the Rugby Football Union. Major international matches are played on its hallowed turf, including Six Nations home games. The Museum of Rugby features the "Twickenham Experience", a guided tour of 14 exhibition rooms.

WIMBLEDON GREYHOUND STADIUM

Plough La., SW17 0BL. ⊖ Tooting Broadway; Wimbledon. ✆0870 840 8905. www.lovethedogs.co.uk. London's only surviving dog track is open on weekend evenings for greyhound racing.

© Richard Heathcote/The FA/Getty Images

Wembley Stadium

The new stadium – the UK's new national football stadium opened its doors in 2007 and has a capacity of 90,000. The Stadium features a retractable roof, 34 bars and unobstructed views from every seat. In addition to hosting the FA's flagship events including all England's international home matches plus the semi-finals and final of the FA Cup, Wembley is also home to Rugby League's Carnegie Challenge Cup final and a diverse range of additional sports, music and entertainment events throughout the year.

History – Wembley started life as Wembley Park Leisure Grounds in the 19C. In 1889, to encourage more people to use the new railways, the chairman of the Metropolitan Railway decided to build an attraction here, linked by railway to the city. Money later ran out and it was never finished. At the end of the First World War in 1918 the Government made plans for a British Empire Exhibition, with a national sports ground as its centrepiece. The first Wembley Stadium took just 300 days to complete and opened in 1923, hosting its first football match, the FA Cup final between Bolton Wanderers and West Ham United, on 28 April. A crowd of 300,000 fans turned up, far exceeding the Stadium's capacity of 125,000 and promoting a crowd-clearing exercise by mounted police, one on a light-coloured horse – the match has since become known as the "White Horse" final. The Stadium was later added to *(floodlights in 1955; a roof in 1963)* but struggled to cope with the developing needs of sports fans and was completely demolished in 2000, despite local efforts to save its famous twin towers.

⊖Wembley Park or Wembley Stadium Rail or Wembley Central, HA9 0WS. ✆0844 980 8001. www.wembleystadium.com. ∞Tours £16.

INDEX

INDEX

H

I

N

O

P

Q

R

S

Y

Z

INDEX

STAY

EAT

THEMATIC MAPS

MAPS AND PLANS

MAP LEGEND

Monuments and Sights

- Ecclesiastical building
- Mosque
- Synagogue
- Monastery - Lighthouse
- Viewpoint
- Historic house, castle - Ruins
- Dam - Cave
- Fountain - Megalithic sight
- Genoese tower - Windmill
- Temple - Greco-Roman remains
- Temple : Buddhist - Hindu
- Other sight of interest, summit
- Distillery
- Palace, villa, dwelling
- Cemetery : Christian-Muslim-Jewish
- Olive grove - Orange grove
- Mangrove swamp

Sports and Leisure

- Swimming pool - Outdoor, Indoor
- Beach - Stadium
- Marina - Sailing
- Diving - Surfing
- Refuge - Hiking trail
- Horse riding
- Golf course - Leisure activities
- Theme park
- Animal park, zoo
- Garden, arboretum
- Bird reserve
- Windsurfing, kitesurfing
- Sea or sport fishing
- Canyoning, rafting
- Campsite - Hostel
- Bull ring
- Activity base
- Canoeing, kayaking
- Boat trips

Practical Information

- Tourist information
- Car park
- Railway - Bus/Coach station
- Railway
- Tramline
- Underground
- Funicular, rack railway
- Cablecar
- Tourist train
- Car and passenger ferry
- Passenger ferry
- Petrol station - Shop
- Post Office - Telephone
- Internet
- H — Town hall - Bank, Bureau de change
- J — Court - Police station
- T U M — Theatre - University - Museum
- Hospital
- Covered market
- Airport
- Parador, Pousada
- D — Provincial council
- G — District government
- Spa
- Hot spring

Additional Symbols

- Motorway or main road
- Junction
- Road
- Pedestrianised road
- Steps - Trail - Ski slope

Topographical Features

- Active volcano - Coral reef
- Marshland - Desert
- Border - Natural park

COMPANION PUBLICATIONS

REGIONAL MAPS

Michelin map 504 – South East England, The Midlands, East Anglia (Scale 1 : 400 000 – 1cm = 4km – 1in : 6.30 miles) covers the main regions of the country, the network of motorways and major roads. It provides information on shipping routes, distances in miles and kilometres, plan of London, services, sporting and tourist attractions and an index of places.

COUNTRY MAPS

The **Atlas Britain 2008** (Scale 1: 200 000) covers the whole of Great Britain. It provides information on route planning, distances in miles and kilometres, town plans, services, sporting and tourist attractions and an index of places.

INTERNET

Users can access personalised route plans, Michelin mapping on line, addresses of hotels and restaurants featured in The Red Guides and practical and tourist information through the Internet: **www.travel.viamichelin.com** and **www.viamichelin.com**

The Michelin Adventure

It all started with rubber balls! This was the product made by a small company based in Clermont-Ferrand that André and Edouard Michelin inherited, back in 1880. The brothers quickly saw the potential for a new means of transport and their first success was the invention of detachable pneumatic tires for bicycles. However, the automobile was to provide the greatest scope for their creative talents. Throughout the 20th century, Michelin never ceased developing and creating ever more reliable and high-performance tires, not only for vehicles ranging from trucks to F1 but also for underground transit systems and airplanes.

From early on, Michelin provided its customers with tools and services to facilitate mobility and make traveling a more pleasurable and more frequent experience. As early as 1900, the Michelin Guide supplied motorists with a host of useful information related to vehicle maintenance, accommodation and restaurants, and was to become a benchmark for good food. At the same time, the Travel Information Bureau offered travelers personalised tips and itineraries.

The publication of the first collection of roadmaps, in 1910, was an instant hit! In 1926, the first regional guide to France was published, devoted to the principal sites of Brittany, and before long each region of France had its own Green Guide. The collection was later extended to more far-flung destinations, including New York in 1968 and Taiwan in 2011.

In the 21st century, with the growth of digital technology, the challenge for Michelin maps and guides is to continue to develop alongside the company's tire activities. Now, as before, Michelin is committed to improving the mobility of travelers.

MICHELIN TODAY

WORLD NUMBER ONE TIRE MANUFACTURER

- 70 production sites in 18 countries
- 111,000 employees from all cultures and on every continent
- 6,000 people employed in research and development

Moving for a world

Moving forward means developing tires with better road grip and shorter braking distances, whatever the state of the road.

CORRECT TIRE PRESSURE

- Safety
- Longevity
- Optimum fuel consumption

- Durability reduced by 20% (- 8,000 km)

- Risk of blowouts
- Increased fuel consumption
- Longer braking distances on wet surfaces

forward together
where mobility is safer

It also involves helping motorists take care of their safety and their tires. To do so, Michelin organises "Fill Up With Air" campaigns all over the world to remind us that correct tire pressure is vital.

WEAR

DETECTING TIRE WEAR

The legal minimum depth of tire tread is 1.6mm. Tire manufacturers equip their tires with tread wear indicators, which are small blocks of rubber moulded into the base of the main grooves at a depth of 1.6mm.

Tires are the only point of contact between the vehicle and road.

The photo below shows the actual contact zone.

NEW TIRE

WORN TIRE
(1,6 mm tread)

If the tread depth is less than 1.6mm, tires are considered to be worn and dangerous on wet surfaces.

Moving forward means sustainable mobility

INNOVATION AND THE ENVIRONMENT

By 2050, Michelin aims to cut the quantity of raw materials used in its tire manufacturing process by half and to have developed renewable energy in its facilities. The design of MICHELIN tires has already saved billions of litres of fuel and, by extension, billions of tons of CO2.

Similarly, Michelin prints its maps and guides on paper produced from sustainably managed forests and is diversifying its publishing media by offering digital solutions to make traveling easier, more fuel efficient and more enjoyable!

The group's whole-hearted commitment to eco-design on a daily basis is demonstrated by ISO 14001 certification.

Like you, Michelin is committed to preserving our planet.

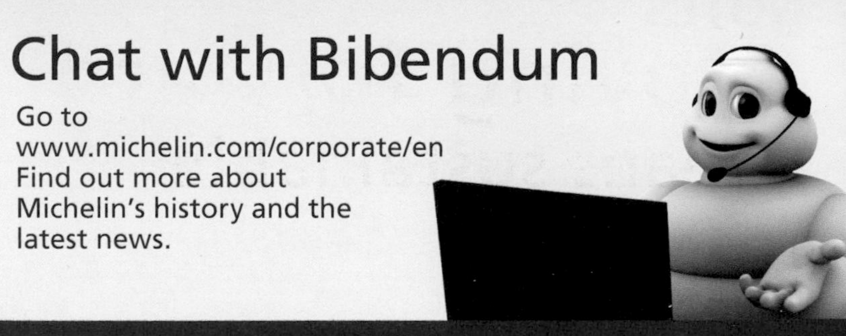

Chat with Bibendum

Go to
www.michelin.com/corporate/en
Find out more about
Michelin's history and the
latest news.

QUIZ

Michelin develops tires for all types of vehicles.
See if you can match the right tire with the right vehicle...

A B C D E F G

1 2 3 4 5 6 7

Solution : A-6 / B-4 / C-2 / D-1 / E-3 / F-7 / G-5

NOTES

NOTES

NOTES

Michelin Travel Partner

Société par actions simplifiées au capital de 11 629 590 EUR
27 cours de l'Ile Seguin - 92100 Boulogne Billancourt (France)
R.C.S. Nanterre 433 677 721

ISBN 978-2-067188-17-4
Printed: March 2013
Printed and bound in France : Imprimerie CHIRAT, 42540 Saint-Just-la-Pendue - N° 201304.0220